HANDBOOK OF

PSYCHOSOMATIC MEDICINE

International Universities Press
Stress and Health Series

Edited by
Leo Goldberger, Ph.D.

Monograph 9

Handbook of

Psychosomatic Medicine

edited by

G. A. Fava

and

H. Freyberger

International Universities Press, Inc.
Madison   Connecticut

Copyright © 1998, International Universities Press, Inc.

INTERNATIONAL UNIVERSITIES PRESS and IUP (& design) ® are registered trademarks of International Universities Press, Inc.

Library of Congress Cataloging-in-Publication Data

Handbook of psychosomatic medicine / edited by G.A. Fava and H. Freyberger.
    p.   cm. — (International Universities Press stress and health series ; 9)
   Includes bibliographical references and index.
   ISBN 0-8236-2302-5
   1. Medicine, Psychosomatic—Handbooks, manuals, etc. I. Fava, Giovanni A. (Giovanni Andrea) II. Freyberger, Hellmuth.
III. Series: Stress and health series ; monograph 9.
RC49.H328 1997
616.08—dc21   97-27749
                                        CIP

Manufactured in the United States of America

This book is dedicated to the memory of Robert Kellner (1922–1992), outstanding clinician and researcher. Psychosomatic medicine owes him key concepts in the field of somatization and hypochondriasis. His last paper is included in the volume.

Contents

Contributors

Tim A. Ahles, Center for Psycho-Oncology Research, Dartmouth Medical School, and The Norris Cotton Cancer Center, Lebanon, New Hampshire.

Jambur Ananth, University of California at Los Angeles (UCLA) and Harbor UCLA Medical Center, Torrance, California.

Per Bech, Psychiatric Institute, Frederiksborg General Hospital, Hillerød, Denmark.

Diane S. Berry, Southern Methodist University, Dallas, Texas.

M. Biondi, Psychiatric Clinic III, University of Rome "La Sapienza," Rome, Italy.

Barry Blackwell, Department of Psychiatry, University of Wisconsin Medical School, Milwaukee Clinical Campus, Sinai Samaritan Medical Center, Milwaukee, Wisconsin.

Manuela Burgmeier-Lohse, Department of Psychiatry, Hamburg University, Germany.

Barrie R. Cassileth, University of North Carolina at Chapel Hill, North Carolina.

George N. Christodoulou, Department of Psychiatry, Eginition Hospital, University of Athens, Greece.

Jean Cottraux, Department of Psychiatry and Medical Psychology, Hôpital Neurologie, Lyon, France.

Nicholas A. Covino, Departments of Psychiatry, Beth Israel Hospital and Harvard Medical School, Boston, Massachusetts.

Koen Demyttenaere, Departments of Obstetrics and Gynecology, and Psychiatry, Catholic University of Leuven, Belgium.

Thalia G. Dragonas, Department of Preschool Education, University of Athens, Greece.

Douglas A. Drossman, University of North Carolina at Chapel Hill, North Carolina.

Paul M. G. Emmelkamp, Department of Clinical Psychology, Academic Hospital, University of Groningen, The Netherlands.

George L. Engel, Departments of Psychiatry and Medicine, University of Rochester School of Medicine, Rochester, New York.

Fabio Facchinetti, Department of Obstetrics and Gynecology, University of Modena, Italy.

Giovanni A. Fava, Affective Disorders Program, Department of Psychology, University of Bologna, Italy. Also, Department of Psychiatry, State University of New York at Buffalo, and Veterans Administration Medical Center, Buffalo, New York.

Loredana Fioroni, Department of Obstetrics and Gynecology, University of Modena, Italy.

Fred H. Frankel, Departments of Psychiatry, Beth Israel Hospital and Harvard Medical School, Boston, Massachusetts.

Harald J. Freyberger, Department of Psychiatry, Medical University, Lübeck, Germany.

Hellmuth Freyberger, formerly Department of Psychosomatics, Center of Psychological Medicine, Hannover Medical School, Hannover, Germany.

Andrea R. Genazzani, Department of Obstetrics and Gynecology, University of Modena, Italy.

Robert Kellner, Department of Psychiatry, University of New Mexico, School of Medicine, Albuquerque, New Mexico.

Erwin K. Koranyi, Royal Ottawa Hospital, University of Ottawa, Ontario, Canada.

Ulrich Lamparter, Abteilung Psychosomatik und Psychotherapie, Medizinische Klinik, Universitätskrankenhaus Eppendorf, Hamburg, Germany.

Thomas J. Lane, Departments of Medicine and Psychiatry, School of Medicine, University of Connecticut Health Center, Farmington, Connecticut.

Andrew B. Littman, Behavioral Medicine Service of the Cardiovascular Health Center, Department of Psychiatry, Massachusetts General Hospital, and Harvard Medical School, Boston, Massachusetts.

Peter Manu, Departments of Medicine and Psychiatry, School of Medicine, University of Connecticut Health Center, Farmington, Connecticut.

Dale A. Matthews, Departments of Medicine and Psychiatry, School of Medicine, University of Connecticut Health Center, Farmington, Connecticut.

Richard Mayou, University Department of Psychiatry, Warneford Hospital, Oxford, U.K.

Myriam Van Moffaert, Department of Psychiatry and Psychodermatology, University Hospital, Ghent, Belgium.

Murray A. Morphy, Department of Psychiatry, State University of New York at Buffalo, and Veterans Administration Medical Center, Buffalo, New York.

Isabella Neri, Department of Obstetrics and Gynecology, University of Modena, Italy.

Patricia van Oppen, Department of Psychiatry, Amsterdam Psychiatric Center, Free University, Amsterdam, The Netherlands.

James W. Pennebaker, Southern Methodist University, Dallas, Texas.

A. Picardi, Psychiatric Clinic III, University of Rome "La Sapienza," Rome, Italy.

Issy Pilowsky, Department of Psychiatry, The University of Adelaide, Royal Adelaide Hospital, Adelaide, Australia.

Walter M. Potoczny, Geriatric Day Hospital, Royal Ottawa Hospital, University of Ottawa, Ontario, Canada.

Hans-Ulrich Schmidt, Abteilung Psychosomatik und Psychotherapie, Medizinische Klinik, Universitätskrankenhaus Eppendorf, Hamburg, Germany.

Tom Sensky, Charing Cross & Westminster Medical School, West Middlesex University Hospital, Isleworth, U.K.

Peter M. Silberfarb, Center for Psycho-Oncology Research, Dartmouth Medical School, and The Norris Cotton Cancer Center, Lebanon, New Hampshire.

Philip Snaith, Academic Unit of Psychiatry, Leeds University, Leeds, U.K.

Nicoletta Sonino, Department of Psychiatry, State University of New York at Buffalo, and Veterans Administration Medical Center, Buffalo, New York.

Bernhard Strauss, Department of Psychotherapy and Psychosomatics, Kiel University, Germany.

Töres Theorell, National Institute of Psychosocial Factors and Health and the Karolinska Institute, Stockholm, Sweden.

Denise M. Tope, Center for Psycho-Oncology Research, Dartmouth Medical School, and The Norris Cotton Cancer Center, Lebanon, New Hampshire.

Jenifer Wilson-Barnett, Department of Nursing Studies, King's College, London, U.K.

Thomas N. Wise, Department of Psychiatry, Georgetown University School of Medicine, Georgetown, Virginia.

Acknowledgments

The papers listed below were previously published in *Psychotherapy and Psychosomatics*, and are reprinted by permission.

Introduction: G.L. Engel. How much longer must medicine's science be bound by a seventeenth century worldview? 57: 3–16.

Fundamental Trends: T. Theorell, Critical life changes: A review of research. 57: 108–117. R. Mayou, Somatization. 59: 69–83. D.S. Berry, J.W. Pennebaker, Nonverbal and verbal emotional expression and health. 59: 11–19. B. Blackwell, Sick role susceptibility: A commentary on the contemporary database (1989– 1991) and classification system. 58: 79–90. I. Pilowsky, Aspects of abnormal illness behavior. 60: 62–74. R. Kellner, Psychosomatic syndromes, somatization, and somatoform disorders. 61: 4–24. G.A. Fava, The concept of psychosomatic disorder. 58: 1–12. E. Koranyi, W.M. Potoczny, Physical illness underlying psychiatric symptoms. 58: 155–160. G.N. Christodoulou, T.G. Dragonas, Role of early developmental factors in susceptibility to disease. 58: 32–39. P. Bech, Quality of life measurements in chronic disorders. 59: 1–10. T.N. Wise, Teaching psychosomatic medicine: Utilizing concurrent perspectives. 59: 99–106.

Clinical Issues: B.R. Cassileth, D.A. Drossman, Psychosocial factors in gastrointestinal illness. 59: 131–143. A.B. Littman, A review of psychosomatic aspects of cardiovascular disease. 60: 148–167. T. Sensky, Psychosomatic aspects of end-stage renal failure. 59: 56–68. G.A. Fava, N. Sonino, M.A. Morphy, A psychosomatic view of endocrine disorders. 59: 20–33. D.M. Tope, T.A. Ahles, P.M. Silberfarb, Psycho-Oncology: Psychological well-being as one component of quality of life. 60: 129–147. M. Van Moffaert, Psychodermatology: An overview. 58: 125–136. F. Facchinetti, K. Demyttenaere, L. Fioroni, I. Neri, A.R. Genazzani, Psychosomatic disorders related to gynecology. 58: 137–154. U. Lamparter, H.U. Schmidt, Psychosomatic medicine and otorhinolaryngology.

61: 25–40. P. Manu, A.J. Lane, D.A. Matthews, Chronic fatigue syndromes in clinical practice. 58: 60–68. M. Biondi, A. Picardi, Temporomandibular joint pain–dysfunction syndrome and bruxism: Etiopathogenesis and treatment from a psychosomatic integration viewpoint. 59: 84–98. P. Snaith, Body image disorders. 58:119–124. J. Wilson-Barnett, Psychological reactions to medical procedures. 57: 118–127.

Treatment: J. Cottraux, Behavioral psychotherapy applications in the medically ill. 60: 116–128. N.A. Covino, F.H. Frankel, Hypnosis and relaxation in the medically ill. 60: 75–90. P.M.G. Emmelkamp, P. van Oppen, Cognitive interventions in behavioral medicine. 59: 116–130. J. Ananth, Psychopharmacological agents in physical disorders. 58: 13–31. B. Blackwell, Compliance. 58: 161–169. H. Freyberger, H.J. Freyberger, Supportive psychotherapy. 61: 132–142. B. Strauss, M. Burgmeier-Lohse, Inpatient and ward psychosomatic psychotherapy: Concepts, effectiveness, and curative factors. 59: 144–155.

Appendix: G.A. Fava, H.J. Freyberger, P. Bech, G. Christodoulou, T. Sensky, T. Theorell, T.N. Wise, Diagnostic criteria for use in psychosomatic research. 63: 1–8.

Preface

GIOVANNI A. FAVA, HELLMUTH FREYBERGER

The history of psychosomatic medicine as a reformist movement against biomedical reductionism is relatively recent (the early 1930s), despite much more ancient roots. Its official start is often ascribed to the foundation of a journal, *Psychosomatic Medicine,* in 1939 and of the American Psychosomatic Society three years later.[1] The aim of the journal was to study the interrelation of psychological and physiological aspects of all normal and abnormal bodily functions and thus to integrate somatic therapy and psychotherapy. From the very beginning, the psychosomatic movement had an international and antidogmatic connotation. Many of its supporters were "people interested in ideas in the forefront, or on the fringes, of generally accepted thought. They were adventurers and experimenters, unafraid of the untried or the unproven"[1] (p. ix).

The establishment of university departments of psychosomatic medicine in Germany in the sixties was another historical landmark, which was the harbinger of growth of consultation–liaison psychiatry in North America in the seventies and throughout Europe in the eighties.[2]

When the fundamental psychosomatic nature of a clinical problem is poorly understood—as most, if not all, interactions of biological and psychosocial factors in health and disease were—the research strategies that investigators bring to bear are strongly influenced by the prevailing climate of interest and success in the behavioral sciences.[3] Not surprisingly, the first phase of development of psychosomatic medicine (1930–1960) was largely dominated by psychoanalytic and psychophysiological approaches.

xvii

Both applications clearly derived from the success such disciplines had within psychiatry and psychology during that period and endorsed a simple, unifactorial model of pathogenesis. Such models tended to perpetuate an obsolete notion of psychogenesis—one incompatible with the doctrine of multicausality, which constitutes a core postulate of psychosomatic medicine.[4] In the early sixties, however, considerable methodological refinements took place in psychosomatic research, involving both data collection and research designs.[3] They concerned the assessment of stressful life events, illness behavior, personality, and psychological distress. Such converging developments found a suitable conceptual framework within a newly developed unified concept of health and disease,[5] later subsumed by George Engel under the rubric of biopsychosocial model. The third edition of Hill's *Modern Trends in Psychosomatic Medicine*, published in 1976, included an overview by Lipowski[6] which offered a lasting definition of psychosomatic medicine: as a science of the relationships between psychological and biological variables as they pertain to human health and disease; as an approach to the practice of medicine that advocates the inclusion of psychosocial factors in the study, prevention, diagnosis, and management of all diseases; as clinical activities at the interface of medicine and the behavioral sciences. Hill's book included chapters on areas of psychosomatic medicine which would have further developed subsequently, such as psychoneuroendocrinology, pain, eating disorders, and alexithymia. One year after, Weiner[7] published his study of six disorders (peptic ulcer, essential hypertension, bronchial asthma, Graves' disease, rheumatoid arthritis, and ulcerative colitis). On this basis he accomplished the unique, invaluable, and indispensable task of reviewing and synthesizing all of the known social, psychological, and biological facts relevant to them. In the same year a book edited by Lipowski, Lipsitt, and Whybrow,[8] based on a collection of papers, appeared in the *International Journal of Psychiatry in Medicine*, offered another appraisal of a rapidly expanding field. In the eighties, Cheren provided another update of theory, physiology, and practice of psychosomatic medicine.[9]

We thought that a reassessment of the psychosomatic field in the nineties was overdue. This was justified by further developments in the "classic" areas of psychosomatic research, as well as by the emergence of new paradigms in the eighties, such as the renaissance of psychiatric diagnosis and the rise of the neurosciences. We invited leading psychosomatic researchers to write review articles for our journal *Psychotherapy and Psychosomatics*. We are glad to present these contributions in this volume. The book, which consists of three parts, opens with the thoughts of one of the fathers of psychosomatic medicine, George Engel.

The first section deals with fundamental trends in the field (vulnerability to developmental factors and life events, somatization, illness behavior, psychosomatic syndromes, organic psychiatry, quality of life, and teaching of psychosomatic medicine).

The second section deals with clinical issues, reviewing the role of psychosocial factors in various organ systems, as well as topics such as chronic fatigue syndrome, body image disorders, and psychological reactions to medical procedures.

The third section is concerned with treatment issues and encompasses various approaches, both of psychotherapeutic and pharmacologic nature. The volume ends with an appendix which includes the new diagnostic criteria for use in psychosomatic research that have been recently proposed. In a way, the book provides the theoretical background for these developments.

This volume is not intended to be an exhaustive treatment of the vast subject of psychosomatic medicine. We simply wanted to offer an overview of recent psychosomatic research, and for reasons of length we had to decide to omit some subjects that have already been extensively written about. For instance, eating disorders are more than amply covered by a number of excellent monographs, and whilst we did not include a separate chapter on that subject, they are covered in a number of chapters, in particular the one on body image disorders.

REFERENCES

1. Levenson D. *Mind, Body, and Medicine.* Baltimore: Williams and Wilkins;1994.
2. Wise TN, Freyberger H, eds. *Consultation–Liaison Throughout the World.* Basel, Switzerland: Karger;1983.
3. Fava GA, Wise TN, eds. *Research Paradigms in Psychosomatic Medicine.* Basel, Switzerland: Karger;1987.
4. Lipowski ZJ. Psychosomatic medicine: Past and present. *Can J Psychiatry.* 1986; 31:2–7.
5. Engel GL. *Psychological Development in Health and Disease.* Philadelphia: Saunders; 1962.
6. Lipowski ZJ. Psychosomatic medicine: An overview. In: Hill OW, ed. *Modern Trends in Psychosomatic Medicine.* 3rd ed. London: Butterworths;1976.
7. Weiner H. *Psychobiology and Human Disease.* New York: Elsevier;1977.
8. Lipowski ZJ, Lipsitt DR, Whybrow PC, eds. *Psychosomatic Medicine. Current Trends and Clinical Applications.* New York: Oxford University Press;1977.
9. Cheren S. *Psychosomatic Medicine, Theory, Physiology, and Practice.* Madison, CT: International Universities Press;1989.

Chapter 1
Introduction: How Much Longer Must Medicine's Science Be Bound by a Seventeenth Century World View?

GEORGE L. ENGEL

In any consideration of a scientific model for medicine that would qualify as a successor to the biomedical model, be it the biopsychosocial or any other, the fundamental issue is whether physicians can in their study and care of patients be scientists and work scientifically in the human domain. Or is medicine's human domain beyond the reach of science and the scientific method, an art, as the biomedical model in effect requires? How that question is answered depends on one's understanding of what is meant by science and the scientific method, and even more so on the form of the scientific paradigm that guides how knowledge is pursued and solutions to problems are sought. The fundamental distinction, we insist, is not between "science" and "art" but between thinking and proceeding scientifically and not so thinking and proceeding.

This is a question with which I found myself confronted very early in my life, in childhood actually, though obviously at so tender an age I was not yet aware that a problem existed and certainly

1

not what the problem was. Let me explain. My two brothers and I were raised in the house of an uncle, Emanuel Libman (1872–1946), an eminent physician and scientist of the day. Our mother, who had undertaken to manage the household for her bachelor brother and widowed father, married late, and so it came to pass that in 1906 the Engel family became established in Libman's house, a four-story brownstone in mid-Manhattan, and that we three boys grew up in a setting dominated by Libman's professional activities. It was a scene of constant, at times frenetic, activity day and night. His office suite, including a library and laboratory, occupied the entry floor, the basement was a museum of pathology, his bedroom–living room, where he often entertained visitors, was on the fourth floor, next to our own bedrooms. Libman's fame could hardly for long remain unknown to his nephews. All three of us soon enough found ourselves preoccupied with figuring out just what it was he did and why he was so famous and sought after. Not only did his patients number noted figures of the day, but visitors who came to the house to confer with him included the major figures of medicine (and science) from all over the world, William Welch, Ludwig Aschoff, Alexis Carrel, Simon Flexner, Albert Einstein, on and on.

The family, of course, assumed we would in due course all become doctors, "like Uncle Manny." But Lewis (1909–1978) already by the time he was 10 or 11 insisted otherwise. He would become a scientist, not a doctor. And indeed he did, singlemindedly devoting himself to chemistry, beginning with Chemcraft sets in a makeshift basement laboratory, his younger brothers serving as assistants. The bulk of his career was spent at the Harvard Medical School as an American Cancer Society Professor of Biological Chemistry and finally as chairman. My twin Frank (1913–1963) and I, however, vacillated. We read voraciously about science and scientists, medical and otherwise. Lew and his fellow graduate students in biochemistry teased us mercilessly for even considering so unscientific a life's work as that of a doctor. Yet here was Libman, renowned the world over as a clinician, possessed of extraordinary clinical skills and diagnostic acumen. But his scientific reputation rested not on that but on his work in the pathology and bacteriology laboratories. At the bedside he was the wizard, capable of astonishing diagnostic feats, at least according to family legend. In time I learned how often these were verified at postmortem, which at least lent to the family folklore a measure of credibility.

But why were these accomplishments with patients any less "scientific" than what he was doing in the laboratory? Frank and I used to puzzle over this together, but the answer eluded us. Both of us as early as 19 had begun working summers at the Marine Biological Laboratory at Woods Hole, Massachusetts. There we learned first-hand how to proceed scientifically in the laboratory.[1-3] There surely must be the answer, to exercise the same care to be accurate, thorough, reliable, relevant, and comprehensible with patients as we had learned to do when working in the laboratory. And so we proceeded to do; and when we reached the clinical years, it paid off handsomely. Already by our fourth year at Johns Hopkins, we had both earned the respect of our instructors for our not inconsiderable clinical skill and diagnostic acumen. Evidently Flexner's confidence in the laboratory as adequate preparation for a scientific approach at the bedside was sound after all.

And there the matter may have rested had it not happened, entirely by chance, that in 1941 I became involved in a research project on delirium with psychiatrist John Romano, the upshot of which was that I was over the next several years introduced not just to the human psychosocial dimensions of medicine, but even more importantly to what constituted the primary data of that realm and how to gain access thereto. The key proved to be a human relationship with dialogue the medium, and the interview, the scientific instrument for investigation of the human realm. Indeed, in my view, the interview is the most powerful, encompassing, sensitive, and versatile instrument available to the physician and serves many different purposes. Yet none of us ever had any instruction in its use, much less in its underlying principles. From that time on my whole outlook, professional and scientific, was never again to be the same. The human dimensions of medicine had for me at last become accessible to scientific inquiry, just as had the heavens by the invention of the telescope. One could be scientific at the bedside after all!

To learn how this could be, we must first return to the question of what science is and what it means to be scientific. We begin with Charles Odegaard's[4] definition: "Science represents man's most persistent effort to extend and organize knowledge by reasoned efforts that ultimately depend on evidence that can be consensually validated." Note that this definition places no limits on what phenomena may be the subject of scientific inquiry.

The scientific method is complete in the sense that there do not exist phenomena in nature which, in principle, cannot be examined by application of the scientific method of valid data accumulation and verification.[5]

Advances in science depend on developing means and techniques of inquiry that are appropriate for the phenomena under investigation and the conditions and circumstances under which such can be studied. Viruses are not to be studied with the naked eye at absolute zero. By the same token scientific study of human phenomena requires human means and human circumstances.

What is meant by scientific "paradigm" or "model"? Paradigms are constituted from the concepts, assumptions, and rules that guide workers in their pursuit of knowledge and the solution of problems in a given field. Paradigms gain status to the extent that they are successful in solving problems, and they lose status as paradoxes multiply.[6]

Paradigms powerfully influence what scientists select to study and how they go about doing so. The paradigm acts subtly both as a value judgment and as a motivator to proceed in one way or another. Scientists are not necessarily fully aware of the paradigm they are using and how it may influence their judgments and motivation. Paradigms that become part of the scientist's cultural background risk becoming dogma. Kuhn[6] captures the power of paradigms in the following: "The proponents of competing paradigms . . . see different things when they look from the same point in the same direction . . . what cannot even be demonstrated to one group of scientists may seem intuitively obvious to another."

This statement exemplifies the conflict confronted by medicine over the past three centuries. While hardly anyone disputes the extent to which medicine is "concerned with all the various aspects of man's humanness," as René Dubos[7] so aptly put it, medicine's adherence to a 17th century paradigm predicated on the mechanism, reductionism, determinism, and dualism of Newton and Descartes automatically excludes what is distinctively human from the realm of science and the scientific.

The 17th century paradigm is a system of thought in which scientists as objective observers are to regard nature as independent from themselves and unaffected by their act of observation. Developed as an approach to nature as it surrounds man, such a paradigm provides no means to accommodate human processes, and never was intended to. In medicine this has become entrenched in the biomedical view that what is human about medicine and its practice constitutes but an art. Accordingly, the physician has come to be seen as operating scientifically and medicine judged to be properly scientific only when dealing with bodily processes, not when dealing with patients as people.

Yet for almost a century the classical model of physics on which such a way of thinking is based has increasingly been undermined. In the course of the development of relativity theory and quantum mechanics, physics has been obliged to reintroduce the human being into the scientific equation.[8-11] Pure objectivity and total detachment of the investigator from his material no longer constitute inviolable criteria for what is to be accepted as science or scientific, not even ideally. The influence of the investigator has become a factor to be reckoned with, not one that can ever be completely corrected for. Thus relativity theory was formulated around the notion of an observer, while quantum mechanics promoted the observer to a participator who in the very process of investigating affects the outcome of his observations. The scientist and the object of his investigation, it turns out, are not separable precisely because every observational act in itself embodies an element of subjectivity, namely, the observer's decisions as to what to observe and how.[8] The new physics not only shatters the illusion of the scientist as totally detached, it also documents the interconnectedness and interdependence of all levels of organization of natural systems.

The fundamental contrast between the 17th and 20th century paradigms goes well beyond the old philosophic controversy between "realism" and "idealism." Though derivative from experimental studies in physics, the 20th century paradigm in fact establishes the indispensability of including what is human in the explanatory system; it acknowledges that science is a human activity, and that what the scientist does cannot be separated from what is being inquired into. Let us contrast the 17th and 20th century paradigms in a schematized and obviously oversimplified way. The 17th century paradigm (Newton, Descartes): What is being studied exists external to and independent of the scientist, who discovers and characterizes its properties and behavior. This is the essence of the objectivity that is required if one is to be considered a scientist.

Nobelist chemist Marie Curie[12] early in this century left no doubt what she considered to be the scope of science. "Science deals with things not people," she bluntly put it. And of course she was correct. The science she knew never was intended to encompass human affairs—and it doesn't! That is precisely the issue confronting medicine and which medicine has yet to face.

In contrast, let us consider the changes in our understanding of science wrought in the 20th century. The 20th century paradigm (Einstein, Heisenberg): "What is being studied is inseparable from the scientist, who devises mental constructs of his/her experiences with it as a means of characterizing his/her understanding of its properties and behavior."[8]

In this view scientists are not studying a world external to themselves but rather those particular interactions taking place at the moment between themselves and the phenomena in question and under whatever conditions they are being studied. Heisenberg[13] put it: "What we observe is not nature itself, but the interplay between nature and ourselves; science describes nature as exposed to our way of questioning." Delbruck[8] acknowledged the irony of this discovery:

The observational act is a unitary deed of which our choice is an active subjective component . . . in the drama of existence we play the dual rule of actor and observer! How bizarre . . . that this realization, . . . so antithetical to the conceptual foundations of science, should be forced upon us by atomic physics.

Actually this is nothing new for clinicians working with patients. We have always been aware of the difficulty of defining objectively what we are learning from our patients and of doing so independently of the subjective means we employ for our observations. Rather than dismissing such an approach as outside of science, it now appears that the same limitation holds for all of science; it does not constitute a criterion whereby the scientific is to be differentiated from the nonscientific.

Seen from this perspective, the clinical encounter, which defines the conditions and setting in which scientific work with patients proceeds, constitutes not an obstacle to objectivity, but rather another mode of data collection, one the consistency and reliability of which can be perfected once it is recognized wherein the scientific study of one person by another differs from the study of nonhuman material or phenomena. In the latter, be the material an enzyme, organ, or an experimental animal, it is acted on and reacts to the investigator, but itself can neither initiate nor control the process of investigation, much less give an account thereof. The human subject can do all of these and in so doing not only becomes an active participator in his own study, but also provides access to an inner world of experience not possible in lower forms of life. Accordingly, in the clinical setting the scientific effort actually becomes a joint undertaking to be negotiated between physician and patient (or surrogate), one which requires the physician as scientist to be operating concurrently in two modes, one observational, the other relational.

The two modes address quite different categories of data and with different criteria. The observational mode is suited for phenomena that can be observed with the senses (or extensions thereof), e.g., the color of the skin, manifest behavior, heart rate, or level of serum bilirubin. These are the classical data of empirico-analytic inquiry, often capable of precise mensuration as well as accurate description, which, if necessary, can be ascertained without the patient's active participation.

In contrast, a relational mode is required to deal with data in the uniquely human realm of articulated language, symbols, thoughts, and feelings by means of which what we privately experience is organized and communicated and relationships established and managed. In this mode dialogue serves to clarify the meaning and verify the information that is being reported.[14] It is through dialogue that the physician learns the nature and history of the patient's experiences and clarifies on the one hand what they mean for the patient, and on the other, what they might mean in terms of other systems of the natural hierarchy, be they biochemical and physiological, or psychological and social. This is the process of clinical reasoning. It is a mode in which clarification of meaning and of establishment of veracity take precedence over measurement.

By tradition the observational mode, as represented by the empirico-analytic approach, is accorded scientific status, while the relational mode, as dialogue, is not. Yet in clinical practice the physician always operates in both modes at the same time, making observations while engaging in dialogue and vice versa. The two processes thus not only are complementary and supplementary with respect to the results achieved, they are also interdependent in operation. Information being obtained in one mode may not be accessible in the other but may be clarified, elaborated, verified, or refuted by access to the other mode, sometimes simultaneously. Anxiety verbally denied may be verified by demonstrating tachycardia and cold sweaty hands. The meaning of "OK" in response to "How are you?" may be questioned if a gesture of helplessness is observed to accompany it. A patient's report of "palpitation" may be elaborated through direct examination or electronic recordings. Accordingly, the two modes constitute not alternative, but a single integrated means for data disclosure, clarification, and interpretation in the clinical realm. Rather than a combination of one scientific and one nonscientific (or unscientific) approach, they represent a single approach that has evolved logically out of the historical fact that inquiry into the nature of illness and patienthood has always had to depend both on what the patient can communicate verbally and nonverbally and on what the physician can observe.[15–18] Only the constraints of the classical 17th century paradigm exclude the relational from the category of the scientific, as Marie Curie[12] so bluntly informed us.

Dialogue is in fact the only means whereby the patient can acquaint the physician with those inner experiences which had led him to consider himself ill in the first place, and therefore to solicit medical help. By the same token dialogue enables the physician to reconstruct with the patient a plausible sequence of events ("history") from which hypotheses may be developed, which in turn may be explored by further dialogue as well as by other means. As every clinician well knows, the reasoning process (clinical reasoning) proceeds actively and concurrently with the data collecting procedures of observation and dialogue, not seriatim as more commonly is the case with laboratory experiments. As an integral component of the process whereby the clinician gains knowledge of the patient's condition, it is thus clear that *dialogue is truly foundational to scientific work in the clinical realm.*

Once the foundational character of dialogue is acknowledged, the essential complementarity of the human and the scientific premised by the 20th century paradigm becomes apparent. This is inherent in the fact that dialogue as a means of data collection and processing is itself regulated by conditions that determine human relationships. Accordingly, completeness and accuracy of the data are correspondingly enhanced by optimizing those human circumstances which are most likely to facilitate dialogue. The physician has no alternative but to behave in a humane and empathic manner, i.e., to understand and be understanding, if the patient is to be enabled to report clearly and fully, only then can the physician proceed scientifically. To be humane and empathic is not merely a prescription for compassion, as medical educators would like us to believe; it is a requirement for scientific work in the clinical realm.

Biomedicine's rejection of dialogue as a genuinely scientific means of data collection is evident in the neglect of instruction and supervision in interviewing, not to mention in clinical data collection altogether, and in the preference for the case presentation as a method of clinical teaching, one in which students may display their ability to organize and discuss findings, but not reveal the methods and skills whereby they had come by the data in the first place, least of all their interpersonal engagement with the patient.[19-23] Such pervasive inattention to the conditions and requirements for reliable data collection in itself constitutes nothing less than an antiscientific attitude.

The paradox is apparent. Physician and patient alike would agree, that the judgments, decisions, and recommendations made by physicians as far as possible should be based on demonstrated scientific principles and on evidence, i.e., on data that are accurate, complete, and obtained through methods of demonstrated reliability. Reliance on the 17th century paradigm, however, excludes from that requirement information that is only accessible through the medium of human exchange on the grounds that it is "subjective" and by inference thereby "inherently unreliable." In a current journal appears a typical example of dialogue bypassed in favor of direct recourse to diagnostic procedures. The following are direct quotations, but the emphasis is added:

We describe a condition—"liqueur lung"—in which hemoptysis was produced by the aspiration of Bucca . . .

A 22-year-old healthy nonsmoking man presented after coughing up a cup of bright-red blood. *The initial history and physical examination were unrevealing.* A chest roentgenogram, arterial blood gas levels, the complete blood count, indexes of coagulation, the platelet count, and the blood urea nitrogen concentration were all normal.

Bronchoscopy with a flexible fiberoptic instrument was performed within 24 h, since the hemoptysis totaled 75 ml of blood. The trachea and right mainstem bronchus were erythematous and friable and contained a small quantity of fresh blood. No infectious organisms or neoplastic cells were found in the tracheobronchial specimens submitted for analysis. *The bronchoscopic findings prompted additional questioning of the patient.* He revealed that he had experienced a coughing paroxysm the previous evening. He had been at a party and had "guzzled from a bottle of Bucca." While drinking in this manner he began to choke and cough repeatedly. A few hours later, frank hemoptysis began.[24]

"The initial history [was] unrevealing!" There may have been some unusual extenuating circumstance accounting for the failure to learn of the aspiration on first contact with this man, but in my experience it is more likely accounted for by the physician's low valuation of what patients have to report coupled with lack of skill in eliciting information in the first place.

Similar disregard for the applicability of a scientific approach is revealed by the resident who upon coming to the bedside of a new patient in the emergency room immediately requested the three visitors clustering around the bed to leave.* Queried on what she had based such a decision, she could only respond that such was customary; at least so she had been led to believe by her mentors. She had never before seriously considered systematically examining its rationale. In that realm her otherwise well-practiced "inquiring and scientific mind" simply was not operative.[25]

And what about the medical grand rounds patient applauded by the audience for his good fortune at having been in the emergency room rather than still on the street when his cardiac arrest occurred? Only the medical student, whose earlier tape-recorded interview I listened to, had learned how tremendously upset the man had become when the housestaff, failing in their effort to insert an arterial line, had left him alone in the cubicle; the arrest occurred a few minutes later.[26] At the rounds it was the student who voiced curiosity about the possibility of a connection between the man's emotional state and the arrest; no one else did.[27] Here an "inquiring scientific mind" was at work, and that because this student had a scientific model in mind which facilitated his access to the data from which such a question could logically be framed.

To appreciate relationship and dialogue as requirements for scientific study in the clinical setting highlights the natural confluence of the human and the scientific in the clinical encounter

---

* In my teaching rounds how the student or resident engages with the patient is an integral and indispensable part of the exercise. To facilitate that process, we do not rely on the usual case presentation method. The person who knows the patient acts as a resource, responding to questions, but not otherwise participating. The rest of the group, including the faculty member, are to know nothing in advance about the patient. The exercise begins with one member demonstrating for all of us for 5 to 10 minutes how he or she initiates and pursues contact with a patient totally unknown and being seen for the first time.[21]

itself. It is not just that science is a human activity, it is also that the interpersonal engagement required in the clinical realm rests on complementary and basic human needs, especially the *need to know and understand* and *the need to feel known and understood.* The first, to know and understand, obviously is a dimension of being scientific; the second, to feel known and understood, is a dimension of caring and being cared for. Both may be seen as derivative and emergent from biological processes critical for survival in the phylogenetic as well as ontogenetic senses. The need to know and understand originates in the regulatory and self-organizing capabilities of all living organisms to process information from an ever-changing environment in order to assure growth, development, self-regulation, adjustment, and survival.[28] In turn, the need to feel known and understood originates, in man at least, in the transition from the biological mutuality of intrauterine life to the social mutuality of neonatal life that inaugurates the corresponding life-long need to feel socially connected with other humans. In the course of development fulfillment of both needs comes in a complementary fashion to equate with a personal sense of confidence, security, and belonging. The need to know and to understand ultimately achieves its most advanced development in the disciplined curiosity that characterizes scientific thinking. The need to feel known and understood manifests itself in the continuity of human relationships and in the social complementarity between perceived helplessness and the urge to help. Herein then converge the scientific and the caring (samaritan, pastoral) roles of the physician.

Falling ill typically involves for the patient a disruption in that unique continuity of knowing and understanding and of feeling known and understood that ordinarily characterizes health and well-being. Typically a patient comes for help because he is experiencing something strange, different, discomforting, or disabling which he does not understand and/or does not know how or feel able to handle by himself. At the same time he believes, or hopes, the doctor does understand and does know how to handle the situation. The largest part of what the patient feels disturbed by is known only to himself and will remain so unless and until communicated. Two considerations loom large in the patient's decision to share such information and to entrust himself and his care to a physician. The first is confidence that the physician is competent; the second is the expectation, or at least the hope, that the physician will be understanding and that he, the patient, will feel understood. Thereby is the patient motivated to relinquish autonomy and share privacy, often to a degree greater than may be true of almost any other human relationship.

For the patient, to feel understood by the physician means more than just feeling that the physician understands intellectually, that is, "comprehends," what the patient is reporting and what may be wrong, critical as these are for the physician's scientific task.[29] Every bit as important is it that the physician display understanding about the patient as a person, as a fellow human being, and about what he is experiencing and what the circumstances of his life are. "Do my doctors know who I am, who I have been, who I still want to be? Do they understand what I am going through, my suffering, my pain, my distress? Do they understand my hopes and aspirations, my fears and shames, my vulnerabilities and strengths, my needs and obligations and my values? Above all, do they sense my personhood and my individuality? Do they acknowledge my humanity? Do they care?"

The physician's need to know and understand at first glance may seem more exclusively cognitive. But while scientific understanding does mean getting all the facts and getting them straight, every bit as important is for the physician to display that human understanding which is so necessary if the patient is to feel understood. Again, the two are complementary. For when expression of human understanding on the part of the physician is not forthcoming and the patient does not feel understood, then trust and confidence may be impaired and with it the patient's capacity and willingness to collaborate—critical if the physician's scientific aims are to be accomplished.

Let me illustrate these principles with an experience I once had as a visiting professor asked to conduct a medical grand rounds. My aim was to demonstrate the requirements for a scientific approach to a patient with and about whom I had no prior relationship or knowledge. The setting was a large amphitheater on the stage of which I was to work with the patient.

The patient, a man in his mid-40s, arrived in a wheelchair. After an introduction by the resident, I first asked whether the exercise had been explained to him. He at once angrily complained that not only had no one explained the exercise, he had been left unattended in a cold drafty corridor outside the auditorium; altogether no one seemed to care what happened to him. To my awkward efforts at commiseration and apology, he broke eye contact and turned away. He shrugged indifferently when I asked if he would be willing to tell the doctors something about the illness. My "How have you been feeling?" evoked a sarcastic "How would you feel?" We were already at an impasse.

For me to establish my role with him as samaritan, to say nothing of my role as scientist, would require us first somehow to touch one another's individuality, to meet each other as fellow beings. As the physician, the task was mine, not his, and the instrumentality would be dialogue. Only through the give and take of dialogue could we begin to take a measure of each other. Under the circumstances in which we found ourselves, inquiry about his illness seemed the most appropriate entree, awkward as that was.

And as I had anticipated, his initial responses were laconic and limited to symptoms; he said virtually nothing about himself. To try to broaden our engagement beyond those narrow confines, I repeatedly interjected into his bare symptom reporting such questions as, "Where were you when that happened?" "What were you doing?" "Who else was there?" Bit by bit he began to add a few personal details. Then, quite unexpectedly one particular item caught my attention. A vegetable garden! It was while tending a vegetable garden that he first developed chest pain. Here at last was something uniquely personal. Surely having a vegetable garden in the midst of the squalor and congestion of the urban ghetto where he lived must say something of the man behind the angry facade. My curiosity and surprise were genuine, and he must have felt it, for he at once responded to my echoing query, "You were gardening?" with a willingness to elaborate which had not been evident until then. In surprisingly few minutes quite another human being began to emerge, a man with a life story all his own.

Now I was getting to know a former migrant field worker who had successfully established himself as an auto worker in Detroit, only to lose his job in the recession after almost a dozen years of steady employment. Health insurance lapsed, savings melted away, his home and car were repossessed, and his wife and his children finally went back South to her parents' farm. He remained behind still hoping for reemployment, living alone in a rooming house. The garden he had scratched out of the rubble of a vacant lot was one last effort to sustain his image of himself as self-sufficient and responsible. Falling ill and being hospitalized in a large public hospital was the last blow.

As this story began to emerge, we all moved closer, the patient and I and the grand rounds audience, drawn together by shared feelings of despair and concern, pride and admiration, anger and frustration, until all was silence but for the patient's now soft but engaging voice and my occasional sound or word of concern or encouragement. Finally he fell silent, his head lowered, eye contact broken, the upper lid line angled, his eyes moist, his hands resting motionless on his thighs. I knew he was close to tears. Hardly aware of it, I had already pulled my chair closer to his. I placed my hand on his and, squeezing it gently, said softly, "It's been a tough time for you, hasn't it?" At once tears formed. Still silent, he wiped them away with the tissue I had offered him. Then with a faintly apologetic smile, he raised and let fall his hand in the gesture of helplessness, adding "What else could I do?" I nodded and said nothing. Nothing needed to be said. We both now knew we understood each other. After but a brief pause we resumed the exploration of his illness. In short order, I could be confident that I had all the pertinent facts about his illness and about himself and his circumstances to justify the presumptive diagnosis of myocardial infarction and to consider plans for his further study and care. Most of all mutual confidence and trust had been established between us. Yet our total acquaintanceship had spanned but 18 minutes. When I reluctantly brought the interview to a close, we shook hands. This time it was he who squeezed my hand. "Thank you, doctor," he said, though surely he knew we would never meet again.

In this example the requirement to be human in order to be scientific is evident at many levels. In my role as scientist merely the exercise of an inquiring scientific mind would not be enough. I had also to make possible the conditions without which my inquiring scientific mind could not have access to the material required for my task; that is, I had to promote a productive dialogue. To gain access I had also to establish myself in the samaritan role. Through behavior alone I had to achieve in a few minutes, and with a complete stranger, and a hostile one at that, the mutuality of understanding necessary if one person is to entrust life and well-being to another. But my ability to do so was not merely a matter of intuition, common sense, and experience, important as these may be. Quite to the contrary, it rested on a body of knowledge and a set of principles about human behavior and relationships arrived at through systematic inquiry; that is, scientifically.

To illustrate such application of scientific thinking in the human domain, let us focus on the 2 or 3 minutes which culminated in the patient's crying. During the first minutes of our meeting, he hardly impressed me as a man likely to cry. But once he began his litany of losses and frustrations, crying became not just a possibility, but a possibility the risks and benefits of which I had to weigh. On the one hand, crying and being comforted by me could facilitate my goal of engendering a feeling of understanding between us; on the other, it might evoke shame and embarrassment, even anger and loss of control, especially for this man in the public glare of teaching rounds. In addition, I also had to keep in mind possible medical contraindications to crying, as might occur had the patient just had eye surgery, for example. Thus even the task of establishing myself in the samaritan role itself called for a scientific approach. It would not do for me simply to rely on my own impulses or intuitions. My judgments as to whether I should encourage or inhibit his crying had to be based on evidence reliably elicited and on knowledge and principles scientifically arrived at; not only that, the decision had to be reached while a choice was still possible. How did I do so?

First, while actively engaging in dialogue, I was at the same time monitoring the likelihood of his crying. This I did by paying attention to signs known to presage crying, such as facial expressions (e.g., angling of the upper lid), gestures (e.g., helplessness), body movements and positions (e.g., sagging of his shoulders), behaviors (e.g., bringing a finger to his eye), and what he was having to say and how (e.g., sad content, a "catch" in his voice).[30-35]

Second, I watched and listened for indications of physical and emotional movement toward or away from me, as sustaining or breaking eye contact, inclining his body toward or away from me, or sharing or withholding intimacies.

Third, I noted his responses to my behavior, as when I moved closer, spoke more softly, or indicated sympathy with his plight. All of these each of us knows more or less intuitively, but we are not necessarily aware that we know, or what it is we know, which informs us that crying may be imminent. Here the scientific process involves examining and analyzing the intuitive, establishing its validity through means the reliability of which can be assayed, and deriving principles the generalizability of which can be tested by other means and/or by other investigators.

Einstein once characterized science as "nothing more than a refinement of everyday thinking."[36] Wherein was my approach here any more scientific than how I might have behaved in everyday life? What is perhaps most obvious is that not only was I prepared in my mind for the possibility that the patient might cry—patients do cry, after all, even those least expected to—I also had an agenda covering what issues might need to be addressed in his case were crying to loom as a possibility; and I had a design in mind for how to do so.

Further, from information derived from scientific study I had learned reliable signs whereby to monitor with minimal, even subliminal, attention to the prospects of his crying. Such cognitive monitoring is one of the refinements Einstein alluded to, namely the establishment and use of uniform and agreed upon criteria to identify and characterize natural phenomena. By recourse to such a taxonomy of crying, in addition to my own intuitive sensitivity,[31] I was able to track this man's progress toward crying at the same time I was processing the data which would determine whether I should try to encourage him to cry or whether I should try to forestall it, also a process for which criteria exist. In so proceeding, I remained fully conscious of and deliberately attentive to the collaborative nature of my work with the patient; I was not simply being a cold, detached observer of another's distress. Nor was I distracted from our overall agenda by the necessity to address his distress. On the contrary, I used my human inclination to assuage distress as a means to forge ties with the patient and to engender thereby the mutual understanding required for the patient and me together to pursue our emerging scientific agenda.

We have defined science in its broadest historical sense as man's most persistent effort to extend and organize knowledge by reasoned efforts that ultimately depend on evidence that can be consensually validated.[4, 37, 38] Note that this characterization of science—and scientific—is independent of any particular paradigm. Paradigms by their very nature serve to create a frame of mind receptive to answering some questions and sanctioning certain methods while discouraging and ruling out others. Often operating as silent assumptions taken fully for granted, we have seen how in medicine's adherence to the 17th century paradigm of physics has in the clinical realm actually engendered attitudes that are antiscientific and behaviors that are unscientific. Science and being scientific have increasingly come to be defined in terms of that paradigm. As a result, the human realm either has been excluded from accessibility to scientific inquiry or the scientific approach to human phenomena has been required to conform to the reductionistic, mechanistic, dualistic predicates of the biomedical paradigm. To do so constitutes misapplication of that paradigm.[39] What the advocates of the universality of the biomedical model have failed to appreciate is that, like its 17th century counterpart in classical physics, the biomedical model represents a limiting case the utility of which is in no way diminished as long as its use is restricted to the phenomena for which it was designed. The biomedical model needs no defense, neither with respect to its past accomplishments nor to its future utility, as long as that rule is applied. But to do otherwise is to be *unscientific*; to advocate doing otherwise is to promote dogma and become *antiscientific*. To become more fully scientific, medicine requires a paradigm capable of encompassing the human domain. The 20th century paradigm of physics assumes the human dimension as a given for all scientific endeavor and in that sense eliminates an obstacle to paradigm development in medicine. As Einstein poetically expressed it, the relationship of the successor paradigm, whether called systems or biopsychosocial, with its predecessor, the biomedical, depends on accepting the latter's limitations:

> Creating a new theory (paradigm) is not like destroying an old barn and erecting a skyscraper in its place. It is rather like climbing a mountain, gaining new and wider views, . . . but the point from which we started out still exists and can be seen, although it appears smaller and forms a tiny part of our broad view gained . . . on our way up.
>
> From the new theory it is clear in which cases classical physics is valid and wherein its limitations lie.[40]

CONCLUSIONS

(1) The biomedical model, like the model of classical physics, represents a limiting case; it cannot be used as a criterion for science (or "scientific") in medicine. (2) Application of the biomedical model outside its limits is unscientific; advocacy of such application promotes dogma and is antiscientific. (3) Scientific medicine requires a paradigm capable of encompassing the human domain. The 20th century paradigm of physics assumes the human dimension as a given for all scientific endeavor and hence meets that requirement for paradigm development in medicine. (4) The general systems theory derived biopsychosocial model and the more fully articulated infomedical model of Foss and Rothenberg[45] are promising candidates for successor paradigms to the biomedical model.[26, 41–44]

REFERENCES

1. Engel GL, Chao I. The comparative distribution of organic phosphorus compounds in the cardiac and striated muscles of limulus polyphemus. *J Biol Chem.* 1935;108:389–393.
2. Engel GL, Gerard RW. The phosphorus metabolism of invertebrate nerve. *J Biol Chem.* 1935;112:379–392.
3. Webster MD, Engel FL, Lang EP, Amberson WR. The influence of pH upon the elimination of hemoglobin by the perfused frog's kidney. *J Cell Comp Physiol.* 1934;5:399–412.
4. Odegaard CE. *Dear Doctor. A Personal Letter to a Physician.* Menlo Park, CA: Henry J Kaiser Family Foundation; 1986.
5. Zimmerman DW. A note on the completeness of the scientific method. *Psychol Rec.* 1984;34:175–179.
6. Kuhn TS. *The Structure of Scientific Revolutions.* 2nd ed. Chicago: University of Chicago Press; 1970: p 159.
7. Dubos R. Hippocrates in modern dress. *Proc Inst Med, Chicago.* 1965;25:242–251.
8. Delbruck M. *Mind from Matter? An Essay on Evolutionary Epistemology.* Palo Alto, CA: Blackwell Scientific; 1986: p 289.
9. Comfort A. On physics and biology. Getting our act together. *Perspect Biol Med.* 1985;29:1–9.
10. Bernstein J. John Archibald Wheeler. *Johns Hopkins Mag.* 1985;37:(5)23–33.
11. Morowitz HJ. Myasthenia gravis and arrows of fortune. *Hosp Pract.* 1986;21:(3)179–192.
12. Curie M. Cited by: Goodfield J: Humanity in science: A perspective and a plea. *Science.* 1977;198:580–585.
13. Heisenberg W. *Physics and Philosophy, the Revolution in Modern Science.* New York: Harper;1958: p 81.
14. Wiggins OP, Schwartz MA. Techniques and persons. Habermasean reflections on medical ethics. *Hum Stud.* 1986;9:365–377.
15. Engel GL. Clinical observation. The neglected basic method of medicine. *JAMA.* 1965;192:842–852.
16. Engel GL. Enduring attributes of medicine relevant to the education of the physician. *Ann Intern Med.* 1973;78:587–593.
17. Engel GL. Commentary on Schwartz & Wiggins: Science, humanism and the nature of medical practice. *Perspect Biol Med.* 1985;28:362–365.
18. Reiser SJ. *Medicine and the Reign of Technology.* Cambridge, U.K.: Cambridge University Press; 1978.
19. Reichsman F, Browning FE, Hinshaw JR. Observation of undergraduate clinical teaching in action. *J Med Educ.* 1964;39:147–163.
20. Payson HE, Barchas JD. A time study of medical teaching rounds. *N Engl J Med.* 1965;273:1468–1471.
21. Engel GL. Some limitations of the case presentation method for clinical teaching. An alternative approach. *N Engl J Med.* 1971;284:20–24.
22. Engel GL. Are medical schools neglecting clinical skills? *JAMA.* 1976;236:861–863.

23. Shankel SW, Mazzaferri EL. Teaching the resident in internal medicine. Present practices and suggestions for the future. *JAMA*. 1986;256:725–729.
24. Conetta R, Tamarin FM, Wogalter D, Brandstetter RD. Liqueur lung. *N Engl J Med*. 1987;316:348–349.
25. Engel GL. Physician-scientists and scientific physicians: Resolving the humanism-science dichotomy. *Am J Med*. 1987;82:107–111.
26. Engel GL. The clinical application of the biopsychosocial model. *Am J Psychiatry*. 1980;137:535–544.
27. Engel GL. Sudden and rapid death during psychological stress. Folklore or folk wisdom? *Ann Intern Med*. 1971;74:771–782.
28. Riedl R. *Biology and Knowledge. The Evolutionary Bases of Reason*. New York: Wiley;1984.
29. Evans DA, Block MR, Steinberg ER, Penrose AM. Frames and heuristics in doctor–patient discourse. *Soc Sci Med*. 1986;22:1027–1034.
30. Engel GL. The care of the patient: Art or science? *Johns Hopkins Med J*. 1977; 140:222–232.
31. Engel GL. Signs of giving up. In Troup SB, Greene WA, eds. *The Patient, Death and the Family*. New York: Scribner's;1974: pp 43–69.
32. Darwin C. *The Expression of the Emotions in Man and Animals* (1872). New York: Appleton;1896.
33. Schmale AH. Needs, gratifications and the vicissitudes of the self-representation. A developmental concept of psychic object relationships. *Psychoanal Study Soc*. 1962;2:9–41.
34. Schmale AH, Tinling D, Eby L. Experimental induction of affects. *Acta Med Psychosom*. 1967;1:1–8.
35. Engel GL. Grief and grieving. *Am J Nursing*. 1964;64:93–98.
36. Einstein A. *Out of My Later Years*. New York: Philosophical Library;1950, p 59.
37. Flexner A. *Medical Education. A Comparative Study*. New York: Macmillan;1925.
38. Harrison AS. Common elements and interconnections. *Science*. 1984;224:939–942.
39. Engel GL. Misapplication of a scientific paradigm. *Integra Psychiatry*. 1985;3:9–11.
40. Einstein A, Infeld L. *The Evolution of Physics*. New York: Simon & Schuster;1938, p 159.
41. Brody H. The systems view of man: Implications for medicine, science and ethics. *Perspect Biol Med*. 1978;17;71–92.
42. Engel GL. The need for a new medical model: A challenge for biomedicine. *Science*. 1977;196:129–136.
43. Engel GL. The biopsychosocial model and the education of health professionals. *Ann NY Acad Sci*. 1978;310:169–181.
44. Schwartz MA, Wiggins OP. Systems and the structuring of meaning: Contributions to a biopsychosocial medicine. *Am J Psychiatry*. 1986;143:1213–1221.
45. Foss L, Rothenberg K. *The Second Medical Revolution. From Biomedicine to Infomedicine*. Boston: Shambhala/New Science Library;1987.

Part I

Fundamental Issues

Chapter 2
Critical Life Changes:
A Review of Research

TÖRES THEORELL

In the present review, my goal is not to give a comprehensive description of all life event research that has been published in the literature but rather to describe approaches and general ideas in the field. For instance, I will not cover all kinds of illnesses systematically. My own interests have been primarily in cardiovascular illness.

TWO TRADITIONS

Systematic research on distressing life changes has been going on since the 1950s. The interest in life change research increased dramatically when Holmes and Rahe[1] published their "schedule of recent experiences" in 1967. This was an effort to produce weights given to different life events by the average person in the normal population. Such weights have subsequently been used in the study of associations between life events and illnesses as well as between life events and physiological reactions. During later years, however, research on life events has been developing according to two contrasting traditions.

1. The first of these two traditions is a sociological one which emphasizes the characteristics of the event itself and the conditions under which it occurs. According to Brown et al. who represent this tradition,[2] it is very important to know the circumstances. For instance, the death of a spouse is a very different matter for a person who has experienced the spouse's suffering during a long-lasting chronic illness as compared to a person whose spouse dies suddenly and unexpectedly. A pregnancy is a very different event for a woman who wants a baby and who lives under good social circumstances with a husband, as compared to a woman who did not expect a baby and who lives alone under poor economic conditions.

In order to explore the environmental impact of an event, one has to do a thorough interview regarding the context. Only after such an interview, does it become possible to judge the importance in terms of the threat that the event may impose. The person's perception of the change is not important, however.

2. A psychological tradition which emphasizes the perception that the individual has of the life change. According to this tradition, the life change does not have any importance in itself. It is only the individual's appraisal of and attitude to the change that is important. The individual himself is asked to rate the possibility to control the change and to anticipate it in advance, desirability, gain/loss, and exit/entrance.[3]

If we want to decide which life changes are distressing enough to merit our interest in the clinical situation, it is not sufficient to pay attention either to the event itself or to the individual appraisal of or attitude to it.

If we disregard the individual and decide to start a program for increased support during distressing life changes, and define the life change situations that we should work with only on the basis of the characteristics of the event, we may start supporting people who do not need support. Or conversely, for a few very sensitive persons even life changes that seem completely trivial to others may elicit serious illness episodes such as schizophrenia, and these people may need our support.

On the other hand, if we disregard the characteristics of the event and only listen to the person's way of describing his reactions to it, we may face the difficulty that some persons deny the importance of certain events, and this denial could be associated with increased risk of illness in itself. Or conversely, we may run the risk that the description is distorted by a tendency to exaggerate that may not be associated with illness. As a consequence, we may support someone who does not need the support. Another unwanted consequence of such an individual-oriented approach is that there could be unlimited acceptance of extremely bad circumstances, leading to a situation where people are taught to accept any type of terrible situation.

During periods of calm and peace, a society may have time to organize support for its citizens. Sweden has been in this situation for many years, which in part may explain why there has been considerable interest in developing supportive structures to improve the livelihood of people surviving difficult life change situations. In such a climate the sociological tradition becomes important, and it was also during such periods and societal circumstances that measuring and characterizing the life changes themselves began (the sociological tradition).

During times of crisis and war, when large numbers of people are exposed to markedly threatening life conditions, the individual may feel that his own way of coping with distressing life changes is the only relevant factor. It was exactly in such a climate that the scientific interest in coping with difficulties arose. This is when a military psychologist in Israel, Ben Shalit,[4] created his coping wheel for measuring coping style and predicting successful performance among soldiers in the Arab–Israeli wars of the 1960s. And this is the condition that created the interest in sense of coherence in Aaron Antonovsky when he had studied the long-term consequences of having survived a period in a concentration camp.[5]

We have to come to the conclusion that the group of people to concentrate on in efforts to help with distressing life changes has to be defined by means both of characteristics of the event and individual perception.

In line with the psychological strategy for recording life events is the use of self-rated scores of various aspects of the importance of the life change that the person has reported. The initial concept used was the required amount of adaptation.[*] Other aspects have been recorded such as degree of upset that the change has caused,[6] the amount of gain or loss involved,[6] whether in general it was negative or positive, totaling negative and positive scores,[7] and the possibility of anticipating and controling the event.[3] Finally, there is also a methodology for recording anything that the person may perceive as a life change, even very trivial things. According to this method, a diary is used in which the person may record all the "hassles and uplifts" in life.[8]

PERSONAL CHARACTERISTICS

In this case, we get to know the person by means of clinical contacts or by means of a structured method, such as a questionnaire, in order to find out whether this person is coping well or less well with events. A person who has poor coping ability may need support, even in rather trivial life changes. Several standardized methods are available. For instance, Lazarus and Folkman[9] presented their coping inventory which, in its original version, has 67 questions. Another example is Shalit's coping wheel.[4]

A method that we have been using in our own studies consists of a central question: What do you do when your boss treats you badly? There are several preconstructed response alternatives to this question. The same procedure is repeated with a

---

[*]A recently updated version of the life change questionnaire, which includes self-ratings of the required amount of adaptation, can be ordered from R. H. Rahe, Nevada Stress Center, University of Nevada School of Medicine, 1000 Locust Street, Reno, Nevada 89520.

work mate instead of the boss. In our own research, we have found that factor analysis of this short questionnaire provides us with two independent factors. The first one essentially describes overt coping (I go directly to my boss and discuss it with him) and the other one covert coping (I do not say anything, but I plan revenge). The added scales of open and covert coping, respectively, contain eight items each. The scales have acceptable internal validity.[11] These two coping strategies are examples of coping strategies that were described by Lazarus and Folkman.[9] People who cope successfully with life changes have been described as people with a strong sense of coherence in life[5] and with hardiness.[10]

It may also be helpful to try to characterize the emotional coping strategies. This is more difficult and requires more indirect methods. It is mostly impossible to ask a person to describe his or her emotional coping strategy, so more thorough interviews are required. A method for describing emotional coping has been described in a study by our group. It builds upon a semistructured interview going through each one of four emotions (joy, sadness, anger, and anxiety). The subject is asked to describe an extreme situation for each particular emotion. Subsequently, the person is asked about the conditions, how he really felt, and how people in the environment reacted. Afterwards, an independent person rates various aspects of the emotional coping strategy that is observable during the interview. Does the person really have contact with the feeling? How often does the emotional reaction occur? Does the person deal with the emotion in a constructive way? How do people in the network react? Does the person allow him or herself to have this feeling? Is the person able to differentiate different affects from one another? This study shows that a nonconstructive emotional coping strategy may be associated with the development of early-stage hypertension in young men[12] and with therapy resistance in clinically overt hypertension.[13] Other researchers have found that the relationship between emotional coping and illness risk is complex.

PHYSIOLOGICAL MONITORING

Sometimes, subjects deny both the occurrence and the importance of life changes that they are going through. The only way of recording whether a life change has had importance in such a subject is to measure changes in physiological functions. For instance, studies have shown that plasma cortisol and prolactin increase during unemployment.[14] Plasma prolactin increases during the weeks after a subway train driver has killed or seriously injured somebody while driving the train.[15] Plasma cortisol increases during the terminal phase of the cancer illness of a close relative.[16, 17] Cellular immune function is affected by the death of a spouse[18] and by unemployment. In general, the accumulation of several life changes during a week[19] or a month[20] is associated with increasing urinary excretion of adrenaline although the amount of reaction and the strength of the association vary markedly between subjects. In a study of weekly variations in life change units in patients who had been rehabilitated after a myocardial infarction, it was found that a doubling of the amount of life change units from one week to the next was associated on average with a 50% increase in urinary adrenaline output during working hours.

On the other hand, it has also been shown that the pattern of endocrine reactions during the course of a reaction to a critical life change is associated with the way in which the subject is coping with the situation. Plasma prolactin change may be a good example of this. Plasma prolactin tended to be lower in women who received special supportive attention from the ward personnel in a cancer ward during their relative's cancer illness than in a control group of women who did not receive such attention during the same experience.[16] It has been hypothesized that plasma prolactin levels increase particularly during episodes of passive coping during a crisis and may accordingly, both in women and in men, mirror a withdrawn passive giving-up attitude.[21] Similarly, in studies of parents of children with cancer, it was shown that marked plasma cortisol elevation was only observed in parents with ineffective coping patterns.[17]

PHYSIOLOGICAL MONITORING
DURING TALK ABOUT LIFE CHANGES

It has been shown in several studies that one way of elucidating the importance of a potentially distressing life change may be to discuss the life change with the person while physiological functions are being recorded. This could be seen as a way of making the person reexperience the event symbolically. Two examples will be described. In the first case, a 39-year-old researcher described a markedly threatening build-up of life changes with marked difficulties with the boss, difficulties in getting research funded, and a divorce within the 3 months preceding the infarction. The discussions were associated with successively increasing heart rate, increased stroke volume (according to the ballistocardiography), and decreasing finger pulse volume (which may parallel increased vessel resistance in the arms), and finally, as a result of all of this, markedly and progressively rising blood pressure during the interview (systolic blood pressure rising from 135 to 180 mm Hg). The attitude that this patient had during the conversation was that he had failed and that he was markedly frustrated. In the second case, a 40-year-old clerk who had been forced by his supervisor to do excessive overtime work despite protests and whose son had been in a traffic accident, the discussions were associated with less marked changes: decreasing heart rate, increased stroke volume, and increased finger pulse volume, and, as a result, very small changes in blood pressure (systolic blood pressure rising from 125 to 130 mm Hg). This patient had the attitude during the interview that his myocardial infarction was not his fault; he blamed his boss whom he had even forewarned ("If you force me I shall develop a myocardial infarction"). Accordingly, the patient's self-esteem was not threatened.[22] These two cases illustrate the fact that different attitudes and, possibly, coping strategies may be associated with markedly different cardiovascular reaction patterns during discussion of the event, and accordingly, possibly also during the life changes themselves. In the first case, psychological support during rehabilitation was much more important than in the second case, since the coping pattern indicated by the patient's attitude to the changes that he described was much less healthy.

How Important Are Distressing Life Changes to Health?

The literature describing associations between life changes and health is enormous. There have been descriptions of defined changes in relation to a specific diagnosis. One example is the incidence of pregnancy hypertension during war time which has been shown to increase.[23] Another demonstrates an increase in hypertension after migration[24]; a third, cardiovascular deaths after bereavement,[25] and a fourth depression in relation to unemployment.[26] Another kind of association that has been described is the one between life changes in general and during illness. This literature is extensive. The reader is referred to reviews by Rahe,[27] Brown and Harris,[28] Dohrenwend and Dohrenwend,[3] de Faire and Theorell,[22] Henry and Stephens,[29] and Sarason et al.[30] Several of the articles published could be criticized on the ground that self-administered questionnaires have been used both in order to describe the life changes and the illnesses. Especially in cross-sectional studies this is problematic, since personal characteristics influence the way questionnaires are filled out and could influence both life change descriptions and illness reports. Accordingly, false-positive relationships could arise. However, when illness reports based upon hospitalization or objective recording of illness episodes have been used, it has been possible to establish relationships between an accumulation of life changes and the near-future onset of illness. Most authors agree that life changes are not very good predictors of illness episodes by themselves but that the predictions are greatly improved by information on coping or related factors. One example from my own research is the following.

Seven thousand middle-aged construction workers were asked about life changes during the past year. Life change total units were calculated for this year based upon the amount of upset that each change on the list caused to subjects in the normal population. These units were used for a prediction of episodes of hospitalization causing at least 1 month of continuous work absenteeism or death during 1 year of follow-up. For myocardial infarction, a follow-up of 2 years was used. It turned out that the predictions were not very successful with the exception of episodes of psychiatric illness, which could be significantly predicted by means of the life change totals. However, for certain categories of life changes, associations were observed with certain illness categories. Changes in the family structure, in many cases clearly caused by illness in the spouse, were of importance in the onset of low back pain or other degenerative joint diseases.[31] Changes or strain at work were of importance to the near future risk of myocardial infarction.[32] Similar observations have been made with the Brown-Birley technique for rating life changes with regard to the risk of developing mental illness. Markedly threatening life events could facilitate the onset of a clinical depression with a "brought-forward time" of several weeks, whereas even minor life changes could trigger an episode of schizophrenia within a very short time—days or even hours.[2]

The study of construction workers also showed that predictions of illness were greatly facilitated by the concomitant use of indicators of chronic stress factors (which may have been associated with coping strategies also although they were not measured at this time). Thus, most of the episodes of illness in the near future occurred in the group that had had both an accumulation of life changes during the last year and a high discord score.[33]

How to Intervene

There are many articles in the literature regarding ways of coping with difficult life situations. Many articles have made the point that persons who have a positive outlook, even when a crisis occurs, are more likely than others to cope well with difficult life changes. This has been labeled *stamina*.[34] During conditions of long-term war, the resources available for coping diminish, and distressing life events are found to affect children adversely. An emotional coping style was found to correlate with depressive symptomatology during such conditions.[35] In Israeli soldiers exposed to combat, it was found that posttraumatic stress disorder with the end of the war was associated with the occurrence of negative life events during follow-up and choice of coping strategies 1 and 2 years later. Authors of such articles have speculated about how to improve coping under such adverse conditions. It has been proposed that one should start with the emotional coping itself.[36] The role of social support has been stressed in such reports, both in the sense that the individual's seeking for social support seems to be an important and beneficial coping strategy and also in the sense that the existence of good social support is protective in itself. Very few programs for improving coping skills in difficult situations have been evaluated in controlled studies. There are, however, a few examples. One of the first published ones was a study of newly bereaved people.[37] All women in this situation in a given geographical area during a defined period of time were offered special professional support. A control group was followed in the evaluation. The researchers were able to show that psychiatric illness following this disastrous life change in a person's life was less frequent and less long-lasting in the group which had been offered such support.

In a study of students who had experienced an accumulation of life events during a given period, they were offered a program of 10 1.5-hour group sessions. In the first sessions, the group leader (an experienced psychologist/social worker) was active in presenting examples of how to solve crisis situations. In the following sessions, the participants were active in role playing and other ways of illustrating how to solve problems during crises. The two intervention groups reported declines in the number of illness episodes and number of disability days over the two semesters of study. The control group did significantly worse on these measures than the intervention groups.[38] These should only be seen as examples. The author will describe an example in which he was involved in designing and implementing the evaluation of a program designed to help relatives of cancer patients to cope more effectively with the situation.

The study was initiated by a nurse teacher[39] who had been struck by the fact that relatives of cancer patients are frequently neglected psychologically by healthcare personnel. In fact, it is quite possible that cancer ward staff may prevent serious mental illness in relatives by taking care of them in a more effective way. Previous experiences of relatives of patients in a hospice, has pointed in this direction.[40] The program included several components, and it is difficult to know which one was effective. First of all, relatives were allowed to spend more time than normal in this special cancer ward. This was facilitated by means of meals offered to them and improved parking facilities at the hospital. Second, special information meetings with discussions were organized every week for relatives. The themes of these meetings were structured and covered various subjects such as normal psychological reactions to a cancer illness in close relatives and the therapies offered in the ward. Third, the relatives were taught how to take responsibility for some parts of the care, such as feeding, etc.

There were components in the program that were not regarded as positive by some participants. For instance, some relatives felt pressure to take the patient from the hospital for home care. The program personnel regarded the program as something very positive, but a follow-up indicated that they were more afraid of learning new things than they had been before the program started. This may be an indication that they felt overburdened by a new set of tasks which they had never considered before and which they realized that they had insufficient education and resources to undertake.

The effects of the program were evaluated in the relatives who were offered the program as well as in a control group of relatives, who were comparable with regard to age, gender, and relatives' kind and degree of cancer illness, by means of neuroendocrine measurements (plasma cortisol and prolactin), recordings of the coping wheel, and structured observations regarding signs of depression, anxiety, and mental status. The coping wheel was used in order to explore the various ways of coping that the relatives were using during the process. All these examinations were made at intervals of 3 to 4 weeks. About half of the patients died during the months that the study was going on. Accordingly, we were able to study psychiatric and neuroendocrine state as well as coping patterns after the death of the patient. Such follow-up observations were made after 1 month, 2 months, and 1 year.

The results indicated that relatives in the special program had been much more prepared for the death of the patient.[41] They showed less evidence of disturbed mental state during the terminal stage of the patient's illness as well as during the whole follow-up period than the relatives in the control group. There was also less evidence of depression 1 year after the death of the patient, but before that there had been no difference between the groups. Interestingly, it was in the group of relatives who had been offered the activation program that the plasma cortisol levels were elevated during the terminal stage of the illness.[39] Further, they tended to have lower plasma prolactin levels during the treatment of the patient, which may be consistent with a more active coping pattern in this crisis situation. This was also confirmed by results from the coping wheel, which indicated that relatives who had been offered the activation program were much more active in seeking contact and discussing issues with relatives outside the immediate family during the terminal phase of the illness than relatives in the control group.

This example seems to show (1) that it is possible to create active programs which may prevent or at least shorten depressive reactions after the death of a close relative from cancer; (2) that increased information increases awareness of the coming death, which may be a very important reason why relatives who were offered the activation program had less severe and less long-lasting psychiatric reactions after the death of the patient. Thus, increased anticipation and controllability have decreased the adverse consequences of this distressing life change.

Another example is the study of subway drivers who had experienced a person under train (PUT) incident.[15] Three weeks after the PUT incident, a significantly increased sleep disturbance score and elevated plasma prolactin was observed. This acute psychophysiological reaction, however, had no association with the increased risk of long-term sick leave in the interval 3 months to 1 year after PUT. Instead, two independent predictors of long-term sick leave were a high depression score 3 weeks after PUT as well as a high plasma cortisol concentration during this period. Neither of these two predictors was significantly elevated, however. The pattern of associations did indicate that the PUT event was important in triggering long-term sick leave (which was higher than in the control group of subway drivers), but that those who suffered long-term illness were those who were in a bad psychological state when the event occurred. The accident as such had importance: those who killed or only mildly hurt the victim did not run any increased risk of long-term sick leave, whereas those who injured the victim seriously did. This may point to the importance of keeping the driver informed about the medical condition of the victim for a long period after the event.

EVENTLESSNESS

An important empirical observation from studies of our group is that low numbers of life events may be indicative of illness risk as well. It has been observed in longitudinal studies that blood pressure rises when people are exposed to difficult crisis situations. However, men with asymptomatic blood pressure elevation, observed in screening of a population, report few life events.[42] The interpretation of this finding is difficult. Do blood-pressure sensitive people tolerate life events less well than others and therefore deliberately avoid them? Do they report fewer events as part of an alexithymia syndrome which makes them less interested in events they experience? These are only a few of the possible questions that might be raised.

CONCLUSION

Life event research has expanded substantially during the last two decades. Physiologists, psychologists, and sociologists all contribute to the field. For some conditions, it is not necessarily excessive numbers of life events that create the most problems, eventless lives may be just as dangerous.

REFERENCES

1. Holmes TH, Rahe RH. The social readjustment rating scale. *J Psychosom Res.* 1967;11:213–218.
2. Brown GW, Sklair F, Harris TO, Birley JLT. Life events and psychiatric disorders. 1. Some methodological issues. *Psychol Med.* 1973;3:74–87.
3. Dohrenwend BS, Dohrenwend BP, eds. *Stressful Life Events, Their Nature and Effects.* New York: Wiley;1974.
4. Shalit B. *Report No. 1: The Instrument, Design Administration and Scoring. Report No. 2: Validation, Reliability of the Instrument. Report No. 3: Empirical Results and the Validation of the Application of the Instrument. FOA Rapport.* Stockholm, Sweden: Försvarets Forskningsanstalt;1978.
5. Antonovsky A. Unraveling the Mystery of Health. San Francisco, Jossey-Bass;1987.
6. Paykel ES. Recent life events and clinical depression. In: Gunderson EKE, Rahe RH, eds. *Life Stress and Illness.* Springfield, IL: Thomas;1974: pp 135–150.
7. Myers JK, Lindenthal JJ, Pepper MP. Social class, life events and psychiatric symptoms, a longitudinal study. In: Dohrenwend BS, Dohrenwend BP, eds. *Stressful Life Events, Their Nature and Effects.* New York: Wiley;1974: pp 191–206.
8. De Longis A, Coyne JC, Dakof G, Folkman S, Lazarus RS. Relationship of daily hassles, uplifts, and major life events to health status. *Health Psychol.* 1982;1:119–136.
9. Lazarus RS, Folkman S. *Stress, Appraisal, and Coping.* New York: Springer;1984.
10. Kobasa SC. Barriers to work stress. II. The hardy personality. In Doyle Gentry W, Benson H, de Wolff CJ, eds. *Behavioral Medicine: Work, Stress and Health.* Dordrecht, Netherlands: Nijhoff;1985: pp 181–204.
11. Theorell T, Michelsen H, Nordemar H. *MUSIC Books. 3. Validity and Reliability of Methods* (in Swedish). Stockholm; Sweden: Work Environment Research Institute;1992.
12. Knox S, Svensson J, Theorell T, Waller D. Emotional coping and elevated blood pressure. *Behav Med.* 1988;14:52–58.

13. Isaksson H, Konarski K. The psychological and social condition of hypertensives resistant to pharmacological treatment. *Soc Sci Med.* Provisionally accepted.
14. Brenner SO, Levi L. Long-term unemployment among women in Sweden. *Soc Sci Med.* 1987;25:153–161.
15. Theorell T, Leymann H, Jodko M, Konarski-Svensson J, Norbeck HE, Eneroth P. Person under train incidents: Medical consequences for the driver. *Psychosom Med.* Provisionally accepted.
16. Theorell T, Häggmark C, Eneroth P. Psychoendocrinological reactions in female relatives of cancer patients. Effects of an activation programme. *Acta Oncol.* 1987;26:419–424.
17. Wolff CT, Friedman SB, Hofer MA, Mason JW. Relationship between psychological defenses and mean urinary 17-hydroxycorticosteroid excretion rates. 1. A predictive study of parents of fatally ill children. *Psychosom Med.* 1964;26:576–591.
18. Ader R. Psychosomatic and psychoimmunologic research. *Psychosom Med.* 1980;42:307–321.
19. Theorell T, Lind E, Fröberg J, Karlsson CG, Levi L. A longitudinal study of 21 coronary subjects—Life changes, catecholamines and related biochemical variables. *Psychosom Med.* 1972,34:505.
20. Chadwick J, Chesney M, Black GW, Rosenman RM, Sevelius GG. *Psychological Job Stress and Coronary Heart Disease.* Menlo Park, CA: Stanford Research Institute;1979.
21. Theorell T, Perski A, Alerstedt T, Sigala F, Ahlberg-Hultén G, Svensson J, Eneroth P. Changes in job strain in relation to changes in physiological state. *Scand J Work Environ Health.* 1988;14:189–196.
22. de Faire U, Theorell T. *Life Stress and Coronary Heart Disease.* St. Louis, KY: Green;1984.
23. Rofe Y, Goldberg J. Prolonged exposure to a war environment and its effects on the blood pressure of pregnant women. *Br J Med Psychol.* 1981;56:305–311.
24. Beaglehole R, Eyles E, Prior I. Blood pressure and migration in children. *Int J Epidemiol.* 1979;8:5–10.
25. Parkes CM, Benjamin B, Fitzgerald RG. Broken hearts: A statistical study of increased mortality among widowers. *Br Med J.* 1969;1:740–743.
26. Hall EM, Johnson JV. Depression in unemployed Swedish women. *Soc Sci Med.* 1988;12:1349–1355.
27. Rahe RH. Life change and subsequent illness reports. In: Gunderson EKE, Rahe RH, eds. *Life Stress and Illness.* Springfield, IL: Thomas;1974, pp 58–78.
28. Brown GW, Harris T. *Social Origins of Depression—A Study of Psychiatric Disorders in Women.* London: Tavistock;1978.
29. Henry JP, Stephens PM. *Stress, Health and the Social Environment: A Sociobiological Approach to Medicine.* New York: Springer;1977.
30. Sarason IG, Johnson JH, Siegel JM. Assessing the impact of life changes. Development of the life experiences survey. *J Consult Clin Psychol.* 1978;44:127–139.
31. Theorell T, Floderus B, Lind E. The relationship of disturbing life-changes and emotions to the early development of myocardial infarction and other serious illnesses. *Int J Epidemiol.* 1975;4:281–296.
32. Theorell T, Flodérus-Myrhed B. "Work-load" and risk of myocardial infarction: A prospective psychosocial analysis. *Int J Epidemiol.* 1977;6:17–21.

33. Theorell T. Selected illnesses and somatic risk factors in relation to two psychosocial stress indices—A prospective study of middle-aged building construction workers. *J Psychosom Res.* 1976;20:7.
34. Colerick EJ. Stamina in later life. *Soc Sci Med.* 1985;21:997–1006.
35. Bryce JW, Walker N, Ghorayeb F, Kanj M. Life experiences, response styles and mental health among mothers and children in Beirut, Lebanon. *Soc Sci Med.* 1989;28:685–695.
36. Solomon Z, Mikulincer M, Flum H. Negative life events, coping responses, and combat-related psychopathology: A prospective study. *J Abnorm Psychol.* 1988;97:302–307.
37. Parkes CM. Bereavement counseling: Does it work? *Br Med J.* 1980;iii:281.
38. Marx MB, Somes GW, Garrity TF, Reeb AC Jr, Maffeo PA. The influence of a supportive, problem-solving group intervention on the health status of students with great recent life change. *J Psychosom Res.* 1984;28:275–278.
39. Häggmark C. *Invitation to Relatives to Participate in the Care of the Cancer Patient at the Hospital. Effects of an Activation Programme.* Karolinska Institute, Stockholm;1989. Thesis.
40. Cameron J, Parkes CH. Terminal care: Evaluation of effects on surviving family of care before and after bereavement. *Postgrad Med J.* 1983;59:73–78.
41. Häggmark C, Bachner M, Theorell T. Factors predicting psychological, physiological, and social outcome in relatives of cancer patients one year after the patient's death. Effects of an activation programme. *Acta Oncol.* In press.
42. Theorell T, Svensson J, Knox S, Waller D, Alvarez M. Young men with high blood pressure report few life events. *J Psychosom Res.* 1986;30:243–249.

Chapter 3
Somatization

RICHARD MAYOU

For over 200 years doctors have been aware of the difficulties of distinguishing the causes of physical symptoms which may have physical or psychological explanations.[1-3] In the 19th and early 20th century, there were acrimonious controversies about the *nervous patient*, and syndromes such as *soldier's heart* and *shell-shock* and many physical pathologies were proposed. However, over the past 60 years anxiety disorders and depression have become well defined as a cause of many somatic symptoms, and it has become increasingly accepted that psychological factors contribute to many of the nonspecific physical symptoms that are frequent in primary and hospital care. Even so, there are continuing arguments about possible physical causes of syndromes such as noncardiac chest pain, nonulcer dyspepsia, low back pain, and chronic fatigue. Rival specialists continue to claim proof for rival etiologies.

Although many newly presenting nonorganic physical symptoms are easily managed by appropriate investigation and reassurance, a sizable proportion of patients suffer persistent or recurrent symptoms which may be associated with marked impairment of quality of life and considerable use of medical resources. The management of these patients is generally seen to be difficult, and primary care practitioners, physicians, and psychiatrists are often pessimistic about the opportunities for successful treatment of chronic complaints. There is, however, increasingly persuasive evidence that the early recognition of these patients and their appropriate management by general practitioners and hospital

41

doctors, by specialist psychiatrists and clinical psychologists can lead to a successful outcome both in terms of quality of life for patients and their relatives, but also in terms of the reduction and use of medical and other health services.[3-5]

DEFINITIONS

Terminology has, as so often in psychiatry, been a considerable obstacle to understanding. Traditional syndromes, such as *neurasthenia* and *hypochondriasis*, have been variously described within specialist psychiatric practice.[1,3] The term *somatization* also has a long and complex history. Introduced by Stekel in 1908, it is very widely used by psychiatrists and psychologists. Although somatization has not only been variously defined, it usually implies a process of expression of psychological distress in somatic rather than physical terms. Lipowski's[6] widely quoted definition states that somatization is a "transient or persistent tendency to experience and communicate psychological distress in the form of somatic symptoms and to seek medical help for them." Similarly, Bridges and Goldberg's[7] operational definition of somatization requires both presentation with a physical complaint and evidence of a DSM-III psychological disorder. Neither version, therefore, includes the large number of patients who present in primary care with medically unexplained somatic symptoms which are not accompanied by an overt psychological symptom. We need a general term to cover the whole range of clinical problems encountered in everyday medical practice, whether or not they are attributable to underlying primary psychiatric disorder. Indeed some are entirely understandable. There are advantages in general terms such as *nonorganic physical symptoms* or *medically unexplained symptoms*. Kellner[8] has favored the term *functional somatic symptoms*, which has less theoretical implications than somatization, even though there are problems about the varying uses of the word *functional.*

Problems of terminology have been perpetuated, even exacerbated, by the creation in DSM-III of *somatoform disorders*. The subcategories have names derived from long established but highly unsatisfactory terms such as *conversion disorder, hypochondriasis,* and *somatization disorder*. Conversion disorder is separated from dissociation. Somatization disorder is an excessively narrow derivation of arbitrary so-called Briquet's syndrome. Psychogenic pain is a confession of ignorance. Hypochondriasis, now defined by both DSM and ICD in narrow terms, was formerly often a much more general concept. Indeed, Kellner has continued to use the term, describing transient and recurrent hypochondriasis and making a distinction between primary and secondary hypochondriasis.[3, 9] Overall, laudable attempts by the authors of international classifications to promote greater precision have provided no more than a preliminary sketch which have not been implemented in ICD-10 or DSM-IV. It is also unfortunate that the use of the category *somatoform disorders* has confused many of those who do not understand that it is but one of the psychiatric correlates of unexplained medical symptoms.

This review prefers to use terms such as *medically unexplained symptoms* and to avoid words (such as the title of this paper) which are laden with inappropriate theoretical implications. It considers in turn the epidemiology of medically unexplained symptoms, their clinical significance, etiology (including association with psychiatric disorder), and treatment. It aims to be comprehensive, in that it covers the whole range of clinical problems (Tables 3.1, 3.2) in primary and hospital care: specific problems, such as nonulcer dyspepsia and chronic fatigue, and more complex syndromes, such as persistent multiple complaints (for example somatization disorder) and the various forms of chronic pain of the type frequently encountered in pain clinics. It covers symptoms for which there is no organic basis, those which may result from the interaction of physical and psychological factors, and also the occurrence of unexplained somatic symptoms in association with major physical illness. We do not cover the very frequent occurrence of similar problems in childhood[10] for which similar principles apply. Lack of evidence prevents adequate review of symptoms in the elderly,

TABLE 3.1
Symptoms

Pain	Dysphonia
Abdominal	Dysphagia
Chest	Nausea
Muscle and joint	Diarrhoea
Low back	Food allergy
Headache	Dizziniess
Facial	Headache
Pelvic	Incontinence and urgency
Neuropathic	Tremor
Fatigue	Concern about appearance
Breathlessness	Worry about benign tissue
Palpitations	lumps and inconsistencies
Tinnitus	Pruritus

where there are extra difficulties in determining the role of occult physical etiologies of nonspecific symptoms.

EPIDEMIOLOGY

GENERAL POPULATION

Everyone in the general population regularly experiences a wide variety of minor physical sensations.[11, 12] Such symptoms are usually accepted as being normal and of little significance, and only a small proportion result in consultation with doctors. Even so, surveys which have attempted to define the severity of such symptoms in the general population indicate sizable numbers of people suffering symptoms which are disabling and distressing. For example, Von Korff et al.[11] surveyed a sample of members of a large health maintenance organization in Seattle and reported 41% of subjects reported back pain in the previous 6 months, 26%

TABLE 3.2
Syndromes

Multiple symptoms –
    somatization disorder
Chronic pain
Accident or compensation neurosis
Post-traumatic symptoms
Dysmorphophobia

---

headache, 17% abdominal pain, 12% chest pain, and 12% facial pain. Most of these complaints were longstanding and recurrent. Although they were mainly of no more than mild to moderate intensity and did not usually limit activities, many subjects reported periods of several days during the 6-month period when they had been unable to carry out their usual activities because of the pain. It is evident in this and other studies that the greater the number of physical complaints, the higher the proportions suffering from current and lifetime psychiatric disorder.[13] A small percentage of those in the general population fulfill the criteria of a somatization disorder and a larger number satisfy abridged definitions of somatization disorder.[14]

PRIMARY CARE

The determinants of consultation with doctors are unclear but have been well studied for several symptoms, for example the irritable bowel syndrome.[15] Recurrent abdominal pain is experienced by most people in the general population, but only a small proportion of patients consult doctors and describe major limitations of their quality of life. Those who consult seem to have a general tendency to consult doctors and to be more anxious.

A substantial proportion of new consultations in primary care relate to somatic symptoms for which no specific cause can be found. Kroenke,[16–18] in a series of reports from a primary care internal medicine clinic at a U.S. Army medical center, has described the considerable frequency of 14 common nonspecific symptoms, with small minorities of each being given an organic diagnosis, the considerable dissatisfaction at not receiving "helpful" therapy, and the substantial consultation and investigation costs of such complaints.

Psychiatric research in primary care has shown that the majority of those with emotional disorders present with physical symptoms. Bridges and Goldberg[7] classified mode of presentation for 500 consecutive episodes of psychiatric disorder in urban general practice. Only 17% of subjects presented with psychological symptoms ("psychologizers") whilst 27% had psychiatric disorder in association with physical illness, 56% were "somatizers" (somatic presentation plus DSM psychological disorder), of which 24% were described as "facultative" since they readily admitted to psychological symptoms on specific enquiry. In contrast 32% were "pure somatizers" who saw their complaints as having physical origins and were unwilling to accept psychological explanations. The usual medical response to such symptoms and negative investigation in primary care is reassurance, sometimes accompanied by a symptomatic prescription.

Long-term outcome has not been well described. Although it is clear that many complaints are transient, an important minority are persistent and associated with disability and continuing consultation. A conspicuous subgroup of primary care patients consult very regularly over long periods of time, for either the same symptom or varying physical complaints.

HOSPITAL OUTPATIENT CLINICS

Nonspecific physical complaints are among the commonest reasons for referral from primary care to British hospital outpatient clinics.[19] Medically undiagnosed symptoms are frequent in many general hospital outpatient clinics.[3, 6, 20] Inevitably, they are particularly common in the selected population referred to pain clinics.[21] Follow-up studies suggest that negative physical findings fail to reassure many clinic attenders. It is difficult to determine from a widely dispersed literature what proportions of patients with particular types of symptoms are reassured, and how many suffer persistent or recurrent problems. However, it is clear that many patients with many types of specific complaint suffer persistent disability, and that the subgroup of patients with a multiple somatic complaint use very considerable amounts of general hospital care over long periods of time.[22]

Hospital Inpatients

Nonspecific symptom diagnoses are made for a small minority of discharges of inpatients, between 1 and 2% of all discharges in Oxford. Such patients frequently report persistent symptoms and have a greater than expected use of subsequent psychiatric care, as has been particularly well demonstrated following normal coronary angiograms.[23] We found in a linked case register study that patients discharged from general hospitals with several types of nonspecific physical diagnoses used psychiatric services at rates considerably greater than that expected for the population in the year before and in the year following the index of general hospital admission.[24] In a series of Danish case register studies Fink[25, 26] has documented the extensive medical and surgical assessment and treatment resources by a relatively small number of people who have multiple admissions to the hospital for which no physical diagnoses are recorded. A fifth of persistent somatizers had been admitted at least once for a factitious illness.

Consultation Liaison and Behavioral Medicine

All reports of series of consecutive attenders at consultation-liaison (CL) services[27, 28] have noted that the assessment of unexplained physical symptoms is among the commonest reasons for referral. Such symptoms are most commonly associated with anxiety and depression and somatoform diagnoses are made much less frequently.[27-29] However, most CL units concentrate on inpatients, whereas medically unexplained symptoms are most numerous amongst medical outpatients. There have been few accounts of

CL outpatient series. Behavioral medicine, principally practiced by clinical psychologists,[30] is becoming well established but rather little has been published describing the characteristics of referrals, apart from the large literature on chronic pain.

SPECIALIST PSYCHIATRY

It is uncertain to what extent somatization problems present to specialist psychiatric services as the principal or secondary complaint. Kellner[9] points out that secondary hypochondriasis is common as a feature of many psychiatric disorders but that its clinical and economic significance has been neglected.

CLINICAL SIGNIFICANCE

Epidemiological research demonstrates a high prevalence of medically unexplained physical symptoms in the general population. Although only a minority consult doctors, such symptoms are frequent in all medical settings. It remains difficult to obtain a fully comprehensive view of epidemiology. Surveys concentrate on particular types of specific symptoms or on multiple symptoms. There is remarkably little dialogue between those interested in particular symptoms and in the heterogeneous problems that are referred to as "chronic pain," and which are often defined by the highly unsatisfactory criterion of attendance at a pain clinic. While most research has concentrated on adults below the age of 65, it appears that similar clinical problems are common in children[10] and in the elderly.

Evidence of course and outcome is even less satisfactory than for prevalence but indicates a generally good prognosis in the general population. In contrast, there is a progressively poorer outlook (in terms of symptoms, associated emotional disorder, and disability) as the patient is seen in primary care, in hospital outpatient clinics, and as an inpatient. Associations with psychiatric disorder are most conspicuous in those with multiple symptoms and in those seen in specialist hospital settings.

The minority of symptoms that are persistent or recurrent are associated with very considerable morbidity and use of medical services. All efforts to estimate the cost of persistent symptoms suggest a very considerable proportion of medical budgets, and in addition, largely uncosted consequences for work and other aspects of quality of life.[31, 32] It is likely that effective interventions could be highly cost effective in that the extra costs of greater psychological input would be "offset" by reduction of unnecessary health costs.[33] We are faced, therefore, with the clinical problems of providing: (1) more effective early reassurance to new consulters, and (2) identifying and offering much more effective help to those who have persistent problems. Since medically unexplained symptoms are so prevalent in every area of medical practice, these are clinical issues which must be faced by all doctors and not just by those with specialist expertise. Improved care requires better and earlier routine care in general practice and in general hospitals, together with earlier and easier access to specialist psychiatric and psychological services. It is unfortunate that therapeutic nihilism remains common throughout medicine. Many primary care doctors and physicians have concluded that psychological treatments have little to offer and most psychiatrists appear to agree. Even CL services give low priority to such patients. Recent growing research interest in the epidemiology and etiology of such problems and many individual's clinical initiation must lead to the development of more effective treatments, to means of delivering to large numbers of patients, and to the better training of doctors (including psychiatrists) and all those involved in care.

ETIOLOGY

Controversy about etiology has been fueled by the excessively narrow standpoints of clinicians and research workers whose experience has been limited to selected groups of subjects. It is essential to avoid such generalizations from specialist experience, and to view the particular clinical problems encountered in any medical setting with an awareness of wider epidemiology. Barsky and Klerman,[34] in an important review classified four types of concepts of hypochondriasis: psychiatric syndrome, psychodynamic process, amplifying cognitive style, and socially learned illness behavior. It seems likely that all these types of explanation are of significance.[35, 36] It is certain that there is no single type of etiology for the whole range of somatization symptoms. For example, Kirmayer and Robbins[37, 38] have emphasized that three basic approaches to the definition of somatization in fact correspond with three rather different groups of patients commonly encountered in medical practice. Their research definitions were in a study of 685 patients attending family medicine clinics: (1) high levels of functional somatic distress, as measured by the Somatic Symptom Index of the Diagnostic Interview Schedule; (2) hypochondriasis measured by high scores on a measure of illness worry and the absence of evidence for serious illness; (3) exclusively somatic clinical presentations among patients with current major depression or anxiety. They concluded that these three forms of somatization were associated with different sociodemographic and illness behavior characteristics and reported that a majority of patients met criteria for only one type of somatization. They argued that the distinct pathogenic processes may be involved in each of the three types of somatization. Most studies of etiology of particular symptoms have concentrated on single etiological factors. There have been few comprehensive studies and these have found it difficult to draw conclusions from large numbers of interrelated variables. It is unfortunate that the result has been unproductive controversies about the etiology of specific factors, for example panic disorder, esophageal spasm, and microvascular angina as explanations for noncardiac chest pain. Rival researchers have shown little understanding of other viewpoints and little inclination to consider multicausal explanations. Nevertheless, it is probable that in clinical populations multicausal interactive etiologies are usual and that all factors that have been widely mentioned play some role.

TABLE 3.3
Etiology

Physiological + pathological factors
Minor physical pathology
Benign tissue lumps and inconsistencies
Arousal: autonomic and hormonal
Muscle tension
Hyperventilation
Inactivity
Poor sleep
Physiological consequences of food and drink
Side effects of medication

Psychological
Knowledge, beliefs
Psychiatric disorder
Personality
Experience of illness – self and others

Reactions of others
Relatives and friends
Medical care
Other therapists

There has been too little awareness of the ways in which patients develop their understanding of medical problems,[39, 40] and of the ways in which cultural and social factors influence presentation, understanding, and management. It is essential to recognize the wide variety of factors contributing to etiology.[35, 36] Table 3.3 groups these as physiological and pathological, psychological, and the reactions of others. Awareness of normal physiological processes or of medically minor pathology appears to underlie many, but not all, of somatization complaints.[41, 42] Psychological factors may determine the ways in which such perceptions are both perceived and interpreted.[37] They may also be the direct primary or secondary causes of somatic symptoms. Thus, current stress and tension may make an individual more aware of a benign subcutaneous lump or of long-standing awareness of heart rhythm. This is especially likely if there is particular reason to be currently aware of physical illness and its consequences in other people, or if past experience of medicine has been unsatisfactory.

Superimposed on predisposing and precipitating factors, the reactions of others, and especially the experience of medical care, act as maintaining factors. For example, a middle-aged man with a bad family history of heart disease may present with chest wall pain which he has misinterpreted as evidence of heart failure shortly after hearing of the death of a close friend from a heart attack. Family anxiety is likely to exacerbate the problem, and symptoms may well become worse if the general practitioner prescribes trinitrin and arranges referral to a cardiologist. Thereafter, even negative investigation may be inadequate to persuade the patient that continuing symptoms do not have a sinister cause.

The contribution of iatrogenic factors must not be underestimated, and the patients' illness behavior[43] must be seen alongside medical behavior. Many patients find it difficult to tolerate uncertainty and ambiguity. They readily misinterpret medical information, drawing erroneous conclusions from past experience, the media, and the reaction of friends and relatives. Very frequently, doctors remain unaware of the patients' idiosyncratic misinterpretation.

The association of nonorganic physical symptoms with undoubted physical disorder is complex but important. Patients who have suffered a myocardial infarction or who have undergone coronary artery surgery frequently complain of chest pain and palpitations which do not have a physical cause.[44, 45] A substantial proportion of patients with chronic pain describe symptoms which are partly, but not wholly, explicable by organic disorder.[46] It is evident that in a multicausal interactive etiology of nonorganic symptoms there is a range of clinical syndromes from those in which there is no underlying physiological and pathological process (e.g., illness phobias) to those in which major physical illness is an important factor. Lishman[47] has pointed out the ways in which physiogenic and psychogenic factors contribute to the genesis of the postconcussional syndrome so that "organic factors are chiefly relevant in the early stages, whereas long-continued symptoms are perpetuated by second-ary neurotic developments, often of a complex nature." Compen-sation, which is often seen as a major etiological factor in lower back pain and "accident neurosis," should be interpreted in this manner and seen as one of a variety of psychological and social determinants.[48]

THE ROLE OF PSYCHIATRIC DISORDER

Physicians have often ignored psychiatric causes of somatic symptoms. Psychiatrists have often overestimated the significance of overt psychiatric disorder as defined by standard criteria, and underestimated the wider significance of the psychological processes, described above. Patients may describe worrying nonorganic physical symptoms, yet not have any diagnosable psychiatric disorder. Even so, psychiatric disorder is undoubtedly significant in etiology of somatic symptoms (especially those that are most serious and persistent) and may predispose to precipitate or maintain symptoms.

Somatization may be associated with almost any form of psychiatric disorder, but most commonly with *anxiety* and *depression*.[3] The unsatisfactory groupings of *somatoform disorder* have proved difficult to apply. Criteria are arbitrary and lack precision through having no clear boundaries. For example, the diagnosis of hypochondriasis requires patients that are not reassured by appropriate investigation and explanation. This leaves unclear what should be regarded as "appropriate" medical discussion and reassurance. In clinical practice, to draw the distinction between appropriate concern and psychiatric disorder is often unclear. It is impossible to determine whether patients have had the appropriate explanation, discussion, and reassurance that are required to make somatoform diagnosis. Persistent somatic symptoms may often be understandable reactions to uncertainty that have been made worse by the reactions of others, uncertainty, and lack of explanation by doctors. In many instances the underlying misinterpretations derive not only from the patient's misconceptions but from the doctor who has not provided either an alternative explanation or an answer to the patient's particular anxieties, and indeed may have contributed to the misunderstanding by inconsistent or ambiguous advice or behavior. If in such circumstances we make a somatoform diagnosis we confer an impression of substance and understanding when, in fact, underlying mechanisms and their significance are entirely obscure.

Somatoform pain disorder is no more than an admission of ignorance, hardly an acceptable basis for diagnosing a psychiatric disorder. The definition of *somatization disorder* deriving from highly artificial and narrow subtyping remains arbitrary; indeed, proposals for an abridged version to demonstrate the need to distinguish between patients with specific symptoms and those with multiple recurrent symptoms. Many patients with either facultative or pure somatization symptoms (to use Goldberg's distinction) will admit that they are frequently inclined to worry about their health. This tendency cannot usually be regarded as a *hypochondriacal personality disorder*, but in a minority of frequent consulters health anxiety is so disabling as to constitute a disorder of personality.[49] Indeed, it is probably more appropriate to regard somatization disorder as an abnormality of personality rather than a somatoform disorder. Delusions of illness cause little diagnostic problem as part of psychiatric syndrome but, occasionally, monosymptomatic hypochondriacal disorders cause difficulties in diagnosis and management.[50]

Factitious disorder is uncommon but underdiagnosed. It results in considerable morbidity and substantial health costs.[51] It is not considered further in this paper.

Comparisons of evidence relating to different types of nonorganic physical symptoms suggest that there may be somewhat different patterns of association with types of psychiatric disorder. Chest pain and palpitations are strongly associated with panic and general anxiety whereas headache and a variety of chronic pain syndromes are more likely to be associated with depression.[52] Depression is also frequently comorbid with somatization disorder[53] and there remains argument about the significance of pain as depressive equivalent.

TABLE 3.4
General Principles of Management

Physical and psychological history
Appropriate physical investigation
Explanation of symptoms
Opportunity for discussion of patients' beliefs
Emphasize role of psychological factors from outset
Avoid reinforcing patient's erroneous beliefs
Control medical care
Agree treatment plan

GENERAL PRINCIPLES OF MANAGEMENT

Management is concerned with routine measures to prevent iatrogenic complications, the early recognition of problems, simple early intervention and specialist interventions for patients with severe and chronic complaints. The general principle for assessment and treatment listed in Table 3.4 are fundamental to effective early treatment, the minimization of the iatrogenic causes of persistent symptoms and disability, and efficient use of medical resources. It is essential to combine taking the symptoms seriously and appropriate investigation with an awareness of the possible significance of psychological and social factors.[54] Avoidance of a dualist approach in which physical explanations are first sought and psychological explanations are only suggested when all else has proved negative, is likely to make a comprehensive treatment plan more acceptable to the patients and more effective. It is also essential that patients feel they have an adequate explanation of their symptoms, and that they have the opportunity to discuss their worries. At first presentation, reassurance is important and frequently successful. However, repeated simple reassurance that the problem is not serious is inadequate and perhaps harmful in management of continuing symptoms and of patients' fears that doctors have neglected a

TABLE 3.5
Treatment in Primary Care and General Outpatient Clinics

Assessment – physical and psychological
Show interest in the reality of symptoms
Treat any physical problems
Provide explanation
Opportunity for discussion of beliefs and worries
Simple specific psychiatric treatment
   (e.g. antidepressants)
Advice: practical. behavioural
Follow-up

serious and occult medical condition.[55] Offering an opportunity for full discussion can often deal with misunderstandings, and also provide a psychological explanation in form that is understandable and acceptable. Goldberg et al.[56] have described the general principles of such an approach in primary care, and have been able to put forward specific techniques for use by general practitioners (feeling understood, changing the agenda, making the link). This general model of training needs further development and wider application in hospital care. Table 3.5 summarizes the principal stages of treatment in primary and general medical care and in specialist psychiatric or psychological practice.

SPECIALIST TREATMENT

The specific aims of treatment will vary with the individual and should be clearly specified before treatment begins.[57] There are four general aims: reduction of distress; decreased disability; improvement of symptoms; limitation of inappropriate use of medical care. The treatment approaches described here are collaborative, much

TABLE 3.6
Specific Treatment Procedures

Treatment of underlying minor
  pathology
Psychotropic medication
Education
Psychotherapy
Cognitive behavioural treatment
Control of medical care
In-patient programmes

---

of the work being done by the patients between sessions as "homework." Some patients find this immediately attractive while others need considerable explanation and encouragement. The use of specific treatment techniques (Table 3.6) should not detract from the importance of "nonspecific" factors common to all forms of psychotherapy. It is essential to establish a working relationship with the patient which offers hope for recovery, an acceptable rationale for the treatment, and the opportunity for discussion of worries and frustrations. The treatment should help patients to rebuild their self-esteem and sense of control over their lives. Many of the patients seen in psychiatric practice have already consulted numerous doctors and may be attending several other specialists as well as their own general practitioner. Simplification and clarification of medical care is essential so that it is clear who has primary clinical responsibility, and possible sources of confusion and misunderstanding are eliminated or minimized.

REFERRAL

Failure to attend the first assessment interview is a major cause of treatment failure. To minimize this problem, the referring doctor must explain there is no evidence of serious disease, without seeming dismissive of the patient's symptoms or implying they are "imaginary." He should explain that even though he has no physical treatment to offer, the patient is suffering from a common and well-recognized condition, and he has a colleague with special treatment expertise in this area. The referring doctor should then explain that, as in all medical conditions, reducing stress and learning ways of coping with, or controlling symptoms is helpful. On receipt of the referral the therapist should set up an early appointment, preferably for a general hospital clinic. Joint consultation with the referring doctor is only rarely feasible but is particularly effective.

ASSESSMENT

The aims of assessment are: to ensure that all appropriate steps have been taken to exclude physical disease, to identify any psychiatric disorder, and to produce a positive formulation of the problem in cognitive, behavioral, and physiological terms. The medical and psychiatric notes should be reviewed before the patient is seen. One of the therapist's first tasks in the interview is to ask the patients about their reactions to the referral, to correct misconceptions, and to allow questions. A standard psychiatric history should include details of physical symptoms, current occupational or social adjustment, with a particular emphasis on behavior avoided because of fear of harmful consequences or exacerbation of symptoms. A detailed history of past illness and consultations, and of beliefs about any investigations and treatment, is essential.[4] Previous doctors may have seemed dismissive of the patient's physical symptoms, and showing a genuine interest and sympathy will help establish a useful working relationship. Great caution should be exercised in suggesting that psychological factors, or psychiatric illness play a role in the etiology of their symptoms. For many patients such suggestions imply that they are imagining symptoms, are at fault for being ill, or are even going mad. Therefore rather than abruptly rejecting beliefs about physical causes, common ground can be established by discussing the role of "stress" in all medical conditions. It is desirable to use the patient's own vocabulary; for example, using the words *tension* and *stress* rather than *anxiety*. Once trust has been established most patients are willing to engage in an explicitly pragmatic treatment approach.

Failure to Engage in Treatment

When patients fail to attend the first assessment appointment, the referring doctor should be asked to contact the patient to encourage attendance on another occasion. It is often helpful to discuss the importance of positive referral with the general practitioner or hospital doctor.

Dropouts

Patients who drop out of treatment should be contacted and the reasons for their discontinuation discussed. This often reveals the issues which need to be included in a revised treatment plan. It is often possible to renegotiate treatment once the misunderstandings which led to its breakdown are clarified.

Poor Response to Treatment

Some patients will fail to improve despite apparently accepting the treatment. In such cases, the psychological formulation should be reviewed. Sometimes, a medical reassessment for occult disease may be appropriate.

Physical Treatments

It is important to treat any physical factor that is contributing to etiology. For example, patients with noncardiac chest pain, drug treatment for esophagitis[58] may be valuable whilst in irritable bowel syndrome, medical prescription is a fundamental part of specialist care.[15] In chronic pain appropriate analgesics, or even surgical or nerve block techniques, are fundamental to management of the subjective and behavioral difficulties. Not only are such interventions directly helpful, but they also demonstrate to the patient that his symptoms have been taken seriously.

PSYCHOTROPIC MEDICATION

Drug treatment is indicated for specific psychiatric disorders, notably depression. Antidepressants are also widely effective in a number of conditions in which depressive symptoms are not prominent, such as atypical facial pain, some chronic pain,[46] and other problems. Although the mechanism of action may be unclear, the trial of an antidepressant is often valuable. Anxiolytic medication has been widely recommended in patients with associated generalized anxiety or panic.[59] It is unclear as to how their effectiveness compares with psychological interventions and immediate and long-term impact. An example is the use of antidepressant and anxiolytic drugs in the treatment of noncardiac chest pain associated with panic or general anxiety. However, it is important to be aware that many patients with noncardiac chest pain do not suffer from anxiety and panic disorder and cannot be expected to respond to such medication.

PSYCHOTHERAPY

Psychotherapy in all its forms has been widely practiced.[1, 3] Several studies suggest that it may be effective. It is probable that the important ingredients are therapists' interest and concern, acceptance of the reality and significance of the symptoms, the exploration of alternative explanations to the patients' own erroneous beliefs, and discussion of ways of coping with symptoms and disability more effectively. Reassurance has often been seen as having a role, but as a simple repetitive response to insistent patient demands it is almost certainly harmful to patients with chronic symptoms.[55]

INPATIENT CARE

Inpatient programs have been widely reported for chronic pain, but have been used less frequently for other chronic syndromes.[60, 61] It is probable that they do have an important role in establishing new and more appropriate behaviors in patients with chronic problems. Removal from normal surroundings and the factors reinforcing symptoms may give the opportunity for changes that would not otherwise be possible.

COGNITIVE BEHAVIORAL TREATMENT

According to the cognitive behavioral model a patient's symptoms,[57] distress, and disability are perpetuated by an interaction between psychological and physiological processes. Central to the model is the way the person *thinks* about bodily sensations. Thus if benign bodily sensations are regarded by the patient as being symptomatic of disease, several consequences ensue. First, the patient will experience emotional distress, which may cause further bodily sensations. Second, increased attention will be paid to these sensations. Third, the type of behaviors adopted to cope with the symptoms may be "dysfunctional" in that they act to exacerbate the problem rather than relieve it. Fourth, other people, including doctors, may respond to the patient in a way that intensifies, rather than reduces their concern with disease, attention to bodily sensations, and dysfunctional coping. *Cognition* refers to the patient's thinking about the bodily sensations, and includes *thoughts* (e.g., the thought "it must be a brain tumor" in response to headache), more enduring *beliefs* (e.g., "brain tumors run in my family so I'm likely to get one"), and lifelong underlying *assumptions* (e.g., "all symptoms indicate disease"). Assumptions have their origin in the patient's family's response to symptoms and the patient's own previous personal experience of illness. These cognitions are the determinants of the behavioral, emotional, and attentional responses to bodily sensations. *Behavior* in response to functional somatic symptoms (FSS) may be "dysfunctional" in that it maintains, rather than resolves the problem. New dysfunctional behaviors include repeated checking of physical signs and reading of medical literature. Such behaviors increase preoccupation with bodily sensations and encourage a sinister misinterpretation of them. The seeking of medical investigation and treatment may also reinforce preoccupation with disease, and detract from behaviors more likely to resolve psychosocial problems that gave rise to the initial distress. The converse of new dysfunctional behavior is a reduction in previous normal behavior. Hence, activity is avoided for fear of provoking symptoms: time is taken off work, exercise reduced, and social contact diminished. The patient's awareness of this occupational, physical, and social disability serves to strengthen concern about physical disease. Furthermore, the persistent avoidance of activity may result in physiological changes that actually reduce physical capacity for activity. *Interpersonal factors* are also important. The behavior of relatives, friends, and fellow sufferers, and both medical and nonmedical practitioners, may cause or reinforce emotional distress, preoccupation with disease, and symptom-maintaining behaviors. The giving of repeated reassurance by other persons also tends to maintain morbid concerns.

SPECIAL PROBLEMS

MULTIPLE SYMPTOMS

Patients with hypochondriasis and somatization disorder are particularly demanding to treat, and the aim may have to be "damage limitation" (control of medical care, reducing disability, help for relatives) rather than cure.[4, 62]

CHRONIC PAIN

Severe chronic pain may have both physical and psychological etiologies. Antidepressant medication, behavioral and cognitive behavioral programs have all been shown to be of value.[21, 46]

HYPOCHONDRIASIS

A variety of procedures have been suggested for hypochondriasis. All require detailed assessment, a clearly agreed plan for frequent treatment sessions, and strenuous efforts to control medical care. Warwick[55] and Salkovskis[63] have described a cognitive and behavioral technique which appears to have had promising results. It is probable that the elements in this treatment have much in common with the psychotherapeutic methods described by Kellner[3] and others.

DYSMORPHOPHOBIA

It is a poorly defined syndrome which is often very difficult to treat. At times, dysmorphophobia is part of a psychotic syndrome and requires neuroleptic medication. A proportion of patients with relatively realistic expectations do well with surgery. Despite a number of promising case reports it is unclear to what extent psychological methods can be successful for the patients who have nonpsychotic dysmorphophobia.[64]

CONCLUSION

Medically unexplained symptoms are common in all medical practice but often have a good prognosis. It is essential that we take a comprehensive view of *clinical problems* and that we do not restrict our research or clinical series to patients with diagnosable psychiatric disorder. Persistent symptoms can pose great problems in management, but it is evident that modern psychological methods hold out a great promise for effective intervention. There remains an urgent need to evaluate treatment of the wide range of clinical problems and to devise methods of efficient delivery. So substantial is the overall clinical problem that we need to devise methods which can be used early in routine primary and hospital care. These routine symptom methods need to be supplemented by more intensive and individual care for patients with severe complaints that do not respond to straightforward methods. This means not only access to specialist psychiatric and psychological services, but probably also increased provision of specialist nurses who have been trained in the cognitive, behavioral, and other psychological methods which are shown to be effective. The more that such specialists can be incorporated into the routine organization of general practice and of hospital clinics, the more the treatments will be acceptable to patients and their families, and the more likely they are to be effective. The availability of the treatment described is currently severely limited by a shortage of skilled therapists. Few general practitioners and physicians have these skills, and clinical psychologists and nurse therapists are in short supply. Many, perhaps most, general psychiatrists do not have the interest or skills to offer this type of psychological management, and the number of specialist liaison psychiatrists remains grossly inadequate. Although some economy in treatment time may be possible if treatment is given in groups, this way of giving psychological treatment only goes a small way to bridging the gap between need and availability. Better training and improved facilities (especially for inpatient treatment) would greatly improve patient care. In view of the enormous current use of medical resources by these patients such investment would prove to be not only effective in improving outcome for patients and their families, but also costeffective.

References

1. Kellner R. The treatment of hypochondriasis: To reassure or not to reassure? The ease for reassurance. *Int Rev Psychiatry*. 1992;4:71–75.
2. Oppenheim J. *Shattered Nerves. Doctors, Patients and Depression in Victorian England*. New York: Oxford University Press;1991.
3. Kellner R. *Psychosomatic Syndromes and Somatic Symptoms*. Washington, DC: American Psychiatric Press;1991.
4. Bass C. *Somatization: Physical Symptoms and Psychological Illness*. Oxford, U.K.: Blackwell;1990.
5. Creed F, Mayou RA, Hopkins A. *Medical Symptoms Not Explained by Organic Disease*. London: The Royal College of Psychiatrists & The Royal College of Physicians;1992.
6. Lipowski ZJ. Somatization: The concept and its clinical application. *Am J Psychiatry*. 1988;145:1358–1368.
7. Bridges KW, Goldberg DP. Somatic presentation of DSM-III psychiatric disorders in primary care. *J Psychosom Res*. 1985;29:563–569.
8. Kellner R. *Somatization and Hypochondriasis*, New York: Praeger;1986.
9. Kellner R. Diagnosis and treatments of hypochondriacal syndromes. *Psychosomatics*. 1992;33:278–289.
10. Goodman JE, McGrath PJ. The epidemiology of pain in children and adolescents: A review. *Pain*. 1991;46:247–264.
11. Von Korff M, Dworkin SF, Le Resche LL, Kruger A. An epidemiologic comparison of pain complaints. *Pain*. 1988;32:173–183.
12. Crook J, Rideout E, Browne G. The prevalence of pain complaints in a general population. *Pain*. 1984;18:299–314.
13. Simon GE, Von Korff M. Somatization and psychiatric disorder in the NIMH epidemiologic catchment area study. *Am J Psychiatry*. 1991;148:1494–1495.
14. Bridges K, Goldberg D, Evans B, Sharpe T. Determinants of somatization in primary care. *Psychol Med*. 1991;21:473–483.
15. Drossman DA, Thompson WG. The irritable bowel syndrome: Review and a graduated multicomponent treatment approach. *Ann Int Med*. 1992; 116:1009–1010.
16. Kroenke K, Arrington ME, Mangelsdorff D. The prevalence of symptoms in medical out-patients and the adequacy of therapy. *Arch Intern Med*. 1990; 150:1685–1689.
17. Kroenke K, Mangelsdorff D. Common symptoms in ambulatory care: Incidence, evaluation, therapy and outcome. *Am J Med*. 1989;86:262–266.
18. Kroenke K. Symptoms in medical patients: An untended field. *Am J Med*. 1992;92(1A):3–6.
19. Bradlow J, Coulter A, Brooks P. *Patterns of Referral. A Study of Referrals to Out-Patient Clinics from General Practices in the Oxford Region*. Oxford, U.K.: Health Services Research Unit;1992.
20. Mayou RA, Hawton KE. Psychiatric disorder in the general hospital. *Br J Psychiatry*. 1986;149:172–190.

21. Keefe FJ, Dunsmore J, Burnett R. Behavioral and cognitive-behavioral approaches to chronic pain: Recent advances and future direction. *J Consult Clin Psychol.* 1992;60:528–536.
22. Katon W, Lin E, Von Korff M, Russo J, Lipscomb P, Bush T. Somatization: A spectrum of severity. *Am J Psychiatry.* 1991;148:34–40.
23. Chambers JB, Bass C. Chest pain and normal coronary anatomy: Review of natural history and possible aetiologic factors. *Prog Cardiovasc Dis.* 1990;33: 161–184.
24. Mayou RA, Seagroatt V, Goldacre M. Use of psychiatric services by patients in a general hospital. *Br Med J.* 1991;303:1029–1032.
25. Fink P. Surgery and medical treatment in persistent somatizing patients. *J Psychosom Res.* 1992;36:439–447.
26. Fink P: Physical complaints and symptoms of somatizing patients. *J Psychosom Res.* 1992;36:125–136.
27. Slavney PR, Teitelbaum ML. Patients with medically unexplained symptoms: DSM-III diagnoses and demographic characteristics. *Gen Hosp Psychiatry.* 1985; 7:21–25.
28. Katon W, Ries RK, Kleinman A. Part II: A prospective DSM-III study of 100 consecutive somatization patients. *Compr Psychiatry.* 1984;25:305–314.
29. Snyder S, Strain JJ. Somatoform disorders in the general hospital inpatient setting. *Gen. Hosp Psychiatry.* 1989;11:288–293.
30. Agras WS. Some structural changes that might facilitate the development of behavioural medicine. *J Consult Clin Psychol.* 1992;60:499–504.
31. Shaw J, Creed F. The cost of somatization. *J Psychosom Res.* 1991;35:307–312.
32. Kellner R. Somatization: The most costly comorbidity? In: Maser ID, Cloninger CR, eds. *Comorbidity of Mood and Anxiety Disorders.* Washington, DC: American Psychiatric Press;1990: pp 239–252.
33. Van Korff M, Katon W, Lin E. Psychological distress, physical symptoms, utilization and the cost-offset effect. In: Sartorius N, Goldberg D, De Girolamo G, Costa e Silva L, Lecrubier Y, Wittchen U. *Psychological Disorders in General Medical Settings.* New York: Hogrefe & Huber, 1990; pp 159–169.
34. Barsky AJ, Klerman GL. Overview: Hypochondriasis, bodily complaints, and somatic styles. *Am J Psychiatry.* 1983;140:273–283.
35. Barsky A. Amplification, somatization, and the somatoform disorders. *Psychosomatics.* 1992;33:28–34.
36. Sharpe M, Bass C. Pathophysiological mechanisms in somatization. *Int Rev Psychiatry.* 1992;4:81–97.
37. Kirmayer L, Robbins JM. *Current Concepts of Somatization. Research and Clinical Perspectives.* Washington, DC: American Psychiatric Press;1991.
38. Kirmayer LJ, Robbins JM. Three forms of somatization in primary care: Prevalence, co-occurence, and sociodemographic characteristics. *J Nerv Ment Dis.* 1991;179:647–655.
39. Hunt LM, Jordan B, Irwin S. Views of what's wrong: diagnosis and patients' concepts of illness. *Soc Sci & Med.* 1989;28:945–956.
40. Hadlow J, Pitts M. The understanding of common health terms by doctors, nurses and patients. *Soc Sci Med.* 1991;32:193–196.
41. Mayou RA. Editorial. Medically unexplained physical symptoms. *Br Med J.* 1991;303:534–535.

42. Mayou RA. The nature of bodily symptoms. *Br J Psychiatry.* 1976;129:55–60.
43. Mayou RA. Illness and behaviour and psychiatry. *Gen Hosp Psychiatry.* 1989; 11:307–312.
44. Mayou RA. Invited review: Atypical chest pain. *J Psychosom Res.* 1989;33:373–406.
45. Mayou RA. Patients' fears of illness, chest pain and palpitations. In: Creed F, Mayou RA, Hopkins A, eds. *Medical Symptoms Not Explained by Organic Disease.* London: Gaskell;1991.
46. France RD, Krishnan KRR. *Chronic Pain.* Washington, DC: American Psychiatric Press;1988.
47. Lishman WA. Physiogenesis and psychogenesis in the post-concussional syndrome. *Br J Psychiatry.* 1988;153:460–469.
48. Philips HC, Grant L. The evolution of chronic back pain problems: A longitudinal study. *Behav Res Ther.* 1991;29:435–441.
49. Tyrer S. Psychiatric assessment of chronic pain. *Br J Psychiatry.* 1992;160:733–741.
50. Munro A. Phenomenological aspects of monodelusional disorders. *Br J Psychiatry.* 1991;159:62–64.
51. Sutherland AJ, Rodin GM. Factitious disorders in a general hospital setting: Clinical features and a review of the literature. *Psychosomatics.* 1990;31:392–414.
52. Lipowski ZJ. Somatizaton and depression. *Psychosomatics.* 1990;31:13–21.
53. Smith GR. The epidemiology and treatment of depression when it coexists with somatoform disorders, somatization, or pain. *Gen Hosp Psychiatry.* 1992; 14:265–272.
54. Editorial. Negative investigations. *Lancet.* 1992;340:213.
55. Warwick H. The treatment of hypochondriasis: To reassure or not to reassure? Provision of appropriate and effective reassurance. *Int Rev Psychiatry.* 1992;4:76–80.
56. Guest GH, Drummond PD. Effect of compensation on emotional state and disability in chronic back pain. *Pain.* 1992;48:125–130.
57. Sharpe M, Peveler R, Mayou RA. Invited review. The psychological treatment of patients with functional somatic symptoms: A practical guide. *J Psychosom Res.* 1992;36:515–529.
58. Clouse RE. Psychopharmacologic approaches to therapy for chest pain of presumed esophageal origin. *Am J Med.* 1992;92:106S–113S.
59. Beitman BD, Basha IM, Trombka LH, Jayaratna MA, Russell BD, Tarr SK. Alprazolam in the treatment of cardiology patients with atypical chest pain and panic disorder. *J Clin Psychopharmacol.* 1988;8:127–130.
60. Lipowski ZJ. An in-patient programme for persistent somatizers. *Can J Psychiatry.* 1988;33:275–278.
61. Shorter E, Abbey SE, Gillies LA, Singh M, Lipowski ZJ. Inpatient treatment of persistent somatization. *Psychosomatics.* 1992;33:295–301.
62. Smith GR, Miller LM, Monson RA. Consultation-liaison intervention in somatization disorder. *Hosp Community Psychiatry.* 1986;37:1207–1210.
63. Salkovskis P. Psychological treatment of non-cardiac chest pain: The cognitive approach. *Am J Med.* 1992;92:114S.
64. Hollander E, Neville D, Frenkel M, Josephson S, Liebowitz MR. Body dysmorphic disorder. Diagnostic issues and related disorders. *Psychosomatics.* 1992;33:156–165.

Chapter 4
Nonverbal and Verbal Emotional Expression and Health

DIANE S. BERRY, JAMES W. PENNEBAKER

Beginning with Darwin,[1] many theorists have proposed a biological link between the experience and expression of the primary emotions.[1-4] To the extent that this helps to ensure the effective communication of affect, the adaptive value of such a link is clear. A reasonably reliable one-to-one correspondence between internal states and patterns of expression is necessary for the maintenance of parent–infant relationships, peer communication within a group, and communication between different groups of individuals. In most species, the modes of emotional expression are limited to variations in facial display, body movement, gesture, and nonverbal utterances such as screams and cries. In humans, emotional experience can also be vividly conveyed in language.

The purpose of this paper is to explore the links between the verbal and nonverbal expression of emotion and physiological activity. (In this paper, the terms *nonverbal* and *verbal* are used in a manner consistent with the nonverbal communication literature. In particular, nonverbal expression embraces all nonlinguistic aspects of communication regardless of channel. These include factors such as facial behaviors, gesture, and gaze, as well as vocal qualities such as intonation and paralinguistic cues.

Verbal expression refers to the process of translating the message into words, whether in the written or spoken channel.) We begin with a discussion of the different dimensions of emotional expression. We then examine the relation between individual differences in emotional expression and autonomic nervous system activity. In the third section, we evaluate recent findings concerning expressivity and physical health. Finally, we propose that, in humans, it is critical to distinguish between verbal and nonverbal emotional expression when considering their links to physical and mental health.

Individual Differences in the Expression of Emotion

In 1984, Buck[2] summarized his research on emotional expressiveness by categorizing nonverbal behaviors as either spontaneous or symbolic. Spontaneous communications are those universal patterns of nonverbal behaviors that specify internal states or traits. These communications reveal internal qualities with which they share a reliable, biologically based relationship.[1, 5-7] For example, placing one's hand on a hot stove will elicit a fairly predictable and easily recognizable facial and vocal response from most of us. Such spontaneous communications are automatic and thus difficult, albeit not impossible, to simulate or suppress.

A second category of expressive behaviors, referred to as symbolic communications, are learned and under varying degrees of conscious control. This form of emotional expression is socially and culturally mediated and generally thought to be poorly correlated with one's internal state. For example, the tendency to mask negative affect through the modulation of facial behaviors in accordance with socially sanctioned display rules has been observed in children as young as 1 or 2 years.[8] Whereas the spontaneous communication system is functional at birth and apparent throughout the lifespan, the symbolic communication system begins to interact with and modify spontaneous communication at a very young age. The precise nature of this interaction varies as a function of one's gender, culture, and specific social environment, yielding individual differences in expressive style.[9-11]

Traditionally, the concepts of spontaneous and symbolic communication styles have been applied to nonverbal rather than verbal (i.e., word-based) behaviors. This reflects, in part, different research traditions and methods among researchers interested in nonverbal communication and those studying language and cognitive processes. Although verbal expressivity would typically be categorized as a symbolic rather than spontaneous style, it is of interest to determine if symbolic nonverbal and verbal behaviors work in comparable ways. This would be particularly relevant for our understanding of individual differences in biological correlates of expressivity.

Verbal and nonverbal emotional communication styles share a number of characteristics. In particular, both are stable over time and can be viewed as meaningful individual difference factors. To some extent, these differences are probably related to temperament. Differences in facial animacy, for example, are observed in infants as soon as 36 hours after birth,[12] and stable individual differences in facial behaviors are displayed by age 2.[13] Similarly, behavioral studies with young children indicate that both verbal and nonverbal markers of shyness are readily apparent by age 3 and are highly reliable over time.[14] Social experience also seems to play an important role in determining expressivity. For example, some researchers report that abused children are less facially expressive and more verbally inhibited than are their nonabused peers. Presumably, these children learn to inhibit their facial displays and speech as a method of avoiding maltreatment.[15]

Both verbal and nonverbal patterns of emotional expressiveness appear to be socially shared within families. For example, Burrowes and Halberstadt,[16] and Halberstadt[17] have revealed that people from families that are high in nonverbal expressivity are more facially expressive than individuals from low-expressive families. Data from studies of naturally occurring emotional communications have further indicated that people from families that are low in expressivity are more accurate decoders of emotional expressions than are people from high-expressive families. Conversely, it is more difficult to read the natural, unposed emotional expressions exhibited by individuals from families that are low in expressivity than it is to read those of people from high-expressive families.

Halberstadt's interpretation of these findings is that individuals who grow up in families in which emotions are not overtly expressed become attuned to very subtle indicators of internal states, yielding high decoding accuracy. On the other hand, it is especially difficult to identify the emotional communications of people from low-expressive backgrounds because they have been taught to actively inhibit nonverbal displays of emotion. Interestingly, there is no difference in the ability of people from high- and low-expressive families to produce readable posed expressions. This argues against the alternative explanation that individuals from low-expressive families are difficult to read because they do not know how to successfully produce expressions of affect. Instead, they seem to refrain from using their skills in this domain during the course of their daily lives.

NONVERBAL EXPRESSIVENESS AND AUTONOMIC ACTIVITY

Individual differences in temperament, social experiences, and familial influence may contribute to the development of what researchers have labeled internalizing and externalizing styles of emotional expressivity.[1, 18] When confronted with an emotion-inducing stimulus, internalizers show little if any overt response, whereas externalizers are much more likely to openly express their reactions. For example, a number of studies have examined people's ability to identify the content of the slides that stimulus persons are viewing (e.g., pleasant versus unpleasant) from observing their facial behaviors. Judges are less often accurate in their identifications of the stimuli presented to internalizers than in their judgments of what externalizers are viewing.[19] Moreover, internalizers exhibit fewer actual facial behaviors when observing these stimuli than do externalizers.[20] Internalizers and externalizers are further characterized by different patterns of physiological response. In particular, internalizers show higher levels of skin conductance than do externalizers when exposed to emotionally charged stimuli.[21, 22] Internalizers also show increases in heart rate under these conditions, whereas externalizers do not.[1]

A number of studies suggest that the heightened autonomic responses of internalizers may reflect the work of behavioral inhibition. Specifically, internalizers work to actively suppress emotional expression. Fowles,[23] for example, summarized several studies that consistently demonstrated that when individuals were forced to inhibit or suppress their own behavior, specific increases in electrodermal activity occurred. Indeed, he concluded that electrodermal activity (e.g., skin conductance levels and phasic responses) served as a marker for behavioral inhibition. Consistent with this view, changes in physiological response have been observed within a given individual as a function of variations in overt expressiveness. For example, Pennebaker and Chew[24] found that when people engaged in a guilty knowledge task in which they attempted to inhibit spontaneous facial behaviors, their skin conductance levels increased from baseline. These findings, together with those dealing with internalizers, suggest that when such nonverbal responses are suppressed, they in effect go underground and are expressed covertly through increased autonomic arousal.

VERBAL EXPRESSIVENESS
AND AUTONOMIC ACTIVITY

Just as there are stable individual differences in the extent to which people exhibit nonverbal displays of their feelings, there are differences in the extent to which people are willing to verbally disclose personal information about traumatic, emotional events that they have experienced. Moreover, the physiological profiles that characterize high versus low disclosers parallel those that differentiate individuals with externalizing and internalizing patterns of emotional expression.[25] For example, Pennebaker et al.[26] asked subjects to talk into a tape recorder about their most traumatic personal experiences. These responses were recorded while the subjects were alone in an experimental cubicle. The subjects were then categorized as high or low disclosers on the basis of independent judges' ratings of how personal and stressful these descriptions sounded. It was found that low disclosers exhibited higher skin conductance levels than high disclosers when describing the traumatic event. Moreover, the autonomic levels among the high disclosers were significantly lower during their talking about traumatic topics than when they talked about relatively trivial control topics. Low disclosers exhibited higher levels of skin conductance when instructed to talk about a traumatic topic than when discussing a trivial topic.

Other studies have revealed similar patterns of data. In an in-depth interview project, 33 Holocaust survivors talked about their personal experiences during World War II while skin conductance level and heart rate were continuously measured.[27] Those subjects who benefited most from the experience in terms of long-term health and self-reports of well-being also evidenced significant drops in skin conductance while talking about particularly traumatic personal events. These data suggest that the disclosure of negative emotions may reduce physiological activity and stress whereas the active inhibition of such thoughts and feelings may prolong or exacerbate bodily activation.

INHIBITION OF EMOTIONAL EXPRESSIVENESS AND HEALTH

People who continuously inhibit the expression of their internal feelings thus experience higher baseline levels of physiological arousal than other persons. What might the long-term effects of such active inhibition be? Much research has documented that the inhibition of negative emotions via failure to disclose or discuss traumatic events is associated with heightened physiological arousal and health-related problems. Conversely, talking or writing about personal traumas brings about lower levels of physiological arousal and yields both short- and long-term improvements in health.[25] These data come from both correlational and experimental research.

In a series of questionnaire studies, several hundred college students and corporate employees were asked to rate the degree to which they had, either recently or in childhood, experienced each of several traumatic events (e.g., death of relative, divorce of parents, sexual trauma). In addition, participants rated the degree to which they had talked with others about each trauma they had experienced. Across samples of subjects who reported at least one such event, those who had not disclosed the trauma were more likely to have been diagnosed with cancer, high blood pressure, ulcers, and other major and minor health problems than were subjects who had confided about the event. Further, the college student subjects in this trauma–nonconfiding group were twice as likely to go to the student health center for illness during their freshman year than students who had not had a trauma or who had had traumas about which they had confided.[25, 28] Among adult samples, failing to disclose a childhood trauma was associated with an increased incidence of hospitalizations and physician visits.[29] Moreover, these effects held after statistically controlling for gender, age, and social class.

A series of laboratory studies provide further support for a link between verbal disclosure and health. In this research, subjects are typically assigned to a condition in which they write about extremely traumatic events or about relatively superficial control topics for 15 to 20 minutes per day for three to five consecutive days, depending on the specific study. Assessments of the participants' health status are obtained prior to the experiment as well as several weeks or months subsequent to its conclusion. In general, this work reveals that the health of those subjects who disclose traumatic experiences during the course of a study evidence significant reductions in physician visits during the 2 to 4 months after its completion.[30, 31] Furthermore, data obtained from blood samples taken before and after the 4-day writing phase of one experiment reveal that such disclosure enhances immune function.[32] Together, these findings point to links among the verbal inhibition of thoughts and feelings about traumatic personal experiences, physiological arousal, and physical health. In particular, people who do not disclose negative events appear to be under greater physical stress and are ultimately at greater risk for a variety of minor and major health problems than are high disclosers.

There is a marked similarity between the relation of physiological response to the verbal disclosure of emotionally traumatic events, and to the disclosure of emotion via nonverbal expression. To the extent that the active ongoing inhibition of nonverbal expression influences autonomic activity and places continual stress on the body, it would follow that nonverbal expressivity will also be related to health. Although we would expect links between nonverbal expressiveness and health, we do not make the blanket prediction that all individuals identified as low in expressiveness will be less healthy than all people identified as highly expressive. Rather, a number of variables should moderate the relation between expressiveness and health. Consistent with this view, the available data do not reveal simple linear relations between most measures of expressivity and physical status. For example, Friedman and Booth-Kewley[33] found no correlation between scores on a self-report measure of expressiveness, the Affective Communication Test (ACT), and the prevalence of heart disease in a sample of middle-aged males. Similarly, King and Emmons[34] found no relation between scores on either the ACT or a survey assessing general expressivity, the Emotional Expressiveness Questionnaire, and self-reports of undergraduates' daily symptoms or health center visits.

Under what conditions would one expect to find a relation between nonverbal expressivity and health? One relevant variable may be the extent to which a person expresses negative as opposed to positive feelings. The research on verbal disclosure and health previously described has most clearly revealed a relationship between inhibiting the disclosure of negative events and physical health. Thus, one might predict the inhibition of nonverbal expressions of negative affect to be especially stressful, and most likely to predict health status. Because individuals' nonverbal expressiveness of positive affect is unrelated to how expressive they are of negative feelings,[16] this would suggest that only measures of negative expression should predict health status. Therefore, indices such as the ACT which explicitly assess positive expression would indeed be expected to be uncorrelated with self-reports of negative expressivity, as previously reported.[16]

A second factor that needs to be considered when examining the relation of nonverbal expressivity and health is the specific nature of the measuring instruments used to assess expressivity. Much of the work on the development of individual differences in nonverbal behavior, as well as on the relations between expressivity and physiological activity, conceptualize expressivity in terms of variables such as facial animacy, vocal intonation, and encoding accuracy. For example, researchers who have studied internalizing and externalizing expression styles and their physiological correlates typically differentiate externalizers from internalizers on the basis of criteria such as how accurately judges can decode their facial movements. On the other hand, researchers studying the links between expressive style and health tend to assess the self-reported likelihood of performing particular behaviors related to openness about feelings rather than focusing on measures of actual physical expressivity. The Emotional Expressivity Questionnaire described earlier, for example, includes items such as, "If a friend surprised me with a gift, I wouldn't know how to act," and "I apologize when I have done something wrong."

These self-report measures appear to be tapping into a personality style that may or may not be isomorphic with actual indices of facial or vocal expressivity. Indeed, the ACT has been described as a measure of personal charisma or social popularity and is correlated with measures of extroversion.[35] Validation studies do reveal significant relations between measures such as facial behavior and ACT scores, but these relations tend to be modest in size.[36] Moreover, other studies have failed to document relations between measures of expressive style and measures of facial behavior. For example, Berry[37] found no relations between the frequency, speed, or complexity of people's facial behaviors and their self-reported general expressiveness. Together, these data call into question the overlap of the different measures of expressivity used in these programs of research, and suggest that more direct measures of expression than self-report items may be better predictors of health status.

Some support for this is provided by a recent study by Malatesta et al.[38] who videotaped women's facial behaviors while they described recent vivid emotional events. These clips were then played back without sound to naive judges, who rated the amount of facial expressiveness exhibited by the subjects. It was found that women who were judged to be facially inexpressive when describing negative emotional events reported more physical symptoms than did facially expressive women. Additional support for the link between nonverbal expressivity and health is provided by research with individuals exhibiting clinical alexithymia. One of the characteristics of this disorder is a low level of nonverbal expressiveness. These people are also more likely to experience somatic disorders than are other members of the population.[39]

A third question that warrants consideration is whether low expressivity, however measured, is by necessity indicative of inhibition. Pennebaker's model,[25] which generated the line of thought outlined here, specifically focused on a conflict between the desire to verbally disclose previous traumas and the inhibition of that desire. Research on the socialization of expressivity suggests that such learned inhibition of nonverbal expressive displays can indeed contribute to a low expressive style. However, other factors that are unrelated to inhibition also may contribute to variations in expressivity. For example, evidence of stable variations in the facial expressivity of 2-day-old infants lends support to a role of innate temperament differences that influence expression style.[13]

In all likelihood, then, there are some individuals who are naturally low in expressivity and experience neither conflict nor health problems as a result. On the other hand, individuals who are inexpressive because they have learned to inhibit their natural expressive tendencies may be at higher risk for health problems. Some support for this is provided by King and Emmons' finding[34] that self-reports of ambivalence over emotional expressiveness predict health status, whereas self-reports of general expressivity do not. This proposal is also consistent with the study by Friedman et al.[40] of the joint effects of expressiveness and type A or B classification on health. These researchers found that some low-expressive males were especially at risk for heart disease. These men were described by Friedman et al. as tense, overcontrolled, and actively inhibiting strong emotions. On the other hand, other men who were equally low in expressiveness were comparatively quite healthy. These men were described as quiet and relaxed individuals who were naturally low in expressivity. Finally, it should be noted that the nature of one's personal history may play an important role in determining a relation between expressiveness and health. For example, inexpressive persons who have experienced turbulent personal lives may be at greater risk for health problems than equally inexpressive people with more tranquil pasts.

Verbal versus Nonverbal Emotional Expression and Health

Clearly, there are several striking parallels between the nonverbal and verbal disclosure of emotional state. In most cases, emotional expressivity is linked with immediate drops in autonomic activity, especially electrodermal activity. In both the verbal and nonverbal modes, individual differences in expressivity moderate immediate changes in autonomic levels. Specifically, those who are classified as highly expressive (externalizers in the nonverbal literature; high disclosers in the verbal studies) evidence the greatest autonomic reductions during emotion-laden laboratory tasks.

In addition to the similarities outlined here, however, there are some important differences between the nonverbal and verbal modes of emotional expression. In particular, these forms of expression differ in the causal mechanisms that link them to long-term health. Pennebaker[25] has identified two independent processes by which expression may influence health. First, the active, ongoing inhibition of either verbal or nonverbal expressions of emotion requires sustained effort, can produce baseline increases in physiological arousal, and thus serves as a significant source of physical stress. Therefore, when low levels of either verbal or nonverbal expressivity signal the presence of ongoing inhibition, the emergence of related health problems is likely.

Second, translating an event into language, either by writing or talking, affects the way the experience is organized and encoded in the mind. The mere act of putting a trauma into words changes the memory of it. It evolves from being a large, diffuse, chaotic emotional experience into a coherent narrative or story, with a beginning, middle, and an end. Once the event is organized, it can more readily be assimilated and set aside.[41] The inhibition or the suppression of thoughts and emotions about the event then becomes unnecessary. Thus, health benefits due to verbal expression may further accrue as a result of this assimilation process.

Evidence for the specific health benefits of putting stressful experiences into words is accumulating from a variety of sources. In reanalyses of earlier studies, Harber and Pennebaker[42] found that subjects who wrote essays on traumatic subjects that were rated as organized or that evidenced increased organization over the course of the 4-day study were most likely to exhibit improved physical health and/or immune function. In another study, subjects were randomly assigned to write about either the emotions and facts surrounding a traumatic experience or, in one control condition, write about only their emotions concerning a trauma. Both groups wrote for four consecutive days. The results revealed that the process of organizing the event led to greater long-term health benefits than did simply venting emotions related to the event. Thus, both verbal and nonverbal expressivity may predict health status by virtue of their relations to inhibition. Verbal expressiveness should additionally influence health by helping individuals to cognitively reorganize and assimilate aversive emotional events. As discussed above, there is growing evidence from our laboratory and others that writing about traumatic experiences or discussing them in a clinical setting is associated with improvements in physical health and immune function as well as reduced reliance on medical facilities. Although no such studies have been conducted using induced nonverbal emotional expression, we suspect that they would reveal parallel albeit less powerful effects. This would seem to be an important issue for researchers to address in the future.

These lines of research have direct implications for psychotherapy and physical health. We suspect that therapeutic interventions that rely solely on the nonverbal expression of emotion (e.g., dance, art, music, or venting therapies) will likely yield immediate beneficial changes in autonomic activity, and perhaps other physiological improvements. These changes, however, may be greatly enhanced when therapy clients are additionally given the opportunity to translate their experiences into words. We believe that there is sufficient evidence to suggest that improvements in psychosomatic conditions will most likely be achieved by allowing individuals to express their traumatic experiences with both words and behaviors.

References

1. Darwin C. *The Expression of the Emotions in Man and Animals* (1872). New York: Philosophical Library;1972.
2. Buck R. *The Communication of Emotion.* New York: Guilford;1984.
3. Izard CE. *Human Emotions.* New York: Plenum;1977.
4. Tompkins S. *Affect, Imagery and Consciousness.* New York: Springer;1962.

5. Berry DS. What can a moving face tell us? *J Pers Soc Psychol.* 1990;58:1004–1014.
6. Berry DS. Child and adult sensitivity to gender information in patterns of facial motion. *Ecol Psychol.* 1991;3:349–366.
7. Gibson JJ. *The Ecological Approach to Visual Perception.* Boston: Houghton-Mifflin;1979.
8. Cole PM. Display rules and the socialization of affect displays. In: Zivin G, ed. *The Development of Expressive Behavior.* New York: Academic;1985: pp 269–290.
9. Ekman P, Friesen WV. *Unmasking the Face.* Englewood Cliffs, NJ: Prentice-Hall;1975.
10. Halberstadt AG. Family socialization of emotional expression and nonverbal communication styles and skills. *J Pers Soc Psychol.* 1986;51:827–836.
11. Hall JA. *Nonverbal Sex Differences.* Baltimore: Johns Hopkins Press;1984.
12. Field T. Neonatal perception of people: Maturational and individual differences. In: Field T, Fox N, eds. *Social Perception in Infants.* Norwood, NJ: Ablex, 1985; pp 31–52.
13. Malatesta CZ, Culver C, Tesman JR, Shepard B. The development of emotion expression during the first 2 years of life. *Monogr Soc Res Child Dev.* 1989;54:1–104.
14. Kagan J, Reznick JS, Snidman N. Biological bases of childhood shyness. *Science.* 1988;240:167–171.
15. Gaensbauer TJ, Sands K. Distorted affective communications in abused/neglected infants. *J Am Acad Child Psychiatry.* 1979;18:236–250.
16. Burrowes BD, Halberstadt AG. Self and family expressiveness styles in the experience and expression of anger. *J Nonverb Behav.* 1987;11:254–268.
17. Halberstadt AG. Family expressive styles and nonverbal communication skills. *J Nonverb Behav.* 1983;8:14–26.
18. Jones HE. The study of patterns of emotional expression. In: Reymert M, ed. *Feelings and Emotions.* New York: McGraw-Hill;1950.
19. Buck R, Savin VJ, Miller RE, Caul WF. Nonverbal communication of affect in humans. *J Pers Soc Psychol.* 1974;23:362–371.
20. Buck R, Miller RE, Caul WF. Sex, personality and physiological variables in the communication of emotion via facial expression. *J Pers Soc Psychol.* 1974;30:587–596.
21. Buck R. Individual differences in nonverbal sending accuracy and electrodermal responding: The externalizing–internalizing dimension. In: Rosenthal R, ed. *Skill in Nonverbal Communication.* Cambridge, U.K.: Oelgeschlager, Gunn & Hain;1979.
22. Lanzetta JT, Kleck RE. Encoding and decoding of nonverbal affect in humans. *J Pers Soc Psychol.* 1970;16:12–19.
23. Fowles DC. The three arousal model: Implications of Gray's two-factor learning theory for heart rate, electrodermal activity, and psychopathy. *Psychophysiology.* 1980;17:87–104.
24. Pennebaker JW, Chew CH. Deception, electrodermal activity and inhibition of behavior. *J Pers Soc Psychol.* 1985;49:1427–1433.
25. Pennebaker JW. Confession, inhibition, and disease. *Adv Exp Soc Psychol.* 1989;22:211–244.
26. Pennebaker JW, Hughes C, O'Heeron RC. The psychophysiology of confession: Linking inhibitory and psychosomatic process. *J Pers Soc Psychol.* 1987;52: 781–793.

27. Pennebaker JW, Barger SD, Tiebout J. Disclosure of traumas and health among Holocaust survivors. *Psychosom Med.* 1989;51:577–589.
28. Pennebaker JW. *Opening Up: The Healing Power of Confiding in Others.* New York: Morrow;1990.
29. Pennebaker JW, Susman JR. Disclosure of traumas and psychosomatic processes. *Soc Sci Med.* 1988;26:327–332.
30. Pennebaker JW, Beall SK: Confronting a traumatic event: Toward an understanding of inhibition and disease. *J Abnorm Psychol.* 1986;95:274–281.
31. Pennebaker JW, Colder M, Sharp LK. Accelerating the coping process. *J Pers Soc Psychol.* 1990;58:528–537.
32. Pennebaker JW, Kiecolt-Glaser JK, Glaser R. Disclosure of traumas and immune function: Health implications for psychotherapy. *J Consult Clin Psychol.* 1988;56:239–245.
33. Friedman HS, Booth-Kewley S. Personality, type A behavior and coronary heart disease: The role of emotion expression. *J Pers Soc Psychol.* 1987;53:783–792.
34. King LA, Emmons RA. Conflict over emotional expression: Psychological and physical correlates. *J Pers Soc Psychol.* 1990;58:864–877.
35. Riggio RE, Friedman HS. Impression formation: The role of expressive behavior. *J Pers Soc Psychol.* 50:421–427.
36. Riggio RE, Friedman HS. Individual differences and clues to deception. *J Pers Soc Psychol.* 1983;45:899–915.
37. Berry DS. *Perceiving Faces: Contributions of Dynamic Information.* Brandeis University, Waltham;1987. Thesis.
38. Malatesta CZ, Jomas R, Izard CE. The relation between low racial expressivity during emotional arousal and somatic symptoms. *Br J Med Psychol.* 1987;60:169–180.
39. Taylor GJ, Bagby RM, Parker JDA. The alexithymia construct: A potential paradigm for psychosomatic medicine. *Psychosom Med.* 1991;32:153–164.
40. Friedman HS, Hall JA, Harris MJ. Type A behavior, nonverbal expressive style, and health. *J Pers Soc Psychol.* 1985;48:1299–1315.
41. Horowitz MJ. *Stress Response Syndromes.* New York: Jasob Aronson;1986.
42. Harber KD, Pennebaker JW. Overcoming traumatic memories. In: Christianson SA, ed. *The Handbook of Emotion and Memory.* New York: Guilford Press;1993.

Chapter 5
Sick-Role Susceptibility: A Commentary on the Contemporary Database (1989–1991) and Classification System

BARRY BLACKWELL

THE SICK-ROLE CONCEPT

The distinction between the objective biomedical domain of disease and the more subjective psychosocial concept of illness or sickness was first made by the Swiss medical historian Henry Sigerist and later elaborated by the American sociologist Talcott Parsons in what he designated "the sick role."[1] The way in which this social role was enacted by the individual was defined by Mechanic and Volkart,[2] who introduced the term *illness behavior*. Later on, this concept was further amplified by the Australian psychiatrist Pilowsky,[3] who coined the term *abnormal illness behavior* to describe individuals whose chronic disability was disproportionate to demonstrable disease. The concept of illness behavior has attracted considerable attention in the last decade, with two international conferences, the first in Australia (1984) and the second in Canada (1985). This interest undoubtedly reflects societal concern

85

about what Barsky[4] has called the "paradox of health"—a rising preoccupation with sickness and disability despite objective improvements in health status and overall declining mortality. The manifestations of this preoccupation can be observed at the individual and societal level.[5] Patients are displaying and doctors are treating an expanding panoply of fashionable disorders, categorized by Stewart[6] as the changing faces of somatization. As shown in Table 5.1, these new illnesses can be added to the old, more traditional manifestations of the sick role cataloged by Katon.[7]

From a societal perspective, what Barsky calls the medicalization of daily life and the commercialization of health have resulted in escalating national expenditures. One particular manifestation of the increasing social burden of sick-role behavior has been concern about the number of individuals receiving Social Security Disability for chronic symptoms, particularly pain, that are not adequately accounted for by objective medical evidence. The "purging" of the Disability rolls at the beginning of the Reagan Administration and the subsequent public reaction resulted in Congress appointing a commission to address this topic. This in turn led to an Institute of Medicine Committee on Pain, Disability and Chronic Illness Behavior. In its 1987 report,[8] the Committee firmly rejected the use of the term *illness behavior* as either a disease or diagnosis, and they categorized it as a misleading attempt to lump together conditions and concepts best considered separately. This denunciation was reflective of concerns increasingly expressed in the literature. Criticism has focused mainly on the self-evident conclusion that illness behavior is an eye-of-the-beholder phenomenon, and that too often the eye is that of a physician. The principle instrument developed by Pilowsky to measure illness behavior is saturated with neuroticism, a dimension related to excessive medical complaints which cannot be equated with illness behavior unless there is a concurrent, objective assessment of the medical condition.[9] This has led to the tongue-in-cheek conclusion that the abnormal illness behavior is often not that of the patient but that of the referring or treating physician.[10] Support for this unhappy contention comes from a study comparing patients'

TABLE 5.1
Medical Specialties and Their Problem Patients (adapted from Katon[7])

Allergy	food allergies
Cardiology	atypical chest pain
Dentistry	TMJ syndrome
Emergency room	Munchausen syndrome
ENT	tinnitus
Endocrinology	hypoglycemia
Gastroenterology	irritable bowel
Internal medicine	chronic fatigue syndrome, vitamin deficiency
Neurology	dizziness, headache
Obsterics/Gynecology	pelvic pain, premenstrual syndrome
Occupational medicine	multiple chemical sensitivity
Orthopedics	low back pain
Psychiatry	somatization, conversion disorders
Pulmonary	hyperventilation, dyspnea
Rehabilitation	closed head injury
Rheumatology	fibromyalgia

with physicians' perceptions of emotional factors in the presentation of medical problems in primary care.[11] In this study, the physician's assessment of an emotional contribution was completely unrelated to the patient's self-reports of psychological symptoms, and was most influenced by the physician's estimate of lack of medical severity and the patient's dissatisfaction with care. Put simply, illness behavior in this study was a disgruntled patient whom the physician was unable to diagnose. Such a conclusion is not confined to primary care since similar findings of inexplicable amounts of suffering have been noted on a neurology ward.[12]

What becomes clear is that the illness behavior label is a blunt instrument in the hands of an unsophisticated physician. Pilowsky[3] himself has pointed out that to understand this diagnosis is "a difficult task and a heavy responsibility." It requires a commitment to the kind of semiotic perspective which views symptoms not simply as icons or indices of disease, but as symbolic statements of suffering which can only be fully interpreted through an empathic inquiry into the patient's attributions and beliefs.[13]

Whatever the problems of definition or measurement may be, there remain compelling reasons why, in 1992, we must continue to grapple with the paradox of sick-role susceptibility. People who believe they are sicker than the doctor does are not only expensive to treat and maintain, but there is reason to suppose that at both the individual and societal level illness behavior influences mortality. People who rate their own health as poor are more likely to die sooner for reasons that remain unexplained.[14] A society like Sri Lanka appears to have low mortality rates because there is a greater sensitivity to disease or the risk of dying associated with a highly efficient cultural use of curative services.[15]

CONTEMPORARY DATABASE

My personal interest in the sick role began 20 years ago with the development of a cognitive behavioral approach to the treatment of patients on the psychosomatic unit at Cincinnati General Hospital.[16] Over the years a database was accumulated and made available to others as an Illness Behavior Bibliography.[17] A burgeoning and diffuse literature made it difficult to maintain this project, and several years ago it was allowed to lapse. The invitation to participate in a workshop at the semicentennial annual meeting of the American Psychosomatic Society sparked a new look at this field of inquiry. A Medline search was initiated under the Index Medicus key phrase *sick role*. For the 5 years 1987 through 1991, there were 1118 English-language citations. This was reduced to a more manageable 526 citations for the three most recent years, 1989 through 1991. After a review of titles, topics, and journals a total of 148 citations were selected for detailed review as the basis for this update. The size of the database is intimidating and is widely dispersed through different disciplines and journals.

COMMENTARY

Before proceeding to evaluate the areas of inquiry and trends in the field, there are a number of methodologic questions concerning the database.

MEASUREMENT ISSUES

Of the papers reviewed, 81 contained elements of experimental design and used a bewildering variety of rating scales, inventories, questionnaires, surveys, checklists, schedules, indices, and lists. Table 5.2 shows the 65 measuring instruments used in these articles. With so many rating scales of uncertain validity, it is not surprising that terms are often confusing, poorly defined, or potentially duplicative. For example, one study[18] using the Somatosensory Amplification Scale and the Whitely Index found strong correlations between the scales, and questioned the independence of somatization and hypochondriasis. But another study using different rating scales and different terminology came to an opposite conclusion. Patients with fibromyalgia and rheumatoid arthritis were studied for increased body awareness (which some people call *somatization*) and illness worry (which others might term *hypochondriasis*). In this study, the distinction seemed valid and useful since disability in fibromyalgia (but not in rheumatoid arthritis) was more determined by illness worry than by body awareness.[19]

Even when terms are agreed upon and the scales that measure them appear valid, there is significant uncertainty about the independence of some variables. Central to the entire issue of illness behavior is the influence of medical disorders on psychological measures. The capability to determine the extent to which disability is disproportionate to detectable disease requires that there be objective measures of both disability and disease that are truly independent of one another. Historically, the way in which such measures may be confounded is illustrated by elevation in the first three scales of the Minnesota Multiphasic Personality Inventory

TABLE 5.2
Illness Behavior Evaluations (Rating Scales, Inventories, and Questionnaires) cited in 81 Experimental Studies, 1989–1991

Body awareness
SCL-90 somatization
Somatosensory amplification
Private body consciousness
Seriousness of illness
Whitely index
Belloc health questionnaire
Sickness impact profile
Hopkins symptom checklist
Health status questionnaire
Illness distress scale
Severity of illness-disease course
Psychosomatic symptoms checklist
SMU health questionnaire
Pennebaker PILL

Coping/behavior
Arthritis impact
Coping strategy
Self-efficacy inventory
Ways of coping
Habitual response to illness
Self help in chronic illness
Billings and Moore coping questionnaire
Activities of daily living
Illness behavior questionnaire
Health opinion survey
Illness behavior assessment schedule

Affect
Beck depression
GHQ
Brief symptom inventory
MMPI
Hamilton depression
CES-D
Zung depression
Carroll depression
Diagnostic interview schedule

Affect (continued)
Mental health inventory
Positive affect scale
State-trait anxiety
Clinical interview schedule

Social support
Louisville social support
UCLA loneliness scale
Social problem questionnaire
Dyadic adjustment scale
Inventory of socially supportive behaviors

Stress
Holmes-Rahe
Life experience survey
Hassles scale
Daily stress inventory

Attitudes/cognitions
Health locus of control
Children's health care attitudes
Recovery locus of control
Mischel uncertainty illness
Northouse fear of recurrence
Demoralisation scale
Toronto alexithymia scale
Bond questionnaire (defensive style)
Psychosocial adjustment to illness
Crumbaugh purpose in life
Expanded attributional style
Alienation from self
Alienation from work
Hackett-Cassem denial
Life orientation test
Thematic apperception
Models of diabetes
Inflammatory bowel disease concerns

(MMPI) (hysteria, depression, and hypochondriasis). Although named "the psychosomatic triad" because of their ubiquitous elevation in a variety of disorders thought to display illness behavior, these scales are also sensitive to unequivocal medical conditions.[20] A similar contemporary finding has occurred with the concept of alexithymia, with recent studies[21, 22] reporting that scores on the Toronto Alexithymia Scale were elevated among medical patients and correlated with a lower quality of life. The authors named this "secondary" or "trait" alexithymia, and postulate that it develops as a defense to ward off suffering due to disease.

In the psychological domain, there is continued uncertainty of the extent to which measures of various attributes are truly independent of one another. This is particularly true of the role that mood may play as a modifier of other measures such as somatization,[23–25] illness behavior,[26] patient concerns,[27] alexithymia or denial.[28] One review[29] proposes a unifying concept of "negative affectivity" which plays a central role as a universal contaminant of self-report health measures. Another study[30] arrives at a similar conclusion but coins the term *pessimistic explanatory style*. Given the plethora of scales, it is particularly valuable that a book has appeared which reviews all the instruments used for measuring health.[31]

RESEARCH DESIGN

The majority of studies are cross-sectional rather than longitudinal. This feature yields correlational findings that contribute to the difficulty of distinguishing one cognitive concept from another, or separating cause from effect. A rare exception is a longitudinal study of labeling in hypertension[32] which did not support the findings of earlier studies[33] that patients newly diagnosed with high blood pressure show increased absenteeism from work. However, prospective studies such as this one may yield spurious negative results because the high level of scrutiny involved induces compliance.

The populations observed have been various, and generalizability is inevitably restricted. Some authors study a single disease such as diabetes,[34] myocardial infarction[35] or Crohn's disease,[36] while others include heterogeneous medical disorders.[18, 37] A few studies contrast conditions that are assumed to be either functional or structural. Such comparisons include irritable and inflammatory bowel disease,[27] fibromyalgia and rheumatoid arthritis,[19] or dyspepsia and peptic ulcer.[38] Other populations involve not diseases but symptoms, such as chronic pain[39] or tinnitus.[40] Another source of variance has been the timeline of research. Some studies focus on the early stages of health-seeking behavior in primary-care medical settings,[41–43] while others deal with the later stages of chronic disease. One study compared response to an acute with response to a chronic condition, in this case wrist fracture with stroke.[44] An interesting methodologic innovation has been attention to a critical juncture in the natural history of a disorder in order to observe the "at risk" role,[45] for example following detection of a lump in the breast or recurrence of myocardial infarction.[46]

One important emphasis has been the widespread use of experimental designs to study cognitive factors in response to the threat of illness. Like much research involving experimental manipulation of psychological variables, many of these studies make use of healthy volunteers, often students.[28, 47]

AREAS OF INQUIRY, AND TRENDS

In a previous presentation on this topic to the American Psychosomatic Society in 1982, a conceptual model was presented that considered illness behavior or sick-role susceptibility to be the end product of a process by which bodily sensations were filtered and given valency or meaning by biological, psychological, or social and cultural factors (Fig. 5.1). This model will be used to break down and discuss the contemporary database.

Biological Factors. Table 5.3 summarizes the biological factors thought to influence susceptibility to sick-role behavior. Recent research has added little to this list, and only three citations were identified in the literature review. A Swedish study of hypochondriasis[48] found a correlation between alexithymia scores and increased concentrations of homovanillic acid in the

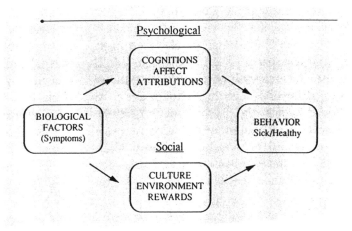

Figure 5.1 Biopsychosocial Influences on Sick-Role Behavior.

cerebrospinal fluid. This finding conflicts with Nemiah's hypothesis that implied diminished dopaminergic activity in the mesolimbic pathways of patients with alexithymia. Most studies of sick-role susceptibility have focused on chronic disease, but an interesting Italian project[49] explored the illness attitudes of women during pregnancy and found a progressive increase in hypochondriacal fears and disease phobia with each trimester. This study resonates with interest in the "at risk" role.[45, 50] It may have important preventative implications because focusing on attitudes, beliefs, and behaviors at times of new diagnosis or recurrence may provide insights into strategies that reduce sick-role susceptibility later in the course of a disease.

Psychological Factors.   Table 5.4 summarizes the psychological factors that influence sick-role susceptibility, and the bulk of citations in the current review involve such influences. As the field has evolved, it has incorporated new concepts and theories. A major shift has been away from an interest solely in medical settings and vulnerability factors to include people who shun traditional care,[41, 51, 52] utilize alternative medicine,[53–56] or possess

TABLE 5.3
Biological Influences

Primary	Secondary
Autonomic reactivity	Deconditioning
Response specificity	Drug dependence
Pain threshold	'At risk' transitions
Disease characteristics	
Chronic	
Intermittent	
Etiologically obscure	
Poorly controlled	
Cortico-limbic dysjunction	

psychological attributes and coping strategies which buffer them from the sick role. Such attributes include the hardiness concept involving commitment, control, and challenge in the face of disease.[57–59] Self-help[60, 61] or active coping[62, 63] can be contrasted with helplessness,[64] self-handicaping,[65] or emotion-focused coping,[66, 67] and optimism[68, 69] can be contrasted with pessimism or negative affectivity.[23, 29] This range of protective influences adds significantly to the traditional role of denial[29, 35, 70] in reducing sick-role susceptibility. The interest in positive or protective factors is reflected in an overall concern for quality of life[71] and minimization of the sick role.

Particular emphasis and research on psychological factors has been placed on cognitive adaptation to bodily change[72] or response to life-threatening events.[61] A popular explanatory model has become the so-called commonsense representation of illness[73, 74] with emphasis on the individual's personal view of their particular condition.[34] One interesting review[75] conceptualizes hypochondriasis as "health anxiety" and likens reassurance seeking to the anxiety-reducing function of a compulsive ritual.

Social and Cultural Factors. Table 5.5 lists the social and cultural factors thought to influence sick-role susceptibility. In the contemporary

TABLE 5.4
Psychological Influences

	Cognitive	Affective	Behavioral
State (transient)	New symptom attribution Cognitive impairment (age, psychosis)	Depression Anxiety	Developmental stage

Trait (enduring)	Hypochondriasis
	Denial
	Locus of control
	Self handicapping
	Health beliefs
	Belief in physicians
	Religious beliefs
	Hardiness
		Alexithymia
		Pessimistic/optimistic style
		Negative affectivity
			Somatization
			Pain tolerance
			Learned helplessness
			Coping style
			   Active vs. avoidant
			   Emotion vs. problem focused
			Affiliative tendencies

TABLE 5.5
Social, Environmental, and Cultural Influences

Stress levels
Social support/significant others
Gender role
Labelling (social sanction)
Contagion ('mass hysteria')
Modelling (especially childhood)
Conditioning
Culture
Migration
Marital status/satisfaction
Employment status/satisfaction
Socioeconomic status
Financial rewards (entitlements/compensation/
  litigation)
Medical investigation and treatment

literature, the social dimension has particularly emphasized developmental influences across the age spectrum[37, 71] from childhood[76] to old age.[77–80] Special attention is being paid to parental influences that may shape the later development of illness behavior.[81–85] Interest in gender roles continues.[42, 43, 86] At least superficially it appears as if women view themselves as healthier, have a tendency to behave sicker and live longer, while men tend to see themselves as sicker, shun health care, and die younger. One review[87] cautions against such glib generalizations. Research on social support and particularly on the role of the spouse with a sick person is paying more sophisticated attention to the nuances of interactions,[39, 88, 89] including the gender of the afflicted partner, the quality of the relationship, and the timing of support relative to the onset of illness.[90] The role of social stress from either major life events or daily hassles has been studied with regard to such mediating influences as chronicity, controllability,[91] and personal perception.[36, 38] Although monetary gain is an important reinforcement in sick-role adoption, only a single study[92] addresses this topic with an exploration of how the resolution of litigation influences psychological symptoms.

Broader cultural factors continue to be explored, and include the effects of migration[93] and descriptions of culture-bound syndromes such as Figa in the Yemen[94] and Kesambet in Bali.[95] Ethnographic depictions of cultural variation in sick-role behavior[53, 54, 96] contrast sharply with the conclusion from a review of all the experimental studies to date on pain[97] which fails to find support for any cultural component to either pain threshold or behavior.

Finally, there is an interesting report of an outbreak of epidemic hysteria[98] which demonstrates the role of contagion, modeling, and personal vulnerability in the acute adoption of the sick role.

CLASSIFICATION AND TREATMENT

Two particularly striking features of this literature are the absence of treatment interventions and the lack of any unifying system of classification. The descriptive parsimony and nonetiologic sterility of the *Diagnostic and Statistical Manual* (DSM) completely fail to provide a framework around which to organize this large and expanding area of inquiry. While one can sympathize with the Institute of Medicine's rejection of the concept of illness behavior, the current systems of classification are equally unsatisfactory and fail to do justice to the evolving data. The category of somatoform disorders is particularly unsatisfactory.[99] It makes untenable distinctions between hypochondriasis and somatization, and the subcategory of somatoform pain disorders places undue emphasis on the single symptom of pain, ignoring the many other singular or syndromal manifestations of somatic preoccupation encountered in this review. The conversion category is equally unsatisfactory because it departs from a nonetiologic stance in the area of conflict or primary gain that is particularly difficult to define. The classification "Psychological Factors Affecting a Physical Condition" is virtually ignored by clinicians and one might well ask, "Where have all the psychosomatic disorders gone?" None of these subdivisions of the diagnostic and statistical manual do justice to the information in the literature.[99, 100]

On the basis of many years of clinical study and research, my colleagues and I proposed a unifying syndrome with seven features[16] and later described a treatment strategy with matching interventions.[101] Table 5.6 shows this model which is capable of assimilating any of the biological, psychological, and social variables dealt with in the existing and evolving database on sick-role susceptibility. We hope that the model can be useful to others who strive for clarity in a confusing field and are interested in conceptually based treatments.

As a final thought-provoking suggestion, I propose that the seven features of this syndrome be given the classificatory title of *Biopsychosocial Factors Affecting Disability Due to Medical Disorders*. This unifying concept might become the only somatoform diagnosis. This would have the following advantages:

(1) It requires concurrent biomedical and psychosocial assessment and therefore avoids the dualism implicit in current categorizations.

(2) It unifies the existing somatoform disorders and psychological factors affecting a medical condition. This avoids the often impossible task of deciding whether or not there is an adequate physiological basis for any particular disorder.

(3) This classification is descriptive but not reductionistic, and incorporates all of the features of somatoform disorders present in the current classification.

(4) It is etiologic but remains atheoretical since it requires a consideration of all the biological, psychological, social and cultural factors which may be involved.

(5) It encourages conceptually based treatment choices and discourages the contemporary "Chinese menu" approach to the treatment of chronic pain and various other forms of sick-role behavior.

(6) Finally, this conceptualization makes it possible to reconcile a vast literature with a classificatory system.

TABLE 5.6
Features and Management of Sick-Role Behavior:
Biopsychosocial Factors Affecting Disability Due to Medical Disorders

Features of syndrome		Management strategy	
1	Disability disproportionate to detectable disease	1	Thorough disease assessment
2	Search for disease validation	2	Redefinition of symptoms without challenging reality
3	Appeal to physician responsibility	3	Patient responsibility
4	Attidudes of vulnerability; helplessness	4	Symptom control; self management
5	Avoidance of healthy role (primary gain)	5	Enhancement of healthy role
6	Environmental rewards for sick role (secondary gain)	6	Redeployment of environmental rewards
7	Interpersonal behaviors that sustain sick role	7	Physician behavior to minimize sick role

References

1. Susser M. Disease, illness, sickness; impairment, disability and handicap. *Psychol Med.* 1990;20:471–473.
2. Mechanic D, Volkart EH. Stress, illness behavior, and the sick role. *Am Sociol Rev.* 1961;26:51–58.
3. Pilowsky I. The concept of abnormal illness behavior. *Psychosomatics.* 1990;31: 207–213.
4. Barsky AJ. The paradox of health. *N Engl J Med.* 1988;318:414–418.
5. Barsky AJ. *Worried Sick: Our Troubled Quest for Wellness.* Boston: Little Brown;1988.
6. Stewart DE. The changing faces of somatization. *Psychosomatics.* 1990;31: 153–158.
7. Katon WJ. The development of a randomized trial of consultation–liaison psychiatry trial in distressed high utilizers of primary care. *Psychiatr Med.* 1991;9:577–591.
8. Osterweis M, Kleinman A, Mechanic D, eds. *Pain and Disability.* Washington, DC: National Academy Press;1987.
9. Zonderman AB, Heft MW, Costa PT Jr. Does the illness behavior questionnaire measure abnormal illness behavior? *Health Psychology.* 1985;4:425–436.
10. Mayou R. Illness behavior and psychiatry. *Gen Hosp Psychiatry.* 1989;11: 307–312.
11. Jones LR, Mabe PA, Riley WT. Physician interpretation of illness behavior. *Int J Psychiatry Med.* 1989;19:237–248.
12. Creed F, Firth D, Timol M, Metcalfe R, Pollock S. Somatization and illness behaviour in a neurology ward. *J Psychosom Res.* 1990;34:427–437.
13. Priel B, Rabinowitz B, Pels RJ. A semiotic perspective on chronic pain. Implications for the interaction between patient and physician. *Br J Med Psychol.* 1991;64:65–71.
14. Idler EL, Kasl S. Health perceptions and survival: Do global evaluations of health status really predict mortality? *J Gerontol.* 1991;46:S55–S65.
15. Caldwell J, Gajanayake I, Caldwell P, Peiris I. Sensitization to illness and the risk of death: An explanation for Sri Lanka's approach to good health for all. *Soc Sci Med.* 1989;28:365–379.
16. Wooley S, Blackwell B, Winget C. A learning theory model of chronic illness behavior: Theory, treatment and research. *Psychosom Med.* 1978;40:379–401.
17. Blackwell B, Gutmann M. An illness behavior bibliography. *Psychiatr Med.* 1987;5:171–176.
18. Barsky AJ, Wyshak G, Klerman GL. The Somatosensory Amplification Scale and its relationship to hypochondriasis. *J Psychiatr Res.* 1990;24:323–334.
19. Robbins JM, Kirmayer W, Kapusta MA. Illness worry and disability in fibromyalgia syndrome. *Int J Psychiatry Med.* 1990;20:49–63.
20. Blackwell B, Merskey H, Kellner R. Somatoform pain disorders. In: *Treatments of Psychiatric Disorders: A Task Force Report of the American Psychiatric Association.* Washington, DC: American Psychiatric Press;1989.
21. Wise TN, Mann LS, Mitchell JD, Hryvniak M, Hill B. Secondary alexithymia: An empirical validation. *Compr Psychiatry.* 1990;31:284–288.

22. Wise TN, Mann LS, Hryvniak M, Mitchell JD, Hill B. The relationship between alexithymia and abnormal illness behavior. *Psychother Psychosom.* 1990;54:18–25.
23. Noyes R Jr, Kathol RG, Debelius-Enemark P, Williams J, Mutgi A, Suelzer MT, Clamon GH. Distress associated with cancer as measured by the Illness Distress Scale. *Psychosomatics.* 1990;31:321–330.
24. Billings CK. Anxiety and physical illness. *Psychiatr Med.* 1990;8:149–162.
25. Brown FW, Golding JM, Smith GR Jr. Psychiatric comorbidity in primary care somatization disorder. *Psychosom Med.* 1990;52:445–451.
26. Grassi L, Rosti G, Albieri G, Marangolo M. Depression and abnormal illness behavior in cancer patients. *Gen Hosp Psychiatry.* 1989;11:404–411.
27. Drossman DA, Leserman J, Li Z, Mitchell CM, Zagami EA, Patrick DL. The rating form of IBD patient concerns. A new measure of health status. *Psychosom Med.* 1991;53:701–712.
28. Flannery RB Jr, Perry JC. Self-rated defense style, life stress, and health status: An empirical assessment. *Psychosomatics.* 1990;31:313–320.
29. Watson D, Pennebaker JW. Health complaints, stress, and distress: Exploring the central role of negative affectivity. *Psychol Rev.* 1989;96:234–254.
30. Lin EH, Peterson C. Pessimistic explanatory style and response to illness. *Behav Res Ther.* 1990;28:243–248.
31. McDowell I, Newell C. *Measuring Health: A Guide to Rating Scales and Questionnaires.* New York: Oxford University Press;1987.
32. Moum T, Naess S, Sorensen T, Tambs K, Holmen J. Hypertension labelling, life events and psychological well-being. *Psychol Med.* 1990;20:635–646.
33. Alderman MH, Lamport B. Labelling of hypertensives: A review of the data. *J Clin Epidemiol.* 1990;43:195–200.
34. Hampson SE, Glasgow RE, Tooben DJ. Personal models of diabetes and their relations to self-care activities. *Health Psychol.* 1990;9:632–646.
35. Trijsburg RW, Bal JA, Parsowa WP, Erdman RAM, Duivenvoorden HJ. Prediction of physical indisposition with the help of a questionnaire for measuring denial and overcompensation. *Psychother Psychosom.* 1989;51:193–202.
36. Garrett VD, Brantley PJ, Jones GN, McKnight GT. The relation between daily stress and Crohn's disease. *J Behav Med.* 1991;14:87–96.
37. Chaturvedi SK, Bhandari S. Somatisation and illness behaviour. *J Psychosom Res.* 1989;33:147–153.
38. Hui WM, Shiu LP, Lam SK. The perception of life events and daily stress in nonulcer dyspepsia. *Am J Gastroenterol.* 1991;86:292–296.
39. Saarijarvi S. A controlled study of couple therapy in chronic low back pain patients. Effects on marital satisfaction, psychological distress and health attitudes. *J Psychosom Res.* 1991;35:265–272.
40. Kirsch CA, Blanchard EB, Parnes SM. Psychological characteristics of individuals high and low in their ability to cope with tinnitus. *Psychosom Med.* 1989;51:209–217.
41. Murray J, Corney R. Not a medical problem? An intensive study of the attitudes and illness behavior of low attenders with psychosocial difficulties. *Soc Psychiatry Psychiatr Epidemiol.* 1990;25:159–164.
42. Vazquez-Barquero JL, Wilkinson G, Williams P, Diez-Manrique JF, Pena C. Mental health and medical consultation in primary care settings. *Psychol Med.* 1990;20:681–694.

43. Corney RH. Sex differences in general practice attendance and help seeking for minor illness. *J Psychosom Res.* 1990;34:525–534.
44. Partridge C, Johnston M. Perceived control of recovery from physical disability: Measurement and prediction. *Br Clin Psychol.* 1989;28:53–59.
45. Cella DF, Mahon SM, Donovan MI. Cancer recurrence as a traumatic event. *Behav Med.* 1990;16:15–22.
46. Loveys B. Transitions in chronic illness: The at-risk role. *Holistic Nurs Pract.* 1990;4(3):56–64.
47. Croyle RT, Ditto PH. Illness cognition and behavior: An experimental approach. *J Behav Med.* 1990;13:31–52.
48. von Scheele C, Nordgren L, Kempi V, Hetta J, Hallborg A. A study of so-called hypochondriasis. *Psychother Psychosom.* 1990;54:50–56.
49. Fava GA, Grandi S, Michelacci L, Saviotti F, Conti S, Bovicelli L, Trombini G, Orlandi C. Hypochondriacal fears and beliefs in pregnancy. *Acta Psychiatr Sand.* 1990;82:70–72.
50. Hilton BA. The relationship of uncertainty, control, commitment, and threat of recurrence to coping strategies used by women diagnosed with breast cancer. *J Behav Med.* 1989;12:39–54.
51. Murray J, Corney R. Locus of control in health: The effects of psychological well-being and contact with the doctor. *Int J Soc Psychiatry.* 1989;35:361–369.
52. Demers RY, Altamore R, Mustin H, Kleinman A, Leonardi D. An exploration of the dimensions of illness behavior. *J Fam Pract.* 1980;11:1085–1092.
53. Fabrega H Jr. The concept of somatization as a cultural and historical product of western medicine. *Psychosom Med.* 1990;52:653–672.
54. Semmes CE. Nonmedical illness behavior: A model of patients who seek alternatives to allopathic medicine. *J Manipulative Physiol Ther.* 1990;13:427–436.
55. Tonai S, Maezawa M, Kamei M, Satoh T, Fukui T. Illness behavior of housewives in a rural area in Japan: A health diary study. *Cult Med Psychiatry.* 1989;13:405–417.
56. El-Islam MF, Abu-Dagga SI. Illness behaviour in mental ill-health in Kuwait. *Scand J Soc Med.* 1990;18:195–201.
57. Kobasa SC, Maddi SR, Kahn S. Hardiness and health: A prospective study. *J Pers Soc Psychol.* 1982;42:168–177.
58. Kobasa SC. The hardy personality: Toward a social psychology of stress and health. In Suls J, Sanders G, eds. *Social Psychology of Health and Illness.* Hillsdale, NJ: Erlbaum;1982.
59. Drory Y, Florian V. Long-term psychosocial adjustment to coronary artery disease. *Arch Phys Med Rehabil.* 1991;72:326–331.
60. Braden CJ. A test of the self-help model: Learned response to chronic illness experience. *Nurs Res.* 1990;39:42–47.
61. Taylor SE. Adjustment to threatening events. *Am Psychol.* 1983;38:1161–1173.
62. Jensen MP, Turner JA, Romano JM. Self-efficacy and outcome expectancies: Relationship to chronic pain coping strategies and adjustment. *Pain.* 1991;44:263–269.
63. Ehmann TS, Beninger RJ, Gawel MJ, Riopelle RJ. Coping, social support, and depressive symptoms in Parkinson's disease. *J Geriatr Psychiatry Neurol.* 1990;3:85–90.

64. Spinhoven P, Jochems PA, Linssen ACG, Bogaards M. The relationship of personality variables and patient recruitment to pain coping strategies and psychological distress in tension headache patients. *Clin J Pain.* 1991;7:12–20.
65. Organista PB, Miranda J. Psychosomatic symptoms in medical outpatients: An investigation of self-handicapping theory. *Health Psychol.* 1991;10:427–431.
66. Davis-Berman J. Physical self-efficacy, perceived physical status, and depressive symptomatology in older adults. *J Psychol.* 1990;124:207–215.
67. Bomardier CH, D'Amico C, Jordan JS. The relationship of appraisal and coping to chronic illness adjustment. *Behav Res Ther.* 1990;28:297–304.
68. Desharnais R, Godin G, Jobin J, Valois P, Ross A. Optimism and health-relevant cognitions after a myocardial infarction. *Psychol Rep.* 1990;67: 1131–1135.
69. Scheier MF, Magovern GJ Sr, Abbott RA, Matthews KA, Owens JF, Lefebvre RC, Carver CS. Dispositional optimism and recovery from coronary artery bypass surgery: The beneficial effects on physical and psychological well-being. *J Pers Soc Psychol.* 1989;57:1024–1040.
70. Levenson JL, Mishra A, Hamer RM, Hastillo A. Denial and medical outcome in unstable angina. *Psychosom Med.* 1989;51:27–35.
71. Ebrahim S, Brittis S, Wu A. The valuation of states of ill-health: The impact of age and disability. *Age Ageing.* 1991;20:37–40.
72. Cioffi D. Beyond attentional strategies: A cognitive-perceptual model of somatic interpretation. *Psychol Bull.* 1991;109:25–41.
73. Baumann LJ, Cameron LD, Zimmerman RS, Leventhal H. Illness representations and matching labels with symptoms. *Health Psychol.* 1989;8:449–469.
74. Lau RR, Bernard TM, Hartman KA. Further explorations of common-sense representations of common illnesses. *Health Psychol.* 1989;8(2):195–219.
75. Warwick HM, Salkovskis PM. Hypochondriasis. *Behav Res Ther.* 1990;28:105–117.
76. Band EB. Children's coping with diabetes: Understanding the role of cognitive development. *J Pediatr Psychol.* 1990;15:27–41.
77. Tran TV, Chatters L, Wright R Jr. Health, stress, psychological resources, and subjective well-being among older Blacks. *Psychol Aging.* 1991;6:100–108.
78. Zautra AJ, Maxwell BM, Reich JW. Relationship among physical impairment, distress, and well-being in older adults. *J Behav Med.* 1989;12:543–557.
79. Haug MR, Wykle ML, Namazi KH. Self-care among older adults. *Soc Sci Med.* 1989;29:171–183.
80. Gottlieb GL. Hypochondriasis: A psychosomatic problem in the elderly. In: Billig N, Rabins PV, eds. *Issues in Geriatric Psychiatry. Adv Psychosom Med.* Basel: Karger;1989;19:67–84.
81. Hackworth SR, McMahon RJ. Factors mediating children's health care attitudes. *J Pediatr Psychol.* 1991;16:69–85.
82. Schechter NL, Bernstein BA, Beck A, Hart L, Scherzer L. Individual differences in children's response to pain: Role of temperament and parental characteristics. *Pediatrics.* 1991;87:171–177.
83. Quadrel MJ, Lau RR. A multivariate analysis of adolescents' orientations toward physician use. *Health Psychol.* 1990;9:750–773.
84. Cappelli M, McGrath PJ, MacDonald NE, Katsanis J, Lascelles M. Parental care and overprotection of children with cystic fibrosis. *Br J Med Psychol.* 1989;62:281–289.

85. Osborne RB, Hatcher JW, Richtsmeier AJ. The role of social modeling in unexplained pediatric pain. *J Pediatr Psychol.* 1989;14:43–61.
86. MacIntyre S, Pritchard C. Comparisons between the self-assessed and observer-assessed presence and severity of colds. *Soc Sci Med.* 1989;29: 1243–1248.
87. Kandrack MA, Grant KR, Segall A. Gender differences in health related behaviour: Some unanswered questions. *Soc Sci Med.* 1991;32:579–590.
88. Baider L, Perez T, De-Nour AK. Gender and adjustment to chronic disease. *Gen Hosp Psychiatry.* 1989;11:1–8.
89. Manne SL, Zautra AJ. Spouse criticism and support: Their association with coping and psychological adjustment among women with rheumatoid arthritis. *J Pers Soc Psychol.* 1989;56:608–617.
90. Fontana AF, Kerns RD, Rosenberg RL, Colonese KL. Support, stress, and recovery from coronary heart disease: A longitudinal causal model. *Health Psychol.* 1989;8:175–193.
91. Gannon L, Pardie L. The importance of chronicity and controllability of stress in the context of stress–illness relationships. *J Behav Med.* 1989;12:357–372.
92. Binder RL, Trimble MR, McNiel DE. The course of psychological symptoms after resolution of lawsuits. *Am J Psychiatry.* 1991;148:1073–1075.
93. de Bruyn M. Turkish migrants and somatic fixation in the Netherlands: Research in Amsterdam. *Soc Sci Med.* 1989;29:897–898.
94. Swagman CF. Fija: Fright and illness in highland Yemen. *Soc Sci Med.* 1989; 28:381–388.
95. Wikan U. Illness from fright or soul loss: A North Balinese culture-bound syndrome? *Cult Med Psychiatry.* 1989;13:25–50.
96. Moore R. Ethnographic assessment of pain coping perceptions. *Psychosom Med.* 1990;52:171–181.
97. Zatzick DF, Dimsdale JE. Cultural variations in response to painful stimuli. *Psychosom Med.* 1990;52:544–557.
98. Small GW, Propper MW, Randolph ET, Eth S. Mass hysteria among student performers: Social relationship as a symptom predictor. *Am J Psychiatry.* 1991;148:1200–1205.
99. Stoudemire A, Hales RE. Psychological and behavioral factors affecting medical conditions and DSM-IV. *Psychosomatics.* 1991;32:5–13.
100. King SA, Strain JJ. Revising the category of somatoform pain disorder. *Hosp Community Psychiatry.* 1992;43:217–219.
101. Blackwell B, Gutmann M. The management of chronic illness behaviour. In: McHugh S, Vallis M, eds. *Illness Behavior.* New York: Plenum;1987.

Chapter 6
Aspects of Abnormal
Illness Behavior

ISSY PILOWSKY

THE CONCEPT

As mentioned in an earlier version of this paper[1] in September 1984 at the 15th European Conference on Psychosomatic Research held in London, a session was set aside for the presentation and discussion of papers on abnormal illness behavior (AIB). A lively interchange of views occurred during which the late Dr. Heinz Wolff made the perceptive statement: "This is a dangerous idea!" A consideration of the definition of AIB soon makes evident why the idea is not only "dangerous," but also necessary.

AIB is defined as:

The persistence of a maladaptive mode of experiencing, perceiving, evaluating, and responding to one's own health status, despite the fact that a doctor has provided a lucid and accurate appraisal of the situation and management to be followed (if any), with opportunities for discussion, negotiation and clarification, based on adequate assessment of all relevant biological, psychological, social and cultural factors.

The various parts of this definition are worthy of detailed examination.

1. *The persistence of an inappropriate or maladaptive mode of perceiving, evaluating, or acting in relation to one's own state of health.*

Comment: The second half of this sentence (mode . . . health) is a description of "illness behavior" (a concept first introduced by Mechanic and Volkart[2]) which indicates that it does not refer to overt behavior alone, but also includes the nature of the individual's subjective experience of his health status. The importance of this is that when a psychiatric diagnosis is made, it is the subjective experience and way of thinking about illness, i.e., the phenomenology, which is crucial to the making of distinctions between the various forms of AIB. Indeed, it is unfortunate that the term *AIB*, based as it is on the term *illness behavior*, has led some to take a purely behavioral approach to diagnosis.

2. *Despite the fact that the doctor (or other appropriate social agent) has offered an accurate and reasonably lucid explanation of the nature of the illness and the appropriate course of management to be followed (if any).*

Comment: As mentioned above, this spells out what is meant by *medical reassurance.* Nonetheless, the criticism that the doctor could be wrong in his opinion may be valid. There are two points to be made here. The first is that the patients being discussed are invariably nonresponsive to the opinions of any number of doctors. The second is that if the doctor is wrong, then the diagnosis cannot be made. Thus this definition of AIB has the effect of making the doctor self-reflective and cautious about making the diagnosis. Actually, this may hardly be necessary when one considers Beaber and Rodney's[3] finding that the family physicians they studied never recorded such a diagnosis in a series of patients, some of whom scored extremely high on the Whitely Index of Hypochondriasis.[4] Nonetheless, it should also be said that a doctor cannot adopt an attitude of absolute certainty about an opinion or recommendation, and it is the patient with AIB who manifests what is regarded as an unjustified certainty as to the diagnosis. Thus, in presenting any diagnosis, a doctor should be prepared to acknowledge the possibility that he may not be accurate in his advice, and this brings us to the next part of the definition.

3. *With opportunities for discussion, negotiations and clarification.*

Comment: Here the definition takes into account the fact that diagnoses and plans of management are not infrequently a basis for negotiation between doctor and patient; and rightly so, since in the course of negotiation, the doctor will discover if his communications require further clarification and elaboration. In particular, patient and doctor need to work toward congruence in their ways of conceptualizing the etiology, pathology, diagnosis, treatment, and prognosis of the condition under discussion. Here the doctor will need to take pains to allow the patient to feel that his lay opinions are respected and welcomed, an issue which arises in the last part of the definition.

4. *Based on an adequate assessment of all biological, psychological, social, and cultural factors.*

Comment: Whatever the doctor has to say to the patient should be based on a proper clinical evaluation, i.e., one which considers all aspects of the patient's functioning. The word *adequate* is used to indicate that no assessment is perfect, but in this context should be the type of assessment most peers would regard as appropriate to the circumstances. It is appreciated, of course, that this part of the definition sets high standards, higher perhaps than many doctors could meet. If so, it reminds us to what extent the conditions under the rubric of AIB serve to act as a challenge to the medical profession to review its standards of medical care and education, particularly if unusually large numbers of patients in a particular population are being diagnosed as manifesting AIB. The psychological factors referred to in this definition include cognitive, attitudinal, and emotional issues. For example, a patient may be excessively concerned about a symptom because of insufficient or inaccurate information about its significance, and the AIB may promptly disappear once he has been provided with the facts. On the other hand, the condition from which he suffers may be correctly labeled with a psychiatric diagnosis, such as *anxiety disorder* or *depressive disorder*, and on being so informed, the inappropriate illness behavior does not persist, and indeed, the patient accepts a psychological or psychiatric approach to the illness. In many instances, it may be necessary to explain to the patient that his illness includes both somatic and emotional elements, which the patient may also accept. In other words, this definition rests on the premise that AIB cannot be established with confidence, unless the doctor has proceeded in an appropriate fashion and the patient has shown an ability to negotiate or to accept the doctor's view.

Social and cultural factors also need to be emphasized, because a person's sociocultural background leads to belief systems about illness and its treatment, which may not be shared by the doctor. These differences must be acknowledged, and the patient's views respected. The experience of many doctors working in cultures other than their own, suggests that under these circumstances, different belief systems can coexist in harmony for the individual patient, who may feel quite comfortable about using a doctor, a diviner, and a herbalist at the same time or, similarly, an orthopedic surgeon, an osteopath, and an acupuncturist. Finally, it goes without saying that where the doctor and patient do not share a common language, professional interpreters should be used. The problem is more difficult where differences are sociolinguistic, and this requires particular sensitivity on the doctor's part.

Finally, we may recall the doctor's special social role in establishing to whom the sick role may be granted. As Parsons[5] has described, in order to be accorded the sick role, the patient is obliged to cooperate with an appointed agent of society (usually a doctor), or the role and its privileges will not be granted.

It will be appreciated that a distinction must be drawn between illness behavior which is normal, that which is discordant (or anomalous), that which is atypical, and finally the abnormal forms. These distinctions are not easy to make, particularly when we lack solid information about the range of illness behaviors to be expected in relation to various illnesses.

It is acknowledged of course, that it may not be possible to carry out all the requirements listed for the definitive diagnosis of AIB despite the fact that one has good reason to believe from the patient's attitude to his health, that such a condition exists. For example, the patient may report preoccupation with illness and fears about possible diseases which he might develop. At such an early stage of the assessment, one might reasonably make a provisional diagnosis of AIB, or perhaps more specifically, of hypochondriasis or somatoform pain disorder.

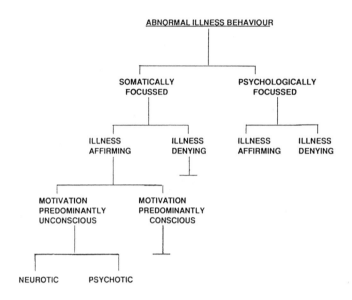

Figure 6.1. Classification of AIB.

In previous papers I have suggested a classification of AIBs based on whether motivation is predominantly conscious or unconscious, whether illness is affirmed or denied, and whether the focus is somatic or psychological (Figure 6.1). Syndromes which are subsumed under the various categories of AIB are listed in Tables 6.1 and 6.2.

It will be appreciated that not all such syndromes are considered part of official classifications, but they are, nonetheless, of clinical significance.

Most attention in this area has been paid to illness affirming, somatically focused AIB, e.g., hypochondriasis.[4, 6, 7] Very little interest has been shown in conditions where illness is denied or where the focus is a psychological disorder, e.g., the denial of schizophrenia, depression, or anorexia nervosa.

TABLE 6.1
Somatically Focused AIB

Illness affirming	Illness denying

A *Motivation predominantly conscious*
  1 Malingering
  2 Chronic factitious syndrome with physical symptoms (Munchausen syndrome)
  3 Factitious disorder with physical symptoms
 	
B *Motivation predominantly unconscious*
  1 Neurotic (somatoform disorders)
    Somatization disorder
    Conversion disorder
    Somatoform pain disorder
    Hypochondriasis
    Body dysmorphic disorder
  2 Hypochondriacal delusions associated with:
    (a) Major depressive disorder with mood-congruent psychotic features
    (b) Schizophrenic disorder
    (c) Monosymptomatic hypochondriacal psychoses
	A *Motivation predominantly conscious*
	  1 Denial to obtain employment
	  2 Denial to avoid feared therapies
	  3 Denial of illness (e.g. VD) due to shame and guilt
	
	B *Motivation predominantly unconscious*
	  1 Neurotic, e.g.:
	    (a) Noncompliance following myocardial infarction
	    (b) Counterphobic behaviour in haemophilia
	    (c) Noncompliance with antihypertensive therapy
	  2 Psychotic
	    Denial of somatic pathology, e.g. as part of hypomanic or schizophrenic disorder
	
	C *Neuropsychiatric*
	    Anosognosia

TABLE 6.2
Psychologically Focused AIB

Illness affirming	Illness denying
A *Motivation predominantly conscious*	A *Motivation predominantly conscious*
1 Malingering	Denial of psychotic symptomatology to avoid stigma, hospital admission, or to gain discharge from care
2 Factitious disorder with psychological symptoms (ganser syndrome)	Denial of psychotic illness to avoid discrimination by health care professionals or employers
B *Motivation predominantly unconscious*	B *Motivation predominantly unconscious*
1 Neurotic	Neurotic: refusal to accept 'psychological' diagnosis or treatment in the presence of neurotic illness, personality disorder or dependency syndromes (alcohol, opiates, etc.)
'Psychic hypochondriasis'	
'Phrenophobia'	
Dissociative reactions	
Psychogenic amnesia	
2 Psychotic	Psychotic: denial of illness ('lack of insight') in psychotic depression, manic states and schizophrenia syndromes
Delusions of memory loss or loss of brain function	Neuropsychiatric: confabulatory reaction in Korsakoff's psychosis and other organic brain syndromes

There has recently been a significant development in this regard, since Strauss et al.[8] have proposed a new diagnostic category for DSM-IV of "maladaptive denial of physical disorder" as a subtype of adjustment disorder. They were led to this suggestion by their experience with the use of DSM-III-R in a consultation–liaison psychiatry setting, where they found "many patients for whom maladaptive denial of physical illness was the focus of clinical attention." In their paper they propose a descriptive text for DSM-IV and also a persuasive discussion in support of this new diagnosis. They provide eight clinical vignettes which illustrate aspects of the diagnosis including the major issue of noncompliance. They suggest that:

This category should be used when, as a reaction to the symptoms, signs, or diagnosis of a physical illness, the predominant response is persistent denial of having a physical disorder that exposes the individual to a significantly higher risk of serious physical illness or death.

The denial takes the form of the individual asserting that he or she does not have the physical disorder or of behaving in a way that indicates that he or she minimizes the significance of the disorder. This occurs in the face of obvious physical manifestations of the disorder or in spite of the patient's having been adequately informed of its presence by a doctor.

This category does not include instances where the individual not only denies having the disorder, but is delusional in other ways. It also does not include situations where the individual refuses treatment or lifestyle changes that caregivers believe are optimum after having made an informed and considered evaluation of the risks and benefits of these changes. The category also does not include situations in which the individual refuses treatment because it violates religious or some cultural belief systems [p. 1171].

DIAGNOSIS AND MANAGEMENT

In discussing the diagnosis and management of AIB, I will be focusing particularly on the somatoform disorders, such as hypochondriasis, conversion disorders, and somatoform pain disorders (DSM-III-R).

The need for an integrated approach to management is particularly important in these patients and is exemplified by the functioning of the multidisciplinary pain clinic.

Before any management can be instituted it is important, as always, to clarify the nature of the problem and establish rapport. As the definition of AIB implies, a thorough clinical assessment is mandatory. By "clinical" is meant an assessment which includes all aspects of biological, psychological, and social functioning. Having carried this out, it is necessary to convey one's findings to the patient in a way which is comprehensible.

"Somatologia" and "Thymologia"

It is well known that patients frequently do not inhabit the same language-world as the doctor and for this reason may seem inarticulate or uncooperative. It would be unfortunate if the patient who has a somatic view of his distress and was reluctant to adopt a psychological perspective, was too readily labeled alexithymic. It would be more appropriate, I feel, to speak of "somatologia" and "thymologia" since the use of a somatic language does not necessarily imply a lack of a psychological and emotional frame of reference. It may simply be the case, that for certain individuals, somatic complaints have a built-in emotional connotation which, in the patient's sociolinguistic niche, is not customarily spelled out. Thus if a person says he is suffering excruciating pain, he may find it strange to be asked if he is anxious or depressed, as though these could be independent emotions. Furthermore, patients being interviewed by psychiatrists often feel that their somatic experiences are being doubted, and as a consequence are suspicious of questions which imply the presence of emotional disturbance. On the other hand, they are usually prepared to acknowledge that the pain has caused depression, anxiety, and anger. I have elaborated this issue because of a concern that the concept of alexithymia may result in some patients being regarded as unsuitable for any form of psychotherapy when, indeed it may be quite appropriate provided the therapist is prepared to be flexible in his approach.

The aim of the evaluative process is not only to make a categorical diagnosis but also to achieve a dimensional view of the patient's illness behavior. The dimensions of illness behavior were investigated by Pilowsky and Spence[9] using the Illness Behavior Questionnaire. This is a 62-item self-administered instrument[10] which explores the patient's attitudes to illness, amongst other issues.

As a result of a principal component analysis, seven factors emerged, which formed the basis of seven scales. The stability of virtually all factors has been demonstrated in subsequent studies by Large and Mullins[11] and Zonderman et al.[12]

The seven scales are named General (Phobic) Hypochondriasis, Disease Conviction, Psychological versus Somatic Focusing, Affective Inhibition, Affective Disturbance, Denial and Irritability. These clearly represent important dimensions of illness behavior and it will be useful to describe them in greater detail.

The General (Phobic) Hypochondriasis scale assesses a fearful attitude to illness with some insight into its excessive nature. It is very similar to the phobic factor found by Pilowsky[4] in the factor analysis of the Whitely Index of Hypochondriasis. Generally speaking, pain clinic patients show little of this attitude which is commoner in association with anxiety and phobic disorders, although a high score may be an early sign of a schizophrenic illness.

The Disease Conviction scale reflects a firm belief that a somatic disorder is present and a reluctance to accept reassurance. The focus is on bodily symptoms and sensations, and sleep is disturbed. Pain clinic patients tend to score higher on this scale than any other clinical population.

The Psychological versus Somatic Focusing scale is interesting in that it is a bipolar one. A high score indicates that the patient is prepared to adopt a psychological perspective, while a low score indicates a tendency to reject the possibility of a psychological dimension to the condition and a focus on somatic problems. Pain clinic patients invariably achieve a very low score on this scale, while psychiatric patients obtain higher scores.

The next two scales are related to feelings and emotions and the capacity to communicate them. The Affective Inhibition scale is scored so that a high score indicates an inability to communicate feelings (especially negative ones). The Affective Disturbance scale assesses the presence of anxiety, depression, and tension.

The Denial scale indicates a tendency to deny life stresses and also (perhaps more importantly) to attribute all current difficulties to a somatic disorder. In other words, high scorers seem to believe that all their troubles would be over if they were cured of the physical problems. On the other hand, low scorers are indicating that they have ongoing life problems which would continue even if they were physically well.

"Irritability" is the label attached to the seventh scale. A high score indicates the presence of interpersonal friction.

These scales reflected dimensions of AIB which need to be taken into account when assessing a patient's problems and planning treatment; they cannot be regarded as replacing clinical diagnosis but can serve as a screening instrument.

The Illness Behavior Questionnaire profile of a "typical" pain clinic is shown in Figure 6.2. The clinical diagnosis of hypochondriasis is not easy and presents a problem for researchers seeking comparability between studies. The problem stems from the fact that the diagnosis emerges from a development in the doctor–patient relationship, whereby the doctor and patient cannot arrive at an agreement as to the latter's health status, because of a strong belief that disease is present on the part of the patient, which cannot be justified by the "objective data." This is not something which can be established satisfactorily by a questionnaire or a nonmedical research assistant. However, matters might be improved by diagnostic criteria which were consistently phenomenological, such as: (1) an uncomfortable awareness of bodily events most of the time; (2) fears and concerns about health and disease which are present most of the time; (3) an awareness of an inability to accept reassurance from doctors who have offered clear information, associated with the concern that doctors have not done everything possible to detect disease or are withholding information and/or treatment which could be helpful; and

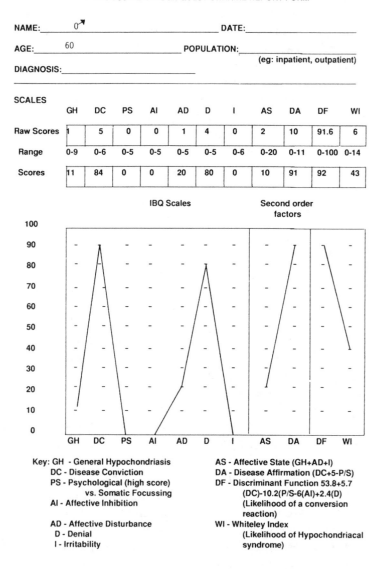

Figure 6.2   Illness Behavior Questionnaire Report Form

(4) an awareness of inability to accept the suggestion that non-physical, i.e., psychosocial, factors may be relevant to one's condition, and marked emotional discomfort when this possibility is raised.

Thus the patient may be able to say "I worry about my health all the time. I notice things in my body such as pains or palpitations and I think I might have cancer or I'm going to have a heart attack or a stroke. Sometimes I think I'm silly, but I still go on worrying. Even though my doctor has investigated everything very thoroughly, I can't accept what he says about there being nothing to worry about, at least not for long. When he says it may be a mental problem and that we should talk about some of the difficulties in my life, with my family or job, I get very upset and worry about my health even more."

As mentioned above, the treatment of somatoform disorders and especially psychogenic pain is best undertaken by a multidisciplinary team. The main treatments available are: (1) pharmacological; (2) somatic; (3) behavioral, cognitive-behavioral, cognitive-educational; and (4) psychotherapeutic, i.e., (a) individual, (b) group, (c) marital, (d) family, and (e) hypnotherapy.

PHARMACOLOGICAL TREATMENTS

The tricyclic antidepressants have been widely used in the treatment of chronic pain and they are singularly effective when a reasonably distinct depressive syndrome can be demonstrated. However, it has also been proposed that the tricyclics may modulate the pain experience by enhancing the activity of the endogenous pain suppression system (which is dependent on both serotonin and noradrenaline).

Despite the wide use of these agents, relatively few controlled trials have been carried out on their effectiveness. Pilowsky et al.[13] conducted a double-blind placebo-controlled trial of amitriptyline in patients referred to a pain clinic who were deemed suitable for such treatment. Patients were given 6 weeks of amitriptyline, or placebo, in a fixed dosage schedule rising to 150 mg daily if tolerated, in order to achieve blood levels which would be regarded in the therapeutic range for the treatment of depression. At the 6 weeks' point the patient was switched to the other tablet (amitriptyline or placebo). The results showed that patients recorded lower levels of pain on a visual analog scale at 2 and 4 weeks on amitriptyline than on placebo. However, at 6 weeks there was no significant difference on the visual analog scores or on global assessments of pain and coping. The changes in pain scores were not related to changes in depression scores.

It was felt that the dropping off of the advantage to amitriptyline by the sixth week may have been due to the high dosage of drug used, and that lower doses might be more effective. It was also a clinical impression that these patients were singularly sensitive to side effects. However, the work of Edelbrock et al.[14] does not offer support for this possibility.

SOMATIC TREATMENTS

We have found somatic treatments such as muscular relaxation, physiotherapeutic massage, and transcutaneous nerve stimulation to be helpful in providing some patients with a degree of relief. In addition, these treatments help to convince the patient that the somatic dimension of the pain experience is being taken seriously and thus helps to establish rapport. As yet the precise role of these treatments in the management of chronic pain has not been systematically evaluated. Nonetheless, there is considerable clinical experience which supports the importance of the role of the physiotherapist in any pain management team.[15] The role of acupuncture will not be discussed in detail, but the reader may refer to the paper of Melzack[16] for an excellent overview. As yet there appears to be no good evidence to suggest that it has any special advantage over other similar methods of intense sensory stimulation, nor that specific acupuncture points are relevant to its effectiveness.

BEHAVIORAL METHODS

The purpose of these approaches is to modify the individual's pain-related illness behaviors, including the ways in which he thinks about the pain, its consequences, and his own capacity to cope with it. The use of what has come to be known as the cognitive–behavioral approach, typically requires a 3- to 6-week inpatient stay, and participation in a highly structured program involving graduated exercises and activities, cognitive restructuring, individual psychotherapy, and family therapy. It is most important that patients are well prepared for the program and show motivation for change. Fordyce[17] who pioneered this approach has described the methods well. Excellent reviews of the effectiveness of these approaches have been presented by Turner and Chapman[18] and Tan.[19] It is clear that further work is required to delineate the specific ingredients which are effective in these forms of treatment. Nonetheless, clinical experience suggests that the cognitive–behavioral approach is particularly helpful in patients who have become inactive due to pain, and are spending many hours of the day sitting or lying down.

Recent reports have described treatment approaches to hypochondriasis which may have wider relevance. Barsky et al.[20, 21] describe a cognitive–educational treatment for hypochondriasis based on the idea of somatosensory amplification. Four factors are considered to amplify somatic symptoms: (1) attention and expectation; (2) symptom attribution and appraisal; (3) the context used for interpreting the symptoms; and (4) disturbing affect and dependency needs.

Groups of six to eight patients meet for six consecutive weeks for a "course" on the perception of physical symptoms. The educational component is stressed in order to reduce patient resistance and the "stigma attached to psychiatric treatment." Patients are introduced to techniques for reducing somatic "hypervigilance," such as attention and relaxation exercises and distraction techniques. A good deal of didactic material is presented, and this approach to hypochondriasis seems to be acceptable to patients and to be helpful in offering a logical, internally consistent model with which to gain a sense of mastery over their AIB. The need for a "rigorous, controlled, intervention trial to assess its efficacy" is stressed by the authors, who suggest that since the therapy can be specified in detail, it should be possible to identify the essential ingredients.

Hypochondriacal patients are approached somewhat differently by House[22] who has reported on 100 patients referred to a district general hospital in the United Kingdom for help with the treatment of hypochondriasis. House describes in detail his assessment of patients. Again, the need to establish credibility during a transition phase by behaving as a conscientious open-minded clinician is described. In fact, with this approach, the doctor acquires credibility which is truly deserved. Amongst other components of the treatment, the discussion of attitudes to medical management, physical investigation, and psychiatric referral are explored. It is interesting that 20 patients did not attend after the initial assessment. The therapy is short term, flexible, and based on a cognitive–behavioral approach. It was found that 80% of those who attended showed a marked or moderate improvement. Patients with a major depression had the best prognosis. A worse outcome was seen in younger patients, those with a past psychiatric history, and those receiving state benefits. Interestingly, the question of the outcome of treatment in patients with low back pain in relation to compensation showed that patients on unlimited disability compensation were less likely to return to work than those on time-limited or no compensation.

The cognitive–behavioral approach has been used widely in the treatment of somatoform pain disorders, especially in North America. Benjamin[23] has reviewed the psychological treatment of chronic pain and concluded that the various approaches may well be complementary. He urged that approaches should be eclectic, be free of dogmatism, and use only methods which have been shown to work. In common with many others, he called for more research in this area. While these are highly commendable objectives, it is inevitable that, for the present, clinicians are influenced in their choice of treatment package by factors such as the context in which the service is being delivered (teaching hospital, district hospital, urban or rural) cultural and language issues, and the availability of trained personnel.

PSYCHOTHERAPEUTIC APPROACHES

In many patients with AIB of the somatoform type, it is extremely difficult to institute psychotherapy if a conventional approach is taken.[24] As mentioned above, this is because rapport can only be established on the basis of an initial acceptance of the patient's pain as evidenced by the use of physical therapies.

We have found that an assessment by a multidisciplinary panel and the use of physiotherapeutic methods results in very little resistance to the suggestion of a psychiatric approach, provided it is made clear that this does not imply a total disregard or abandonment of any somatic approach.

A number of psychotherapeutic approaches may be taken, including individual, group, marital, and family. We have focused particularly on the brief individual psychotherapeutic approach.[24] In a pilot study on a small group of chronic pain patients, we found that dynamically orientated psychotherapy consisting of 12 weekly 45-minute sessions produced better results as regards global functioning, when compared to 6 fortnightly 15-minute supportive sessions.[25] In the course of our experience with the use of individual psychotherapy we have found that reduction in pain complaints cannot be regarded as the only index of improvement. Indeed, patients may report that their pain is unchanged or worse, but that they feel generally better and are less disabled.

The use of group psychotherapy has been well described by Pinsky[26] working at the City of Hope Medical Center. In any program where patients are admitted in cohorts for fixed periods, groups have a part to play in facilitating information exchange and therapeutic modeling.

It is crucial that the role of the spouse and family not be overlooked in the management of abnormal or discordant illness behaviors. This is certainly the case in the somatoform disorders and chronic pain in particular. As Jeans and Rowat[27] have written, "learning to live with chronic pain is a family affair." They emphasize the need for professionals and family to collaborate in order to achieve mutually agreed goals.

Hypnotherapy is an approach which has been poorly evaluated for its contribution to the treatment of somatoform disorders in general, but it would appear to have a role in pain control when used for certain individuals in appropriate contexts.[18, 28, 29]

Combination Therapy

In practice most patients are treated with combinations of therapies. Pilowsky and Barrow[30] have reported on a controlled evaluation of brief psychotherapy and amitriptyline (AMI). The study involved four treatment groups, namely: (1) AMI + psychotherapy (n = 26); (2) AMI + support (n = 26); (3) placebo + psychotherapy (n = 26); and (4) placebo + support (n = 24).

Outcome was independently assessed in terms of "categorical" variables (pain, well-being, and activity) and a number of "continuous" variables (intensity of pain, amount of time in pain, and "productivity," i.e., ability to carry out usual tasks and duties). Analysis of the categorical data showed significant findings only for "activity" in that patients receiving supportive psychotherapy (i.e. 6, 15-minute fortnightly sessions) did better with AMI than with placebo. Further, those on AMI did better without psychotherapy (12, 45-minute, weekly sessions). Overall, those on AMI showed improved activity levels. An interesting finding which emerged is that patients on psychotherapy and placebo reported a significant increase in pain intensity, but also a significant increase in productivity.

This finding is supported by clinical observations of patients who report that they feel better and more active even though the pain is worse. This is something to be borne in mind when managing somatically focused illness-affirming disorders in general since it draws attention to the fact that a change in physical symptomatology may not correlate positively with other indices of outcome.

Overview

The purpose of this paper has been to emphasize the need for an integrated approach to diagnosis and therapy in the treatment of AIB, especially in the context of chronic, intractable pain. The approach involves a comprehensive clinical assessment and a readiness to communicate and negotiate with the patient in a manner which respects his capacity to understand, as well as his personal theories concerning his state of health. It must be acknowledged that the precise nature of the multidisciplinary approach will vary from setting to setting, depending on the human resources available. Nonetheless, the principles of collaborative medicine and interprofessional respect are the same no matter how great or small the number of participants. For certain patients, it is the most appropriate and efficient method of management.

Furthermore, the need for a suitable "transition phase" or management which allows the patient to adopt a psychological perspective in addition to a somatic perspective is also emphasized.

REFERENCES

1. Pilowsky I. Abnormal illness behaviour (dysnosognosia). *Psychother Psychosom.* 1986;46:76–84.
2. Mechanic D, Volkart EH. Illness behaviour and medical diagnosis. *Health Hum Behav.* 1960;1:86–94.
3. Beaber R, Rodney W. Underdiagnosis of hypochondriasis in family practice. *Psychosomatics.* 1984;25:39–46.
4. Pilowsky I. Dimensions of hypochondriasis. *Br J Psychiatry.* 1967; 113:89–93.
5. Parsons T. *Social Structure and Personality.* North Ryde, NSW: Collier-Macmillan;1964.
6. Pilowsky I. Abnormal illness behaviour. *Br J Med Psychol.* 1969;42:347–351.
7. Pilowsky I. A general classification of abnormal illness behaviours. *Br J Med Psychol.* 1978;51:131–137.
8. Strauss DH, Spitzer RL, Muskin PR. Maladaptive denial of physical illness: A proposal for DSM-IV. *Am J Psychiatry.* 1990;147:1168–1172.
9. Pilowsky I, Spence ND. Patterns of illness behaviour in patients with intractable pain. *J Psychosom Res.* 1975;19:279–287.
10. Pilowsky I, Spence ND. *Manual for the Illness Behaviour Questionnaire.* 2nd ed. Adelaide, Australia: University of Adelaide;1983.
11. Large R, Mullins P. Illness behaviour profiles in chronic pain: The Auckland experience. *Pain.* 1981;10:231–239.
12. Zonderman AB, Heft MW, Costa PT Jr. Does the Illness Behaviour Questionnaire measure abnormal illness behaviour? *Health Psychol.* 1985;4:425–436.
13. Pilowsky I, Hallett EC, Bassett DL, Thomas PG, Penhall RK. A controlled study of amitriptyline in the treatment of chronic pain. *Pain.* 1982;14:169–179.

14. Edelbrock PM, Lenssen ACG, Zitman FG, Rooymans HGM, de Wolff FA. Analgesic and antidepressive effects of low dose amitriptyline in relation to its metabolism on patients with chronic pain. *Clin Pharmacol Ther.* 1986;39: 156–162.
15. Paris SV. The role of the physical therapist in pain control programmes. *Clin Anaesthesiol.* 1985;3:155–167.
16. Melzack R. Hyperstimulation analgesia. *Clin Anaesthesiol.* 1985;3:81–92.
17. Fordyce WE. *Behavioral Methods for Chronic Pain and Illness.* St Louis: Mosby;1976.
18. Turner J, Chapman CR. Psychological intervention for pain: A critical review. I + II. *Pain.* 1982;12:1–46.
19. Tan S-Y. Cognitive and cognitive–behavioural methods for pain control: A selective review. *Pain.* 1982;12:201–228.
20. Barsky AJ, Geringer E, Wood CA. A cognitive–educational treatment for hypochondriasis. *Gen Hosp Psychiatry.* 1988;10:322–327.
21. Barsky AJ, Goodson JD, Lane RS, Cleary PD. The amplification of somatic symptoms. *Psychosom Med.* 1988;50:510–519.
22. House A. Hypochondriasis and related disorders: Assessment and management of patients referred for a psychiatric opinion. *Gen Hosp Psychiatry.* 1989;11:156–165.
23. Benjamin S. Psychological treatment of chronic pain: A selective review. *J Psychosom Res.* 1989;33:121–131.
24. Pilowsky I, Bassett DL. Individual dynamic psychotherapy for chronic pain. In: Roy A, Tunks P, eds. *Chronic Pain: Psychosocial Factors in Rehabilitation.* Baltimore: Williams & Wilkins;1982.
25. Bassett D, Pilowsky I. A study of brief psychotherapy for chronic pain. *J Psychosom Res.* 1985;29:259–264.
26. Pinsky JJ. Chronic, intractable, benign pain. *J Hum Stress.* 1978;4:17–21.
27. Jeans ME, Rowat KM. Counselling the patient and family. In: Wall PD, Melzack R, eds. *Textbook of Pain.* 2nd ed. Edinburgh: Churchill-Livingstone; 1989.
28. Barber J, Adrian C. *Psychological Approaches to the Management of Pain.* New York: Brunner/Mazel;1982.
29. Chapman SL. Behaviour modification for chronic pain states. *Clin Anaesthesiol.* 1985;3:111–142.
30. Pilowsky I, Barrow CG. A controlled study of psychotherapy and amitriptyline used individually and in combination in the treatment of chronic intractable "psychogenic" pain. *Pain.* 1990;40:3–19.

Chapter 7
Psychosomatic Syndromes, Somatization, and Somatoform Disorders

ROBERT KELLNER

The studies that are reviewed herein suggest that psychosomatic syndromes are common, cause a great deal of suffering and disability, and are a major public health problem. The present article is aimed at presenting the main conclusions on the extent of the contributions of biological and psychological factors, discussing the role which these syndromes play in the processes of somatization and somatoform disorders, and discussing the implications of the findings for the treatment of somatoform disorders.

For the purposes of the present article the term *psychosomatic* indicates any mind–body relationship. A psychosomatic disorder is defined as a physical disorder or disease in which psychological processes play a substantial role in at least some patients with this syndrome.

The emphasis in the present article is on syndromes that are common or may be distressing. Most are classified in the DSM-III-R in the category of psychological factors affecting physical conditions (316.00). I have tried to classify symptoms of ill health by the use of the traditional dichotomy into those caused by tissue pathology and those which belong to the realm of physiology or psychiatry. Many symptoms and syndromes, however, cannot be confidently placed into one or other of these categories for various reasons which are discussed below. I have not addressed in this review the psychological aspects of physical diseases in which emotional factors may influence the course of the disease such as in peptic ulcer or coronary artery disease. The etiology, life expectancy, and treatments are different and a discussion of these diseases lies beyond the scope of the present survey.

In all psychosomatic syndromes, physical diseases which can cause similar symptoms but require substantially different treatments need to be carefully excluded by the usual diagnostic procedures. The medical differential diagnoses are not discussed here. A more extensive review of the literature and a description of the studies on which the conclusions are based has been presented elsewhere.[1]

PSYCHOSOMATIC SYNDROMES

This section contains a brief description of common psychosomatic syndromes. Unless otherwise indicated the conclusions are based on controlled studies which yielded significant results.

FIBROMYALGIA

The symptoms of fibromyalgia are predominantly muscular aches, pains, and stiffness, and there are tender points at various anatomical sites. The patients have low muscle pain threshold not merely at the classical tender points.[2] Some authors distinguish between fibromyalgia and the myofascial pain syndrome which have somewhat different manifestations.[3]

Prevalence. About 6 to 11% of patients in medical clinics present with fibromyalgia.[4] The prevalence depends to a large extent on the diagnostic criteria; muscle pains and incomplete syndromes are more common.[5]

The rate of hospitalization is higher than for rheumatoid arthritis. Days lost from work are similar to those for low back pain and double that for osteoarthritis.[6]

Etiology. The etiology of fibromyalgia is complex. Several studies have shown impaired sleep in fibromyalgia. In an experimental study, increased muscle tenderness was induced by deprivation of NREM sleep but not of REM sleep. The sleep architecture of patients with fibromyalgia is similar to that of the chronic fatigue syndrome, but differs from that of dysthymic disorder. The findings suggest that nonrestorative sleep may be one of the causes of fibromyalgia.[7, 8]

Special techniques of investigation suggest altered muscle physiology and pathology in primary fibromyalgia,[9–11] at least in some patients, and this includes low levels of free tryptophan.[12] A subgroup of patients shows evidence of a connective tissue disorder (secondary fibromyalgia).[13]

Psychological and Psychiatric Studies. Patients with fibromyalgia who attend rheumatology clinics have more psychopathology than other patients.[14] This did not apply to patients with fibromyalgia who attended a general medical clinic because of other diseases but had not sought treatment for fibromyalgia[15]; they may have either suffered from a less severe disorder, or because of less psychopathology they may have chosen not to seek treatment for fibromyalgia.

The findings on depression have not been uniform. Some studies show substantially more depression in patients with fibromyalgia than in other medical patients.[14] One study showed a higher prevalence of primary affective disorder in relatives of patients with fibromyalgia than those with rheumatoid arthritis.[16]

Comments. Although there is evidence that some of the patients with fibromyalgia have physiological abnormalities or tissue pathology, the extent to which this occurs is unknown. The pathology and psychobiology of fibromyalgia is not fully understood. The current findings suggest a process as follows: various factors can cause stage 4 sleep anomaly and these include physical disease, psychopathology, and low serotonin concentration. This, in turn, decreases pain threshold, and induces the characteristic features of fibromyalgia. Other unknown biochemical or immune mechanisms may be involved.[10, 17] The characteristics of many of the patients are similar to those of somatizing patients and similar psychological processes may be involved.[18] The role of various etiologic factors differs probably from one individual to the next.

Treatments. Various drugs have been used in the treatment of fibromyalgia.[19] Cyclobenzaprine is more effective than placebo.[20] Amitriptyline in small doses is more effective than placebo and naproxen.[21] Injections of local anesthetics are being frequently used and there is some evidence for short-term relief,[22] but their efficacy on follow-up has not been tested in controlled studies.

In one study of medically unexplained muscular pains, psychotherapy combined with physiotherapy was substantially more effective than physiotherapy alone.[23] In a small controlled study, EMG biofeedback was more effective than placebo treatment.[24] In one study, cardiovascular fitness training was more effective than a control treatment.[25]

FATIGUE

Fatigue, tiredness, and lack of energy are common symptoms. The prevalence varies with the method of study and ranges from 20 to over 40%.[26, 27]

Etiology. The symptom of fatigue is unrelated to age. It is more common in people who are physically inactive[28]; the cause of this association is unknown. Experimental studies with fatigued individuals show that in some there is an impairment in the rate of recovery after muscular exertion and they appear to have an increased perception of effort.[29, 30] The major experiments on the physiology and psychology of chronic fatigue have been surveyed by Kennedy.[31]

Fatigue as a symptom needs to be distinguished from the chronic fatigue syndrome. This syndrome has several characteristic features which include a sudden onset, chronic or recurrent debilitating fatigue aggravated after exertion, sore throat, lymph node pain and tenderness, headache, myalgia and weakness, and psychiatric symptoms such as depression.[32] There is evidence to suggest that the chronic fatigue syndrome is caused, in a substantial proportion of patients, by an immunological complication of viral infections.[33, 34] Recent studies suggest that a retrovirus infection may be the cause of such a reactivation.[35] A few studies suggest involvement of the central nervous system. Findings on cognitive deficits have been conflicting.[36, 37]

Psychological and Psychiatric Studies. Several studies have shown that the symptom of fatigue is associated with depression as well as anxiety.[1] In a study of patients who were chronically fatigued, about two-thirds had psychiatric disorders which were considered to be the main cause of their fatigue.[38] That depression can cause fatigue is demonstrated by the contrast of psychomotor retardation in the depressive phase and the endurance and energy in the manic phase of bipolar disorder. In the early stages after viral infections, physical causes for symptoms predominate whereas psychological factors become more prominent in later stages.[39]

Comments. The studies suggest that there are various causes for chronic fatigue.[39-42] In patients with the chronic fatigue syndrome there is evidence to suggest an immunological complication of a viral infection. Other patients have a viral infection and postviral fatigue induces them to avoid physical activity; this could lead eventually to impaired fitness and excessive tiredness caused in part by inactivity.[43] Other patients have a psychiatric disorder, usually depression, and in yet others, physical disease and psychiatric disorder coexist and the assessment of their relative contribution is not feasible.[44] Some patients have neither evidence of physical disease nor of conspicuous psychiatric disorder, and fatigue and exhaustion are their main complaints. The proportion of patients in these categories has not been established with certainty.

Treatments. In patients with the chronic fatigue syndrome the effects of acyclovir on fatigue and laboratory findings did not differ from those of placebo.[45] Two controlled studies of immunoglobulin therapy have yielded conflicting results.[46, 47] A recent study has shown substantial improvement in several patients treated with ampligen which is, at present, an experimental drug.[48, 49]

There are no published controlled studies on the psychological or psychiatric treatment of this syndrome. Wessely et al.[50] treated patients with severe chronic postviral fatigue syndrome by a combination of methods which included explanation, education, gradual realistic increase in physical activity, cognitive therapy, and antidepressant drugs when necessary. The proportion of patients who improved appeared substantially larger than those with conventional treatments.[51]

ESOPHAGEAL MOTILITY DISORDERS

Various kinds of motility disturbances of the esophagus range from absent to excessive peristalsis. These may be associated with abnormal functioning of either the upper or the lower esophagus. Manometric findings show either nonspecific abnormalities of characteristic syndromes: aperistalsis, achalasia, diffuse esophageal spasm, nutcracker esophagus, and hypertensive lower esophageal sphincter. In some patients, it takes elaborate laboratory investigations to detect and to determine the kind of esophageal motility disorder. These disorders are not all distinct and some change their character with the passage of time.[52]

Etiology. Esophageal motility is found in 10 to 30% of patients who have noncardiac chest pain. These disorders are one of the causes of dysphagia. Across studies chest symptoms are associated with motor abnormalities, but the findings are complex, inconsistent, and the correlations are low.[53] In most cases, pain is not caused by muscle spasm.[54] In many of the older studies of chest pain, some of the causes of cardiac pain such as microvascular angina were not excluded by current diagnostic methods.

The source of chest pain at times of stress has not been determined. One study suggests that the pain may be caused by esophageal ischemia because rewarming after experimental cooling takes longer in patients with nutcracker esophagus than normal controls.[55] Experimental distension of the esophagus causes more pain in patients with chest pain than in other patients, so the former appear to have a lower sensation threshold.[56, 57]

Psychological and Psychiatric Studies. The relationship of esophageal motility to psychological factors has been examined in several studies.[58, 59] Measurable changes in contraction of the esophagus can be demonstrated in the laboratory with stressful stimuli including complicated cognitive tasks.[60] Abnormal manometric findings in conjunction with pain are associated with lifetime prevalence of psychiatric diagnoses but not with current distress as measured with self-rating scales. The psychiatric disorder may have initiated the motility disorder which then persisted; conversely, the esophageal dysfunction may have led to introspection and anxiety.[61, 62] Psychological tests that purport to measure psychopathology have yielded conflicting results.[56, 62] There are, to date, too few studies to reach definite conclusions on the reasons for these discrepancies.

Treatments. There are no controlled studies of psychological treatments of esophageal motor abnormalities. Explanation and reassurance constitute apparently adequate treatment for the majority.[63] In uncontrolled studies and case reports successes have been reported in chronic cases with progressive muscular relaxation,[64] hypnosis,[65] and systematic desensitization or biofeedback.[66] Some patients are able to learn to increase lower esophageal pressure with biofeedback,[67] but its usefulness in the treatment of esophageal reflux has not been determined.

Various drug treatments have been used in motility disorders.[68] Many patients respond to placebo which confounds the evaluation of specific drug effects. The results of studies with nifedipine are conflicting; in one study, nifedipine was superior to placebo[69] but not in others.[70] Other calcium channel blockers have been recommended but there are, to date, no adequate controlled studies. Trazodone was more effective than placebo on chest pain but the drug had no effect on manometric abnormalities.[71] Drug treatment of esophageal reflux (which is not a psychosomatic disorder) is beyond the scope of this survey.

NONULCER DYSPEPSIA

Nonulcer dyspepsia (NUD) may manifest itself with various symptoms of the upper gastrointestinal tract including epigastric or retrosternal discomfort or pain, a burning sensation in the epigastrium, nausea and vomiting without evidence of organic pathology.

Prevalence. About 20% of random employees endorse on a questionnaire "stomach pains" as well as "sick, nauseated" in any one week.[26] NUD is a common disorder that causes substantial distress and disability and involves great costs. The severity of symptoms and disability are, on the average, as great or greater than that of duodenal ulcer.[72]

Clinical Features. The diagnosis cannot be made without careful exclusion of other causes of dyspepsia.[73] Various types of NUD have been proposed by a working party of gastroenterologists[74] depending on the kind of symptoms: gastroesophageal-refluxlike dyspepsia, ulcerlike dyspepsia, dysmotility-type, dyspepsia with aerophagia, and idiopathic.

Etiology. There is an inconsistent relationship between symptoms and detected abnormalities such as gastritis and duodenitis.[75] Several reviewers concluded that it is a group of heterogeneous conditions. "Gastric acid may play a role in a few cases, for example, those associated with reflux, whereas in others, abnormal motility, and infection with *Campylobacter pylori* [. . .] may be other causes.[74]

Psychological and Psychiatric Studies. Self-rating scales of distress in patients with NUD yielded scores similar to those of neurotic psychiatric patients.[76] Psychiatric diagnoses, predominantly anxiety disorders, are more common in patients with NUD than in other gastroenterology patients.[77, 78] In a community study, abdominal symptoms in general (not merely NUD) were strongly associated with psychiatric symptoms.[79] Severe threatening or traumatic life events are more common in several studies of functional abdominal pain than in other patients[80] and as common as in patients who have taken overdoses of drugs.[81]

Treatments. In general, neither antacids nor H_2 receptor antagonists are more effective than placebo.[1] In some studies, there was a relationship between the type of NUD and response to drugs: in the gastroesophageal–refluxlike NUD and in the ulcerlike NUD, cimetidine was found to be effective,[82] whereas in the dysmotilitylike NUD, metoclopramide and domperidone were more effective than placebo.[83] In a placebo-controlled crossover study, lorazepam and diazepam relieved functional gastrointestinal symptoms, including in a few patients with NUD.[84]

Psychological treatment which included applied relaxation and group psychotherapy was combined with medical care in the treatment of NUD. The psychotherapy group had fewer episodes of pain than controls who had only routine medical care.[85]

The rate of gastric secretion can be reduced by visual biofeedback.[86, 87] It is unknown whether biofeedback is effective in NUD.

IRRITABLE BOWEL SYNDROME

The primary symptoms of irritable bowel syndrome (IBS) are diarrhea, constipation, or both; abdominal pain and gaseousness are present to a variable degree. Various subsyndromes have been described.[88] Symptoms that occur more often in IBS than in organic disease are: pain relieved by defecation, more frequent stools with pain onset, looser stools with pain onset, abdominal distension, mucus in stool, and feeling of incomplete evacuation after defecation.[89]

Irritable bowel syndrome patients who seek treatment have also noncolonic gastrointestinal symptoms such as nausea, dyspepsia, and esophageal symptoms.[90] They also tend to have nongastrointes-tinal symptoms such as bladder symptoms, back pain, and tiredness.[91]

Prevalence. The 1-year prevalence of IBS is about 20%.[92] The ma-jority of subjects with IBS do not seek treatment. Between 20 and 50% of all gastrointestinal consultations are because of IBS.

Etiology. There are several authoritative reviews of the etiology of IBS.[58, 93] In IBS the bowel is more sensitive to experimental stretch and probably also to distension by gas and feces, which causes pain.[94, 95] Experimental distension leads to increase in bowel mo-tility which is larger in IBS than in normal controls.[95, 96] Various biochemical abnormalities have been reported in IBS but their significance is unknown.[97] There is an increased prevalence of IBS in first-degree relatives.[91] Lactose malabsorption causes simi-lar symptoms but is an unrelated disorder.[58, 98]

Psychological and Psychiatric Studies. Numerous studies found that patients with IBS who are seeking medical treatment have higher distress scores on distress scales and psychological inventories mea-suring psychopathology than patients with gastrointestinal dis-eases of organic origin and normal controls.[58, 99, 100] They have substantially more psychiatric disorders than other patients.[101, 102] Intestinal motility increases in patients with IBS as well as in nor-mal subjects after emotional stress.[103] A large proportion of pa-tients with IBS report stressful events such as losses preceding either the onset or the exacerbation of symptoms.[104] Psychosocial stress appears to be one of the factors that induces abnormal motility as well as symptoms.

When subjects in community surveys who have symptoms of IBS but have not sought treatment (particularly when restrictive diag-nostic criteria for IBS are used) are compared with controls who have no abdominal symptoms, the difference between the two groups on self-rating scales of distress is either small or nonexistent. This would suggest that the majority of noncolonic symptoms, including symptoms of psychiatric ill health, are associated with seeking medi-cal help rather than being an integral part of the IBS syndrome.[105]

There is some evidence from retrospective studies that the symptoms of IBS are, in part, learned. For example, patients with IBS report that in childhood they had more parental attention and more treats when ill than other patients.[106]

Comments. Patients who attend for treatment with IBS have a more responsive alimentary tract to various stimuli which include mechanical as well as psychosocial stressors.[58] Some patients because of their emotional distress appear to be less capable of coping with their abdominal symptoms.

The results of various studies suggest that the psychopathology of patients with IBS is not uniform. The degree of physiological abnormality as well as the role and nature of psychological factors and social stressors differ from one individual to the next.

Treatments. None of the drugs used in the treatment of IBS has been uniformly effective.[107] Patients who are predominantly constipated may benefit from substances which increase bulk,[108] whereas those who have predominantly diarrhea are likely to benefit from tricyclic antidepressants; the initial doses are substantially lower than those used for the treatment of depression. There is at present no evidence that one tricyclic antidepressant is better than another.[109, 110] Antispasmodics, which are widely used, have a logical appeal but their benefits have not been adequately supported in controlled studies and they should not be the drug of first choice.[107] Overall, there is little evidence to date that supports treatment with antianxiety drugs unless they are needed for the treatment of coexisting anxiety. The evidence for other drugs at present is sparse but a few of the new drugs are promising.[1]

Explanation, reassurance, and support constitute adequate treatment in some patients. Several psychological treatments have been found effective in IBS in controlled studies.[100] Psychotherapy combined with medical treatment has been found substantially more effective than routine medical care in two studies.[111, 112] Hypnosis was strikingly effective in a study in patients with severe IBS who had failed to respond to all previous treatments.[113] Other effective psychological treatments include psychotherapy combined with autogenic training,[114, 115] and a stress management program.[116] The controlled studies of relaxation treatment alone have yielded inconclusive results.

URETHRAL SYNDROME

The urethral syndrome consists of dysuria and urgency, and is a common complaint in medical practice. The syndrome has various causes.

Prevalence. Urinary symptoms in adult women are among the most common complaints in medical practice[117] and may cause substantial distress. About half the women attending with dysuria have shown no evidence of current urinary tract infection.[118]

Etiology. The role of infection in women with sterile urine has not been determined with certainty.[118] The proportion of patients in whom no recent infection can be detected varies across studies[119]; many women with urethral symptoms show histological evidence of previous infections, even in the absence of current infection.[120] In some women there is evidence of spasticity of the urethral musculature which may cause or contribute to symptoms of urethral irritation,[121] and in some there is pelvic floor hyperactivity.[122] There is increased urethral closure pressure and instability of urethral pressure at rest; autonomic mediated spasms explain these symptoms in part.[123] Other possible mechanisms have been reviewed by Brumfitt et al.[118]

Psychological and Psychiatric Studies. Women with the urethral syndrome attending a urology clinic had elevated MMPI scores.[124] In a family practice, patients with the urethral syndrome who had no evidence of current infection were more anxious and had more tranquilizers prescribed in the previous year[125] and had more psychosocial problems on follow-up than those who had urinary infections.[126] In another study, in family practice women with the urethral syndrome had no more psychiatric ill health than those with urinary tract infections.[118]

Comments. Infection is the commonest cause for urethral symptoms. The few psychological and psychiatric studies in patients with chronic urethral syndrome have yielded conflicting results. It is uncertain to which extent psychopathology is a contributing factor. In a few, emotional distress probably plays a role. These patients either perceive their urethral symptoms more or are more distressed by them. Since abnormal tension in the bladder and in the striated muscle of the urethra appear to contribute to the syndrome, in some patients emotional arousal perhaps induces or aggravates the spasm.

Treatments. Urinary tract infections require the appropriate treatment. Studies of treatment of the urethral syndrome with antibiotics have yielded conflicting results.[125] One study suggests that urethral dilation may be helpful.[127]

Diazepam was found to relieve symptoms in uncontrolled studies[122, 128] and in another, some patients improved with prazosin or other a-blocking drugs.[123] In an uncontrolled study of 15 patients referred for unspecified psychiatric treatment, 13 were reported to have recovered.[129]

PHYSIOLOGICAL DISTURBANCES INDUCED BY BEHAVIORS

There are various behaviors that may induce physiological or pathological changes which, in turn, can cause bodily symptoms. The disorders discussed herein are hyperventilation and aerophagy.

HYPERVENTILATION

In severe anxiety, hyperventilation is often striking, with the patient feeling a lack of air. In other patients it may be inconspicuous and the patient may be unaware of breathing excessively.[130, 131]

About 13% of random subjects who replied to a questionnaire stated that they had breathing difficulties or not enough air during the past week; in neurotic outpatients the prevalence was about 40%.[26]

The fall in pCO_2 and consequent alkalosis may cause symptoms of tetany and reduced cerebral oxygenation may cause faintness or dizziness. Hyperventilation occurs in severe anxiety and panic attacks. Many patients report that all symptoms of panic appear suddenly and simultaneously. In others, hyperventilation appears to be a consequence of panic[132]; the somatic symptoms of hyperventilation aggravate panic if these are perceived as unpleasant and are interpreted in a catastrophic fashion such as symptoms of serious disease.[133, 134] Subsequently, the fear becomes more severe and induces more hyperventilation.

In hyperventilating patients, the true nature of the disorder may not be recognized. Deliberate hyperventilation may reproduce the symptoms the patient usually experiences.

Treatments. There is evidence that retraining of breathing combined with explanatory and cognitive therapy decreases the incidence of panic attacks.[135] Retraining of breathing increases resting pCO_2[136] and decreases the number of recurrences of agoraphobia treated with exposure.[137]

AEROPHAGIA

The excessive swallowing of air may cause gastrointestinal symptoms such as dyspepsia, distension, and flatus. The patients may swallow more frequently or may be observed gulping air; they are often unaware of the habit. It occurs more commonly in hiatal hernia and peptic ulceration as one of the likely causes is an attempt to relieve symptoms.[138] Conversely, aerophagia appears to be one of the causes of NUD. Other causes are frequent swallowing and habits that cause hypersalivation such as chewing tobacco. Excessive swallowing may trigger bowel peristalsis because of distension by air and may contribute to the symptoms of IBS.[139]

Psychological Factors. There are no systematic studies exploring the psychological factors in aerophagia, only a few published case reports. There are several case histories of the treatment of aerophagia in the mentally retarded. Antianxiety drugs have been found to be effective, which suggests that anxiety is one of the causes of this habit.

Treatments. A small study suggests that audiofeedback with a microphone that amplifies swallowing noises combined with habit reversal techniques decreases the rate of swallowing as well as relieving dyspeptic symptoms. Training in muscular relaxation also reduced symptoms, but to a lesser degree.[140] There are a few case histories and small uncontrolled series in children and retarded institutionalized patients in which various operant conditioning and contingency management techniques decreased or eliminated air swallowing.[141-143] In crossover trials, lorazepam, medazepam, and diazepam were decidedly more effective than placebo.[144, 145]

PAIN SYNDROMES

STRIATED MUSCLE CONTRACTION

Contraction of voluntary muscle is a common source of physiological activity that gives rise to somatic symptoms. Such activity is one of the causes of regional pain. In other patients, reflex contraction is a response to pain.

There is increased activity of striated muscle as measured by EMG during emotion including during experimental stress. EMG levels in anxious patients tend to be higher than in controls.[146, 147] The return to baseline levels after experimental stress is slower in anxious patients than in normal controls.[146]

EMG potentials are larger in neck muscles during experimental stress in patients who complain of headaches than in other psychiatric patients.[148] EMG activity of the temporalis muscle is significantly higher in patients with muscle contraction headaches than in normal controls; there are no significant differences, however, in EMG activity of patients who have headache at the time of measurements and those who do not[149]; some of the headache patients have lower tension than the controls. Muscle tension is higher in parts of the body that are aching or painful compared to other parts of the body.[150] Patients with headaches or neck pain develop greater EMG activity during experimental pain inflicted on the forearm than other patients.[151] Some patients with low backache have elevated EMG levels in paravertebral muscles,[152] particularly when emotionally stressed.[146, 153]

Treatments. There is consistent evidence that muscle contraction headaches are relieved by relaxation training, biofeedback, antidepressant drugs and analgesics.[154, 155] These treatments are likely to be effective in other types of muscle contraction pain as well.[156]

NONCARDIAC CHEST PAIN

There are numerous causes of noncardiac chest pain.[157] About 100,000 people in the United States evaluated each year because of chest pain have normal coronary arteriograms; many others are investigated for cardiac disease by noninvasive procedures.[158]

Psychiatric disorders, particularly panic disorder, depression, and hyperventilation, are substantially higher in patients with normal arteriograms than in patients with coronary artery disease.[157] Hyperventilation can cause chest pain as well as electrocardiographic changes that resemble myocardial ischemia.[159] During panic attacks the tension in intercostal muscles increases.[160]

Treatments. A controlled study of cognitive–behavioral therapy suggests at least the short-term efficacy of such treatments. With this therapy chest pain was reduced, mood improved, activities increased, and the patients now accepted that psychological factors had been the major cause of their symptoms.[161, 162]

PELVIC PAIN

Complaints of chronic pelvic pain are common in gynecological patients. The pain can be extremely distressing and incapacitating.

Etiology. Laparoscopies in women with chronic pelvic pain reveal normal tissue in one-third to three-quarters of cases.[163] The various causes that have been proposed include chronic pelvic infections, nerve entrapment, and localized areas of hypersensitivity with referred pain.[164] Varicosities and vascular abnormalities are more common than in other women.[165]

Psychiatric and Psychological Studies. On the average, women with this syndrome show more evidence of psychiatric ill health than other patients, including those who have pelvic pain caused by organic disease such as endometriosis. A substantial proportion believe that they have an undiagnosed disease.[166] Patients with pelvic pain had experienced substantially more sexual abuse in childhood as well as in adult life; they had a history of depression and drug abuse that preceded the onset of the pain.[167] The patients with this syndrome appear to be psychologically heterogeneous with about one-half scoring in the normal ranges on distress scales.[168]

Comments. The definite causes of this syndrome remain unknown. Vascular abnormalities tend to be more common, thus, congestion appears to be a factor in some patients. Ovarian hormones tend to dilate pelvic veins, which may explain the occurrence of the pain during the reproductive years.[169] In some, pain appears to originate with severe sexual trauma in childhood and is accompanied by disturbed adult sexuality; in others, psychological distress appears to be the consequence of severe chronic pain.

Treatment. Numerous treatments have been suggested and reported in uncontrolled studies.[170] In a controlled study, suppression of ovarian activity with medroxyprogesterone acetate relieved pain.[171] Cognitive behavior therapy combined with relaxation training was found superior in outcome to that in a control group in which patients received explanation only.[172] In another study, there was an interaction effect of five sessions of psychotherapy and medroxyprogesterone acetate, but no evidence on follow-up of efficacy of brief psychotherapy alone.[171]

OTHER CHRONIC PAIN SYNDROMES

There are several other chronic pain syndromes, most of which are classified in the DSM-III-R under Somatoform Pain Disorder. There is a formidable literature on the nature and treatment of chronic pain.[156, 173, 174]

PSYCHOSOMATIC SYNDROMES AND SOMATIZATION

BIOLOGICAL AND PSYCHOSOCIAL FACTORS

The prevalence studies show that psychosomatic syndromes afflict a large proportion of people. The findings from the studies also suggest that in most, if not all, syndromes there is a biological as well as psychosocial contribution. There appear to be substantial differences among the syndromes; for example, in hyperventilation psychiatric causes are paramount; the physiological changes are secondary; whereas in IBS, an abnormal responsiveness of the colon which leads to a disturbance in motor activity is a crucial etiological factor. There are also substantial differences among individuals with the same symptom or syndrome. For example, fatigue can be caused by psychomotor retardation with a severe depression in a physically healthy individual, or can be a consequence of a viral infection in a person who has no psychiatric illness.

Even when the etiology of a syndrome is known, there may be uncertainty whether a particular symptom is caused by a physiological or pathological process. A symptom as well as a physiological response may be the final common path with various possible causes. A simple example of a process that may be psychophysiological is the shedding of tears. An overflow of tears may be caused by pathological processes such as infections, allergies, injuries, tumors, by anatomical abnormalities such as a blocked nasolacrimal duct, and by psychophysiological processes, for example, grief and laughter, and other emotions such as gratitude. The same symptom or response may have different causes in different individuals and in the same individual at different times. A bulky meal may cause an attack of diarrhea in a patient with an irritable bowel syndrome on one occasion, whereas severe anxiety may precipitate an attack at another time. In several of the psychosomatic disorders, the causation is usually far more complex than in these simple examples, with several etiological factors interacting and summating.

SOMATIZATION

In the DSM-IV the disorders that have traditionally been labeled as *somatization* are classified largely in the categories of somatoform disorders, and some belong to the category of psychological factors affecting physical conditions. In the *International Classification of Diseases* (ICD-10)[175] somatization syndromes are classified among the somatoform disorders (F45), the dissociative (conversion) disorders (F44), neurasthenia (480), and a few in the category of behavioral syndromes and medical disorders associated with physiological dysfunction (F50).

There is incomplete agreement among authors on the definition of somatization. For example, Katon et al.[176] define it as "an idiom of distress in which patients with psychosocial and emotional problems articulate their distress primarily through physical symptomatology." Kleinman and Kleinman[177] define it as "the expression of personal and social distress in an idiom of bodily complaints with medical helpseeking." Ford[178, 179] defined it as the use of somatic symptoms for psychological purposes. Bridges and Goldberg[180] chose operational criteria for somatization that consist of consulting behavior; the patient attributes the somatic manifestations to a physical problem, but it is a psychiatric illness and responds to psychiatric treatment. Lipowski[181] defined it as the experience and communication of psychological distress in the form of physical symptoms. Several authors concluded that somatization is neither a discrete clinical entity, nor the result of a single pathological or psychological process and that somatization cuts across diagnostic categories.[134, 182, 183]

For the purposes of the present overview I have chosen a broad definition of somatization that is in accord with one of the criteria from the DSM-IV. It is part of the criteria for undifferentiated somatoform disorder and, with slight variations, for some of the other somatoform disorders. Somatization indicates one or more physical complaints, e.g., fatigue, gastrointestinal or urinary complaints, and either (1) appropriate evaluation uncovers no organic pathology or pathophysiologic mechanism (e.g., a physical disorder or effect of injury) to account for the physical complaints, or (2) when there is related organic pathology, the physical complaints or resulting social or occupational impairment are grossly in excess of what would be expected from the physical findings.

BOUNDARIES OF DIAGNOSTIC CATEGORIES

There is a close relationship and a blurred boundary between the psychosomatic syndromes surveyed herein and some of the somatoform disorders. For example, somatization disorder of the DSM-III-R and the more common undifferentiated somatoform disorder include symptoms as follows: abdominal pain, nausea, bloating, diarrhea, back pain, joint pain, pain in extremities, pain during urination, other pain (excluding headaches), shortness of breath when not exerting oneself, palpitation, chest pain, dizziness, fatigue and loss of appetite, difficulty in swallowing, urinary retention or difficulty urinating and pseudoneurologic symptoms. The criteria, furthermore, stipulate that appropriate evaluation uncovers no organic pathology or pathophysiologic mechanism [...] to account for the physical complaints and when there is related organic pathology, the physical complaints

[. . .] or resulting social or occupational impairment are grossly in excess of what would be expected from the physical findings.

It may be exceedingly difficult in clinical practice as well as in clinical research, particularly in epidemiological studies with lay interviewers, to classify accurately a symptom or a group of symptoms among the somatoform disorders (300.70) or in the category psychological factors affecting physical conditions (316.00). All of the symptoms of undifferentiated somatoform disorders and most of the symptoms listed under somatization disorder may be caused by the psychosomatic syndromes listed above. For example, the irritable bowel syndrome is classified as code 316. Persistent abdominal complaints, however, in which the physiology may be the same, but not all the characteristic symptoms and signs are present that warrant the IBS diagnosis might be classified under code 300.70. The ICD-10 shares some of the same problems.

The DSM-IV stipulates that appropriate evaluation discovers no organic pathology or pathophysiologic mechanism. The classification may hinge on the interpretation of what constitutes "appropriate evaluation." In medical practice, as opposed to research, the appropriate evaluation is limited to the exclusion of substantial physical disease, but does not pursue investigations to detect the mechanism responsible for each symptom of a somatizing patient.

Etiology. The survey of the psychosomatic syndromes revealed diverse etiological factors. Many of these factors are shared by somatization in general. These common roots are relevant to the discussion of the relationship of psychosomatic syndromes to some of the somatoform disorders.

Clustering. In patients with psychosomatic disorders, there is a tendency for clustering of syndromes. That is, a person with a psychosomatic syndrome is at risk of acquiring another one. For example, patients with fibromyalgia are more likely than other patients to have also an irritable bowel syndrome and chronic fatigue,[184] and patients with an irritable bowel syndrome are more prone than others to have noncolonic functional syndromes as well as symptoms unrelated to the gastrointestinal tract.[185, 186] Since there is also a positive correlation between psychic or cognitive symptoms of anxiety and depression and the number and severity of somatic symptoms, clustering appears to be, in part, a function of the severity of the emotional disturbance. In part, clustering appears to be caused by a person's tendency to react to stress with physiological changes in various systems or somatization or both. In a recent study, Kirmayer and Robbins[187] found that the pattern of symptom reporting of somatizers was better characterized by several functional syndromes (or psychosomatic syndromes) than by a single disorder of somatization. In some patients, the functional symptoms of somatizers can be explained by clustering of psychosomatic syndromes, albeit often in atypical forms.

Seeking Care. Whether an individual seeks treatment for his or her symptoms will be influenced by several factors.[188–192] In several of the disorders described in previous sections, for example, in the irritable bowel syndrome, clustering, neurotic symptoms, and abnormal personality traits were predominantly associated with *patient status.* This term has been used by several authors to describe the symptoms of a self-selected group of people who sought treatment (as opposed to individuals with the same disorder who do not seek medical care). Only a part of a patient's emotional symptoms, however, are exclusively associated with patient status; functional somatic symptoms are also extremely common in people who do not seek medical care, and there is also a robust correlation of these symptoms with anxiety and depression in people who do not seek treatment.

Psychiatric Diagnosis. The clustering of psychosomatic syndromes has implications for diagnosis. A patient may complain of chronic tiredness, muscle pains, nausea, abdominal cramps, and difficulty in swallowing, and routine medical investigations have excluded physical disease. This patient might be labeled by a psychiatrist as a somatizer and classified among one of the somatoform disorders, depending how the instruction in the DSM-III-R (e.g., those for Undifferentiated Somatoform Disorder) are interpreted. Yet, if the patient is referred to several nonpsychiatric specialists the diagnoses might be fibromyalgia, NUD, IBS, and pseudodysphagia. Psychosomatic syndromes can occur in any degree of severity. For example, Masi and Yunus[5] describe various manifestations of fibromyalgia which range from mild muscular pains to the severe and characteristic syndromes. It may be advantageous to conceptualize a somatizing patient as someone in whom psychosomatic syndromes have clustered. The extensive research on psychosomatic syndromes may enhance the understanding of the somatizing process and this conceptualization allows a rational choice of treatment which will be discussed below.

Physiological Changes. Many of the symptoms of somatoform disorders can be explained as consequences of the physiological activity described in the section on psychosomatic syndromes; for example, endocrine changes during sympathetic adrenergic arousal, increase in striated muscle tension and smooth muscle activity, changes in blood flow, and the effects of overbreathing. Individuals have a characteristic pattern of physiological responses to stress.[192] In patients who are morbidly anxious or complain primarily of somatic symptoms, the symptoms correlate highly with physiological changes.[193] The evidence across studies is consistent. Strong emotions, particularly anxiety, depression, and hostility induce changes in a physiological activity, induce or aggravate somatic symptoms, as well as psychosomatic syndromes.[1]

Low Pain Threshold. A lower pain threshold has been found in several groups of people with bodily complaints. Patients with fibromyalgia have a low pain threshold, not only at tender points, but at other parts of the muscle as well.[2] Some of the patients with esophageal chest pain are more sensitive to distension of the esophagus than those without pain.[56, 57, 194] Patients with the "tender heart syndrome" experience pain during catheterization of coronary arteries.[195] Conversely, patients with silent myocardial ischemia tend to have a high pain threshold.[196, 197] Patients with IBS have a lower pain threshold to distension, their bowel reacts more when distended, yet they do not have a low pain threshold to cutaneous pain.[95]

Severely hypochondriacal patients[198] and patients with disease phobia[199] have low pain thresholds, and these two diagnostic groups are strongly associated with somatization. In subjects who have an abnormally low threshold for sensations, even slight changes in physiologic activity such as an increase in striated muscle tension or physiological distension of the viscera may give rise to distressing sensations. The degree of distress and the propensity to seek medical care may be influenced by a low sensation threshold.

Other Etiological Factors. The nature of the psychosocial contribution to psychosomatic syndromes and somatoform disorders is similar. The syndromes for which extensive empirical data are available show most of the etiological features found in studies of somatization.

A partial list of the remaining etiological factors in somatization includes as follows: genetic factors,[200, 201] depression,[176, 202] anxiety,[193] selective perception,[203] fear of diseases, or a false belief of having a disease,[134] amplification of bodily symptoms,[204] learning,[134] including maladaptive learning in a stressful home environment,[205] abuse of various kinds in childhood,[206, 207] low socioeconomic class and poor education,[208] the effects of culture and subculture,[177, 209] gain and social reinforcement[210, 211] and alexithymia.[212, 213]

The psychosocial factors may influence the extent of the physiological changes, determine whether these changes or sensations from other causes are perceived and modulate the degree of distress they cause. Finally, they determine whether or not a person will seek medical care. These factors have been surveyed by several authors.[1, 176, 178, 182, 204, 208, 214–216]

TREATMENT OF SOMATIZATION

There are no adequate controlled studies of the treatment of somatization in general, only studies of the treatments of individual syndromes. Several of the psychosomatic syndromes may require specific treatments; these treatments may also be used effectively in patients with somatoform disorders if the underlying syndrome is recognized. Since psychosomatic syndromes differ in prognosis and respond differently to treatments,[1] the recognition that somatization may be the manifestation of a specific syndrome may also help the clinician to reach a better estimate of the prognosis.

Acknowledgments

Various sections of earlier versions of this manuscript were critically reviewed by several psychiatric and nonpsychiatric physicians as follows: Drs. Dennis McCarthy, Frederick Koster, Wolfgang Schmidt-Novarra, David Benahum, John Slocumb, Diana Keller, E. H. Uhlenhuth, Vladan Starcevic, Laura Lane, and Tina Walch. Ms. Elynn Cowden edited the manuscript. Ms. Betty Bierner and Ms. Heidiliza Hunt provided secretarial assistance.

References

1. Kellner R. *Psychosomatic Syndromes and Somatic Symptoms*. Washington, DC.: American Psychiatric Press;1991.
2. Quimby LG, Block SR, Gratwick GM. Fibromyalgia: Generalized pain intolerance and manifold symptom reporting. *J Rheumatol.* 1988;15:1264–1270.
3. Wolfe F. Fibrositis, fibromyalgia, and musculoskeletal disease: The current status of the fibrositis syndrome. *Arch Phys Med Rehabil.* 1988;69:527–531.
4. Wolfe F, Cathey M. Prevalence of primary and secondary fibrositis. *J Rheumatol.* 1983;10:965–968.
5. Masi AT, Yunus MB. Concepts of illness in populations as applied to fibromyalgia syndromes. *Am J Med.* 1986;81(suppl 3A):19–25.
6. Cathey MA, Wolfe F, Kleinheksel SM, Hawley DJ. Socioeconomic impact of fibrositis: Study of 81 patients with primary fibrositis. *Am J Med.* 1986;81(suppl 3A):78–84.

7. Gupta MA, Moldofsky H. Dysthymic disorder and rheumatic pain modulation disorder (fibrositis syndrome): A comparison of symptoms and sleep physiology. Can J Psychiatry. 1986;31:608–616.

8. Moldofsky H, Scarisbrick P. Induction of neurasthenic musculoskeletal pain syndrome by selective sleep state deprivation. Psychosom Med. 1976;38:35–44.

9. Bennett RM. The fibrositis/fibromyalgia syndrome. Proceedings of a Symposium. Am J Med. 1986;81 (suppl 3A):1–4.

10. Bennett RM. Current issues concerning management of the fibrositis/ fibromyalgia syndrome. Am J Med. 1986;81 (suppl 3A):15–18.

11. Goldenberg DL. Fibromyalgia syndrome: An emerging but controversial condition. JAMA. 1987;257:2782–2787.

12. Moldofsky H, Warsh JJ. Plasma tryptophan and musculoskeletal pain in nonarticular rheumatism ("fibrositis syndrome"). Pain. 1978;5:65–71.

13. Dinerman H, Goldenberg DL, Felson DT. A prospective evaluation of 118 patients with the fibromyalgia syndrome: Prevalence of Raynaud's phenomenon, sicca symptoms, ANA, low complement, and Ig deposition at the dermal-epidermal junction. J Rheumatol. 1986;13:368–373.

14. Goldenberg DL. An overview of psychologic studies in fibromyalgia. J Rheumatol. 1989;16 (suppl 19):12–14.

15. Clark S, Campbell SM, Forehand ME, Tindall EA, Bennett RM. Clinical characteristics of fibrositis. II. A "blinded," controlled study using standard psychological tests. Arthritis Rheum. 1985;28:132–137.

16. Hudson JI, Hudson MS, Pliner LF, Goldenberg DL, Pope HG Jr. Fibromyalgia and major affective disorders: A controlled phenomenology and family history study. Am J Psychiatry. 1985;142:441–446.

17. Yunus MB. Fibromyalgia syndrome: New research on an old malady. Br Med J. 1989;298:474–475.

18. Kirmayer JL, Robbins JM, Kapusta MA. Somatization and depression in fibromyalgia syndrome. Am J Psychiatry. 1988;145:950–954.

19. Miller DR, Seifert RD. Management of fibromyalgia, a distinct rheumatologic syndrome. Clin Pharm. 1987;6:778–786.

20. Bennett RM, Gatter RA, Campbell SM, Andrews RP, Clark SR, Scarola JA. A comparison of cyclobenzaprine and placebo in the management of fibrositis. Arthritis Rheum. 1988;31:1535–1542.

21. Goldenberg DL, Felson DT, Dinerman H. A randomized, controlled trial of amitriptyline and naproxen in the treatment of patients with fibromyalgia. Arthritis Rheum. 1986;29:1371–1377.

22. Fine PG, Milano R, Hard BD. The effects of myofascial trigger point injections are naloxone reversible. Pain. 1988;32:15–20.

23. Draspa LJ. Psychological factors in muscular pain. Br J Med Psychol. 1959;32: 106–116.

24. Ferraccioli G, Ghirelli L, Scita F, Nolli M, Mozzani M, Fontana S, Scorsonelli M, Tridenti A, De Risio C. EMG-biofeedback training in fibromyalgia syndrome. J Rheumatol. 1987;14:820–825.

25. McCain GA, Bell DA, Francois MM, Halliday PD. A controlled study of the effects of a supervised cardiovascular fitness training program on the manifestations of primary fibromyalgia. Arthritis Rheum. 1988;31:1135–1141.

26. Kellner R, Sheffield BF. The one-week prevalence of symptoms in neurotic patients and normals. *Am J Psychiatry.* 1973;130:102–105.
27. Chen MK. The epidemiology of self-perceived fatigue among adults. *Prev Med.* 1986;15:74–81.
28. Hughes JR, Crow RS, Jacobs DR Jr, Mittelmark MB, Leon AS. Physical activity, smoking, and exercise-induced fatigue. *J Behav Med.* 1984;7:217–230.
29. Lloyd AR, Hales JP, Gandevia SC. Muscle strength, endurance and recovery in the post-infection fatigue syndrome. *J Neurol Neurosurg Psychiatry.* 1988;51: 1316–1322.
30. Stokes MJ, Cooper RG, Edwards RHT. Normal muscle strength and fatigability in patients with effort syndromes. *Br Med J.* 1988;297:1014–1017.
31. Kennedy HG. Fatigue and fatigability. *Br J Psychiatry.* 1988;153:1–5.
32. Holmes GP, Kaplan JE, Gantz NM, Komaroff AL, Schonberger LB, Strauss SE, Jones JF, Dubois RE, Cunningham-Rundles C, Pahwa S, Rosato G, Zegans LS, Purtilo DT, Brown N, Schooley RT, Brus I. Chronic fatigue syndrome: A working case definition. *Ann Intern Med.* 1988;108:387–389.
33. Gratzner HG, Johnson TS, Hermann WJ, Steinbach TL, De Herrera R. Assessment of stress-induced immune function in chronic fatigue syndrome patients. In: Plotnikoff N, Murgo A, Faith R, Wybran J, eds. *Stress and Immunity.* Boca Raton, FL: CRC Press;1991: pp 247–257.
34. Lloyd AR, Wakefield D, Boughton CR, Dwyer JM. Immunological abnormalities in the chronic fatigue syndrome. *Med J Aust.* 1989;151: 122–124.
35. DeFreitas E, Hilliard B, Cheney PR, et al. Retroviral sequences related to human T-lymphotropic virus type II in patients with chronic fatigue immune dysfunction syndrome. *Proc Natl Acad Sci.* 1991;88:2922–2926.
36. Bastien S. Neuropsychological deficits in chronic fatigue syndrome. Presented at the International Conference, Epstein Barr Virus: The first 25 Years, April 1989;Oxford.
37. Altay HT, Toner BB, Brooker H, Abbey SE, Salit IE, Garfinkel PE. The neuropsychological dimensions of postinfectious neuromyasthenia (chronic fatigue syndrome): A preliminary report. *Int J Psychiatry Med.* 1990;20: 141–149.
38. Manu P, Matthews DA, Lane TJ. The mental health of patients with a chief complaint of chronic fatigue. *Arch Intern Med.* 1988;148:2213–2217.
39. White PD. Fatigue and chronic fatigue syndromes. In: Bass C, ed. *Somatization: Physical Symptoms and Psychological Illness.* Oxford, U.K.: Blackwell Scientific Publications;1990: pp 104–140.
40. Wessely S. The history of postviral fatigue syndrome. In: Behan P, Goldberg D, Mowbray J, eds. *British Medical Bulletin (Postviral Fatigue Syndrome).* New York: Churchill Livingstone;1991.
41. Krupp LB, Mendelson WB, Friedman R. An overview of chronic fatigue syndrome. *J Clin Psychiatry.* 1991;52:403–410.
42. Kendell RE. Chronic fatigue viruses, and depression. *Lancet.* 1991; 337:160–162.
43. Woods TO, Goldberg DP. Psychiatric perspectives: An overview. *Br Med Bull.* 1991;47:908–918.
44. David AS, Wessely S, Pelosi AJ. Postviral fatigue syndrome: Time for a new approach. *Br Med J.* 1988;296:696–701.

45. Strauss SE, Dale JK, Tohi M, Lawley T, Preble O, Blaese RM, Hallahan C, Henle W. Acyclovir treatment of the chronic fatigue syndrome. *N Engl J Med.* 1988;319:1692–1698.
46. Lloyd A, Hickie I, Wakefield D, Boughton C, Dwyer J. A double-blind, placebo-controlled trial of intravenous immunoglobulin therapy in patients with chronic fatigue syndrome. *Am J Med.* 1990;89:561–568.
47. Peterson PK, Shepard J, Macres M, Schenck C, Crosson J, Rechtman D, Lurie N. A controlled trial of intravenous immunoglobulin G in chronic fatigue syndrome. *Am J Med.* 1990;89:554–560.
48. American Society for Microbiology. Experimental drug held effective for chronic fatigue, immune dysfunction. *Conf J.* 1991;i:1–3.
49. Cotton P. Treatment proposed for chronic fatigue syndrome; Research continues to compile data on disorder. *JAMA.* 1991;266:2667–2668.
50. Wessely S, Butler S, Chalder T, David A. The cognitive behavioural management of the postviral fatigue syndrome. In: Jenkins R, Mowbray J, eds. *The Postviral Fatigue Syndrome.* Chichester, U.K.: John Wiley;1990.
51. Butler S, Chalder T, Ron M, Wessely S. Cognitive behaviour therapy in chronic fatigue syndrome. *J Neurol Neurosurg Psychiatry.* 1991;54:153–158.
52. Dalton CB, Castell DO, Richter JE. The changing faces of the nutcracker esophagus. *Am J Gastroenterol.* 1988;83:623–628.
53. Blackwell JN, Castell DO. Oesophageal chest pain: A point of view. *Gut.* 1984;25:1–6.
54. Reidel WL, Clouse RE. Variations in clinical presentation of patients with esophageal contraction abnormalities. *Dig Dis Sci.* 1985;30:1065–1071.
55. MacKenzie J, Belch J, Land D, Park R, McKillop J. Oesophageal ischaemia in motility disorders associated with chest pain. *Lancet.* 1988;ii: 592–595.
56. Richter JE, Barish CF, Castell DO. Abnormal sensory perception in patients with esophageal chest pain. *Gastroenterology.* 1986;91:845–852.
57. Edwards DAW. Tender oesophagus: A new syndrome (abstract). *Gut.* 1982;23: A919.
58. Whitehead WE, Schuster MM. *Gastrointestinal Disorders.* New York: Academic Press;1985.
59. Richter JE, Obrecht WF, Bradley LA, Young LD, Anderson KO. Psychological comparison of patients with nutcracker esophagus and irritable bowel syndrome. *Dig Dis Sci.* 1986b;31:131–138.
60. Anderson KO, Dalton CB, Bradley LA, Richter JE. Stress induces alteration of esophageal pressures in healthy volunteers and non-cardiac chest pain patients. *Dig Dis Sci.* 1989;34:83–91.
61. Clouse RE, Lustman PJ. Psychiatric illness and contraction abnormalities of the esophagus. *N Engl J Med.* 1983;309:1337–1342.
62. Clouse RE, Lustsman PJ. Value of recent psychological symptoms in identifying patients with esophageal contraction abnormalities. *Psychosom Med.* 1989;51:570–576.
63. Ward BW, Wu WC, Riehter JE, Hackshaw BT, Castell DO. Non-cardiac chest pain: Is diagnosis of esophageal etiology helpful (abstract)? *Gastroenterology.* 1985;88:1627.
64. Jacobson E. Spastic esophagus and mucous colitis: Etiology and treatment by progressive relaxation. *Arch Intern Med.* 1927;39:433–445.

65. Cerny M, Setka J, Jarolimek M, Tuma P. Self-regulation of esophageal activity. *Activ Nerv Sup* (Praha). 1988;30:181–182.
66. Latimer PR. Biofeedback and self-regulation in the treatment of diffuse esophageal spasm: A single-case study. *Biofeedback Self Regul.* 1981; 6:181–189.
67. Schuster MM, Nikoomanesh P, Wells D. Biofeedback control of lower esophageal sphincter contraction. *Rendiconti Gastroenterol.* 1973;5:14–18.
68. Traube M, McCallum RW. Primary oesophageal motility disorders. Current therapeutic concepts. *Drugs.* 1985;30:66–77.
69. Nasrallah SM, Tommaso CL, Singleton RT, Backhaus EA. Primary esophageal motor disorders. Clinical response to nifedipine. *South Med J.* 1985;78: 312–315.
70. Richter JE, Dalton CB, Bradley LA, Castell DO. Oral nifedipine in the treatment of noncardiac chest pain in patients with the nutcracker esophagus. *Gastroenterology.* 1987;93:21–28.
71. Clouse RE, Lustman PJ, Eckert TC, Ferney DM, Griffith LS. Low-dose trazodone for symptomatic patients with esophageal contraction abnormalities. A double-blind, placebo-controlled trial. *Gastroenterology.* 1987;92:1027–1036.
72. Nyrén O, Adami HO, Gustavsson S, Lööf L. Excess sick-listing in nonulcer dyspepsia. *J Clin Gastroenterol.* 1986;8:339–345.
73. Editorial. Data base on dyspepsia. *Br Med J.* 1978;i:1163–1164.
74. Colin-Jones DG (chairman). Management of dyspepsia: Report of a working party. *Lancet.* 1988;i:576–579.
75. Johnsen R, Bernersen B, Straume B, Forde OH, Bostad L, Burhol PG. Prevalences of endoscopic and histological findings in subjects with and without dyspepsia. *Br Med J.* 1991;302:749–751.
76. Magni G, Di Mario F, Aggio L. Psychological distress in non-ulcerous dyspepsia (letter). *Gastroenterol Clin Biol.* 1985;9:86.
77. Magni G, Di Mario F, Bernasconi G, Mastropaolo G. DSM-III diagnoses associated with dyspepsia of unknown cause. *Am J Psychiatry.* 1987;144:1222–1223.
78. Talley NJ, Fung LH, Gilligan IJ, McNeil D, Piper DW. Association of anxiety, neuroticism, and depression with dyspepsia of unknown cause. *Gastroenterology.* 1986;90:886–892.
79. Johnsen R, Jacobsen BK, Forde OH. Associations between symptoms of irritable colon and psychological and social conditions and lifestyle. *Br Med J.* 1987;292:1633–1635.
80. Canton G, Santonastaso P, Fraccon IG. Life events, abnormal illness behaviour and appendectomy. *Gen Hosp Psychiatry.* 1984;191–195.
81. Farmer R, Creed FH. Life events, hostility and deliberate self-harm. *Br J Psychiatry.* 1992;161:145–153.
82. Johannessen, Fjosne U, Kleveland PM, Halvorsen T, Kristensen P, Loge I, Hafstad PE, Sandbakken P, Petersen H. Cimetidine responders in non-ulcer dyspepsia. *Scand J Gastroenterol.* 1988;23:327–336.
83. DeLoose F. Domperidone in chronic dyspepsia: A pilot open study and a multicentre general practice crossover comparison with metoclopramide and placebo. *Pharmatherapeutica.* 1979;2:140–146.
84. Baume P, Tracey M, Dawson L. Efficacy of two minor tranquilizers in relieving symptoms of functional gastrointestinal distress. *Aust NZ J Med.* 1975;5: 503–506.

85. Bates S, Sjödén PO, Nyrén O. Behavioral treatment of non-ulcer dyspepsia. *Scand J Behav Ther.* 1988;17:155–165.
86. Whitehead WE, Renault PF, Goldiamond I. Modification of human gastric acid secretion with operant-conditioning procedures. *J Appl Behav Anal.* 1975;8:147–156.
87. Whitehead WE, Drescher VM. Perception of gastric contractions and self-control of gastric motility. *Psychophysiology.* 1980;17:552–557.
88. Thompson WG. The irritable bowel. *Gut.* 1984;25:305–320.
89. Manning AP, Thompson WG, Heaton KW, Morris AF. Towards positive diagnosis of the irritable bowel. *Br Med J.* 1978;ii:653–654.
90. Watson WC, Sullivan SN, Corke M, Rush D. Globus and headache: Common symptoms of the irritable bowel syndrome. *Can Med Assoc J.* 1978;118:387–388.
91. Whorwell PJ, McCallum M, Creed FH, Roberts CT. Non-colonic features of irritable bowel syndrome. *Gut.* 1986;27:37–40.
92. Thompson WG, Heaton KW. Functional bowel disorders in apparently healthy people. *Gastroenterology.* 1980;79:283–288.
93. Read NW. *Irritable Bowel Syndrome.* New York: Grune & Stratton;1985.
94. Ritchie J. Pain from distension of the pelvic colon by inflating a balloon in the irritable colon syndrome. *Gut.* 1973,14:126–132.
95. Whitehead WE, Engel BT, Schuster MM. Irritable bowel syndrome: Physiological and psychological differences between diarrhea-predominant and constipation-predominant patients. *Dig Dis Sci.* 1980;25:404–412.
96. Chasen R, Tucker H, Palmer D, Whitehead W, Schuster M. Colonic motility in irritable bowel syndrome and diverticular disease (abstract). *Gastroenterology.* 1982;82:1031.
97. Lennard-Jones JE. Functional gastrointestinal disorders. *N Engl J Med.* 1983; 308:431–435.
98. Arvanitakis C, Chen GH, Folscroft J, Klotz AP. Lactase deficiency. Comparative study of diagnostic methods. *Am J Clin Nutr.* 1977;30:1597–1602.
99. Blanchard EB, Radnitz CL, Evans DD, Schwarz SP, Neff DF, Gererdi MA. Psychological comparisons of irritable bowel syndrome to chronic tension and migraine headache and nonpatient controls. *Biofeedback Self Regul.* 1986; 11:221–230.
100. Creed F, Guthrie E. Psychological factors in the irritable bowel syndrome. *Gut.* 1987;28:1307–1318.
101. Fava GA, Pavan L. Large bowel disorders. II. Psychopathology and alexithymia. *Psychother Psychosom.* 1976/1977;27:100–105.
102. Ford MJ, Miller PM, Eastwood J, Eastwood MA. Life events, psychiatric illness and the irritable bowel syndrome. *Gut.* 1987;28:160–165.
103. Chaudhary NA, Truelove SC. Human colonic motility: A comparative study of normal subjects, patients with ulcerative colitis, and patients with the irritable colon syndrome. *Gastroenterology.* 161;40:1036.
104. Fava GA, Pavan L. Large bowel disorders. I. Illness configuration and life events. *Psychother Psychosom.* 1976/1977;27:93–99.
105. Whitehead WE, Bosmajian L, Zonderman AB, Costa PT Jr, Schuster MM. Symptoms of psychologic distress associated with irritable bowel syndrome. *Gastroenterology.* 1988;95:709–714.

106. Whitehead WE, Winget C, Fedoravicius AS, Wooley S, Blackwell B. Learned illness behavior in patients with irritable bowel syndrome and peptic ulcer. *Dig Dis Sci.* 1982;27:202–208.
107. Klein KB. Controlled treatment trials in the irritable bowel syndrome: A critique. *Gastroenterology.* 1988;95:232–241.
108. Lucey MR, Clark ML, Lowndes J, Dawson AM. Is bran efficacious in irritable bowel syndrome? A double-blind placebo-controlled crossover study. *Gut.* 1987;28:221–225.
109. Myren J, Lövland B, Larssen SE, Larsen S. Psychopharmacologic drugs in the treatment of the irritable bowel syndrome. *Ann Gastroentérol Hépatol* (Paris). 1984;20:117–123.
110. Greenbaum DS, Mayle JE, Vangeren LE, Jerome JA, Mayor JW, Greenbaum RB, Matson RW, Stein GE, Dean HA, Halvorsen NA, Rosen LW. Effects of desipramine on irritable bowel syndrome compared with atropine and placebo. *Dig Dis Sci.* 1987;32:257–266.
111. Svedlund J, Ottosson J, Sjödin I, Dotevall G. Controlled study of psychotherapy in irritable bowel syndrome. *Lancet.* 1983;ii:589–592.
112. Guthrie E, Creed F, Dawson D, Tomenson B. A controlled trial of psychological treatment for the irritable bowel syndrome. *Gastroenterology.* 1991;100: 450–457.
113. Whorwell PJ, Prior A, Faragher EB. Controlled trial of hypnotherapy in the treatment of severe refractory irritable bowel syndrome. *Lancet.* 1984;i:1232–1233.
114. Voirol MW, Hipolito J. Anthropoanalytical relaxation in irritable bowel syndrome: Results 40 months later. *Schweiz Med Wochenschr.* 1987;117:1117–1119.
115. Berndt H, Maercker W. Psychotherapy of irritable colon. *Z Gesamte Inn Med.* 1985;40:107–110.
116. Bennett P, Wilkinson S. A comparison of psychological and medical treatment of the irritable bowel syndrome. *Br J Clin Psychology.* 1985;24:215–216.
117. Latham RH, Stamm WE. Urethral syndrome in women. *Urol Clin N Am.* 1984;11:95–101.
118. Brumfitt W, Hamilton-Miller JMT, Gillespie WA. The mysterious "urethral syndrome." *Br Med J.* 1991;303:1–2.
119. Editorial: Can Kasstigation beat the truth out of the urethral syndrome? *Lancet.* 1982;ii:694-695.
120. Tait J, Peddie BA, Bailey RR, Arnold EP, Russell GL, Bishop VA, Burry AF. Urethral syndrome (abacterial cystitis). Search for a pathogen. *Br J Urol.* 1985;57:552–556.
121. Schmidt RA, Tanagho EA. Urethral syndrome or urinary tract infection? *Urology.* 981;18:424–427.
122. Kaplan WE, Firlit CF, Schoenberg HW. The female urethral syndrome: External sphincter spasm as etiology. *J Urol.* 1980;124:48–49.
123. Barbalias GA, Meares EM Jr. Female urethral syndrome: Clinical and urodynamic perspectives. *Urology.* 1984;23:208–212.
124. Carson CC, Osborne D, Segura JW. Psychologic characteristics of patients with female urethral syndrome. *J Clin Psychol.* 1979;35:312–313.
125. O'Dowd TC, Smail JE, West RR. Clinical judgment in the diagnosis and management of frequency and dysuria in general practice. *Br Med J.* 1984;288: 1347–1349.

126. O'Dowd TC, Pill R, Smail JE, Davis RH. Irritable urethral syndrome: Follow-up study in general practice. *Br Med J.* 1986;292:30–32.
127. Bergman A, Karram M, Bhatia NN. Urethral syndrome. A comparison of different treatment modalities. *J Reprod Med.* 1989;34:157–160.
128. Firlit CF, Cook WA. Voiding pattern abnormalities in children. *Urology.* 1977; 10:25–29.
129. Carson CC, Segura JW, Osborne DM. Evaluation and treatment of the female urethral syndrome. *J Urol.* 1980;124:609–610.
130. Brashear RE. Hyperventilation syndrome. *Lung.* 1983;161:257–273.
131. Gardner WN, Meah MS, Bass C. Controlled study of respiratory responses during prolonged measurement in patients with chronic hyperventilation. *Lancet.* 1986;ii:826–830.
132. Bass C, Lelliott P. Hyperventilation in the aetiology and treatment of anxiety disorders. In: Emmelkamp PMG, Everaerd WT, Kraimat F, Van Son MJ, eds. *Fresh Perspectives on Anxiety Disorders.* Lisse, Netherlands: Swets & Zeitlinger;1989.
133. Clark DM. A cognitive approach to panic. *Behav Res Ther.* 1986;24:461–470.
134. Kellner R. *Somatization and Hypochondriasis.* New York: Praeger;1986.
135. Clark DM, Salkovskis PM, Chalkley AJ. Respiratory control as a treatment for panic attacks. *J Behav Ther Exp Psychiatry.* 1985;16:23–30.
136. Salkovskis PM, Jones DRO, Clark DM. Respiratory control in the treatment of panic attacks: Replication and extension with concurrent measurement of behaviour and pCO_2. *Br J Psychiatry.* 1986;148:526–532.
137. Bonn JA, Readhead CPA, Timmons BH. Enhanced adaptive behavioural response in agoraphobic patients pretreated with breathing retraining. *Lancet.* 1984;ii:665–669.
138. Roth JL, Bockus HL. Aerophagia: Its etiology, syndromes and management. *Med Clin N Am.* 1957;41:1673–1696.
139. Calloway SP, Fonagy P, Pounder RF. Frequency of swallowing in duodenal ulceration and hiatus hernia. *Br Med J.* 1982;285:23–24.
140. Calloway SP, Fonagy P, Pounder RE, Morgan MJ. Behavioural techniques in the management of aerophagia in patients with hiatus hernia. *J Psychosom Res.* 1983;27:499–502.
141. Barrett RP, McGonigle JJ, Ackles PK, Burkhart JE. Behavioral treatment of chronic aerophagia. *Am J Ment Defic.* 1987;91:620–625.
142. Gauderer MWL, Halpin TC, Izant JR. Pathologic childhood aerophagia: A recognizable clinical entity. *J Pediatr Surg.* 1981;16:301–305.
143. Holburn CS, Dougher MJ. Effects of response satiation procedures in the treatment of aerophagia. *Am J Ment Defic.* 1986;91:72–77.
144. Baume P, Cuthbert J. The effect of medazepam in relieving symptoms of functional gastrointestinal distress. *Aust NZ J Med.* 1973;3:457–460.
145. Baume P, Tracey M, Dawson L. Efficacy of two minor tranquilizers in relieving symptoms of functional gastrointestinal distress. *Aust NZ J Med.* 1975;5: 503–506.
146. Malmo RB, Shagass C, Davis JF. A method for the investigation of somatic response mechanisms in psychoneurosis. *Science.* 1950;112:325–328.
147. Goldstein IB. Physiological responses in anxious women patients: A study of autonomic activity and muscle tension. *Arch Gen Psychiatry.* 1964;10:382–388.

148. Malmo RB, Shagass CC. Physiologic study of symptom mechanisms in psychiatric patients under stress. *Psychosom Med.* 1949;11:25–29.
149. Fujii S, Kachi T, Sobue I. Chronic headache: Its psychosomatic aspect. *Jpn J Psychosom Med.* 1981;21:411–419.
150. Sainsbury P, Gibson JG. Symptoms of anxiety and tension and the accompanying physiological changes in the muscular system. *Neurol Neurosurg Psychiatry.* 1954;17:216–224.
151. Malmo RB, Wallerstein H, Shagass C. Headache proneness and mechanisms of motor conflict in psychiatric patients. *J Pers.* 1953;22:163–187.
152. Dolce JJ, Raczynski JM. Neuromuscular activity and electromyography in painful backs: Psychological and biomechanical modes in assessment and treatment. *Psychol Bull.* 1985;97:502–520.
153. Flor H, Turk DC, Birbaumer N. Assessment of stress-related psychophysiological reactions in chronic back pain patients. *J Consult Clin Psychol.* 1985;53:354–364.
154. Blanchard EB, Andrasik F, Ahles TA, Teders SJ, O'Keefe D. Migraine and tension headache: A meta-analytic review. *Behav Ther.* 1980;11:613–631.
155. Getto CJ, Ochitill H. Psychogenic pain disorder. In: Jefferson JW, Greist JH, Spitzer R, eds. *The Treatment of Mental Disorders of the DSM-III.* New York: Oxford University Press;1982, pp 277–286.
156. Blackwell B, Merskey H, Kellner R. Somatoform pain disorders. In: Karasu T, ed. *Treatments of Psychiatric Disorders.* Washington, DC: American Psychiatric Press;1989:pp 2120–2138.
157. Mayou R. Illness behavior and psychiatry. *Gen Hosp Psychiatric.* 1989;11:307–312.
158. Kemp HG, Kronmal RA, Vlietstra RE, Frye RL. Seven-year survival of patients with normal or near normal coronary arteriograms: ACASS registry study. *J Am Co Cardiol.* 1986;7:479–483.
159. Lary D, Goldschlager N. Electrocardiogram changes during hyperventilation resembling myocardial ischemia in patients with normal coronary arteriograms. *Am Heart J.* 1974;87:383–390.
160. Lynch P, Bakal DA, Whitelaw W, Fung T. Chest muscle activity and panic anxiety: A preliminary investigation. *Psychosom Med.* 1991;53:80–89.
161. Limes I, Mayou RA, Pearce MJ, Klimes I. Psychological treatment for atypical non-cardiac chest pain: A controlled evaluation. *Psychol Med.* 1990;20:605–611.
162. Pearce MJ, Mayou RA, Klimes I. The management of atypical noncardiac chest pain. *Q J Med.* 1990;76:991–996.
163. Liston WA, Bradford WP, Dowie J, Kerr MG. Laparoscopy in a general gynecological unit. *Am J Obstet Gynecol.* 1972;113:672–677.
164. Editorial: Enigmatic pelvic pain. *Br Med J.* 1978;ii:1041–1042.
165. Beard RW, Pearce S, Highman JH, Reginald PW. Diagnosis of pelvic varicosities in women with chronic pelvic pain. *Lancet.* 1984;i:946–949.
166. Kellner R, Slocumb JC, Rosenfeld RC, Pathak D. Fears and beliefs in patients with the pelvic pain syndrome. *J Psychosom Res.* 1988;32:303–310.
167. Walker E, Katon W, Harrop-Griffiths J, Holm L, Russo J, Hickok LR. Relationship of chronic pelvic pain to psychiatric diagnoses and childhood sexual abuse. *Am J Psychiatry.* 1988;145:75–80.
168. Slocumb JC, Kellner R, Rosenfeld RC, Pathak D. Anxiety and depression in patients with the abdominal pelvic pain syndrome. *Gen Hosp Psychiatry.* 1989;11:48–53.

169. Beard RW, Reginald PW, Wadsworth J. Clinical features of women with chronic lower abdominal pain and pelvic congestion. *Br J Obstet Gynaecol.* 1988;95:153–161.
170. Renaer M. *Chronic Pelvic Pain in Women.* Heidelberg, Germany: Springer;1981.
171. Farquhar CM, Rogers V, Franks S. A randomized controlled trial of medroxyprogesterone acetate and psychotherapy for the treatment of pelvic congestion. *Br J Obstet Gynaecol.* 1989;96:1153–1162.
172. Beard RW, Reginald PW, Pearce S. Psychological and somatic factors in women with pain due to pelvic congestion. *Adv Exp Med Biol.* 1988;245:413–421.
173. Merskey H, Spear FG. *Pain: Psychological and Psychiatric Aspects.* London: Balliere, Tindall & Cassell;1967.
174. Melzak R. *The Puzzle of Pain.* New York: Basic Books;1973.
175. World Health Organization. *International Classification of Diseases,* 10th revision. Geneva: World Health Organization;1990.
176. Katon W, Kleinman A, Rosen G. Depression and somatization: A review. Part I. *Am J Med.* 1982;72:127–135.
177. Kleinman A, Kleinman J. Somatization. The interconnections among culture, depression experiences, and the meaning of pain. In: Kleinman A, Good B, eds. *Culture and Depression.* Berkeley: University of California Press;1986: pp 429–490.
178. Ford CV. *The Somatizing Disorders: Illness as a Way of Life.* New York: Elsevier;1983.
179. Ford CV. The somatizing disorders. *Psychosomatics.* 1986;27:327–337.
180. Bridges KW, Goldberg DP. Somatic presentation of DSM-III psychiatric disorders in primary care. *J Psychosom Res.* 1985;29:563–569.
181. Lipowski ZJ. Somatization: Medicine's unsolved problem (editorial). *Psychosomatics.* 1987;28:294–297.
182. Mayou R. The nature of bodily symptoms. *Br J Psychiatry.* 1976;129:55–60.
183. Kirmayer L. Somatization and the social construction of illness experience. In: McHugh S, Vallis TM, eds. *Illness Behavior: A Multidisciplinary Model.* New York: Plenum;1986: pp 111–133.
184. Yunus MB, Masi AT, Aldag JC. A controlled study of primary fibromyalgia syndrome: Clinical features and association with other functional syndromes. *J Rheumatol.* 1989;16(suppl 19):62–71.
185. Drossman DA, Sandler RS. Irritable bowel syndrome: The role of psychosocial factors. In: Read NW, ed. *Irritable Bowel Syndrome.* Orlando, FL: Grune & Stratton;1985: pp 67–74.
186. Cann PA, Read NW. A disease of the whole gut? In: Read NW, ed. *Irritable Bowel Syndrome.* Orlando, FL: Grune & Stratton;1985: pp 53–60.
187. Kirmayer LJ, Robbins JM. Functional somatic syndromes. In: Kirmayer LJ, Robbins JM, eds. *Current Concepts of Somatization.* Washington, DC: American Psychiatric Press;1991: pp 79–106.
188. Mechanic D. Social psychologic factors affecting the presentation of bodily complaints. *N Engl J Med.* 1972;286:1132–1139.
189. Pilowsky I. Abnormal illness behavior. *Br J Med Psychol.* 1969;42:347–351.
190. Blackwell B. Illness behaviour labeling and compliance. *Clin Invest Med.* 1981;4:209–214.
191. Bridges K, Goldberg D, Evans B, Sharpe T. Determinants of somatization in primary care. *Psychol Med.* 1991;21:473–483.

192. Anderson CD. Expression of affect and physiological response in psychosomatic patients. *J Psychosom Res.* 1981;25:143–149.
193. Tyrer P. *The Role of Bodily Feelings in Anxiety.* London: Oxford University Press;1976.
194. Barish CF, Castell DO, Richter JE. Graded esophageal balloon distention: A new provocative test for noncardiac chest pain. *Dig Dis Sci.* 1986;31:1292–1298.
195. Cannon RO III, Leon MB, Watson RM. Chest pain and "normal" coronary arteries: Role of small coronary arteries. *Am J Cardiol.* 1985;55:50B–60B.
196. Droste C, Roskamm H. Experimental pain measurement in patients with asymptomatic myocardial ischemia. *J Am Coll Cardiol.* 1983;1:940–945.
197. Glazier JJ, Chierchia S, Brown MJ, et al. Importance of generalized defective perception of painful stimuli as a cause of silent myocardial ischemia in chronic stable angina pectoris. *Am J Cardiol.* 1986;58:667–672.
198. Merskey HA, Evans PR. Variations in pain complaint threshold in psychiatric and neurological patients with pain. *Pain.* 1975;1:73–79.
199. Bianchi GN. Origins of disease phobia. *Aust NZ J Psychiatry.* 1971;5:241–257.
200. Cloninger CR. *Somatoform and Dissociative Disorders.* Philadelphia: WB Saunders; 1986.
201. Kendler KS, Health AC, Martin NG. Symptoms of anxiety and symptoms of depression. *Arch Gen Psychiatry.* 1987;44:451–457.
202. Cadoret RJ, Widmer RB, Troughton EP. Somatic complaints: Harbinger of depression in primary care. *J Affective Disord.* 1980;2:61–70.
203. Pennebaker JW, Watson D. The psychology of somatic symptoms. In: Kirmayer LJ, Robbins JM, eds. *Current Concepts of Somatization.* Washington, DC: American Psychiatric Press;1991: pp 21–35.
204. Barsky AJ, Goodson JD, Lane RS. The amplification of somatic symptoms. *Psychosom Med.* 1988;50:510–519.
205. Bohman M, Cloninger CR, von Knorring AL. An adoption study of somatoform disorders. III. Cross-fostering analysis and genetic relationship to alcoholism and criminality. *Arch Gen Psychiatry.* 1984;41:872–878.
206. Kellner R, Schneider-Braus K. Distress and attitudes in patients perceived as hypochondriacal by medical staff. *Gen Hosp Psychiatry.* 1988;10:157–162.
207. Drossman DA, Leserman J, Nachman G, Li AM, Gluck H, Toomey TC, Mitchell CM. Sexual and physical abuse in women with functional or organic gastrointestinal disorders. *Ann Intern Med.* 1990;113:828–833.
208. Kirmayer LJ. Culture, affect, and somatization. Part I. *Transcult Psychiatr Res Rev.* 1984;21:159–188.
209. Escobar JI, Burnam A, Karno M. Somatization in the community. *Arch Gen Psychiatry.* 1987;44:713–720.
210. Better SR, Fine PR, Simson D. Disability benefits as disincentives to rehabilitation. *Health Soc.* 1979;57:412–427.
211. Bishop ER Jr, Torch EM. "Dividing hysteria": A preliminary investigation of conversion disorder and psychalgia. *J Nerv Ment Dis.* 1979;167:348–356.
212. Fava GA, Baldaro B, Osti RMA. Towards a self-rating scale for alexithymia. *Psychother Psychosom.* 1980;34:34–39.
213. Taylor GJ, Bagby RM, Parker JDA. The alexithymia construct: A potential paradigm for psychosomatic medicine. *Psychosomatics.* 1991;32:153–164.

214. Lipowsky ZJ. Somatization: The concept and its clinical application. *Am J Psychiatry.* 1988,145:1358–1368.
215. Bass C. *Somatization: Physical Symptoms and Psychological Illness.* Oxford: Blackwell Scientific Publications;1990.
216. Robbins JM, Kirmayer LJ. Cognitive and social factors in somatization. In: Kirmayer LJ, Robbins JM, eds. *Current Concepts of Somatization.* Washington, DC: American Psychiatric Press;1991: pp 107–141.

Chapter 8
The Concept
of Psychosomatic Disorder

GIOVANNI A. FAVA

A critical appraisal of current developments in clinical medicine is likely to underscore some limitations that technological advances have not been able to avoid. Somatization, defined by Lipowski[1] as the tendency to experience and communicate psychological distress in the form of physical symptoms and to seek medical help for them, is a widespread clinical phenomenon that may involve up to 30 to 40% of medical patients. A significant proportion of problems presenting to a primary-care physician cannot be assigned a suitable diagnostic rubric in the International Classification of Diseases.[2] Further, the need to include consideration of function in daily life, productivity, performance of social roles, intellectual capability, emotional stability, and well-being—subsumed under the rubric of quality of life[3]—in assessing medical and surgical treatments has achieved wide currency, particularly in chronic diseases where cure cannot take place.

Such converging developments should pave the way for an upsurge of interest (if not a renaissance) in psychosomatic medicine. This does not seem to be the case. Eisenberg[4] identifies several barriers to a more widespread incorporation of humanistic and psychologically responsive care into medical practice: (1) acquired insensitivity (psychological responsiveness costs money and seems to reduce efficiency); (2) skepticism about the reality of psychosocial factors in the pathogenesis and course of disease; (3) misattribution of therapeutic effects (limited

161

knowledge on the part of physicians regarding the powerful nonspecific effects of the patient-doctor relationship); (4) difficulty in learning new skills, and (5) the current social context of medical practice. His list thus includes medical barriers to implementation of the psychosomatic approach. However, it is also fair to wonder whether psychosomatic medicine has any responsibilities in these failures.

Engel[5] remarks that:

[T]he "falling ill typically involves for the patient a disruption in that unique continuity of knowing and understanding and of feeling known and understood that ordinarily characterizes health and well-being. . . . The largest part of what the patient feels disturbed by is known only to himself and will remain so unless or until it is communicated.

Feinstein[6] notes that clinical medicine tends to rely on "hard data," preferably expressed in the dimensional numbers of laboratory measurements, excluding "soft information" such as data about a patient's spectrum of symptoms, severity of illness, disability, and all the distinctly human reactions (love, hate, joy, sorrow, etc.). These exclusions have "diverted attention from the clinician's traditional obligation to offer relief and comfort, not just cure."[6] The challenge of a new humanistic clinical science would be—according to Feinstein—to translate these soft data into valid and sensible clinical measurements.

In this context, one may wonder what was the role of psychosomatic medicine in refining the methods whereby clinicians may assess psychosocial aspects of disease. Certainly the last decade has witnessed a renaissance in psychiatric diagnosis, and this progress has been most impressive in the field of affective disorders. A substantial improvement in their definition and assessment has resulted in a potentially higher likelihood of their detection in medical practice, even though the skills of physicians as to this aspect are still poor.[7] If we consider any functional disorder, whether gastrointestinal,[8] neurologic,[9] or cardiologic,[10] we may find that in many cases the label *somatization* is simply part of the clinical manifestations of an affective disorder, such as a major depressed episode in irritable bowel syndrome[8] or panic disorder with agoraphobia in cardiac neurosis.[10] The DSM-IV[11] provides a helpful diagnostic tool for such differentiation, as well as in case of predominantly physical pathology.[7] However, depressive and anxiety disturbances account only for part of psychological distress in the medically ill.[9, 10]

Psychosomatic investigators have shown very little interest in a nosologic approach to their field, as if it were a useless exercise in labeling.[12] Weiner[13] exemplifies this disdainful attitude toward diagnosis: "If the term 'psychosomatic medicine' has any meaning at all, it is a medicine of sick persons not of their diseased organs. Therefore, our future efforts should be extended on studying persons in ill-health not their symptoms, or how these might cluster" (pp. 154–155).

While we may agree on the humanistic approach to the patient advocated by Weiner,[13] as well as on the necessity to move from a biomedical to a biopsychosocial approach,[5] it is doubtful whether such holistic and compassionate approach entails a clinical (prognostic and therapeutic) solution to the psychosocial problems of clinical practice in medicine.

As Roth and Kroll[14] remark, from the point of view of advancing knowledge and developing specific therapeutic interventions, a major weakness of the biopsychosocial model is its "tendency to range every type of disorder—neurotic, psychotic, organic, psychosomatic—side by side as though there were nothing to choose between them in the character of the abnormality or in the nature of the etiological factors involved." The heuristic value of phenomenological descriptions of the interactions between bodily and psychological symptoms with their diagnostic translations is undeniable. Yet the issue of psychosomatic diagnosis is neglected by psychosomatic researchers, even by its more clinically oriented investigators (consultation–liaison psychiatrists). These latter seem to be concentrated on concepts borrowed from the marketplace (cost-effectiveness analyses) that result in rationalizing retreat from justice (a humane approach to medical patients).

The DSM-IV is then used, without much discussion, as the tool to characterize psychosocial problems in the medically ill. An analysis of its rubrics most relevant to psychosomatic medicine may reveal its conceptual flaws and clinical inadequacies.

STRESS-RELATED DISORDERS

There is a growing interest in the role of stress in medicine. The short-term effects of acute, experimental stresses have become the focus of a large volume of medical research. The clinical implications of these studies are a source of considerable controversy: the validity of laboratory stressors as models for real-life stressors has been questioned in fields such as endocrinology,[15] and the extension of these results to long-term situations is purely inferential. The general tendency in medicine does not seem that of endorsing the old clinical notion, supported by life event research, that events and situations in a person's life that are meaningful and elicit emotional distress may be followed by physical illness or even death,[16] but seems to be that of creating a subset of functional medical disorders characterized by stress. The DSM-IV diagnosis of adjustment disorder lends support to this tendency. The diagnosis of adjustment disorder with physical complaints is the most relevant from a psychosomatic viewpoint.

The essential features of an adjustment disorder are as follows[11]: (1) a reaction to a recent identifiable psychosocial stressor; (2) a maladaptive reaction to it, resulting in impairment in functioning and/or symptoms in excess of normal reaction; (3) the disturbance is not merely one instance of a pattern of overreaction to stress or an exacerbation of a mental disorder; and (4) the maladaptive reaction has persisted for no longer than 6 months.

As a general model, the diagnosis of adjustment disorder may be of undeniable importance and indeed is frequently used in consultation–liaison psychiatry.[12] However, its clinical translation is rather difficult. First, Kissen[17] discussed over three decades ago the logical fallacies of such categorization, involving the disappearance of somatic symptoms when the stress is removed, while this is not always the case. Second, it reflects a unifactorial obsolete model of disease (external stressor causing illness, not unlike mycobacterium causing tuberculosis) that ignores other interacting agents such as the degree of social support, the psychological significance of stress or injury, personal expectations of performance, and other personality features which influence psychological vulnerability.[18] In a series of classical studies, Mason[19] demonstrated how the psychological significance of the stressful situation rather than the stressor itself produces activation of the hypothalamic–pituitary–adrenal axis.[19] Third, the term *stressor* is poorly specified, while life-events research has identified uncontrolled and undesirable events as the most threatening challenges, particularly when it was clearly an event of major importance to the patient and resulted in major changes in the patient's work, social or family circle, or living conditions.[20] Finally, the DSM-IV tends to ignore the longitudinal (prodromal, acute, subacute, residual) development of disorders.[21] When the premorbid adjustment to stressful circumstances (including physical illness) is explored with phenomenological accuracy, it becomes likely that the disturbance is merely one instance of a pattern of overreaction to stress. If a more selective definition of stressor is chosen, then adjustment disorders may be quite rare in the medically ill.[10] The category of adjustment disorder may simply be a cross-sectional, superficial appraisal of neurotic—as recently redefined[21]—or psychosomatic disturbances.

PSYCHOLOGICAL FACTORS AFFECTING PHYSICAL CONDITION

"Psychosomatic disorder" is currently used by many physicians to refer to a physical illness or symptom believed to be caused by psychological factors. The definition of psychophysiologic disorder included in the DSM-I in 1952[22] and the DSM-II in 1968[23] largely derived from the concept of psychosomatic disorder that was prevalent during the first phase of development of psychosomatic medicine (1930–1960). Psychophysiological disorders were "characterized by physical symptoms that are caused by emotional factors and involve a single organ system, usually under autonomic nervous system innervation."[23]

The term *psychosomatic disorder* was strongly criticized by several psychosomatic researchers, notably Lipowski[16] and Engel.[24] The latter author wrote that the term *psychosomatic disorder* (or disease) is misleading, since it implies a special class of disorders of psychogenic etiology and by inference, therefore, the absence of a psychosomatic interface in other diseases. "Strictly speaking, there can be no 'psychosomatic diseases,' just as there can be no 'biochemical' or 'physiological diseases.' Rather diseases have their psychosomatic and biochemical and physiological components or aspects"[24] (p. 6). Lipowski[16] criticized the concept of psychosomatic disorder, since it tended to perpetuate the obsolete notion of psychogenesis—one incompatible with the doctrine of multicausality, which constitutes a core postulate of current psychosomatic medicine. Further, it should be noted that the term *psychosomatic disorder* may be imprecise, since it might refer to organic diseases in which psychological factors are reputed to play a necessary role (e.g., ulcerative colitis) or to functional disturbances in which the organic etiology is not clearly established (e.g., irritable bowel syndrome).[25]

Such criticisms were taken into account in DSM-III, as part of a multiaxial approach to psychiatric diagnosis. A category, not a diagnosis, entitled "psychological factors affecting physical condition" was introduced in DSM-III[26] and retained in DSM-IV.[11] This category enables the physician to note that psychological factors contribute to the initiation or exacerbation of a physical disorder or symptom. The physical disorder can be noted on axis III. The judgment that psychological factors are affecting the physical disorder requires evidence of a temporal relationship among the environmental stimulus, the meaning given to it, and the initiation or exacerbation of the physical disorder.[11]

Such categorization was aimed at increasing collaboration among specialists (avoiding etiologic inferences) and at providing the psychiatrist with a better description of emotional components of medical practice.[27] However, internists and surgeons still talk about (and often resent) psychosomatic disorders, and psychiatrists do not use this new category more than the previous diagnosis of "psychophysiologic disorder," i.e., very little.[12]

Is the concept of psychosomatic disorder so useless and dangerous? Recently, the concept of neurosis underwent a critical appraisal,[21] and similar considerations may apply to psychosomatic disorders. An interesting discussion about the psychosomatic concept took place in 1945. James Halliday[28] defined psychosomatic affection as "a bodily disorder whose nature can be appreciated only when emotional disturbances, i.e., psychological happenings, are investigated in addition to physical disturbances, i.e., somatic happenings." He listed six characteristics of diseases "signable" to the psychosomatic category: (1) emotion as a precipitating factor (life event); (2) personality type; (3) sex ratio (a marked disproportion in sex incidence); (4) association with other psychosomatic affections ("when one affection played Hamlet, the other usually left the stage"); (5) family history; and (6) phasic manifestations (temporal relationships between psychologically meaningful events and remissions or recurrences of illness).

The concept of psychosomatic affection, Halliday[28] remarks:

[B]rings together a large number of seemingly unrelated facts. The outlook gained shows that many "localized diseases," the names of which have hitherto been found scattered through textbooks of medicine under the headings of the various anatomical systems, may now be grouped under a unifying etiological category. The term psychosomatic affection is therefore a valid symbol which provides a new instrument for thinking, for investigation and for the direction of action [p. 244].

If one thinks of pathological entities such as fibrositis and chronic fatigue syndrome in the functional realm, the heuristic value of the concept cannot be dismissed. However, it contained a basic conceptual flaw: consideration of diseases as homogeneous entities. Careful appraisal of current medical literature leads to the opposite direction, i.e., recognition of their multifactorial and heterogeneous components.[13, 25] Kissen,[29] however, about two decades later, while discussing the significance of syndrome shift in psychosomatic medicine (consecutive replacement of one type of functional disturbance by another), provided a better specification of the term *psychosomatic.* "It would appear possible for an illness generally thought of as being 'psychosomatic' to be 'non-psychosomatic' in certain individuals. Likewise an illness not generally thought as 'psychosomatic' may be psychosomatic in some individuals" (p. 40). This is not different from what Lipowski,[30] an outspoken critic of the concept of psychosomatic disorder, later wrote:

It is generally agreed now that all diseases, physical and mental, are multifactorial in origin. . . . There is growing evidence that the psychological and social variables are a class of etiologic factors in all diseases. Their relative weight may vary considerably from illness to illness, from individual to individual, and from one episode to another of the same illness in the same person [p. 483].

Cushing's syndrome provides a helpful illustration of this phenomenon. In a preliminary study,[31] it was found that patients with Cushing's syndrome reported significantly more stressful life events—collected by means of a standardized method[20]—than healthy control subjects matched for sociodemographic variables. When the sample of patients was expanded, however, it was found that this excess of events pertained to the hypothalamic–pituitary forms of illness and not to the adrenal or ectopic ones.[32]

The hope of Halliday[28] to acquire unifying phenomenological aids that may allow identification of psychosomatic distress across different somatic disorders (whether of functional or organic nature) is still an appealing one. Yet, do we have adequate methods for this clinical assessment?

Bech,[33] in a recent paper, remarkably identifies a major conceptual innovation in the concept of quality of life: the importance attributed to the measurement of well-being, as opposed to the traditional emphasis on psychological distress and psychopathology. Similarly, a neglect of subclinical, prodromal, and residual psychiatric symptoms and the paucity of psychometric instruments to reliably detect milder psychiatric symptomatology have been underscored.[21] Bech[33] outlines the dynamic interaction between well-being, discomfort, and distress (identified in terms of traditional psychopathology) in clinical assessment, and the heuristic values of concepts such as that of demoralization of Frank and Frank,[34] i.e., the patient's consciousness of having failed to meet his or her own expectations or those of others or being unable to cope with some pressing problems. Another clinical concept that may be opposed to traditional psychopathology is that of alexithymia,[35] a characteristic inability to express emotions, either as a personality trait or an acquired inability secondary to medical illness or life stresses.

In a naive conceptualization, yet the one implicitly endorsed by the DSM-IV,[11] well-being, discomfort, and distress may be seen as mutually exclusive (e.g., well-being is lack of distress). Yet, there is psychosomatic evidence to call such views in question. When, for instance, Kellner's Symptom Questionnaire,[36] probably the best-validated self-rating scale for the simultaneous assessment of psychological distress and well-being, was used in psychosomatic medicine and clinical psychiatry, different psychometric patterns emerged. At times, the two dimensions were inversely proportional, i.e., when well-being increased, distress decreased. Other times, however, they were not. In pregnancy, a significant decrease in distress took place after the simple performance of prenatal diagnostic procedures such as amniocentesis, yet well-being increased only when patients learned about their favorable outcome.[36] Some psychometric properties of the Symptom Questionnaire also suggest interesting differentiations: the test–retest reliability of the distress scores (anxiety, depression, somatization, hostility) in normal subjects is very high, whereas the well-being scores (relaxation, contentment, physical well-being, friendliness) reflect short-lived mood states.[36] There are also clinical exemplifications of the complex interdependence of well-being, discomfort, and distress. During antidepressant treatment, appearance of isolated instances of well-being, despite persistence of depressed mood and symptoms, may be an early sign of recovery.[37] Discomfort, in the form of mild symptoms, was found to precede the onset of panic attacks, a disabling, acute form of psychological distress.[38] Disappearance of episodes of well-being may result in poor tolerance to discomfort and may be a sign of impeding distress.

The psychosomatic prospects of Halliday[28] and Kissen[29] may thus be reinterpreted in the light of current psychometric research, i.e., there is potential for psychosomatic specificity. This is not in the form of disease specificity (as postulated by Halliday), but in the form of specific patterns of interactions of psychological well-being, discomfort, and distress, with somatic symptoms that can be recognized across different diseases. Kellner,[39] for instance, outlines specific psychological clusters, but also similarities across different functional medical disorders, such as fibromyalgia, fatigue, and dyspepsia. To the same extent that clinical syndromes of depression may have different manifestations in the medically ill, and yet retain some unitary characteristics (e.g., organic mood syndromes), there may be specific psychosomatic patterns characterized by psychological phenomena, such as alexithymia[35] or irritable mood[40] or defective coping[18] or demoralization,[34] that tend to be expressed largely in the form of physical symptoms. Careful appraisal of Halliday's characteristics of psychosomatic affections throughout the different phases of illness (prodromal, acute, subacute, chronic, residual) with appropriate psychometric instruments (including assessment of well-being and discomfort) may shed some light on these psychosomatic phenomena and provide a phenomenological ground for a century of psychodynamic observations.

SOMATOFORM DISORDERS

This heading in DSM-IV[11] lists several distinct yet ostensibly related disorders: (1) body dysmorphic disorder (dysmorphophobia); (2) conversion disorder; (3) hypochondriasis; (4) somatization disorder (recurrent and multiple somatic complaints); (5) pain disorder; and (6) undifferentiated somatoform disorder.

This classification has been seriously questioned.[41] It "reflects mind–body dualism and perpetuates the questionable dichotomy of organic versus psychogenic disorders and symptoms"[41] (p. 1365). For instance, the diagnosis of somatization disorder is cumbersome and difficult to be used or found in medical populations. A conceptual framework for "somatoform" is missing, even though one description frequently recurs across disorders: "the person's concern is grossly excessive" (body dysmorphic disorder); "social or occupational impairment is grossly in excess of what would be expected from the physical findings" (somatization disorder); "the complaint of pain . . . is grossly in excess of what would be expected from physical findings" (somatoform pain disorder), etc. All disorders refer to normative patterns, yet these are never clearly outlined. We may then wonder whether a more comprehensive frame of reference might be of clinical value. Lipowski[41] attributes such value to the concept of somatization, reducing the group to two disorders: somatization disorder and partial (or restricted) somatization disorder. Yet, in a previous paper,[30] he had remarkably stressed the importance of illness behavior:

[O]nce the symptoms of a somatic disease are perceived by the same person, or he has been told by a doctor that he is ill even if symptoms are absent, then this disease-related information gives rise to psychological responses which influence the patient's experience and behavior as well as the course, therapeutic response and outcome of a given illness episode [p. 483].

Lewis,[42] well before the concept of illness behavior was formulated, remarked how "it is commonly assumed that the ordinary person with a physical illness has 'complete insight,' i.e., that he views his symptoms objectively as another person would. But everybody knows that this is not so and that people vary widely and inevitably in this respect" (p. 438). He made a plea for the systematic study of psychopathology of insight, whether accompanied by mental or bodily symptoms or both. This plea was answered by the concept of Pilowsky[43] of abnormal illness behavior, defined as the persistence of a maladaptive mode of perceiving, experiencing, evaluating, and responding to one's health status, despite the fact a doctor has provided a lucid and accurate appraisal of the situation and management to be followed (if any), with opportunities for discussion, negotiation, and clarification, based on adequate assessment of all relevant biological, psychological, social, and cultural factors.

Pilowsky differentiates somatically and psychologically focused abnormal illness behavior. Within the somatically focused there are two broad categories: illness affirming and illness denying.

The illness-affirming abnormal behavior involves (1) motivation predominantly conscious (malingering, Münchhausen syndrome, factitious disorder with physical symptoms), and (2) motivation predominantly unconscious (somatization disorder, conversion disorder, psychogenic pain disorder, hypochondriasis, and the hypochondriacal delusions associated with other psychiatric disorders).

The illness-denying category involves (1) motivation predominantly conscious, such as denial of an illness to obtain employment; (2) motivation predominantly unconscious (e.g., noncompliance, counterphobic behavior, denial secondary to a psychiatric disorder such as mania); and (3) anosognosia. This implies lack of awareness of disease and is most commonly shown for left hemiplegic limbs where it represents a focal derangement of the body schema, dependent on subtle defects of sensory experience and higher order defects of intellectualization.[44]

Many psychosomatic situations occurring in medical and surgical settings fall within the concept of abnormal illness behavior.[9, 12, 45] Strauss et al.,[46] for instance, described several cases of maladaptive denial of physical illness including lack of compliance. They proposed that DSM-IV include a subtype of adjustment disorder called "with maladaptive denial of physical disorder." It is really unclear why such commonly observed phenomena should be subsumed under the rubric of adjustment disorder (where illness is the stressor), as if compliance were a problem shortly following illness onset and likely to improve later, instead of the reverse sequence. Or as if illness denial (e.g., counterphobic behavior of a patient who resumes strenuous work after myocardial infarction) and illness amplification (e.g., psychological invalidism of a patient who suffered from the same heart problem) were totally unrelated behaviors, instead of the ends of the spectrum of illness behavior, potentially sharing intrapsychic mechanisms.

Recently, some phenomenological justifications for a further refinement of the concept of Pilowsky[43] of abnormal illness behavior have been outlined.[47] These proposals were mainly based on research evidence that accumulated with the use of Kellner's Illness Attitude Scales, self-rating scales that measure attitudes, fears, and beliefs associated with abnormal illness behavior.[48] The category of illness-affirming abnormal behavior could further be specified in the subdivision which Pilowsky characterizes as influenced by predominantly unconscious motivations. Illness-affirming behaviors could be then divided into primary and secondary forms. These latter would be the direct consequence of a major psychiatric illness, such as major depressive disorders[49] or panic disorder,[50] and should be chronologically superimposed on those. There is no evidence to suggest abnormal illness behavior in schizophrenia,[51] yet occasional instances of hypochondriacal delusions may occur and remit upon treatment of schizophrenia.[52] It would, however, be unwise to classify all psychotic hypochondriacal delusions as secondary. Monosymptomatic hypochondriacal psychoses provide a good example. Similar considerations apply to secondary forms of illness denial (such as anosognosia). The contribution of a coexisting mood disorder to secondary illness-affirming behaviors may be of paramount importance.

In medical practice, any undue concern about bodily function is often labeled as hypochondriacal. As a result, hypochondriasis may be seen primarily as an amplification of somatic sensations[53] or not substantially different from health anxiety.[54] There is preliminary evidence to suggest that the following distinctions are worthy of clinical attention and may entail prognostic and therapeutic implications[47]:

1. Hypochondriasis: The DSM-IV[11] definition of hypochondriasis includes only probably the most severe end of the spectrum: the preoccupation with the fear of having, or the belief that one has, a serious disease when appropriate physical examination does not support the diagnosis of any physical disorder that can account

for the patient's symptoms. The most distinct characteristic is, however, the resistance to medical reassurance. A patient may become extremely worried about his health, and yet his fears may be eliminated by a satisfactory medical examination.[47]

2. Disease phobia: Bianchi[55] defined disease phobia as a "persistent, unfounded fear of suffering from a disease, with some doubt remaining despite examination and reassurance" (p. 241). There are two differential characteristics from hypochondriasis. One is the phobic quality of the fears that tend to manifest themselves in attacks rather than in constant, chronic worries. In this sense, the relationship of disease phobia to hypochondriasis is similar to the one of panic disorder to generalized anxiety. The other characteristic is the longitudinal specificity of symptoms (i.e., some patients who are convinced that they suffer from heart disease and do not transfer their fears to other organ systems).[47]

3. Thanatophobia: Ryle's description of the sense of impending death[56]—with resulting conviction of dying soon (even though there is no objective medical reason for such fear)—was associated by Kellner[48] with the fear of news which reminds of death, such as funerals or obituary notices. A strong association with cardiac disease—outlined in a lucid, autobiographic account by Ryle[57]—may suggest the presence of secondary forms that are devoid of psychopathological inferences. Thanatophobia was found to be frequently associated with nosophobia and panic attacks.[47, 58]

4. Health anxiety: This term was defined as encompassing nonspecific dimensions of abnormal illness behavior, such as generic worry about illness (that may readily respond to reassurance) and concern about pain and bodily preoccupations (a tendency to amplify somatic sensations). These forms of health anxiety may be short-lived (unlike hypochondriasis, disease phobia, and thanatophobia that tend to persist), as in women undergoing medical procedures and as a reaction to life-threatening illness, such as myocardial infarction.[47]

5. The DSM-IV differentiates somatization disorder from conversion (an alteration or loss of physical functioning).[11] The distinction is mainly based on the number of symptoms instead of more precise clinical features. Engel,[59] for instance, does not

operate such differentiation. Instead, he provides more stringent criteria for the diagnosis of conversion symptoms that include confirmatory criteria (precipitation of symptoms by psychological stress, the association of which the patient is unaware; demonstration of the determinants of the symptom choice, in terms of body language, physical symptoms previously experienced by the patient, symptoms observed in someone else, symptoms wished on someone else, primary and secondary gains). Suggestive criteria include the ambivalent manner in which the symptom is reported, inconsistency with somatic processes, hysterical personality features. Lipowski[30] remarks the association between conversion symptoms and organic diseases, particularly those of the central and peripheral nervous system and the special senses. The case of "conversion symptoms" that are prodromes of a major medical illness that manifests itself at a later stage is a well-known clinical example of this association. Conversion symptoms are thus a difficult diagnostic subgrouping of abnormal illness behavior. They tend to be diagnosed as an exclusion rubric (when organic causes for the disturbances are ruled out) and yet require positive criteria for determination, as those outlined by Engel.[59] They may be also associated with other forms of abnormal illness behavior (e.g., hypochondriasis) or affective disorder (e.g., panic disorder with agoraphobia). In these cases, conversion symptoms more than a coexisting diagnostic group often represent a secondary, even though not negligible, manifestation.

6. Body-dysmorphic disorder appears to be an important and long-recognized, disturbance—at least since Morselli's classical description in 1891.[60] Morselli himself emphasized the phobic avoidance associated with the disorder. In a controlled study on the quality of life of hirsute women, it was found that social fears and avoidance were the most distinct psychological characteristics of these patients.[61] In the DSM-IV, however, in one of the several unsubstantiated statements devoid of doubt, it is written that the classical term *dysmorphophobia* is a misnomer, "since the disturbance does not involve phobic avoidance." Another diagnostic statement is that the defect should be imagined or only "slight." What happens when the defect is not "slight" (such as in hirsutism

according to standardized criteria), and yet women react in a very different way to it (from normal functioning to strict seclusion)? As for other forms of abnormal illness behavior, dysmorphophobia lends itself to a primary/secondary distinction. Secondary forms may be a consequence of another psychiatric disturbance. (Dysmorphophobia may be the most obvious and yet not the most severe symptom of a generalized social phobia or may result from a schizophrenic illness, thus reaching delusional intensity.) Actually, dysmorphophobia is only one form of body image disorder, some of which may be of organic nature, such as unilateral unawareness and neglect of a limb (that sometimes foreshadows the development of a hemiparesis), autotopagnosia (the inability to recognize, name, point, or command various parts of the body, usually seen in conjunction with diffuse bilateral lesions of the brain), and illusions of transformation and displacement.[44] These disorders, however, are seldom seen in the absence of marked impairment of consciousness and do not necessarily involve preoccupation. As a result, *dysmorphophobia* is a more specific term than *body-dysmorphic disorder*, and the two terms are not mutually exclusive or equivalent.

7. The DSM-IV[11] lists two other somatoform disorders. One is undifferentiated somatoform disorder that has been criticized in detail elsewhere[12] and that probably may be subsumed under the nonspecific rubric of health anxiety. The other is pain disorder. While Pilowsky[43] acknowledges the presence of "psychogenic pain disorder" as a separate entity (and indeed patients with chronic pain frequently display abnormal illness behavior), one may wonder whether detection of a coexisting affective disorder such as depression,[7] or more specific forms of abnormal illness behavior may be more clinically fruitful.

CONCLUSION

Unlike Weiner,[13] I believe that future psychosomatic efforts should be expended on studying psychological symptoms and how these might cluster with the somatic ones in the medically ill. Categories that are too vague or ill conceived, as the current DSM-IV criteria related to psychosomatic medicine, are of little heuristic value for the clinician working at the interface between medicine and the behavioral sciences. When psychiatrists or physicians qualified in psychosomatic medicine are asked to provide their opinion to their colleagues, certainly they are not very daring in stating that the patient has psychological problems or that the functional symptoms are undifferentiated. The concept of psychosomatic disorder in its various clinical hypotheses may undergo validation following the guidelines provided by Robins and Guze[62] for psychiatric diagnosis: (1) clinical description along syndromal lines that remain constant across different diseases; (2) laboratory studies[63]; (3) delimitation from affective and other psychiatric disorders; (4) follow-up study; and (5) family study, i.e., the occurrence of specific psychosomatic patterns in first-degree biological relatives.[64]

The concept of abnormal illness behavior should probably supplant the somatoform disorders rubric and provide a conceptual framework for disorders that would otherwise be scattered and unrelated in the DSM-III-R or that would not find room (such as denial of illness). A considerable body of research evidence may already be used in this direction.[43, 47]

A better psychosomatic diagnosis may entail prognostic and therapeutic implications, both in terms of psychopharmacology and psychotherapy. As Lewis[65] commented: "instead of making psychogenesis the touchstone—the unreliable touchstone—of psychosomatic illness, and psychopathology the major object of research in such disorder" (trying, for instance, to demonstrate that functional medical illness is nothing but misdiagnosed psychiatric illness), the emphasis should be placed "on the varieties of associated somatic and mental responses that the human organism may offer to life situations."

References

1. Lipowski ZJ. Somatization. *Psychother Psychosom.* 1987;47:160–167.
2. White KL. *The Task of Medicine.* Menlo Park, CA: Kaiser Foundation;1988.
3. Fava GA. Methodological and conceptual issues in research on quality of life. *Psychother Psychosom.* 1990;54:70–76.
4. Eisenberg L. Science in medicine: Too much or too little and too limited in scope? In: White KL, ed. *The Task of Medicine.* Menlo Park, CA: Kaiser Foundation;1988: pp 190–217.
5. Engel GL. How much longer must medicine's science be bound by a seventeenth century world view? *Psychother Psychosom.* 1992;57:3–16.
6. Feinstein AR. The intellectual crisis in clinical science. *Perspect Biol Med.* 1987;30:215–230.
7. Fava GA. Depression in medical settings. In: Paykel ES, ed. *Handbook of Affective Disorders.* 2nd ed. London: Churchill Livingstone;1992: pp 667–685.
8. Walker EA, Roy Byrne PP, Katon WJ. Irritable bowel syndrome and psychiatric illness. *Am J Psychiatry.* 1990;147:565–572.
9. Creed F, Firth D, Timol M, Metcalf R, Pollock S. Somatization and illness behaviour in a neurology ward. *J Psychosom Res.* 1990;34:427–437.
10. Conti S, Savron G, Bartolucci G, Grandi S, Magelli C, Semprini F, Saviotti FM, Trombini G, Fava GA, Magnani B. Cardiac neurosis and psychopathology. *Psychother Psychosom.* 1989;52:88–91.
11. American Psychiatric Association. *Diagnostic and Statistical Manual of Mental Disorders* (DSM-IV). Washington, DC: American Psychiatric Press;1994.
12. Fava GA. Psychosomatic diagnosis. *Psychosomatics.* 1987;28:549–550.
13. Weiner H. Some unexplored regions of psychosomatic medicine. *Psychother Psychosom.* 1987;47:153–159.
14. Roth M, Kroll J. *The Reality of Mental Illness.* Cambridge, U.K.: Cambridge University Press;1986: p.65.
15. Vingerhoets AJJM, Assies J. Psychoneuroendocrinology of stress and emotions. *Psychother Psychosom.* 1991;55:69–75.
16. Lipowski ZJ. Psychosomatic medicine: Past and present. *Can J Psychiatry.* 1986;31:14–21.
17. Kissen DM. A scientific approach to clinical research in psychosomatic medicine. *Psychosom Med.* 1960;22:118–126.
18. Lazarus RS, Folkman S. *Stress, Appraisal, and Coping.* New York: Springer; 1984.
19. Mason JW. A review of psychoendocrine research on the pituitary-adrenal cortical system. *Psychosom Med.* 1968;30:576–607.
20. Paykel ES. Methodology of life events research. In: Fava GA, Wise TN, eds. *Research Paradigms in Psychosomatic Medicine.* Basel, Switzerland: Karger;1987: pp 13–29.
21. Fava GA, Kellner R. Prodromal symptoms in affective disorders. *Am J Psychiatry.* 1991;148:823–830.
22. American Psychiatric Association. *Diagnostic and Statistical Manual of Mental Disorders.* Washington, DC: American Psychiatric Association;1952.

23. American Psychiatric Association. Diagnostic and Statistical Manual of Mental Disorders. 2nd ed. Washington, DC: American Psychiatric Association;1968.
24. Engel GL. The concept of psychosomatic disorder. *J Psychosom Res.* 1967;11:3–9.
25. Fava GA, Wise TN. Methodological issues in psychosomatic research. In: Fava GA, Wise TN, eds. *Research Paradigms in Psychosomatic Medicine.* Basel, Switzerland: Karger;1987: pp 1–12.
26. American Psychiatric Association. *Diagnostic and Statistical Manual of Mental Disorders* (DSM-III). Washington, DC: American Psychiatric Association;1980.
27. Looney JG, Lipp MR, Spitzer RL. A new method of classification for psychophysiologic disorders. *Am J Psychiatry.* 1978;135:304–308.
28. Halliday JL. The significance of the concept of a psychosomatic affection. *Psychosom Med.* 1945;7:240–245.
29. Kissen DM. The significance of syndrome shift and late syndrome association in psychosomatic medicine. *J Nerv Ment Dis.* 1963;136:34–42.
30. Lipowski ZJ. Physical illness and psychopathology. *Int J Psychiatry Med.* 1974;5: 483–497.
31. Sonino N, Fava GA, Grandi S, Mantero F, Boscaro M. Stressful life events in the pathogenesis of Cushing's syndrome. *Clin Endocrinol (Oxf).* 1988;29:617–623.
32. Fava GA, Sonino N, Pagotto U, Fallo F, Boscaro M. Stressful life events may play a role in the pathogenesis of Cushing's disease (abstract). *J Endocrinol Invest.* 1990;13(suppl 2):147.
33. Bech P. Measurement of psychological distress and well-being. *Psychother Psychosom.* 1990;54:77–89.
34. Frank JD, Frank JB. *Persuasion and Healing.* Baltimore: Johns Hopkins University Press;1991.
35. Nemiah JC, Freyberger H, Sifneos PE. Alexithymia: A view of the psychosomatic process. In: Hill OW, ed. *Modern Trends in Psychosomatic Medicine.* London: Butterworth;1976: pp 430–439.
36. Kellner R. A symptom questionnaire. *J Clin Psychiatry.* 1987;48:268–274.
37. Fava GA. Psychotherapy research: Clinical trials versus clinical reality. *Psychother Psychosom.* 1986;46:6–12.
38. Fava GA, Grandi S, Canestrari R. Prodromal symptoms in panic disorder with agoraphobia. *Am J Psychiatry.* 1988;145:1564–1567.
39. Kellner R. *Psychosomatic Syndromes and Somatic Symptoms.* Washington, DC: American Psychiatric Press;1991.
40. Fava GA. Irritable mood and physical illness. *Stress Med.* 1987;3:293–299.
41. Lipowski ZJ. Somatization: The concept and its clinical applications. *Am J Psychiatry.* 1988;145:1358–1368.
42. Lewis AJ. The psychopathology of insight. *Br J Med Psychol.* 1934;14:332–348.
43. Pilowsky I. Abnormal illness behaviour. *Psychother Psychosom.* 1986;46:76–84.
44. Lishman WA. *Organic Psychiatry.* Oxford: Blackwell;1987.
45. Wise TN. Psychosomatic medicine. *Psychother Psychosom.* 1986;46:85–95.
46. Strauss DN, Spitzer RL, Muskin PR. Maladaptive denial of physical illness. *Am J Psychiatry.* 1990;147:1168–1172.
47. Fava GA, Grandi S. Differential diagnosis of hypochondriacal fears and beliefs. *Psychother Psychosom.* 1991;55:114–119.
48. Kellner R. *Somatization and Hypochondriasis.* New York: Praeger;1986.

49. Kellner R, Fava GA, Lisansky J, Park S, Perini GI, Zielezny M. Hypochondriacal fears and beliefs in DSM-III melancholia. *J Affect Disord.* 1986;10:21–26.

50. Fava GA, Kellner R, Zielezny M, Grandi S. Hypochondriacal fears and beliefs in agoraphobia. *J Affect Disord.* 1988:14:239–244.

51. Fava GA, Molnar G, Zielezny M: Health attitudes of psychiatric inpatients. *Psychopathology.* 1987;20:180–186.

52. Molnar G, Fava GA. Intercurrent medical illness in the schizophrenic patient. In: Stoudemire A, Fogel BS, eds. *Principles of Medical Psychiatry.* Orlando, FL: Grune & Stratton;1987: pp 451–461.

53. Barsky AJ, Wyshak G. Hypochondriasis and related health attitudes. *Psychosomatics.* 1989;30:412–420.

54. Warwick HM, Salkovskis PM. Hypochondriasis. *Behav Res Ther.* 1990;28:105–117.

55. Bianchi GN. Origins of disease phobia. *Aust NZ J Psychiatry.* 1971;5:241–257.

56. Ryle JA. Angor animi, or the sense of dying. *Guys Hosp Rep.* 1928;78:230–235.

57. Ryle JA. The sense of dying. A postscript. *Guys Hosp Rep.* 1949;99:224–235.

58. Fava GA, Grandi S, Saviotti FM, Conti S. Hypochondriasis with panic attacks. *Psychosomatics.* 1990;31:351–353.

59. Engel GL. Conversions symptoms. In: MacBryde CM, Blacklow RS, eds. *Signs and Symptoms.* Philadelphia: Lippincott;1970: pp 650–659.

60. Morselli E. Sulla dismorfofobia e sulla tafefobia. *Boll Reale Accad Med Genova.* 1891;6:5–14.

61. Sonino M, Fava GA, Mani E, Belluardo P, Boscaro M. Quality of life of hirsute women. *Postgrad Med J.* 1993;69:186–189.

62. Robins E, Guze SB. Establishment of diagnostic validity in psychiatric illness. *Am J Psychiatry.* 1970;126:107–111.

63. Bloch M. Psychophysiological methods in psychosomatic research. In: Fava GA, Wise TN, eds. *Research Paradigms in Psychosomatic Medicine.* Basel, Switzerland: Karger;1987: pp 134–166.

64. Lotstra F, Sevy S, Mendlewicz J. Genetic and biological markers in psychosomatic research. In: Fava GA, Wise TN, eds. *Research Paradigms in Psychosomatic Medicine.* Basel, Switzerland: Karger;1987: pp 252–264.

65. Lewis AJ. Aspects of psychosomatic medicine. *Recenti Prog Med.* 1954;16:434–453.

Chapter 9
Physical Illnesses Underlying Psychiatric Symptoms

Erwin K. Koranyi, Walter M. Potoczny

Symptoms of aberrant behavior, mood, perception, and thinking modalities are observed not only within the domain of psychiatry proper. They regularly accompany the widest varieties of physical illnesses and toxic states as well. In many instances such symptoms can represent the first manifestation of a physical illness and can precede other signs or clinical display by years. Thus, such symptoms can be entirely unspecific in nature. This is why it happens so many times that patients with an underlying and unrecognized physical illness are shunted to psychiatric clinics or to private psychiatrists or are mistakenly self-diagnosed by the patients themselves, while the hidden physical pathology remains unknown.[1] It should be sufficient to leaf through any textbook of internal medicine, neurology, or a pharmacopeia to discover that prominently emotional symptomatology—ranging from depression, anxiety, uncontrolled behavior, sleep disorder, sexual dysfunction, hallucinations, to change in customary personality features—share the boundaries of all medicine with the classical field of psychiatry. In fact, no psychiatric symptoms exist that at times cannot be caused or aggravated by a variety of medical illnesses.[2, 3]

CLINICAL PRESENTATIONS

Given that all symptoms, whether physical or psychiatric, occur within the context of a patient's total life situation, at times the psychosocial consequence of the symptom may result in a misleading clinical presentation. For example, a very high proportion of patients with adult-onset diabetes will gradually develop sexual dysfunction before other, more pathognomonic, symptoms appear.[4] This will not only take the form of an erectile impotence but can lead to regressive sexual behavior with disastrous marital and social consequences as the patient resorts to more esoteric sexual stimuli. Numerous cases like that have been referred to us for martial therapy.[1] There is no obligation on the patient to pronounce his symptoms in compliance with the current textbook of medicine, to the contrary, being a layman, he is free to judge and evaluate his symptoms and presumptions entirely subjectively. Not so the physician.

Psychiatric manifestations almost regularly accompany cases of systemic lupus erythematosus[5-7] and they are in fact one of the official diagnostic criteria of that condition. A variety of thyroid diseases[8-10] are notoriously chaperoned by disordered mood or behavior, while there may be a paucity of physical signs at the early stages of the disease. Psychiatric manifestations of temporal lobe epilepsy,[11-13] the most common form of epilepsy, are often not recognized. Numerous drugs can cause bona fide psychiatric symptoms such as hallucinations, depression, and cognitive impairment.[14-17] A depression caused by administration of reserpine or by lupus erythematosus is not distinguishable clinically from a sui generis endogenous depression.

With failure to detect the hidden somatic pathology, the treatment will be exclusively psychopharmacological or psychotherapeutic and therefore futile. Such instances will only lend a bad reputation to psychiatry and psychosomatic medicine.

So far nothing new has been stated here. The rate of undiagnosed physical illnesses in the psychiatric patient population has been well studied for decades. Appreciation of the findings, however, regretfully remains insufficient.

Keeping with the principles of some of the ancient medical literature, Osler[18] always emphasized the emotional components accompanying medical illnesses, and writing on the issue of neurasthenia he raises the important question, "Has the patient an organic disease?" Bonhoeffer,[19] discussing organic pathology, frequently portrayed the emotional aspects of the disease and highlighted that physical morbidity and mortality rates were disproportionately high in psychiatric patients. Malzberg's[20] study confirmed this observation some two decades later. Subsequently, Rorsman[21] found two and Babigian and Odoroff[22] three times higher rates of mortality among psychiatric patients. In a study on large ambulatory patient population Koranyi[23] found that all modalities of death, including accidents, suicides, and natural causes, were indeed remarkably higher when compared to that in the general population, and that life expectancy of psychiatric patients was some 20 years shorter than in the population at large.

Physical Illness in Psychiatric Patients

The first author dealing specifically with physical illnesses found concurrently in psychiatric patients was Phillips[24] in 1937. He investigated 164 psychiatric patients and found a rate of 45% with medical illnesses. Furthermore, in 24% of the instances the presenting psychiatric symptoms could be explained by the patient's physical condition. In a preliminary prospective study of 100 consecutive ambulatory psychiatric patients in a large general hospital, Koranyi[25] found a total of 49 patients who suffered from a variety of medical illnesses. Analyzing the missed diagnoses and the source of referrals, this study highlighted that referring physicians other than psychiatrists were unaware of these conditions in 30% of the cases, while psychiatrists and psychiatric institutions missed the physical diagnoses in 50% of their patients. Social agency and self-referred patients remained undiagnosed as to their medical conditions in 86% of the instances. In a larger study at the same institution involving 2090 psychiatric clinic patients Koranyi[1] found that 43% suffered from at least one significant medical condition and 46% remained undiagnosed by the referring source. Nonpsychiatric medical practitioners failed to diagnose the physical illnesses in 32% of cases in this sample, psychiatrists 48%, while social agencies and self-referrals failed to suspect the presence of an underlying physical disorder in 83 and 84%, respectively, of the instances. A substantial proportion of the physical illnesses, 18%, appeared to have a causative relation to the psychiatric symptoms. In other instances the medical condition aggravated the psychiatric illness (51%), while in some others (31%) it merely coincided with the psychiatric morbidity.

Since 1937 some 21 epidemiological studies have appeared in the literature in Canada, the United States, and in Europe on the subject, embracing a combined population of over 9199 patients (one early paper did not provide the sample size). I find it useful to present the relevant data in Table 9.1.

In the 19 studies that list exactly the rate of physical illnesses, an average of 50.1% was found. Of these, 16 studies yielded a rate between 33 and 60%; a single study showed a low rate of 17% and two of them as high as an 80% rate. Despite the different geographical locations and times, involving a multiform demographical population and unequal methodology, there is significant concordance concerning the high rates of medical illnesses in the psychiatric patient population.

There are two questions to be addressed. Why are medical illnesses so often missed in psychiatric patients? Why is the rate of medical illnesses higher in the psychiatric patient population?

There appear to be a number of factors responsible for the missed medical diagnoses. Medical practitioners may not insist on physical examination of cases that appear to be overtly psychiatric in nature or in some instances where the patient has poor hygiene. They may find patients poor communicators, particularly

TABLE 9.1
Comparative Results of 21 Studies

Authors	Year	Number of patients	Rate of physical illnesses, %	Direct relation to psycho-pathology, %	Priorly un-diagnosed %
Phillips [24]	1937	164	45	24	?
Marshall [26]	1949	?	44	?	?
Herrige [27]	1960	209	50	?	?
Davies [28]	1965	36	58	42	?
Maguire and Granville-Grossman [29]	1968	200	33	?	49
Johnson [30]	1968	250	60	12	80
Koranyi [25]	1972	100	49	20	71
Burke [31]	1972	202	43	?	?
Eastwood [32]	1975	124	? 'high'	?	?
Etamad [33]	1978	3,542	50	?	?
Burke [34]	1978	133	50	?	?
Hall et al. [35]	1978	658	?	9	46
Koranyi [1]	1979	2,090	43	18	46
Buckley et al. [36]	1980	200	52	?	?
Hall et al. [37]	1980	100	80	46	46
Ferguson and Dudleston [38]	1986	650	17	?	?
Marcil et al. [39]	1987	50	56	?	?
Pary and Barton [40]	1988	110	54	?	?
Honig et al. [41]	1989	218	80	46	46
Knutsen and DuRand [42]	1991	78	56	?	56
Mahendru et al. [43]	1991	85	32	?	84
Total		9.199	50.10	27.12	58.22

those with organic illness or with schizophrenia.[40] Patients may focus more on the psychosocial consequences of his or her illness rather than the actual symptoms.[1] Physicians often find it difficult to separate the medical complaints from the symptoms of mood and behavior. Patients having had previous psychiatric treatment may prejudice the clinical judgment of the physician. When psychiatric patients are referred to medical specialists for "routine" consultation, the workup often remains insufficient and the physician may perceive the situation to rule out contraindications for psychiatric treatment or for psychotropic medications.

Psychiatrists are frequently used by unscreened patients as primary physicians. Some psychiatrists are of the opinion that the patient's somatic condition is not their concern. They may fail to raise the question, what else than the "obvious" may be responsible for the patient's symptoms? Some psychiatrists do not like to perform a physical examination or they feel that they have lost their competence to do so. In some settings psychiatrists do not have adequate facilities for a physical examination. Women are often not examined by psychiatrists because of fear of false accusations of sexual improprieties. Elderly patients may take too long to dress or undress. Despite these concerns, Dercole et al.[44] found that women and the elderly still have a higher rate of physical illnesses.

PSYCHIATRIC PATIENTS AND PHYSICAL ILLNESS SUSCEPTIBILITY

Do psychiatric patients have a higher susceptibility to physical illness? The answer is unequivocally yes. Fink[45] found high utilization of medical hospital beds in a psychiatric patient population. The mechanism as to why psychiatric patients show increased morbidity from medical causes is not well understood. One of several contributing factors is probably the higher level of stress. Heightened stress deriving either from physical or from mental sources acts like a stone thrown upon the calm surface of a lake, the consequential ripples travel far into the lagoon.

Selye's[46] early research found that atrophy of the spleen and the thymolymphatic system in animals following physical stress was due to elevated corticosteroids. Not only do the cortisol levels rise in stress but also catecholamines, ACTH, prolactin, growth hormone, and other substances, each with their respective physiological and behavioral consequences. The elevation of these biologically active compounds occurs regardless of whether the stress is psychogenic in origin or derived from physical illnesses or organic causes. A propensity to high cortisol levels is the cornerstone of the dexamethasone suppression test which will be abnormal in a proportion of cases of clinical depression. But the elevation of cortisol will patently suppress T lymphocyte immunocompetence in response to mitogenic stimulation. The anecdotal observation of Parkes et al.[47] that widows frequently die during the first year of bereavement ("broken heart syndrome") gained more scientific proof with the work of Bartrop et al.[48] who demonstrated proportional impairment of T cell competence and impaired immunity over the time during bereavement. Subsequent similar studies have well demonstrated the direct relationship between stress, elevated levels of corticosteroids, and a reduction of immunocompetence.[49-51] Animal research on social stress and social isolation in mice was found to favor tumor growth by Sklar et al.[52] Prolonged competition for basic life needs under difficult conditions or in the face of predictable failure was found to heighten the risk for atherosclerosis, kidney failure, hypertension, or cerebrovascular accidents in animals as described by Gottschalk.[53] Results of stress research were summarized recently.[51] It has been demonstrated that increased sympathetic activity will induce the rate-limiting enzyme, tyrosine hydroxylase and thus catecholamines in the brain. Stress-related elevation of antidiuretic hormone suppresses sodium levels, particularly in the elderly, and may lead to subclinical delirium.

Thus stress, or rather stress response may be one bridge whereby physical illnesses may cause psychiatric symptomatology on the one hand and disturbed emotions may result in medical illnesses on the other. These observations may explain only some but not all of the reasons why excess rates of physical illnesses occur in psychiatric patient populations. Further explanations, no doubt, will emerge with future research. Meanwhile, the need for careful medical scrutiny of all psychiatric patients can only be strongly emphasized along with the fact that the evaluation of psychiatric patients is a medical responsibility.

References

1. Koranyi EK. Morbidity and rate of physical illnesses in a psychiatric clinic population. *Arch Gen Psychiatry.* 1979;36:414–419.
2. Koranyi EK. Undiagnosed physical illnesses in psychiatric patients. *Annu Rev Med.* 1982;33:309–316.
3. Koranyi EK. Introduction. In: Koranyi EK,ed. *Physical Illnesses in the Psychiatric Patient.* Springfield, IL: Charles C Thomas;1982: pp 3–8.
4. Goldman JA, Schecter A, Eckerling B. Carbohydrate metabolism in infertile and impotent males. *Fertil Steril.* 1970;21:397–401.
5. Denko JD. Problems in diagnosis and treatment of lupus psychosis. *Am J Psychother.* 1977;1:125–136.
6. Feinglass EJ, Dorsch CA, Zizik TM, Stevans MB. Neuropsychiatric manifestations of systemic lupus erythematosus: Diagnosis, clinical spectrum and relationship to other features of the disease. *Medicine.* 1976;4:323–339.
7. Koranyi EK, Dewar A. Neuropsychiatric features of drug induced and spontaneous systemic lupus erythematosus. *The Psychiatr J Univ Ottawa.* 1986;2:52–57.
8. Schiffer RB, Klein RF, Sider RC. *The Medical Evaluation of Psychiatric Patients.* New York: Plenum Med;1988.
9. Carney MWP, MacLeod S, Sheffield BF. Thyroid function screening in psychiatric patients. *Br J Psychiatry.* 1981;138:154–156.
10. Sandhu HS, Cohen LM. Endocrine disorders. In: Charen S, ed. *Psychosomatic Medicine: Theory, Physiology and Practice.* Madison, CT: International Universities Press;1989;2:661–706.
11. Blumer D. Temporal lobe epilepsy and its psychiatric significance. In: Benson FD, Blumer D, eds. *Psychiatric Aspects of Neurological Disease.* New York, Grune & Stratton;1975;1:171–198.
12. Delgrado-Escueta AV. The epilepsies: New developments of the 1980's. In: Appel SH, ed. *Current Neurology.* Chicago: Year Book Medical Publication;1986: pp 235–288.
13. Scheinberg P. *Modern Practical Neurology.* New York: Raven Press;1981.
14. Shader RI. *Psychiatric Complications of Medical Drugs.* New York: Raven Press; 1972.

15. Lapierre YD, Oyeweumi LK. "Psychiatric" adverse effects of psychotherapeutic drugs. In: Koranyi EK, ed. *Physical Illnesses in Psychiatric Patients.* Springfield, IL: Charles C Thomas;1982: pp 101–118.
16. Hansten PD. *Drug Interactions.* 5th ed. Philadelphia: Lea & Febiger;1985.
17. Abramowitz M. Drugs that cause psychiatric symptoms. *Med Lett.* 1984;26:75–78.
18. Osler WM. *Selected Aphorisms.* Birmingham: Classics of Medicine Library;1985.
19. Bonhoeffer K. Die Psychosen im Gefolge von akuten Infektionen, allgemeinen Erkrankungen und inneren Erkrankungen. In: Aschaffenburg GL, ed. *Handbuch der Psychiatrie.* Leipzig, Germany: Deuticke;1912;3:1–60.
20. Malzberg B. *Mortality among Patients with Mental Disease.* Utica, NY: New York State Hospital Press;1934.
21. Rorsman B. Mortality among psychiatric patients. *Acta Psychiatr Scand.* 1974;50: 354–375.
22. Babigian HM, Odoroff CHP. The mortality experience of a population with psychiatric illness. *Am J Psychiatry.* 1969;126:470–481.
23. Koranyi EK. Fatalities in 2,070 psychiatric outpatients. *Arch Gen Psychiatry.* 1977;34:1137–1142.
24. Phillips RG. Physical disorder in 164 consecutive admissions to a mental hospital: The incidence and significance. *Br Med J.* 1937;2:363–366.
25. Koranyi EK. Physical health and illness in a psychiatric outpatient department population. *Can Psychiatr Assn J.* 1972;17(suppl):109–116.
26. Marshall H. Incidence of physical disorders among psychiatric inpatients. *Br Med J.* 1949;2:468–470.
27. Herrige CF. Physical disorders in psychiatric illness. *Lancet.* 1960;ii:949–951.
28. Davies WD. Physical illness in psychiatric outpatients. *Br J Psychiatry.* 1965;111:27–37.
29. Maguire GP, Granville-Grossman KL. Physical illness in psychiatric patients. *Br Med J.* 1968;115:1365–1369.
30. Johnson DAW. The evaluation of routine physical examination in psychiatric cases. *Practitioner.* 1968;200:686–691.
31. Burke AW. Physical illness in psychiatric hospital patients in Jamaica. *Br J Psychiatry.* 1978;133:22–27.
32. Eastwood MR. *The Relation between Physical and Mental Illness.* Toronto, Canada: University of Toronto Press;1975.
33. Etamad B. The role of medicine in psychiatry. *Arch Gen Psychiatry.* 1978;35:904–905. Letter.
34. Burke AW. Physical disorder among day hospital patients. *Br J Psychiatry.* 1978;133:22–27.
35. Hall RCW, Popkin MK, Devault RA. Physical illness presenting as psychiatric disease. *Arch Gen Psychiatry.* 1978;35:1315–1320.
36. Buckley P, Karasu TB, Berkman I, Charles E. Unrecognized physical illness and psychiatric care, from Albert Einstein College of Medicine. Paper presented at the Annu Congr APA, San Francisco;May 1980.
37. Hall RCW, Gardner ER, Stickney SK, LeCann AF, Popkin MK. Physical illness manifesting as psychiatric disease. *Arch Gen Psychiatry.* 1980;37:989–995.
38. Ferguson B, Dudleston K. Detection of physical disorder in newly admitted psychiatry patients. *Acta Psychiatr Scand.* 1986;5:485–489.
39. Marcil R, Leung P, Bloom JD. The use of DSM III axis III in recording physical illness in psychiatric patients. *Am J Psychiatry.* 1987;11:1484–1486.

40. Pary RJ, Barton SN. Communication difficulty of patients with schizophrenia and physical illness. *South Med J.* 1988;4:489–490.
41. Honig A, Pop P, Tan ES, Philipsen H. Physical illness in chronic psychiatric patients from a community psychiatric unit: The implication for daily practice. *Br J Psychiatry.* 1989;155:58–64.
42. Knutsen E, DuRand C. Previously unrecognized physical illnesses in psychiatric patients. *Hosp Community Psychiatry.* 1991;2:182–186.
43. Mahendru RK, Gupta AK, Bahal DK. Physical illness in psychiatric patients. *Indian J Psychiatry.* 1987;3:269–273.
44. Dercole A, Scodol AE, Struening E, Curtis J, Millman J. Diagnosis of physical illnesses in psychiatric patients using axis III and a standardized medical history. *Hosp Community Psychiatry.* 1991;4:395–400.
45. Fink P. Physical disorders associated with mental illness, a register investigation. *Psychol Med.* 1990;4:829–834.
46. Selye H. *The Stress of Life.* 2nd ed. New York: McGraw-Hill;1976.
47. Parkes CM, Benjamin B, Fitzgerald RG. Broken heart: A statistical study of increased mortality among widowers. *Br Med J.* 1969;1:740–743.
48. Bartrop RW, Luckhurst E, Lazarus L, Kiloh LG, Penny R. Depressed lymphocyte function after bereavement. *Lancet.* 1977;1:834–836.
49. Kiecolt-Glaser JK, Glaser R. Stress and the immune system. In: Tassman A, Riba MB, eds. *Review of Psychiatry.* Washington, DC.: American Psychiatric Press;1992;11:123–238.
50. Irwin M, Pattertson T, Smith TL. Reduction of immune function in life stress and depression. *Biol Psychiatry.* 1990;27:22–30.
51. Koranyi EK. Physiology of stress reviewed. In: Cheren S, ed. *Psychosomatic Medicine.* Madison, CT: International Universities Press;1989;1:241–278.
52. Sklar LS, Anisman H. Stress and coping factors influence tumor growth. *Science.* 1979;513–515.
53. Gottschalk LA. Vulnerability and immune response. Paper presented at the 135th annual meeting of the APA, Toronto;1982.

Chapter 10
Role of Early Developmental Factors in Susceptibility to Disease

George N. Christodoulou, Thalia G. Dragonas

In trying to account for developmental deviances in the realm of psychopathology, we have shifted from an exclusive focus on constitutional factors to a broader attention to the behavioral characteristics of the child. In recent years, a number of studies, longitudinal in the main, have expanded their attention to the complexity of the environmental contexts within which children develop—contexts which simultaneously shape and are being shaped by the developing children in an interactional fashion.

Although some categories of problems have roots almost exclusively in the biological–constitutional condition of the child, these refer to only a small proportion of children. Reviews of studies of children suffering from a variety of reproductive risk factors point out that, except for the most severely damaged children, environmental factors play an important role in determining developmental outcomes.[1, 2] Yet it is nonetheless true that children vary genetically in their responses to diverse rearing conditions. There exist individual differences in development under similar rearing conditions as well as an average level of development under varying environmental conditions.[3]

In this paper we choose to focus on the very early developmental factors, the influence of which has been implicated in infancy and subsequently has adverse outcome. We adopt an orientation which emphasizes both the interplay between constitutional and environmental factors and the mutual interaction between the child and its environment.

Pre- and Perinatal Factors

The prenatal risk factors responsible for the greatest majority of adverse outcome in infants refer both to genetic factors, such as chromosomal irregularities, and environmental parameters causing organic dysfunction, such as maternal viruses, malnutrition, poor quality of intrauterine life, and the effect of chemicals. They are less easily detected and prevented than are perinatal factors such as hazards at the time of birth or preterm birth.

Research has focused greatly on the biological risk factors at the prenatal and perinatal periods. Yet the problem gets infinitely more complex because the biological risk inevitably interacts with social, psychological, and psychosocial risk, such as low socioeconomic status, family size, increased number of stressful life events, lack of social support, mental illness of the parent, marital discord, emotional difficulties at large.

Moreover, there is evidence that a relationship does exist between mother and infant during pregnancy. This early relationship serves on the one hand as a blueprint for the type of interaction that will take place after birth, and, on the other, it impinges upon the parent's subsequent ability to represent development adaptively to the infant. In other words, the antenatal relationship with the infant has predictive validity.[4]

Studies which focus on the mother's physiologic changes during the gestational period offer some tentative findings correlating these changes with the kind of relationship which is eventually forged with the infant. It has been shown, for example, that peak pregnancy blood pressure was associated with fetal growth retardation and lower fetal heart rate which in turn was associated with greater crying and irritability in the newborns.[5] Other studies have investigated the relationship between maternal pregnancy complications and subsequent psychiatric disturbance or maladaptive behavioral syndromes in preschool or older children. Conflicts between pregnant women's reproductive function and their status as mothers were associated with reports of enuresis and other adaptational problems in the children.[6] Significantly more pregnancy delivery complications were found for emotionally disturbed children than were found for controls or for their siblings.[7-9] It seems that in instances of a difficult pregnancy the mother's representational abilities may be impaired to the extent that forging an interactional bond with the infant becomes problematic. It is a feedback process whereby the mother's emotional status can affect her physiological status which in turn affects her psychological capacities, such as her ability to differentiate from the infant and to envision development. This impacts so much on the fetal outcome as to the very early parent–infant relationship.

Preterm birth seems to be the risk factor studied with the greatest methodological sophistication.[10] A high-risk and disabled infant mobilizes a number of emotional and psychological reactions in parents. Parents have been found to experience feelings of guilt,[11, 12] to manifest a high level of defensive attribution and self-blame,[13] to feel a deep sense of failure,[14] and to express grief and mourning responses[15, 16] accompanied by depression.[17] Feelings of love and investment are often withheld to protect the parent from grief in case the infant dies.[18, 19] Ambivalent feelings of anger and distress may rise as well.[20]

In high-risk cases, both parents and infants are usually deprived of the very early contact experiences which facilitate the establishment of an adaptive relationship.[21] Parents often feel ill prepared for the infant's care upon hospital discharge[22] and may experience delays of several days or even months in developing feelings of warmth and strong affection for their child.[23, 24] A high-risk infant may have a disorganizing and negative impact on the marital system,[25-27] or the sharing of strong emotions may alternatively strengthen the marital relationship.[28]

Research findings point out that the interactive pattern between high-risk infants and their parents is affected, owing as much to the properties of the infants themselves as to those of their parents. These infants spend less time in an alert state, they are less responsive, allowing thus for more limited interaction, and they are more difficult to soothe.[29-31] As some infants improve, certain parents' reactions may remain the same in continuing to act as if the child runs still a medical risk.[32, 33] Yet other parent–child systems may set into motion more responsive alterations creating thus a dynamic environment.[1, 31] Nonetheless, overall findings suggest that serious perinatal risk jeopardizes the development of a consistent, well-functioning relationship.

There seem to be considerable differences in parent–child interaction patterns between high-risk and healthy infants. Yet these differences do not necessarily imply developmental deficiencies. Mothers are often able to adapt and compensate for these differences in infants.[34] Many studies on developmental outcome during the first two years of life reveal that at risk infants at birth can develop secure attachments to their parents in infancy.[10, 23, 34-36]

Less positive developmental outcomes are also reported. The incidence of sudden infant death syndrome is six times greater among high-risk preterm babies.[37, 38] Moreover, increased numbers of nonorganic failure to thrive and of abused and neglected infants are all found among high-risk preterm infants.[30, 39, 40] It is the behavioral repertoire of the poorly organized infant that may provoke violent reactions on the part of the caregiver. With increasing severity of perinatal stress, an increase in the proportion of 2-year-olds was found to be below normal in physical, intellectual, and social development.[41]

However, perhaps the most challenging finding is that single early events are often not sufficient for increased pathological incidences. It is their combination with characteristics of the environment that can turn outcome toward one or the other direction.[42] The importance of the benefits of a good early home environment in minimizing the disadvantages of severe pre- and perinatal risk is emphasized in several studies. Developmental adaptation depends greatly on the characteristics of the infant as well as on the quality of the caregiving environment.

Effect of Maternal Mental Illness

The study of mother–infant interaction during the 1st year of the child's life shows how sensitive infants are to their mothers' communications and how selectively they respond to human qualities. Infants can discriminate subtle variations in maternal behavior; they engage in persistent efforts when they seek communication, and they protest and show their distress or withdrawal when the mother behaves inappropriately. Studies on detailed observation reveal that in their relationship with their infant, mothers with psychopathological disorders may fail to show the subtle adaptations[43] which are characteristic of ordinary maternal communication. The infant may become distressed and withdrawn, and its adaptation to its disturbed mother may become an established and inappropriate pattern of relating to people other than the mother and to the mother too after she has recovered, thus limiting subsequent experience.[44]

Research on mother–infant relationships where the mother is psychopathologically disturbed is rather limited and is based on either maternal reports or laboratory-based and naturalistic direct observation. Evidence concerning the effect of adverse early mother–child interaction on subsequent development is still scanty, mainly because we lack relevant longitudinal data. Stern[44] proposes that in the absence of the maternal adaptations characterizing early interaction, the establishment of a stable and enduring sense of a "core self" is threatened. Moreover, Trevarthen[45] suggests that brain structure and functioning may be influenced by the activation of specific motivational states and in turn the quality of experience. Yet both of these hypotheses are difficult to trace in terms of developmental progress, since environmental and/or self-repairing functions may moderate the effects of earlier damage.

The main bulk of the literature focuses on the two broad groups of mental disorders: schizophrenia and affective disorders. Another distinction is made on whether the illness antedates the pregnancy or whether it appeared for the first time during pregnancy or after birth. The relationship between nature and timing of the disorder and the consequent disturbances of the mother–infant interaction are best understood when placed in the personal and social context.

There seem to be contradictory findings regarding the schizophrenic mother–infant interactions. Schizophrenic mothers were found to be less able than controls to interpret infant cues properly and to attribute intentionality to the infant. They did not regard the establishment of a reciprocal relationship as very important and played less with their infants.[46] Similarly, schizophrenic mothers of infants who showed emotional disorder at 18 months of age were found to play little with their infants, to engage in limited joyful interaction, and to express curtailed positive affect.[47] Yet, another study[48] revealed that schizophrenic mothers tended to be more affectionate and responsive to their infants than controls, possibly as a result of increased anxiety. Results from the Rochester Longitudinal Study pointed out that seriously ill mothers engaged in less spontaneous, happy, and talkative interactions with their infants at 1 year of age. The infants as well appeared to be less spontaneous. However, they were not different from controls in their attachment behavior.[49] In contrast, a major Swedish longitudinal study[50] revealed anxious patterns of attachment at the same age. The diversity of these findings is attributed by Melhuish et al.[51] to the diversity in the employed methodology.

Children of schizophrenic mothers showed extreme apathy or excessive irritability during infancy, relating to emotional impairment in later childhood;[52, 53] poor sensorimotor functioning[54] and poor conceptual development[55] at 1 year of age.

The data from the Rochester Longitudinal Study[42] indicate that children of schizophrenic mothers are a high-risk sample, but no more so than samples of children of other severely ill mothers. Moreover, low socioeconomic class and minority status are even greater risk factors for an unfavorable developmental outcome than is maternal mental illness. The combined risk of both factors naturally produces the worst outcomes— outcomes, however, which do not necessarily lead to schizophrenia.[42] Thus, the importance of the characteristics of the environment and their mediating effect are becoming increasingly apparent.

There seems to be a great need for longitudinal studies with repeated observations in naturalistic settings, focusing on the total caregiving environment of the child, and for a better understanding of the relationship between maternal schizophrenia and developmental outcome.

The incidence of mental illness during pregnancy is much lesser than that after childbirth, and comparisons of outcome of disorders arising in pregnancy as opposed to postnatally suggest that only disorders which persist into the puerperium are likely to affect the developing child.[56] Little is known about the possible effects on infant development of maternal affective disorders occurring in the puerperium. Moreover, there are inconsistencies in research findings, and some of the overall few prospective studies suffer from methodological limitations.[57] Most of the information concerning children is derived from maternal reports which may be colored by the mother's emotional state.[58]

Studies of children whose mothers had been depressed at some point during the year or so following childbirth reveal, at the ages of 19 months to 4 years, consistent evidence of differences in children which are related to the maternal emotional state.[57] Mothers who had been depressed after birth were found to give more negative descriptions of their children at 2 and 4 years[59] and to report more behavior problems at the same age[60] than did controls. Maternal depression during the first 3 months after birth was associated with poor cognitive functioning at 4 years,[56] and depression 14 months after birth was associated with child behavior problems at 42 months.[61]

Clinical reports and more systematic observation studies reveal a general picture of less positively expressed affect and reciprocity toward the infant. Studies with simulated depression in the mother[43, 62] investigated the infant's reactions. The sensitivity of the infants to the affective state of the mother suggested that depressive styles of interaction are transmitted to the infant already during the very first months. Children of mothers suffering from major affective disorders were found to exhibit insecure attachment, involving avoidance of and resistance to the mother when reunited with her after brief separations.[63] Similar results are also reported by Gaensbauer et al.[64] for children aged 12 to 18 months. Yet patterns of attachment were not found to differ for infants of mothers with an affective disorder either in the Rochester Longitudinal Study[49] or in the study by Naslund et al.[50] In the former, the mothers were found to hold their 4-month-old infants less and to be less playful, happy, and vocal with them.

Inconsistencies in results and differences in child outcome may be attributed either to the illness itself, the nature and the timing of the depressive disorder, or to the consequences of the illness. Important differences in interactive style were noted within the distinct subgroups of depressed populations. For example, mothers with extensive previous depression would either show little emotion and leave the child unoccupied or would be less controlling.[65] On the other hand, where depression was precipitated by recent stressful life events, women's mothering was not affected and hence their offspring suffered little impact.[60] Weissman and Paykel[66] have shown that in mothers with long-term problems, even when depressive symptomatology has remitted, communication continues to be inhibited, and deficits in relation to the children persist. Thus differences in child outcome are not a function of only current depressive symptomatology. It seems they are also associated with the child's involvement with a long-term disturbed parent that threatens its stability.[67]

The greater the diversity of the research findings, the more we realize that the understanding of the depressed mother–infant relationship as a contributor to future psychopathology is a more complex undertaking whereby we need to know the hereditary predisposition of the child, the depressive symptomatology of the mother, the quality of communication, the role played by the behavioral pattern of the mother, as well as the possible contribution of a variety of other subtle intervening variables which have as yet not been thoroughly investigated.

CONCLUSION

In unraveling the role of early developmental factors in relation to adverse outcome in the child, we are faced with the nature of the developmental model which best befits the dynamic process of risk. If we adopt a model stressing the discontinuity of development, we would assume that problems at an older age may not be directly related to an earlier period. Conversely, the assumption behind models which allow for immediate and direct effects is that the mother–infant interaction is molded on the principle of a feedback loop. Such a model would point to the possibility of a critical disruption. Yet it would also leave room for subsequent experiences which may mitigate outcome.

The challenge we are faced with is to apply the research findings from those of the studies mentioned, which have revealed reliable and applicable information, in order to realign the mother's relationship with the infant into an interaction that is more conducive to adaptive development.

Finally, two points should be stressed: (1) the assessment of the long-term consequences of early influences is a complicated issue because of the difficulties in eliminating intervening influences,[68] and (2), as pointed out by Neuton,[69] in order to be prophylactically effective, an intervention must eliminate not only the hypothesized deleterious factor (e.g., an isolated stress), but also the surrounding circumstances which are responsible for it. This latter task is probably of equal or even greater prophylactic importance.

REFERENCES

1. Sameroff AJ, Chandler MJ. Reproductive risk and the continuum of caretaking casualty. In: Horowitz FD, Hetherington M, Scarr-Salapatek S, Siegel G, eds. *Review of Child Development Research.* Chicago: University of Chicago Press;1975: vol 4.
2. Wilson RS. Risk and resilience in early mental development. *Dev Psychol.* 1985;21:795–805.
3. Scarr S, Weinberg RA. The Minnesota adoption studies: Genetic differences and malleability. *Child Dev.* 1983;54:260–267.
4. Trad PV. *Infant Previewing: Predicting and Sharing Interpersonal Outcome.* New York: Springer;1990.
5. Woodson RH, Jones NG, da CostaWoodson E, Pollock S, Evans M. Fetal mediators of the relationships between increased pregnancy and labour blood pressure and newborn irritability. *Early Hum Dev.* 1979;3:127–139.
6. Nilsson A, Almgren PE, Kohler EM, Kohler L. Enuresis: The importance of maternal attitudes and personality. A prospective study of pregnant women and a follow-up of their children. *Acta Psychiatr Scand.* 1973;49:114–130.
7. McNeil TF, Wiegerink R, Dozier JE. Pregnancy and birth complications in the births of seriously, moderately, and mildly behaviorally disturbed children. *J Nerv Ment Dis.* 1970;151:24–34.
8. McNeil TF, Wiegerink R. Behavioral patterns and pregnancy and birth complication histories in psychologically disturbed children. *J Nerv Ment Dis.* 1971;152:315–323.
9. Mura EL. Perinatal differences: A comparison of child psychiatric patients and their siblings. *Child Psychiatr Q.* 1974;48:239–255.
10. Easterbrooks MA. Effects of infant risk status on the transition to parenthood. In: Michaels GY, Goldberg WA, eds. *The Transition to Parenthood.* New York: Cambridge University Press;1988.
11. Howard J. The influence of children's developmental dysfunctions on marital quality and family interaction. In: Lerner R, Spanier G, eds. *Child Influences on Marital and Family Interaction.* New York: Academic Press;1978.
12. Callahan EJ, Brasted WS, Granados JL. Fetal loss and sudden infant death: Grieving and adjustment for families. In: Callahan EJ, McCluskey KA, eds. *Life-Span Developmental Psychology: Nonnormative Life Events.* New York: Academic Press;1983.
13. Tennen H, Affleck G, Gershman K. Self-blame among parents of infants with perinatal complications: The role of self-protective motives. *J Pers Soc Psychol.* 1986;50:690–696.
14. Seashore MJ, Leifer AD, Barnett CR, Leiderman PH. The effects of denial of early mother-infant interaction on maternal self-confidence. *J Pers Soc Psychol.* 1973;27:369–378.
15. Klaus MH, Kennell JH. *Maternal-Infant Bonding: The Impact of Early Separation or Loss on Family Development.* St Louis: Mosby;1976.
16. D'Arcy E. Congenital defects: Mother's reaction to first information. *Br Med J.* 1968;iii:796–798.

17. Solnit A, Stark M. Mourning and the birth of a defective child. *Psychoanal Study Child.* New York: International Universities Press;1961:16:523-537.
18. Kaplan D, Mason EA. Maternal reactions to premature birth viewed as an acute emotional disorder. *Am J Orthopsychiatry.* 1960;30:539.
19. Borg S, Lasker J. *When Pregnancy Fails.* Boston: Beacon Press;1981.
20. Heisler V. *A Handicapped Child in the Family.* New York: Grune & Stratton;1972.
21. Klaus MH, Kennell JH. *Parent-Infant Bonding.* St Louis: Mosby;1982.
22. Jeffcoate JA, Humphrey ME, Lloyd JK. Role perception and response to stress in fathers and mothers following pre-term delivery. *Soc Sci Med.* 1979;13A: 139–145.
23. Harmon RJ, Culp AM. The effects of premature birth on family functioning and infant development. In: Berlin I, ed. *Children and Our Future.* Albuquerque, NM: University of New Mexico Press;1981.
24. Robson K, Kumar R. Delayed onset of maternal affection after childbirth. *Br J Psychiatry.* 1980;136:347–353.
25. Pawl JH, Petarsky JH. Infant–parent psychotherapy: A family in crisis. In: Provence S, ed. *Infants and Parents.* New York: International Universities Press;1983.
26. Simon R. *After the Tears.* Denver, CO: Children's Museum of Denver;1985.
27. McIntyre MN. Need for supportive therapy for members of a family with a defective child. In: Lubs A, de la Crez F, eds. *Genetic Counseling.* New York: Raven Press;1977.
28. Korn SL, Chess S, Fernandez P. The impact of children's physical handicaps on marital quality and family interaction. In: Lerner R, Spanier G, eds. *Child Influences on Marital and Family Interaction.* New York: Academic Press;1978.
29. Field TM. Interaction patterns of preterm and full-term infants. In: Field TM, Sostek AM, Goldberg S, Shuman HH, eds. *Infants Born at Risk.* New York: Spectrum Press;1979.
30. Lester BM, Zeskind PS. The organization and assessment of crying in the infant at risk. In: Field TM, Sostek AM, Goldberg S, Shuman HH, eds. *Infants Born at Risk.* New York: Spectrum Press;1979.
31. Di Vitto B, Goldberg S. The effect of newborn medical status on early parent-infant interaction. In: Field TM, Sostek AM, Goldberg S, Shuman HH, eds. *Infants Born at Risk.* New York: Spectrum Press;1979.
32. Crnic KA, Ragozin AS, Greenberg MT, Robinson NM, Basham RB. Social interaction and developmental competence of preterm and full-term infants during the first year of life. *Child Dev.* 1983;54:1199–1210.
33. Minde K, Marton P, Manning D, Hines B. Some determinants of mother-infant interaction in the premature nursery. *J Am Acad Child Psychiatry.* 1980;19:1–21.
34. Goldberg S, Perrotta M, Minde K. *Maternal Birthweight and Attachment in Low Birthweight Twins and Singletons.* Unpublished manuscript. Hospital for Sick Children;1983.
35. Field TM, Hallock N, Ting E, Dempsey G, Dabiri C, Shuman HH. A first-year follow-up of high-risk infants: Formulation of a cumulative risk index. *Child Dev.* 1978;49:119–131.
36. Wasserman GA. Affective expression in normal and physically handicapped infants: Situational and developmental effects. *J Am Acad Child Psychiatry.* 1986;25:393–399.

37. Guilleminault C, Peraita T, Souquet M, Dement WC. Apneas during sleep in infants: Possible relationship with sudden infant death syndrome. *Science.* 1974;190:677–679.
38. Kattwinkel J. Neonatal apnea: Pathogenesis and therapy. *J Pediatr.* 1977;90: 342–347.
39. Belsky J. Three theoretical models of child abuse: A critical review. *Int J Child Abuse Negl.* 1978;2:37–49.
40. Hunter RS, Kilstrom N, Kraybill EN, Loda F. Antecedents of child abuse and neglect in premature infants: A prospective study in a newborn intensive care unit. *Pediatrics.* 1978;61:629–635.
41. Werner E, Simonian K, Bierman JM, French FE. Cumulative effect of perinatal complications and deprived environment on physical, intellectual, and social development of preschool children. *Pediatrics.* 1967;39:490–505.
42. Sameroff A, Seifer R, Zax M, Barocas R. Early indicators of developmental risk: The Rochester Longitudinal Study. Manuscript.
43. Field TM. Early interactions between infants and their post partum depressed mothers. *Infant Behav Dev.* 1984;7:517–522.
44. Stern DN. *The Interpersonal World of the Infant: A View from Psychoanalysis and Developmental Psychology.* New York: Basic Books;1985.
45. Trevarthen CB. Brain science and the human spirit. *Zygon.* 1986;21:161–200.
46. Cohler B, Weiss J, Grunebaum H. Child-care attitudes and emotional disturbances in mothers of young children. *Genet Psychol Monogr.* 1970;82:3–47.
47. Sobel D. Children of schizophrenic parents: Preliminary observations on early development. *Am J Psychiatry.* 1961;118:512–517.
48. Schachter J, Elmer E, Ragins N, Wimberly F. Assessment of mother–infant interaction: Schizophrenic and non-schizophrenic mothers. *Merrill Palmer Q.* 1977;23:183–205.
49. Sameroff AJ, Seifer R, Zax M. Early development of children at risk from emotional disorders. *Monogr Soc Res Child Dev.* 1982;47:199.
50. Naslund B, Persson-Blennow I, McNeil TF, Kaij L, Malmqvist-Larsson A. Offspring of women with non-organic psychosis: Infant attachment to the mother at one year of age. *Acta Psychiatr Scand.* 1984; 69:231–241.
51. Melhuish EC, Gambles C, Kumar R. Maternal mental illness and the mother-infant relationship. In: Kumar R, Brockington IF, eds. *Motherhood and Mental Illness.* London: Wright;1988: vol 2.
52. Fish B, Alpert M. Abnormal states of consciousness and muscle tone in infants born to schizophrenic mothers. *Am J Psychiatry.* 1962;119:439–445.
53. Fish B, Hagin R. Visual-motor disorders in infants at risk for schizophrenia. *Arch Gen Psychiatry.* 1973;28:900–905.
54. Marcus J, Auerbach J, Wilkinson L, Burack CM. Infants at risk for schizophrenia. *Arch Gen Psychiatry.* 1981;38:703–713.
55. Gamer E, Gallant D, Grunebaum H. An evaluation of one-year-olds on a test of object permanence. *Arch Gen Psychiatry.* 1976;33:311–317.
56. Cogill S, Caplan H, Alexandra H, Robson K, Kumar R. Impact of postnatal depression on the developing child. *Br Med J.* 1986;i:1165–1167.
57. Murray L. Effects of postnatal depression on infant development: Direct studies of early mother–infant interactions. In: Kumar R, Brockington IF, eds. *Motherhood and Mental Illness.* London: Wright;1988: vol 2.

58. Fergusson DM, Horwood LJ, Gretton ME, Shannon FT. Family life events, maternal depression and maternal and teacher descriptions of child behaviour. *Pediatrics.* 1985;75:30–35.

59. Zajicek E, de Salis W. Depression in mothers of young children. *Child Abuse Negl.* 1979;3:833–835.

60. Pound A, Cox A, Puckering C, Mills M. The impact of maternal depression on young children. In: Stevenson JE, ed. *Recent Research in Developmental Psychopathology.* Oxford: Pergamon Press;1985.

61. Ghodsian M, Zajicek E, Wolkind S. A longitudinal study of maternal depression and child behaviour problems. *J Child Psychol Psychiatry.* 1984;25:91–109

62. Cohn JF, Tronick EZ. Three-month-old infants' reaction to simulated maternal depression. *Child Dev.* 1983;54:185–193.

63. Radke-Yarrow M, Cummings EM, Kuczynski L, Chapman M. Patterns of attachment in two and three year olds in normal families and families with parental depression. *Child Dev.* 1985;56:884–893.

64. Gaensbauer TJ, Harmon RJ, Cytryn L, McKnew DH. Social and affective development in infants with a manic-depressive parent. *Am J Psychiatry.* 1984; 141:223–229.

65. Mills M, Puckering C, Pound A, Cox A. What is it about depressed mothers that influences their children's functioning? In: Stevenson JE, ed. *Recent Research in Developmental Psychopathology.* Oxford: Pergamon Press;1985.

66. Weissman MM, Paykel ES. *The Depressed Woman.* Chicago: University of Chicago Press;1974.

67. Rutter M, Quinton D. Parental psychiatric disorder: Effects on children. *Psychol Med.* 1984;14:873–880.

68. Christodoulou GN. Prevention of psychopathology with early interventions. *Psychother Psychosom.* 1991;55:201–207.

69. Neuton J. Prevention in childhood. In: Neuton J, ed. *Preventing Mental Illness.* London: Routledge & Kegan Paul;1988.

Chapter 11
Quality of Life
Measurements
in Chronic Disorders

P. BECH

HEALTH-RELATED QUALITY OF LIFE

From a historical point of view quality of life was a political concept. As discussed elsewhere,[1] it was Lyndon B. Johnson who, in 1964, introduced the concept by declaring that "goals cannot be measured in the size of our bank balance. They can only be measured in the quality of the lives that our people lead. . . ." At the same time the ecological ("green") movement started as a reaction against the uncritical use of pesticides. This movement became a psychological, ecological, and philosophical movement often with references to the "limits to growth" sponsored by the Club of Rome indicating that Nature is often irreplaceable. Slogans such as "things are interconnected" or "think globally, act locally" illustrate the ecological aspect of quality of life.

In medicine, publications on quality of life increased significantly in the late seventies.[1] In principle health-related quality of life is the trade-off between the raw health outcomes as defined by doctors and the impact of the therapies on the patients themselves. This balance can best be illustrated by the traditional procedure in controlled clinical trials. In the standard protocol of controlled clinical trials it is often stated: "patients who consented to participate in the trial were randomly allocated to the different treatments. . . . This was done by use of sampling with replacement. . . ." When measuring raw health data in clinical trials (in medicine often with reference to laboratory data or other "objective" measurements; in psychiatry with reference to symptom rating scales such as the Hamilton scales) no patient is considered to be indispensable. However, when measuring quality of life data every patient might be considered as irreplaceable.

As discussed elsewhere,[2] Eysenck, who throughout his scientific work has constructed scales to compare patients across age, sex, and culture (so-called nomothetic scales), realized that:

[I]n writing one's autobiography, one inevitably has to take the idiographic path of trying to see regularities in one's own life, look for behaviour patterns that repeat themselves, and try to discover variables that are important for oneself, even though they might not be of general interest. . . .[2]

Health-related quality of life is to consider what is of idiographic importance for the individual patient; what in a sense is irreplaceable for him or her from a treatment point of view.

When making an overview of the attempts to measure quality of life in medicine[1, 3] some issues have emerged which had a general interest across patient variables. In the following, quality of life will be considered as a relevant indicator for at least two approaches to the measurement of health, namely a multidimensional approach to medical disorders[1] and a one-dimensional patient-perceived improvement approach for treatment outcome.[3]

Raw health data was organized by DSM-III[4] into a multiaxial system. The different axes in DSM-III have also been found relevant when describing the quality of life of patients, often referred to as the PCASEE model,[2] where P refers to physical, C to cognitive, A to affective, S to social problems, E to economic stressors, and E to ego functions.

ILLNESS INDICATORS

Illness refers to the clinical symptoms of a disease. According to the WHO classification[5] "impairment" is defined as the biological disturbance of a disease and "disability" is defined as the manifestation of the clinical disorder, the illness, often in terms of the patient's performance or behavior. According to WHO, "handicap" is defined as the subjective disadvantage of being ill and is included in the concept of health-related quality of life, the impact of ill-being on well-being.

As discussed by Wood,[6] illness indicators are dependent on the type of illness. Thus, acute illness indicators are recovery or death, because an acute illness is often life threatening: the outcome is unequivocal; either a return to health or death. The interventions have the immediate objective to add years to life. On the other hand, if the returning to health is only partial, the illness has been chronic. Among chronic illness indicators the severity of illness is, of course, the most relevant. However, the measurement of severity of illness is not always simple. Disagreements between doctors and their patients or between the patients and their relatives might emerge. In chronic illness the objective of treatment interventions is to add quality of life to years. Health-related quality of life has therefore its main applicability in chronic disorders. Feinstein[7] has differentiated between an ailment-oriented index in chronic disorders (the disability which is the characteristic focus of attention in the daily clinical practice) and disorder-specific indices (the extent to which the disability clinically has diagnostic properties). The ailment-oriented index covers the patient's self-care, activities of daily life (ADL), which is a health-status indicator closer to the concept of quality of life than the disorder-specific index.

Patients with chronic disorders often consult their family doctor because of stressful life events rather than because of illness problems.[8]

QUALITY OF LIFE AND COPING STRATEGIES: PREDICTIVE QUALITY OF LIFE SCALES

Quality of life can, inter alia, be considered as an attempt to exclude the classical medical model (organic impairment, clinical disability, ADL problems) as shown in Table 11.1. Quality of life is often identified with the stress model in which the chronic illness is considered as an enduring stressor (Table 11.1). From the stress model point of view quality of life includes psychosocial defense mechanisms and coping strategies.

The concept of coping with illness was defined by Lipowski[9] as including all the cognitive and motor activities which an ill person employs to preserve his bodily and psychic integrity, to compensate as much as possible for any irreversible impairment. In this definition Lipowski integrates the psychological elements of Lazarus[10] and the sociological elements of Mechanic.[11]

Although psychosocial defense mechanisms are unconscious intrapsychic processes (and therefore most appropriately should be tested by dynamic instruments like the Thematic Apperception Test),[12, 13] attempts have been made to develop self-rating scales measuring such constructs as denial, regression, repression, projection. Among the most frequently used scales in this field are the Eysenck Neuroticism Scale[14] and the Life Style Index.[15] For further discussion see Olff and Endresen.[16]

Table 11.2 shows predictive scales for outcome of treatment in chronic disorders. The scales have been classified not only according to stress, coping, and defense mechanisms, but also

TABLE 11.1
Health-Related Quality of Life

Medical model (etiological causation)	Stress model (stimulus response)	Demoralisation model (teleological holism)
Organic impairment →	illness as pysychosocial stressor →	helping the patient to define his or her goals →
Clinical disability →	psychosocial defense mechanisms →	expressing the distance between the current situation and the wished goals →
ADL handicaps (self-care) →	coping strategies	individual, health-related quality of life

TABLE 11.2
Predictive Scales for Outcome of Treatment

1	Personality (generic)	Eysenck Neuroticism Scale [14]
2	Personality (disease-specific)	type A behaviour [34]
3	Defense mechanisms (generic)	Life Style Index [15]
4	Coping with illness (generic)	psychosocial adjustment to illness [35]
5	Coping with illness (disease-specific)	mental adjustment of cancer [36]
6	Stress resistance (hardiness against illness)	commitment, control, challenge [37]

concerning whether they are disease-specific (e.g., type A behavior in chronic heart disorders or mental adjustment to cancer in breast cancer) or generic (i.e., can be applied regardless of the disease being investigated).

QUALITY OF LIFE AS AN OUTCOME MEASUREMENT: THE MULTIDIMENSIONAL PCASEE MODEL

The PCASEE model should be considered as an attempt to use the multidimensional DSM-III approach at the level of quality of life measurement. In Table 11.1, quality of life was identified with the demoralization model in which the patients from a teleological point of view holistically are helped to define their goals of life by expressing the distance between their current situation and these goals. This approach has been accepted by Sartorius[17] from WHO and he added that the measurement of quality of life is subject to no other difficulties than those inherent in all measurements of emotions.

In Table 11.3 an attempt is made to describe the PCASEE model in the language of symptoms at different levels from illness indicators to quality of life indicators.

Among the first to construct quality of life scales were Parloff et al.[18] who developed the Symptom Check List. They tried to find another language than symptoms because symptoms are so closely related to illness, but they failed. In a nonpatient study on quality of life, "the inner American," Veroff et al.[19] concluded that "symptoms are interesting and important indicators of psychological experience. . . . They represent the presenting complaints people have, ones that they commonly use in conversations about the every day stressors and strains of modern living. . . ."

One of the coworkers to the Parloff paper was Frank who introduced the term *demoralization* for emotional discomfort or distress[20]:

[D]emoralization describes the states of candidates for psychotherapy, whatever their diagnostic label. They are conscious of having failed to meet their own expectations or those of others, or being unable to cope with some pressing problem. They feel powerless to change the situation themselves. Their life space is constricted, both in space and time . . . the demoralized person is prey to anxiety and depression (the two most common complaints of persons seeking psychotherapy).

Quality of life in chronic disorders, therefore, is a grid as shown in Table 11.3 where the PCASEE dimension by the language of symptoms are described both for disability (indicators of illness) and for quality of life problems (emotions and demoralization).

When discussing Food and Drug Administration perspectives on quality of life, Johnson[21] considered the whole range of symptoms of depressed mood. This symptom can be an indicator of primary depression, of a systemic disease (e.g., severity of cancer), or of quality of life (e.g., demoralization).

The concept of improvement during treatment refers not only to improvement of disability but, in chronic disorders especially, to improvement of the occasion or the hour. Unlike primary depression (which has a syndrome duration of at least 2 weeks according to DSM-III), emotions of quality of life last from hours to days. As shown in Table 11.3, it is therefore appropriate to

TABLE 11.3
Content Validity of Health Status and Quality of Life Measurements (PCASEE domains or axes)

Points of view	P Physical	C Cognitive	A Affective	S Social	E Economy	E Ego functions
Health status (syndromes)	somatic	organic mental	functional mental	activity of daily life	psychosocial stressors	personality
DSM-III axes	3	1	1	5	4	2
Health status (symptoms)	tiredness	concentration	depression	interpersonal sensitivity	degree of freedom	self-control
	sleep	memory	anxiety			self-acceptance
Health-related quality of life	subjective health	decision making	feeling warmth with others	doing things well	feeling economic basis good	playing useful part in things, commitment

TABLE 11.4.
Outcome Scales, Health-Related Quality of Life (generic)

1	Demoralization (monothetic)	Hopkins Symptom Checklist [18]
2	Distress (monothetic)	General Health Questionnaire [38]
3	Well-being (monothetic)	PGWB [22]
4	Combined health status quality of life (monothetic)	Health status quality of life (SF-36) [39]
5	Individually perceived quality of life (idiographic)	Repertory grid (PCASEE) [31]

ask such questions as, "how often have you been depressed?" at the quality of life level, whereas "how long and severe has your depression been?" is an appropriate question at the major depression level. At the demoralization level questions as to how bad versus how good are most appropriate.

There are many generic quality of life outcome scales and a few of them are shown in Table 11.4. Among these scales the Psychological General Well-Being Scale (PGWB)[22] is the most appropriate taking the PCASEE model into account. This scale had the highest discriminant validity in the first comprehensive, multidimensional, quality of life study on chronic disorders accepted by the *New England Journal of Medicine* in 1986.[23] Table 11.5 shows how the many scales used in this study fit into the PCASEE model. The PGWB scale is here placed as an affective scale, but as shown in Table 11.6, the PGWB when placed in the PCASEE model is taking both the dimension and the symptom level (disability vs. quality of life) into account.

The psychometric description of the PGWB is shown in Table 11.7.

QUALITY OF LIFE AS A ONE-DIMENSIONAL OUTCOME INDICATOR

The PGWG scale can, as shown in Table 11.7, be used as a one-dimensional outcome indicator, by its total score, although the scale includes both symptoms of disability and of quality of life items. The use of subscales or of many different scales as in the Croog study[23] (Table 11.5) might give statistical problems because of multiple endpoint measures. The use of one index (e.g., a visual analog scale or a global improvement scale) has often been recommended to overcome this problem. Multiple dimensions are often referred to as profiles and one-dimensional measurements as index. Both approaches should be used.

TABLE 11.5
Quality of Life Assessment[23] in Patients with Hypertension

P Physical	C Cognitive	A Affective	S Social	E Econonomic-social stress	E Ego functions
Physical Symptom Distress Index	Wechsler Memory Scale [43]	SCL-53 [45]	Work Performance and Satisfaction [46]		Life Satisfaction Social Roles [48]
Hypertension Detection Program [40]					
Sleep Dysfunction Scale [41]	Reitan Trait-Making Test [44]	PGWB Index [22]	Social Participation Index [47]		
Sexual Symptom Distress [42]					

TABLE 11.6

Repertoire of PCASEE in the Psychological General Well-Being Schedule (PGWB[22])

PGWB schedule	P Physical	C Cognitive	A Affective	S Social	E Economic-social stressors	E Ego-functions
Symptoms 'observer'	(2) general health (6) energy (21) exhausted		(3) depressed mood (5) nerves (7) blue (8) tense (11) hopeless (17) anxious mood (19) restless			
Indicators of quality of life 'patient'	(10) subjective health (12) satisfied with sleep (13) preoccupied with health	(4) control (14) losing control	(1) general spirits (18) emotional sure of yourself (20) cheerful	(15) engaged in social life (16) social active	(22) feeling under stress	(9) satisfied with personal life

TABLE 11.7
Psychological General Well-Being Schedule (PGWB),
Its Psychometric Properties

Administration	self-rating
Type	generic
Applicability	outcome of treatment
Number of items	22
Item definition	Likert (0–5)
	5 = absent
	0 = maximum
Content validity	PCASEE (components)
	symptom/quality of live
	(level)
Construct validity	Cronbach alpha
	= 0.92
Discriminant validity	Croog et al. [23]
Concurrent validity	SCL-90: –0.77 (Hopkins)
Statistics	total score: index
	subscore: profile

WHO IS THE NATURAL QUALITY OF LIFE DECISION MAKER?

One of the most simple lexicographical definitions of quality of life is the one stipulated by Joyce[24] who defines health-related quality of life as "what the patient says it is." Consequently, the natural decision makers are the patients themselves. However, the reliability of self-reported statements is often questioned for such chronic disorders as dementia, schizophrenia, substance use disorder, or alcoholism. In most quality of life trials patients with these disorders are excluded and these patients' relatives are then considered as the natural decision makers. This problem has been discussed elsewhere for schizophrenia and alcoholism.[25, 26]

Studies correlating the patient's, the relative's, and the treating doctor's assessment of the patient's quality of life are rather few. The most interesting finding in this field is the study by Jachuck et al.[27] in patients with mild to moderate hypertension. While the doctors all found that the quality of life of the 75 patients examined in the study was unchanged or increased, only half of the patients agreed, and only 1 of the 75 relatives agreed. Recently, Frimodt-Møller et al.[28] replicated this study showing a higher concordance between the patients and their relatives, but the correlation coefficients were only around 0.50. In patients with cancer diseases, Slevin et al.[29] found correlation coefficients between the patients and their doctors around 0.50 as well.

When relying on the patient's own assessment it is of major importance to use individually perceived scales rather than traditional group-oriented scales. An attempt to use the PCASEE model as background for an individually perceived quality of life assessment has recently been made.[30] In patients with chronic anxiety disorders (generalized anxiety disorders) it was found that the individually perceived PCASEE assessment had higher validity than the traditional, group-orientated scales (e.g. the General Health Questionnaire) to discriminate between treatments.[31]

GENERIC VERSUS DISEASE-SPECIFIC QUALITY OF LIFE SCALES

In Table 11.2 both generic (disease-independent) and disease-specific scales with predictive validity for quality of life were shown. In Table 11.4 only generic scales to measure outcome of treatment were shown. The Karnofsky Performance Status Scale[32] was originally designed as a cancer-specific scale but has since been used as a generic scale for quality of life index (it is, however, a performance health status scale and not a health-related quality of life scale). Recently a "living with asthma" questionnaire has been released[33] which is an example of a disease-specific quality of life scale.

Individually perceived (patient-related) and disease-specific quality of life (disease-related) scales are (Table 11.8) considered

TABLE 11.8
Generic versus Disease Specific Scales: Advantages and Disadvantages

Statistical power (primary research)	Outcome of treatment (sensitivity to change)	Ability to generalize (secondary research)
Mild	generic scales (norms across disease)	great
Moderate	disease specific (norms for individual disease)	moderate
Great	patient specific (important only for the individual patient)	limited

to have the highest validity when discriminating between treatments. Such scales (Table 11.8) have, of course, a limited ability to generalize, i.e., to make comparisons to other research findings, which often is an important feature of secondary research.[2]

SUMMARY

The application of health-related quality of life measurements is in patients with chronic disorders where the objective of interventions is to add quality of life to years. The multidimensional aspects of quality of life are congruential to the multidimensional aspects of illness, taking physical, congitive, affective, social, economic, and personal factors into account. The quality of life measurements are in the context the patient's own subjective statements.

In this overview scales predictive for coping strategies as well as scales measuring outcome of treatment have been considered. Generic scales as well as disease-specific scales have been discussed. Because quality of life essentially is an attempt to make a global or holistic assessment on the part of the patient, one-dimensional well-being indicators have been contrasted to multiple-endpoint measurements or profiles.

REFERENCES

1. Bech P. Quality of life in psychosomatic research. A psychometric model. *Psychopathology.* 1987;20:169–179.
2. Bech P. *Rating Scales for Psychopathology, Health Status, and Quality of Life. A Compendium on Documentation with Reference to the DSM-III-R and WHO Systems.* Berlin: Springer;1993.
3. Bech P. Measurement of psychological distress and well-being. *Psychother Psychosom.* 1990;54:77–89.
4. American Psychiatric Association. *Diagnostic and Statistical Manual (DSM-III).* 3rd ed. Washington, DC: American Psychiatric Association;1980.
5. World Health Organization. *International Classification of Impairments, Disabilities, and Handicaps* (ICIDH/WHO). Geneva, Switzerland: WHO;1980.
6. Wood PHN. The international classification of impairments, disabilities, and handicaps of the World Health Organization. In: Leidel R, Potthoff P, Schwefel D, eds. *European Approaches to Patient Classification Systems.* Berlin: Springer;1990: pp 83–101.
7. Feinstein AR. *Clinimetrics.* New Haven, CT: Yale University Press;1987.
8. White KL. The ecology of medical care. *N Engl J Med.* 1981;265:885–892.
9. Lipowski I. Physical illness, the individual and the coping process. *Int J Psychiatry Med.* 1970;1:91–102.
10. Lazarus RS. *Psychological Stress and Coping Process.* New York: McGraw-Hill;1966.
11. Mechanic D. *Medical Sociology.* New York: Free Press;1968.
12. Groth-Marnat G. *Handbook of Psychological Assessment.* New York: Wiley; 1990.
13. Olff M. *Defence and Coping: Self-Reported Health and Psychological Correlated.* Utrecht, Netherlands: ISOR;1991.
14. Eysenck HJ, Eysenck SBG. *Psychoticism as a Dimension of Personality.* London: Hodder & Stoughton;1976.
15. Plutchik R, Kellerman H, Conte HR. A structural theory of ego defences and emotions. In: Izard CE, ed. *Emotions and Psychopathology.* New York: Plenum;1979.
16. Olff M, Endresen I. The Dutch and Norwegian translations of the Plutchik questionnaire for psychological defence. In: Olff M, Godaert G, Ursin H, eds. *Qualification of Human Defence Mechanisms.* Heidelberg: Springer;1991.
17. Sartorius N. Cross-cultural comparisons of data about quality of life. Sample of issues. In: Aaronson NK, Beckmann J, eds. *The Quality of Life of Cancer Patients.* New York: Raven Press;1987: pp 19–24.

18. Parloff MB, Kelman HC, Frank JD. Comfort, effectiveness, and self-awareness as criteria of improvement in psychotherapy. *Am J Psychiatry.* 1954;111:343–351.
19. Veroff J, Douran E, Kulka RA. *The Inner American.* New York: Basic Books;1981.
20. Frank JD. *Persuasion and Healing.* New York: Schocken;1974: p. 48.
21. Johnson JR. A regulatory view. In: Walker SR, Rosser RM, eds. *Quality of Life Assessment: Key Issues in the 1990s.* Dordrecht, Netherlands: Kluwer Academic Publishers;1992.
22. Dupuy HJ. The psychological General Well-Being (PGWB) Index. In: Wenger NK, Mattson ME, Furberg CD, Elinson J, eds. *Assessment of Quality of Life in Clinical Trials of Cardiovascular Therapies.* New York: Le Jacq Publishing;1984: pp 184–188.
23. Croog SH, Levine S, Testa M. The effects of antihypertensive therapy on the quality of life. *N Engl J Med.* 1986;314:1657–1664.
24. Joyce CRB. Need for new models and methods assessing health-related quality of life. *Int J Methods Psychiatry Res.* In press.
25. Bech P, Hjortsø S. Problems in measuring quality of life in schizophrenia. *Nord Psykiatr Tidsskr,*1990;44:23–27.
26. Bech P, Tørning J. Alkokolisme. Psykopatologiske og behandlingsmæssige overvejelser i spektret mellem livskvalitet, depression, angst og aggressivitet. *Månedsskr Prakt Lægegern.* 1992;70:785–793.
27. Jachuck SJ, Brierly H, Jachuck S, Willcox PM. The effect of hypotensive drugs on quality of life. *J R Col Gen Pract.* 1982;32:103–105.
28. Frimodt-Møller J, Loldrup Poulsen D, Kornerup HJ, Bech P. Quality of life, side effects and efficacy of lisinopril compared with metoprolol in patients with mild to moderate essential hypertension. *J Hum Hypertens.* 1991;5:215–221.
29. Slevin ML, Plant H, Lynch D, Drinkwater J, Gregory WM. Who should measure quality of life, the doctor or the patient? *Br J Cancer.* 1988;57:109–112.
30. Thunedborg K, Allerup P, Bech P, Joyce CRB. Development of the repertory grid for measurement of individual quality of life in clinical trials. *Int J Methods Psychiatry Res.* In press.
31. Thunedborg K, Allerup P, Bjerrum H, Joyce CRB, Bech P. Discrimination between treatments of generalized anxiety disorder by assessment of health related and individual patient-perceived quality of life. In preparation.
32. Karnofsky DA, Burchenal JH. The clinical evaluation of chemotherapeutic agents in cancer. In: MacLeod CM, ed. *Evaluation of Chemotherapeutic Agents.* New York: Columbia University Press;1949: pp 191–205.
33. Hyland ME, Finnis S, Irvine SH. A scale for assessing quality of life in adult asthma sufferers. *J Psychosom Res.* 1991;35:99–110.
34. Bortner RW. A short scale as a potential measure of pattern A behavior. *J Chronic Dis.* 1969;22:87–91.
35. Derogatis LR. The psychological adjustment to illness (PAIS). *J Psychosom Res.* 1986;30:77–91.
36. Watson M, Greer S, Young J, Inayat Q, Burges C, Robertson B. Development of a questionnaire measure of adjustment to cancer: The MAC scale. *Psychol Med.* 1988;18:203–209.
37. Kobasa S, Maddi SR, Kahn S. Hardiness and health: A prospective study. *J Pers Soc Psychol.* 1982;42:168–177.

38. Goldberg D. *The Detection of Psychiatric Illness by Questionnaire.* Oxford: Oxford University Press;1972.
39. Wells KB, Stewart A, Hays RD, et al. The functioning and well-being of depressed patients. Results from the medical outcomes study. *JAMA.* 1989;262:914–919.
40. Hypertension Detection and Follow-up Program Cooperation Group. The effect of treatment on mortality in "mild" hypertension: Results of the Hypertension Detection and Follow-up Program. *N Engl J Med.* 1982;307:976–980.
41. Jenkins CD, Stanton BA, Savageau JA, Denlinger P, Klein MD. Coronary artery bypass surgery: Physical, psychological, social, and economic outcomes six months later. *JAMA.* 1983;250:782–788.
42. Jogan MJ, Wallin JD, Baer RM. Antihypertensive therapy and male sexual dysfunction. *Psychosomatics.* 1980;21:234–237.
43. Wechsler D. A standardized memory scale for clinical use. *J Psychol.* 1945;17:87–95.
44. Reitan RM. *Trial Making Manual for Administration, Scoring, and Interpretation.* Indianapolis: Indiana University Medical Center;1958.
45. Derogatis LR, Spencer PM. *The Brief Symptom Inventory, Administration, Scoring Procedures.* Baltimore: Johns Hopkins University School of Medicine;1982.
46. House JS. *Work Stress and Social Support.* Reading, MA: Addison-Wesley;1981.
47. Croog SH, Levine S. *Life after a Heart Attack: Social and Psychological Factors Eight Years Later.* New York: Human Sciences Press;1982.
48. Campbell A, Converse PE, Rodgers WL. *The Quality of American Life.* New York: Russell Sage Foundation;1976.

Chapter 12
Teaching Psychosomatic Medicine: Utilizing Concurrent Perspectives

THOMAS N. WISE

Teaching psychosomatic medicine is a serious challenge in our contemporary medical environment where both time and technology are premium commodities. Time is an important variable in medical practice due to economic pressures that demand increased physician productivity. Primary care physicians average anywhere from 5 to 15 minutes per visit.[1] Concurrently technology has revolutionized the management strategies of disease so that body CT scanning is often more relevant than observation, palpation, and auscultation. In this setting emotional factors in medical care are devalued, thereby making the task of teaching psychosomatic medicine difficult. To further compound the problem, the exact nature of psychosomatic medicine itself is not clear. What are its boundaries? Early pioneers such as Alexander, Dunbar, and Groddeck suggested linear relationships between psychopathology and disease.[2] Current understanding of the interplay between psychological factors and disease causation recognizes the nonlinear multivariant relationships that characterize psychosomatic problems.[3] Furthermore, medicine is taught as an empirical discipline thereby making it difficult to emphasize the subjective nature of psychological phenomena. George Engel[4]

223

has emphasized the dichotomy between the humanism of medicine, which is considered an essential element of the profession, and the objective empiricism of the medical model. Teaching students to tolerate and understand the different logic of the subjective experience of illness versus the empirically observed signs of disease states is a pedagogic challenge.

WHAT IS THE MESSAGE
OF PSYCHOSOMATIC MEDICINE?

Psychosomatic medicine is best conceptualized as understanding health and illness from a multifactorial perspective that includes biological, psychological, and social factors.[5] This approach is the biopsychosocial model of Engel[6] and Reading.[7] Modern medicine is beginning to understand the complexity of disease causality as molecular biology illuminates biologic heterogeneity. Physicians, however, still ignore or devalue the psychosocial aspects involved in their patients' maladies. The physician treating a patient with neoplastic disease will objectify the tumor and externalize the disorder by speaking of the neoplasm in the third person, thereby minimizing the subjective suffering of the patient.[8] The essential task of psychosomatic education is integration of psychosocial issues into clinical evaluation and treatment. Unfortunately psychosomatic aspects of disease are often denigrated because psychosocial issues appear less clinically relevant; e.g., to suggest that stress necessarily causes coronary artery disease. Furthermore, psychosomatic medicine is often correlational with treatment approaches that can be ancillary to the main treatment of the disease. Recent data, however, suggests that social buffering is an important element in compliance and reoccurrence of medical disease.[9] The burden of depression and inadequate treatment of emotional disorders is increasingly documented as a serious problem. Wells et al.[10] and Hoeper et al.[11] have shown that the burden of depressed patients is greater than a variety of chronic medical illnesses. The biopsychosocial model reminds us of the need to integrate biologic, social, and psychological issues but does not clearly offer a methodology. Two important books on psychiatry offer a methodology that will help structure psychosomatic education for students at all levels of training. McHugh and Slavney[12] and Slavney and McHugh[13] elucidate the various perspectives utilized in psychiatry. This approach offers a logical and systematic method to teach psychosomatic concepts. The four perspectives important in psychiatry and psychosomatic medicine can be emphasized in consultation–liaison settings. They are the medical model, the life history method, the intersubject differences, and the role of motivated behaviors. Each of these methodologies is utilized in the rest of clinical medicine but they are rarely discussed as unique approaches to the patient. Each perspective has inherent strengths and weaknesses. The perspectives approach avoids issues and arguments about correlation versus causality in psychosomatic medicine. The first perspective, *the disease model*, is the most familiar to all physicians. Via syndromal identification, categories are developed that are reliable.[14] Research is required to demonstrate these disorders to be valid. The approach to understanding the validity of such categories via coherent course, similar response to treatment, genetic influences, and biologic causes is similar to that found in the rest of medicine. Thus the new taxonomy, whether it be DSM-IV or ICD-10, is an essential element to teach.[15] Students must understand that psychiatry does involve serious clinical assessment with rigorous diagnostic categorization that ideally will lead to pathophysiologic correlation. As better understanding of chronic fatigue syndrome evolves, the need to first define an entity and then try to understand pathologic issues can evolve. The development of the Centers for Desease Control (CDC) criteria for chronic fatigue syndrome will allow investigators to better select patients with this cluster of symptoms and signs.[16] The overlap with depression is also interesting but is as yet a "correlation" not a "cause" of this vexing clinical entity. First reliability is needed then the search for validation.

By operationally defining depression and teaching the use of rating scales, the reliability and validity of mood disorders can be emphasized to students. Unfortunately many students and physicians see depression in the medically ill as an "understandable reaction" to an illness. By focusing upon the syndromal and disease model of depression, the concept of medical comorbidity can be taught. Only then can appropriate treatment be initiated. Unfortunately a recent study by Katon et al.[17] documented that primary care physicians still undertreat depression even when such disorders are clearly identified by a psychiatrist. Other studies have indicated that rating scales are not fully appreciated by seasoned primary care physicians who tend to dismiss such data when making clinical judgments.[18, 19] The challenge for psychosomatic educators is to highlight the disease model of psychiatry as valid within medical populations such as seen in both primary care settings as well as hospital patients.

A 61-year-old man with a left hemisphere infarct was evaluated in a medical clinic for complaints of insomnia. The patient's negativism and irritability had thwarted efforts for physical rehabilitation and frustrated his wife. The medical students felt that his demoralization was understandable in view of his disability. Nevertheless the fact that he was suffering from a poststroke depression was overlooked. Treatment with nortriptyline improved his mood and facilitated rehabilitation efforts. The teacher was able to emphasize how the students' empathy after listening to the patient's narrative was essential to understand his frustration, but that consideration of the medical model was also necessary. Did this patient have a definable disease? In fact he fulfilled criteria for a DSM-IV mood disorder due to an organic factor and was treated for such. The use of multiple perspectives in such cases illuminates the psychosomatic approach in a systematic manner.

The next perspective is *the life history narrative* which is maybe the most interesting to students but often dismissed as common sense or nonscientific. In fact, Jaspers[20] and others have demonstrated that phenomenologic assessment of patients is an important and systematic methodology. By using empathic ability, the physician apprehends emotionally significant events.[21] The patient awaiting open heart surgery whose two siblings have died of similar procedures can be terrified, and such life history understanding is essential to manage such patients. Nevertheless patients may also have a definable psychiatric disorder.

An 80-year-old man was seen due to persistent anxiety following recurrent defibrillation from an implanted ventricular defibrillator. It was initially assumed that he had developed such anxiety from the expectation that he would experience the uncomfortable physical "shock" following the electrical pacing. Careful evaluation revealed that he was a remarkably alert man who had previously experienced a cardiac arrest prior to his defibrillator implant. He thought that each defibrillation was a similar arrest and he was terrified that he experience a minideath at each "shock." When the physicians clarified this misconception his anxiety disappeared and he tolerated the physical discomfort of subsequent pacing.

Thus the "meaning" of phenomena can only be gleaned by careful interviewing that focuses upon the unique meaning of events to the individual. This is the essential strength of the life history method. The understanding of patients' life histories and the connection with their present emotional status illuminates our understanding of patients but does not confidently allow us to say that there is a "causal connection" as in the medical model. Nevertheless it must be constantly emphasized that failure to understand a patient's life history will result in noncompliance, anxiety depression, and potential difficulties in the patient's mortality and morbidity.

The next perspective of *intersubject differences* is easy for students to understand if the teacher can illustrate that the dimensional approach to blood pressure or a laboratory value for blood urea nitrogen is similar to the dimensional approach of intelligence, height, weight, or dimensions of personality. Thus intersubject differences easily lend themselves to teaching of personality. Individuals may be classified as more or less prone to anxiety and depression, i.e., neuroticism or more or less outgoing, i.e., extraverted.[22] Such dimensions of personality are essential in managing patients. Allowing medical students to utilize simple personality questionnaires such as the Eysenck Personality Inventory on medical patients will further demonstrate the utility of such understanding of personality.[23] Understanding the clinical management of such personality styles is essential.[24] To demonstrate the need for the obsessional patient to have information and control exemplifies the use of such a perspective. Finally the concept of *motivated behaviors* helps to demonstrate why the study of substance abuse, eating disorders, and sleep disorders may be important in managing patients in any

medical specialty. Goal direct behavior to reduce tension via ingesting potentially addicting substances whether alcohol or morphine
needs to be an ever present area of concern to all physicians.

Such perspectives seem simplistic but provide a clear model that
includes biologic, psychological, and social areas. They provide a
logic that recognizes both strengths and weaknesses of each approach. Thus psychosomatic medicine is an "approach" to clinical
medicine more than to a specific group of diseases. Questions still
remain. Is it necessary to partition psychosomatic diseases from the
concept of psychological factors in health and disease? Should psychosomatic training focus upon causal aspects of a disease or should
it emphasize the inherent psychosocial aspects issues surrounding
an illness such as quality of life, reaction to illness, problems with
medicine compliance, and comorbid conditions that affect course
and cost of an illness? The introduction of behavioral medicine and
health psychology challenges the psychosomatic model since psychiatric pathology is often ignored. Psychosomatic medicine is not
a recognized specialty in North America. Fortunately consultation–
liaison psychiatry has become the clinical derivative of psychosomatic
medicine. The consultation–liaison psychiatrist is most often the
messenger of the biopsychosocial approach, while family practitioners and general internists have increasingly taught this approach.

A 34-year-old woman was evaluated due to complaints of fatigue, depression, difficulty in sleeping, and the belief that she had an immune deficiency that was part of a chronic fatigue syndrome. The patient had recently
seen a variety of physicians, one of whom had told her that she had a systemic yeast infection and began treating her with a variety of unorthodox
approaches including daily coffee ground enemas. The patient's husband
demanded she seek further evaluation and she was hospitalized on a medical service. The patient's history revealed her to be a very intelligent woman
whose professional career was interrupted by the birth of a son 4 years before. The patient admitted she was ambivalent about having a child but due
to her husband's wishes gave up her career and subsequently moved from
an urban setting to a suburb which would be easier for the child. Prior history revealed her to have been a worrier who felt vulnerable to a variety of ills
and tended to be depressed. Medical evaluation revealed no systemic disorders and there was no evidence that she had an autoimmune abnormality or
a systemic infection. The patient was presented in consultation–liaison

rounds to demonstrate how an individual's abnormal illness beliefs could be transformed into the fixed belief that she had chronic fatigue syndrome, although she did not fulfill the operational criteria that the CDC has established. Using a medical model, the patient categorically qualified for a major mood disorder. Her life history narrative revealed her professional life to have been in conflict with her role as a mother and wife. Such a conflict concurs with Abbey and Garfinkle's[25] recent discussion of chronic fatigue syndrome to represent a health metaphor for contemporary role conflicts of women. She meaningfully connected her anger at having to move to a suburb and avoiding the city life which she loved. Her personality was high in neuroticism and gave her a tendency to worry, be depressed, and feel vulnerable and self-conscious. She demonstrated no motivated behaviors because she did not have a drug or alcohol history, but did have a sleep disorder that was part of her depressive syndrome. The patient readily admitted she was depressed but did not fully give up the idea that she had an immune deficiency. Thus, she persisted in her illness beliefs. Vigorous treatment for her depression, however, focusing upon the sleep disorder and her energy level yielded some improvements. Ongoing therapy was directed toward trying to get her to resolve some of her conflicts about work versus mothering.

This case demonstrates the utility of the perspectives and its need to think of a multivariant course of illness that could be labeled *psychosomatic.* Although this patient did not have a miraculous recovery, she was described in an understandable and systematic manner which allowed physicians to have a rational treatment approach. Perspectivism offers such a structure and is a useful vehicle for teaching physicians at all levels of education.

WHO ARE THE STUDENTS?

Psychosomatic education in North America is primarily in the form of consultation–liaison psychiatry which suggests that psychosomatic medicine on this continent is basically a psychiatric discipline, taught by psychiatrists. Undergraduate medical students are often recipients of this education. There are two basic goals in teaching undergraduate medical students.[26] The first is to impart knowledge about basic psychiatric syndromes that include the major psychoses, both functional and organic, as well as the role of character disorders and other psychiatric categories. Students must understand basic concepts of psychiatric diagnosis and treatment. The consultation psychiatrist can teach such basic constructs in a clinical arena that is generalizable to students who will not enter psychiatry. A second element is that of imparting the need for psychosocial variables in the practice of other medical disciplines. Demonstrating depression in the medically ill can be done in such settings. This pedagogic task is difficult because medical students are faced with a bewildering array of scientific data as modern medicine becomes more focused upon molecular biology with the vast array of treatments that have evolved from such knowledge. The second cohort of individuals who are consumers of such education include residents in both psychiatry and other medical disciplines. Both of these groups need to understand the multivariant approach to disease. Unfortunately they are often focused upon other tasks such as learning the skills of their specialty, whether it be surgery or long-term psychotherapy. The final group of individuals who are often targets for consultation–liaison psychiatry are practicing physicians. Such individuals are more receptive to the psychosomatic message because they have seen the effects of psychosocial pathology within their patient populations. It is the task both of the educator as well as the psychiatric practitioner to develop proper role models for educating such mature physicians. The message must be practical and nondemeaning. Thus at every level of educational progress the consultation–liaison psychiatrist must impart data that is coherent and relevant.

There exists a variety of resistances that interfere with acceptance of psychosocial education.[27] The consultation–liaison psychiatrist should understand the various critiques that have arisen regarding psychiatrists. These include fears that patients may get angry if referred to a psychiatrist, the spectra of stigmatization, the issue of excessive cost, prior bad experiences, and poor communication with psychiatrists.[28] The fears that patients will not accept psychiatric referral and view it as a punishment of stigma must be discussed. Prior difficult experiences with psychiatrists should also be understood as a common problem in teaching psychiatry. Fear of therapeutic control and issues of cost must also be understood.[29] Steinberg et al.[30] have directly confronted physicians in such resistances and found that this is an effective way to enhance both referral rates but also demonstrate the utility of psychiatric consultation. Physicians' inherent discomfort with psychopathology may arouse dysphoric uncomfortable emotions within themselves or harks back to earlier personal memories. Another common complaint is the devaluation of psychiatry as a soft discipline not like "real medicine." Each of these resistances must be directly confronted. Psychiatry has abetted such criticisms by isolating itself in separate institutions. The use of consultation psychiatry as a primary vehicle for education avoids such isolation. The individual consultation note can be an effective didactic tool, but must be regularly repeated.[31] This demands that the consultation psychiatrist be practical and available.

LOCUS OF TRAINING

There are a variety of sites available for teaching psychosomatic medicine. The traditional forum has been the medical–surgical hospital ward.[32] Such units can be mixed or specialized for a specific population such as a burn unit, cardiovascular program, intensive care, or oncology cohort. Such settings allow for students to observe psychiatric consultations as well as liaison endeavors. The general medical setting is useful to demonstrate acute psychological problems caused by or a reaction to physical illness. Unfortunately problems not clearly identified as psychiatric may be missed if referrals are restricted to obviously identified psychiatric populations. This has been referred to as the "numerator problem" in that the "denominator," i.e., all patients on a ward are not accessible for evaluation. Liaison psychiatry has been offered as a solution but its funding and implementation have been difficult.[33] Another arena is the psychosomatic unit. This setting has been described by Freyberger et al.[34] and Kohle.[35] These units treat patients denoted as suffering from psychosomatic disorders and in Hannover utilize student therapists as health care providers. Developing an inpatient psychosomatic unit is difficult in North America because of the ambiguity of what patients should be admitted. Instead the med-psych unit also provides an excellent arena for combined medical and psychiatric problems.[36] The medical psychiatric unit offers a variety of advantages for such training and can evolve into both an inpatient and ambulatory setting. In such settings, clinical phenomena such as chronic pain, abnormal illness behaviors, and classic psychosomatic disorders can be managed. Another setting which is becoming increasingly popular has been the specialized ambulatory medical clinic.[37] The primary care ambulatory clinic is an excellent setting to see somatization problems in particular hypochondriacal states as described by Barsky et al.,[38] which are rarely referred to a formal psychiatric setting. A final arena that has not been fully utilized in teaching psychosocial aspects of medical disorders is the emergency room.[39] Whether dealing with the suicidal patient, the somatizing patient who seeks emergency care for a fundamental psychiatric issue or the effects upon family of acute trauma, the emergency room arena is a remarkable vehicle for teaching psychiatry. Previous studies have indicated a low recognition rate of both depression and organic disorders in the emergency services. The use of emergency rooms for such education is difficult since scheduling is unpredictable. There are advantages and disadvantages to each of these settings.

Conclusion

In summary, psychosomatic education is best conceptualized as the role of consultation–liaison psychiatry in teaching the importance of psychosocial variables in medical practice to students and physicians at various stages of their careers. The biopsychosocial approach of Engel reminds us of such variables whereas perspectivism allows us to logically partition these perspectives with the inherent grammar and logic of each. By understanding the psychiatric taxonomy the medical model in psychiatry is reified; i.e., "what" disorder does the patient have. The life history method is essential to understanding "who" each patient is; i.e., a unique subjective individual. Intersubject differences offer a method to teach personality differences whereas the role of behavior and motivated behaviors to reduce tension helps explain why some patients seek addicting substances to reduce painful dysphoric states.

The use of perspectives demystifies both psychosomatics and biopsychosocial constructs. Each perspective requires a logic and grammar that must be taught by a trained physician. It directly confronts the devaluation of critics who feel that the psychosocial elements within patient care are either merely common sense or less important. The noncompliant patients may be so depressed that they feel taking antihypertensive medication is worthless or so fearful due to a previous event in their life that they do not comply. Only by careful assessment can patients be evaluated. By careful elucidation the various perspectives that comprise both psychiatry and psychosomatic medicine can this essential discipline be taught.

ACKNOWLEDGMENTS

The author gratefully acknowledges the seminal ideas and support of Drs. Phillip R. Slavney and Paul R. McHugh.

REFERENCES

1. Hannay D, Usherwood T, Platts U. Workload of general practitioners before and after the new contract. *Br Med J.* 1992;304:615–618.
2. Lipowski ZJ. Psychosomatic concepts in historical perspective. In: Lacey JD, Sturgeon DA, eds. *Proc 15th Eur Conf Psychosom Res.* London: Libbey;1986: pp 1–5.

3. Weiner H. *Psychobiology and Human Disease.* New York: Elsevier;1977.
4. Engel GL. Physician-scientists and scientific physicians resolving the humanism-science dichotomy. *Am J Med.* 1987;82:107–111.
5. Lipowski ZJ. Psychosomatic medicine in the seventies. *Am J Psychiatry.* 1977;134: 233–244.
6. Engel GL. The need for a new medical model: A challenge for biomedicine. *Science.* 1977;196:129–136.
7. Reading AJ. Illness and disease. *Med Clin North Am.* 1977;61:703–710.
8. Wise TN. The physician and his patient with cancer. *Primary Care.* 1974;1:373–382.
9. Case RB, Moss AJ, Case N, McDermott M, Eberley S. Living alone and the risk for recurrence of a cardiac event. *JAMA.* 1992;267:515–519.
10. Wells KB, Stuart A, Hays RD, Burman MA, Rogers W, Daniels M, Berry S, Greenfield S, Ware J. The functioning and well-being of depressed patients. *JAMA.* 1989;262:914–1919.
11. Hoeper EW, Nycz GR, Kessler LG, Burke JB, Pierce WE. The usefulness of screening for mental illness. *Lancet.* 1984;i:33–35.
12. McHugh PR, Slavney PR. *The Perspectives of Psychiatry.* Baltimore: Johns Hopkins University Press;1986.
13. Slavney PR, McHugh PR. *Psychiatric Polarities.* Baltimore: Johns Hopkins University Press;1987.
14. Robins E, Guze SB. Establishment of diagnostic validity in psychiatric illness. *Am J Psychiatry.* 1970;126:107–111.
15. American Psychiatric Association. *Diagnostic and Statistical Manual and Mental Disorders.* 3rd ed. rev. Washington, DC: American Psychiatric Press;1987.
16. Holmes GP, Kaplan JE, Gantz NM, Komaroff AL, Schonberger LB, Straus SE, Jones JF, Dubois RE, Cunningham-Rundles C, Pahwa S, Tosato G, Zegans LS, Purtilo DT, Brown N, Schooley RT, Brus I. Chronic fatigue syndrome, a working case definition. *Ann Intern Med.* 1988;108:387–389.
17. Katon W, von Korff M, Lin E, Bush T, Ormel J. Adequacy and duration of antidepressant treatment in primary care. *Med Care.* 1992;30:67–76.
18. Moore JT, Simimperi DR, Bobula JA. Recognition of depression by family medicine residents. The impact of screening. *J Fam Pract.* 1978;7:509–516.
19. Shapiro S, German PS, Skinner EA, von Korff M, Turner RW, Klein LE, Teitelbaum ML, Kramer M, Burke JD, Burns BJ. An experiment to change detection and management of mental morbidity in primary care. *Med Care.* 1987;25:327–336.
20. Jaspers K. *General Psychopathology.* Chicago: University of Chicago Press;1972: pp 301–363.
21. Slavney PR, McHugh PR. Life stories and meaningful connections: Reflections on a clinical method in psychiatry and medicine. *Perspect Biol Med.* 1984;27:279–288.
22. Costa PT, McCrae RR. Neuroticism, somatic complaints, and disease: Is the bark worse than the bite? *J Pers.* 1987;55:299–316.
23. Eysenck HJ, Eysenck SB. *Manual of the Eysenck Personality Inventory.* London: London University Press;1964.
24. Kahana RJ, Bibring GL. Personality types in medical management. In: Zinberg NE, ed. *Psychiatry and Medical Practice in a General Hospital.* New York: International Universities Press;1964: pp 108–123.

25. Abbey SE, Garfinkle PE. Neurasthenia and chronic fatigue syndrome: The role of culture in the making of a diagnosis. *Am J Psychiatry.* 1991;148:1638–1646.

26. O'Shanick GJ, Levenson JL, Wise TN. The general hospital as a center of biopsychosocial training. *Gen Hosp. Psychiatry.* 1986;8:365–371.

27. Wise TN, Mann LS, Berlin RM, Berenbaum I. Mental health referral patterns by family medicine educators. *Compr Psychiatry.* 1984;25:465–469.

28. Mezey AG, Kellett JM. Reasons against referral to the psychiatrist. *Postgrad Med J.* 1967;47:315–319.

29. Hull J. Community phyiscans. Perceptions of their role in treating psychiatric disorders. *Int J Psychiatry Med.* 1980/81;10:9–21.

30. Steinberg H, Torem M, Saravay SM. The analysis of physician resistance to psychiatric consultation. *Arch Gen Psychiatry.* 1980;37:1007–1012.

31. Garrick TR, Stotland NL. How to write a psychiatric consultation. *Am J Psychiatry.* 1982;139:849–855.

32. Gomez J. *Liaison Psychiatry.* New York: Free Press;1987.

33. Levitan SJ, Komfeld DS. Clinical and cost benefits of liaison psychiatry. *Psychiatry.* 1981;138:790–793.

34. Freyberger H, Nordmeyer J, Klunsebeck HW, Lempa W, Avenarius JH, Wellmann W, Liedtke R, Schlol R. Clinical and educational activities of a psychosomatic division. *Adv Psychosom Med.* 1983;11:166–175.

35. Kohle K. The psychosomatic unit. *Adv Psychosom Med.* 1983,11:176–190.

36. Fava GA, Wise TN, Molnar G, Zielezny M. The medical psychiatric unit: A novel psychosomatic approach. *Psychother Psychosom.* 1985;43:194–201.

37. Epstein SA, Gonzales JJ. Outpatient consultation–liaison psychiatry: A valuable addition to the training of advanced psychiatry residents. *Proc 38th Annu Meet Acad Psychosom Med.* 1991; p 46.

38. Barsky AJ, Wyshak G, Klermon GL. Transient hypochondriasis. *Arch Gen Psychiatry.* 1990;47:746–752.

39. Litovitz GL, Hedberg M, Wise TN, White JD, Mann LS. Recognition of psychological and cognitive impairments in the emergency department. *Am J Emer Med.* 1985;3:400–402.

Part II

Clinical Issues

Chapter 13
Psychosocial Factors
in Gastrointestinal Illness

BARRIE R. CASSILETH, DOUGLAS A. DROSSMAN

Gastroenterologists have long recognized the role of psychosocial factors in their patients' disorders. In the past decade, research has supported this clinical impression, and the links among physiologic systems that enable reciprocal interactions among psychosocial and organic processes have been documented. Gastrointestinal (GI) disorders represent a paradigm of psychosomatic medicine. This chapter is devoted to that paradigm. It explores the interconnected nature of psychosocial factors and gastrointestinal function, disease and outcome.

CONCEPTUAL PERSPECTIVE

A model or construct of disease is not just a theoretical abstraction of philosophical interest. Indeed, it is instead the very foundation on which illness is understood and medicine practiced. A change in the commonly accepted model produces analogous changes in clinical assumptions and patient care.

For the past century, the traditional understanding of illness and disease in Western civilization has been the *biomedical model*.[1] Its major premise is that any illness can be reduced to a single cause, and that identifying and modifying that etiologic agent will explain the cause, and ultimately produce a cure. The model also incorporates the Cartesian view that illness is either an "organic" disorder with an objectively defined pathophysiology, or a "functional" disorder, with no specifically identifiable pathophysiology. This dualism enforces a distinction between medical or organic illnesses, versus psychologic or functional illnesses.

This biomedical, Cartesian perspective is inconsistent not only with the experience of gastroenterologists, but also with the clinical experience of internists generally, where failure to find a specific diagnosis is more common than not. In a study of 1000 internal medicine patients,[2] for example, only 16% of 567 new complaints were attributable eventually to an organic cause, and an additional 10% were given psychiatric diagnoses. Further, patients who received psychiatric or nonorganic (functional) diagnoses did not benefit from standard symptomatic treatment.

Such results are familiar in gastroenterology. Over 40% of patients have functional diagnoses,[3] and patients commonly complain of symptoms such as abdominal cramps and loose stools that have coexisting organic (e.g., inflammatory bowel disease) and functional (e.g., irritable bowel) etiologies.[4] Further, GI diseases result from the interaction of several factors. Finally, the presence of a functional GI disorder does not necessarily define psychopathology any more than a documented organic GI disorder automatically excludes such an association.[5]

These factors, and their analogs in other medical subspecialties, show that the biomedical model does not fully explain the known realities of illness. A more appropriate construct, the biopsychosocial model of illness,[6, 7] increasingly has come to replace the older construct. This model incorporates the reality of mutual interaction not only among bodily systems (genetic, endocrinological, neural, psychosocial, immunological), but also across levels of systems—from the subcellular through the environmental.

The biopsychosocial or systems model allows illness to be viewed as a result of interacting systems at the cellular, tissue, organismal, interpersonal, and environmental levels.[7-9] A subcellular level change, for example, such as the development of AIDS, now can be understood for its potential to affect organ function, the person, the family, and society. Similarly, a change at the interpersonal level, such as the death of a spouse, can affect psychologic status, midbrain function, cellular immunity, and, ultimately, disease susceptibility.

With this approach, biological and behavioral processes operate simultaneously, thus explaining why biological factors such as oncogene alteration can vary in clinical expression and produce different biological responses, illness experiences, and reactions to treatment.

External Stress and GI Physiology

The interaction between "stress"[10] and GI function has peppered the literature for centuries,[11, 12] and is supported by clinical observations[13] as well as laboratory studies. For example, small doses of thyrotropin-releasing hormone (TRH) injected into nuclei of the hypothalamus and brainstem of laboratory animals produce gastric secretion and motility via the vagus nerve.[14] The reciprocal relationship between TRH and other local peptides appears to modulate the development of gastroduodenal ulcers.[15] A clinical relationship between mood changes and altered gastric physiology and ulcers is further supported by reports of increased CNS levels of TRH in patients with depression.[13, 16, 17] Similar effects occur in other areas of the GI tract.[18–20]

Reciprocal effects from gut to brain also have been demonstrated. These effects are enabled by the richly innervated nerve plexes and neuroendocrine associations of the enteric nervous system, and its connections with the spinal, autonomic and CNS.[21] Through neural connections, extrinsic or enteroceptive (including mental) information can affect GI secretion and motility. These viscerotropic effects reciprocate by influencing pain perception, mood, and other mental functions.[22]

The bidirectional nature of these processes explains the presence of abnormalities in afferent sensation as well as motor function in the functional GI disorders.[23, 24] Disturbances in the function of any subsystem can lead to a variety of brain–gut system effects including altered pain sensation, dysmotility, and mood disturbance.

Modulation of the brain–gut system also occurs via neurotransmitters such as vasoactive intestinal polypeptide, TRH, 5-hydroxytryptamine and its congeners, substance P, cholecystokinin, the enkephalins, and so on. These substances act variously on GI function and human behavior depending upon their location.[25–28] Interactions such as these, through documentation of relevant pathways, lay the groundwork for consideration of clinical concerns.

PSYCHOSOCIAL FACTORS
AND THE DEVELOPMENT OF GI ILLNESS

Although methodologically adequate data are yet to come, observations suggest that conditioning experiences may influence physiological functioning and, possibly, the development of psychophysiologic disorders. Visceral functions such as the secretion of digestive juices and motility of the gallbladder, stomach, and intestine, can be classically conditioned.[29]

Because abstract rewards such as gaining approval or attention are positive reinforcers, family interactions have the potential to modify GI physiology. For example, consider the child who awakens on the day of a dreaded examination with anxiety and "flight–fight" symptoms of tachycardia, diaphoresis, abdominal cramps, and diarrhea. The parent keeps the child home because of a stomachache, allowing him to stay in bed and watch TV. Days later, as the child is about to leave for school, the symptoms recur.

The patient's interpretation of the abdominal discomfort as an illness requiring school absence allowed the child to avoid the feared situation. Repetition of this pattern favors the development of similar symptoms in future distressing circumstances.[30] Such conditioning experiences during childhood may encourage a predilection to develop a psychophysiologic reaction, and may also influence the person's attitudes and behaviors toward illness.[31]

A related question is whether there are specific personality types associated with gastroenterologic disease. Research supports a role for psychological disturbance, in the presence of relevant biological predispositions, as a conditional stressor in the exacerbation of disease. However, the concept of a disease-specific personality has not been confirmed. Contemporary research and understanding of the multifactorial etiology of disease suggest that such a notion probably is overly simplistic.

Mixed results describe research on stressful life events as contributing to the development of GI disease in humans and other animals. Colitis in the cotton-topped tamarin may be related to the change from freedom to captivity,[32] and increased prevalence of peptic ulcer disease was found in the early 1970s for people working at the high pressured job of air traffic controller.[33]

The results of more recent studies are ambivalent. A positive association between life stress and clinical presentation was reported for duodenal ulcer patients in one investigation,[34] but in another, ulcer patients and controls showed similar numbers of negative life events, although patients perceived their events to be more negative.[16] Data are similarly at odds for inflammatory bowel disease.[35–37]

An explanation for the mixed results may lie with the growing evidence that peptic ulcer, as an example, is a heterogeneous disorder with multiple biologic predispositions that interact in various combinations. Contributing factors include genetic susceptibility, *Helicobacter pylori* infection,[38] cigarette smoking, and nonsteroidal analgesic use, to name a few. On this basis, the role of psychosocial factors in the etiology of peptic ulcer disease, by definition, would be limited or minor.

Analogous research on the genetic front challenges the idea of a strong role for psychosocial factors in at least some colorectal cancers: People who inherit a mutant APC gene have nearly a 100%

probability of developing colon cancer.[39, 40] Since 1989, growing evidence indicates that the mutated p53 gene is central to the development of cancers not only of the colon, but also of the breast, brain, kidney, and bone,[41, 42] suggesting a more modest role for psychosocial factors in the etiology of cancer than has been proposed. Overall, there is no unifiable role for psychosocial factors across GI illnesses, although they may play a role in the timing or severity of symptom onset, or in the patient's response to illness.

FUNCTIONAL GI DISORDERS

Psychosocial components are more clearly evident in the functional GI disorders, for which diagnostic criteria recently were developed.[43] Patients with functional GI disturbances describe a wide variety of symptoms affecting regions of the entire GI tract, as indicated below in Table 13.1. The irritable bowel syndrome, functional dyspepsia, and chronic abdominal pain comprise the functional GI illnesses of greatest concern to physicians. These disorders are of special interest because they are difficult to treat. Patients can present with idiosyncratic problems and with variable degrees of concurrent psychosocial disturbance, depending on clinical circumstances.

The discussion that follows addresses chronic functional abdominal pain as a prototypic functional GI disorder. Although it is relatively uncommon even in the gastroenterologist's office, issues surrounding functional abdominal pain are relevant to the other functional disorders as well. Further discussion can be found elsewhere for the irritable bowel syndrome[44] and for functional dyspepsia.[45]

Common behavioral features typically characterize patients with chronic functional abdominal pain.[46] These include the patient's presentation of symptoms urgently and intently; conflicting pain behaviors (e.g., stoic yet dependent) as the illness becomes the focus of life for the patient; no explanatory medical diagnosis

TABLE 13.1
Functional Gastrointestinal Disorders

Functional esophageal disorders
  Globus
  Rumination syndrome
  Functional chest pain of presumed esophageal origin
  Functional heartburn
  Functional dysphagia
  Unspecified functional esophageal disorder
Functional gastroduodenal disorders
  Functional dyspepsia
    Ulcer-like dyspepsia
    Motility-like dyspepsia
    Unspecified functional dyspepsia
  Aerophagia
Functional bowel disorders
  Irritable bowel syndrome
  Functional constipation
  Functional diarrhea
  Burbulence
  Unspecified functional bowel disorder
Chronic functional abdominal pain
Functional biliary pain
  Sphincter of Oddi dyskinesia
Functional anorectal symptoms
  Functional incontinence
  Functional anorectal pain
    Levator syndrome
    Proctalgia fugax
  Pelvic floor dyssenergia
  Unspecified functional anorectal disorder

following numerous visits and tests; narcotic dependency; and a history of psychosocial trauma.

Chronic functional abdominal pain is best understood within the biopsychosocial framework. This illness then can be seen in terms of interactions among biologic and psychosocial factors, all of which require attention in the treatment process. In chronic pain, tissue pathology is unlikely and signs of autonomic arousal associated with acute pain do not occur. Although patients with this disorder tend to minimize a role for psychosocial factors, they typically have a history of unresolved loss, emotional trauma, and disrupted social support. There is also high incidence of comorbid psychiatric disorder among patients with chronic functional abdominal pain.[46]

COPING AND REACTION TO GI DISEASE

Among gastroenterologic patients as a group, psychological reactions range widely from normal to disabling. Similarly, psychological disturbances vary in etiology and severity from mild, transient difficulties, to medical illnesses that are amenable to support and reassurance, to primary psychiatric diagnoses. Because psychiatric illness in the medical setting is common,[47] and because it aggravates medical disease, the identification and treatment of psychiatric comorbidity is clinically important.

Once any disease is experienced as illness, the patient responds psychologically. The perception that one is ill is accompanied by emotional reactions that vary across and within patients. Impairment in health-related quality of life—a global construct that includes the patient's perceptions, illness experience, and functional status[48]—and the adaptations required of patients with chronic disease are considerable.

The meaning of illness, the perceived alterations in body image such as occur with colostomy, social acceptability, the degree of functional impairment and its implications in terms of future function at work and at home, and the likelihood of surgery or untimely death, must all be managed by the patient. It is therefore, not surprising that patients with inflammatory bowel disease, for example, experience greater impairment of psychosocial than physical function.[48] Predominant disturbances occur in work, sleep and rest, recreation, social interaction, and emotional state.

How the patient adapts, and the physician's assistance in achieving adaptation can be crucial to the patient's psychologic well-being and clinical course. It is not surprising that some chronically ill patients regress and behave dependently. The continued symptoms, restrictions in activity, and caretaking that patients must undergo may tax family, friends, and physicians as well, all of whom may feel helpless and unable to provide adequate emotional or medical assistance.

Conversely, some patients resist the help of others to avoid acknowledging their imposed dependence. The family must deal with feelings of guilt and anger, the expressions of which, although possibly unavoidable, are usually socially unacceptable. It is often the physician who bears not only the brunt of such feelings in the patient and family, but also the burden of reconciling difficulties among the various parties.

In most instances, problems resolved and the patient establishes a pattern of coping, typically reverting to previous coping styles. However, if the individual has limited capacity to cope, if the disorder is particularly incapacitating, or if the interpersonal family relationships remain unstable, more physician and ancillary effort are required to achieve satisfactory adjustment. Ancillary assistance is available through social work or social service agencies, psychologic counseling, and peer support groups.

EFFECTS ON CLINICAL OUTCOME

Psychosocial factors contribute not only to the experience of disease as illness and to subsequent illness behaviors, but also, ultimately, to clinical outcome. Outcome comprises the patient's general well-being and daily function, or health related quality of life; symptom severity; health care use including physician visits, hospitalizations and surgeries; and the course of the disease and its possible complications. In keeping with a biopsychosocial or systems model, outcomes may have reciprocal effects on preceding determinants.

An outcome measure relevant to clinicians is the frequency of health care visits. Although a higher frequency of visits is associated with greater disease activity or physiological dysfunction, studies now show that psychological distress and psychosocial disturbance also and independently influence the seeking of health care in gastrointestinal illness.[5, 47, 49]

In addition, the seeking of health care per se may be associated with psychological difficulties. In a study of 767 high utilizers of health care at a health maintenance organization medical clinic in Seattle,[50] major depression or dysthymic disorder was seen in 40%, generalized anxiety disorder in 22%, and somatization disorder in 20%. For most patients, identification of these formal psychiatric diagnoses led to improved treatment.

The effect of a history of physical or sexual abuse on health status measures recently was examined among female gastroenterology outpatients at a university medical center.[51]

A history of abuse was reported in 44% of the sample: 53% for functional diagnoses, 37% for organic diagnoses. This history was known by treating physicians in only 17% of patients. After controlling for medical diagnosis and background variables, patients with a history of abuse, compared to those who did not reveal abuse, reported more frequent abdominal pain, a history of pelvic pain, more nonabdominal symptoms such as headache and fatigue, and more lifetime surgeries. The seemingly high frequency of abuse reported in this population may relate to the nature of a university gastroenterology practice where many patients with refractory illness are referred.[51]

These data suggest that the severity or activity of gastrointestinal disease is not always sufficient to explain patients' health status and health outcome. It is clinically relevant for physicians to seek out and attend to possible contributing psychosocial factors. This is particularly important for patients with unexplained, severe, or refractory GI symptoms and a high health care use rate, for whom medical plus psychologic or psychopharmacologic treatment will improve clinical outcome.

CLINICAL APPLICATIONS

Despite uncertainty regarding the degree to which psychosocial processes affect disease onset, activity, and complications, the pathophysiologic substrate for this association clearly exists. More clearly documented is the influence of psychosocial factors on GI dysfunction and on the experience and psychosocial consequences of illness. Data in support of these influences are more than sufficient to justify the need for physicians to skillfully obtain, organize, and integrate psychosocial information in order to provide optimal patient care.

Recommendations concerning psychosocial diagnosis and care of patients with GI complaints are discussed below. These suggestions are particularly relevant for patients with chronic illness or predominant psychosocial difficulties. A more comprehensive discussion is found elsewhere.[52]

OBTAINING INFORMATION FROM THE PATIENT

The physician's dialogue with the patient is the most important asset to diagnosis, treatment, and the ensuing physician–patient relationship. Unfortunately, this clinical skill often is underdeveloped or underutilized. The medical history is best obtained through a patient-centered, nondirective interview, in which the patient is encouraged to tell the story in his or her own way so that the events contributing to the illness unfold naturally.[53] Open-ended questions are best avoided initially as a means of generating hypotheses, and additional information should be obtained with use of facilitating expressions, such as, "Can you tell me more?" or by repeating the patient's previous statements, head nodding, or silent pauses with an expectant look.

Closed-ended (yes-no) questions are appropriate only later to further characterize the symptoms. Multiple choice or leading questions also should be avoided initially because the patient's desire to comply may bias the responses. The traditional "medical" and "social" histories should be elicited together, so that the medical problem can be described in its psychosocial context.

Information about the setting of symptom onset or exacerbation should be obtained. Questions should communicate the physician's interest and willingness to address both biologic and psychologic aspects of the illness. The interview approach also encourages patient self-awareness, and it may suggest a need for behavioral interventions such as stress reduction techniques or counseling, to ameliorate symptom flare-ups in the future.

Historical information should be obtained from the perspective of the patient's understanding of the illness. Important questions to ask include, "What do you think is causing this problem?"; "Why did it happen now?"; "What kind of treatment do you think you should receive?" and "What do you fear most about your illness?"[54]

EVALUATION AND DIAGNOSIS

The relative influence of biologic, psychologic, and social dimensions on the illness must be assessed in order to develop a good diagnostic and treatment plan. Both medical and psychologic hypotheses should be considered. It is just as inappropriate (and possibly harmful) to subject a patient with "functional" illness to unneeded diagnostic studies while failing to explore psychologic determinants, as it is to obtain a psychiatric consultation in a patient presenting with fulminant colitis and toxic megacolon. A negative medical evaluation is not sufficient for making a psychosocial diagnosis.

To establish a diagnosis, additional studies may be needed. Deciding which tests to order requires considering their usefulness within the clinical context. Is it safe? Cost-effective? Will the results make a difference in treatment? Patients who are persistent in their complaints or who challenge the physician's competence may tempt the physician to schedule unneeded studies or surgery out of uncertainty, or just to "do something." This behavior has been called "furor medicus."[55] It can be avoided by basing decisions on careful and objective evaluation of data, such as blood in the stool, fever, and abnormal serum chemistries, rather than solely on the patient's illness behavior.

Patients with persistent, unexplained abdominal pain are familiar to gastroenterologists. One may be tempted to continue testing to pursue the search for structural disease. However, studies of patients with chronic unexplained abdominal pain indicate that, given adequate initial evaluation, the likelihood of finding an overlooked etiology is exceedingly low.[56] In such instances, the appropriate clinical goal is not medical diagnosis, but psychosocial assessment plus treatment of the chronic pain.

There are several factors known to be associated with chronic pain symptoms. These include: (1) a recent disruption in the family or social environment, such as a child leaving home; (2) a major loss or anniversary of a loss; (3) a history of sexual or physical abuse; (4) the onset or worsening of depression or other psychiatric diagnosis; and (5) a "hidden agenda," such as narcotic seeking behavior, laxative abuse, pending litigation or disability. Eliciting information about any of these factors may help in planning treatment. Although psychiatric consultation and treatment may be needed, it is also important for the physician to continue follow-up care and to remain vigilant to the possible development of new findings.

ESTABLISH A THERAPEUTIC RELATIONSHIP

A therapeutic relationship is accomplished when the physician validates the patient's beliefs, concerns, and expectations; offers empathy, clarification of misunderstandings, and education; and negotiates with the patient to plan treatment.[53] The strategy for accomplishing these goals must be individualized because patients vary in the degree of negotiation and participation they prefer. In all cases, the physician should be nonjudgmental and show interest in the patient's well-being regardless of cause.

When the patient is unwilling or unable to accept the role of psychosocial factors in illness, the physician can still obtain such information indirectly, by inference, and should not attempt to provide the patient with "insight." If asked whether the problem is "in my head," the physician can explain that illness is rarely one or the other, and that it is important to understand all factors, including the patient's feelings. The physician may indicate that many chronic conditions can be associated with depression or unrealistic fears.

TREAT WITH REASSURANCE AND UNDERSTANDING OF PATIENT NEEDS

Patients with fears or concerns need to be reassured. However, premature or inappropriate reassurance will be perceived by patients as insincere, or as a lack of thoroughness on the part of the physician. Although physicians should respond to the patient's needs and requests with empathy, patients' requests should be pursued only when that is in the patient's best interests. For example, disability is a disincentive to helping the patient reestablish "wellness" and return to gainful employment. If the patient does not qualify for disability, this should be stated clearly and firmly.

Illness is associated with certain benefits, including increased attention and support, release from usual responsibilities, and possibly social and financial compensation. For some patients more may be lost than gained by giving up the state of illness. The physician must accept that clinical improvement in these situations may take a long time, but may be advanced if help is also directed toward improving the psychosocial concomitants of the illness, such as improving coping strategies.

Reinforce Healthy Behaviors

Particularly for patients with abnormal illness behaviors, a focus on symptoms and suffering can be used as an attention-seeking device. The physician unwittingly may reinforce these behaviors by attending to patient complaints to the exclusion of other issues, acting on each complaint by ordering diagnostic studies or prescribing medication, or by assuming total responsibility for the patient's well-being. The patient may then learn that the physician's interest is contingent on continued illness behavior rather than on clinical improvement, and this will lead the patient to maintain a passive and compliant manner.

When these factors are recognized, efforts can be made to minimize diagnostic studies and to work toward reinforcing the patient's health-promoting behaviors. Patients should be given responsibility for their care, for example, selecting among several indicated medications such as high-fiber diet or psyllium seed preparation for constipation, or designing their own exercise program.

When the physician rewards these efforts with praise and attention, patients learn that becoming healthier can lead to personally meaningful rewards. The physician should also pay attention to other aspects of the patient's life, while limiting discussion about symptoms to no more than is needed to satisfy medical concerns. This technique of differential attention reinforces a more adaptive form of social communication. Finally, as with all chronic illness, the physician's efforts should be directed toward achieving psychosocial adaptation, rather than searching for cure.

Psychopharmacologic Medication

Psychopharmacologic medications are indicated for treatment of an associated primary psychiatric disorder, but can also be used adjunctively in treating selected patients with chronic GI complaints.

In the latter case, this decision is based on the patient's functional and behavioral status as much as on any specific mood alteration.

The tricyclic antidepressants and in some cases, the monoamine oxidase inhibitors are of benefit for treating chronic pain (through endorphin activation and excitation of corticofugal pain inhibitory pathways), panic attacks, eating disorders, primary depression, and secondary depressive symptoms associated with chronic GI illness.[52] Any of these syndromes in the presence of deterioration in daily function such as inability to work or "vegetative" activities, poor appetite, weight loss, sleep disturbance, decreased energy or libido (subserved by central brain monoamine function), are reasonable indications for a therapeutic trial.

Therapy should be considered even if the patient denies feelings of sadness, a state termed *masked* depression. Treatment should be instituted up to full therapeutic levels over 2 to 3 weeks and maintained for 3 to 6 months. A poor clinical response may relate to the tendency for physicians to use inadequate dosages.[57]

Anxiolytic agents, particularly the benzodiazepines, are frequently used to ameliorate anxiety disorders or acute anxiety, particularly if it is associated with stress-induced flare-ups of bowel disturbance. The benefits of these drugs should be balanced with the long-term risks of sedation, drug interactions, habituation, and withdrawal rebound. Newer antianxiety agents such as buspirone may have fewer short- and long-term side effects.[58] Overall, its efficacy for patients with chronic GI disturbances has not been established as well as is the case for the antidepressant class of drugs.

Antipsychotic drugs, or neuroleptics include the phenothiazines (e.g., chlorpromazine) and butyrophenones (e.g., haloperidol) are used primarily for treating disturbances of thought, perception, and behavior in psychotic patients. They may be used to treat acute episodes of agitation, alcohol withdrawal, or psychotic (somatic) delusional disorders presenting as a GI disorder, but psychiatric consultation is recommended. Opiate drugs have little role in treating patients with chronic pain or psychosocial disturbance because of their potential for abuse and dependency.

PSYCHOTHERAPY AND BEHAVIORAL TREATMENTS

Adjunctive psychologic care by a psychiatrist, psychologist, or other mental health professional should be sought when the illness produces personal, social, and economic hardship. The need for such therapy rests less on a psychiatric diagnosis than on the probability that therapy will improve function, mood, or coping style. The patient must see psychiatric care as relevant to personal needs.

Psychotherapy must be individualized. For the psychologically minded and motivated patient, *insight-oriented psychotherapy* can be recommended. The patient experiencing interpersonal difficulties or who has limited finances might benefit from group therapy. *Cognitive–behavioral treatment* is effective for patients with bulimia and other compulsive disorders. It involves the patient in identifying stressors and thoughts that increase mental distress. Patients learn new ways of coping by restructuring these thoughts. *Crisis intervention* is designed to get the individual over a particularly difficult period in a few sessions.

Family or marital counseling is indicated when family disruption contributes to the illness or to the patient's maladaptive behavior. Finally, *behavioral treatments* (e.g., relaxation training, generalized biofeedback, meditation, hypnosis) are safe, noninvasive, and cost-effective methods designed to reduce anxiety levels, teach health-promoting behaviors, give patients greater responsibility and control in their health care, and improve pain control.

PHYSICIAN-RELATED CONCERNS

The provision of care for medical patients having psychosocial difficulties at times may impact upon physician's needs, attitudes, and behaviors. If not recognized, they can adversely affect the patient's care. Particularly with patients who have unexplained complaints, demand a diagnosis, or are inclined to be litigious, the hazard of overdoing the diagnostic evaluation or instituting unneeded or harmful treatments should be weighed. Some patients develop interpersonal conflicts with their physicians. They become controlling, overdependent, or demanding, and physicians may react with blame or stigmatization. Physicians must understand these behaviors in terms of the patient's psychological traits or the medical illness, rather than as a personal failure. In our role as physicians, we may have expectations for rapid relief with displays of gratitude from patients. However, some patients will resist improvement, and may be unable or unwilling to acknowledge our efforts. Here, it is best to refocus treatment from cure to improvement in daily function despite continued symptoms. Personal gratification can be derived from the personal effort rather than from the patient's comments. Finally, each physician must set personal limits on time and energy spent with especially challenging patients. Limiting the length of office visits, allocating part of the care to other health care workers when necessary, and saying no, are important methods for achieving a balance between personal needs and patient benefits.

REFERENCES

1. Reading A. Illness and disease. *Med Clin North Am.* 1977;61:703–706.
2. Kroenke K, Mangelsdorff AD. Common symptoms in ambulatory care: Incidence, evaluation, therapy, and outcome. *Am J Med.* 1989;86:262–266.
3. Mitchell CM, Drossman DA. Survey of the AGA membership relating to patients with functional gastrointestinal disorders. *Gastroenterology.* 1987;92: 1282–1284.
4. Bayless TM. Inflammatory bowel disease and irritable bowel syndrome. *Med Clin North Am.* 1990;49:21–28.
5. Drossman DA, McKee DC, Sandler RS, Mitchell CM, Cramer EM, Lowman BC, Burger AL. Psychosocial factors in the irritable bowel syndrome. A multivariate study of patients and nonpatients with irritable bowel syndrome. *Gastroenterology.* 1988;95:701–708.
6. Engel GL. The need for a new medical model: A challenge for biomedicine. *Science.* 1977;196:129–136.
7. Von Bertalanffy L. *General System Theory.* New York: Braziller;1968.
8. Daruna JH, Morgan JE. Psychosocial effects on immune function: Neuroendocrine pathways. *Psychosomatics.* 1990;31:4–12.

9. Kiecolt-Glaser JK, Glaser R. Psychosocial moderators of immune function. *Ann Behav Med.* 1989;9:16–20.
10. Hinkle LE. The concept of "stress" in the biological and social sciences. In: Lipowski ZJ, ed. *Psychosomatic Medicine. Current Trends and Clinical Applications.* New York: Oxford University Press;1977: pp 27–49.
11. Wolf S. The psyche and the stomach. *Gastroenterology.* 1981;80:605–608.
12. Cannon WB. The movements of the intestine studied by means of roentgen rays. *Am J Physiol.* 1902;6:251–284.
13. Wolf S, Wolff HG. *Human Gastric Function.* New York: Oxford University Press;1943.
14. Tache Y, Stephens RL Jr, Ishikawa T. Central nervous system action of TRH to influence gastrointestinal function and ulceration. *Ann NY Acad Sci.* 1989;553:269–285.
15. Hernandez DE. Neurobiology of brain-gut interactions: Implications for ulcer disease. *Dig Dis Sci.* 1989;34:1809–1816.
16. Feldman M, Walker P, Green JL, Weingarden J. Life events stress and psychosocial factors in men with peptic ulcer disease—a multidimensional case-controlled study. *Gastroenterology.* 1986;91:1370–1379.
17. Kirkegard C, Faber J, Hummer L, Rogowski P. Increased levels of TRH in cerebrospinal fluid from patients with endogenous depression. *Psychoneuroendocrinology.* 1979;4:227–235.
18. Young LD, Richter JE, Anderson KO, Bradley LA, Katz PO, McElveen L, Obrecht WF, Dalton C, Snyder RM. The effects of psychological and environmental stressors on peristaltic esophageal contractions in healthy volunteers. *Psychophysiology.* 1987;24:132–139.
19. Valori RM, Kumar D, Wingate DL. Effects of different types of stress and/or "prokinetic" drugs on the control of the fasting motor complex in humans. *Gastroenterology.* 1986;90:1890–1900.
20. Almy TP, Hinkle LE Jr, Berle B, Kern F Jr. Alterations in colonic function in man under stress. III Experimental production of sigmoid spasm in patients with spastic constipation. *Gastroenterology.* 1949;12:437–451.
21. Mayer EA, Raybould HE. Role of visceral afferent mechanisms in functional bowel disorders. *Gastroenterology.* 1990;99:1688–1704.
22. Svensson TH. Peripheral, autonomic regulation of locus coeruleus noradrenergic neurons in brain: Putative implications for psychiatric and psychopharmacology. *Psychopharmacology.* 1987;92:1–7.
23. Clouse RE, Lustman PJ, McCord GS, Edmundowicz SA. Clinical correlates of abnormal sensitivity to intraesophageal balloon distention. *Dig Dis Sci.* 1991;36:1040–1045.
24. Whitehead WE, Holtkotter B, Enck P, Hoelzl R, Holmes KD, Anthony J, Shabsin HS, Schuster MM. Tolerance for rectosigmoid distention in irritable bowel syndrome. *Gastroenterology.* 1990;98:1187–1192.
25. Geracioti TD Jr, Liddle RA. Impaired cholecystokinin secretion in bulimia nervosa. *New Engl J Med.* 1988;319:683–688.
26. Shavit Y, Martin FC. Opiates, stress and immunity: Animal studies. *Ann Behav Med.* 1987;9:11–15.
27. Burks TF, Galligna JJ, Hirning LD, Porreca F. Brain, spinal cord and peripheral sites of action of enkephalins and other endogenous opioids on gastrointestinal motility. *Gastroenterol Clin Biol.* 1987;11:44B–51B.

28. Drossman DA. Clinical research in the functional digestive disorders. *Gastroenterology.* 1987;92:1267–1269.
29. Miller NE. Effect of learning on gastrointestinal functions. *Clin Gastroenterol.* 1977;6:533–546.
30. Miller NE. Learning of visceral and glandular responses. *Science.* 1969;163: 434–439.
31. Drossman DA. Patients with psychogenic abdominal pain: Six years' observation in the medical setting. *Am J Psychiatry.* 1982;139:1549–1557.
32. Drossman DA. Is the cotton-topped tamarin a model for behavioral research? *Dig Dis Sci.* 1985;30:24S–27S.
33. Cobb S, Rose RM. Hypertension, peptic ulcer and diabetes in air traffic controllers. *JAMA.* 1973;224:489–496.
34. Jess P, van der Lieth L, Matzen P, Madsen P, Krag E, Knigge U, Hjgaard L, Dejgard A, Christiansen PM, Bonnevie O. The personality pattern of duodenal ulcer patients in relation to spontaneous ulcer healing and relapse. *J Intern Med.* 1989;226:395–400.
35. Drossman DA. Psychosocial aspects of ulcerative colitis and Crohn's disease. In: Kirsner JB, Shorter RG, eds. *Inflammatory Bowel Disease,* 3rd ed. Philadelphia: Lea & Febiger;1988: pp 209–226.
36. North CS, Alpers DH, Helzer JE, Spitznagel EL, Clouse RE. Do life events or depression exacerbate inflammatory bowel disease? *Ann Intern Med.* 1991;114:381–386.
37. Fava GA, Pavan L. Large bowel disorders. I Illness configuration and life events. *Psychother Psychosom.* 1976;27:93–99.
38. Graham DY, Lew GM, Klein PD, Evans DG, Evans DJ, Saeed ZA, Malaty HM. Effect of treatment of Helicobacter pylori infection on the long-term recurrence of gastric or duodenal ulcer. *Ann Intern Med.* 1992;116:705–708.
39. Kinzler KW, Nilbert MC, Vogelstein B, Bryan TM, Levy DB, Smith KJ, Preosonger AC, Hamilton SR, Hedge P, Markham A, Carlson M, Hoslyn G, Groden J, White R, Miki Y, Miyoshi Y, Nishisho I, Nakamura Y. Identification of a chromosome 5q21 gene that is mutated in colorectal cancers. *Science.* 1991;251:1366–1370.
40. Grogen J, Thliveris A, Samowitz W, Carlson M, Gelbert L, Albertsen H, Joslyn G, Stevens J, Spiro L, Robertson M, Sargeant L, Krapcho K, Wolff E, Burt R, Hughes JP, Warrington J, McPherson J, Wasmuth J, Le Paslier D, Abderrahim H, Cohen D, Leppert M, White R. Identification and characterization of the familial adenomatous polyposis coli gene. *Cell.* 1991;66:589–600.
41. Toguchida J, Yamaguchi T, Dayton SH, Beauchamp RL, Herrara GE, Ishizaki K, Yamamuro T, Meyers P, Little JB, Sasaki MS, Weichselbaum RR, Yandell DW. Prevalence and spectrum of germline mutations of the p53 gene among patients with sarcoma. *N Engl J Med.* 1992;326:1301–1308.
42. Malkin D, Jolly KW, Barbier N, Look T, Friend SH, Gebhardt MC, Andersen TI, Borresen A-L, Li FP, Garber J, Strong LC. Germline mutations of the p53 tumor-suppressor gene in children and young adults with second malignant neoplasms. *N Engl J Med.* 1992;326:1309–1315.
43. Drossman DA, Funch-Jensen P, Janssens J, Talley NJ, Thompson WG, Whitehead WE. Identification of subgroups of functional bowel disorders. *Gastroenterol Int.* 1990;3:159–172.

44. Drossman DA, Thompson WG. The irritable bowel syndrome: Review and a graduated, multicomponent treatment approach. *Ann Intern Med.* 1992;116: 1009–1016.
45. Drossman DA. Psychosocial factors in functional dyspepsia. *Eur J Gastroenterol Hepatol.* 1992;4:608–614.
46. Drossman DA. Psychosocial factors in chronic functional abdominal pain. In: *Pain Research and Clinical Management.* New York: Elsevier;1993.
47. Whitehead WE, Bosmajian L, Zonderman AB, Costa PT Jr, Schuster MM. Symptoms of psychologic distress associated with irritable bowel syndrome. Comparison of community and medical clinic samples. *Gastroenterology.* 1988; 95:709–714.
48. Drossman DA, Patrick DL, Mitchell CM, Zagami EW, Appelbaum MI. Health related quality of life in inflammatory bowel disease: Functional status and patient worries and concerns. *Dig Dis Sci.* 1989;34:1379.
49. Drossman DA, Leserman J, Mitchell CM, Li Z, Zagami EA, Patrick DL. Health status and health care use in persons with inflammatory bowel disease. A national sample. *Dig Dis Sci.* 1991;36:1746–1755.
50. Katon W, Von Korff M, Lin E, Lipscomb P, Russo J, Wagner E, Polk E. Distressed high utilizers of medical care: DSM-III-R diagnoses and treatment needs. *Gen Hosp Psychiatry.* 1990;12:355–362.
51. Drossman DA, Leserman J, Nachman G, Li Z, Gluck H, Toomey TC, Mitchell CM. Sexual and physical abuse in women with functional or organic gastrointestinal disorders. *Ann Intern Med.* 1990;113:828–833.
52. Drossman DA. Psychosocial factors in the care of patients with gastrointestinal diseases. In: Yamada T, ed. *Textbook of Gastroenterology.* Philadelphia: Lippincott;1991; pp 546–561.
53. Lipkin M Jr. The medical interview and related skills. In: Branch WT, ed. *Office Practice of Medicine.* 2nd ed. Philadelphia: Saunders;1987: pp 1287–1306.
54. Barsky AJ. Hidden reasons some patients visit doctors. *Ann Intern Med.* 1981;94:492–498.
55. Devaul RA, Faillace LA. Persistent pain and illness insistence—A medical profile of proneness to surgery. *Am J Surg.* 1978;135:828–833.
56. Klein KB. Chronic intractable abdominal pain. *Semin Gastro Dis.* 1990;1:43–56.
57. Cakkues AL, Popkin MK. Antidepressant treatment of medical-surgical inpatients by nonpsychiatric physicians. *Arch Gen Psychiatry.* 1987;44:157–160.
58. Rakel R. Assessing the efficacy of antianxiety agents. *Am J Med.* 1987;82(suppl 5A):1–6.

Chapter 14
A Review
of Psychosomatic Aspects
# of Cardiovascular Disease

ANDREW B. LITTMAN

This article outlines recent advances in understanding the interface between psychiatric and cardiovascular medicine. While the early pioneers in this area offered astute insights from their clinical experience, the hypotheses underlying their insights never underwent scientific scrutiny. As these insights began to be critically tested, however, somewhat global concepts regarding psychosomatic causality became increasingly differentiated and specifically explicated. In the last decade, the knowledge base in this area has been greatly expanded by a wide range of basic research studies and clinical intervention trials. Most recently, researchers have enhanced their understanding of various psychosomatic processes through the use of psychiatric diagnostic phenomenology. Consequently, a greater understanding of the neurobiologic basis of emotional states is emerging.

SMOKING CESSATION

Cigarette smoking is the single most avoidable cause of death in our society.[1] Recent studies indicate that patients with coronary artery disease who stop smoking have a lower mortality from all causes of death and a less frequent occurrence of myocardial infarction in particular than those who continue to smoke.[2] Other research has found, not surprisingly, that there is a greater survival rate for patients who have myocardial infarctions and have smoked if they quit after their first myocardial infarction.[3] Public awareness of the health benefits of smoking cessation has stimulated many individuals to stop smoking. In the United States over the last 40 years, there has been a dramatic decline of over 30% in the percentage of adults in the general population who smoke.[5] Among those individuals who have experienced myocardial infarction, approximately 50% have quit smoking.[4] Despite this overall positive trend in the decline of adult smokers in this country, the proportion of smokers who have failed to quit, continue to smoke heavily, and are addicted to nicotine has increased.[1] Historically, most organized treatments designed to assist in smoking cessation have been behaviorally or psychologically based. Long-term quit rates associated with these programs have averaged 30%.[5] Pharmacologic approaches have more recently been developed to provide adjunctive means to help smokers quit. Randomized trials, including double-blind placebo-controlled studies with nicotine chewing gum—the most widely used pharmacologic agent for smoking cessation, indicate that the use of nicotine gum improves long-term quit rates.[6] The efficacy of the gum seems to be due to its ability to relieve symptoms of nicotine withdrawal, including irritability, anxiety, difficulty concentrating, and restlessness.[7]

The efficacy of nicotine gum in smoking cessation, however, appears to be partly a function of whether or not the gum is used in conjunction with the patient's having new learning experiences, and the specific nature of these learning experiences. When nicotine gum is used by an individual to stop smoking independent of a specialized smoking cessation clinic, its effect has been shown to be minimal.[8] Typically, the individual attempting to quit on his own lacks support, as well as instructions on the correct usage of the gum. It is important to note, however, that the differences observed in treatment outcome for those individuals who are using nicotine gum on their own versus those who use it in the context of an organized program, may in part be a function of sociodemographic or psychiatric differences between these two groups. The use of nicotine gum in the context of a clinic-based smoking cessation treatment program appears to significantly increase treatment efficacy. Furthermore, increased treatment efficacy with nicotine gum appears to be maximized when it is combined with specific behavioral skills training, rather than a standard didactic approach.[9]

Transdermal nicotine patches are now being used for smoking cessation and have recently become available to the general public.[10] The advantage of this form of therapy is the constant delivery system of nicotine into the bloodstream. This constant delivery offers an individual nicotine without the regular reinforcing behaviors of cigarette smoking or nicorette use. Cardiac patients are cautioned to discontinue smoking while using the nicotine patch, as well as not to use the highest dosage patch. Only preliminary efficacy data is currently available. Initial clinical practice at Massachusetts General Hospital suggests that the effectiveness of treatment depends in part on whether the nicotine patch is used in conjunction with a behavioral treatment program. In addition, it appears that a sizable number of nicotine patch-treated patients develop various affective symptoms, including hostility and depressive disorders, or profound sleep disturbances, in the process of tapering the patch dosage, and relapse.

Another pharmacologic agent that has been studied in the treatment of smoking has been clonidine. Glassman et al.[11] found in a 6-month follow-up of a placebo-controlled smoking cessation trial that clonidine offered a significant beneficial effect in women only compared to placebo. Findings from several studies suggest that there is a relationship between depression and cigarette smoking. Glassman et al. found in the course of their study on the efficacy of clonidine in the treatment of cigarette smoking that there was an unusually high prevalence (61%) of past major depression in the sample. A history of regular smoking was found more frequently among individuals who had a history of major depressive disorder than among those who never had a major depression or those who never had a psychiatric diagnosis.[11] Another study of patients with coronary artery disease found significantly higher smoking rates among patients who had major depressive disorder compared to those who were euthymic.[13] In a study of adolescents, depressive mood during adolescence was predictive of heavy cigarette use in adulthood.[14]

A recent result of considerable importance to our understanding of how to effectively treat individuals who smoke is the finding that many patients who have difficulty in quitting smoking have a past history of major depression. Glassman's[11] study on the efficacy of clonidine found that a past history of major depression in individuals attempting to quit smoking was predictive of a poor response to treatment, independent of whether the subject received the active drug or the placebo. An epidemiologic study by Glassman et al.[12] also found that smokers with major depression were less successful in their attempts to quit than were those without a history of major depression or a psychiatric diagnosis. In addition to the finding that many smokers who have difficulty smoking have a past history of major depression, it has been noted that when a patient with a history of depression quits smoking, depressive symptoms or major depressive symptoms may ensue.[12] Further analysis by Covey et al.[15] has shown that during the first week of smoking cessation, subjects who were ultimately unsuccessful at quitting experienced craving, depressive mood, and difficulty concentrating more intensely than those who were ultimately successful at smoking cessation. It has been suggested that drug treatments that are specifically designed to treat depressive symptoms evident while smoking or which have developed subsequent to smoking cessation, may improve smokers' success rates in quitting.[16] A recent double-blind study of the use of doxepin as an adjunct to smoking cessation supports this view.[17]

Other mood states in addition to depression appear to play a role in the maintenance of smoking behavior and successful treatment. Findings from several studies suggest that smoking to relieve negative symptoms such as anger, poor frustration tolerance, and tension is related to greater difficulty in quitting smoking.[18] Individuals with baseline elevated levels of these symptoms, or individuals who develop these symptoms in the midst of a quit attempt, may benefit from treatment. Two recent studies, one open and one placebo-controlled, with buspirone, a serotonergic antianxiety agent, have shown reductions in craving, anxiety, irritability, restlessness, and sadness during withdrawal from nicotine.[19, 20] It is currently unclear whether these improvements in withdrawal intensity will translate into increased long-term smoking cessation rates.

Significant inroads have recently been made in our understanding of smokers who have had difficulty quitting, as well as the range and mix of potential therapeutic avenues available to them. Continued research is needed to evaluate the efficacy of these diverse treatments for smoking cessation in relation to the possible differential effects of these various treatments in various symptomatic populations.

PHYSICAL ACTIVITY

A review of the impact of cardiac rehabilitation programs, primarily consisting of exercise programs, after the development of symptomatic coronary artery disease, indicated a 25% reduction in death from all causes including cardiovascular mortality.[21] However, the review also found a statistically nonsignificant increase in nonfatal infarction in those groups that began cardiac rehabilitation within 8 weeks after myocardial infarction, suggesting that exercising vigorously prematurely may be hazardous. In the Multiple Risk Factor Intervention Trial (MRFIT) study, subjects were classified into tertiles of low, moderate, and high levels of leisure time physical activity. Moderate levels of leisure time physical activity were associated with 63% less cardiovascular deaths and 70% less total deaths than the low leisure time physical activity group. Interestingly, mortality rates for the high leisure time physical activity group were similar to those of the moderate leisure time physical activity group. The study found that 30 to 69 minutes of predominantly light and moderate-intensity activities on a daily basis was the optimal level of activity to reduce cardiovascular risk for the study patients.[22] There has been little systematic study of the impact of exercise on elderly or female patients with coronary artery disease. One recent study conducted on an elderly population indicated similar physiologic benefits of exercise in the elderly as in younger patients with coronary artery disease.[23]

Physical activity appears to have a protective function in the primary prevention of coronary artery disease as well. The U.S. Centers for Disease Control (CDC) reviewed existing observational studies and found a significant and graded relationship between physical inactivity and the risk of coronary artery disease.[24] A recent study conducted by the Cooper Clinic, based on data from over 13,000 subjects, showed a strong, stepwise, and consistent inverse relationship between physical fitness and mortality. The major burden of increased risk for morbidity and mortality was evident primarily in the lowest quintile of fitness, with the risk being sharply reduced thereafter.[25] The role of physical constitution can complicate the analysis of the extent to which physical activity is protective against the development of coronary artery disease. A study by Paffenbarger et al.[26] sheds some light on this issue, finding that the protective effect of having been a college athlete, and possibly constitutionally superior, disappears over time after graduation. This study also demonstrates the protective impact of moderate levels of physical activity, and strongly suggests that moderate physical activity and not constitution is the relevant protective behavior.

No studies have examined the influence of discrete depressive disorders or other mood states on the level of physical activity of patients with coronary artery disease. This is especially relevant in light of the steep increase in risk of the lowest quintile of physical activity for cardiac patients. One study was able to take into account depressive symptomatology in cardiac rehabilitation patients, and showed that the level of a patient's depression is not predictive of the level of exercise functioning prior to a course of cardiac rehabilitation. At the end of a course of supervised exercise therapy, however, patients with moderate to severe levels of depressive symptoms do not achieve a statistically significant training effect, as measured by the improvement on postprogram exercise testing in comparison to preprogram exercise testing. In contrast, a robust training effect was found in control subjects who were psychiatrically asymptomatic or had mild depressive symptoms.[27, 28] This study suggests that depressive symptoms may block a patient's capacity to benefit from exercise therapy.

Attempts to validate or quantify the impact of exercise training programs on psychosocial functioning in patients with coronary artery disease have been fraught with contradictory results. The contradictory findings are based partly on the variation in medical severity, psychosocial distress, and psychiatric diagnosis in the heterogeneous populations studied.[29] In a normal population, moderate exercise training, in contrast to placebo or high exercise training, has been shown to improve mental well-being.[30] One controlled study compared the impact of aerobic exercise to group counseling in anxious and/or depressed postmyocardial infarction patients. It found that exercise improved work capacity, independence and sociability, and diminished fatigue and anxiety-depression. Compared to exercise, counseling reduced depression, decreased interpersonal friction, and increased friendliness. The control group showed no substantial change on any measured factor.[31]

Studies evaluating the impact of exercise on type A behavior show a reduction of type A behavior in healthy middle-aged men who undergo an exercise program. Both exercise and strength and flexibility programs show a reduction in overt and self-report of type A behavior, but only exercise reduced the cardiovascular (heart rate, blood pressure, and MVO2) and sympathoadrenal responses to mental stress.[32, 33] Other physiological and psychological benefits of exercise have been found in addition to the benefits of exercise listed above. These benefits include: (1) improved life pattern characterized by more regulated eating patterns, longer and more restful sleep, decreased anxiety-depression, improved sexual adjustment, and a greater ease in handling daily stress; (2) substantial reduction in systolic blood pressure and heart rate at rest and comparable levels of submaximal work; (3) substantial increases in peak oxygen uptake; (4) substantial decreases in myocardial work at rest and submaximal work; (5) substantial changes in body composition, i.e., reduced fat and increased muscle mass; (6) changes in the central and peripheral circulation comparable with those observed in otherwise physically active subjects[34]; and (7) improvement in lipid parameters. Exercise appears to have equal efficacy as does dieting in reducing plasma lipids in overweight sedentary men. High density lipoproteins and triglycerides both diminished significantly in both exercise and diet groups with no changes in total cholesterol or low density lipoproteins.[35, 36]

CHOLESTEROL AND BEHAVIOR

Considerable evidence exists documenting the association between increased serum cholesterol and a heightened risk for coronary artery disease. Dietary and pharmacologic primary and secondary prevention trials to lower serum cholesterol have been found to reduce the incidence of coronary artery disease.[37] As a consequence of these findings, public health recommendations have been made to the general public in both Europe and America to reduce total dietary fat intake in order to reduce serum cholesterol concentrations.[38, 39] Despite the reduction of serum cholesterol in primary prevention trials and the reduction in incidence of coronary heart disease events, survival has not been found to be extended in any study thus far. A meta-analysis of these primary prevention trials of cholesterol lowering revealed a reduction in mortality from coronary heart disease, no decrease in total mortality, and a significant increase in death unrelated to illness. Interestingly, this significant increase in deaths was found in the study groups receiving treatment to lower cholesterol concentrations, and was due to accidents, suicide, or violence. The explanation for the increased accidents, suicide, and violence in study subjects exposed to cholesterol lowering interventions is unclear. In reviewing studies which investigate these relationships, a group in Edinburgh stated, "it is not clear whether the effect on behaviour is due to low absolute concentrations of cholesterol or to the change in subjects' normal cholesterol concentrations, or whether it is a side-effect of dieting or drug therapy or due to some other phenomenon"[40] [p. 997]. A relationship between serum cholesterol and aggressiveness or hostility in the Whitehall study of U.K. civil servants,[41] or between serum cholesterol and accidental or violent deaths in long-term studies, has not been demonstrated.[42–45] In a prison population in Finland, inmates with aggressive conduct disorders or antisocial personalities had lower serum cholesterol concentrations than inmates without such disorders.[46, 47] While further research is clearly needed to elucidate the relationship between deaths from noncardiac causes and cholesterol lowering, it is possible that such a relationship may appear at points of marked reductions of cholesterol, in individuals with extremes of aggressivity, or in individuals with a predisposition to develop mood disorders.

In an attempt to further understand the phenomenon of increased death from noncardiac causes associated with cholesterol lowering, the social behavior of monkeys was monitored in one of two dietary conditions, high fat or prudent.[48] Criteria for the prudent condition were based on the American Heart Association recommendation of obtaining 30% of daily caloric intake from fat. The only difference found between the high fat and prudent groups was that more contact aggression was initiated in the prudently fed monkey group. Interestingly, this same dietary fat manipulation produced lower central nervous system serotonergic activity in the prudently fed monkeys in comparison to the monkeys on the high fat diet. This finding points to the possibility of a biobehavioral basis for the increased aggression seen in the prudently fed group.[48] Engelburg[49] has suggested that a fall in serum cholesterol concentration causes a decrease in brain serotonin, producing less suppression of aggressive behavior. A meta-analysis was conducted of studies investigating the effect of dietary versus drug interventions in cholesterol lowering trials in excess mortality from aggression. This analysis identified an increased risk of death from violence and suicide only for subjects undergoing drug interventions to reduce cholesterol concentrations.[50] This finding suggests that violent and aggressive behavior is in some way related to low serum cholesterol concentrations or the reduction of serum lipids. Further research is needed to clarify the clinical relevance of these findings.

DEPRESSION AND HEART DISEASE

Numerous studies have demonstrated a high incidence of psychiatric symptomatology in general, and depressive symptoms in particular, in patients with coronary artery disease. Between 20 and 40% of patients with coronary artery disease have been found to exhibit depressive symptoms.[51-57] Wishnie[57] studied psychiatric symptomatology in 24 patients in the early phase of their recovery. Twenty-one of the 24 patients studied rated themselves as anxious or depressed, 18 were assessed to require either a sedative or an antidepressant, 15 reported sleep disturbances, and 18 reported disruptive family quarrels. Another study found 33% of a sample of postmyocardial infarction patients exhibited signs of severe depression as much as 18 months after infarction.[54] In addition, two groups have reported that at least half of their sample of patients describing psychiatric symptoms after their myocardial infarction had described experiencing similar symptoms predating the infarction.[53, 57]

Drawing conclusions from studies investigating the association between psychiatric and depressive symptomatology and coronary artery disease has been limited by the various criteria and methods used to define both psychiatric morbidity and depressive symptoms. These diverse methods include self-report, clinical diagnosis, and symptom checklist. The methodological issues which have arisen in the definition and measurement of mood disorders in the physically ill are reviewed by House.[58] One such issue is the question of whether depressive symptoms should be viewed as a continuous dimension or as a typology. One problem in using a typology in assessing depressive symptoms is that "subsyndromal" depressive symptoms, which have not met more rigorous criteria for depressive disorder, have generally been considered to be "self-limited," transient, and of minimal significance.[59, 60] Data from the Medical Outcome Study, however, indicate that patients with major depressive disorder, as well as patients with depressive symptoms in the absence of major depressive disorder tended to have worse physical, social, and role functioning, and worse perceived current health, than did patients with no chronic conditions.[61] The poor functioning uniquely associated with depressive symptoms, with or without depressive disorder, was worse than eight major chronic medical conditions. The only chronic medical condition which was associated with worse functioning was chronic cardiac disease. In addition, depression and chronic medical conditions appeared to have additive effects on patient functioning.[61]

Klerman[62] believed that the medical community tends to view major depression as "biologic," while viewing patients presenting with only depressive symptoms as less severely ill, or perhaps not ill at all. Depressive symptoms tend to be called either secondary depression, demoralization, or neurotic depression, implying that this is "less" a biologic illness than major affective disorder. Related to this minimization of the clinical significance of depressive symptoms is the fact that there are few, if any, controlled trials of treatment for depressive symptoms. This lack of investigation in this area is surprising, given the morbidity associated with these symptoms. It is also surprising in light of the finding that depressive symptoms in cardiac patients has an adverse effect on patient motivation. Two groups have shown a lower rate of adherence to treatment in coronary artery disease patients manifesting depressive symptoms.[63, 64] Although we do not know the impact of depressive symptoms on the mortality of patients with coronary artery disease, several studies have demonstrated that patients with major depression have a higher than expected rate of mortality from natural causes, and specifically from cardiovascular disease.[65–68]

Two recent studies have evaluated the incidence of major depressive disorder in patients with coronary artery disease, as well as the extent of diagnosis and treatment for these disorders. One group found an 18% incidence of current major depression in coronary artery patients undergoing a diagnostic cardiac catheterization. Only 20% of these depressed patients had been diagnosed and received treatment prior to the study.[69] Another group found a 15% incidence of major depressive disorder in patients in the second week after a myocardial infarction. Less than 10% of those with major depression received treatment during the course of the study.[70] Another study on the relationship between depressive disorder and cardiac events showed that major depression was the best predictor of major cardiac events (myocardial infarction, bypass surgery, angioplasty, or death) in the year following diagnostic catheterization in coronary artery disease patients, controlling for severity of disease, left ventricular ejection fraction, and smoking status.[69] Finally, one study showed that the rate of myocardial infarction was significantly greater in inadequately treated depressed patients compared with the adequately treated patients.[68] This finding is consistent with the interpretation that adequate treatment of depression reduces the risk of death conferred by the depressive disorder itself. However, no study has been conducted to date that evaluates the impact of treatment of major depression in coronary artery disease patients on morbidity and mortality.

The lack of effective diagnosis and treatment of depression in cardiac patients is due to several factors. First, depression is considered by many to be a normal concomitant of coronary artery disease and, until very recently, not widely recognized as a cause of increased morbidity and mortality in these patients. Second, many clinicians view these depressions as exogenous or secondary and not requiring treatment. Third, some physicians believe secondary depressions are not amenable to treatment. Fourth, the symptoms of depression are commonly misattributed as symptoms of the coronary disease itself. Fifth, many clinicians are concerned about adverse cardiovascular effects of psychotropics in patients with coronary artery disease, and are concomitantly reluctant to consider the appropriateness of their use. Given an understanding of the pharmacotherapy of depressive disorder, psychotropic agents can be safely and effectively given. The pharmacotherapy of depression in cardiac patients is covered in the following section. The treatment of depressive symptoms and distress, as well as the psychotherapy of depressive disorder, will be discussed under the treatments of stress, hostility, and type A behavior.

Pharmacotherapy of Depression

The mode of therapeutic action of antidepressants and their adverse side effects are not precisely understood, but are known to be based on their activity at peripheral and central serotonergic, adrenergic, cholinergic and histaminergic sites. The cardiovascular effects of tricyclic antidepressants have been widely studied. These clinically significant side effects include tachycardia, orthostatic hypotension, conduction delays, effects on cardiac rhythm, and myocardial contractility.[71] Although a tricyclic-induced tachycardia of 10 to15 beats/minute is commonly noted by clinicians, robust effects are rarely seen.[72] This increase in heart rate is considered to be an anticholinergic side-effect. It is persistent and generally not of clinical significance. Patients who have ventricular decompensation with shortened diastolic filling times may have an exacerbation of their congestive heart failure. Occasional symptomatic tachycardia with heart rates of 120 to 140 do occur. This phenomenon appears to occur most often in young women.[73] Desipramine is the least anticholinergic tricyclic compound.[74]

Orthostatic hypotension is one of the most common serious cardiovascular side effects of tricyclic antidepressants.[75-77] The occurrence of this side effect appears to be unrelated to age and sex.[76] An 8% incidence of orthostatic hypotension was observed in a sample of medically healthy depressed patients treated with imipramine, compared to a 50% incidence of hypotension in depressed patients with congestive heart failure.[78, 79] Nortriptyline produced orthostatic hypotension in only 5% of patients with heart failure, and consequently appears to be the tricyclic of choice in the treatment of depressed cardiac patients.[80] Tricyclic antidepressants have been reported to produce, at toxic levels, all types of supraventricular and ventricular arrhythmias.[81] These drugs were thought to be possibly arrhythmogenic and contraindicated in patients with arrhythmias.[81] Studies of imipramine and nortryptyline have demonstrated a clinically significant antiarrhythmic effect of these drugs.[82, 83] Tricyclics have been shown to have characteristics of class 1A antiarrhythmic compounds such as quinidine and procainamide.[84] The tricyclic antidepressants in therapeutic dosages have a "quinidinelike" effect. Consistent with this effect is the finding of an increase in the P-R and Q-T intervals, QRS segment, and a diminishment of T-wave height with tricyclic usage.[72] Mild conduction delays are common and of little concern. However, preexisting defects involving the His-Purkinje conduction system, such as bundle-branch blocks, put patients at risk for more serious second- or third-degree heart block.[85] Twenty-five percent of patients who had preexisting P-R or QRS abnormalities and were treated with tricyclic antidepressants had second- or third-degree heart block.[85] Only patients with preexisting conduction defects developed heart block. Another investigation showed a 9% development of second-degree atrioventricular block in patients with preexisting bundle branch blocks who were treated with tricyclics, compared to a 0.7% development in patients with normal pretreatment electrocardiograms. The one patient with a normal pretreatment electrocardiogram who developed second degree AV block was found to have an abnormal His-Purkinje conduction system on further evaluation.[86] Therapeutic levels of tricyclic antidepressants do not impair left ventricular function, even in patients with moderate to severe impairment in cardiac output. Imipramine, doxepin, and nortriptyline have all been shown to have no negative effect on left ventricular function.[78, 87, 88] As noted above, patients with congestive heart failure have a very high incidence of orthostatic hypotension.

The monoamine oxidase inhibitors (MAOIs) have been used for the treatment of depression for many years. Recently, MAOIs have been used to treat atypical depression and anxiety disorders.[89, 90] MAOIs are used infrequently with patients with cardiovascular disease because of the likelihood of marked orthostatic hypotension. In addition, there is a possibility of hypertensive crisis when tyramine-containing foods or sympathomimetic drugs are ingested, although the incidence of hypertensive episodes is in fact fairly rare.[91]

Other newer antidepressants have been made available for clinical use. While the cardiovascular effects of tricyclic antidepressants are better known, these drugs have side effects and toxicity profiles that suggest that there may be an advantage of some of these newer agents in treating cardiac patients with psychiatric disorders. Amoxapine may produce extrapyramidal effects due to its dopamine blocking.[92] Conduction abnormalities and atrial arrhythmias have been reported as well.[93] Maprotiline has been reported to cause torsade de pointes at the high end of the therapeutic range, despite having a drug side effect profile quite similar to desipramine.[72] Trazodone has little effect on cardiac conduction at routine dosages.[93] It has been demonstrated to produce beneficial hemodynamic changes such as mild reduction of pulse and blood pressure and improved left ventricular function.[94] Trazodone has been reported to rarely exacerbate ventricular ectopy.[95, 96] Bupropion has no cardiotoxic or anticholinergic effects, but causes seizures at high normal therapeutic dosages.[97, 98] Fluoxetine appears to have little cardiotoxicity and no anticholinergic effects.[99] In addition, it has virtually no effect on the electrocardiogram[100] and seems to have no cardiovascular effects at toxic concentrations.[101] Despite the considerable potential advantages of some of the newer antidepressants to treat cardiac patients, controlled clinical trials evaluating the safety of these compounds in subjects with arrhythmia, congestive heart failure, conduction disturbances, and preexisting orthostatic blood pressure findings will be needed to demonstrate the real benefits of these agents.

Psychostimulants have been used to treat depression in medically ill patients[102] and patients who become depressed after cardiac surgery.[103] Agents such as dextroamphetamine and methylphenidate have been found to be effective when other antidepressants cannot be safely used, as for example in patients with profound heart failure or conduction abnormalities. The lack of anticholinergic side effects and the absence of orthostatic hypotension, as well as the rapid onset of action, are very useful features. Despite the low dosages used to treat these patients (5–20 mg per day by mouth) however, hypertension, tachycardia, arrhythmias, and coronary vasospasm can occur in rare circumstances, necessitating close cardiac monitoring. Psychostimulants are possibly contraindicated in patients with unstable angina, significant hypertension, psychosis, delirium, and current use of medications such as alphamethyl-dopa, monoamine oxidase inhibitors, and bronchodilators.

Lithium carbonate is primarily used as the mainstay of the treatment of manic–depressive disorder. Additionally, it has been used at low dose in recent years to augment the antidepressant response of depressed patients who have not responded to an antidepressant trial. At therapeutic levels, lithium appears to be safe for the majority of patients receiving treatment. Lithium commonly produces flattening or even inversion of T waves, although electrocardiographic changes are of minimal significance.[104] Cases of syncope due to sinus node dysfunction, as well as ventricular arrhythmias, have been observed.[105] Patients with cardiac disease are more at risk to develop lithium toxicity than patients without cardiac disease. Lithium is a salt and is excreted completely by the kidney, primarily in the proximal renal tubule. The presence of congestive heart failure, renal insufficiency, salt restriction, and thiazide diuretics, all contribute to an elevated lithium level and the possibility of lithium toxicity.[106]

The antipsychotic agents are useful in the treatment of psychosis, delirium, and uncontrolled emesis. The antipsychotic drugs with low potency of dopamine blockade, the so-called low-potency agents, are chlorpromazine, thioridazine, and mesoridazine. These low-potency antipsychotic drugs have significantly more anticholinergic, alpha-adrenergic blocking, and quinidinelike effects than the high-potency antipsychotic agents, and are therefore associated with more cardiotoxicity.[107] Thus, low-potency antipsychotic agents are relatively contraindicated in cardiac patients. The high-potency antipsychotics, such as haloperidol, trifluperazine, fluphenazine, and perphenazine, are considered to rarely cause clinically significant adverse cardiac effects.

Psychiatric Risk Factors for Coronary Artery Disease

Observations regarding the presence of intense emotional states, such as anger, impatience, worry, and emotional distress in patients with coronary artery disease are well documented.[108, 109] In addition, there has been an abundance of clinical reports that suggest that these emotional states have some impact on the precipitation of cardiac events. The first of these factors to be scientifically studied was stressful life events. It is now recognized that exposure to a stressful situation per se is probably not sufficient to induce the pathophysiological changes of coronary artery disease.[110] Individual predisposition or vulnerability to the health effects of a particular stressor is most likely required.[111] Inadequate psychological and social resources for coping have been hypothesized to contribute to this vulnerability.[112]

Beginning in 1959, Drs. Meyer Friedman and Raymond Rosenman[113] advanced the hypothesis that the type A behavior pattern is independently associated with a higher risk for the development of coronary artery disease. Type A behavior was defined as a behavior pattern exhibited that results from the interactions of individual predispositions with situations that are considered by the individual to be stressful. Those who manifest this behavior pattern operate with a sense of time urgency, competitiveness, easily provoked annoyance, and aggression.[114] The Western Collaborative Group Study (WCGS),[115] a prospective study following 3154 healthy men for 8½ years, demonstrated that persons with type A behavior had twice the risk of acquiring coronary artery disease, independent of other known risk factors, than individuals exhibiting type B behavior. In addition, type A behavior was a good predictor of subsequent reinfarction in this population.[116] The early studies of three distinct populations demonstrated that patients with type A behavior had more extensive coronary artery disease as measured by angiography than those with type B behavior, even controlling for standard coronary risk factors in two of the studies.[117–119] In 1981, the Review Panel on Coronary Prone Behavior and Coronary Heart Disease of the National Heart Lung and Blood Institute[120] recognized type A behavior as an independent risk factor for coronary artery disease. In contrast to these earlier studies, which found type A behavior to be associated with increased morbidity and mortality from coronary artery disease, research conducted since 1981 on this relationship had had more mixed results. There have been a large number of negative findings, including the MRFIT,[121] Aspirin Myocardial Infarction Study,[122] and Multicenter Postinfarction Program.[123] These studies show no effect of type A behavior in patients followed prospectively.

Two critical review articles provide some perspective on the ideologic fervor that has surrounded these more recent findings.[124, 125] The authors of these articles suggest that the discrepant findings in type A research are due to the different methods used in diagnosing type A behavior.[124, 125] One method used to diagnose type A behavior is the semistructured interview, which is thought to be the gold standard in the assessment of type A behavior. Another method is the self-administered questionnaire, of which there are many examples. Although the questionnaires have more frequently been found to be associated with negative findings than the interview, studies using the interview have also frequently been shown to have negative findings.

Another question raised by the set of findings of no effect of type A behavior is whether or not researchers have consistently measured the salient feature of the "coronary-prone personality." There is increasing evidence that hostility is the specific component of type A behavior that is most predictive of increased risk for coronary artery disease.[125, 126] Reevaluation of the WCGS and MRFIT data showed that the potential for hostility does turn out to be a particularly strong predictor of coronary events.[126, 127] Even in angiographic studies where type A behavior was unrelated to the extent of atherosclerosis, reanalysis of this data showed hostility to be significantly correlated with coronary artery disease demonstrated via angiography.[128] Hostility and cynicism, as measured by the Cook-Medley subscale of the Minnesota Multiphasic Personality Inventory (MMPI),[129] has been shown to be predictive of morbidity and mortality from coronary artery disease.[130, 131] While there has been considerable improvement in predictive capability with various measures of hostility over the past decade,[132] the most effective means of quantifying hostility is as yet unclear.[133]

Social influences have been shown to have a significant impact on patients with coronary artery disease. Social support, occupational stress, and socioeconomic status all appear to have fairly powerful influences on the morbidity and mortality of individuals with coronary artery disease.[134] Increased mortality was observed among persons identified as having fewer friends and social relationships in the Alameda Country study. This finding was also found at three other sites.[135] Ruberman et al.[136] have shown that social isolation impacts negatively on the mortality of patients after myocardial infarction, and Case et al.[137] have shown that living alone does this as well. Socioeconomic status has been shown to be inversely related to coronary artery disease mortality in Marmot's[138] study of civil servants in London. The effect of low social and economic resources on survival in coronary artery disease patients has recently been demonstrated.[139] Finally, Karasek et al.[140] have shown repeatedly that the interaction of very demanding work with few opportunities to control one's job situation, sometimes called job strain, results in coronary artery disease signs, symptoms, prevalence, and mortality.[134]

Numerous mechanisms appear to link stress, type A behavior, depression, and hostility to the pathophysiology of coronary artery disease, including sudden cardiac death, silent ischemia, and atherosclerosis. The most studied of these mechanisms is the link between emotional states and sudden cardiac death.[141] Animal studies have shown that stressed[142] or angered dogs[143] have a lower cardiac threshold for ventricular fibrillation than control animals. Personally relevant mental stress appears to be an important precipitant of silent myocardial ischemia.[144] Mental stress-induced ischemia may be due to excessive coronary vasoconstriction.[145] An exaggerated heart rate and blood pressure response is also displayed by some individuals who exhibit a more generalized heightened adrenergic response to stress.[146] Evidence that anger can induce myocardial ischemia by coronary vasoconstriction comes from a study which showed that angering an animal by food deprivation can consistently produce myocardial ischemia and coronary vasoconstriction in the immediate postanger period.[147] Another finding of importance is that reduced vagal tone or high sympathetic activity, as measured by power spectral analysis of heart rate variability, has been shown in various studies to correlate with angiographic severity,[148] risk of ventricular fibrillation,[149] type A behavior,[150] and possibly depression.[151]

Finally, hostility, social stress, and physiologic responsiveness to psychological challenge have been shown to interact to effect the rate of progression and extent of atherosclerosis in monkey models.[152] A review of the neuroendocrine correlates of stress and the role of stress in atherosclerosis has been conducted.[153] In addition, evidence for hostility as the critical factor of type A behavior that is associated with extent of atherosclerosis in angiographic studies in humans comes from numerous studies.[152] In summary, there is a great deal of evidence to implicate hostility as a pathogenic factor in the development of atherosclerosis, precipitation of silent myocardial ischemia, induction of coronary vasospasm by mental stress, reduction of parasympathetic-to-sympathetic autonomic balance, risk of sudden cardiac death by ventricular fibrillation, and the continuation of cigarette smoking.

Treatment of Hostility, Stress, and Type A Behavior

A 1981 National Heart, Lung, and Blood Institute review panel recognized the type A behavior pattern as an independent risk factor for coronary artery disease. Since there were few controlled studies on psychologic treatments and no somatic treatments available to reduce the type A behavior pattern, however, the panel concluded that there was no evidence that the type A behavior pattern could be modified, or that its modification might decrease risk or outcome for patients with coronary artery disease.[120] Numerous studies have been conducted to attempt to reduce type A behavior. Most of these studies have design flaws, such as the use of unvalidated, subjective instruments, small sample size, and the lack of hard end-points in the measurement of outcomes. Despite these flaws, it has been shown that psychologic treatment can significantly modify the type A behavior pattern in healthy individuals,[154] as well as patients with coronary artery disease.[155] In a meta-analysis of the literature on the psychologic treatment for the type A behavior pattern,[156] a wide variety of treatment types demonstrated efficacy. These included yoga, emotional support, community-wide public health efforts, and more standard group therapy interventions. It appeared that the treatments that were most successful in reducing type A behavior, however, were part of a multifaceted comprehensive treatment approach. The most efficacious of these comprehensive approaches was the combination of an educational intervention, a coping method utilizing either a relaxation or cognitive orientation, and a behavioral intervention.[156]

The Recurrent Coronary Prevention Project is the largest project to date to evaluate the efficacy of the group treatment of type A behavior. This study, consisting of 862 postmyocardial infarction patients, investigated the impact of the treatment of type A behavior on the rate of recurrence of myocardial infarction and cardiac death.[155, 157, 158] At 4½ years following the start of the study, type A behavior was markedly reduced in 35.1% of those receiving type A reduction treatment, compared to 9.8% of those who received standard care alone. The rate of cardiac recurrence was significantly less in the type A behavior modification group (12.9%) compared to the control group (21.2%). In addition, there was a significant reduction in the number of cardiac deaths in the group receiving treatment of type A behavior.

Frasure-Smith and Prince[159] conducted a long-term stress reduction study of 461 men with acute myocardial infarction. Study subjects participated in a 1-year randomized, controlled trial of a program consisting of monthly monitoring of psychological stress levels, and additional counseling visits by nurses for highly stressed patients. The program significantly reduced stress scores, had a marginal impact on cardiac mortality during the first postinfarct year, and significantly reduced long-term recurrences of acute myocardial infarction. The author has subsequently shown that the highly stressed patients in this study had a 3-fold increase in risk of cardiac mortality over a 5-year follow-up period. Those patients who were highly stressed but received the 1-year program of stress monitoring and intervention, however, did not experience any significant long-term increase in risk. Low-stress patients did not experience any benefit from the stress monitoring program.[159]

The meta-analysis of type A reduction treatment studies in cardiac patients has also demonstrated a 3-year reduction of 50% for combined mortality and recurrent myocardial infarction.[156] Ornish et al.[160] conducted a study utilizing a multifaceted treatment approach to reduce coronary atherosclerosis, and found regression of coronary atherosclerosis in 82% of the treatment group in 1 year. In contrast, the control group showed progression of their disease. The treatment approach used by Ornish et al. combined a low-fat vegetarian diet, stress management training, including yoga, meditation, and group therapy, and moderate exercise. In addition, patients were required to abstain from cigarette smoking in order to enter the study. The extent of regression was best predicted by overall adherence to the treatment intervention. Unfortunately, it is impossible to separate out the possible differential effects of the various components of the intervention in this study.

PHARMACOTHERAPY OF STRESS, HOSTILITY, AND TYPE A BEHAVIOR

Research findings suggest that psychopharmacologic treatments may be effective in modifying type A behavior and related hostility syndromes and may thereby reduce the morbidity and mortality of coronary artery disease. In individuals who do not respond to behavioral approaches to reduce stress, hostility, and type A behavior, the use of pharmacologic agents may become a viable treatment option. Beta-blockers were originally thought to be an effective treatment of type A behavior.[161] Follow-up studies of the use of betablockers to treat type A behavior have found inconsistent results and "modest at best" effects.[162] Benzodiazepines have been thought to be helpful in treating type A behavior and ameliorating the stress response. Alprazolam reduces plasma catecholamine levels in response to exercise stress,[163] and has been shown to effect cortisol and blood pressure responses to acute mental stress in type A subjects.[164] In addition, a recent preliminary study showed that treatment with alprazolam resulted in a significant, 70% reduction in the duration of silent ischemia in a small sample of coronary patients.[165] However, a group of studies exist which indicate that benzodiazepines can produce a paradoxical, aggression-enhancing or "disinhibiting" effect.[166]

Low levels of central serotonin have been found to be reduced in mood and personality disorder patients with a history of suicide or impulsive aggression. Evidence exists that central serotonergic activity is more closely associated with a tendency toward aggressive behavior, rather than the frank expression of aggression itself. More specifically, low central serotonin activity may be more associated with a lowered threshold for aggressive responses to noxious stimuli than aggression itself.[167] Low levels of central serotonin has been correlated with the urge to act out hostility in normal volunteers as well.[168] The phenomenon concerning the "urge to act out hostility" described in this literature appears quite similar to the constellation of characteristics identified as the salient features of coronary prone behavior.

Lowered central serotonergic activity has been shown to have a direct impact on the pathophysiology of sudden cardiac death. Rabinowitz and Lown[169] showed that central serotonin modulates autonomic neural activity and sympathetic input from the brain to the heart. An increase in central serotonergic activity was shown to inhibit the flow of arrhythmogenic sympathetic nerve traffic from the brain to the heart.[169] Lithium raises central serotonergic activity, and was the first drug shown to reduce human aggression.[170] The use of a central serotonin 1a agonist, buspirone, to reduce type A behavior and hostility, was studied in an open trial of 10 men with coronary artery disease, type A behavior, easily provoked hostility, and no axis I diagnosis by standard clinical diagnostic interview. This study used a battery of psychological tests and videotyped structured interviews to measure type A behavior, and demonstrated a significant reduction of type A behavior and hostility after treatment with buspirone.[171]

In summary, the body of literature previously described suggests three important findings. First, stress, type A behavior, and hostility can be reduced through the use of behavioral approaches. Second, reduction of these factors in patients with coronary artery disease decreases their morbidity and mortality. Third, central serotonergic activity appears to be a central biological mechanism for hostility, and pharmacologic agents that raise central serotonergic activity appear to reduce type A behavior and hostility. Continued research is needed to elucidate those relationships in order that clinical interventions can be specifically targetted to appropriate patients.

REFERENCES

1. Shopland D. *The Health Consequences of Smoking: Chronic Obstructive Lung Disease: A Report of the Surgeon General.* USDHEW Publication PHS-84-50205. Washington, DC: Government Printing Office;1984.
2. Vlieststra RE, Kronmal RA, Oberman A, Frye RL, Killip T. Effect of cigarette smoking on survival of patients with angiographically documented coronary artery disease. *JAMA.* 1986;255:1023–1027.
3. Sparrow D, Dawber TR. The influence of cigarette smoking on prognosis after a first myocardial infarction. *J Chronic Dis.* 1978;31:425–432.
4. Burling TA, Singleton EG, Bigelow GE, Baile WF, Gottlieb SH. Smoking following myocardial infarction: A critical review of the literature. *Health Psychol.* 1984;3:83–96.
5. Schwartz JL. *Review and Evaluation of Smoking Cessation Methods: The United States and Canada. 1978–1985.* US DHHS Public Health Service, NIH Publication No. 87-2940 Washington, DC: US Government Printing Office; 1987.
6. Hughes JR, Miller SA. Nicotine gum to help stop smoking. *JAMA.* 1984;252: 2855–2858.
7. Hughes JR, Hatsukami D. Signs and symptoms and tobacco withdrawal. *Arch Gen Psychiatry.* 1986;43:289–294.
8. Hughes JR, Gust SW, Keenan RM, Fenwick JW, Healey ML. Nicotine vs placebo gum in general medical practice. *JAMA.* 1989;261:1300–1305.
9. Goldstein MG, Niaura R, Follick MJ, Abrams DB. Effects of behavioral skills training and schedule of nicotine gum administration on smoking cessation. *Am J Psychiatry.* 1989;146:56–60.
10. Abelin T, Buehler A, Muller P, Vesanen K, Imhof PR. Controlled trial of transdermal nicotine patch in tobacco withdrawal. *Lancet.* 1989;i:7–10.

11. Glassman AH, Stetner F, Walsh BT, Raizman PS, Fleiss JL, Cooper TB, Covey LS. Heavy smokers, smoking cessation, and clonidine. *JAMA*. 1988; 259:2863–2866.

12. Glassman AH, Helzer JE, Covey LS, Cottler LB, Stetner F, Tipp JE, Johnson J. Smoking, smoking cessation, and major depression. *JAMA*. 1990;264:1546–1549.

13. Carney RM, Rich MW, TeVelde A, Saini J, Clark K. The relationship between heart rate, heart rate variability, and depression in patients with coronary artery disease. *J Psychosom Res*. 1988;31:4981–4988.

14. Kandel DB, Davies M. Adult sequelae of adolescent depressive symptoms. *Arch Gen Psychiatry*. 1986;43:255–262.

15. Covey LS, Glassman AH, Stetner F. Depression and depressive symptoms in smoking cessation. *Compr Psychiatry*. 1990;31:350–354.

16. Glassman AH, Covey LS. Future trends in the pharmacologic treatment of smoking cessation. *Drugs*. 1990;40:1–5.

17. Edwards NB, Murphy JK, Downs AD, Ackerman BJ, Rosenthal TL. Doxepin as an adjunct to smoking cessation: A double-blind pilot study. *Am J Psychiatry*. 1989;146:373–376.

18. Pomerleau OF, Adkins DM, Pertschuk M. Predictors of outcome and recidivism in smoking-cessation treatment. *Addict Behav*. 1978;3:65–70.

19. Gawin F, Compton M, Byck R. Potential use of buspirone as treatment for smoking cessation: A preliminary trial. *Fam Pract Recert*. 1989;11:74–78.

20. Hillerman DE, Mohuiddin SM, Del Core MG, Sketch MH. Effect of buspirone on withdrawal symptoms associated with smoking cessation. *Arch Intern Med*. 1992;152:350–352.

21. Oldridge NB, Guyatt GH, Fischer ME, Rimm AA. Cardiac rehabilitation after myocardial infarction; combined experience of randomized clinical trials. *JAMA*. 1988;260:945–950.

22. Leon AS, Connett J, Jacobs DR, Rauramaa R. Leisure-time physical activity levels and risk of coronary heart disease and death: The multiple risk factor intervention trial. *JAMA*. 1987;258:2388–2395.

23. Lavie C, Milani R, Littman A. Benefits of cardiac rehabilitation and exercise training in secondary coronary prevention in the elderly. *J Am Coll Cardiol*. In press.

24. Powell KE, Thompson PD, Casperson CJ, Kendrick JS. Physical activity and the incidence of coronary artery disease. *Annu Rev Publ Health*. 1987;8:253–287.

25. Blair SN, Kohl HW, Paffenbarger RS, Clark DG, Cooper KH, Gibbons LW. Physical fitness and all-cause mortality: A prospective study of healthy men and women. *JAMA*. 1989;262:2395–2401.

26. Paffenbarger RS, Hyde RT, Wing AL, Steinmetz CH. A natural history of athleticism and cardiovascular health. *JAMA*. 1984;252:491–495.

27. Downing J, Littman A, Scheer J, Pegg B. Depressive symptoms in cardiac rehabilitation patients correlates with blunted training effect. *J Am Coll Cardiol*. 1992;19:257A.

28. Milani R, Littman A, Lavie C. Depressive symptoms predict functional improvement following cardiac rehabilitation and exercise program. *J Cardiopulm Rehabil*. In press.

29. Taylor CB, Houston-Miller N, Ahn DK, Haskell W, DeBusk RF. The effects of exercise training programs on psychosocial improvement in uncomplicated postmyocardial infarction patients. *J Psychosom Res.* 1986;30:581–587.
30. Moses J, Steptoe A, Mathews A, Edwards S. The effects of exercise training on mental well-being in the normal population: A controlled trial. *J Psychosom Res.* 1989;33:47–61.
31. Stern MJ, Gorman PA, Kaslow L. The group counselling v exercise therapy study: A controlled intervention with subjects following myocardial infarction. *Arch Intern Med.* 1983;143:1719–1725.
32. Blumenthal JA, Fredikson M, Kuhn CM, Ulmer RL, Walsh-Riddle M, Appelbaum M. Aerobic exercise reduces levels of cardiovascular and sympathoadrenal responses to mental stress in subjects without prior evidence of myocardial ischemia. *AJC.* 1990;65:93–98.
33. Blumenthal JA, Emery CF, Walsh MA, Cox DR, Kuhn CM, Williams RB, Williams RS. Exercise training in healthy Type A middle-aged men: Effects on behavioral and cardiovascular responses. *Psychosom Med.* 1988;50:418–433.
34. Naughton JP. Physical activity and coronary heart disease. In Wilson PK, ed. *Adult Fitness and Cardiac Rehabilitation.* Baltimore: University Park Press; 1975: pp 3–8.
35. Hubert HB, Feinleib M, McNamara PM, Castelli WP. Obesity as an independent risk factor for cardiovascular disease: A 26-year follow-up of participants in the Framingham Heart Study. *Circulation.* 1983;67:968–977.
36. Wood PD, Stefanick ML, Dreon DM, Frey-Hewitt B, Garay SD, Williams PT, Superko HR, Fortmann SP, Albers JJ, Vranizan KM, Ellsworth NM, Terry RB, Haskell WL. Changes in plasma lipids and lipoproteins in overweight men during weight loss through dieting as compared with exercise. *N Engl J Med.* 1988;319:1173–1179.
37. Muldoon MF, Manuck SB, Matthews KA. Lowering cholesterol concentrations and mortality: A quantitative review of primary prevention trials. *Br Med J.* 1990;301:309–314.
38. Study Group of the European Atherosclerosis Society. Strategies for the prevention of coronary heart disease: A policy statement of the European Atherosclerosis Society. *Eur Heart J.* 1987;8:77–88.
39. Consensus Conference. Lowering blood cholesterol to prevent heart disease. *JAMA.* 1985;253:2080–2086.
40. Fowkes FGR, Leng GC, Donnan PT, Deary IJ, Riemersma RA, Housley E. Serum cholesterol, triglycerides, and aggression in the general population. *Lancet.* 1992;340:995–998.
41. Brunner E, Davey Smith G, Pilgrim J, Marmot M. Low serum cholesterol and suicide. *Lancet.* 1992;339:1001–1002.
42. Pekkanen J, Nissinen A, Punaar S, Karnonen MJ. Serum cholesterol and risk of accident or violent death in a 25 year follow up: The Finnish cohorts of the seven countries study. *Arch Intern Med.* 1989;149:1589–1591.
43. Davey Smith G, Shipley MJ, Marmot MG, Rose G. Plasma cholesterol concentrations and mortality: The Whitehall study. *JAMA.* 1992;267:70–76.
44. Frachi G, Menotti A, Conti S. Coronary risk factors and survival probability from coronary and other causes of death. *Am J Epidemiol.* 1987;126:400–408.

45. Kromhout D, Katan MB, Menotti A, Keys A, Bloemberg B. Serum cholesterol and long-term death rates from suicide, accidents, or violence. *Lancet.* 1992;340:317.
46. Vikkunen M. Serum cholesterol in anti-social personality. *Neuropsychobiology.* 1979;5:27–30.
47. Vikkunen M, Pentinnen H. Serum cholesterol in aggressive conduct disorder: A preliminary study. *Biol Psychiatry.* 1984;19:435–439.
48. Muldoon MF, Kaplan JR, Manuck SB, Mann JJ. Effects of dietary fat on central nervous system serotonergic activity (abstract.) *Psychosom Med.* 1991;53:216.
49. Engelburg H. Low serum cholesterol and suicide. *Lancet.* 1992; 339:727–729.
50. Davey Smith G, Pekkanen J. Should there be a moratorium on the use of cholesterol lowering drugs? *Br Med J.* 1992;304:431–434.
51. Kurosawa H, Shimiza Y, Nishimatsu Y, Horose S, Takamo T. The relationship between mental disorders and physical disorders in patients with acute myocardial infarction. *Jpn Circ J.* 1983;47:723–725.
52. Wynn A. Unwarranted emotional distress in men with ischaemic heart disease. *Med J Aust.* 1967;ii:847–851.
53. Cay EL, Vetter N, Philip AE, Dugand P. Psychological status during recovery from an acute heart attack. *J Psychosom Res.* 1972;16:425–435.
54. Kavanaugh IT, Shephard RJ, Tuck JA. Depression after myocardial infarction. *Can Med Assn J.* 1975;113:23–27.
55. Stern JJ, Pascale L, Ackerman A. Life adjustment post myocardial infarction: Determining predictive variables. *Arch Intern Med.* 1977;137:1680–1685.
56. Wishnie HA, Hackett TP, Cassem NH. Psychological hazards of convalescence following myocardial infarction. *JAMA.* 1971;215:1292–1296.
57. Lloyd GG, Cawley RH. Psychiatric morbidity in men one week after first acute myocardial infarction. *Br Med J.* 1978;ii:1453–1454.
58. House A. Mood disorders in the physically ill—problems of definition and measurement. *J Psychosom Res.* 1988;32:345–353.
59. Hackett TP. Depression following myocardial infarction. *Psychosomatics.* 1985;25(suppl):23–28.
60. Cassem NH, Hackett TP. Psychological rehabilitation of myocardial infarction patients in the acute phase. *Heart Lung.* 1973;2:383–385.
61. Wells KB, Stewart A, Hays RP, Burnam MA, Rogers W, Daniels MS, Berry S, Greenfield S, Ware J. The function and well-being of depressed patients—Results from the medical outcome study. *JAMA.* 1989;262:914–919.
62. Klerman GL. Depressive disorders—further evidence for increased medical morbidity and impairment of social functioning. *Arch Gen Psychiatry.* 1989;46:856–858.
63. Blumenthal JA, Williams RS, Wallace AG, Williams RB, Needles TL. Physiological and psychological variables predict compliance to prescribed exercise therapy for inpatients recovering from myocardial infarction. *Psychosom Med.* 1982;44:519–527.
64. Finnegan DL, Suler JR. Psychological factors associated with maintenance of improved health behaviors in postcoronary patients. *J Psychol.* 1985;119:81–94.
65. Malzberg B. Mortality among patients with involution melancholia. *Am J Psychiatry.* 1937;93:1231–1238.

66. Murphy JM, Monson RR, Oliver DC, Sobol AM, Leighton AH. Affective disorders and mortality. *Arch Gen Psychiatry.* 1987;44:473–480.
67. Rubins PV, Harris K, Koven S. High fatality rates of late life depression associated with cardiovascular disease. *J Affective Disord.* 1985;9:165–167.
68. Avery D, Winokur G. Mortality in depressed patients treated with electroconvulsive therapy and antidepressants. *Arch Gen Psychiatry.* 1976;33: 1029–1037.
69. Carney RM, Rich MW, Friedland KE, Saint J, TeVelde A, Simeone C, Clark K. Major depressive disorder predicts cardiac events in patients with coronary artery disease. *Psychosom Med.* 1988;50:627–633.
70. Schleifer SJ, Macani-Hinson MM, Coyle DA. The nature and course of depression following myocardial infarction. *Arch Intern Med.* 1989;149:1785–1789.
71. Cassem NH. Cardiovascular effects of antidepressants. *J Clin Psychiatry.* 1982;43(sec 2):22–29.
72. Giardina EG, Bigger JT, Glassman AH. The electrocardiographic and antiarrhythmic effects of imipramine hydrochloride at therapeutic plasma concentrations. *Circulation.* 1979;60:1045–1052.
73. Roose SP, Glassman AH, Dalack GW. Depression, heart disease, and tricyclic antidepressants. *J Clin Psychiatry.* 1989;50:(suppl):7–16.
74. Baldessarini RJ. *Chemotherapy in Psychiatry.* Cambridge, MA: Harvard University Press;1985: pp 156–157.
75. Glassman AH, Bigger JT, Giardina EV, Kantor SJ, Perel JM, Davies M. Clinical characteristic of imipramine-induced orthostatic hypotension. *Lancet.* 1979;1:468–472.
76. Roose SP, Glassman AH, Siris SG, Walsh BT, Bruno RL, Wright LB. Comparison of imipramine- and nortryptyline-induced orthostatic hypotension: A meaningful difference. *J Clin Psychopharmacol.* 1981;1:316–319.
77. Glassman AH, Roose SP, Giardina EGV. Cardiovascular effects of tricyclic antidepressants. In: Meltzer HY, ed. *Psychopharmacology: The Third Generation in Progress.* New York: Raven Press;1987: pp 1437–1442.
78. Glassman AH, Johnson LL, Giardina EGV. The use of imipramine in depressed patients with congestive heart failure. *JAMA.* 1983;250:1997–2001.
79. Roose SP, Glassman AH, Giardina EGV. Cardiovascular effects of imipramine and buproprion in depressed patients with congestive heart failure. *J Clin Psychopharmacol.* 1987;7:247–251.
80. Roose SP, Glassman AH, Giardina EGV. Nortriptyline in depressed patients with left ventricular impairment. *JAMA.* 1986;256:3253–3257.
81. Williams RB, Sherter C. Cardiac complications of tricyclic antidepressant therapy. *Ann Intern Med.* 1971;74:395–398.
82. Giardina EGV, Bigger JT. Antiarrhythmic effect of imipramine hydrochloride in patients with ventricular premature complexes without psychological depression. *Am J Cardiol.* 1982;50:172–179.
83. Giardina EGV, Barnard T, Johnson LL. The antiarrhythmic effect of nortriptyline in cardiac patients with ventricular premature depolarizations. *J Am Coll Cardiol.* 1986;7:1363–1369.
84. Weld FM, Bigger JT. Electrophysiological effects of imipramine on ovine cardiac Purkinje and ventricular muscle fibers. *Circ Res.* 1980;46:167–175.

85. Glassman AH, Bigger JT. Cardiovascular effects of therapeutic doses of tricyclic antidepressants: A review. *Arch Gen Psychiatry.* 1981;38:815–822.
86. Roose SP, Glassman AH, Giardina EGV. Tricyclic antidepressants in depressed patients with cardiac conduction disease. *Arch Gen Psychiatry.* 1987;44:273–275.
87. Veith RC, Raskind MA, Caldwell JH. Cardiovascular effects of tricyclic antidepressants in depressed patients with chronic heart disease. *N Engl J Med.* 1982;306:954–959.
88. Roose SP, Glassman AH, Giardina EGV. Cardiovascular effects of imipramine and buproprion in depressed patients with congestive heart failure. *J Clin Psychopharmacol.* 1987;7:247–251.
89. Davidson JRT, Miller RD, Turnbull CD. Atypical depression. *Arch Gen Psychiatry.* 1982;39:527–534.
90. Sheehan DV. Delineation of anxiety and phobic disorders responsive to monoamine oxidase inhibitors: Implications for classification. *J Clin Psychiatry.* 1984;457(sec 2):29–32.
91. Kronig MH, Roose SP, Walsh BT, Woodring S, Glassman A. Blood pressure effects of phenelzine. *J Clin Psychopharmacol.* 1983;3:307–310.
92. Pi EH, Simpson GM. New antidepressants: A review. *Hosp Formulary.* 1985; 20:580–583.
93. Byrne JE, Gomoll AW. Differential effects of trazodone and imipramine on intracardiac conduction in the anesthetized dog. *Arch Int Pharmacodyn.* 1982;259:259–270.
94. Hames TK, Burgess CD, George CF. Hemodynamic responses of trazodone and imipramine. *Clin Pharmacol Ther.* 1982;12:497–502.
95. Janowsky D, Curtis G, Zisook S, Kuhn K, Resovsky K, LeWinter M. Ventricular arrhythmias possibly aggravated by trazodone. *Am J Psychiatry.* 1983;140: 796–797.
96. Vlay SC, Friedling S. Trazodone exacerbation of VT. *Am Heart J.* 1983;105:604. Letter.
97. Wenger TL, Cohn JB, Bustrack J. Comparison of the effects of bupropion and amitryptyline on cardiac conduction in depressed patients. *J Clin Psychiatry.* 1983;44:174–175.
98. Peck AW, Stem WC, Watkinson C. Incidence of seizures during treatment with tricyclic antidepressants and bupropion. *J Clin Psychiatry.* 1983;44:197–201.
99. Feighner JP. Clinical efficacy of the newer antidepressants. *J Clin Psychopharmacol.* 1981;1:23–28.
100. Fisch C. Effect of fluoxetine on the electrocardiogram. *J Clin Psychiatry.* 1985;46:42–44.
101. Cooper GL. The safety of fluoxetine: An update. *Br J Psychiatry.* 1988;153(suppl 3):77–86.
102. Woods SW, Tesar GE, Murry GB, Cassem NH. Psychostimulant treatment of depressive disorders secondary to medical illness. *J Clin Psychiatry.* 1986; 47:12–15.
103. Kaufman MW, Cassem NH, Murray GB, Jenike MA. The use of methylphenidate in depressed patients after cardiac surgery. *J Clin Psychiatry.* 1984;45:82–85.
104. Lydiard RB, Gelenburg AJ. Hazards and adverse effects of lithium. *Annu Rev Med.* 1982;33:327–344.

105. Schou M. Electrocardiographic changes during treatment with lithium and with drugs of the imipramine-type. *Acta Psychiatr Scand.* 1963;169:258–259.
106. Jefferson JW, Kalin NH. Serum lithium levels and long-term diuretic use. *JAMA.* 1979;241:1134–1136.
107. Fowler NO, McCall D, Chou T, Holmes JC, Hanenson IB. Electrocardiographic changes and cardiac arrhythmias in patients receiving psychotropic drugs. *Am J Cardiol.* 1976;37:223–230.
108. Hunter J. *A Treatise on the Blood and Gun Shot Wounds with a Short Account of the Author's Life.* London: Richardson;1794.
109. Osler W. Angina pectoris. Delivered before the Royal College of Physicians of London. *Lancet.* 1910;i:839–840.
110. Reich P. How much does stress contribute to cardiovascular disease? *J Cardiovascular Med.* 1983;8:825–831.
111. Kobasa SC. Stressful life events, personality, and health: An inquiry into hardiness. *J Pers Soc Psychol.* 1979;37:1–11.
112. Gentry WD, Kobasa SC. Social and psychological resources mediating stress-illness relationships in humans. In: Gentry WD, ed. *Handbook of Behavioral Medicine.* New York: Guilford;1984.
113. Friedman M, Rosenman RH. *Type A Behavior and Your Heart.* New York: Knopf;1974.
114. Friedman M, Ulmer D. *Treating Type A Behavior and Your Heart.* New York: Fawcett Crest;1984: pp 33–46.
115. Rosenman RH, Brand RJ, Jenkins CD, Friedman M, Straus R, Wurm M. Coronary heart disease in the Western Collaborative Group Study: Final follow-up experience of 8.5 years. *JAMA.* 1975;233:872–877.
116. Jenkins CD, Zyzanski SJ, Rosenman RH. Risk of new myocardial infarction in middle-aged men with manifest coronary heart disease. *Circulation.* 1976;53:342–347.
117. Zyzanski SJ, Jenkins CD, Ryan TJ, Flessas A, Everist M. Psychological correlates of coronary angiographic findings. *Arch Intern Med.* 1976;136:1234–1237.
118. Blumenthal JA, Williams RGJ, Kong Y, Schanberg SM, Thompson LW. Type A behavior pattern and coronary atherosclerosis. *Circulation.* 1978; 58:634–639.
119. Frank KA, Heller SS, Kornfeld DS, Sporn AA, Weiss MB. Type A behavior pattern and coronary angiographic findings. *JAMA.* 1978; 240:761–763.
120. The Review Panel on Coronary-Prone Behavior and Coronary Heart Disease: Coronary-prone behavior and coronary heart disease: A critical review. *Circulation.* 1981;63:1199–1215.
121. Shekelle RB, Hulley SB, Neaton JD. The MRFIT behavior pattern study. II. Type A behavior and incidence of coronary heart disease. *Am J Epidemiol.* 1985;122:559–570.
122. Shekelle RB, Gale M, Norusis M. Type A score (Jenkins Activity Survey) and risk of recurrent coronary heart disease in the aspirin myocardial infarction study. *Am J Cardiol.* 1985;56:221–225.
123. Case RB, Heller SS, Case NB. Type A behavior and survival after acute myocardial infarction. *N Engl J Med.* 1985;312:737–741.
124. Dimsdale JE. A perspective on type A behavior and coronary artery disease. *N Engl J Med.* 1988;318:111–112.

125. Matthews KA, Haynes SG. Type A behavior pattern and coronary disease risk: Update and critical evaluation. *Am J Epidemiol.* 1986;123:923–960.

126. Matthews KA, Glass DC, Rosenman RH, Bortner RW. Competitive drive, pattern A, and coronary heart disease: A further analysis of some data from the Western Collaborative Group Study. *J Chronic Dis.* 1977;30:489–498.

127. Dembroski TM, MacDougall JM, Costa PT. Components of hostility as predictors of sudden death and myocardial infarction in the multiple risk factor intervention trial. *Psychosom Med.* 1989;51:514.

128. MacDougall JM, Dembroski TM, Dimsdale JE, Hackett TP. Components of type A, hostility, and anger. Further relationships to angiographic findings. *Health Psychol.* 1985;4:137–152.

129. Cook WW, Medley DM. Proposed hostility and pharisaic virtue scales for the MMPI. *J Appl Psychol.* 1954;38:414–418.

130. Barefoot JC, Dahlstrom WG, Williams RB. Hostility, CHD incidence, and total mortality: A 25-year follow-up study of 255 physicians. *Psychosom Med.* 1983;45:59–63.

131. Williams RB, Haney TL, Lee KL, Kong Y, Blumenthal J, Whalen R. Type A behavior, hostility, and coronary atherosclerosis. *Psychosom Med.* 1980;42:539–549.

132. Barefoot JC, Dodge KA, Peterson BL, Dahlstrom WG, Williams RB. The Cook-Medley hostility scale: Item content and ability to predict survival. *Psychosom Med.* 1989;51:46–57.

133. Smith TW. Hostility and health: Current status of a psychosomatic hypothesis. *Health Psychol.* 1992;11:139–150.

134. Tyroler HA, Haynes SG, Cobb LA, Irvin CW, James SA, Kuller LH, Miller RE, Shumaker SA, Syme LA, Wolf S. Environmental risk factors in coronary artery disease. *Circulation.* 1987;76(suppl I):139–144.

135. Syme SL. Coronary artery disease: A sociocultural perspective. *Circulation.* 1987;76(suppl I):112–116.

136. Ruberman W, Weinblatt E, Goldberg JD, Chaudary BS. Psychosocial influences on mortality after myocardial infarction. *N Engl J Med.* 1984;311:552–559.

137. Case RB, Moss AJ, Case N, McDermott M, Eberly S. Living alone after myocardial infarction: impact on prognosis. *JAMA.* 1992;267:515–519.

138. Marmot MG. Stress, social and cultural variations in heart disease. *J Psychosom Res.* 1983;27:377–384.

139. Williams RB, Barefoot JC, Califf RM, Haney TL, Saunders WB, Pryor DB, Hlatky MA, Siegler IC, Mark DB. Prognostic importance of social and economic resources among medically treated patients with angiographically documented coronary artery disease. *JAMA.* 1992;267:520–524.

140. Karasek R, Baker D, Marxer F, Ahlbom A, Theorell T. Job decision latitude, job demands, and cardiovascular disease: A prospective study of Swedish men. *Am J Public Health.* 1981;71:694–705.

141. Frank C, Smith S. Stress and the heart: Biobehavioral aspects of sudden cardiac death. *Psychosomatics.* 1990;31:255–264.

142. Lown B, Verrier RL, Corbalan R. Psychologic stress and threshold for repetitive ventricular response. *Science.* 1973;182:834–836.

143. Verrier RL, Lown B. Behavioral stress and cardiac arrhythmias. *Annu Rev Physiol.* 1984;46:155–176.

144. Rozanski A, Bairey CN, Krantz DS, Friedman J, Resser KJ, Morell M, Hilton-Chalfen S, Hestrin L, Bietendorf J, Berman DS. Mental stress and the induction of silent myocardial ischemia in patients with coronary artery disease. *N Engl J Med*. 1988;318:1005–1012.
145. Yeung AC, Vekshtein VI, Vita JA, Fish RD, Krantz DS, Ganz P, Selwyn AP. Vasomotor response of coronary arteries to mental stress (abstract). *Circulation*. 1989;80(suppl II):591.
146. Specchia G, de Servi S, Falcone C, Gravazzi A, Angoli L, Bramucci E, Ardissino D, Mussini A. Mental arithmetic stress testing in patients with coronary artery disease. *Am Heart J*. 1984;108:56–63.
147. Verrier RL, Hagestad EL, Lown B. Delayed myocardial ischemia induced by anger. *Circulation*. 1987;75:249–254.
148. Hayano J, Sakakibara Y, Yamada M, Ohte N, Fujinami T, Yokoyama K, Watanabe Y, Takata K. Decreased magnitude of heart rate spectral components in coronary artery disease: Its relation to angiographic severity. *Circulation*. 1990;81:1217–1224.
149. Billman GE, Hoskins RS. Time-series analysis of heart rate variability during submaximal exercise: Evidence for reduced cardial vagal tone in animals susceptible to ventricular fibrillation. *Circulation*. 1989;80:146–157.
150. Kamada T, Miyake S, Kumashiro M, Monou H, Inoue K. Power spectral analysis of heart rate variability in type As and type Bs during mental workload. *Psychosom Med*. 1992;54:462–470.
151. Carney RM, Rich MW, TeVelde A, Saini J, Clark K, Freedland KE. The relationship between heart rate, heart rate variability and depression in patients with coronary artery disease. *J Psychosom Res*. 1988;32:159–164.
152. Clarkson TB. Personality, gender and coronary artery atherosclerosis of monkeys. *Arteriosclerosis*. 1987;7:16–23.
153. Fava M, Littman A, Halperin P. Neuroendocrine correlates of the type A behavior pattern: A review and new hypothesis. *Int J Psychiatry Med*. 1987; 17:289–307.
154. Gill JJ, Price VA, Friedman M, Thoresen CE, Powell LH, Ulmer D, Brown B, Drews FR. Reduction in type A behavior in healthy middle-aged American military officers. *Am Heart J*. 1985;110:503–514.
155. Friedman M, Thoresen CE, Gill JJ, Powell LH, Ulmer D, Thompson L, Price VA, Rabin DD, Breall WS, Dixon T, Levy R, Bourg E. Alteration of type A behavior and reduction in cardiac recurrences in postmyocardial infarction patients. *Am Heart J*. 1984;108:237–248.
156. Nunes EV, Frank KA, Kornfeld DS. Psychologic treatment for the type A behavior pattern and for coronary heart disease: A meta-analysis of the literature. *Psychosom Med*. 1987;48:159–173.
157. Friedman M, Thoresen CE, Gill JJ, Ulmer D, Powell LH, Price VA, Brown B, Thompson L, Rabin DD, Breall WS, Bourg E, Levy R, Dixon T. Alteration of type A behavior and its effect on cardiac recurrences in post myocardial infarction patients: Summary results of the recurrent coronary prevention project. *Am Heart J*. 1986; 112:653–663.
158. Friedman M, Powell L, Thoresen CE, Ulmer D, Price VA, Gill JJ, Thompson L, Rabin DD, Brown B, Breall WS, Levy R, Bourg E. Effect of discontinuance of type A behavioral counseling on type A behavior and cardiac

recurrence rate of postmyocardial infarction patients. *Am Heart J.* 1987;114: 483–490.

159. Frasure-Smith N, Prince R. Long-term follow-up of the Ischemic Heart Disease Life Stress Monitoring Program. *Psychosom Med.* 1989;51:485–513.

160. Ornish D, Brown SE, Scherwitz LW, Billings JH, Armstrong WT, Ports TA, McLanahan SM, Kirkeeide RL, Brand RJ, Gould KL. Can lifestyle changes reverse coronary heart disease? *Lancet.* 1990;336:129–133.

161. Krantz DS, Contrada RJ, Durel LA, Hill R, Friedler E, Lazar JD. Comparative effects of two beta-blockers on cardiovascular reactivity and type A behavior in hypertensives. *Psychosom Med.* 1988;50:615–626.

162. Schmiedler R, Friedrich G, Neus H, Rudel H, von Eiff AW. The influence of beta blockers on cardiovascular reactivity and type A behavior pattern in hypertensives. *Psychosom Med.* 1983;45:417–423.

163. Stratton JR, Halter JB. Effect of benzodiazepine (alprazolam) on plasma epinephrine and norepinephrine levels during exercise stress. *Am J Cardiol.* 1985;56:136–139.

164. Williams RB, Schanberg SM, Kuhn CM, Lane JD. Influence of alprazolam on neuroendocrine and cardiovascular response to stress in type A men. Annu Meet Am Coll Neuropsychopharmacol, Washington, DC;1986.

165. Shell WE, Swan HJC. Treatment of silent myocardial ischemia with transdermal nitroglycerine added to beta-blockers and alprazolam. *Cardiol Clin.* 1986;4:697–704.

166. Wilkinson CJ. Effects of diazepam (valium) and trait anxiety on human physical aggression and emotional state. *J Behavioral Med.* 1985;8:101–114.

167. Coccaro E. Central serotonin and impulsive aggression. *Br J Psychiatry.* 1989;155:52–62.

168. Roy A, Adinoff B, Linnoila M. Acting out hostility in normal volunteers: Negative correlation with levels of 5-HIAA in cerebrospinal fluid. *Psychiatry Res.* 1989;24:187–194.

169. Rabinowitz S, Lown B. Central neurochemical factors related to serotonin metabolism and cardiac ventricular vulnerability for repetitive electrical activity. *Am J Cardiol.* 1978,41:516–522.

170. Sheard MH. Effect of lithium on human aggression. *Nature.* 1971; 230:113.

171. Littman A, Fava M, McKool K, Lamon-Fava S, Pegg E. The use of buspirone in the treatment of stress, hostility, and type A behavior in cardiac patients: An open trial. *Psychother Psychosom.* 1993;59:107–110.

Chapter 15
Psychosomatic Aspects of End-Stage Renal Failure

Tom Sensky

Across Europe, approximately 50 to 80 people per million develop end-stage renal disease (ESRD) each year, requiring some form of renal replacement therapy.[1] In the United States, more than 100,000 people receive treatment for ESRD.[2] Renal hemodialysis first became available in the mid-1940s. Until relatively recently, the limited availability of dialysis machines resulted in some selectivity in the age of patients, and the types of disease, accepted for renal replacement therapy. More recently, numerous innovations have considerably increased the availability and success of dialysis and transplantation. While previously patients had to come to a specialist unit for regular dialysis, many more now have the facilities to dialyse in their own homes. Other treatment advances have had a considerable impact on people who dialyse, notably the recent introduction of erythropoietin therapy.[3, 4] The development of continuous ambulatory peritoneal dialysis (CAPD) in Canada in the mid-1970s marked a further breakthrough; CAPD does not involve the complex technology of hemodialysis. Patients not only benefit by being free of the dialysis machine, but CAPD also offers more sustained control of uremia and allows a more liberal dietary and fluid intake regime. Many nephrologists favor CAPD for their young or elderly patients, although the long-term effects of CAPD are not yet as well established as those of hemodialysis. The age range of dialysis patients has risen steadily, as has the proportion of patients over 65 years old.[2, 5] For many patients with ESRD, the favored treatment is renal transplantation. Here also, considerable advances have been made in the last decade; for example, through improved immunosuppressive techniques. This has led to improved success rates of transplantation[6] and a consistent decline in mortality (gross mortality among European renal transplant recipients fell from 4.2 to 2.4% during the years 1980 to 1987.[1] The psychosocial aspects of ESRD must be seen in the context of these treatment advances. While many psychosocial factors described in the early literature on renal replacement therapy remain significant today, their importance relative to other factors might have altered considerably. One other disease-related factor is particularly relevant to the adequate understanding of the psychosocial aspects of ESRD. A sizable proportion of patients receiving renal replacement therapy also have diabetes. People with diabetes constitute more than a quarter of those who start renal replacement therapy in the United States, although this proportion is substantially lower in Europe.[5] These people have to cope not only with their renal replacement therapy but also with diabetes, which leads to a significantly worse prognosis in ESRD.[2, 5] However, the recent introduction of combined kidney–pancreas transplantation promises a better outcome for this group of patients.[7, 8] There have been numerous comprehensive reviews of psychosocial aspects of ESRD.[9–14] Rather than duplicate these, the present paper will focus on selected questions relevant to clinicians working with people with ESRD, and assess critically to what extent published research provides answers for these. Attention will be confined to adults with ESRD—the psychosocial aspects of ESRD in children will not be discussed.

ESRD—A "TYPICAL" CHRONIC PHYSICAL ILLNESS?

Chronic physical illness, whatever its origin, taxes the individual's ability to cope and demands adjustments to behavior and emotions from patient and family alike. However, ESRD is more than just another chronic illness, for several reasons. There are few if any parallels to the experience of hemodialysis. Twice or three times weekly, the person becomes a patient, completely dependent on a machine for survival. This dependence extends to renal unit staff, or to family members where patients dialyse at home. In many instances, home dialysis is only possible because of the active help of family members. In such cases, the dialysis sessions often become part of the family routine. By contrast, between dialysis, the person often shows no signs of "illness." Renal unit staff and family alike may put pressure on the individual to lead a "normal" life, placing the individual into a form of *double bind*.[15] Hemodialysis therefore represents an extreme form of the *sick role cycle*.[16]

Many patients at some stage of their illness have a *choice* of renal replacement treatments. In terminal heart or liver failure, death is inevitable without transplantation. Patients with ESRD can often choose between having a transplant and remaining on dialysis. Despite the evidence of improved health and life satisfaction, which is possible with a successful transplant, some patients elect to remain on dialysis.[17] The decision to join the waiting list for transplantation is difficult, particularly because many patients will have experience of a rejected graft, either personally or through talking to others in the clinic or the dialysis unit. Having joined the transplant list, other pressures arise. For example, when a donor kidney becomes available, several potential recipients are called into the transplant unit. Although this procedure is intended to find the most suitable match between the donor kidney and the potential recipients, patients and their families often perceive the process differently, sometimes attributing their failure to be selected for the transplant to personal factors, such as being unmarried, or not complying as well as they should have done with their diet. Although transient, such stressors are important, and occur frequently in all transplant units. The possibility of using live donors also distinguishes renal transplantation from other forms of transplant surgery. The use of live donors is controversial.[18–21] However, it is generally accepted that while the demand for kidney transplants outstrips the supply of cadaveric organs, live related donors will continue to be required.[22] The percentage of transplants from live donors ranges from approximately 6% in Australia to more than 25% in the United States.[22]

These and other aspects of ESRD which arguably make it a unique condition have attracted comment, particularly from a psychodynamic perspective.[23–29] However, they have been subjected to very little systematic investigation, with the exception of the role of patients' families in general, and live donors in particular (see below).

PSYCHIATRIC MORBIDITY

As in other chronic physical illness, the predominant psychiatric diagnoses in ESRD are depression and anxiety.[30, 31] Approximately 5% of transplant recipients experience psychotic symptoms in the postoperative period,[32, 33] although this prevalence may have dropped with the less enthusiastic use of steroids for immunosuppression. Uremic encephalopathy presents as a typical acute brain syndrome, which is usually alleviated by dialysis, and relieved by transplantation.[34] In addition to uremia, parathyroid hormone probably has an etiological role. Hyperparathyroidism alone can produce a similar clinical presentation, and in dialysands with encephalopathy, parathyroidectomy can lead to clinical improvement.[35] Patients on dialysis may develop a chronic brain syndrome, sometimes associated with aluminum toxicity,[36] but not always so.[35] The incidence of the dialysis disequilibrium syndrome, in which cerebral edema is thought to have a contributing role,[35] has been reduced following refinements in dialysis technique. Aside from such gross presentation of organic brain syndromes, patients on dialysis and their families sometimes report changes in cognitive functioning and mood in relation to time after dialysis. While these changes may be too subtle for clinicians to observe with confidence, formal psychometric testing reveals, for example, improvements in memory, and possibly also attention, immediately after dialysis sessions.[37] The possible impact of such fluctuations in intellect and emotions on the responses of dialysis patients to questionnaires or interviews is unknown, having been almost entirely ignored in research work to date.

Reported prevalence rates of depression vary from zero to 100%.[38] This wide range of results can be accounted for by the choice in many studies of inappropriate measures of depression or psychiatric morbidity, such as the Beck Depression Inventory[39–41] or the General Health Questionnaire.[42, 43] Not only is it inappropriate to use these *screening* questionnaires as *case-finding* instruments, but they overestimate prevalence rates in the physically ill, where somatic symptoms may be due to the underlying physical illness(es) rather than to depression.[38] For example, in one patient sample, 47% of patients rated as depressed on the Beck Depression Inventory, but only 5% fulfilled DSM-III criteria for depression.[38] Where rigorous methods of diagnosis have been applied, more consistent prevalence rates of depression have been reported, of 30% or less.[30, 31, 44–46]

Numerous investigators have attempted to compare rates of depression, or of psychiatric morbidity, associated with different forms of renal replacement therapy. Unfortunately, few such studies have paid adequate attention to matching the patient groups.[47] For example, compared with people who come to hospital for dialysis, those who dialyse at home are more likely to be less disabled by their physical symptoms, have good family support, and be employed. For this reason, patients on home dialysis might be expected to have lower prevalence rates of depression than those who dialyse in hospital. Some studies have presented results for all dialysis patients in their sample, without distinguishing between home or hospital dialysis, or CAPD.

Similar problems arise in comparing psychiatric morbidity amongst those on dialysis and those who have received transplants. While some studies have reported lower rates of psychiatric morbidity after transplantation,[30] others have found little difference between transplant recipients and dialysands in this respect.[42] With a few exceptions,[31, 48–50] these studies have been limited by their cross-sectional design. Prospective, longitudinal investigations have suggested that successful transplantation is indeed associated with a lower rate of psychiatric symptomatology.[31, 48] However, transplant recipients whose grafts fail tend to do badly.[51]

Depressive symptoms are more common in those with a past history of depression,[31, 50, 52] and may decline with duration of treatment.[30, 52, 53] The results of several studies[30, 31, 52] indicate that in ESRD, as in other chronic physical illnesses,[54, 55] symptoms of depression are transient. Symptoms of depression or hopelessness have been associated in some studies with cognitive factors such as appraisal of poor control over health[31, 40, 56] or of the intrusiveness of the illness.[57] Mood disturbance has also been associated with the failure to use adaptive avoidance as a coping strategy.[58]

Numerous authors have stressed the problems in accurately diagnosing depression in ESRD.[59–62] Symptoms which are particularly helpful in discriminating between depressed and nondepressed people with ESRD include depressed mood, hopelessness, worthlessness, guilt, and suicidal ideation.[46, 52] Fatigue and sleep disturbance are unhelpful in this respect.[63] As in any other physical illness, it is important that depression be recognized and adequately treated, with antidepressants[64–66] and/or psychological interventions such as cognitive therapy.[55, 67] One reason for this is that depression may in some instances be associated with poor compliance with, or withdrawal from, active treatment (dialysis, dietary restrictions, immunosuppression therapy etc.)[68] (see below). This in turn is life-threatening. High rates of suicidal behavior as well as completed suicide have been reported both for people on dialysis[69] and after transplantation.[70] However, accurate ascertainment of suicide or suicidal ideation is difficult in this patient group. It has been suggested that the crucial factor influencing some patients to choose to discontinue their treatment is the patient's perception of his prognosis,[71] which may be very different from (objective) disease status.[54, 55] More generally, the possible impact of depression on overall outcome in ESRD is unclear. Some have suggested that depression is associated with a poor outcome (notably a higher mortality rate),[39, 72–75] but others have failed to confirm this finding.[41, 76]

A further complication in the recognition and management of psychiatric disturbance in ESRD is the possible role of denial. Although it has been suggested that denial may be an adaptive coping strategy in this group of patients,[58, 76] especially after a failed transplant,[77] this appears to be contradicted by reports of successful group interventions,[78–80] in which the influence of denial has presumably been minimized. Denial has also been described among the families of patients with ESRD (see below).

PATIENT ADHERENCE
TO THE MEDICAL REGIME

Poor adherence is a problem in transplant recipients as well as those on dialysis, although it has been studied much more extensively in the latter group. The observation that those patients who show poor adherence after transplantation are more likely to have shown a similar pattern while on dialysis,[81] is particularly worrying because in some instances, very poor adherence while on dialysis is one factor used to determine the patient's priority for transplantation. Among dialysands, despite the considerable literature on factors possibly influencing adherence to dietary and fluid restrictions, firm conclusions are impossible because of the contradictory results of published work. Thus while some reports have associated satisfactory compliance with good social supports,[82] others have described the opposite effect.[83] Similarly, satisfactory compliance has been linked with internal locus of control in some studies[84–86] but not others.[84, 87] Other cognitive factors, such as the individual's capacity for self-control, may also be important.[88] Despite the reports that psychiatric morbidity might lead to a worse overall prognosis in ESRD (see above), studies of adherence have, with few exceptions,[76, 89, 90] disregarded possible effects of depression and other psychiatric disturbance. Most reports are subject to one or more of three major methodological problems, which together could account for the inconsistent published results. First, researchers have commonly

examined a limited range of psychosocial variables, ignoring others which may be relevant to their chosen model. To some extent,
this must be inevitable in this field of research, where comprehensive models are seldom practicable. However, some studies may have
adopted models of adherence which are too simple. For example,
locus of control beliefs may be influenced by depression,[67, 91] and
their impact on adherence may depend on the individual's social
supports. Second, very few studies have considered male and female
patients separately. There is not a priori reason why men and women
should cope in the same way. In fact, intuitively, arguments can be
made that particular psychosocial variables are likely to influence
the two sexes differently (see below).[92] The third methodological
problem in most studies relates to their definitions of adherence
or compliance. The variables most commonly chosen as measures
of compliance have been interdialysis weight gain and predialysis
serum potassium levels. A 2 kg weight gain between dialysis is more
significant when the patient's mean postdialysis weight is 50 kg than
with a mean weight of 80 kg. Thus the interdialysis weight gain
should be measured as a fraction of ideal weight, or mean weight,[93]
rather than using arbitrary cut-off points between "low" and "high"
weight gain.[84, 85, 87, 89, 90, 94, 95] Where researchers have adopted measures based on both serum potassium and weight gain, there have
been poor correlations between these,[89, 93] casting doubt on the
validity of composite measures of compliance, which have been
widely adopted.[84, 85, 96] With few exceptions,[86, 87, 93] researchers have
also failed to record the residual urine volume of the patients they
have studied. Most samples of dialysands include a proportion of
patients whose 24-hour urine output exceeds 500 ml, and this will
in turn influence the accuracy of the chosen adherence measures.

QUALITY OF LIFE

This has been the focus of much research, particularly to compare
the impact of the different forms of renal replacement therapy.

While there have been some reports that transplant recipients fare better than those on dialysis,[97–100] other studies have reported little measurable benefit from transplantation, particularly when compared with home dialysis.[101–103] Patients who dialyse at home consistently fare better than those who dialyse in hospital or in dialysis units.[102] Self-reported quality of life is also consistently improved by treating those on dialysis with erythropoietin.[104–106] Among transplant recipients, greater improvements in physical and social well-being have been reported when patients are treated with cyclosporin rather than other immunosuppressive therapy,[99] although others have found the opposite.[105] Patients who have to return to dialysis following a failed transplant have a particularly poor outlook according to some reports,[99, 102] but not others.[97]

Results from published studies are no more conclusive even when considering discrete aspects of life quality, such as sexual function, or employment. There is a high prevalence of sexual dysfunction among people who dialyse. Although psychological factors are important in the etiology of sexual dysfunction in ESRD,[107] important organic contributors include low testosterone levels and hyperprolactinemia,[108] possibly associated with zinc deficiency.[109] These physiological factors are often reversed by transplantation.[108] While some researchers have reported that sexual function improves after transplantation[48], others have failed to confirm this.[110–113] A similar picture emerges for employment. Although some studies have reported a higher proportion of patients able to work after transplantation,[100] many others show very little difference between transplant recipients and those on dialysis.[97, 98, 102, 103, 112] However, it is important to distinguish being employed and being *capable* or working.[114]

To summarize, patients with viable grafted kidneys express more satisfaction with their lives than those on dialysis, and there are sound clinical reasons why they should do so. However, the *objective* evidence for an improvement in quality of life due to transplantation is relatively weak. The main reason for this apparent paradox lies in the nature and definition of *quality of life*. This is a highly complex concept,[115, 116] with no agreed operational definition. Numerous researchers have measured quality of life using simple measures of life satisfaction, such as Campbell's Quality of Life scales or similar instruments.[3, 97, 99, 100, 102, 117] Such instruments were developed for use in community samples, and have never been properly validated in the physically ill. In fact, ratings on Campbell's scales correlate highly with measures of depression.[118] In effect, such simple quality of life instruments are little more than measures of affective disturbance. While depression clearly influences subjective quality of life, its occurrence in ESRD, as in physical illness generally, is usually independent of the severity of the disease.[54, 55] Thus someone with ESRD might report low life satisfaction either because of the impact of the disease despite treatment, or because of depression. Studies using more complex measures of quality of life have chosen general instruments, such as the Psychosocial Adjustment to Illness Scale,[58, 119] the Karnovsky Index[3, 120, 121] or the Sickness Impact Profile.[3, 40, 122] It is possible that such scales are less sensitive to the changes expected from therapeutic interventions in ESRD than specific scales,[116, 123] designed especially for use in ESRD.[53, 98, 106, 124]

Another important contributing factor to the discrepant results described above is the different case-mix of patient groups in many comparisons. As noted above, there can be marked sociodemographic and clinical differences between dialysis and transplant samples, between those on home and unit hemodialysis, and between those on CAPD and hemodialysis. Equally important to rehabilitation and quality of life are the expected differences in outcome between diabetic and nondiabetic patients. Some researchers have overcome this by more carefully matching patient groups,[113] or attempting to control for relevant variables statistically.[98, 102] However, many others have ignored this problem. The optimal solution, seldom reported to date, is to undertake prospective longitudinal studies, following up patients from dialysis through transplantation.[48, 125]

IMPACT OF ESRD ON FAMILIES

Diaylsis, particularly for those who dialyse at home, becomes a way of life for the whole family. People on dialysis frequently report changes in their roles within the family. Even if the patient is restored to good health by transplantation, established family roles may endure,[98] even though there may be less family disruption after transplantation than before.[99] Spouses have high rates of anxiety and depression,[30, 126–128] and children often have behavioral problems and difficulties at school.[129] Where family communications and support are inadequate, patients may choose against dialysing at home.[130] High levels of denial have been reported.[131–134] Patients and spouses sometimes avoid expression of concern or doubt, even when these may be obvious.[131, 132] The significance of such denial is unclear. Among families training to do home dialysis, one report has suggested that denial predicts failure,[135] another suggested the opposite.[136] Equally, it may be that patients and partners deny the extent of marital discord because the burden of dialysis eclipses all other problems they have to face.[133] In view of such denial it is paradoxical that there is close agreement between patients and spouses in attitudes and adjustment.[132, 137, 138] Others have suggested that intimacy and good support between marital partners are key factors in minimizing psychological distress.[139] Another paradoxical finding is that patients on dialysis appeared to have a significantly worse prognosis when their families were well integrated—when the family had a strong belief that they must face up to difficulties as a family rather than as individuals.[83] It has been suggested that this result may be due to the fact that "strong" families tend to persevere in trying to cope without calling on professional help as often as do "weak" families.

Again, as with adherence and quality of life, a major flaw in most of these studies has been the failure to consider the possible relevance of the patient's sex. Where this has been examined, both patient and spouse are more likely to have psychiatric symptoms and difficulties in adjustment if the patient is female.[137, 139] Psychological distress may be associated in particular with marital role strain—a discrepancy between role expectations and perceived roles.[139] These findings have been interpreted in terms of the assumed different predominant roles which men and women have in society[92]—while women tend to have predominantly nurturant roles, which require them to be flexible in response to the needs of others, men's roles are more likely to be fixed. It has been suggested that the overall role demands on women are more stressful than on men, and become much harder to satisfy when a woman falls ill,[139] although others have argued the opposite.[138] Equally, it may be that, because the nurturant role is acknowledged as flexible, there is often an expectation that this role will be sustained despite illness, whereas it is easier to sacrifice a fixed role (such as "breadwinner") to illness.

Another criticism applicable to many of these studies is that they lacked appropriate control groups, with which the ESRD families could be compared.[140] Such families may appear "pathological" relative to others which do not have to shoulder the burden and uncertainties of a chronic illness, but this could reflect an adaptive response to their circumstances. In any case, signs of apparent family pathology, as with psychiatric disorder in general in the physically ill,[141] do not necessarily indicate the need for specialist intervention.

One exceptional family influence in ESRD is the possibility for a close relative to become a live kidney donor. As noted above, live donation is controversial. While some have argued strongly against living related donors,[18] others have gone as far as suggesting that depriving someone who wishes to donate a kidney of the opportunity to do so could itself be psychologically harmful.[19] In most instances, donation of a kidney by a living relative has a good psychological outcome for both donor and recipient,[48, 142, 143] even when the graft has been unsuccessful.[48] The process by which a potential donor comes forward is complex. In many instances, the patient does not canvas among family members for a potential donor[143–145] or may couch the request for a donor in such a vague way that others fail to understand it.[146] Older patients are less likely to solicit for a related donor than younger ones, and also more likely to take responsibility for the decision themselves.[144] In some cases, a family member reaches the decision to become a donor rapidly, without much discussion either with the family[143, 145] or with renal unit staff,[145] casting doubt on the adequacy of the donor's informed consent for the operation. However, in a follow-up of a large sample of donors, 84% indicated that they had received adequate information beforehand.[143] If live related donation is to be encouraged, renal unit staff have an important role to play in ensuring that patients and their families are adequately informed, and possibly also in fostering discussion of possible live donation at the appropriate time.[144]

IMPACT ON RENAL UNIT STAFF

Staff on dialysis units work very closely with their patients, in some instances over long periods. Working in this way makes emotional demands on staff. For many patients, the renal unit becomes an important focus of their lives, sometimes stretching the boundary which staff attempt to make between professional and private life. Through prolonged contact with their patients, staff develop an investment in the patients' prognoses.[147] The extensive knowledge which many patients acquire about their illness and its treatment can sometimes be perceived as threatening, especially by less experienced staff, and can also lead patients to be quite demanding regarding details of their care.[148, 149] Equally, it is often very difficult to work with patients who are perceived to persistently abuse their diets or other aspects of their treatment. On every renal unit, staff also have to face the complex ethical and emotional problems associated with deciding to stop treatment.[150] All these factors can predispose staff to emotional exhaustion or burnout.[151] Staff may attempt to deal with these difficulties using denial, which may adversely affect patient care.[53, 96, 147, 152] Although this has been cited as a reason for increased involvement with patients of specialists (psychologists or psychiatrists),[53] a more satisfactory approach is to help staff to increase their competence and confidence in the management of stress, both their own and that of their patients. Staff acknowledge these difficulties, as well as the likely benefits of further training and support.[149]

Conclusions

Much of the research effort in this field has been devoted thus far to comparisons of psychosocial factors between different forms of treatment for ESRD. The overall aim of much of this work has been to seek confirmation, from a psychosomatic perspective, of the relative efficacy of particular types of treatment. Rapid technological and clinical advances over recent years have not only made redundant the findings of some studies published even a decade ago, but are also likely to enhance further the potential differences in outcome between available interventions. Comparison of psychosocial or psychosomatic factors between dialysis and transplantation then becomes much less clinically relevant. The predominant conclusion from research to date is that, in terms of rehabilitation, adjustment, or quality of life, some people do better than others, regardless of the type of treatment. This conclusion is likely to stand, even allowing for the methodological inadequacies of much of the research. In ESRD, as in other chronic physical illnesses,[54, 67] it is unsafe to assume that "rehabilitation," "adjustment," or "quality of life" accurately reflect the *physical* outcome of treatment. Rather, these measures of outcome are influenced by cognitive and psychosocial as well as biological factors. Particularly because of the huge investment in resources and time required in the treatment of ESRD, researchers in psychosomatic medicine have a responsibility to identify such influences and the patients in whom they are likely to be significant, and to use the results of this work to develop interventions to optimize the overall outcome of treatment.

References

1. Brunner FP, Selwood NH. Results of renal replacement therapy in Europe, 1980 to 1987. *Am J Kidney Dis.* 1990;15:384–396.
2. Eggers PW. Mortality rates among dialysis patients in Medicare's end-stage renal disease program. *Am J Kidney Dis.* 1990;15:414–421.

3. Evans RW, Rader B, Manninen DL. The quality of life of hemodialysis recipients treated with recombinant human erythropoietin. Cooperative Multicenter EPO Clinical Trial Group. *JAMA.* 1990;263:825–830.

4. Wolcott DL, Marsh JT, La Rue A, Carr C, Nissenson AR. Recombinant human erythropoietin treatment may improve quality of life and cognitive function in chronic haemodialysis patients. *Am J Kidney Dis.* 1989;14:478–485.

5. Held PJ, Brunner FP, Odaka M, Garcia JR, Port FK, Gaylin DS. Five-year survival for end-stage renal disease patients in the United States, Europe and Japan, 1982 to 1987. *Am J Kidney Dis.* 1990;15:451–457.

6. Terasaki PI, Perdue S, Sasaki N, Mickey MR, Whitby L. Improving success rates of kidney transplantation. *JAMA.* 1983;250:1065–1068.

7. Nathan DM, Fogel H, Norman D, Russell PS, Tolkoff-Rubin N, Delmonico FL, Auchincloss H Jr, Camuso J, Cosimi AB. Long-term metabolic and quality of life results with pancreatic/renal transplantation in insulin-dependent diabetes mellitus. *Transplantation.* 1991;52:85–91.

8. Piehlmeier W, Bullinger M, Nusser J, König A, Illner WD, Abendroth D, Land W, Landgraf R. Quality of life in type 1 (insulin-dependent) diabetic patients prior to and after pancreas and kidney transplantation in relation to organ function. *Diabetologia.* 1991;34(suppl 1):150–157.

9. Levy NB. *Psychonephrology I. Psychological Factors in Hemodialysis and Transplantation.* New York: Plenum;1981.

10. Blodgett C. A selected review of the literature of adjustment to hemodialysis. *Int J Psychiatry Med.* 1981;11:97–124.

11. Levy NB. *Psychonephrology II: Psychological Problems in Kidney Failure and Their Treatment.* New York: Plenum;1983.

12. House RM, Thompson TL. Psychiatric aspects of organ transplantation. *JAMA.* 1988;260:535–539.

13. Shanteau J, Harris RJ. *Organ Donation and Transplantation.* Washington, DC: American Psychological Association;1990.

14. Shanteau J, Harris RJ, VandenBos GR. Psychological and behavioral factors in organ donation. *Hosp Community Psychiatry.* 1992;43:211–212.

15. Alexander L. The double-bind theory and haemodialysis. *Arch Gen Psychiatry.* 1976;33:1353–1356.

16. Goldstein B, Dommermuth P. The sick role cycle: An approach to medical sociology. *Sociol Soc Res.* 1960;46:36–47.

17. Callender CO, Jennings PS, Bayton JA, Flores JC, Tagunicar H, Yeager C, Bond O. Psychologic factors related to dialysis in kidney transplant decisions. *Transplant Proc.* 1989;21:1976–1978.

18. Kreis H. Why living related donors should not be used whenever possible. *Transplant Proc.* 1985;17:1510–1514.

19. Ogden D. Consequences of renal donation in man. *Am J Kidney Dis.* 1983; 11:501–511.

20. Sutherland DER. Living related donors should be used whenever possible. *Transplant Proc.* 1985;17:1503–1509.

21. Caplan AL. Risks, paternalism, and the gift of life. *Arch Intern Med.* 1985; 145:1188–1190.

22. Bonomini V, Gozzetti G. Is living donation still justifiable? *Nephrol Dial Transplant.* 1990;5:407–409.

23. Viederman M. On the vicissitudes of the need for control in patients confronted with hemodialysis. *Compr Psychiatr.* 1978;19:455–467.
24. Dansak DA. Secondary gain in long-term hemodialysis patients. *Am J Psychiatry.* 1972;129:352–355.
25. Muslin HL. On acquiring a kidney. *Am J Psychiatry.* 1971;127:1185–1188.
26. Freedman A. Psychoanalysis of a patient who received a kidney transplant. *J Am Psychoanal Assn.* 1983;31:917–956.
27. Basch SH. The intrapsychic integration of a new organ: A clinical study of kidney transplantation. *Psychoanal Q.* 1973;42:364–384.
28. Eisendrath RM. The role of grief and fear in the death of kidney transplant patients. *Am J Psychiatry.* 1969;126:381–387.
29. Viederman M. Psychogenic factors in kidney transplant rejection. A case study. *Am J Psychiatry.* 1975;132:957–959.
30. House A. Psychosocial problems of patients on the renal unit and their relation to treatment outcome. *J Psychosom Res.* 1987;31:441–452.
31. Sensky T. Psychiatric morbidity in renal transplantation. *Psychother Psychosom.* 1989;52:41–46.
32. Blazer DG, Petrie WM, Wilson WP. Affective psychoses following renal transplant. *Dis Nerv Syst.* 1976;37:663–667.
33. Chambers M. Psychological aspects of renal transplantation. *Int J Psychiatry Med.* 1982;12:229–236.
34. Teschan PE, Arieff AI. Uremic and dialysis encephalopathies. In: McCandless DW, ed. *Cerebral Energy Metabolism and Metabolic Encephalopathies.* New York: Plenum;1985: pp 263–286.
35. Fraser CL, Arieff AI. Nervous system complications of uremia. *Ann Intern Med.* 1988;109:143–153.
36. Sideman S, Manor D. The dialysis dementia syndrome and aluminum intoxication. *Nephron.* 1982;31:1–10.
37. Osberg JW, Meares GJ, McKee DC, Burnett GB. Intellectual functioning in renal failure and chronic dialysis. *J Chronic Dis.* 1982;35:445–457.
38. Smith MD, Hong BA, Robson AM. Diagnosis of depression in patients with end-stage renal disease. *Am J Med.* 1985;79:160–166.
39. Schulman R, Price JDE, Spinelli J. Biopsychosocial aspects of long-term survival on end-stage renal failure therapy. *Psychol Med.* 1989;19:945–954.
40. Christensen AJ, Turner CW, Smith TW, Holman JM, Gregory MC. Health locus of control and depression in end-stage renal disease. *J Consult Clin Psychol.* 1991;59:419–424.
41. Devins GM, Mann J, Mandin H, Paul LC, Hons RB, Burgess ED, Taub K, Schorr S, Letourneau PK, Buckle S. Psychosocial predictors of survival in end-stage renal disease. *J Nerv Ment Dis.* 1990;178:127–133.
42. Kalman TP, Wilson PG, Kalman CM. Psychiatric morbidity in long-term transplant recipients and in patients undergoing haemodialysis. *JAMA.* 1983;250:55–58.
43. Petrie K. Psychological well-being and psychiatric disturbance in dialysis and renal transplant patients. *Br J Med Psychol.* 1989;62:91–96.
44. Farmer CJ, Snowden SA, Parsons V. The prevalence of psychiatric illness among patients on home haemodialysis. *Psychol Med.* 1979;9:509–514.

45. Lowry MR, Atcherson E. A short-term follow-up of patients with depressive disorder on entry into home haemodialysis training. *J Affective Disord.* 1980;2:219–227.
46. Hinrichsen GA, Lieberman JA, Pollack S, Steinberg H. Depression in hemodialysis patients. *Psychosomatics.* 1989;30:284–289.
47. Plough AL, Salem SR, Shwartz M, Wiler JM, Ferguson CW. Case-mix in end stage renal disease; differences between patients in hospital-based and freestanding treatment facilities. *N Engl J Med.* 1984;310:1432–1436.
48. Simmons RG. Social and psychological posttransplant adjustment. In: Kutner NG, Cardenas DD, Bower JD, eds. *Rehabilitation and the Chronic Renal Disease Patient.* New York: Spectrum;1985: pp 85–98.
49. Muthny FA. Postoperative course of patients during hospitalization following renal transplantation. *Psychother Psychosom.* 1984;42:133–142.
50. Malmquist A. A prospective study of patients in chronic hemodialysis. II. Predicting factors regarding rehabilitation. *J Psychosom Res.* 1973;17:339–344.
51. Rodin G, Voshart K, Cattran D, Halloran P, Cardella C, Fenton S. Cadaveric renal transplant failure: the short-term sequelae. *Int J Psychiatry Med.* 1986; 16:357–364.
52. Craven JL, Rodin GM, Johnson L, et al. The diagnosis of major depression in renal dialysis patients. *Psychosom Med.* 1987;49:482–492.
53. Nichols KA, Springford V. The psycho-social stressors associated with survival by dialysis. *Behav Res Ther.* 1984;5:563–574.
54. Sensky T. Patient's reactions to illness: Cognitive factors determine responses and are amenable to treatment. *Br Med J.* 1990;300:622–623.
55. Sensky T, Wright J. Cognitive therapy with medical patients. In: Wright J, Thase M, Ludgate J, Beck AT, eds. *The Cognitive Milieu: Inpatient Applications of Cognitive Therapy.* New York: Guilford;1992.
56. Devins GM, Binik YM, Gorman P, et al. Perceived self-efficacy, outcome expectancies, and negative mood states in end-stage renal disease. *J Abnorm Psychol.* 1982;91:241–244.
57. Devins GM, Binik YM, Hutchinson TA, Hollomby DJ, Barre PE, Guttman RD. The emotional impact of end-stage renal disease: importance of patients' perceptions of intrusiveness and control. *Int J Psychiatry Med.* 1983;13:327–343.
58. Fricchione GL, Howanitz E, Jandorf L, Kroessler D, Zervas I, Woznicki RM. Psychological adjustment to end-stage renal disease and the implications of denial. *Psychosomatics.* 1992;33:85–91.
59. Wise TN. The pitfalls of diagnosing depression in chronic renal disease. *Psychosomatics.* 1974;15:83–84.
60. Yanagida EH, Streltzer J. Limitations of psychological tests in a dialysis population. *Psychosom Med.* 1979;41:557–567.
61. Israel M. Depression in dialysis patients: A review of psychological factors. *Can J Psychiatry.* 1986;31:445–451.
62. Kutner NG, Fair PL, Kutner MH. Assessing depression and anxiety in chronic hemodialysis patients. *J Psychosom Res.* 1985;29:23–31.
63. Barrett BJ, Vavasour HM, Major A, Parfrey PS. Clinical and psychological correlates of somatic symptoms in patients on dialysis. *Nephron.* 1990;55:10–15.
64. Rosser R. Depression during renal dialysis and following transplantation. *Proc R Soc Med.* 1976;69:832–834.

312 TOM SENSKY

65. Kennedy SH, Craven JL, Rodin GM, Roin GMR. Major depression in renal dialysis patients: An open trial of antidepressant therapy. *J Clin Psychiatry.* 1989;50:60–63.
66. Levy NB. Psychopharmacology in patients with renal failure. *Int J Psychiatry Med.* 1990;20:325–334.
67. Sensky T. Cognitive therapy with patients with chronic physical illness. *Psychother Psychosom.* 1989;52:26–32.
68. Rodin GM, Chmara J, Ennis J, Fenton S, Locking H, Steinhouse K. Stopping life-sustaining medical treatment: psychiatric considerations in the termination of renal dialysis. *Can J Psychiatry.* 1981;26:540–544.
69. Abram HS, Moore GL, Westervelt FB. Suicidal behavior in chronic dialysis patients. *Am J Psychiatry.* 1971;127:1199–1204.
70. Washer GF, Schroter GPJ, Starzl TE, Weil R. Causes of death after kidney transplantation. *JAMA.* 1983;250:49–54.
71. Hirsch DJ. Death from dialysis termination. *Nephrol Dial Transplant.* 1989;4:41–44.
72. Burton HJ, Kline SA, Lindsay RM, Heidenheim AP. The relationship of depression to survival in chronic renal failure. *Psychosom Med.* 1986;48:261–268.
73. Farmer CJ, Bewick M, Parsons V, Snowden SA. Survival on home hemodialysis: Its relationship with physical symptomatology, psychosocial background and psychiatric morbidity. *Psychol Med.* 1979;9:515–523.
74. Richmond JM, Lindsay RM, Burton HJ, Conley J, Wai L. Psychological and physiological factors predicting outcome on home hemodialysis. *Clin Nephrol.* 1982;17:109–113.
75. Zairnik JP, Freeman CW, Sherrard DJ, Calsyn DA. Psychological correlates of survival on renal dialysis. *J Nerv Ment Dis.* 1977;164:210–213.
76. Foster FG, Cohn GL, McKegney FP. Psychobiologic factors and individual survival on chronic renal hemodialysis—a 2 year follow-up. *Psychosom Med.* 1973;35:64–81.
77. Streltzer J, Moe M, Yanagida EH, Siemsen A. Coping with transplant failure: Grief vs denial. *Int J Psychiatry Med.* 1983;13:97–106.
78. Campbell DR, Sinha BK. Brief group psychotherapy with chronic hemodialysis patients. *Am J Psychiatry.* 1980;137:1234–1237.
79. Sorensen ET. Group therapy in a community hospital dialysis unit. *JAMA.* 1972;221:899–901.
80. Buchanan DC. Group therapy for kidney transplant patients. *Int J Psychiatry Med.* 1975;6:523–531.
81. Rodriguez A, Diaz M, Colon A, Santiago Delpin EA. Psychosocial profile of noncompliant transplant patients. *Transplant Proc.* 1991;23:1807–1809.
82. Steidl JH, Finkelstein FO, Wexler JP, Feigenbaum H, Kitsen J, Kliger AS, Quinlan DM. Medical condition, adherence to treatment regimens, and family functioning: Their interactions, in patients receiving long-term dialysis treatment. *Arch Gen Psychiatry.* 1980;37:1025–1027.
83. Reiss D, Gonzalez S, Kramer N. Family process, chronic illness, and death: On the weakness of strong bonds. *Arch Gen Psychiatry.* 1986;43:795–804.
84. Brown J, Fitzpatrick R. Factors influencing compliance with dietary restrictions in dialysis patients. *J Psychosom Res.* 1988;32:191–196.

85. Wenerowicz WJ, Riskind JH, Jenkins PG. Locus of control and degree of compliance in hemodialysis patients. *J Dial.* 1978;2:495–505.
86. Bollin BW, Hart LK. The relationship of health belief motivations, health locus of control and health valuing to dietary compliance of hemodialysis patients. *Am Assn Nephrol Nurs Tech J.* 1982;9:41–47.
87. Blackburn SL. Dietary compliance of chronic hemodialysis patients. *J Am Diet Assn.* 1977;70:36–37.
88. Rosenbaum M, Smira KBA. Cognitive and personality factors in the delay of gratification of hemodialysis patients. *J Pers Soc Psychol.* 1986;51:357–364.
89. Yanagida EH, Streltzer J, Siemsen A. Denial in dialysis patients: Relationship to compliance and other variables. *Psychosom Med.* 1981;43:271–280.
90. Tracey HM, Green C, McCleary J. Noncompliance in hemodialysis patients as measured with the MBHI. *Psychol Health.* 1987;1:411–423.
91. Devins GM, Binik YM, Hollomby DJ, Barre PR, Guttman RD. Helplessness and depression in end-stage renal disease. *J Abnorm Psychol.* 1981;90:531–545.
92. Gove WR. Gender differences in mental and physical illness: The effects of fixed roles and nurturant roles. *Soc Sci Med.* 1984;20:77–91.
93. Manley M, Sweeney J. Assessment of compliance in hemodialysis adaptation. *J Psychosom Res.* 1986;30:153–161.
94. Ferraro KF, Dixon RD, Kinlaw BJR. Measuring compliance among incentre hemodialysis patients. *Dial Transplant.* 1986;15:226–236.
95. Procci WR. Psychological factors associated with severe abuse of the hemodialysis diet. *Gen Hosp Psychiatry.* 1981;3:111–118.
96. Kaplan De-Nour A, Czaczkes JW. Bias in assessment of patients on chronic dialysis. *J Psychosom Res.* 1974;18:267–276.
97. Johnson JP, McCauley CR, Copley JB. The quality of life of hemodialysis and transplant patients. *Kidney Int.* 1982;22:286–291.
98. Koch U, Muthny FA. Quality of life in patients with end-stage renal disease in relation to the method of treatment. *Psychother Psychosom.* 1990;54:161–171.
99. Simmons RG, Abress L. Quality-of-life issues for end-stage renal disease patients. *Am J Kidney Dis.* 1990;15:201–208.
100. Sophie LR, Powers MJ. Life satisfaction and social function: Posttransplant self-evaluation. *Dial Transplant.* 1979;8:1198–1202.
101. Kutner NG, Cardenas DD. Assessment of rehabilitation outcomes among chronic dialysis patients. *Am J Nephrol.* 1982;2:128–132.
102. Evans RW, Manninen DL, Garrison LP, Hart LG, Blagg CR, Gutman RA, Hull AR, Lowrie EG. The quality of life of patients with end-stage renal failure. *N Engl J Med.* 1985;312:553–559.
103. Kaplan De-Nour A, Shanan J. Quality of life of dialysis and transplanted patients. *Nephron.* 1980;25:117–120.
104. Barany P, Pettersson E, Bergstrom J. Erythropoietin treatment improves quality of life in hemodialysis patients. *Scand J Urol Nephrol.* 1990;131(suppl):55–60.
105. Evans RW. Recombinant human erythropoietin and the quality of life of end-stage renal disease patients: A comparative analysis. *Am J Kidney Dis.* 1991;18:62–70.
106. Laupacis A, Wong C, Churchill D. The use of generic and specific quality-of-life measures in hemodialysis patients treated with erythropoietin. *Controlled Clin Trials.* 1991;12:168S–179S.

107. Alleyne S, Dillard P, McGregor C, Hosten A. Sexual function and mental distress status of patients with end-stage renal disease on hemodialysis. *Transplant Proc.* 1989;21:3895–3898.
108. Foulks CJ, Cushner HM. Sexual dysfunction in the male dialysis patient: Pathogenesis, evaluation and therapy. *Am J Kidney Dis.* 1986;8:211–222.
109. Mahajan SK, Hamburger RJ, Flamenbaum W, Prasad AS, McDonald FD. Effect of zinc supplementation on hyperprolactinaemia in uremic men. *Lancet.* 1985;ii:750–751
110. Morris PL, Jones B. Life satisfaction across treatment methods for patients with end-stage renal failure. *Med J Aust.* 1989;150:428–432.
111. Procci WR, Hoffman KR, Chatterjee SN. Persistent sexual dysfunction following renal transplantation. *Dial Transplant.* 1978;7:891–894.
112. Procci WR. A comparison of psychosocial disability in males undergoing maintenance hemodialysis or following cadaver transplantation. *Gen Hosp Psychiatry.* 1980;2:255–261.
113. Sayag R, Kaplan De-Nour A, Shapira Z, Kahan E, Boner G. Comparison of psychosocial adjustment of male nondiabetic kidney transplant and hospital hemodialysis patients. *Nephron.* 1990;54:214–218.
114. Kutner NG, Brogan D, Fielding B. Employment status and ability to work among working-age chronic dialysis patients. *Am J Nephrol.* 1991;11:334–340.
115. Fava G. Methodological and conceptual issues in research on quality of life. *Psychother Psychosom.* 1990;54:70–76.
116. Guyatt G, Feeny D, Patrick D. Issues in quality-of-life measurement in clinical trials. *Controlled Clin Trials.* 1991;12:81S–90S.
117. Maher BA, Lamping DL, Dickinson CA, Murawski BJ, Olivet DC, Santiago GC. Psychosocial aspects of chronic hemodialysis: The National Cooperative Dialysis study. *Kidney Int.* 1983;23(suppl 13):S50–S57.
118. Sensky T. Measurement of quality of life in end-stage renal failure. *N Engl J Med.* 1988;319:31–53.
119. Kaplan De-Nour A. Psychosocial adjustment to illness scale (PAIS): A study of chronic hemodialysis patients. *J Psychosom Res.* 1982;26:11–22.
120. Parfrey PS, Vavasour HM, Gault MH. A prospective study of health status in dialysis and transplant patients. *Transplant Proc.* 1988;20:1231–1232.
121. Gutman RA, Stead WW, Robinson RR. Physical activity and employment status of patients on maintenance dialysis. *N Engl J Med.* 1981;304:309–313.
122. Rodin GM, Voshart K, Fenton SSA, Cardella C, Cattran DC, Halloran PF. Depression and medical illness: A study of patients with end-stage renal disease. *Mod Med Can.* 1984;39:462–465.
123. Wiklund I, Karlberh J. Evaluation of quality of life in clinical trials: Selecting quality-of-life measures. *Controlled Clin Trials.* 1991;12:204S–216S.
124. Parfrey PS, Vavasour H, Bullock M, Henry S, Harnett JD, Gault MH. Development of a health questionnaire specific for end-stage renal disease. *Nephron.* 1989;52:20–28.
125. McClellan WM, Anson C, Birkeli K, Tuttle E. Functional status and quality of life: Predictors of early mortality among patients entering treatment for end stage renal disease. *J Clin Epidemiol.* 1991;44:83–89.
126. Mlott SR, Allain A. Personality correlates of renal dialysis patients and their spouses. *South Med J.* 1974;67:941–944.

127. Speidel H, Koch V, Balck F, Kneiss J. Problems in interaction between patients undergoing long-term hemodialysis and their partners. *Psychother Psychosom.* 1979;31:235–242.
128. Rideout EM, Rodin GM, Littlefield CH. Stress, social support, and symptoms of depression in spouses of the medically ill. *Int J Psychiatry Med.* 1990;20:37–48.
129. Tsaltas MO. Children of home dialysis patients. *JAMA.* 1976;236:2764–2766.
130. Evans RW. Children of dialysis patients and selection of dialysis setting. *Am J Psychiatry.* 1978;135:343–345.
131. Maurin J, Schenkel J. A study of the family unit's response to hemodialysis. *J Psychosom Res.* 1976;20:163–168.
132. Mass M, Kaplan De-Nour A. Reactions of families to chronic hemodialysis. *Psychother Psychosom.* 1975;26:20–26.
133. Finkelstein FO, Finkelstein SH, Steele TE. Assessment of the marital relationships of hemodialysis patients. *Am J Med Sci.* 1976;271:21–28.
134. Molumply SD, Sporakowski MJ. Family stress in hemodialysis. *Fam Rel.* 1984;33:33–39.
135. Marshall JR, Rice DG, O'Mera M, Shelp WD. Characteristics of couples with poor outcome in dialysis home training. *J Chronic Dis.* 1975;28:378–385.
136. Fishman DB, Schneider CJ. Predicting emotional adjustment in home dialysis patients and their relatives. *J Chronic Dis.* 1972;25:99–106.
137. Soskolne V, Kaplan De-Nour A. The psychosocial adjustment of patients and spouses to dialysis treatment. *Soc Sci Med.* 1989;29:497–502.
138. Gray H, Brogan D, Kutner NG. Status of life areas: Congruence/noncongruence in ESRD patient and spouse perceptions. *Soc Sci Med.* 1985;20:341–346.
139. Chowanec GD, Binik YM. End stage renal disease and the marital dyad. An empirical investigation. *Soc Sci Med.* 1989;28:971–983.
140. Chowanec GD, Binik YM. End stage renal disease (ESRD) and the marital dyad: A literature review and critique. *Soc Sci Med.* 1982;16:1551–1558.
141. Sensky T. The general hospital psychiatrist: Too many tasks and too few roles? *Br J Psychiatry.* 1986;148:151–158.
142. Simmons RG, Klein SD, Simmons RL. *The Gift of Life: The Social and Psychological Impact of Organ Transplant.* New York: Wiley;1977.
143. Smith MD, Kappell DF, Province MA, Hong BA, Robson AM, Dutton S, Guzman T, Hoff J, Shelton L, Cameron E, Emerson W, Glass NR, Hopkins J, Peterson C. Living-related kidney donors: A multicentre study of donor education, socioeconomic adjustment, and rehabilitation. *Am J Kidney Dis.* 1986;8:223–233.
144. Sensky T, Mee AD. Dilemmas faced by dialysis patients in search of a living related kidney donor. *Dial Transplant.* 1989;18:243–249.
145. Fellner CH, Marshall JR. Twelve kidney donors. *JAMA.* 1968;206:2703–2707.
146. Simmons RG, Klein SD. Family noncommunication: The search for kidney donors. *Am J Psychiatry.* 1972;129:687–692.
147. Kaplan De-Nour A, Czaczkes JW. Emotional problems and reactions of the medical team in a chronic haemodialysis unit. *Lancet.* 1968;ii:987–991.
148. Leonard MO. Professional stress and the responses of nurses caring for patients with chronic renal failure. In: Levy NB, ed. *Psychonephrology 1: Psychological Factors in Hemodialysis and Transplantation.* New York: Plenum;1981: pp 35–42.

149. Muthny FA. Job strains and job satisfaction of dialysis nurses. *Psychother Psychosom.* 1989;51:150–155.
150. Kilner JF. Ethical issues in the initiation and termination of treatment. *Am J Kidney Dis.* 1990;15:218–227.
151. Maslach C. The client role in staff burn out. *J Soc Issues.* 1978;34:111–124.
152. Kaplan De-Nour A. Social adjustment of chronic dialysis patients. *Am J Psychiatry.* 1982;139:97–100.

Chapter 16
A Psychosomatic View
of Endocrine Disorders

GIOVANNI A. FAVA, NICOLETTA SONINO,
MURRAY A. MORPHY

Cushing was a pioneer in the psychosomatic approach to endocrine disease. He outlined three major areas of psychosomatic interest in endocrinology: (1, p. 990) the study of the role of "psychic traumas" in the pathogenesis of pituitary disease ("great may be our present difficulty in determining which was the primary factor—the psychic instability or the disturbance of internal secretion"); (2) the psychopathology of endocrine disorders, differentiating the psychic disturbances directly caused by hormonal derangements (nowadays subsumed under the rubric of organic affective disorders) from "a certain functional superstructure" that "builds itself on even minor ailments"; and (3) the endocrine study of psychiatric disorders, which may lead to the development of "some serological tests" that may be "of diagnostic value."[1]

An impressive body of knowledge has accumulated on the relationship of endocrine disease to psychological distress,[2-8] on endocrine dysfunction in psychiatric illness, notably depression,[9-13] and on the limbic-hypothalamic control of hormonal function.[12] On the other hand, the role of stressful life events in increasing vulnerability to endocrine disorders and quality of life issues have been largely neglected.[14]

This report will examine endocrine disorders (Cushing's syndrome, Addison's disease, hyperthyroidism, hypothyroidism, hyperprolactinemia, acromegaly, growth hormone deficiency, hirsutism) with major psychosomatic implications. The psychosomatic aspects of other disorders, such as hyperparathyroidism and diabetes insipidus have been discussed elsewhere.[8] Specific reviews on the psychiatric consequences and quality of life related to diabetes mellitus[15–18] are available.

The relationship between hormonal abnormalities and psychological consequences is complex and should be viewed in a multifactorial frame of reference. For instance, anxiety attacks may be induced by pheochromocytoma. However, Starkman et al.[19] found that none of their 17 patients with active pheochromocytoma described the severe apprehension or fear of panic attacks and agoraphobia. Thus, the elevated levels of catecholamines secreted in this illness did not appear to be sufficient to elicit a major psychiatric disorder. Similarly, in clinical psychiatry, the mere occurrence of panic attacks, in the absence of preexisting phobic avoidance and hypochondriasis, is unlikely to be followed by panic disorder.[20]

CUSHING'S SYNDROME

The relationship of life events to Cushing's syndrome has been suggested by a number of clinical observations,[1, 21–23] but these have lacked structured methods of data collection and control groups. In a controlled study,[24] patients with Cushing's syndrome reported significantly more stressful life events than a normal control group and had significantly more of the following: exits from the social field, undesirable events, uncontrolled events, events that had an objective negative impact, and independent events (unlikely to be a consequence of the illness). When the patient sample was increased,[25] a subdivision between patients with pituitary-dependent Cushing's disease and pituitary-independent Cushing's syndrome, due to adrenal adenoma or carcinoma, primary nodular adrenal hyperplasia, or ectopic ACTH production, could be achieved. Patients with pituitary-dependent Cushing's disease reported significantly more life events than those with pituitary-independent Cushing's syndrome. These findings, awaiting further replication, would suggest that the relationship between stressful life events and Cushing's syndrome pertains to the hypothalamic–pituitary forms of the illness.

The pathogenesis of Cushing's syndrome is still controversial. An etiological role for pituitary factors has been shown in Cushing's disease.[26] However, several findings would also point to what Cushing postulated as "some primary derangement of the nervous system."[1] Life events affect the complex interdependence between immunologic function, brain, and neuroendocrine regulation.[27] A disturbance of the regulatory mechanisms of limbic structures and, particularly, of the biogenic amines which may affect hormonal release, can trigger complex biochemical reactions. Neurotransmitters may control proopiomelanocortin release.[28] On the other hand, corticosteroids may influence beta-adrenergic receptor binding and density.[12] The reciprocal relationship between corticosteroids and the adrenergic and serotonergic pathways[12] may explain the occurrence of intermittent Cushing's disease, the recurrence of illness in some patients after microadenomectomy, and the sporadic therapeutic success of antiserotonergic agents. It may also explain the specific association of Cushing's disease with depression.[8] Whitlock,[4] summarizing 12 studies up to 1980 involving 330 patients, observed that in 45% of cases patients were depressed or suicidal. The severity of depression is difficult to evaluate in the earlier studies though the reports of attempted or completed suicides suggest a significant degree of morbidity. Such studies also noted a wide range of psychiatric disturbances, including schizophrenia and delirium, even though depression was the most common syndrome. Six more recent reports support the association between depression and hypercortisolism. Cohen[23] found varying degrees of depression in 25 of 29 consecutive patients. Kelly et al.[29 30] compared 15 patients with active Cushing's syndrome with 15 other patients who had been treated successfully and 13 patients with other pituitary tumors. Depressive symptoms were significantly severer in patients with active Cushing's syndrome compared to the other groups.[29] Depressive symptoms substantially

improved upon treatment,[30] confirming previous findings. Starkman et al.[31] found that low ACTH levels were significantly associated with milder depressed mood. Haskett[32] used a standardized
assessment of depression and found that 24 of 30 consecutive
patients met the criteria for a major depressive episode, in about
80% of such cases depression reaching melancholic proportions.
Eight of the 24 patients had a bipolar affective disorder, i.e., history of mania or hypomania and depression. Schizophrenic syndromes were not evident. Patients frequently attempted to minimize
or conceal serious psychiatric disturbance, including suicide attempts.[32] Therefore, major psychiatric disturbances other than
affective disorders are infrequent in Cushing's syndrome, and if
psychotic symptoms occur, they are likely to be a complication
of mania or severe depression. Neuropsychological testing, however, has indicated that about two-thirds of patients suffering
from Cushing's syndrome have varying degrees of diffuse bilateral cerebral dysfunction, with impairment in nonverbal, visual–
ideational, visual–memory, and spatial–constructional abilities,
and that there are several correlations between affective symptoms and cognitive impairment.[33] Hudson et al.[34] also found a
very high rate of lifetime diagnosis of mood disorder (81%) in
16 patients with Cushing's disease. The rate of familial mood disorder among these patients was significantly lower than that
found among patients with major depression not associated with
physical illness.

Several studies have noted how depressive symptoms often preceded the physical manifestations of Cushing's syndrome.[8] Murphy
and Brown found that, for women of 50 years or younger, the link
between severe life events and the onset of physical illness was not
direct, but rather mediated by a depressive disorder.[35] Depression
might thus be an intermediate link between life stress and pituitary disease. On the basis of the analogies between Cushing's
disease and depression[8] and of cases of intermittent Cushing's syndrome with depressive symptoms,[36-38] a pathological continuum
between the two conditions was proposed.[39] Several fruitful clinical implications of this psychosomatic perspective have been illustrated by Murphy in a recent review.[13]

ADDISON'S DISEASE

The psychosomatic correlates of adrenal insufficiency have not been studied as extensively as in Cushing's syndrome. Following Addison's original description,[40] however, several studies have noted the occurrence of depression in such patients. Engel and Margolin[41] reported depression in 6 of 15 unselected cases, while Cleghorn[42] found such a disturbance in 12 of 25 cases. Apathy, negativism, social withdrawal, and irritability were most common. Treatment with glucocorticoids induced rapid improvement in psychiatric symptoms,[43, 44] even in a case of agitated depression previously refractory to electroconvulsive therapy.[45] The severity of depression is difficult to evaluate. From Drake's description,[46] a mild degree of symptomatology would seem to be prevalent, yet severe cases have been reported. Depression did not appear to be a common component of Addison's disease in children and adolescents,[47, 48] where inhibitory behavior prevailed.[47] In adults, however, depression is a common manifestation. In the majority of cases described by McFarland,[44] psychotic symptoms were associated with complications such as electrolyte disturbances, hypoglycemia, and convulsions. These studies illustrate the need to consider adrenocortical deficiency as a cause of psychiatric disorder or cognitive impairment including those patients in whom long-term corticosteroids have been recently discontinued.[49] Hypothalamic–pituitary–adrenal axis hypoactivity with subnormal 11-deoxycortisol responses to metyrapone and relatively low morning plasma cortisol levels have been reported in a few depressed patients.[50] However, these were sporadic occurrences and a parallelism between major depression and Addison's disease does not seem to be tenable. Fatigue is, however, a prominent symptom of Addison's disease, and there may be implications from the psychosomatic studies for the neurobiology of the chronic fatigue syndrome. Demitrack et al.[51] in fact found mild glucocorticoid deficiency (reduced basal evening glucocorticoid levels and low 24-hour urinary-free cortisol) in patients suffering from chronic fatigue. This deficiency was thought to be secondary to an impairment of hypothalamic stimuli to the pituitary-adrenal axis.[51]

Hyperthyroidism

The occurrence of life stress preceding the onset of hyperthyroidism is an old clinical observation.[1] Bram in 1927[52] reviewed 3343 cases of exophthalmic goiter. In 85% of these cases, he detected "a clear history of psychic trauma as the exciting cause of the disease." The relationship of stressful life events to hyperthyroidism was supported by subsequent clinical studies.[53-57] These psychosomatic papers, however, have considerable shortcomings, lacking structured methods of data collection and control groups. Contradictory findings have been obtained in epidemiologic surveys[58-60] which also suffered from inadequate methods of assessment. Three studies used standardized methods of life event assessment and a controlled design in hyperthyroidism. Gray and Hoffenberg[61] did not find significant differences between 50 patients with thyrotoxicosis and 50 with nontoxic goiters. Sonino et al.,[62] however, using the same scale for life events, did find significant differences between 70 patients with Graves' disease and a control group of 70 healthy subjects, matched for sociodemographic variables.

There are several explanations for these discrepancies that have been discussed elsewhere.[62] The negative results obtained by Gray and Hoffenberg may be due to methodological flaws, including the fact that nontoxic goiter has also been associated with stress.[63] Winsa et al.[64] mailed a questionnaire about life changes to 219 patients with Graves' disease and 372 matched controls. The patient group reported more negative events. Several factors may contribute to Graves' disease.[65] Stressful life events may affect the regulatory mechanisms of immune function in a number of ways.[27] Within the extreme complexity of the phenomena implicated in the pathogenesis of autoimmune thyroid hyperfunction,[65] there is preliminary evidence to suggest a potential pathogenetic role for emotional stress.

Hyperthyroidism is commonly associated with increased anxiety, hyperactivity, emotional lability, mania, and confusion.[66] However, depression can develop in thyrotoxicosis. Kleinschmidt et al.[67] studied 84 patients suffering from Graves' disease and noted their mixture of anxiety, aggression, and depression which was refractory to psychotherapeutic approaches. Whybrow et al.[68] observed depression in 2 of 10 patients, and provided evidence for an impairment of cognitive function, although not as severe as with hypothyroidism. Apathetic hyperthyroidism, first described by Lahey,[69] is a condition where the typical manifestations of thyroid hyperactivity are absent, while apathy, cardiovascular symptoms, and depression prevail.[70] Such depression may improve dramatically with the correction of thyrotoxicosis[69–72] while it appears not to respond to antidepressants.[71–73] Kathol and Delahunt[74] applied DSM-III criteria to a sample of 32 newly diagnosed patients suffering from hyperthyroidism and found that 10 of them presented with a major depressive episode. Another 15 patients suffered from anxiety disturbances, which in 13 reached the intensity of panic attacks. No psychotic disturbances were noted. Antithyroid therapy induced a significant improvement in the depressive and anxiety symptoms of most of the patients,[75] as was found as well in other subsequent studies.[76, 77] However, this does not resolve the issue as to whether these affective disturbances are simply a consequence of increased thyroid hormone levels or precede the onset of hyperthyroidism and may even represent a risk factor for its development.

For instance, there is a well-known association of hyperthyrodism to phobic symptoms, particularly agoraphobia.[78–80] Achievement of normal thyroid function may result in the disappearance of phobic symptoms in many cases,[78–80] but not in other instances.[14] It is indeed difficult to conceptualize a complex, multifactorial, slow-incubation disturbance such as panic disorder with agoraphobia[20] as being simply the consequence of increased anxiety, depression and irritability due to hyperthyroidism.

Hypothyroidism

Fatigue, memory impairment, lethargy and decreased libido, are well-known clinical manifestations of hypothyroidism. Several studies have described depression as the most frequent psychiatric finding in hypothyroidism.[68, 81–84] Jain[84] found depression in 13 of 30 such patients. Psychotic features may accompany hypothyroidism[84, 85] and may antedate other physical manifestations of the disorder.[86, 87] Depression may result also from hypothyroidism secondary to thyroidectomy,[88] Hashimoto's thyroiditis,[89] and possibly, lithium treatment[90] and isolated TSH deficiency.[91] Gold et al.[92] evaluated thyroid function in 250 patients referred to a psychiatric hospital for treatment of depression or anergia. Twenty of the 250 patients had some degree of hypothyroidism. Half of such patients had subclinical hypothyroidism, which could be detected only by TRH testing.[92] It was suggested[93] on the basis of positive thyroid microsomal antibodies that "symptomless" autoimmune thyroiditis may underlie subclinical hypothyroidism. The behavioral disturbances may then slowly progress to those seen in classical myxedema.[93] There is no evidence, however, that behavioral symptoms associated with subclinical hypothyroidism respond to thyroid replacement. Even depression in frank hypothyroidism does not always respond.[81–84]

In addition to depression, hypothyroidism can present with a wide range of psychiatric manifestations, including personality disturbances and paranoid disorders,[83–86] and severe cognitive impairment.[68, 84, 86] Indeed, hypothyroidism may lead to a degree of inattention, disorientation, and intellectual deficit that may yield the clinical diagnosis of dementia and persist even after adequate hormonal replacement.[94]

The addition of thyroid hormone to antidepressants has yielded contradictory results, even though in some studies it appears to enhance the antidepressant activity of tricyclic drugs in depressed patients with normal thyroid function.[95] What is known is that depressed hypothyroid patients do not respond, by and large, to antidepressant drugs[96] and that patients experience increased sadness and anxiety when they are not taking thyroid hormone replacement.[97] Depression in primary hypothyroidism may be associated with poor compliance[98] and requires a careful psychological approach to assure an appropriate thyroxine treatment.

HYPERPROLACTINEMIA

Even though there is evidence about the relationship of acute stress to prolactin,[99] there are no controlled studies on the relationship of stressful life events to hyperprolactinemia. A biographic and clinical investigation of 101 patients with hyperprolactinemia and/or galactorrhea suggested that exposure during childhood to an environment characterized by an absent or alcoholic, violent father may condition some women to develop hyperprolactinemia and/or galactorrhea later in life as a response to specific environmental changes.[100] These observations were confirmed when sisters of patients with prolactinoma (generally exposed to the same environment as the patients) and a control group were studied.[101] Higher mean serum prolactin concentrations and a higher incidence of hyperprolactinemia and galactorrhea were reported by women with paternal deprivation during childhood.[101] Further, patients with hyperprolactinemic amenorrhea were found to have had functional enuresis during childhood significantly more frequently than women with amenorrhea and normal prolactin levels.[102] The psychosomatic implications of these studies, including the view of idiopathic hyperprolactinemia as a transitional stage toward prolactinoma,[103] have been discussed in detail by Sobrinho.[104]

In 13 patients with postpill galactorrhea-amenorrhea, hyperprolactinemia was found to be associated with high levels of anxiety.[105] In another study, 11 hyperprolactinemic amenorrheic patients showed clear symptoms of depression.[106] A decrease of libido is a frequent symptom in hyperprolactinemic patients,[107] which could be a consequence of a psychological disorder. These psychosomatic studies of hyperprolactinemic states did not employ control groups, and amenorrhea alone, even without hyperprolactinemia, might have been responsible for the symptoms of anxiety and depression.[108] In a study performed in Italy,[109] patients with hyperprolactinemic amenorrhea reported significantly more depression, hostility, and anxiety on a self-rating scale than two control groups (one of normal healthy women and the other of patients with amenorrhea and normal prolactin levels). Six of 18 hyperprolactinemic women were found to suffer from a major depressive disorder[110] according to DSM-III criteria. These results were fully replicated in a subsequent study performed in the United States.[111] Other independent investigations supported the relationship of hyperprolactinemia to depression and hostility in women.[112, 113] Interestingly, hyperprolactinemic males were significantly more depressed than healthy controls, but no more than medical controls and there were no differences in hostility.[114] These results were later confirmed by others,[115] and tentatively suggest that even though sadness, demoralization, and apathy may be present in hyperprolactinemic males, the intensity of a major depressive disorder is seldom reached. The fact that the findings in male patients were substantially different from those in women may also suggest that the behavioral effects of prolactin may depend on its interaction with gonadal hormones.[116] Postpartum women who had high prolactin levels were significantly more hostile than a control group and as hostile as hyperprolactinemic women.[117] It should be mentioned, however, that hostility and irritability are frequently associated with depression in endocrine disease and may be symptoms of depression.[8]

Depression in hyperprolactinemia was found to respond poorly to amitriptyline.[8] In a placebo-controlled cross-over study of bromocriptine in eight hyperprolactinemic patients, self-rated psychological distress decreased and well-being increased in parallel with the bromocriptine-induced fall in prolactin.[118] Psychological distress may be added to the symptom complex of hyperprolactinemic amenorrhea and may be a specific indicator for bromocriptine treatment.[113, 118]

ACROMEGALY

Bleuler[119] in 1951 provided a description of the psychopathology of 28 patients suffering from acromegaly. He observed "moodiness" and personality changes, and illustrated a psychotherapeutic approach to a patient. Two case reports suggested a link of gigantism[120] and acromegaly[121] to depression. Kelly et al.,[29] however, did not find cases of depression in six patients with acromegaly, and Abed et al.[122] found no increase in psychiatric morbidity, including depression, in 41 patients with acromegaly, in comparison with general population and patient samples. The lack of significant psychopathology (organic affective syndromes) cannot be equated to an absence of compromised quality of life in these patients, which awaits appropriate investigation. Cushing himself[1] emphasized the psychological consequences of "feeling acromegalic," and demoralization and psychological disturbances were described in pituitary gigantism.[123]

GROWTH HORMONE DEFICIENCY

The profound psychological implications of growth hormone deficiency in childhood (disturbances in identity formation, social withdrawal, impaired self-esteem, distorted body image) have been emphasized in several investigations.[124-127] A state of functional growth hormone deficiency in childhood may occur also as a result of disruption of social relationship in the neonatal environment. The syndrome, known as psychosocial dwarfism or abuse dwarfism, is characterized by delayed physical, intellectual, and emotional growth, and normalizes rapidly with improvement of psychosocial environment.[128]

Only recently attention has been dedicated to the compromised quality of life of adults with growth hormone deficiency,[129, 130] as well as with multiple pituitary hormone deficiency.[131] Patients with growth hormone deficiency were found to have difficulties leading a normal professional and private life.[132, 133] The educational achievements of these patients were found to be normal, but the rate of employment and marriage were much lower than expected, emphasizing the need to develop strategies that might lead to more satisfactory psychosocial integration in adult life.[134] Social isolation, low interest in pleasurable activities, sexual dysfunction, fatigue, and irritability were reported by patients with growth hormone deficiency compared to a normal control group.[129, 130] Similarly, patients with multiple pituitary hormone deficiencies showed lower openness, lower assertiveness, a greater neuroticism than did control subjects matched for height and sociodemographic variables.[131] Significant psychological improvement upon recombinant growth hormone treatment was reported in double-blind, placebo-controlled, cross-over studies, concerned with growth hormone-deficient adults.[130, 135, 136] These psychological effects together with physical benefits are being evaluated against potential side effects in the long-term management of growth hormone deficiency in adults and might lead to a more widespread indication for such substitution therapy.

HIRSUTISM

For almost a century a significant number of physicians have noted the tremendous emotional impact of idiopathic hirsutism upon patients, even when amounts of hair are small and medically insignificant.[137] The role of physicians is complicated because medical advice about the "normality" of idiopathic hirsutism is inconsistent with societal and commercial conceptualizations and there is no simple commercial or medical treatment.[137, 138] Merivale[139] noted that the onset of hirsutism took place after stressful life events in 4 of 10 women. Bush and Mahesh[140] described the rapid development of hirsutism in an identical twin after emotional stress, and suggested that it was due to an increase in adrenocortical function caused by emotional tension, coupled with a slight inherited abnormality in the ratio of cortisol to androgens. Meyer and Zerssen[141] intensively studied 15 patients from a psychoanalytic viewpoint and found irritability, frigidity, and reduction of emotional contact. Some patients could no longer accept themselves, and a "complex of acceptance" induced a picture of "chronic re-active depression." In a study of 33 hirsute women, however, psychological rating scales to assess neuroticism, introversion, anxi-ety, self-esteem, and aggression did not disclose significant differ-ences with a group of women suffering from a variety of minor dermatologic complaints.[138] Higher levels of anxiety in 15 hirsute women compared to 20 control subjects, were reported by oth-ers.[142] Benzodiazepines, however, had no significant effects on hair growth in women with idiopathic hirsutism.[143] In a controlled study using both observer- and self-rated psychometric methods, hirsute women displayed significantly more hostility and irritable mood than control subjects, even though there were no signifi-cant differences in anxiety and depression.[144] Thus, different meth-ods of assessment seem to yield different results in hirsutism. A possible explanation lies in the fact that hirsutism does not en-tail major affective disturbances, unlike Cushing's syndrome or hyperthyroidism. Quality of life, however, appears to be com-promised, as documented in a recent investigation where 50 hir-sute women reported significantly more social fears than a normal control group.[145] Sexual dysfunction is also reported by hirsute women,[138] and appears to worsen upon antiandrogen treatment.[146]

In hirsutism, as well, it is difficult to establish whether psycho-logical problems are only a simple consequence of excess hair or may act as a predisposing factor associated with stress and other biological vulnerabilities. Hyperandrogenic women displayed a greater cortisol release following mental stress compared to nor-mal women, and this abnormal pituitary–adrenal activation might play a role in the pituitary–ovarian disruption characteristic of the ovarian androgenic syndrome.[147]

CONCLUSION

The psychosomatic approach to the study of endocrine disease has yielded important insights into their mechanisms and characteristics, as well as in the psychobiologic understanding of affective disorders.

1. There is growing interest in the role of stress in clinical endocrinology. Shorter acute, experimental stresses have become the focus of a large volume of endocrine research, but the validity of laboratory stressors as models for real-life stressors has been questioned, and the extension of these results of long-term situations is purely inferential.[148] On the other hand, the issue of chronic stress has been largely neglected, yet its potential to provide conceptual links between laboratory and clinical studies is considerable. It appears that stressful life events may play a role in the onset of illnesses such as Cushing's disease and Graves' disease.

2. Psychological symptoms are often among the prodromes of endocrine disorders. It is not clear whether they represent the first signs of hormonal derangements, due to the sensitivity of the brain to these changes, or they may constitute a predisposing factor for hypothalamic-pituitary activation. Depression in Cushing's syndrome may be an example of the former occurrence. Anxiety and phobic disorders in hyperthyroidism or early neurotic traits in hyperprolactinemia may be examples of the latter case.

3. The concept of organic affective syndromes in DSM-III-R (mood or anxiety disturbances caused by organic factors that remit upon correction of the metabolic derangements) is supported by the psychosomatic study of endocrine disease. In particular, in organic mood disorders the poor response of depression to antidepressant drugs may have important implications for the general issue of depression not responding to standard pharmacological treatments. It is of considerable research interest, in fact, that some drugs used to treat Cushing's disease or Nelson's syndrome have been reported to display antidepressant and/or mood-stabilizing properties in patients not suffering from endocrine disease. Such drugs include cyproheptadine, bromocriptine, and sodium valproate,[8] metyrapone, aminoglutethimide, and ketoconazole,[149] and ritanserin.[150] The category of organic affective syndromes has been removed from DSM-IV.[151] Yet, a considerable body of evidence in endocrinology would lead to retaining its use.

4. Clinical endocrinology seems to depart from other areas of medicine (e.g., cardiology) that have become increasingly concerned with the issue of quality of life. Using Engel's[152] appraisal of current medical education, it appears that the average endocrinologist today:

[C]ompletes his formal education with impressive capabilities to deal with most of the technical aspects of endocrine disease, yet when it comes to dealing with psychosocial aspects of patient care he displays little more than the native ability and personal qualities with which he entered medical school [p. 169].

Further, the considerable body of knowledge about psychoneuroendocrinology that has accumulated over the years is perceived as only marginal and incidental to hormonal disturbances, instead of fostering the biopsychosocial comprehension of endocrine disease.[14]

5. In the past decade, medical–psychiatric units designed for patients too psychiatrically disturbed to be treated in medical wards in conjunction with consultation psychiatry, and too medically ill to be on conventional psychiatric inpatient services, have been established in the United States.[153] The joint presence of a psychiatrist and an internist identifies these units. It may not be too daring to postulate the clinical need and feasibility of psychoendocrine units, with both inpatient and outpatient facilities, where both endocrinologists and psychiatrists should work. Such psychoendocrine units would serve clinical populations that currently defy traditional medical subdivisions.

The clinical and research implications of a psychosomatic view of endocrine disorders are thus considerable and may be crucial for further developments in psychoneuroendocrinology.

ACKNOWLEDGMENT

This work was supported in part by a VA Merit Review funding to M.A.M. and by MURST (Rome, Italy) grants to G.A.F. and N.S. Mrs. Karlene Fox provided expert secretarial assistance.

REFERENCES

1. Cushing H. Psychiatric disturbances associated with the ductless glands. *Am J Insanity.* 1913;69:965–990.
2. Whybrow PC, Hurwitz T. Psychological disturbances associated with endocrine disease and hormone therapy. In: Sachar EJ, ed. *Hormones, Behavior and Psychopathology.* New York: Raven Press;1976: pp 125–143.
3. Jefferson JW, Marshall JR. *Neuropsychiatric Features of Medical Disorders.* New York: Plenum;1981: pp 138–178.
4. Whitlock FA. *Symptomatic Affective Disorders.* Sydney, Australia: Academic Press;1982: pp 85–98.
5. Reus VI. Behavioral disturbances associated with endocrine disorders. *Annu Rev Med.* 1986;37:205–214.
6. Nemeroff CB, Kalivas PW, Golden RN, Prange AJ. Behavioral effects of hypothalamic hypophysiotropic hormones, neurotensin, substance P and other neuropeptides. *Pharmacol Ther.* 1984;24:1–56.
7. Rose M. Psychoendocrinology. In: Wilson JD, Foster DW, eds. *Williams Textbook of Endocrinology.* Philadelphia: Saunders;1985: pp 653–681.
8. Fava GA, Sonino N, Morphy MA. Major depression associated with endocrine disease. *Psychiatr Dev.* 1987;4:321–348.
9. Pepper GM, Krieger DT. Hypothalamic-pituitary-adrenal abnormalities in depression. In: Post RM, Ballenger J, eds. *Neurobiology of Mood Disorders.* Baltimore: Williams & Wilkins;1984: pp 245–270.
10. Arana GW, Baldessarini RJ, Ornsteen M. The dexamethasone suppression test for diagnosis and prognosis in psychiatry. *Arch Gen Psychiatry.* 1985;42:1193–1204.
11. Fava GA, Sonino N. Hypothalamic-pituitary-adrenal disturbances in depression. A discussion of recent studies. *IRCS Med Sci.* 1986;14:1058–1061.
12. Holsboer F. Psychoneuroendocrine strategies. In: Fava GA, Wise TN, eds. *Research Paradigms in Psychosomatic Medicine.* Basel, Switzerland: Karger;1987: pp 185–233.
13. Murphy BEP. Steroids and depression. *J Steroid Biochem Mol Biol.* 1991;38:537–559.
14. Sonino N, Fava GA, Fallo F, Boscaro M. Psychological distress and quality of life in endocrine disease. *Psychother Psychosom.* 1990;54:140–144.
15. Wilkinson DG. Psychiatric aspects of diabetes mellitus. *Br J Psychiatry.* 1981;138:1–9.
16. Lustman PJ, Amado H, Wetzel RD. Depression in diabetes. *Compr Psychiatry.* 1983;24:65–74.
17. Rodin G. Psychosocial aspects of diabetes mellitus. *Can J Psychiatry.* 1983;28:219–223.
18. Rodin G. Quality of life in adults with insulin-dependent diabetes mellitus. *Psychother Psychosom.* 1990;54:132–139.
19. Starkman MN, Zelnik TC, Nesse RM, Cameron OG. Anxiety in patients with pheochromocytomas. *Arch Intern Med.* 1985;145:248–252.

20. Fava GA, Grandi S, Canestrari R. Prodromal symptoms in panic disorder with agoraphobia. *Am J Psychiatry.* 1988;145:1546–1567.
21. Trethowan WH, Cobb S. Neuropsychiatric aspects of Cushing's syndrome. *AMA Arch Neurol Psychiatry.* 1952;67:283–309.
22. Gifford S, Gunderson JG. Cushing's disease as a psychosomatic disorder. *Medicine.* 1970;49:397–409.
23. Cohen SI. Cushing's syndrome. *Br J Psychiatry.* 1980;136:120–124.
24. Sonino N, Fava GA, Grandi S, Mantero F, Boscaro M. Stressful life events in the pathogenesis of Cushing's syndrome. *Clin Endocrinol.* 1988;29:617–623.
25. Fava GA, Sonino N, Pagotto U, Fallo F, Boscaro M. Stressful life events may play a role in the pathogenesis of Cushing's disease. *J Endocrinol Invest.* 1990;13(suppl 2):147.
26. Howlett TA, Rees LH, Besser GM. Cushing's syndrome. *Clin Endocrinol Metab.* 1985;14:911–945.
27. Calabrese JR, Kling MA, Gold PW. Alterations in immunocompetence during stress, bereavement and depression. *Am J Psychiatry.* 1987;144:1123–1134.
28. Krieger DT. Physiopathology of Cushing's disease. *Endocr Rev.* 1983;4:22–43.
29. Kelly WF, Checkley SA, Bender DA. Cushing's syndrome, tryptophan and depression. *Br J Psychiatry.* 1980;136:125–132.
30. Kelly WF, Checkley SA, Bender DA, Mashinter K. Cushing's syndrome and depression. *Br J Psychiatry.* 1983;142:16–19.
31. Starkman MN, Schteingart DE, Schork A. Depressed mood and other psychiatric manifestations of Cushing's syndrome. *Psychosom Med.* 1981;43:3–188.
32. Haskett RF. Diagnostic categorization of psychiatric disturbance in Cushing's syndrome. *Am J Psychiatry.* 1985;142:911–916.
33. Starkman MN, Schteingart DE, Schork MA. Correlation of bedside cognitive and neuropsychological tests in patients with Cushing's syndrome. *Psychosomatics.* 1986;27:508–511.
34. Hudson JI, Hudson MS, Griffing GT, Melby JC, Pope HG. Phenomenology and family history of affective disorder in Cushing's disease. *Am J Psychiatry.* 1987;144:951–953.
35. Murphy E, Brown GW. Life events, psychiatric disturbance and physical illness. *Br J Psychiatry.* 1980;136:326–338.
36. Wolff SM, Adler RC, Buskirk ER, Thompson RH. A syndrome of periodic hypothalamic discharge. *Am J Med.* 1964;36:956–967.
37. Bochner F, Burker CJ, Lloyd HM, Nurmber BI. Intermittent Cushing's disease. *Am J Med.* 1979;67:507–510.
38. Kathol RG, Delahunt JW, Hannah L. Transition from bipolar affective disorder to intermittent Cushing's syndrome. *J Clin Psychiatry.* 1985;46:194–196.
39. Reus VI. Diagnosis and treatment in endocrinology and psychiatry. In: Van Dyke C, Temoshok L, Zegans LS, eds. *Emotions in Health and Illness.* New York: Grune & Stratton;1984: pp 23–34.
40. Addison T. Disease of the suprarenal capsules. In: *Collection of the Published Writings of the late Thomas Addison.* London, MDA: New Sydenham Society;1868.
41. Engel GL, Margolin SG. Neuropsychiatric disturbances in internal disease. *Arch Inter Med.* 1942;70:236–259.

42. Cleghorn RA. Adrenal cortical insufficiency. *Can Med Assn J.* 1951;65:449–454.
43. Cleghorn RA, Pattee CJ. Psychologic changes in 3 cases of Addison's disease during treatment with cortisone. *J Clin Endocrinol Metab.* 1954;14:344–352.
44. McFarland HR. Addison's disease and related psychoses. *Compr Psychiatry.* 1963;4:90–95.
45. Cumming J, Kort K. Apparent reversal by cortisone of an electroconvulsive refractory state in a psychotic patient with Addison's disease. *Can Med Assn J.* 1956;74:291–292.
46. Drake FR. Neuropsychiatric-like symptomatology of Addison's disease. *Am J Med Sci.* 1957;234:106–113.
47. Money J, Russell J. Juvenile Addison's disease. *Psychoneuroendocrinology.* 1977;2:149–157.
48. Rajathurai A, Chazan BI, Jeans JE. Self-mutilation as a feature of Addison's disease. *Br Med J.* 1983;ii:1027.
49. Hassanyeh F, Murray RB, Rodger H. Adrenocortical suppression presenting with agitated depression, morbid jealousy, and a dementia-like state. *Br J Psychiatry.* 1991;159:870–872.
50. Fava GA, Morphy MA, Molnar G, Perini GI. Hypothalamic–pituitary–adrenal axis hypoactivity in depressive illness. *IRCS Med Sci.* 1985;13:954–955.
51. Demitrack MA, Dale JK, Strauss SE, Lane L, Listwak SJ, Kruesi MJP, Chronsos GP, Gold PW. Evidence for impaired activation of hypothalamic-pituitary-adrenal axis in patients with chronic fatigue syndrome. *J Clin Endocrinol Metab.* 1991;73:1224–1234.
52. Bram I. Psychic trauma in pathogenesis of exophthalmic goiter. *Endocrinology.* 1927;11:106–116.
53. Conrad A. The psychiatric study of hyperthyroid patients. *J Nerv Ment Dis.* 1934;79:505–529.
54. Katzenlbogen S, Luton FH. Hyperthyroidism and psychological reactions. *Am J Psychiatry.* 1934–1935;91:969–981.
55. Lidz T, Whitehorn JC. Life situations, emotions and Graves' disease. *Psychosom Med.* 1950;12:184–186.
56. Bennett AW, Cambor CG. Clinical study of hyperthyroidism. *Arch Gen Psychiatry.* 1961;4:160–165.
57. Forteza ME. Precipitating factor in hyperthyroidism. *Geriatrics.* 1973;78:123–126.
58. Bastenie PA. Diseases of the thyroid gland in occupied Belgium. *Lancet.* 1947;i:789–792.
59. Meulengracht E. Epidemiological aspects of thyrotoxicosis. *Arch Intern Med.* 1949;83:119–134.
60. Hadden DR, McDevitt DG. Environmental stress and thyrotoxicosis. *Lancet.* 1974;ii:577–578.
61. Gray J, Hoffenberg R. Thyrotoxicosis and stress. *Q J Med.* 1985;54:153–160.
62. Sonino N, Girelli ME, Boscaro M, Fallo F, Busnardo B, Fava GA. Life events in the pathogenesis of Graves' disease. *Acta Endocrinol.* In press.
63. Seldon WA. The role of psychic stress in the aetiology of non-toxic goiter. *Med J Austr.* 1958;2:443–445.

64. Winsa B, Adami HO, Bergstrom R, Gamstedt A, Dahlberg PA, Adamson U, Jansson R, Karlsson A. Stressful life events and Graves' disease. *Lancet.* 1991; 338:1475–1479.
65. McDougall IR. Graves' disease. *Med Clin N Am.* 1991;75:79–95.
66. Jadresic DP. Psychiatric aspects of hyperthyroidism. *J Psychosom Res.* 1990;34: 603–615.
67. Kleinschmidt HJ, Waxenberg SE, Cukor R. Psychophysiology and psychiatric management of thyrotoxicocis. *J Mt Sinai Hosp.* 1956;23:131–153.
68. Whybrow PC, Prange AJ, Treadway CR. Mental changes accompanying thyroid gland dysfunction. *Arch Gen Psychiatry.* 1969;20:48–63.
69. Lahey FH. Non-activated (apathetic) type of hyperthyroidism. *N Engl J Med.* 1981;204:747–748.
70. Thomas FB, Mazzaferri EL, Skillman TG. Apathetic thyrotoxicosis. *Ann Intern Med.* 1970;72:679–685.
71. Taylor JW. Depression in thyrotoxicocis. *Am J Psychiatry.* 1975;132:552–553.
72. Brenner I. Apathetic hyperthyroidism. *J Clin Psychiatry.* 1978;39:479–480.
73. Folks DG. Organic affective disorders and underlying thyrotoxicosis. *Psychosomatics.* 1984;25:243–249.
74. Kathol RG, Delahunt JW. The relationship of anxiety and depression to symptoms of hyperthyroidism using operational criteria. *Gen Hosp Psychiatry.* 1986;8:23–28.
75. Kathol RG, Turner R, Delahunt J. Depression and anxiety associated with hyperthyroidism: Response to antithyroid therapy. *Psychosomatics.* 1986;27: 501–505.
76. Trzepacz PT, McCue M, Klein I, Greenhouse J, Levey GS. Psychiatric and neuropsychological response to propranolol in Graves' disease. *Biol Psychiatry.* 1988;23:678–688.
77. Paschke R, Harsch I, Schlote B, Vardarli I, Schaaf L, Kammeier S, Teuber J, Usadel KH. Sequential psychological testing during the course of autoimmune hyperthyroidism. *Klin Wochenschr.* 1990;68:942–950.
78. Ficarra BJ, Nelson RA. Phobia as a symptom in hyperthyroidism. *Am J Psychiatry.* 1947;103:831–832.
79. Weller MPI. Agoraphobia and hyperthyroidism. *Br J Psychiatry.* 1984;144: 553–554.
80. Emanuele MA, Brooks MH, Gordon DL, Braithwaite SS. Agoraphobia and hyperthyroidism. *Am J Med.* 1989;86:484–486.
81. Miller R. Mental symptoms from myxedema. *J Lab Clin Med.* 1952;40:267–270.
82. Pitts FM, Guze SB. Psychiatric disorders and myxedema. *Am J Psychiatry.* 1961;118:142–147.
83. Tonks CM. Mental illness in hypothyroid patients. *Br J Psychiatry.* 1964;110: 706–710.
84. Jain VK. A psychiatric study of hypothyroidism. *Psychiatria Clin.* 1972;5: 121–130.
85. Reed K, Bland RC. Masked "myxedema madness." *Acta Psychiatr Scand.* 1977;56:421–426.
86. Asher R. Myxedematous madness. *Br Med J.* 1949;ii:555–562.
87. Logothetis J. Psychotic behavior as an initial indicator of adult myxedema. *J Nerv Ment Dis.* 1963;136:561–568.

88. Libow LS, Durell J. Clinical studies on the relationship between psychosis and the regulation of thyroid gland activity. *Psychosom Med.* 1965;27:377–382.

89. Hall RCW, Popkin MK, deVaul R, Hall AK, Gardner ER, Beresford TP. Psychiatric manifestations of Hashimoto's thyroiditis. *Psychosomatics.* 1982;23: 337–342.

90. Sternbach HA, Pottash ALC, Extein I, Gold MS. Identifying depression secondary to lithium-induced hypothyroidism. *Psychosomatics.* 1984;25:864–866.

91. Nordgren L, von Scheele C. Myxedematous madness without myxedema. *Acta Med Scand.* 1976;199:233–236.

92. Gold MS, Pottash ALC, Extein I. Hypothyroidism and depression. *JAMA.* 1981;245:1919–1922.

93. Gold MS, Pottash ALC, Extein I. "Symptomless" autoimmune thyroiditis in depression. *Psychiatry Res.* 1982;6:261–269.

94. Cummings JL. Treatable dementias. In: Mayeux R, Rosen GW, eds. *The Dementias.* New York: Raven Press;1983: pp 165–183.

95. Joffe RT. A perspective on the thyroid and depression. *Can J Psychiatry.* 1990;35:754–760.

96. Russ MJ, Ackerman SH. Antidepressant treatment response in depressed hypothyroid patients. *Hosp Community Psychiatry.* 1989;40:954–956.

97. Denicoff KD, Joffe RT, Lakshmanan MC, Robbins J, Rubinow DR. Neuropsychiatric manifestations of altered thyroid state. *Am J Psychiatry.* 1990;147: 94–99.

98. Exley P, O'Malley BP. Depression in primary hypothyroidism masquerading as inadequate or excessive L-thyroxine consumption. *Q J Med.* 1989;72: 867–870.

99. Fava M, Guaraldi GP. Prolactin and stress. *Stress Med.* 1987;3:211–216.

100. Nunes MCP, Sobrinho LG, Calhaz-Jorge C, Santos MA, Mauricio JC, Sousa MFF. Psychosomatic factors in patients with hyperprolactinemia and/or galactorrhea. *Obstet Gynecol.* 1980;55:591–595.

101. Sobrinho LG, Nunes MCP, Calhaz-Jorge C, Afonso AM, Pereira MC, Santos MA. Hyperprolactinemia in women with paternal deprivation during childhood. *Obstet Gynecol.* 1984;64:465–468.

102. Fava M, Guaraldi GP, Borofsky GL, Mastrogiacomo I. Childhood's enuresis in the history of women with hyperprolactinemic amenorrhea. *Int J Psychiat Med.* 1989;19:41–46.

103. Pereira MC, Sobrinho LG, Afonso AM, Ferreira JM, Santos MA, Sousa MFF. Is idiopathic hyperprolactinemia a transitional state toward prolactinoma? *Obstet Gynecol.* 1987;70:305–308.

104. Sobrinho LG. Neuropsychiatry of prolactin. *Clin Endocrinol Metab.* 1991;5: 119–142.

105. Tyson JE, Andreasson B, Huth J, Smith B, Zacur H. Neuroendocrine dysfunction in galactorrhea-amenorrhea after oral contraceptive use. *Obstet Gynecol.* 1975;46:1–11.

106. Fioretti P, Corsini GV, Murru S, Medda F, Romagnino S, Genazzani AR. Psychoneuroendocrinological effects of 2-alpha-bromoergocriptine therapy in cases of hyperprolactinemic amenorrhea. In: Carenza L, Pancheri P, Zichella L, eds. *Clinical Psychoneuroendocrinology in Reproduction.* London: Academic Press;1978.

107. Franks S, Nabarro JSM, Jacobs HS. Prevalence and presentation of hyperprolactinemia in patients with functionless pituitary tumors. *Lancet.* 1977;i: 778–780.
108. Fava GA, Fava M. Psychiatric symptomatology in secondary amenorrhea. *Stress Med.* 1986;2:191–193.
109. Fava GA, Fava M, Kellner R, Serafini E, Mastrogiacomo I. Depression, hostility and anxiety in hyperprolactinemic amenorrhea. *Psychother Psychosom.* 1981;36:122–128.
110. Mastrogiacomo I, Fava M, Fava GA, Serafini E, DeBesi L. Correlations between psychological symptoms in hyperprolactinemic amenorrhea. *Neuroendorinol Lett.* 1983;5:117–122.
111. Kellner R, Buckman MT, Fava GA, Pathak D. Hyperprolactinemia, distress and hostility. *Am J Psychiatry.* 1984;141:759–763.
112. Keller SK, Nehaus-Theil A, Quabbe HJ. Psychologic correlates of prolactin secretion. *Acta Endocrinol Suppl.* 1985;267:118–119.
113. Koppelman MCS, Parry BL, Hamilton JA, Alagnia SW, Loriaux DL. Effect of bromocriptine on affect and libido in hyperprolactinemia. *Am J Psychiatry.* 1987;144:1037–1041.
114. Fava M, Fava GA, Kellner R, Serafini E, Mastrogiacomo I. Psychological correlates of hyperprolactinemia in males. *Psychother Psychosom.* 1982;37:214–217.
115. Cohen LM, Greenberg DB, Murray GB. Neuropsychiatric presentation of men with pituitary tumors. *Psychosomatics.* 1984;25:925–928.
116. Kellner R, Buckman MT, Fava GA, Mastrogiacomo I. Prolactin, aggression and hostility. *Psychiatr Dev.* 1984;2:131–138.
117. Mastrogiacomo I, Fava M, Fava GA, Kellner R, Grismondi G, Cetera C. Postpartum hostility and prolactin. *Int J Psychiatry.* 1983;12:289–294.
118. Buckman MT, Kellner R. Reduction of distress in hyperprolactinemia with bromocriptine. *Am J Psychiatry.* 1985;142:242–244.
119. Bleuler M. The psychopathology of acromegaly. *J Nerv Ment Dis.* 1951;113: 497–511.
120. Averty TL. A case of acromegaly and gigantism with depression. *Br J Psychiatry.* 1973;122:599–600.
121. Margo A. Acromegaly and depression. *Br J Psychiatry.* 1981;139:467–468.
122. Abed RT, Clark J, Elbadawy MHF, Cliffe MJ. Psychiatric morbidity in acromegaly. *Acta Psychiatr Scand.* 1987;75:635–639.
123. Whitehead EM, Shalet SM, Davies D, Enoch BA, Price DA, Beardwell CG. Pituitary gigantism: A disabling condition. *Clin Endocrinol.* 1982;17:271–277.
124. Rotnem D, Genel N, Hintz RL, Cohen DJ. Personality development in children with growth hormone deficiency. *J Am Acad Child Psychiatry.* 1977; 16:412–426.
125. Drotar D, Owens R, Gotthold J. Personality adjustment of children and adolescents with hypopituitarism. *Child Psychiatry Hum Dev.* 1980;11:59–66.
126. Gordon M, Crouthamel C, Post EM, Richman RA. Psychosocial aspects of constitutional short stature. *J Pediatr.* 1982;101:477–480.
127. Grew RS, Stabler B, Williams RW, Underwood LE. Facilitating patient understanding in the treatment of growth delay. *Clin Pediatr.* 1985;22:685–690.
128. Green WH, Campbell M, David R. Psychosocial dwarfism. *J Am Acad Clin Child Adolesc Psychiatry.* 1984;23:39–48.

129. Bjork S, Jonsson B, Westphal O, Levin JE. Quality of life of adults with growth hormone deficiency. *Acta Pediatr Scand.* 1989;356(suppl):55–59.
130. McGauley GA. Quality of life assessment before and after growth hormone treatment in adults with growth hormone deficiency. *Acta Pediatr Scand.* 1989;356(suppl):70–72.
131. Stabler B, Turner JR, Girdler SS, Light KC, Underwood LE. Reactivity to stress and psychological adjustment in adults with pituitary insufficiency. *Clin Endocrinol.* 1992;36:467–473.
132. Ranke MB. A note on adults with growth hormone deficiency. *Acta Pediatr Scand.* 1987;331(suppl):80–82.
133. Christiansen J, Jorgensen JO, Pedersen SA, Muller J, Jorgensen J, Moller J, Heickendorf L, Skakkebaek NE. GH-replacement therapy in adults. *Horm Res.* 1991;36(suppl):66–72.
134. Dean HJ, McTaggart TL, Fish DG, Friesen HG. The educational, vocational, and marital status of growth hormone deficient adults treated with growth hormone during childhood. *Am J Dis Child.* 1985;139:1105–1110.
135. Jorgensen JOL, Pedersen SA, Thnesen L, Jorgensen J, Ingemann-Hansen T, Skakkebaek NE, Christiansen JS. Beneficial effects of growth hormone treatment in GH-deficient adults. *Lancet.* 1989;i:1221–1225.
136. Degerblad M, Almkvist O, Grundiz R, Hall K, Kaijser L, Knutsson E, Riugertz H, Thoren M. Physical and psychological capabilities during substitution therapy with recombinant growth hormone in adults with growth hormone deficiency. *Acta Endocrinol.* 1990;123:185–193.
137. Ferrante J. Biomedical versus cultural constructions of abnormality: The case of idiopathic hirsutism in the United States. *Cult Med Psychiatry.* 1988; 12:219–238.
138. Callan AW. Idiopathic hirsutism. In: Dennerstein L, Burrows GD, eds. *Handbook of Psychosomatic Obstetrics and Gynecology.* Amsterdam, Netherlands: Elsevier;1983: pp 413–443.
139. Merivale WHH. The excretion of pregnanediol and 17-ketosteroids during the menstrual cycle in benign hirsutism. *J Clin Pathol.* 1951;4:78–84.
140. Bush IE, Mahesh VB. Adrenocortical hyperfunction with sudden onset of hirsutism. *J Endocrinol.* 1959;18:1–8.
141. Meyer AE, von Zerssen D. Psychologische Untersuchungen an Frauen mit sogenanntem idiopathischem Hirsutismus. *J Psychosom Res.* 1960;4:206–235.
142. Rabinowitz S, Cohen R, LeRoith D. Anxiety and hirsutism. *Psychol Rep.* 1983;19:827–830.
143. Dennerstein L, Callan A, Warne G, Montalto J, Brown J, Burrows G, Fultin A, Notelovitz M. The effects of benzodiazepines on hormones in women with idiopathic hirsutism. *Progr Neuropsychopharmacol Biol Psychiatry.* 1984;8:11–17.
144. Fava GA, Grandi S, Savron G, Bartolucci G, Santarsiero G, Trombini G, Orlandi C. Psychosomatic assessment of hirsute women. *Psychother Psychosom.* 1989;51:96–100.
145. Sonino N, Fava GA, Mani E, Belluardo P, Boscaro M. Quality of life of hirsute women. *Postgrad Med J.* 1993;69:186–189.
146. Appelt H, Strauss B. Effects of antiandrogen treatment on the sexuality of women with hyperadrogenism. *Psychother Psychosom.* 1984;42:177–181.

147. Modell E, Goldstein D, Reyes FI. Endocrine and behavioral responses to psychological stress in hyperandrogenic women. *Fertil Steril.* 1990;53:454–459.
148. Vingerhoets AJJM, Assies J. Psychoneuroendocrinology of stress and emotions. *Psychother Psychosom.* 1991;55:69–75.
149. Murphy BEP, Dhar V, Ghadirian AM, Chouinard G, Keller R. Response to steroid suppression in major depression resistant to antidepressant therapy. *J Clin Psychopharmacol.* 1991;11:121–126.
150. Sonino N, Boscaro M, Fallo F, Fava GA. Potential therapeutic effects of ritanserin in Cushing's disease. *JAMA.* 1992;267:1073.
151. Spitzer RL, First NB, Williams JBW, Kendler K, Pincus HA, Tucker G. Now is the time to retire the term "organic mental disorders." *Am J Psychiatry.* 1992;149:240–244.
152. Engel GL. The biopsychosocial model and the education of health professionals. *Ann NY Acad Sci.* 1978;310:169–181.
153. Fava GA. Medical-psychiatric service. *Psychother Psychosom.* 1987;48:96–100.

Chapter 17
Psycho-Oncology:
Psychological Well-Being
as One Component
of Quality of Life

DENISE M. TOPE, TIM A. AHLES,
PETER M. SILBERFARB

Previous articles that have discussed the role of psychiatry in an oncology setting have argued for the need to define and focus that role. One focus, for example, is to act as consultants on medication issues and in differential diagnosis between psychiatric and pathophysiological disorders.[1] While definition and focus are integral for efficacious clinical intervention and are prerequisites for smooth working of an interdisciplinary team, they need not preclude a foundation of knowledge of the broader impact of cancer on a patient's psychosocial functioning. Efforts to understand the whole cancer experience have begun to address the impact of cancer on a patient's *quality of life*, defined as an individual's subjective sense of well-being derived from his or her current experience of life.[2] The purpose of this article is to present a discussion of the psychological well-being of the cancer patient in the context of a broader model of quality of life, incorporating physical, psychological, social, and spiritual factors into the patient's experience of his or her disease. A theoretical framework of quality of life will be presented with a focus on one component of that model that encompasses psychological well-being. Within the discussion on psychological well-being, topics covered will include prevalence of psychiatric diagnoses among patients diagnosed with cancer, interactions between psychological well-being and other components of the quality of life model (namely physical well-being), interventions designed to impact psychological well-being and quality of life in cancer patients, and, finally, issues of increasing importance in quality of life research in psychological oncology.

QUALITY OF LIFE AND PSYCHOLOGICAL WELL-BEING IN THE CANCER PATIENT

When applied in the context of an individual coping with chronic disease, the construct of quality of life incorporates information from multiple life domains, including disease- and treatment-related physical symptoms, perceptions of personal health, physical functional status, and psychological and social well-being.[3] Recognition of the importance of quality of life in cancer patients has increased sharply over the past 5 years, particularly as treatments have become more effective and the lives of cancer patients have been extended.

Ferrell et al.[4] have outlined a model of four overriding factors that comprise patients' quality of life in their experience of cancer: (1) physical well-being; (2) psychological well-being; (3) social concerns; and (4) spiritual well-being. Physical well-being is affected by both specific disease- and treatment-related symptoms, as well as overall functional status. Psychological well-being is comprised of the presence or absence of negative affect, cognitive phenomena such as maladaptive or catastrophic thinking, and psychiatric phenomena such as depression and anxiety, as well as dementia or delirium. Social concerns include the impact of one's environment, including social support network, on the experience of cancer and the impact of cancer on the patient's own social roles. Finally, spiritual well-being is affected by the patient's personal meaning of the cancer experience, degree of suffering, and his or her religious beliefs. The latter has not been extensively studied, especially in comparison to the former three dimensions, but it is a category that is relevant for many patients faced with a diagnosis of cancer and should be considered in any clinical setting.

Although rather broad, a model of quality of life in the patient with cancer carries at least two points directly relevant to a discussion of the mental health professional in the oncology setting. First, psychological well-being, the concept that traditionally represents the focus for mental health professionals, does not exist in a vacuum. Instead, psychological functioning is interconnected with the other three components that all together form a patient's overall sense of well-being. In the clinical context, this interrelatedness refers in part to correlations that exist among patient- and disease-related variables. For instance, Andersen[5] presented a series of findings that suggest that psychological outcome is a direct function of the magnitude of disease or treatment. Degree of psychological distress has been found to be positively related to extent of disease and physical impairment from treatment in lung cancer patients,[6] extent of treatment in breast cancer patients,[7] and depth of surgical invasion in patients with malignant melanoma.[8] In addition to simple correlation, the interrelatedness among components of quality of life also refers to interaction among those components in creating new symptoms and sharply exacerbating existing ones. The development of conditioned or anticipatory nausea and vomiting in patients undergoing cancer chemotherapy illustrates this interaction clearly. Patients who exhibit high levels of anxiety prior to and during chemotherapy infusion and who, in combination, experience significant nausea and vomiting subsequent to chemotherapy are twice as likely to develop conditioned or anticipatory side effects, in addition to pharmacologically induced ones, than those patients who were anxious only or experienced chemotherapy-induced side effects only.[9] In short, it is simply not realistic to consider one component of the cancer experience without consideration of the others.

A second aspect of the quality of life model that is particularly relevant to a discussion of the role of psychiatry in the oncology setting is that the degree of compromise in a patient's quality of life can range from mild to severe, and that the full range must be recognized. The traditional role of the consultation–liaison psychiatrist is to determine the presence or absence of depression, anxiety, organic disorder such as delirium or dementia, or some other form of psychopathology. In contrast to this inherently dichotomous view (that is, either the patient meets criteria for psychiatric diagnosis or does not), the concept of quality of life allows for a full and continuous range, and even minimal compromises in quality of life can be meaningful and might be addressed psychotherapeutically. The traditional view, in contrast, is less likely to see small disruptions in quality of life as clinically relevant. The need to determine clinically relevent psychiatric diagnoses is certainly important, but a concomitant conceptualization of quality of life broadens that inherently restricted stance.

Given that the stated objective of this article is to present the role of the psychiatrist in the oncology setting within the context of a cancer patient's overall quality of life, the focus will be on the patient's psychological well-being within its larger context of physical, social, and spiritual factors. Due to space limitations, these latter components of the quality of life model will not be discussed extensively. Insightful reviews of the roles of physical factors, social concerns, and spirituality on the patient's experience of cancer are available elsewhere.[10]

PREVALENCE OF PSYCHIATRIC DIAGNOSES AS A MEASURE OF PSYCHOLOGICAL WELL-BEING

The range of the impact of cancer in affecting a patient's quality of life and psychological well-being suggests that some degree of psychopathology may be present in these patients, but clinically elevated distress is not ubiquitous. One of the most comprehensive studies to date of psychiatric problems among cancer patients was conducted by Derogatis et al.[11] These investigators administered a battery of psychological tests and a standardized psychiatric interview to 250 randomly selected cancer patients who had been newly admitted to one of three major cancer centers. Using the criteria outlined in the American Psychiatric Association's *Diagnostic and Statistical Manual-Revised* (DSM-III-R), approximately 47% of the patients met a formal psychiatric diagnosis. However, more than two-thirds of all the patients who received a psychiatric diagnosis were given the diagnosis of adjustment disorder, meaning that the emotional and behavioral disturbance was transient, due to an obvious environmental stressor (such as cancer), and responsive to psychological interventions. Recent studies have replicated the findings of Derogatis et al.[11] and have also concluded that the distress experienced by adult[12, 13] and pediatric[14] cancer patients tends to be transient and situational and not representative of severe psychopathology. For most people, their psychiatric dysfunction will remit in a fairly short period of time, although some patients may need professional help in resolving the problem.

MAJOR DEPRESSION

When distress exceeds the criteria for adjustment disorder and requires diagnosis of a mood, anxiety, or thought disorder, the most common diagnosis provided to cancer patients is major depression. The estimated prevalence of major depression in cancer patients is 13%.[11] The hopelessness and helplessness, increased tearfulness, guilt over past behavior (such as smoking cigarettes), and social withdrawal experienced by many cancer patients can readily reach clinically significant levels. In addition to these psychological or emotional signs of depression, many cancer patients describe multiple somatic or vegetative symptoms of depression, such as excessive fatigue, anorexia, and loss of appetite, and hyposomnia or hypersomnia. Fatigue, loss of appetite, decreased interest in sexual activity, and disturbed sleep are experienced by many cancer patients undergoing rigorous treatment, whether depression is present or not. In fact, it is possible for a cancer patient to satisfy the diagnostic criteria for depression solely through somatic complaints, while reporting little if any mood disturbance. For example, Westin et al.[15] targeted depressive symptoms in a sample of patients with head and neck cancer and found that most of the variance in the diagnosis of depression could be accounted for by patients' nutritional status. Breitbart[16] argued that depression in cancer patients is highly related to cancer-related pain and that all patients suspected of experiencing a major depression should be reevaluated after patients' pain has been significantly controlled or alleviated.

The confound between depression and disease can have at least two direct implications for patient care. First, nondepressed patients who manifest the "vegetative signs" of depression may be unduly pressured to seek supportive counseling without proper attention to the physical origin of the symptoms. Of even more concern is the patient who is clinically depressed, but whose symptoms have been attributed, perhaps even by the patient, to the disease or treatment process. This type of patient may not receive the psychotherapeutic or psychopharmacological intervention to alleviate the depression. Thus, the need exists to accurately measure depression in a chronically ill population.

Kathol et al.[17] compared the sensitivity and accuracy of multiple self-report measures, clinician-administered scales, and the lengthier criteria-based structured diagnostic interviews to assess depression in a group of 152 cancer patients. When the number of patients diagnosed as having major depression was compared across the various measures, the findings differed by as much as 13%. Inspection of the data revealed that the indices differed primarily on the degree to which somatically oriented items differentiated between cancer-related and depression-related symptoms. The authors concluded that two relatively quick and easy measures of depression, the Beck Depression Inventory, and the Hamilton Depression Rating Scale, provide effective screening tools for depression in the oncology setting. However, because scores tend to be inflated due to the presence of somatic symptoms in this population, elevated scores should be investigated on a case-by-case basis through a more thorough patient interview.

Subclinical distress differs from major mood disorders not only in level of severity, but in the breadth of the distress as well. Whereas clinically significant depression is perceived by the patient and clinician as pervasive, so-called "normal" emotional reactions to cancer have been labeled "islands of significant life disruption."[18] The use of the term *islands* emphasizes that they are not global or long-lasting problems in adjustment or psychological functioning and that many of these problems can be addressed quite effectively through simple psychological intervention. Schag and Heinrich,[19] for instance, administered an inventory of problem situations developed especially for a cancer population to identify anxiety in a wide variety of medical situations, such as participating in medical examinations or attending a treatment session, and found that anxiety did indeed vary across these situations and was not global for either male or female patients. Thus, for many patients, cancer-related distress is focused around specific fears or concerns. Such fears include fear of death, pain, disfigurement, disability, and disruption of relationships.[20] For newly diagnosed patients, the novelty and intensity of these fears can initially be overwhelming, and they may speculate on the seemingly unending list of areas of their life that could be impacted by their disease. For instance, Loveys and Klaich[21] conducted semistructured interviews with 79 women newly diagnosed with breast cancer and then performed content analysis to determine patients' perceptions or predictions of illness demands. Results indicated 14 domains that these women saw as affected by the diagnosis of breast cancer, including treatment issues, social interaction, physical appearance, mortality, financial and occupational concerns, and general perceptions of the past, present, and future.

Some have suggested that one major psychological task of the cancer patient that brings about emotional distress, especially dysphoria, is grieving. Grieving a loss may have particular impact on those patients with types of cancer or cancer treatments that entail a loss of a body part, such as removal of a breast or other organ via surgery. Empirical research, however, has not completely supported the assumption that loss of a body part plays a major role in one's emotional response to the diagnosis and treatment of certain cancers. It is often assumed, for example, that mastectomy patients expend much emotional energy grieving the loss of their breast. Several recent studies,[22] however, have indicated that surgery with the primary goal of breast preservation versus breast removal has no impact on overall distress for patients undergoing surgery. In other words, patients who have their breast removed through mastectomy exhibit no more distress than those patients whose breast has been preserved through lumpectomy. While it is unrealistic to interpret these findings as evidence that women do not find removal of their breast upsetting, it does underscore the differences in the relative contribution of multiple sources of distress that the cancer patient faces. According to Van Heeringen et al.,[22] the anticipatory grief reaction to a potentially lethal outcome, experienced by most cancer patients, appears to overwhelm any depressive reaction secondary to loss of a breast. The need to adapt to the loss of a breast or, in the case of other cancers, loss of an important organ or disfigurement, are certainly relevant issues to be addressed in psychosocial treatment of the cancer patient, but these issues may play less of an integral role than general concern over disease process and prognosis.

ANXIETY

The prevalence of clinically significant anxiety disorders among cancer patients is approximately 4%,[11] and consists primarily of panic disorder, simple phobia, and generalized anxiety disorder. These disorders are usually preexisting conditions that are exacerbated by situations associated with the disease and its treatment. As in the case of major depression, the presence of adjustment disorders (moderate to severe reactive anxiety of a transient nature), combined with anxiety symptoms directly attributable to the illness or its treatment, such as from medication side effects, serve to make the prevalence of anxiety in the oncology setting appear much greater than the relatively low prevalence rates might indicate.

When anxiety is experienced by the cancer patient, the most commonly cited source of this emotional distress is the uncertainties of the disease and its treatment, as well as the rigorous nature and discomfort of common treatments. Interestingly, researchers have found that some patients who experience considerable discomfort during prolonged cancer treatments such as chemotherapy will become very anxious upon the termination of treatment, apparently because they fear that once the treatment has stopped, the malignancy may grow again. A second source of anxiety commonly attributed to the patient diagnosed with cancer is so-called "death anxiety." The diagnosis of cancer seems to trigger consideration of one's own mortality in almost all cancer patients, regardless of type of cancer and, like depression, regardless of disease stage. Cella and Tross[23] administered a Death Anxiety Questionnaire to 90 male cancer patients (60 Hodgkin's disease survivors, 30 testicular cancer survivors). The investigators found no differences between the cancer types on death anxiety, nor did they find a relationship with extent of disease or prognosis. A significant relationship did emerge, however, between death anxiety and the time elapsed since diagnosis. Thus, concern about death may increase as the patient assimilates the impact of the diagnosis over time, and, perhaps, as the patient experiences the debilitating effect of cancer treatment. For many patients, changes in functional ability secondary to cancer or its treatment may serve as a poignant reminder of their own mortality.

NEUROPSYCHOLOGICAL IMPAIRMENT

In addition to conditions marked by emotional distress, cancer patients are at high risk for cognitive impairment because of the systemic nature of their illness. Since cancer patients tend to be older, they are predisposed to cognitive dysfunction by virtue of their age, a predisposition that becomes challenged with the addition of chemotherapeutic agents.[24] Delirium is the second most common psychiatric illness found in cancer patients, second only to depression.[11, 25] Approximately 8% of all cancer patients meet criteria for delirium, and as many as 75% of terminally ill cancer patients develop this psychiatric condition,[26] yet delirium is the most frequently misdiagnosed psychiatric illness in cancer patients

by medical residents.[25] The perceptual and behavioral disturbances that are often present in delirium (in combination with
impairment of attention, orientation, and memory) tend to mis-
lead the physician's attention regarding their organic etiology.[24]
Moreover, common symptoms such as slight forgetfulness, complaints of "mental fatigue," difficulty concentrating, and complaints of irritability often go unnoticed by physicians or are
attributed solely to depression or anxiety. In their mildest form,
these symptoms might even be consciously overcome through
efforts by the patient.

Organic impairment in the cancer patient is often multifactorial in etiology.[26] Medications such as narcotics prescribed for
pain control, hypnosedatives provided for insomnia, benzodiazepines prescribed for anxiety, and antiemetics administered to
control nausea and vomiting are commonly associated with cognitive dysfunction. Fevers and infections associated with immunosuppression, and side effects of therapy have all been related
to delirium in the oncology setting to varying degrees, as well as
nutritional, metabolic, or endocrine disorders, either alone or
in combination.[24] Cognitive dysfunction can occur as a result of
the cancer itself, as evident in delirium associated with elevated
blood urea nitrogen, hypercalcemia (prominent in women with
breast cancer), or altered blood gases. Primary tumors in the central nervous system (CNS) or cerebral metastasis from other sites
need not be present for defects in cognition to occur. However,
when metastasis to the CNS has occurred, cognitive deficits are
common.[27] In addition to these organic sources, the individual
struggling with cancer is often exposed to one or more factors
that are well known to facilitate the occurrence of delirium when
organic etiology is present; that is, psychological stress, sleep deprivation, sensory deprivation or sensory overload, and immobi-
lization.[28]

Many chemotherapeutic agents have been implicated in causing
cognitive impairment, but since most are given in combination with
each other and other treatments for cancer, such as radiation, it is
difficult to identify a single causative agent. Methotrexate has traditionally been considered to create cognitive impairment in the

patients who receive it, especially when it is given intrathecally, in children and adults.[29, 30] Other chemotherapeutic agents, perhaps even most of them, have been implicated in causing some degree of cognitive impairment, including adrenal steroids such as prednisone[31] and 5-fluorouracil, commonly administered in the treatment of breast cancer.[32]

Despite the apparent relationship between certain types of chemotherapy and radiation and neuropsychological impairment, few studies exist that prospectively and longitudinally assess longer term neuropsychological changes following treatment for cancer. The vast majority of research in this area is with children who had been treated earlier with intrathecal methotrexate for acute leukemia in combination with cranial irradiation. Neuropsychological effects found in these children include impaired visual motor integration,[33] verbal and visual-spatial learning,[34] and attention and memory.[30] Research with adult cancer patients who have undergone neurotoxic treatments is considerably more limited. Only one study has systematically addressed the question of neuropsychological impact of CNS-directed chemotherapy and cranial irradiation in adults. Tucker et al.[35] reported minimal neuropsychological deficits in a group of 25 adults undergoing treatment for leukemia and lymphoma, suggesting that neuropsychological impact may not be as great in adults as compared to children, whose CNSs are still developing. The certainty of these conclusions, however, is limited by the small sample size of the only existing study and lack of replication.

Appropriately diagnosing delirium when it occurs is important for both the relief of needless suffering and for improved medical compliance. It can be readily diagnosed through simple screening procedures, namely a brief, clinician-administered mental status exam or through an abbreviated questionnaire such as the Mini Mental State Examination.[36] Delirium, by definition, is acute and reversible. Much less common is dementia, marked by intellectual deterioration of a protracted and usually irreversible nature. Dementia has recently begun to be manifest at an earlier than expected age in previously treated childhood leukemics.[37]

Predicting Psychological Well-Being

It is difficult, if not impossible, to predict who will suffer a significant degree of emotional distress during the cancer experience, especially a level significant enough to warrant a formal psychiatric diagnosis. One set of factors that may play a role are disease-related variables. A limited number of studies[38] have found evidence of increased psychiatric morbidity in patients with more advanced disease. Some, on the other hand, have indicated that it is the impact of the disease on physical functioning or lifestyle that is the more powerful predictor of psychological functioning, rather than the actual medical staging of the disease.[39] A second set of factors that may increase a cancer patient's likelihood of developing a psychiatric disorder is, not surprisingly, predisposing factors for those conditions in general. For instance, among patients with comparatively high levels of physical disability, depression was more likely to occur if the patient was in pain, had poor social support, and had a relatively high amount of recent stress in his or her life.[39] In her review of depression in cancer patients, Holland[20] points out that an earlier history of affective disorder or alcoholism may predict the development of depression in cancer patients—as these factors predict the development of depression in all individuals.

Investigations that have attempted to predict which patients will respond to cancer and its treatment with excessively high levels of anxiety have consistently reported two findings: Female cancer patients tend to be more anxious than males and younger cancer patients exhibit, in general, more anxiety than their older counterparts. In their study of variations in anxiety across multiple cancer-related situations, Schag and Heinrich[19] reported that females experienced anxiety in significantly more situations than males and that female patients' anxiety was of reliably greater intensity than males. Regarding age, older cancer patients consistently reported less psychological general distress[40, 41] and less situation-specific anxiety.[42] As Nerenz et al.[43] pointed out,

"Elderly patients are less likely to have pressing job and family demands, more likely to have experienced chronic illness and to have learned ways of coping with them, and more likely to accept cancer as a natural occurrence at their stage of life" (p. 963).

When in the course of diagnosis and treatment will the patient with cancer experience distress? In her thoughtful review of psychological intervention with cancer patients, Anderson[5] suggested that the needs of cancer patients vary dramatically across the experience of cancer. Whereas informational needs, for example, may be prominent early in the process, intensive social support may be paramount in patients with terminal disease. Well-meaning staff and even family members too frequently focus on distress surrounding diagnosis, and remain less aware of residual distress. For instance, referrals for psychological or psychiatric consultation, although proportionately few in number, are more likely to be made immediately following diagnosis than at any other time in the cancer experience.[44] In the months and years following diagnosis, patients do indeed appear to adjust, behaviorally and socially, to having cancer, but psychological distress may not normalize in parallel fashion.[45] Wolberg et al.[13] found that the psychological problems in a sample of breast cancer patients did in fact decrease over time, but difficulties were still evident at least 16 months postsurgery. Spouses of cancer patients are likely to assume that many of the problems faced by their partners have been resolved several months postdiagnosis, whereas the patients themselves continue to rate these same issues as highly problematic. Even patients officially considered "recovered" or "cured" are not without distress. Recovered patients with a history of cancer tend to worry more, in general and about cancer in specific, than individuals who have never been diagnosed with cancer.[46] If and when a patient's cancer does recur, the impact of the second diagnosis or recurrence is likely to be more distressing and even more difficult to adjust to, for the majority of cancer patients, than the initial diagnosis.[47, 48]

Interactions between Physical and Psychological Factors

Another important area of investigation is the interaction between somatic symptoms and psychological factors, and the impact of that interaction on patients' quality of life. It is quite logical to assume that the experience of unpleasant physical symptoms and the limitations in function that they cause will create more intense negative mood states and other psychosocial sequelae than might otherwise be expected. Likewise, interactions can also occur in which psychological factors can heighten physical symptoms or even create new ones. Well-known relationships between psychological and physical factors exist in the development of nausea and vomiting in response to cancer chemotherapy and in the experience of cancer pain.

Conditioned Nausea and Vomiting (CNV) and Anxiety

Anxiety in the cancer treatment setting can influence the degree to which a patient experiences nausea and vomiting associated with chemotherapy. The type of nausea and vomiting that seems to be most readily affected is that caused not pharmacologically, but as a result of an associative learning process. Approximately one-third of all cancer patients undergoing cancer chemotherapy will experience *conditioned*, or learned, side effects,[49, 50] where environmental stimuli associated with the hospital or drugs become paired with drug-induced nausea and vomiting, and eventually come to elicit these symptoms even before the drug is injected. Symptoms can occur prior to chemotherapy (known as "anticipatory" symptoms), as well as during and after chemotherapy administration.

In addition to a general predisposition or proneness to nausea and vomiting that a patient might have, prechemotherapy anxiety level has been empirically shown to be a major predictor for the development of CNV in retrospective[42, 51] and prospective investigations.[52, 53] In fact, the incidence of anticipatory nausea may be twice as great in patients with high, as opposed to mild, pre-treatment anxiety.[9] The facilitating or potentiating role of anxiety in CNV has been attributed to the fact that anxious individuals are more vigilant to their environments, thereby attending more closely to the various clinical stimuli that can readily develop into conditioned stimuli.[54] It is also possible that, because of its association with postchemotherapy nausea and vomiting, anxiety can itself develop into a potent conditioned stimulus for nausea and vomiting, and come to elicit these symptoms by association.

With the advent of powerful new antiemetics and adjustment of maximum doses of chemotherapy needed for effectiveness, the nausea and vomiting associated with cancer chemotherapy is less problematic than it was 10 years ago. Research supports the observation that the severity of conditioned side effects and overall physiological arousal associated with chemotherapy infusion have dropped considerably over the past decade, but the incidence of conditioned side effects appears to have remained relatively unchanged.[55, 56] Thus, conditioned side effects may not represent the clinical problem they once did, but they continue to occur with striking frequency and the phenomenon offers the opportunity to observe a unique interaction between psychological and somatic factors.

Multidimensional Nature of Cancer Pain

As many as 20 to 75% of cancer patients will experience moderate to severe pain related to their disease, depending on stage of disease.[57] Pain can be caused by multiple factors, including disease- and treatment-related variables,[57] yet cancer pain had traditionally been studied from a unidimensional/medical perspective. The unidimensional or medical approach holds pain as a result of and directly proportional to tissue damage. Empirical findings, however, have not supported even this most basic assumption that pain is a direct function of organic pathology. For example, Front et al.[58] found no correlation between the presence and location of bone metastases and the report of pain. This lack of strict association between organic pathology and cancer pain has led investigators to develop more complex, multidimensional models of cancer pain, a process that began with the pioneering work of Melzack and Wall[59] and their gate-control theory of pain. Current conceptualizations of cancer pain[60] present it as comprised of physiological, sensory, affective, cognitive, behavioral, and sociocultural components. Thus, the multidimensional model of cancer pain proposes that multiple factors, including psychological variables, impact the patient's experience of pain.[61]

Ahles and Martin,[60] for instance, have proposed that anxiety may contribute to pain through the elevation of muscle tension and other psychophysiological indices. Self-reported depression is reliably higher in a cancer population with chronic, disease-related pain as compared to cancer patients matched on important disease- and treatment-related variables but without chronic pain.[62, 63] Moreover, a positive relationship exists between degree of depression and the patient's experience of cancer-related pain.[64] Cognitive factors, such as interpreting pain as signs of disease progression[65, 66] and attention to somatic cues,[67] may increase pain ratings. Individuals who exhibit a predisposition to focus on somatic symptoms and who are simultaneously anxious tend to report more areas of pain and rate their pain as higher than those with only one contributing variable (high anxiety or high predisposition to notice bodily sensations) or those with neither variable.[67, 68] Behavioral manifestations of pain, such as guarding, grimacing, verbal expressions, and analgesic intake, can be reinforced by environmental factors such as attention, social support, or avoidance of unpleasant tasks,[69] in benign as well as cancer pain.[70, 71] Finally, sociocultural factors such as ethnic background and gender may have subtle influences on the patient's experience of pain.[63, 72]

It is clear that multiple factors contribute to a cancer patient's experience of pain, and that virtually all the components of quality of life, both the physical and the psychological, must be considered in addressing a patient with pain. Interactions among psychological, physiological, social, and even spiritual factors are certainly not limited to the examples described here. As understanding of these complex processes increases, interactions among variables, as opposed to single variables, will likely emerge as causal factors in most experiential phenomena that comprise patients' quality of life.[49]

INTERVENTION IMPACTING QUALITY OF LIFE IN CANCER PATIENTS

Inclusion of the concept of quality of life in a discussion of intervention emphasizes the need to consider the target problem or symptom in the context of physical, social, and spiritual determinants. Since most patients experience some degree of compromise in quality of life through their experience of cancer, but few experience distress to a debilitating degree, it may be useful to consider these interventions in levels according to the intensity of the targeted problem. Levels of intensity range from clinically relevant psychopathology or severe psychological distress, to subclinical, moderate psychological distress, to somatic complaints and situation-specific distress.

PSYCHOPHARMACOLOGICAL TREATMENT

If a patient meets criteria for a major psychiatric disorder, then psychotropic medications may be appropriate and helpful. Three points relevant to the pharmacological treatment of cancer patients are worth noting. First, the appropriateness of psychopharmacological treatment in this population should not be underestimated. Given the commonly held assumption that depression and anxiety are "normal" in this population, cancer patients in distress may represent an undertreated population. Second, the prescribing clinician should be aware of the psychiatric disorders most common in this population that would be amenable to psychopharmacological treatment, such as depression, anxiety, and delirium. Third, although the medications utilized in this population are not unique to cancer patients, some considerations must be made in treating this particular group of patients. This topic has been thoroughly reviewed and discussed elsewhere,[73] and thus will only be highlighted here.

Neuroleptic medication may be helpful in treating agitation and cognitive disorientation secondary to delirium and organic psychosis, without the sedation and respiratory suppression associated with benzodiazepines.[73] Neuroleptics can cause postural hypotension, especially in patients with low blood volume, and can lower seizure threshold, a characteristic that should be considered in patients with CNS involvement of disease. Antidepressant treatment with tricyclic antidepressants may be beneficial in controlling the symptoms of depression in a cancer population, but this class of medications has also been found to be effective even at subtherapeutic doses to assist in sleep and as an adjunct in analgesia.[74] The anticholinergic effects of tricyclic antidepressants can worsen constipation, a notable problem in patients with cancers of the digestive tract, can cause urinary retention, especially troublesome in patients with genitourinary impairment, and can exacerbate mucositis and stomatitis in patients receiving certain chemotherapies and radiation treatments. Some of the newer antidepressant agents may cause fewer of these side effects. Stimulants have been used for the treatment of depression, particularly in the elderly, as well as to relieve fatigue and pain. Massie and Gorzynski[75] suggested that debilitating anxiety lasting longer than 2 weeks should be addressed pharmacologically. When anxiety is a problem, an anxiolytic such as a benzodiazepine may be an effective short-term treatment.[76] The CNS depression associated with benzodiazepines can create weakness, fatigue, confusion, and other unpleasant symptoms, to which cancer patients may be especially vulnerable due to their existing impaired physical state. As in the pharmacological treatment of any medically ill patient, close coordination with the patient's other physicians should be carefully pursued.

PSYCHOTHERAPEUTIC INTERVENTION

A limited number of studies have implemented comprehensive, intensive, and relatively long-term psychosocial intervention packages with cancer patients that are designed to impact their quality of life (for reviews[77]). One of the most methodologically sound studies was conducted by Gordon et al.[78] The authors embarked on a large-scale, randomized clinical outcome study in which more than 300 cancer patients of various diagnoses were assigned to a comprehensive, individualized treatment package, or to condition receiving only standard medical care. The treatment package under study included patient education, individual counseling, and appropriate community-based referrals, with resources available to patients during their initial inpatient hospitalization for treatment and on an outpatient basis for 6 months following discharge. The results of Gordon et al.'s[78] investigation were generally positive, with treatment patients showing greater reductions in negative affect and a greater likelihood of returning to work. Those in need of the treatment, as determined by scores on pretreatment screening measures, and who received it, seemed to benefit to a significant degree as compared to those in need who received no treatment at all. Also, those with more advanced disease benefited more than those with less advanced disease. The advantages to those patients who, in the screening process, had been determined to be at low risk for psychologic morbidity, were less impressive, especially given the time and money that had been invested. Many of the study participants were already coping well with cancer-related distress at the start of the study and, thus, had little need for formal, intensive intervention and had little room for improvement. Those who had demonstrated need, however, responded to a significant degree.

Another strong and rigorous study that assessed the efficacy of an intensive psychological intervention was reported by Spiegel et al.[79, 80] This group of researchers undertook a randomized and controlled study aimed at improving the quality of life of metastatic breast cancer patients. Eighty-six patients were randomly assigned to either a condition that received group therapy and self-hypnosis or to a condition that received only standard clinic treatment. The group therapy intervention, coled by a professional therapist and a breast cancer survivor, was comprehensive and included psychoeducation, problem solving, and support, and lasted approximately 1 year. The results of the study indicated that the patients who received the psychological intervention had significantly improved quality of life (e.g., they were significantly less depressed, fatigued, confused, and phobic, used more effective coping strategies, and reported suffering less due to pain) than patients in the control group.

Each of these studies nicely illustrates that a comprehensive, well-designed intervention package can be effective in improving the psychological well-being of cancer patients. The Gordon et al.[78] study also emphasizes the importance of matching psychosocial treatment to the needs of the patient. If the match is not a good one, then valuable resources, including those of the patient and the treatment provider, may not be utilized optimally. It might also be noted that the comprehensive treatment package in each of these studies addressed multiple components of quality of life, including physical well-being (behavioral intervention for treatment side effects) and social functioning (social support and mechanisms for environmental change). Most research studies on psychosocial intervention in cancer patients, in fact, have recognized, directly or indirectly, the breadth of impact of cancer on quality of life and have incorporated multicomponent treatment packages,[5, 77] as opposed to single-component interventions. Single-component interventions are more common in the treatment of specific physical symptoms or situational distress, as discussed in the following sections.

Because formal psychological intervention is enormously helpful in many cases and unnecessary in others, formal screening procedures have been implemented in the oncology setting. A screening protocol for psychological distress suggested by Sobel and Worden[81] included the use of standard personality tests such as the Minnesota Multiphasic Personality Inventory (MMPI) and specially developed psychometric instruments. Using strategies such as these, Sobel and Worden reported rates of successful prediction ranging from 75%[81] to 83%.[82] Worden and Weisman[83] then conducted a study targeting only psychologically high-risk cancer patients. In their study, 125 patients who had been judged to be at a high risk for developing psychological disturbance through psychological screening were assigned to one of two treatment interventions, either a nondirective or directive psychotherapy condition. The first approach focused on expression of emotion, identification of problems, and nondirective exploration of solutions to those problems. The directive approach, on the other hand, addressed similar issues, but in a didactic, step-by-step manner. Each treatment was administered in four individual sessions. When compared to high-risk control patients, treatment patients receiving either directive or nondirective therapy reported lower levels of emotional distress, fatigue, and confusion, increased vigor, and increased self-ratings of problem-solving skills. No reliable differences emerged between the two interventions. These strong and positive findings, especially promising given the brevity of treatment, were attributed by the authors to the fact that all the patients who received the treatments were more likely to need and make good use of the interventions offered.

In perhaps the most comprehensive study targeting "normal" or low psychiatric morbidity risk patients, Fawzy et al.[84] conducted a well-controlled study that investigated the effectiveness of a treatment package comprised of multiple components. Sixty-six patients with malignant melanoma were assigned to a condition receiving a comprehensive, psychosocial group intervention package involving weekly meetings for 6 weeks, or to a group receiving only routine medical care. The experimental intervention was comprised of patient education, problem-solving, behavioral stress management with relaxation techniques, and general psychological support. It is important to note that the study included an intervention that was one quarter the length of the treatment in the Gordon et al.[78] study described earlier. At the completion of group program, participants reported increased vigor and heightened active-behavioral coping, both of which were considered by the authors to be positive changes in adaptation to illness. The control group reported no significant change in psychosocial factors. At the 6-month follow-up, differences between the two groups were even more pronounced. Intervention patients showed less depression, fatigue, confusion, and overall mood disturbance, as well as increased vigor 6 months after cessation of treatment.

In addition to being reliably successful in controlling the "normal" distress of patients with cancer, the application of psychosocial intervention, in this case a multimodal treatment package, has led to several additional conclusions with clinical import. First, skills developed through cancer-related psychotherapeutic intervention can and are generalized to address other areas of stress in a patient's life, as illustrated in the Fawzy et al.[84] study described above. The findings offered by Fawzy et al.[84] suggested that the skills learned through the psychosocial intervention package facilitated improvement in coping and adaptation and continued expansion of patients' coping repertoire not only at the time of treatment, but also months following treatment. Finally, the study appears to have contained all the factors that seem to predict positive outcome in intervention with cancer patients experiencing low to moderate to distress: an emotionally supportive context, information about the disease and its treatment, and behavioral and cognitive coping strategies, all of which are provided in a structured (rather than unstructured) format.[57]

Another general problem area faced by the cancer patient is physical or psychological distress confined to certain situations. In attempting to control specific disease- or treatment-related symptoms, such as nausea or pain, traditional or supportive psychotherapy has been largely unhelpful,[85, 86] although the patient undergoing psychotherapy may experience reductions in general psychological distress. A cognitive–behavioral treatment program tailored to meet the needs of the individual patient may be helpful in controlling adverse side effects to cancer treatment, managing cancer-related pain, reducing distress associated with aversive medical procedures, and improving compliance with medical procedures, among others.

One of the most widely researched techniques and likely the most widely applied in cognitive–behavioral intervention with cancer patients is progressive muscle relaxation training (PMRT). Originally developed by Jacobson[87] and modified by others, such as Bernstein and Borkovec,[88] PMRT is a relaxation procedure in which predefined muscle groups are sequentially tensed and relaxed. Inclusion of a tensing component generally defines a procedure as "active"; similar procedures but without the tensing portion are referred to as "passive" relaxation techniques. Among the cognitive–behavioral techniques that have been applied for general or situational distress, PMRT and other relaxation strategies have been shown to significantly reduce patients' negative affect,[89, 90] as well as control aversive side effects to cancer treatments.[90]

Relaxation procedures can be initiated in the actual cancer-related setting, but results are likely to be more potent when the skill is taught earlier in the cancer treatment process, practiced by the patient at home, and then applied in the stressful situation.[89] Other relaxation-based strategies such as hypnosis and systematic desensitization have been used in the treatment of specific anxieties and symptoms. A mild aerobic exercise program, although not extensively investigated to date, has been suggested as a simple behavioral intervention to elevate mood,[91, 92] and, based on preliminary laboratory findings with animals, to help control the loss of appetite associated with cancer and its treatment.[93] Cognitive–behavioral treatments applied in the treatment of chronic pain have recently been applied in the treatment of cancer pain with promising results.[71]

Although these treatments are designed specifically to impact a single symptom within the patient's experience of cancer, some evidence exists that patients may, on their own, generalize skills to target other areas of stress. Burish et al.[94] surveyed a sample of cancer chemotherapy patients approximately 1 year posttreatment who had been taught relaxation training and other cognitive–behavioral strategies specifically to help control chemotherapy-related symptoms. According to the authors, the majority of survey respondents had continued to apply the cognitive–behavioral strategies they had learned to assist in coping with other health-related problems as well as with other general stressors. In short, it appears that the positive changes that occur through cognitive–behavioral intervention designed to help patients cope with their illness may represent healthy alterations in coping that extend beyond the cancer treatment process.

Future Directions in Quality of Life

Many of the concepts in research targeting quality of life in cancer patients are not new. Prevalence of psychiatric disorders in the cancer population, concerns of the cancer patient, and development of appropriate interventions to meet the individual needs of the patient have been addressed by psychosocial researchers for years. Newly emerging emphasis on quality of life in cancer patients merely suggests the need for both breadth and integration of a wide spectrum of factors in considering the impact of cancer on general psychological functioning. The purpose of this article has been to present psychological well-being as one component of quality of life that acts in concert with physical, social, and spiritual well-being in shaping an individual's quality of life and experience of cancer. Research in quality of life is progressive, and several new directions are worth highlighting.

QUALITY OF LIFE ASSOCIATED WITH BONE MARROW TRANSPLANT (BMT)

BMT was developed for the treatment of systemic cancers such as leukemia, but has recently been accepted as a treatment for other cancers such as those involving solid tumors. BMT can be classified as *allogeneic,* in which healthy marrow is donated to the cancer patient and then transfused after the patient's own marrow is removed, or *autologous,* when the patient's own bone marrow is harvested, purged of disease, and replaced. Early in the treatment process, shortly after the patient's bone marrow has been removed, the patient undergoes high-dose chemotherapy and often total-body irradiation, to eliminate existing cancer cells without worry of impairment to the bone marrow. After chemotherapy and irradiation, the healthy bone marrow is transfused, and growth of new blood cells from the marrow is expected within 1 to 2 weeks. The process of engraftment can be hastened dramatically with the aid of "growth factors," only recently developed. Until regrowth has occurred and a safe level of blood cells, especially white blood cells, has been reached, patients are severely immunosuppressed. In addition to severe side effects created by the initial high-dose chemotherapy and intensive radiation treatment, prolonged hospitalization in a sterile and isolated room, knowledge that the treatment itself is high-risk secondary to immunosuppression and numerous other complications, BMT offers a unique set of circumstances that

clearly impact the quality of life of the cancer patients who undergo
the treatment.

INCREASED PARTICIPATION IN DECISION MAKING

Loss of control has been heralded as a major contributor to psychological distress in cancer patients and their families. It has
been a widely held belief that the degree to which patients perceive control over their health outcome impacts their subsequent
mood state.[95] Research in informed decision making has largely
targeted women with breast cancer who are scheduled to undergo
surgical treatment. Women who are to be surgically treated for
breast cancer today face a unique situation virtually unknown to
cancer patients in the past. That is, two different but effective
surgical treatments for breast cancer exist: radical and partial
mastectomy. Radical mastectomy involves removal of the entire
breast, a procedure that raises issues for most women surrounding
lifelong disfigurement, but represents an entire treatment procedure in a single operation. Partial mastectomy as a surgical
treatment does not consistently produce disfigurement but almost always involves months of radiation treatment and possible
chemotherapy, and their subsequent side effects. Depending
upon certain disease criteria and the style of the individual physician, many women are offered a choice between these two treatment alternatives. Recent data have indicated that this option of
choosing treatment is significantly more related to psychological
outcome to cancer and its treatment than other potentially relevant variables, even more than the type of treatment chosen.[96]
Specifically, Morris and Ingham[96] reported that women given a
choice of surgical treatment for breast cancer, as compared to
those not given a choice, showed greater overall adjustment as
measured by ability to return to work, attitude toward the future,
and general psychological functioning. This finding is so strong
that it seems to hold even when women are initially given a choice
and later that choice is revoked, perhaps because medical complications arise that dictate one procedure as more appropriate than
the other. Moreover, women who are aware that their physician

advocates their input in the decision-making process tend to exhibit less negative affect and fewer signs of psychological distress, as compared to those who perceive their physician as desiring little input regarding their preferences, even when disease characteristics preclude actual consideration of the patient's input.[97]

Although much more research needs to be done regarding the potential choice areas that will impact outcome, and perhaps the type and amount of information that patients desire[98] when making important choices, actively increasing patients' role in the decision-making process and perhaps providing structured guidance for the patient in making decisions, hold potential as a simple yet powerful intervention to help patients adjust to their disease and its treatment.

IMPACT OF QUALITY OF LIFE ON SURVIVAL

Of all the research areas addressing quality of life in cancer patients, the topic that has received the most attention in the lay press has been whether psychological interventions can prolong life. In recent years a number of claims have been made about the power of mental phenomena on cancer. Claims have been made for the curative effects of specially designed behavior therapy,[99] mental imaging,[100] positive attitude,[101] and laughter,[102] to name a few. Regrettably, there has not been acceptably rigorous scientific evidence for any of these claims, and as a result most physicians and scientists have remained unconvinced.

A relatively recent study has raised the issue once again that changing patients' quality of life may ultimately impact their survival. Spiegel et al.[103] designed a follow-up investigation to their original study, described in an earlier section, aimed at improving the quality of life of metastatic breast cancer patients through a group psychotherapy intervention. Years later, the research group assessed whether the intervention also affected longevity. They found that patients in the intervention condition lived an average of 18 months longer than control patients as measured from the date of study entry to death, approximately 15 months longer as measured from the date of first metastasis to death, and approximately 13 months longer as measured from the initial medical visit to death. The first two comparisons were statistically as well as clinically significant. These results provide important evidence suggesting that psychological treatment may extend the lives of some cancer patients.

Although promising, these results must be regarded cautiously until several issues can be addressed. For example, it is critical to determine whether the results can be replicated prospectively in other patient populations across multiple institutions. Future research should also determine whether the treatment effect holds if important biological and medical factors are controlled so as to ensure that the disease and the medical treatment are similar (or statistically controlled) in all patients. The assessment of other individual difference factors is also critical so that one can determine whether the treatment helps only a small subset of patients, whether it might actually be detrimental to a small subset of patients, or whether it has fairly generalized positive effects. Finally, if the results can be replicated, the identification of the specific causal mechanism will become of utmost interest and importance. Research on each of these issues and others is currently underway at several different institutions in the United States and elsewhere.

REFERENCES

1. Goldberg RJ, Tull RM, Sullivan N, Wallace S, Wool M. Defining discipline roles in consultation psychiatry: The multi-disciplinary team approach. *Gen Hosp Psychiatry.* 1984;6:17–23.
2. Campbell A, Converse PE, Rogers WL. *The Quality of American Life.* New York: Sage;1976.
3. Aaronson NK. Methodologic issues in assessing the quality of life of cancer patients. *Cancer.* 1991;67:844-850.
4. Ferrell BR, Rhiner M, Cohen MZ, Grant M. Pain as a metaphor for illness. Impact of cancer pain on family caregivers. *Oncol Nurs Forum.* 1991;18: 1303–1309.
5. Andersen BL. Psychological interventions for cancer patients to enhance the quality of life. *J Consult Clin Psychol.* 1992;60:552–568.

6. Cella DF, Orofiamma B, Holland JC, Silberfarb PM, Tross S, Feldstein M, Perry M, Maurer LH, Comis R, Oraz EJ. The relationship of psychological distress, extent of disease, and performance status in patients with lung cancer. *Cancer.* 1987;60:1661–1667.

7. deHaes JCJM, van Oostrom MA, Welvaart K. The effect of radical and conserving surgery on quality of life in early breast cancer patients. *Eur J Surg Oncol.* 1986;12:337–342.

8. Cassileth BR, Lusk EJ, Tenaglia AN. Patients' perceptions of the cosmetic impact of melanoma resection. *Plast Reconstr Surg.* 1983;71:73–75.

9. Nerenz DR, Leventhal H, Easterling DV, Love RR. Anxiety and drug taste as predictors of anticipatory nausea in cancer chemotherapy. *J Clin Oncol.* 1986;4:224–233.

10. Holland JC, Rowland JH. *Handbook of Psychooncology: Psychological Care of the Patient with Cancer.* New York: Oxford University Press;1989.

11. Derogatis LR, Morrow GR, Feting J, Penman D, Piasetsky S, Schmale AM, Henrichs, M, Carnicke CLM. The prevalence of psychiatric disorder among cancer patients. *JAMA.* 1983;249:751–757.

12. Malec JF, Rosmaas EP, Messing EM, Cummings KC, Trump DL. Psychological and mood disturbance associated with the diagnosis and treatment of testis cancer and other malignancies. *J Clin Psychol.* 1990;46:551–557.

13. Wolberg WH, Romsaas EP, Tanner MA, Malec JF. Psychosexual adaptation to breast cancer surgery. *Cancer.* 1989;63:1645–1655.

14. Rait DS, Jacobsen PB, Lederberg MS, Holland JC. Characteristics of psychiatric consultations in a pediatric cancer center. *Am J Psychiatry.* 1988;145:363–364.

15. Westin T, Jansson A, Zenkert C, Hallstrom T, Edstrom S. Mental depression is associated with malnutrition in patients with head and neck cancer. *Arch Otolaryngol.* 1988;114:1449–1453.

16. Breitbart W. Psychiatric management of cancer in pain. *Cancer.* 1989;63: 2336–2342.

17. Kathol RG, Mutgi A, Williams J, Clamon G, Noyes R. Diagnosis of major depression in cancer patients according to four sets of criteria. *Am J Psychiatry.* 1990;147:1021–1024.

18. Andersen BL, Anderson B, DeProsse, C. Controlled prospective longitudinal study of women with cancer. II. Psychological outcomes. *J Consult Clin Psychol.* 1986;57:692–697.

19. Schag CA, Heinrich RL. Anxiety in medical situations: Adult cancer patients. *J Clin Psychol.* 1989;45:20–27.

20. Holland JC. Anxiety and cancer: The patient and the family. *J Clin Psychiatry.* 1989;50:20–25.

21. Loveys BJ, Klaich, K. Breast cancer: Demands of illness. *Oncol Nurs Forum.* 1991;18:75–80.

22. van Heeringen C, Van Moffaert M, de Cuypere G. Depression after surgery for breast cancer: Comparison of mastectomy and lumpectomy. *Psychother Psychosom.* 1989;51:175–179.

23. Cella DF, Tross S. Death anxiety in cancer survival: A preliminary cross-validation study. *J Pers Assess.* 1987;51:451–461.

24. Silberfarb PM. Chemotherapy and cognitive defects in cancer patients. *Annu Rev Med.* 1983;34:35–46.

25. Levine PM, Silberfarb PM, Lipowski ZJ. Mental disorders in cancer patients: A study of 100 psychiatric referrals. *Cancer.* 1978;43:1385–1391.
26. Massie MJ, Holland JC, Glass E. Delirium in terminally ill cancer patients. *Am J Psychiatry.* 1983;140:1048–1050.
27. Wasserstrom WR, Glass JP, Posner JB. Diagnosis and treatment of leptomeningeal metastases from solid tumors: Experience with 90 patients. *Cancer.* 1982;49:759–772.
28. Lipowski ZJ. *Delirium: Acute Brain Failure in Man.* Springfield, IL: Thomas; 1980.
29. Bjorgen JE, Gold LHA. Computed tomographic appearance of methotrexate induced necrotizing leukoencephalopathy. *Radiology.* 1977;122:377–378.
30. Goff JR, Anderson HR, Cooper PF. Distractibility and memory deficits in long-term survivors of acute lymphoblastic leukemia. *J Dev Behav Pediatr.* 980;1:158–163.
31. Whybrow PC, Hurwitz T. Psychological disturbances associated with endocrine disease and hormone therapy. In: Sachar EH, ed. *Hormones, Behavior, and Psychopathology.* New York: Raven Press;1976: pp 125–143.
32. Belt RJ, Stephens R. Phase I–II study of ftorafur and methyl-CCNU in advanced colorectal cancer. *Cancer.* 1979;44:869–872.
33. Meadows AT, Massari DJ, Fergusson J. Declines in IQ scores and cognitive dysfunctions in children with acute lymphocytic leukemia treated with cranial irradiation. *Lancet.* 1981;ii:1015–1018.
34. Brouwers P, Riccardi R, Fediao R. Long-term neuropsychologic sequelae of childhood leukemia: Correlation with CT brain scan abnormalities. *J Pediatr.* 1985;106:723–728.
35. Tucker J, Prior PF, Green CR, Ede GMV, Stevenson JF, Gawler J, Jamal GA, Charlesworth M, Thakkar CM, Patel P, Lister TA. Minimal neuropsychological sequelae following prophylactic treatment of the central nervous system in adult leukemia and lymphoma. *Br J Cancer.* 1989;60:775–780.
36. Folstein MF, Folstein SE, McHugh PR. Mini-mental state. *J Psychiatr Residents.* 1975;12:189–198.
37. D'Angio GJ. The child cured of cancer: A problem for the internist. *Semin Oncol.* 1982;9:143–149.
38. Pettingale KW, Burgess C, Greer S. Psychological response to cancer diagnosis. I. Correlations with prognostic variables. *J Psychosom Res.* 1988;32:255–261.
39. Bukberg J, Penman D, Holland JC. Depression in hospitalized cancer patients. *Psychosom Med.* 1984;436:199–212.
40. Mishel MH, Hosteter T, King B, Graham V. Predictors of psychosocial adjustment in patients newly diagnosed with gynecological cancer. *Cancer Nurs.* 1984;7:291–299.
41. Westbrook MT, Viney LL. Age and sex differences in patients reactions to illness. *J Health Soc Behav.* 1983;24:313–324.
42. Ingle RJ, Burish TG, Wallston KA. Conditionability of cancer chemotherapy patients. *Oncol Nurs Forum.* 1984;11:97–102.
43. Nerenz DR, Love RR, Leventhal H, Easterling DV. Psychosocial consequences of cancer chemotherapy for elderly patients. *Health Serv Res.* 1986;20:961–976.
44. Ramirez AJ. Liaison psychiatry in a breast cancer unit. *J R Soc Med.* 1989;82: 15–17.

45. Northouse LL. A longitudinal study of the adjustment of patients and husbands to breast cancer. *Oncol Nurs Forum.* 1989;16:511–516.

46. Easterling DV, Leventhal H. Contribution of concrete cognition to emotion: Neutral symptoms as elicitors of worry about cancer. *J Appl Psychol.* 1989;74:787–796.

47. Mahon SM, Cella DF, Donovan MI. Psychosocial adjustment to recurrent cancer. *Oncol Nurs Forum.* 1990;17:47–52.

48. Silberfarb PM, Maurer LH, Crouthamel CS. Psychosocial aspects of neoplastic disease. I. Functional status of breast cancer patients during different treatment regimens. *Am J Psychiatry.* 1980;137:450–455.

49. Burish TG, Carey MP. Conditioned aversive responses in cancer chemotherapy patients: Theoretical and developmental analysis. *J Consult Clin Psychol.* 1986;54:593–600.

50. Morrow GR, Black PM. Anticipatory nausea and vomiting side effects experienced by cancer chemotherapy patients undergoing chemotherapy treatment. In: Osaba D, ed. *Effect of Cancer on Quality of Life.* Boston: CRC Press;1991: pp 251–268.

51. van Komen RW, Redd WH. Personality factors associated with anticipatory nausea and vomiting in patients receiving cancer chemotherapy. *Health Psychol.* 1985;4:189–202.

52. Andrykowski MA, Redd WH, Hatfield AK. Development of anticipatory nausea: A prospective analysis. *J Consult Clin Psychol.* 1985;53:447–454.

53. Andrykowski MA, Jacobsen PB, Marks E, Gorfinkle K, Haskes T, Kaufman RJ, Currie VE, Holland JC, Redd WH. Prevalence, predictors, and course of anticipatory nausea in women receiving adjuvant chemotherapy for breast cancer. *Cancer.* 1988;62:2607–2613.

54. Dolgin MJ, Katz ER, McGinty K, Siegel SE. Anticipatory nausea and vomiting in pediatric cancer patients. *Pediatrics.* 1985;75:547–552.

55. Carey MP, Burish TG. Etiology and treatment of the psychological side effects associated with cancer chemotherapy: A critical review and discussion. *Psychol Bull.* 1988;104:307–325.

56. Stefanek ME, Sheidler VR, Fetting JH. Anticipatory nausea and vomiting: Does it remain a significant clinical problem? *Cancer.* 1988;62:2654–2657.

57. Bonica JJ. Cancer pain. In: Bonica JJ, ed. *The Management of Pain.* Philadelphia: Lea & Febiger;1990: pp 400–460.

58. Front D, Schneck SO, Frankel A, Robinson, E. Bone metastases and bone pain in breast cancer: Are they closely associated? *JAMA.* 1979;19:1747–1748.

59. Melzack R, Wall, P. Pain mechanisms: A theory. *Science.* 1965;150:971–979.

60. Ahles TA, Martin JB. Cancer pain: A multidimensional perspective. *Hospice J.* 1992;8:25–48.

61. Turk DC, Fernadez E. On the putative uniqueness of cancer pain: Do psychological principles apply? *Behav Res Ther.* 1990;28:1–13.

62. Ahles TA, Blanchard EB, Ruckdeschel JC. The multidimensional nature of cancer-related pain. *Pain.* 1983;17:272–288.

63. McGuire DB. The multidimensional phenomenon of cancer pain. In: McGuire DB, Yarbro CH, eds. *Cancer Pain Management.* Orlando, FL: Grune & Stratton;1987: pp 1–20.

64. Shacham S, Reinhart LC, Raubertas RF, Cleeland CS. Emotional states and pain. Intraindividual and interindividual measures of association. *J Behav Med.* 1983;6:405–419.
65. Daut RL, Cleeland CS. The prevalence and severity of pain in cancer. *Cancer.* 1982;50:1913–1918.
66. Spiegel D, Bloom J. Pain in metastatic breast cancer. *Cancer.* 1983;52:341–345.
67. Ahles TA, Casens HL, Stalling RB. Private body consciousness, anxiety, and the perception of pain. *J Behav Ther Exp Psychiatry.* 1987;18:215–222.
68. Ahles TA, Pecora J, Riley S. Self-focused attention, psychiatric symptoms and chronic pain: A hypothesis. *South Psychol.* 1987;3:25–28.
69. Fordyce WE. *Behavioral Methods for Chronic Pain and Illness.* St. Louis: Mosby; 1976.
70. Ahles TA. Psychological approaches to the management of cancer-related pain. *Semin Oncol Nurs.* 1985;1:141–146.
71. Ahles TA. Psychological techniques for the management of cancer-related pain. In: McGuire DB, Yarbro CH, eds. *Cancer Pain Management.* Orlando, FL: Grune & Stratton;1987: pp 245–258.
72. Lipton JA, Marbach JJ. Ethnicity and the pain experience. *Soc Sci Med.* 1984;19:1279–1298.
73. Goldberg RJ, Cullen LO. The psychiatrist's role in cancer care. *Cancer Surv.* 1987;6:417–437.
74. Walsh TD. Adjuvant analgesic therapy in cancer pain. In: Foley KM, ed. *Advances in Pain Research and Therapy.* Second International Congress on Cancer Pain. New York: Raven Press;1990;16:155–165.
75. Massie MJ, Gorzynski JG. Managing anxiety in cancer patients. *Your Patient and Cancer.* 1982;March:53–60.
76. Silberfarb PM. Psychiatric problems in breast cancer. *Cancer.* 1984;53:820–824.
77. Trijsburg RW, van Knippenberg FCE, Rijpma SE. Effects of psychological treatment on cancer patients: A critical review. *Psychosom Med.* 1992;54:489–517.
78. Gordon WA, Freidenberg I, Diller L, Hibberd M, Wold C. Levine L, Lipkins R, Ezrachi O, Ludico D. Efficacy of psychosocial intervention with cancer patients. *J Consult Clin Psychol.* 1980;48:743–759.
79. Spiegel D. The use of hypnosis in controlling cancer pain. *CA.* 1985;35:221.
80. Spiegel D, Bloom JR, Yalom I. Group support for patients with metastatic cancer: A randomized outcome study. *Int J Group Psychother.* 1981;28:233–245.
81. Sobel HJ, Worden JW. The MMPI as a predictor of psychosocial adaptation to cancer. *J Consult Clin Psychol.* 1979;47:716–724.
82. Worden JW. Psychosocial screening of cancer patients. *J Psychsoc Oncol.* 1983;1:1–10.
83. Worden JW, Weisman AD. Preventive psychosocial intervention with newly diagnosed cancer patients. *Gen Hosp Psychiatry.* 1984;6:243–249.
84. Fawzy FI, Cousins N, Fawzy N, Kemeny ME, Elashoff R, Morton D. A structured psychiatric intervention for cancer pateints. 1. Changes over time in methods of coping and affective disturbance. *Arch Gen Psychiatry.* 1990; 47:720–725.
85. Lyles JN, Burish TG, Krozely MG, Oldham RK. Efficacy of relaxation training and guided imagery in reducing the aversiveness of cancer chemotherapy. *J Consult Clin Psychol.* 1982;50:509–524.

86. Morrow GR, Morrell C. Behavioral treatment for the anticipatory nausea and vomiting induced by cancer chemotherapy. *N Engl J Med.* 1982;307:1476–1480.
87. Jacobson E. *Progressive Relaxation.* Chicago: University of Chicago Press;1938.
88. Bernstein DA, Borkovec TD. *Progressive Relaxation Training: A Manual for the Helping Professions.* Champaign, IL: Research Press;1973.
89. Burish TG, Carey MP, Krozely MG, Greco FA. Conditioned nausea and vomiting induced by cancer chemotherapy: Prevention through behavioral treatment. *J Consult Clin Psychol.* 1987;55:42–48.
90. Carey MP, Burish TG. Providing relaxation training to cancer chemotherapy patients. A comparison of three methods. *J Consult Clin Psychol.* 1987;55:860–865.
91. Gaskin TA, LoBuglio A, Kelly P, Doss M, Pititz N. STRETCH: A rehabilitative program for patients with breast cancer. *South Med J.* 1989;82:467–469.
92. Johnson JB, Kelley AW. A multifaceted rehabilitation program for women with cancer. *Oncol Nurs Forum.* 1990;17:691–695.
93. Daneryd PL, Hafstrom LR, Karlberg IH. Effects of spontaneous physical exercise on experimental cancer anorexia and cachexia. *Eur J Cancer.* 1990; 26:1083–1088.
94. Burish TG, Vasterling JJ, Carey MP, Matt DA, Krozely MG. Posttreatment use of relaxation training by cancer patients. *Hospice J.* 1988;4:1–8.
95. Deadman JM, Dewey JJ, Owens RG, Leinster SJ, Slade PD. Threat and loss in breast cancer. *Psychol Med.* 1989;19:677–681.
96. Morris J, Inham R. Choice of surgery for early breast cancer. Psychosocial consideration. *Soc Sci Med.* 1988;27:1257–1262.
97. Fallowfield LJ, Hall A, Maguire GP, Baum M. Psychological outcomes of different treatment policies in women with early breast cancer outside a clinical trial. *Br Med J.* 1990;301:575–580.
98. Wallston KA, Smith RA, King JE, Smith MS, Rye P, Burish TG. Desire for control and choice of antiemetic treatment for cancer chemotherapy. *West J Nurs Res.* 1991;13:12–23.
99. Grossarth-Maticek R, Eysenck HJ. Creative novation behavior therapy as a prophylactic treatment for cancer and coronary heart disease. *Behav Res Ther.* 1991;29:1–16.
100. Simonton OC. *The Healing Journey.* New York: Bantam Books;1992.
101. Siegel BS. *Love, Medicine, and Miracles.* New York: Harper & Row;1986.
102. Cousins N. *Anatomy of an Illness as Perceived by the Patient: Reflections on Healing and Regeneration.* New York: Norton;1979.
103. Spiegel D, Bloom JR, Kraemer HC, Gottheil E. Effect of psychosocial treatment on survival of patients with metastatic breast cancer. *Lancet.* 1989;14: 888–891.

Chapter 18
Psychodermatology:
An Overview

MYRIAM VAN MOFFAERT

Dermatology has a distinct relation with psychosomatics because the skin has strong psychological implications. Not only do dermis and psyche share their embryological origin, but they are also closely intertwined functionally. The skin, which is an important organ in tactile receptivity, also responds perceptibly to emotional stimuli. Dermatological disorders thus have an immediate impact on tactile communication, on bodily interaction, and on sexual contact in particular.[1] Because the skin is exposed to view, dermatoses readily elicit reactions from the patient's environment. Furthermore, the easy accessibility of the skin allows patients to interact directly with their lesions, so that behavioral factors (touching, scratching, exaggeration, or neglect of the necessary skin care) are likely to complicate or create further lesions.[2-8]

Dermatology holds a distinct position in psychosomatic medicine mainly because it deals with an organ that can be readily seen and touched. The physiological concomitants of fear, anxiety, shame, as well as of sexual excitation and pleasure are visibly indicated by blushing, hair-rising, or growing pale. Aggression, frustration, or irritation may be expressed in itching, paresthesias, hyperhidrosis, or rash. The intensity with which subjective skin symptoms such as itching or erythema are experienced relates directly with the emotional factors.

The visibility of most dermatoses has psychological consequences. Damaged skin is questionable. It often carries the connotation of contagion or a lack of hygiene, and may cause the patient to feel ostracized. The resulting self-depreciative feelings may lead to social fear and shame. Furthermore, the visibility of dermatoses may be an issue in itself. It appears that in psychopathology such as histrionic personality, exhibitionism may be expressed through skin symptoms. With self-inflicted artifacts the skin is targeted because of its visibility. This more or less conscious choice of a particular target area in function of some symbolic value of different body areas constitutes a distinctive item in psychodermatology.

The skin is the main organ of tactile interaction and its easy accessibility affects behavior. The impact of dermatoses on tactile communication and consequently on bodily interactive behavior and on sexual activity in particular is always immediate and often crucial. The skin is an easily available target organ for any self-touching behavior. Patients have direct access to their skin lesions. Dermatoses which are purely organic in origin are exacerbated by behavioral habits. Touching, scratching, squeezing real, or imaginary comedos, can all cause or aggravate dermatoses. Habitual skin care procedures can become part of an obsessional ritual procedure. As a result of environmental stress or psychopathological features, prescribed skin treatment regimens can result in overtreatment as part of the patient's repetitive compulsive behavior pattern. This makes dermatological disorders a field of choice for research into the suitability of behavioral therapeutic techniques. The patient's behavior toward his lesions offers direct clues for the psychological basis of the skin complaints. Moreover, a large proportion of dermatoses are provoked or perpetuated by direct actions which range from automatic scratching and purposeless squeezing of the skin to conscious provocation of lesions on a skin that physically represents a psychodynamic content. Indeed, various dermatoses are primarily disorders expressed in skin symptoms. Complex and refractory psychiatric problems such as self-destructive tendencies and hypochondriacal fixations are frequently expressed through psychocutaneous problems including trichotillomania, acné excoriée, dermatitis artefacta, parasitosis (delusion of infestation), dysmorphophobia, circumscript skin hypochondriasis, the olfactory reference syndrome, or bromosidrosis.

THE CLINICAL FIELD
OF PSYCHOSOMATIC DERMATOSES

It appears self-evident that psychodermatological syndromes are classified according to the type and degree of causal relationship between the psychological etiology and the dermatosis. Clinically three main categories can be distinguished: the psychocutaneous disorders strictu sensu, i.e., the dermatological symptoms based on an underlying psychiatric problem; the psychosomatic dermatoses, which are mainly caused by stress, and biologically determined dermatological disorders the course of which is codetermined by emotional factors. The issue of secondary psychological reactions to dermatological disorders (e.g., anxiety, depression, social phobia) is best dealt with in this third category.[9]

DERMATOLOGICAL SYNDROMES
BASED ON PSYCHIATRIC PROBLEMS

Most psychocutaneous disorders are a somatization of self-aggressive tendencies or hypochondriacal fixations. Patients who self-inflict cutaneous lesions belong to a broad continuum that ranges from malingerers, who simulate a dermatosis with a definite material gain motive (such as release from prison or a sickness allowance), to patients with no particular deceiving attitude, but whose self-inflicted lesions may be the result of nervous habits such as nail-biting (onychophagy), hair-pulling (trichotillomania, or even trichophagy), or acné excoriée (neurotic excoriation often on a predisposed acne skin).

Dermatitis artefacta comprises a variety of lesions (burns, abrasions, erosions, scratches, ulcers or bullae by application or injection of caustic products) that are to some degree consciously provoked by the patient. Pathomimicry patients may be quite ingenious in simulating well-defined dermatoses.[10, 11] The typical dermatitis artefacta patient has serious personality problems, e.g., borderline personality. The cutaneous lesions are often provoked in a repetitive manner, in order to acquire the sick role and gain the dermatologist's medical attention. Cutaneous self-mutilation is often a tension-reducing habit. The body distribution of the self-provoked cutaneous lesions is an objective and clinically accessible feature, which often carries an ascertainable significance. It has been found that patients with self-inflicted dermatological lesions in the face or in the genital area are willing to accept psychological help and respond well to a combination of psychotropic drugs and psychotherapy, while patients with lesions on the limbs or over the entire body strongly resist any psychological treatment.[12]

Palliative dermatological measures such as occlusive bandages, ointments, or placebo drugs, as well as hospitalization that includes bathing and massaging by nurses, can have a therapeutic impact on the psychiatric problem by symbolizing the medical attention and care that the dermatitis artefacta patient is basically craving for.[13]

Trichotillomania, or hair-pulling, may be either a habit or a tic, or a deliberate, though often benign, form of self-inflicted physical change. More often than is generally believed the patient deliberately selects the part of the scalp to be pulled. The ritualized procedure often includes twisting, scrutinizing, or even eating (trichophagy) the hair after it has been extracted. On the grounds of the presumed psychodynamic content of the hair-plucking, psychotherapy on analytic lines has been tried, with moderate results.[14] Like other dermatological syndromes based on unadapted behavior, trichotillomania often proves resistant to behavioral treatment of any kind.

Neurotic excoriations are lesions that are inflicted by patients who have an irresistible urge to manipulate their skin. As a rule this pathology originates during adolescence, following mild acne. It starts with unconscious picking of small irregularities in the skin, and initially it takes the form of an extension of cleaning procedures for removing comedos. In more pronounced cases, the habit becomes uncontrollable and turns into an imperative urge to dig into the skin in order to remove imaginary foreign substances.[15] Treatment is always difficult and general measures, such as protection against further self-mutilation by local bandaging and antipruritic salves, are recommended in combination with supportive psychotherapy.

Dysmorphic disorder, or dysmorphophobia, is characterized by a subjective feeling of ugliness, cosmetic defect, or deformity in one's appearance.[16] In its milder forms the disorder is limited to a fixation on a nonexisting or a minor skin defect, such as blemishes and red spots. Also normal wrinkles and skin changes as a result of aging may become the focus of an obsession-phobia. These patients have urgent requests for incisive dermatological treatment (laser therapy, transplant) or for cosmetic surgery. Some of them develop delusions, in which case the initial dysmorphophobia has been postulated as an ominous symptom of nascent schizophrenia.[17, 18]

Patients with *hypochondriasis of the skin* are convinced that they are suffering from a disease such as cancer, syphilis, or a grave infection. The intensity of the hypochondriasis is quite variable. Patients with extreme bodily preoccupation and a morbid fear of disease are often nonresponsive to reassurance, and they will insist on being examined over and over again. Patients who retain a fear of disease, e.g., after a benign tumor or a minor venereal disease, may have difficulties in accepting their full recovery, often because of unconscious feelings of guilt that compel them to have a chronic unpleasant bodily feeling.[19, 20]

Patients with *delusions of infestation* are utterly convinced of being infested by parasites. They bring all kinds of skin particles for microscopic examination or they demand intensive disinfection procedures by the health services.[21-24] It is no use arguing against this fixed delusion or trying to persuade the patient there is only house dust in the particles he has brought for examination, as this will only diminish his trust. Of course, it is equally wrong for the dermatologist to go along with the patient's delusion by telling him that he can see the parasites too, or to feed his imagination by explaining the life cycle of his parasites. The physician should accept the patient with his false beliefs without actually sharing them. This acceptance is as important in the overall management of the case as the simultaneous use of neuroleptics (e.g., pimozide) is in lessening the delusions.[16, 25]

Other forms of monosymptomatic hypochondriacal psychosis involving the skin are the olfactory syndrome, i.e., the delusion of emitting an offensive body odor, and the conviction of having skin cancer or a venereal disease.[26] Exceptionally, the delusions of parasitosis are shared by two or more family members or people living closely together, in a *folie partagée* (*folie à deux, folie à trois*).[27]

DERMATOSES WITH PSYCHOSOMATIC ETIOLOGY

Experimental work has confirmed that patients with *psychogenic pruritus* have distinguishing character features such as semipermeability, the inability to manage aggressive tendencies, character armoring, exaggerated cleanliness, and fear of disorder.[28] Strategies for responding to and coping with stress vary individually, which explains why certain individuals suffer from itching in response to stress while others do not.[29] Pruritus anogenitalis and pruritus vulvae are often particularly difficult to treat. When itching is a concomitant of some other skin disorder, the control of the scratching habit alone may serve as an effective treatment of the skin disorder. Different techniques have been used: reinforced inhibition in resistant itching and scratching, or a combination of desensitization and covert modeling.[30, 31]

Chronic hyperhidrosis, or excessive sweating, is generally accepted to be related to psychological stress factors. Clinical improvement has been obtained by the use of biofeedback therapies that aim at reducing the symptoms as well as the underlying anxiety.[32]

DERMATOSES WHOSE COURSE IS AFFECTED BY PSYCHOLOGICAL FACTORS

In dermatoses such as eczema, alopecia, or psoriasis, both nonspecific emotional stress factors and specific life events can trigger a relapse, affect the onset and duration, and influence patient compliance. A direct causal link is difficult to establish, but anti-stress treatment is recommended when emotional factors precipitate specific skin problems. Psychological factors seriously affect the result of the dermatological treatment of the local skin problems. Obviously, when a psoriasis patient refuses PUVA because of "fear of cancer," the dermatologist must deal with this fear.[33]

The primary cause of *atopic dermatitis*, also called neurodermatitis, may be immunological, but psychological factors play a part in precipitating and maintaining the lesions, while emotional elements also have a strong impact on the itch–scratch cycle. The efficacy of a psychosomatic approach, and of psychotherapy and behavioral techniques in particular, is well documented. It appears that psychological methods are at least as effective as the classical medical procedures.[34] Behavioral therapy can influence the maladaptive scratching behavior by selectively presenting the withdrawal of the conditioned reinforcers. Considering that medical intervention in atopic dermatitis is merely palliative and only partially effective, and that the results of psychological and behavioral treatment are quite encouraging, there is now a growing support for the psychosomatic treatment of atopic dermatitis.

The exact pathophysiology of *eczema* is not fully known, but the influence of emotional components is sufficiently acknowledged to motivate psychobehavioral treatment.[35, 36] In infantile eczema the role of emotional factors is beyond question. Maternal or parental rejection in atopic children is crucial. While not all atopic children have rejecting mothers, the fact remains that they are more likely to induce resentment and withdrawal in their parents, precisely because they are typically irritable.[37] A positive attitude toward these children is extremely hard to adopt because of their uncontrollable bouts of scratching. A psychosomatic treatment principle has been effected by lowering the active substances in ointments and thus requiring more frequent applications, resulting in an increase of skin contact and cuddling, which is supposed to have a beneficial effect.[36] Behavioral treatment that concentrates on reducing the scratching bouts which aggravate and maintain the lesions has also had striking results. In cases of dyshidrotic eczema, biofeedback procedures have been effective, as shown in the marked changes in skin conductance and in lower subjective levels of anxiety.[38]

Attacks or relapses of *alopecia areata* are influenced by unspecific stress factors as well as by neurotic personality features.[39] Life events recordings in the 6 months prior to an alopecia areata attack, did not, however, confirm the psychogenesis of alopecia.[40] Some authors remain confident in the effectiveness of psychoanalytic psychotherapy, but their reports have serious shortcomings: the duration of follow-up is inadequately standardized, and both the possible impact of other therapeutic variables, e.g. changes in life circumstances, and the high rate of spontaneous remission of alopecia are disregarded.

Neuro-endocrinological investigations support the hypothesis that *psoriasis* patients experience challenging situations as more stressful than nonpsoriatic control groups.[41] Although this corresponds with the commonly observed stress-induced relapses and progress of psoriatic skin disorders, and thus strongly hints at a psychosomatic component, there is no hard evidence for the usefulness of psychotherapy. Neither the significance of personality characteristics (aggression or hostility) nor the exact role of precipitating life events has been defined in attacks or relapses of psoriasis.[42, 43] All the same, individual and group psychotherapy have been reported as beneficial.

General Clinical Guidelines for the Psychosomatic Management of Dermatoses

The psychosomatic management in dermatology requires a focus beyond the skin, its lesions and complaints, including the observation of nonverbal communication, specific anamnestic techniques, an adaptation of the physician-patient relationship, and specific treatment strategies (psychotherapy, behavior therapy, psychotropics).

Nonverbal Communication
of Dermatological Patients

The patient's general behavior and his specific gestures as he explains his complaints and displays his lesions during the dermatological consultation possess a communicative significance. A great deal can be deduced from observing how the patient handles his diseased skin areas.[44] Avoidance of self-touching or continuous plucking, caressing, or fondling himself in a soothing way, may in fact reveal more about the way the patient experiences his illness than his verbal statements.[45] Tension and anxiety are shown immediately in all kinds of "displacement activities," i.e., automatic gestures that mimic washing, scratching, or self-grooming gestures that eventually become increasingly repetitive and vehement in situations of boredom, tension, or repressed aggression. By anxiously trying to mask his lesions or by displaying them overtly, the patient indicates how he expects others to react to his dermatosis.

Anamnestic Investigation
in Psychosomatic Practice

The anamnestic technique needs to be adapted. Rather than following a strictly structured course, the patient should be interviewed more spontaneously not only in order to register the duration, intensity, and quality of the skin complaints, but also to allow the personal experience to reveal itself.[46, 47] This extended anamnesis should reveal the patient's subjective experience of his complaints: the condition in which he first became aware of this skin problem (often of symbolic significance); an assessment of life situations likely to provoke recurrences or exacerbations of the symptoms; a biographical evaluation of the patient's childhood experiences and relationship with significant people (parents, spouse); and the nature of the patient's personality. This approach seems hardly feasible in a busy medical practice. A high turnover of patients and time-limited consultations leave time for only a few target questions. Therefore, we do not advise a psychosomatically directed anamnesis for the first interview, but as the consultations become repetitive in the chronic management of the complaint, time will gradually be found for the extended anamnesis.

The diagnosis of a psychocutaneous disorder must never be solely based on the absence of an organic explanation and the (fortuitous?) discovery of a psychological stress situation. A psychosomatic diagnosis should not only cover possible hereditary somatic dispositions but also any causal connections between personality traits and conflict situations. The overall approach should be patient-centered and include psychosocial aspects and circumstances, rather than disease-orientated, i.e., following a dermatological classification.

DOCTOR–PATIENT RELATIONSHIP IN PSYCHOSOMATIC DERMATOLOGY

In psychosomatic dermatology the doctor–patient relationship is different from the classical relationship, which is based on the active and decision-making attitude of the doctor and the more passively dependent attitude on the part of the patient, who tends to expect the doctor to try and make the right diagnosis and find the appropriate cure. The clinician working at the interface between dermatology and psychiatry, however, will never gain an insight into the psychodynamics of the patient's problems without the latter's active participation. Without this cooperation it will be impossible to establish the various psychogenic factors, the individual subjective experience, or the effect of the skin problems at a relational level.[48] The somatization constitutes a "coded message" of psychological stress translated into a bodily symptom.[49] This message must be decoded and understood, and reformulated in terms which both patient and doctor can understand. In hysteric patients with conversion symptoms the bodily symbolization of a problem which they cannot express verbally is very direct and clear, e.g., paresis of the legs indicates an inability to accept a situation. In the bodily messages of psychocutaneous patients the symbols are less direct. Although their somatization may include some conversive elements, this coded message is hard to understand, as no semantic link can be established between the somatic symptom and the underlying psychodynamic problem.

Specific Treatment Techniques
in the Management of Psychodermatoses

The effectiveness of *psychotherapy* in general in the psychosomatic treatment of skin disorders and the application of various forms of psychotherapy, psychoanalysis, group psychotherapy, or short-term psychotherapy, have not been adequately assessed. On the whole it appears that the positive outcome of psychotherapy is much more dependent on nonspecific factors and on the therapist's commitment and enthusiasm than on specific treatment variables.[45, 50, 51]

The integration of a psychotherapeutic dimension into the routine operation of a dermatology clinic has been realized in some clinics in Germany. Bosse and Hünecke,[52, 53] Rechenberger,[54, 55] and Rechenberger and Rechenberger[56] have established a psychosomatic approach that ranges from individual to interactional psychodynamics, more in particular to the resistance encountered in dermatological patients with eczema, urticaria, and psoriasis and the parallel resistance in dermatologists. Their work focuses on the management of those patients who are not yet aware of a psychogenetic factor in their dermatosis and on the effects of a disturbed mother–child relationship on diseases such as urticaria, psoriasis, or acné excoriée. In seminars and practical supervisions, dermatologists in training are taught how to deal with the psychosomatic components of their practice.

A similar model of a psychodermatological approach has been developed by Escande[57] in the dermatological department of the Hôpital Tarnier in Paris, where Consoli[58] has considerably modified the classic dermatological approach of diagnosing the lesions without much attention to the totality of the patient, toward a new approach that involves interpreting the patient's discourse in order to detect his general distress. The medical as well as the nursing staff possess a psychoanalytic background. The gap between the somatic approach on the one hand and the psychological treatment on the other is bridged by an organizational integration.

Although behavioral factors exert a particular influence on dermatological syndromes at different levels, there have been only a few systematic *behavioral intervention* studies and the applicability of behavioral techniques in psychodermatology has been insufficiently investigated. More than any other treatment technique, behavioral methods have a direct impact on variables that directly influence skin physiology. Indeed, hypnosis, relaxation, etc., bring about changes in physiological parameters such as skin conductance, skin temperature, and vasomotor reactions, all of which can be decisive in the origin of skin disorders. The importance of the behavioral approach lies in the fact that the patient's gestures strongly affect dermatoses. Indeed, many functional or behaviorally determined disorders are the result of reinforced or maintained behavior and some dermatoses (artifacts, acné excoriée, prurigo with excoriations) are the direct products of the patient's behavior.

It is common knowledge among dermatologists that hospitalization by itself can clear a resistant dermatosis, without any change in the dermatological treatment. It is still unclear whether this beneficial impact of hospitalization resides in the fact of being freed from the daily stress of life as an outpatient or in the regression offered by the stay in hospital. Many patients point to the soothing effect they experience through the nursing procedures. In a psychodynamic respect the bathing, the massaging with ointments and creams, and the bandaging reenact maternal care in early childhood, while on a behavioral level they have a relaxing effect on the skin. All this has not yet been systematically researched.

Diverse behavioral therapeutic strategies have been applied, either separately, mixed or in combination with other psychological techniques. In cases where anxiety is a main causal factor, systemic desensitization can be justified. Dermatoses in which self-touching is the behavioral component are treated more successfully by aversion techniques or token economy. Hypnosis and biofeedback have been used in the treatment of various dermatoses. The association of behavioral methods with biological–cognitive techniques is a therapeutic challenge for the future.

Systemic desensitization techniques are appropriate for the treatment of dermatoses which feature anticipatory anxiety. Dermatological practice has to deal with all sorts of fear caused by normal skin changes and especially by contagious diseases. Sexually transmitted diseases and cancer have long been the favorite targets for skin hypochondriasis. While these skin phobias are readily recognizable, they are particularly treatment-resistant.

Aversion therapy has been used in dermatoses ranging from neurodermatitis to trichotillomania.[59, 60] Dermatological problems that are the result of persistent behavior disturbances, such as compulsive scratching, squeezing of real or imaginary comedos, can be treated by administering a light electric shock whenever the patient displays the unadaptive habit. This technique proves particularly adequate for treating compulsive scratching.

Operant techniques may be applied to various syndromes such as compulsive scratching, trichotillomania, and atopic dermatitis. In this treatment the adaptive behavior is reinforced by a reward, while unadaptive behavior is weakened or eliminated by being neglected or punished.

Assertiveness training is appropriate for patients who do not or cannot express their emotions directly and who experience extreme or considerable social fear. They often also show excessive blushing, symptomatic erythema, erythrophobia, and hyperhidrosis. Patients who bottle up their emotions and who have difficulties in expressing feelings of anger tend to develop autonomic vasomotor responses, the most problematic of which is facial symptomatic erythema because of its visibility. In many cases these symptomatic responses entail a secondary fear of becoming red in the face (erythrophobia). Through conditioning the autonomic vasomotor responses and the erythrophobia lead to aggravation of social fear. Here the behavioral treatment of choice is assertivity training based on reciprocal inhibition. Patients with excessive sweating during mental stress find themselves in a similar vicious circle. Fear of the hyperhidrosis develops and this "sudophobia" in itself causes the autonomous response of excessive sweating, mostly on the palms of the hand and the soles of the feet. A methodological training derived from the Schultz relaxation techniques and autohypnosis can modify physiological parameters such as skin resistance and skin temperature. Biofeedback techniques that regulate the skin temperature have two advantages: the relaxation training is quicker and objectively controlled, the temperature rises and peripheral vasodilation improves. This method has been used in cases of alopecia, pruritus vulvae, herpes, and eczema.[61] Acute anxiety produces vasoconstriction, as demonstrated by finger plethysmography. This may be reversed by relaxation biofeedback or hypnosis.

Early researchers in psychodermatology experimented enthusiastically with hypnosis. Now its use is confined to the treatment of verrucae, the experimental production of blisters and the investigation of vasomotor skin changes.

A variety of *psychotropic drugs* have been used in the treatment of psychosomatic dermatoses. The choice of this treatment depends on the existence of a causal link between the psychodermatological problem and a psychiatric factor.

The efficacy of neuroleptic drugs is well documented in two different psychodermatological categories: dermatological syndromes rooted in psychotic conditions, so-called monosymptomatic hypochondriacal psychoses (moderate to high doses), and in pain and paresthesias (low dosage), such as glossodynia or glossopyrosis. For its specific dopamine antagonistic properties, pimozide is advocated as the drug of choice in delusions of infestation.[62–64]

When anxiety and/or depression are part of the etiology or the consequence of the dermatosis, their reduction by anxiolytic or antidepressant drugs can have an indirect beneficial effect on the dermatosis itself. The same indirect action may be presumed for psychotropic drugs which diminish irritability, tension or dysregulation in self-aggression, all of which lead to dermatitis artefacta.

Depressive symptoms are not uncommon in dermatological practice. Stress-inducing life events, including loss and reactive depression, are commonly accepted as causative or precipitating factors for alopecia areata and psoriasis.[4] Although these dermatoses are very different pathophysiologically, they have in common that they are chronic and visible diseases. It follows that many of the depressive symptoms encountered in both are a response to rather than a cause of the illness. The efficacy of antidepressants in both conditions, however, is doubtful, as the demarcation between depression as an etiological issue and as a reactive consequence is difficult to establish.

Apart from the diagnosis of dermatosis complicated by a depressive syndrome, one should be attentive to the diagnosis of a masked depression, also called depression "sine depressione." Although both monoamine oxidase inhibitors and tricyclic antidepressants are effective in treating depression they are not well tolerated by dermatological patients. They have numerous and serious side effects: dry mouth, micturition difficulties, postural hypotension, cardiovascular effects (tachycardia), changes in the ECG with a risk of ventricular arrhythmias. Overdoses of tricyclic antidepressants are potentially lethal. Second-generation antidepressants such as mianserin, fluvoxamine, and fluoxetine have fewer side-effects and are therefore better tolerated.[65] This is important as dermatological patients already suffer from some somatic discomfort and will show noncompliance if the prescribed drugs have negative side-effects.

When psychological stress, tension, anxiety, hostility or irritation are important factors in a dermatosis, the temporary use of anxiolytic drugs is called for. However, the prescription of an anxiolytic, in particular a benzodiazepine, can never be an isolated therapeutic answer. To reduce his anxiety the patient should also be introduced to nonpharmaceutical alternatives. Furthermore, the prescription period should be limited to a few weeks, covering only the acute anxiety situation, because of the risks of dependency and overcompliance and of the possible rebound of the initial anxiety symptoms and the withdrawal effects on discontinuation. Hydroxyzine hydrochloride is an antihistaminic drug which is often prescribed as a tranquillizer in the dermatological treatment of urticaria.

Finally, reports on the use of psychotropic drugs in dermatology tend to emphasize that the psychopharmacological treatment should always be part of an integrative approach, combining medical and psychobiobehavioral management. It follows that the need for a combined approach with diverse forms of psychotherapy is mandatory in psychosomatic dermatology.[66, 67]

CONCLUDING REMARKS: ECLECTIC MANAGEMENT

The practice of psychodermatology requires an eclectic approach. A monoform treatment of psychosomatic dermatosis is bound to be ineffective. Thus a solely dermatological antipruritus medication in psychogenic pruritus is of limited value because it ignores the influence of psychological conflicts in the etiology.[45] However, the same criticism goes for a purely psychotherapeutic approach. Even when psychotherapy is needed for these patients, there is too large a gap between their somatic complaint and the "one-sided psychic" answer offered by psychotherapy. This gap must be bridged in order to reach a therapeutic working alliance. A mixed procedure is needed which measures the value of each etiological moment and accordingly constructs a combined therapy.[37, 44] The problem is that the dermatologist is often not at ease with treatments that belong to the psychiatric field. Experience with medication only often leads to prejudice against psychotherapy. Yet, clinicians who are apprehensive of incorporating some psychotherapy within their therapeutic framework should realize that their rigid adherence to a solely medical approach is one of the reasons why patients come to have a fixed belief in a fictitious somatic illness. Continuous management by a physician who only wants to diagnose and treat somatic illness will make patients more persistent in their hypochondriacal fixations. Psychotropics can be used in psychodermatology as in any psychiatric practice. The stronger the psychic factor is in a dermatosis, the better the effect of psychotropics will be. It is important to realize that the psychiatric symptoms will decrease before the dermatosis improves.[45]

Psychosomatic dermatological patients should not be referred to a psychiatrist unless a serious psychiatric illness is present or unless the dermatologist feels unable to practice a psychological approach. Clinicians who have been trained in a setting that incorporates a psychiatric liaison service have experienced the scope of their possibilities in treating these patients.[13, 56, 68, 69] They find that they can cope much better with the psychosomatic patient and need to refer to the psychiatrist only in exceptional situations. This practical training in cooperation with the liaison psychiatrist and the willingness to adopt a comprehensive patient approach are the main grounds for a rewarding psychosomatic approach in dermatology.

REFERENCES

1. Renshaw D. Sex and the dermatologist. *Int J Dermatol.* 1980;19:469–471.
2. Wittkower ED, Russel B. *Emotional Factors in Skin Disease.* New York: Hoeber;1953.
3. Musaph H. Psychodermatology. In: Hill OW, ed. *Modern Trends in Psychosomatic Medicine.* London: Butterworths;1976:3.
4. Fava GA, Perini GI, Santonastaso P, Fornasa CV. Life events and psychological distress in dermatologic disorders: Psoriasis, chronic urticaria and fungal infections. *Br J Med Psychol.* 1980;53:277–282.
5. Dunbar HF. *Emotions and Bodily Changes.* New York: Columbia University Press;1983.
6. Panconesi E. The future is there: Cutaneous psychoneuroimmunology as a premise. In: *Stress and Skin Diseases: Psychosomatic Dermatology.* Philadelphia: Lippincott;1984.
7. Macalpine I. Is alopecia areata psychosomatic? *Br J Dermatol.* 1958;70:147–158.
8. Van Moffaert M. The importance of permanent psychiatric consulting in the dermatological clinic. *Arch Belg Dermatol.* 1974;30:215–220.
9. Medansky RS, Handler RM. Dermatopsychosomatics: Classification, physiology, and therapeutic approaches. *J Am Acad Dermatol.* 1981;5:125–135.
10. Yap KB. *Automutilatie.* Deventer, Netherlands: Van Loghum Slaterus;1970.
11. Nielsen H, Fruensgaard K, Hjortshoj A. Controlled neuropsychological investigation of patients with neurotic excoriations. *Psychother Psychosom.* 1980; 34:52–61.
12. Van Moffaert M. Localization of self-inflicted dermatological lesions: What do they tell the dermatologist? *Acta Derm Venereol.* (Stockh). 1991;156:23–27.
13. Van Moffaert M. Training future dermatologists in psychodermatology. *Gen Hosp Psychiatry.* 1986;8:115–118.
14. Greenberg HV, Sarner CA. Trichotillomania. *Arch Gen Psychiatry.* 1965;12: 482–489.
15. Fruensgaard K, Hjortshoj A, Nielsen H. Neurotic excoriations. *Int J Dermatol.* 1979;17:761–767.

16. Koblenzer CS. *Psychocutaneous Disease.* Orlando, FL: Grune & Stratton;1987.
17. Cotterill JA. Dermatological nondisease: A common and potentially fatal disturbance of cutaneous body image. *Br J Dermatol.* 1981;104:611–619.
18. Hay GG. Dysmorphophobia. *Br J Psychiatry.* 1970;116:399–406.
19. Hardy GE, Cotterill IA. A study of depression and obsessionality in dysmorphophobic and psoriatic patients. *Br J Psychiatry.* 1982;140:19–22.
20. Frank OS. Dysmorphophobia. In: Gail RN, et al., eds. *Current Themes in Psychiatry.* Utrecht, Netherlands: Spectrum Publications;1985:257–278.
21. Gould WM, Gragg T. Delusions of parasitosis. *Arch Dermatol.* 1976;112:1745–1748.
22. Sizaret P, Simon JP. Les délires à extoparasites de l'âge avancé: Syn drome d'Ekbom. *Encéphale.* 1976;167–175.
23. Breuillard F, Delplanque M. Un délire hypochondriaque cutané. *Concours Méd.* 1980;5705–5709.
24. Bourgeois M, Nguyen-Lan A. Syndrome d'Ekbom et délires d'infestation cutanée. *Ann Méd Psychol.* 1986;144:21–39.
25. Frithz A. Delusions of infestation: Treatment by depot injections of neurolepitcs. *Clin Exp Dermatol.* 1979;4:485–488.
26. Bishop EM. Monosymptomatic hypochondriacal syndromes in dermatology. *J Am Acad Dermatol.* 1983;9:152–158.
27. Evans P, Merskey H. Shared beliefs of dermal parasitosis. *Br J Med Psychol.* 1972;45:19–26.
28. Musaph H. Psychogenic pruritus. *Semin Dermatol.* 1983;2:217–222.
29. Fjellner B, Arnetz B, Eneroth P, Kallner A. Pruritus during standardized mental stress. *Acta Derm Venereol.* (Stockh). 1985;65:199–205.
30. Dobes RW. Amelioration of psychosomatic dermatosis by reinforced inhibition of scratching. *J Behav Ther Exp Psychiatry.* 1977;8:185–187.
31. Daniels LK. Treatment of urticaria and severe headache by behaviour therapy. *Psychosomatics.* 1973;14:347–351.
32. Duller P, Gentry WD. Use of biofeedback in treating chronic hyperhidrosis: Preliminary report. *Br J Dermatol.* 1980;103:143–146.
33. Whitlock FA. *Psychophysiological Aspects of Skin Diseases.* London: Saunders;1970.
34. Schoenberg B, Carr AC. An investigation of criteria for brief psychotherapy of neurodermatitis. *Psychosom Med.* 1963;25:253–263.
35. Brown DG. Emotional disturbance in eczema: A study of symptom-reporting behavior. *J Psychosom Res.* 1967;11:27–40.
36. Brown DG, Bettley FR. Psychiatric treatment of eczema: A controlled trial. *Br Med J.* 1971;ii:729–734.
37. Beveridge GW. Diseases of the skin: Infantile eczema. *Br Med J.* 1974;i:154–155.
38. Miller RM, Coger RW. Skin conductance conditioning with dyshidrotic eczema patients. *Br J Dermatol.* 1979;101:435–437.
39. Puchalski Z, Szlendak L. Anxiety state and anxiety trait in patients with alopecia areata, rosacea and lichen ruber planus. *Z Hautkr.* 1983;14:1038–1048.
40. Perini GI, Fornasa CV, Cipriani R, Bettin A, Zecchino F, Peserico A. Life events and alopecia areata. *Psychother Psychosom.* 1984;41:48–52.
41. Arnetz BB, Fjellner B, Eneroth P, Kallner A. Stress and psoriasis: Psychoendocrine and metabolic reactions in psoriatic patients during standardized stressor exposure. *Psychosom Med.* 1985;47:528–541.

42. Lyketsos GC, Stratigos J, Tawil G, Psara M, Lyketsos CG. Hostile personality characteristics, dysthymic states and neurotic symptoms in urticaria, psoriasis and alopecia. *Psychother Psychosom.* 1985;44:122–131.
43. Matussek P, Agerer D, Sebt G. Aggression in depressives and psoriatics. *Psychother Psychosom.* 1985;43:120–125.
44. Musaph H. *Jeuk: Een multidisciplinaire benadering.* Haarlem, Netherlands: Bohn;1968.
45. Van Moffaert M. Psychosomatics for the practicing dermatologist. *Dermatologica.* 1982;165:73–84.
46. Bastiaans J. Die Übersetzung der Klage. *Psychother Med Psychol.* 1971;21:167–181.
47. Lipowski ZJ, Lipsitt DR, Whybrow PC. *Psychosomatic Medicine.* New York: New York University Press:1977.
48. Siegrist J. Die Bedeutung von Lebensereignissen für die Entstehung körperlicher und psychosomatischer Erkrankungen. *Nervenarzt.* 1980;51:313–326.
49. Marty P, De M'Uzan M, David C. *L'investigation psychosomatique.* Paris: Presses Universitaires de France;1963.
50. Sarti MG, Cossidenti A. Therapy in psychosomatic dermatology. In: *Stress and Skin Diseases: Psychosmatic Dermatology.* Philadelphia: Lippincott;1984.
51. Stephanos S. Ambulatory analytical psychotherapy for the treatment of psychosomatic patients: A report on the method of "relaxation analytique." *Br J Med Psychol.* 1976;49:305–313.
52. Bosse K, Hünecke P. *Psychodynamik und Soziodynamik bei Hautkranken.* Göttingen, Germany: Verlag für Medizinische Psychologie;1976.
53. Bosse K, Hünecke P. Krankheitsabhängiges Verhalten von Psoriasispatienten. Ärzlen und Pflegepersonal im Krankenhaus. *Acta Derm.* 1982;8:163–166.
54. Rechenberger I. *Tiefenpsychologisch ausgerichtete Diagnostik und Behandlung von Hautkrankheiten.* Göttingen, Germany: Vandenhoeck & Ruprecht;1975.
55. Rechenberger I. Zugang zu psychosomatischen Aspekten in der Dermatologie. *Prax Psychother.* 1977;22:265–270.
56. Rechenberger I, Rechenberger HG. Besonderheiten eines Konsiliardienstes und einer psychosomatische Sprechstunde in einer Universitäts-Hautklinik. *Psychother Med Psychol.* 1976;26:163–168.
57. Escande JP. Organisation institutionnelle d'un service hospitalier de dermatologie pour une prise en charge psychosomatique. *Sem Hôp Paris.* 1984;3: 916–919.
58. Consoli S. Observation au long cours d'une patiente présentant des troubles psychosomatiques et suivie en psychothérapie. *Sem Hôp Paris.* 1984;13:909–915.
59. Ratliff RG, Stein NH. Treatment of neurodermatitis by behavior therapy: A case study. *Behav Res Ther.* 1968;6:397–399.
60. Altman K, Grahs C, Friman P. Treatment of unobserved trichotillomania by attention-reflexion and punishment of an apparent covariant. *J Behav Ther Exp Psychiatry.* 1982;13:337–340.
61. Goldberg S, Woehl M. Biofeedback en dermatologie. *Nouv Dermatol.* 1982;1:6–9.
62. Munro A. Monosymptomatic hypochondriacal psychosis manifesting as delusions of parasitosis. *Arch Dermatol.* 1978;114:940–943.
63. Munro A. Delusional parasitosis: A form of monosymptomatic hypochondriacal psychosis. *Semin Dermatol.* 1983;2:197–202.

64. Lyell A. Delusions of parasitosis. *Br J Dermatol.* 1983;108:485–499.
65. Hendrickx B, Van Moffaert M, Spiers R, Von Frenckell R Jr. The treatment of psychocutaneous disorders: A new approach. *Curr Ther Res.* 1991;49:111–119.
66. Koo JM, Strauss GD. Psychopharmacologic treatment of psychocutaneous disorders: A practical guide. *Semin Dermatol.* 1987;6:83–93.
67. Gould WM, Gragg TM. A dermatology-psychiatry liaison clinic. *J Am Acad Dermatol.* 1983;7:73–77.
68. Van Moffaert M. Factitious affections in dermatology. *Arch Belg Dermatol.* 1974;30:221–224.
69. Van Moffaert M, Vermander F, Kint A. Dermatitis artefacta. *Int J Dermatol.* 1986;24:236–238.

Chapter 19
Psychosomatic Disorders Related to Gynecology

FABIO FACCHINETTI, KOEN DEMYTTENAERE,
LOREDANA FIORONI, ISABELLA NERI,
ANDREA R. GENAZZANI

The interaction between different disciplines is a normal trend in modern medicine and gynecology does not represent an exception. Moreover, in the last decades there have been tremendous developments in gynecology, not solely linked to an increase of knowledge, but also stemming from changing patient demands. Gynecological disorders are often an expression of psychological discomfort and distress that impair daily activities, worsen self-esteem, reduce the sense of well-being, social interactions, etc. On the other hand, psychiatric disorders could manifest themselves through a gynecological dysfunction. Therefore, gynecologists should face clinical problems bearing in mind the above-reported interaction with the psychic world. This is particularly true for disorders linked to reproductive life, that is, menstrual and fertility problems. In this paper we will briefly review current issues on four psychosomatic disorders related to gynecological life: psychogenic amenorrhea, premenstrual symptoms, infertility, and climacteric syndrome. In addition to classification and etiopathogenesis, attention will be paid to psychobiological findings in an effort to elucidate neuroendocrine mechanisms underlying the psychosomatic interaction.

393

Psychogenic Amenorrhea

History

It is well known that irregular bleeding can follow a psychic shock. During the First World War[1] the reason for the "war amenorrhea" was recognized as being due to nutritional deficits. Only during the Second World War did several investigators[2] began to consider these amenorrheas as resulting from emotional factors. In fact, Fremont-Smith and Meigs[3] said: "Evidence has accumulated within the past decade to suggest that menstrual abnormalities may be caused not only by organic, but also by emotional factors" (p. 1044). In addition, emotional factors were believed to affect the mucous membrane of the uterus, not only hormonally, but also neurogenically.[4]

Refeinstein[5] was the first to consider the involvement of the hypothalamus in psychogenic amenorrhea, and Rheingold[6] hypothesized the hypothalamic functions as a sort of relay mediating psychic influences on the menstrual cycle. The involvement of the central nervous system in amenorrhea was reinforced by the changes of EEG observed in anovulatory women.[7] This notion was reinforced by the observation that other psychosomatic symptoms may appear simultaneously with amenorrhea as, for instance, fluctuations of weight.[8]

Psychodynamic and Psychometric Evaluations

The psychodynamic approach to psychogenic amenorrhea brought forth the following major problem areas: (1) rejection of the female role and regression of sexuality[9]; (2) conflicts over pregnancy and motherhood with an infantile regression[6, 10]; (3) fear of mutilation.[9] Deutsch[11] underlined the importance of the emotional impact of menarche. She argued that the first bleeding is always experienced as a trauma: the flow from a sphincterless orifice could be depressing because it cannot voluntarily be controlled. In this way, menstrual bleeding is a stressing event in the process of becoming a woman. Benedek[12] wrote:

Young women, even after menstruation has been established, may suppress the ovarian cycle more or less completely as a defense against natural sexuality. Without having anything to do with the "painful," "dirty," and "dangerous" part of sexuality, they may go on with their adolescent fantasies of life rich in sexual experiences. When these girls become able to accept sexuality, the amenorrhea usually disappears.

Amenorrhea could also be a defense against sexuality in conflict situations. Menninger[13] thought that a woman's desire to be a boy may lead to an open denial of femininity. Amenorrhea would be the most logical outcome of such unconscious rejection of femininity. Also psychometric evaluation offers a particular profile of patients with secondary amenorrhea. On the basis of a psychiatric interview and of the Rorschach test, Kelley et al.[14] observed three features typical of these patients: (1) psychosexual immaturity; (2) oral conflicts; and (3) schizoid thinking. According to the authors, the reason that the autonomous disturbances (in the neurovegetative mechanism) manifested themselves in the form of amenorrhea and not as other functions is an unconscious associative relation between psychic conflict and menstrual function. In the material of Sainsburg,[15] those suffering from menstrual disorders scored the scale of neurocity of Eysenck Inventory like other psychosomatic disorders that is higher than the somatically ill subjects. We confirmed that the personality profile in the patients with significant life events, temporarily related to the onset of amenorrhea, showed high levels in the neurotic area.[16] In Osofsky and Fisher's study,[17] projective tests showed a significant correlation between irregularities of the menstrual cycle and disorders of the body image. All these findings agree with the notion that amenorrhea from psychogenic causes is more frequent in girls having internal conflicts and even personality disorders.

NOSOLOGICAL PROBLEM

After Refeinstein's[5] recognition of hypothalamic amenorrhea, Russel[18] divided psychogenic amenorrheas into three groups: (1) those following extreme dangers and privations (war, air raids, reclusion, fear of extermination); (2) those following minor life changes (initiation of studies, boarding school, military service, fear of pregnancy); (3) those related to severe psychiatric disorders.

Physical exercise, low body weight and weight loss,[19, 20] eating and mood disorders,[21] drug abuse,[22] and a variety of external and personal stresses have been linked to the amenorrhea of psychogenic origin. Berga and Girton[23] used the term of *functional hypothalamic amenorrhea* rather than *psychogenic (or hypothalamic) amenorrhea* because of the multifactorial nature of this state. She narrowed the definition to those women whose amenorrhea was at least of 6 months duration, whose percentile of ideal body weight was greater than 85%, whose weight loss was not more than 25%, and whose exercise regimen did not exceed more than 20 miles per week of running or 10 hours of vigorous activity per week. She also excluded those patients having vomiting episodes or recurrent excess eating that might represent bulimia, as well as those with hyperandrogenism, premature ovarian failure, hyperprolactinemia, drug abuse, thyroid and adrenal disease, or any other evidence of organic disease. In other words, *functional hypothalamic amenorrhea* would be the proposed term for the psychogenic amenorrhea, provided that major behavioral and affective disorders were excluded.

Thus, the various aspects of this menstrual disturbance bring us to consider a multidisciplinary approach with gynecological, endocrinological, and psychiatric supports.

PATHOPHYSIOLOGY

During stressful situations the organism employs behavioral and endocrinological patterns aiming at the removal of physical or psychic "stressors," and the action of the different systems persists as long as the behavioral activation itself continues. On the other hand, an alteration of one of these defensive systems always produces an anatomofunctional change of the others. However, it could happen that psychobiological activation cannot achieve a defensive function and thus remove chronic "stressors." This is evident in psychogenic amenorrhea. It has been reported that the total psychophysic expenditure, the personality and the "coping" mechanisms should be considered in the evaluation of amenorrhea.[24]

In the majority of cases of secondary amenorrhea with low or normal gonadotropins, no organic disease can be found.[25] At the level of the hypothalamus, increasing evidence suggests that the gonadotropin-releasing hormone is subjected to several neurotransmitter controls including dopamine that exert inhibitory effects and norepinephrine which displays facilitatory ones.[26] Furthermore, ß-endorphin and corticotropin-releasing factor[27] may play a role in stress-induced inhibition of reproductive functions. In fact, it has been reported that 60% of patients affected by anovulation and/or secondary amenorrhea show increased opioid tonus.[28] Irrespective of gonadotropin levels, patients with secondary amenorrhea fail to release luteinizing hormone (LH) after naloxone blockade of opiate receptors.[29] The neuroendocrine changes of women with functional hypothalamic amenorrhea also include hypercortisolism,[30] decreased LH pulsatility,[31] decreased prolactin secretion,[32] and amplification of nocturnal melatonin rhythm.[33] Anyway, although these findings could be related to a hypothalamic dysfunction their onset could be looking for suprahypothalamic mechanisms mediating the environmental–emotional stress. Fries et al.[34] found that the onset of secondary amenorrhea was often preceded by stressful life events such as separation from husband or partner, failure at school, or problematic and stressful social relationships. Using the Paykel interview for significant life events and the structured clinical interview for DSM-III-R in 55 patients with hypothalamic amenorrhea, we observed that a psychological disturbance induced a significant and specific change in hypothalamic activity. The presence of a psychiatric diagnosis (depressive one is the most frequent) is accompanied by a significant reduction in pulse amplitude, while the presence of significant life events causes a significant reduction of LH pulse frequency. On the other hand, when both a psychiatric disorder and a life event coexist, there is a significant deceleration of LH pulses whose frequency shows a 50% reduction compared to normally menstruating women (Table 19.1).

TABLE 19.1.
LH Secretory Features (Instantaneous Secretory Rate)
in Hypothalamic Secondary Amenorrhea (mean ± SD)

	Frequency pulses/4 h	Amplitude mIU/ml	Duration min
Group A	3.38 ± 1.61	2.07 ± 1.56	25.2 ± 8.7
Group B	2.66 ± 1.11	1.68 ± 1.38	20.1 ± 7.8
Group C	3.44 ± 1.23	1.20 ± 1.01	21.5 ± 7.5
Group D	2.00 ± 1.04	1.22 ± 0.97	23.2 ± 6.5

Data are obtained evaluating LH plasma levels every 10 min, for 4 h. Plasma concentrations were analyzed using the algorhythm DETECT [31]. Group A = Patients free from psychiatric diagnosis and life events (n = 13); group B = patients with only life events (n = 9); group C = patients with only psychiatric diagnosis (n = 9); group D = patients with both life events and psychiatric diagnosis (n = 12). As far as frequency of pulses is concerned, ANOVA indicates a significant change among groups (F = 2.97, 3/40, p = 0.039).

The issue of psychiatric disorders and amenorrhea still needs elucidation. The frequency of amenorrhea in primary psychiatric illness ranges from 5.8% in a 1933 report[35] to 93% in a study published in 1957.[36] In a series of gynecological patients, recent data[37] reported 28% major depressive disorders and 22% generalized anxiety disorders in patients affected by secondary amenorrhea, according to DSM-III criteria. In our series of 100 consecutive cases of secondary amenorrhea, a relevant psychiatric diagnosis was ascertained in 48.8%. Depressive disorder (66.6%) prevailed over anxiety disorder (4.8%). In particular, diagnosis of dysthymia was the most common (47.6%).

All these above-reported data underline that focusing stressful life events and diagnosing relevant psychopathology are essential parts in the evaluation of hypothalamic amenorrhea.

MENSTRUALLY RELATED DISORDERS (FORMERLY PREMENSTRUAL SYNDROME)

DEFINITION

The occurrence of premenstrual discomfort is a long-standing observation. According to the definition of premenstrual syndrome (PMS), somatic (bloating, migraine, breast tenderness, water retention) and psychological (upset mood, irritability, depression) symptoms start 7 to 10 days prior to menses and are cleared by menstrual flow. A proportion of women (5–10% of the Western population) experience these symptoms to a degree that disrupts normal life and depending on cultural norms, seek medical support.[38, 39] Controversies over the description of symptoms, definition of the syndrome, etiopathogenesis, and treatment make PMS one of the more discussed disorders in the psychosomatic area related to gynecology. This has led to controversies in labeling. In fact, the events included in the term *PMS* are unsatisfactory since (1) symptoms are of different origin and recognize different, still unknown pathogenesis; (2) symptoms could also be present in other periods of the cycle. The American Psychiatric Association[40] narrowed the range of symptoms pertinent to this phenomenon into the term *late luteal phase dysphoric disorder* (LLPDD). However, also this definition seems unsatisfactory in view of the reasons described above. The term *menstrually related disorders* (MRD) seems to be generally acceptable.

DIAGNOSIS

Diagnostic criteria of MRD have now found agreement among many groups: (1) symptoms should be cyclical and recurrent, with a free period at least in the follicular phase and exacerbation at ovulation, in the luteal phase, and/or in the first days of menstrual flow; (2) the fluctuations of symptoms should be prospectively confirmed for at last two cycles, using validated questionnaires; (3) the presence of a major mental or physical disorder whose symptoms exacerbate perimenstrually should not be included into MRD.

However, this last point is open to controversy on the relationships between MRD and psychic disorders.

Although one of the other DSM-III-R criteria for LLPDD states that the diagnosis should not be given if the disturbance is a mere exacerbation of the symptoms of another disorder (e.g., anxiety or mood disorder), it also notes that LLPDD may be superimposed on any of these disorders. In fact, many women seeking help for premenstrual symptoms may suffer from other psychiatric disorders which may be independent of the menstrual symptomatology, as observed by Anderson et al.[41] in a sample of 18 women with premenstrual symptoms. However, women with LLPDD have an extremely high lifetime prevalence of axis I disorders, making it very difficult to decide whether or not the premenstrual symptomatology is just a mere exacerbation of other psychiatric disorders. In fact, lifetime prevalence of major depression was found to be 70% in 86 women with prospectively confirmed LLPDD[42] and lifetime axis I diagnoses were 81% of 123 women with PMS.[43]

Attempts to exclude those patients with known current psychiatric disorders from the diagnosis of LLPDD are likely to generate a bias that favors those patients whose axis I disorder is in partial or complete remission by the time their premenstrual symptomatology is investigated. Despite the fact that Pearlstein et al.[44] excluded women with current psychiatric disorders, they found that 19 (20%) of 97 women meeting criteria for LLPDD had current psychiatric disorders. This was accomplished by using the Schedule for Affective Disorders and Schizophrenia.[45] Our group evaluated anxiety and mood disorders using the Structured Clinical Interview for DSM-III-R[40] in 32 patients with prospectively confirmed LLPDD. Our data show that current anxiety and mood disorders are very common among these patients, involving 66% of the subjects, and that this percentage is significantly higher than observed among healthy, not age-matched, female controls. In particular, anxiety disorders, either alone or with mood disorders, were present in 59% of the LLPDD patients; generalized anxiety disorder, panic disorder, and social phobia appeared to be the most common of all disorders. Neither marital status nor age were associated with these data. This finding partially concurs with a previous study by Stout et al.[43] who evaluated the lifetime prevalence rates of psychiatric diagnoses in a PMS clinic and a community sample. They found that 65% of women in the clinic had met DSM-III criteria for phobia and 16% for obsessive–compulsive disorder, with a greater frequency than women from the community. While none of the 223 women in that study were found to meet criteria for panic disorder, 8 of the 32 patients with LLPDD of our above-reported series (25%) met criteria for this disorder.

When we investigated whether patients with either anxiety or mood disorders had a different premenstrual syndrome profile as measured by the Menstrual Distress Questionnaire, we found that LLPDD patients with anxiety and/or mood disorders displayed a Menstrual Distress Questionnaire profile almost identical to that of LLPDD patients without these disorders. Although the relatively low sensitivity of the instrument used (with a small range of scoring) may account for these findings, this in fact confirms our impression that it is impossible to distinguish, purely on the basis of premenstrual symptomatology, patients with LLPDD alone from those with comorbid anxiety or mood disorders.

PATHOGENESIS

The causes leading to perimenstrual symptoms are a highly discussed matter and till now remain an unsolved problem. Several hypotheses proposed in the past tried to explain perimenstrual symptoms on the basis of increasing or decreasing patterns of peripheral hormone plasma levels.[46] Surgical castration, or, more recently, the temporary and reversible ovariectomy obtained by the chronic administration of gonadotropin-releasing hormone or its analogs[47] have demonstrated that the perimenstrual symptomatology could be completely released when ovarian function is terminated. Nevertheless, the pathophysiologic mechanisms of estrogens and progesterone in determining MRD are still unexplained. This is also because of the intrinsic difficulty of arriving at a correct evaluation of the concentrations of these substances. In fact, the estimate of a single sample is far from significant and even serial blood sampling is hidden by the spontaneous, pulsatile pattern of steroid secretion.[48] This makes the old theories about a "luteal phase defect" or a "relative hyperestrogenism" irrelevant in explaining MRD.[49]

The hypothesis that peripheral hormones condition perimenstrual symptomatology through the modulation of central nervous system activities is needed. The hypothalamus–pituitary–adrenal axis and the limbic–hypothalamic network regulate the physiological stress response and the emotional life, respectively. These are certainly the best known adaptive systems in the human and could represent a target of the ovarian steroids. Classical neurotransmitters as well as peptidergic pathways have been evaluated in subjects with MRD. Main findings are summarized in Table 19.2.

The dopaminergic system has been analyzed through radioimmunoassay of the prolactin plasma levels. These levels are significantly higher in the luteal than in the follicular phase, both in healthy women and in women with MRD.[50] The data so obtained could be explained by a higher stress responsivity (blood drawing) or by an "abnormal" steady-state of the dopaminergic tone. However, no definite results have been reached.

Moreover, the opioid tone has also underlined a hyposensitivity of the hypothalamic receptors in women with MRD. Indeed, naloxone-induced plasma LH release fails in PMS patients when tested in the luteal phase of the cycle. Such a response is modulated by ovarian secretions and represents a functional correlate between the ovary and the brain.[51] At the same time, the sensitivity of the noradrenergic presynaptic receptors decreases significantly a few days before the symptomatic period, inducing a blunted response of ß-endorphin and growth hormone plasma levels to clonidine stimulation.[52] Other studies have demonstrated "abnormal" plasma levels of several substances such as melatonin, serotonin, vasopressin, but these data neither allow any working hypothesis nor demonstrate any close correlation with the symptoms (Table 19.2).

TABLE 19.2.

Substances, Hormones, and Neurotransmitters Having Possible Pathophysiological Implication in PMS

	Demonstrated changes			Hypothesized changes
	decreased	increased	unchanged	
Substances	magnesium PGE$_2$ PGF$_{2\alpha}$ SHBG pyridoxine		SHBG	vitamin A sodium potassium
Hormones	progesterone β-endorphin	estradiol progesterone prolactin ADH	estradiol prolactin	renin angiotensin II α-MSH androgens insulin aldosterone
Neurotransmitters	dopamine endogenous opioids noradrenaline serotonin		melatonin	adrenaline acetylcholine

Changes of each compound in respect to healthy population are reported.

MRD as a Disorder of Adaptation

According to the theory of somatopsychic interactions, peri-menstrual symptoms can be explained as an "abnormal" alarm reaction triggered by physiological–supraphysiological changes (hormones, neurotransmitters). To test this hypothesis we submitted women with MRD to lactate infusion.[53] Changes in physiological variables and symptoms of panic were recorded. Two-thirds of patients with MRD developed a panic attack in response to lactate infusion while only 12% of the control population reacted in this manner. Lactate induced panic in all but 1 MRD patient affected by panic disorder. However, panic attacks were recorded in 14 other patients, half of them with PMS alone and the remnants suffering from PMS with other anxiety–mood disorders. When behavioral, cardiovascular and neuroendocrine responses to lactate were examined in patients with MRD alone, heart rate, panic and mood responses were still of higher magnitude than in controls, thus demonstrating that the increased sensitivity to lactate is a feature of the PMS population, even in the absence of comorbid psychiatric disorders. The sensitivity to lactate is related in some way to the severity of MRD, for which panickers as a whole group reported PMS scores much greater than nonpanickers. The relationships between MRD, anxiety disorders and menstrual cycle are further supported by both the increased levels of anxiety occurring pre-menstrually in patients with PMS and not in those with panic disorder,[54] and the successful control of PMS through the anxiolytic drug alprazolam.[55]

The above-described reactions to lactate thus seem to be linked to personality disorders and/or anxiety trait. Indeed, psychometric evaluations already demonstrated that women with MRD show a "neurotic personality trait" and mostly suffer from anxiety disorders.[56] Cultural beliefs play the main role in determining such traits. It is well known that attitudes toward menses and their associated phenomena are transmitted from mothers. A negative attitude or a refusal of this solid marker of feminity probably leads to anticipation of fear and stress at every menstrual cycle.

Disorders of Ferility

In this chapter, the relationship between psychology and female fertility is reviewed. Anecdotal or psychoanalytical hypotheses, however, are not included. Clinical experiences suggest that infertility is associated with important psychological stress. We will discuss which types of stress are caused by infertility, their intensity, and which types of stress interfere with infertility.

Infertility Influences Psychological Well-being

A range of more or less rational emotions and feelings were described in infertile couples. Infertile women experience themselves as frustrated, they lack self-esteem, feel less feminine, feel guilty and depressed: there is a large discrepancy between the actual and the ideal self.[57] Many infertile women feel empty, incomplete, and less desirable.[58] The feeling of loss of control over bodily processes is extremely stressful.[59] The importance of the stress associated with infertility can be estimated by the importance of infertility as a life event, by the incidence of psychiatric symptomatology in infertile couples, or by administering psychometric tests. The importance of infertility as a life event is illustrated by the finding that the incidence of suicide is doubled in infertile women.[60] Studies investigating the incidence of psychiatric symptomatology (major depressive disorder, anxiety disorder) in infertile versus fertile populations did not demonstrate significant differences.[61] Studies using psychometric tests did not demonstrate increased depression or anxiety test results.[62] The discrepancy between the clinical impression of important psychological stress and the negative psychometric test results are probably due to methodological problems. First, Haseltine et al.[63] demonstrated that infertile couples tend to present high scores on social desirability scales, which indicates high levels of repressed anxiety. Infertile couples' test results tend to be influenced by their fear of being excluded from treatment procedures. Second, most of the available studies include patients at different stages of infertility workup. Since all bereavement processes (including infertility) occur in a phasic manner, anxiety and depression levels could vary significantly with time. A study investigating the use of clomiphene citrate demonstrated that drop-out subjects presented with significantly lower neuroticism scores, suggesting another selection bias in many studies.[64] Third, most studies pool patients with different causes of infertility. Morse and Dennerstein[65] already pointed out this problem when they demonstrated that women with unexplained infertility presented higher neuroticism scores than women with mechanical infertility. Women with a luteinized unruptured follicle syndrome as well as women with luteal phase deficiency present higher trait anxiety levels than women with mechanical infertility or fertile controls.[66] Some other methodological problems should be mentioned. Most studies compare infertile women with fertile controls. Since fertility should be regarded as a variation in conception or pregnancy rates (from supernormal to subnormal, from subfertile to infertile), it seems difficult to define a pure infertile and a pure fertile group of women. An analogous remark should be made concerning the definition of normal versus abnormal psychology. Variations within the normal range already have important psychoendocrinological consequences.

PSYCHOLOGICAL INFLUENCES ON FERTILITY

The direct effect of stress on menstrual cycle has already been reported in the chapter on psychogenic amenorrhea.

There are also indirect arguments for a negative effect of stress upon fertility. In an exploratory study, Sarrel and De Cherney[67] suggested that psychotherapy dealing with pregnancy-related conflicts may affect physiological factors and thereby enhance reproductive potential in couples with unexplained infertility. Research has demonstrated that the normal variation of psychological functioning significantly influences fertility. Research including psychometric tests demonstrated that the trait anxiety level of normal fertile women predicts for 16% how fast they will conceive.[68] High trait anxious women have a lower probability of conception than low trait anxious women. In another investigation, we demonstrated that psychology significantly predicts which women conceive during in vitro fertilization (IVF) treatment.[69] Logistic regression demonstrated that the way women cope with the stress of infertility (and of the infertility treatment), i.e., active coping, avoiding and expression of emotion, as well as the (in)effectiveness of this coping, i.e., a depression score, significantly (prediction of 27%), influence pregnancy rates during IVF.[69] The most contributing factors in the prediction of well or not pregnant are the depression score and active coping, and this needs some further comment since depression and active coping are, at first glance, contradictory variables. Clinical experience learns that the psychometric variable *active coping* cannot differentiate between adaptive coping (facing a problem, looking at it from a different point of view, tackling a problem, deciding to start or stop facing a problem . . .) and maladaptive active coping (infinitely trying again even when it no longer makes sense, never deciding to stop and going on forever, which is much more in accordance with monothematic thoughts-acts found in some depressive disorders). Therefore, we called these women with high depression score and high active coping (with lower pregnancy rates during IVF) *Sisyphuslike women.* Every gynecologist recognizes patients who never give up, who would go on with treatment as long as the doctors agree, and this failing in decision making indeed is often the expression of a depressive mood change rather than of enthusiasm. The intensity of the wish for a child is no guarantee for the normality of it. A healthy wish for a child should be on the level of desire, which can include failure and resignation.

PATHWAYS FOR AN EFFECT OF STRESS ON FERTILITY

Several behavioral and/or psychoneuroendocrinological mechanisms have been suggested in the literature.

Cigarette smoking can be a stress-linked behavior and has adverse effects on fertility. Women smokers have more menstrual irregularities, a higher incidence of secondary amenorrhea, a higher incidence of vaginal infection and pelvic inflammatory disease, and they have a lower age at menopause which is a clearly demonstrated dose-related effect.[70] Associated alcohol or caffeine consumption have synergistic negative effects on fertility. The mechanism of menstrual effect of smoking is not fully understood: a nicotine-dependent increase in vasopressin alters LH-releasing activity, nicotine changes serum levels of adrenocorticotropic hormone and prolactin, nicotine and polycyclic aromatic hydrocarbons may destroy oocytes.[70]

Sexual functioning can be impaired by different levels of stress. Absence of sexual activity can be the cause of infertility.[71] An unconsummated marriage caused by female vaginism, male impotence, or both combined sometimes becomes obvious in the infertility clinic, at times only after advanced investigations and treatments. Midcycle dysfunctions, i.e., the inability to have sexual intercourse in the periovulatory period, have been described.[71] Several factors contributing to the midcycle dysfunctions were mentioned in the literature: "this is the night syndrome" (where the couple is forced to have intercourse in a specific night for fertility purposes; this may arise anxiety, e.g., "If I do not make it tonight, all the efforts will be wasted."), change in purpose of sexual intercourse, stress of clinical testing by third party, self-doubt about adequate future performance. We previously demonstrated that most couples confronted with the stress of infertility present temporary sexual problems (impaired or sometimes increased libido), but that especially in more vulnerable (neurotic) couples this results in dysfunctions.[72] Very recently, it was demonstrated that the quality of the sexual encounter could also influence the probability of conception.[73] The incidence of poor postcoital tests was found to be higher among sexually dissatisfied women than among those who were sexually satisfied. Sexual arousal and satisfaction levels were found to be significant predictors of unfavorable postcoital test results. A likely way in which sexual and physiological factors interact to affect fertility is through the impact of the vaginal environment on spermatozoa. The chemical properties of vaginal fluids that change during sexual arousal affect sperm motility and survival.[74] Sexual arousal influences the fertilization process by creating an adequate environment for sperm survival and migration to the cervical mucus. Important weight changes can be caused by psychological problems and impair fertility chances. Important underweight as well as excessive overweight are often associated with ovulatory dysfunction.[20] Even in a normal population, the deviation toward ideal body weight is significantly associated with the way women cope with daily stress.[69] Excessive physical exercise can result in ovulatory dysfunction and can be a psychopathological behavior. The prevalence of menstrual dysfunction in athletic women is reported to range up to 50%.[22] Much of the variability in published reports can be attributed to differences in the groups under study and perhaps also the level of psychological stress associated with physical exercise. For example, as many as half of the women training for, or competing in the Olympic Games were reported to have amenorrhea. Oligomenorrhea was present in 20 to 30% of long-distance runners. Recreational joggers, who may not be under the same competitive stress, have a much lower incidence of menstrual irregularity.[75] Physical exercise could well have a beneficial as well as an adverse effect on (reproductive) health depending on the intensity and on the associated psychological stress.

Psychoendocrinological Mechanisms

Psychoendocrinological stress responses also could influence fertility chances since, for example, prolactin and cortisol are essential hormones in fertility research and in stress research. It is well documented that moderate and severe hyperprolactinemia cause anovulation and amenorrhea. Recently, more subtle elevations of prolactin and even temporarily elevated prolactin levels (nocturnal, preovulatory, or early follicular) were described to affect follicular maturation, ovulation, fertilization, and corpus luteum function.[76] In most infertility clinics, there remains a group of patients (20%), the idiopathic infertile couples, in whom all generally accepted tests are negative and yet conception does not occur. Some of these women secrete prolactin in an unusual manner: they present "spikes" of prolactin and pregnancy rates are smaller in this subgroup.[77] It was also shown that it is difficult to diagnose reliably moderate hyperprolactinemia because of the frequent occurrence of stress hyperprolactinemia.[78] Daytime noise stress increases nocturnal prolactin levels, for example, and this could be important since it was also demonstrated that women with unexplained infertility as well as women with endometriosis have increased nocturnal prolactin levels.[79] The careful investigation of stress responses demonstrated that prolactin is moderately sensitive to anticipatory arousal: prolactin anticipatory release is more important in higher trait anxious women.[80] Moreover, specific coping mechanisms significantly predict prolactin concentrations during the stressful experience of IVF, women with a high avoiding and with a low palliative coping have higher prolactin levels during stress.[81] These higher prolactin levels were found in women with endometriosis, luteal phase deficiency, or luteinized unruptured follicle syndrome, but these prolactin levels did not influence the outcome of IVF significantly. It was suggested that prolactin is a relative psychoendocrinological barrier against conception: prolactin disturbs spontaneous cycles but IVF overcomes this barrier.[69]

The hypothalamo–pituitary–adrenal axis also affects fertility: a direct gonadal effect of corticoid hormones, a corticosteroid-mediated decrease in pituitary responsiveness to gonadotropin-releasing hormone, and a centrally mediated inhibition of gonadotropin-releasing hormone were described.[28]

For IVF cycles, follicular fluid cortisol levels were found to be higher in stimulated than in spontaneous cycles and they negatively influence fertilization rates.[82] The careful investigation of stress responses demonstrated that cortisol is very sensitive to anticipatory arousal.[80] Moreover, specific psychological features significantly predict cortisol concentrations during the stressful experience of IVF: women with a high depression score and high active coping (Sisyphuslike women) present high anticipatory cortisol concentrations.[81] These high anticipatory cortisol levels negatively influence the outcome of IVF. It was suggested that cortisol is a more absolute psychoendocrinological barrier against conception: even the invasive procedure of IVF does not overcome the cortisol barrier.[69]

Infertility influences the psychological functioning of the woman (and of the couple), and the psychological stress of the woman significantly influences her fertility. Behavioral and psychoendocrinological pathways play an important role. An integrated model of how these factors could affect fertility is reported in Figure 19.1. An unfulfilled wish for a child is a stressful life event for each couple and its specific personal, relational, and transgenerational context will determine the intensity of this stressor (primary appraisal). Moreover, each couple will handle this stress differently, depending on their usual coping style (secondary appraisal). The interaction between this primary and secondary appraisal will thus result in a definite level of effectiveness of coping (e.g., depression score). These different levels of psychological functioning influence fertility through psychoendocrinological stress responses. Even normal variations of psychological functioning and of endocrinological levels significantly influence fertility. These findings invite the gynecologist and the couple to face infertility as a psychobiological unit not (yet) ready for conception rather than as a disease, and to face it in a couple-specific psychoendocrinological context (open system).

CLIMACTERIC SYNDROME

Approaching the time of menopause, the so-called climacterium, many women experience the onset of several discomforts. However, the description of these symptoms do not allow us to ascribe one or more of them specifically to the secession of reproductive activity. Indeed, mood disorders, urogenital problems, and vasomotor instability have been described also in other periods of life, specifically during the reproductive years, e.g., MRD.

Therefore, the definition of the climacteric syndrome is not clear and univocal. Hot flashes are a common symptom associated with menopause, being the most distressing one. Seventy-five percent of postmenopausal women seeking medical consultation have hot

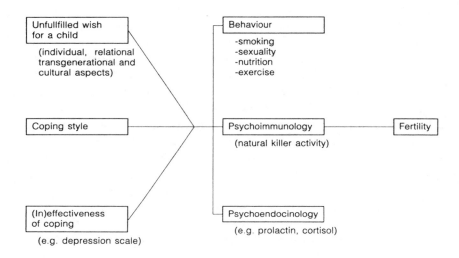

Figure 19.1 Coping Ineffectiveness of Coping and Fertility: An Integrated Model.

flashes. This symptom occurs more frequently at night, often disrupts sleep, and interferes with social activity. In addition, hot flashes are correlated with sweating and other psychosomatic complaints, in particular "feeling tense" and "insomnia," whereas no relationships are present with other somatic, urogenital, and sexual complaints.[83]

The poor definition of climacteric syndrome thus makes it difficult to validate an instrument for measuring symptoms in climacteric women. The best study of a uniform menopausal index is Greene's,[84] which divided the climacteric symptoms into vasomotor, somatic, and psychological (anxiety and depression). On the other hand, Jaszmann et al.[85] defined symptoms as genital or extragenital and Holte et al.[86] divided them into vague somatic complaints, nervousness, mood lability, vasomotor, and urogenital complaints. Collecting all the above data, we believe that symptoms could be divided into two groups: menopause-dependent on

TABLE 19.3
Classification of Climacteric Symptoms with Respect to Their Correlation with Estrogen Failure

Estrogen dependent
Hot flushes
Sweating
Vaginal dryness
Tension-type headache
Stress incontinence

Age dependent
Back pain
Paresthesia
Clinical depression
Cognitive disorders
Loss of libido

Possibly estrogen dependent,
but requiring further studies
Migraine
Dizzyness
Urinary frequency
Upsetting mood
Irritability
Loss of interest
Low self-esteem
Insomnia
Early awakening
Decreased concentration
Increased appetite
Overweight

There is still the need to further studies in order to ascertain if mood disorders pertain to climacteric syndrome.

one hand and age-dependent on the other (Table 19.3). A wide list of symptoms still remain to be classified in one of the above classes and mood disorders are among them.

SOMATIC SYMPTOMS

Many symptoms have been anecdotally ascribed to menopause occurrence, such as changes in sexual behavior and headaches. The physical changes of the genital tissues in estrogen-deprived postmenopausal women lead to symptoms such as burning, dispareunia, and vaginal dryness. Moreover, menopause is a predisposing factor to urinary incontinence. In fact, this symptom is present in a quarter of the population. Besides menopause, previous pelvic surgery and vaginal childbirth are other factors accounting for it.[87] Certainly, estrogen deprivation leads to a pronounced bacteria colonization of the urogenital tract inducing recurrent cystitis: in fact, local hormone treatment reverses this condition.[88] However, the hormonal interpretation is not fully satisfactory and urinary problems at menopause may be referred to a biopsychosocial model.

Traditional assumptions about menopausal women suggest that the above-reported findings induce a deterioration in both sexual interest and activity. At menopause, sexual activity declines among many couples.[89] Whether this problem is related to the decrease in sexual female responsiveness and satisfaction or to the male availability and interest remain to be established. Recent evidence suggests that menopause is really accompanied by a decrease in sexual activity and that there is a real decrease in coital frequency in this period of life.[90] The coital frequency, however, is not necessarily correlated with sexual desire and it is inadequate as a measure of sexual activity. On the other hand, Telinde[91] first drew attention to the importance of the sexual and interpersonal dimension in women complaining of pelvic relaxation and sexual problems. In fact, he states: "in our experience, the problem is rarely due to a local condition, but rather to marital problems."[91] More recently, Bachmann,[92] evaluating 59 women with a mean age of 63 years, found that many continued to engage in sexual intercourse and noted a positive relationship between sexual desire and marital adjustment. It therefore seems that reduction in sexual activity at menopause remains an open problem. Another controversial issue is the role played by the menopause on the course of primary headaches. Confusions arose from the fact that no strict diagnostic criteria were used to define head pain. In a recent study of our group, headache has been found only in the 13.7% of a general population of women who had been menopausal for 2 years.[93] Menopause seems to act differently on the various headache types: it relieves migraine but worsens tension-type headache. Moreover, surgical menopause induces a definite worsening of both headache forms. Looking for correlations between headache and other menopausal complaints using the Kuppermann Index, shows no correlations with somatic symptoms, but a strong one with anxiety and insomnia. This correlation was more prominent with tension-type headache, a headache form that is influenced by the psychic status. In spite of migraine, tension-type headache could really be considered as a climacteric complaint.

MOOD AT MENOPAUSE

The issue of psychological symptoms at menopause is still debated. A review of the literature revealed that cross-sectional studies are unconclusive in this respect. Hunter, in a longitudinal study, demonstrated a small but significant increase of depressed mood in women becoming postmenopausal.[94] However, she indicated that "depression together with cognitive and social factors accounted for 51% of the variance." In a study on general population, both in men and women, it was concluded that a peak of prevalence for psychiatric symptoms occurs just before the mean age of menopause.[95] This finding also agrees with the conclusion of Jaszmann et al.[85] and thus seems to disconfirm possible effects of menopause on affective disorders.

Goldberg,[96] using the General Health Questionnaire, found an increase in depressed mood which was mainly linked to irritability and absence of reward for daily life activities. Similar conclusions were drawn by Ballinger[97] who noticed, however, an increase in anxiety and depression in the women seeking medical help in respect to the general population. She therefore attributes psychological discomfort at menopause to the distress of those women as measured by the increase in negative life events. Despite the fact that the number of life events (mainly exits) did not differ between menopause clinical patients and nonpatients, the former reported a higher negative impact of the life event and reacted with more depressive symptoms.[98] Such negative reaction may be associated to neurotic trait which in turn influences coping behavior. We believe that the evaluation of coping strategies would be the right key to understand the psychological symptoms and the reaction toward somatic symptoms experienced at the menopause. In a preliminary study, we evaluated coping strategies using De Utrechtse Coping List UCL.[69] Such behavior was correlated to affective state in a group of postmenopausal patients seeking medical help. The results indicate that depression scores could be explained through the conditioning of a palliative coping and the inadequacy which originate from depressive coping in the presence of hot flushes. In other words, menopausal symptoms became the origin of the depression only in the presence of a particular coping strategy on the part of the individual (manuscript in preparation). These data indicate that the women with a depressive coping are unable to develop cognitive strategies in respect to biological and social changes occurring at menopause.

Gitlin and Pasnau[99] reviewed the psychiatric syndromes linked to reproductive life. In the past, psychiatry recognized two different types of syndromes associated with the menopause: involutional melancholia and posthysterectomy depression. Longitudinal studies have assessed that the prevalence of depressive disorders is not linked to the loss of reproductive function, while it seems linked to age.[100] In particular, milder psychiatric syndromes seemed to occur in the years preceding the mean age of menopause which, in Western countries, is around 50. On the other hand, the so-called "posthysterectomy depression" recognized by Lindeman[101] does not exist in actual nosology. Indeed, several studies demonstrate that the presence of psychiatric disorders in women undergoing surgical menopause is related to the preoperative psychopathology rather than surgery in itself. On the contrary, a follow-up study in women submitted to hysterectomy show a reduction rather than an increase of psychopathology.[102]

HORMONE REPLACEMENT TREATMENT

The interest of researchers was focused on the possible effects of hormone replacement treatment (HRT; mainly estrogens) on the mood of postmenopausal women. Despite an undefined "mental tonic effect" that estrogens are supposed to display,[103] not much literature exists on this topic.

In several experimental conditions, it has been demonstrated that estrogens are potent neuromodulators, affecting the function of various neurotransmitters, namely serotonin, dopamine, and endogenous opioids. In particular, HRT restores central and peripheral ß-endorphin levels in castrated rats as well as in postmenopausal women, together with an improvement of symptoms.[104]

In a group of oophorectomized women, a prospective study demonstrated that either estrogens or androgens are able to reduce the score of depression which rose again after treatment withdrawal. Placebo was uneffective, thus supporting the specific hormonal effects.[105] Similar results were also reported by other groups confirming that both depression[106] and anxiety[107] at menopause could benefit from HRT. However, it seems that the addition of progestogens to estrogen treatments attenuates the positive effects on mood reported by estrogens alone.[107, 108]

Whether psychological improvement is directly related to hormonal effects or whether it represents a secondary consequence of the somatic well-being (hot flushes and vaginal dryness disappearance) induced by HRT is still an open question. A recent study done by Ditkoff et al.[109] reported that estrogens improve depression scores also in postmenopausal women free of somatic symptoms. These findings therefore suggest the existence of a direct, specific effect exerted by estrogens on mood and well-being perception in postmenopausal women.

References

1. Whitacre FE, Barrera B. War amenorrhea. *J Am Med Assn.* 1944;124:339–344.
2. Sydenham A. Amenorrhea at Stanly Camp, Hong Kong, during internement. *Br Med J.* 1946;2:159–165.
3. Fremont-Smith M, Meigs J. Menstrual dysfunction due to emotional factors. *Am J Obstet Gynecol.* 1948;55:1037–1046.
4. Loeser A. Emotional shock on hormone release and endometrial development. *Lancet.* 1943;i:518–523.
5. Refeinstein EC Jr. Psychogenic or "hypothalamic" amenorrhea. *Med Clin North Am.* 1946;30:1103–1115.
6. Rheingold JD. *The Fear of Being a Woman.* New York: Grune & Stratton; 1964.
7. Bental E, Sharf B, Sharf M, Kuziminsky T. Electroencephalographic changes in anovulatory cycle. *EEG Clin Neurophysiol.* 1969;27:216–221.
8. Holmberg NG, Nylander I. Weight loss in secondary amenorrhea. *Acta Obstet Gynecol Scand.* 1971;50:241–246.
9. Mozley PD. Forced femininity: Opening Pandora's box. *Obstet Gynecol.* 1969;4:414–417.
10. Rosenkotten L, Boor C, Ederly Z, Matthes J. Psychoanalytische Untersuchungen von Patientinnen mit funktioneller Amenorrhö. *Arch Gynaekol.* 1961;207:92–93.
11. Deutsch H. *The Psychology of Women.* New York: Grune & Stratton; 1944:1; 1945:2.
12. Benedek TF. Sexual functions in women and their disturbance. In: Arieti S, ed. *American Handbook of Psychiatry.* New York: Basic Books;1959.
13. Menninger K. Somatic correlations with unconscious repudiation of femininity in women. *J Nerv Ment Dis.* 1939;89:514–517.
14. Kelley K, Daniels G, Poe J, Eassen E, Monroe R. Psychological correlations with secondary amenorrhea. *Psychosom Med.* 1954;16:129–132.
15. Sainsurg B. Neurosis and psychosomatic disorders in outpatients. *Adv Psychosom Med.* 1960;1:259–269.
16. Fioroni L, Facchinetti F, Cerutti G, Nappi G, Genazzani AR. Personality traits in secondary amenorrhea. *J Psychosom Obstet Gynecol.* 1991;11:67–76.
17. Osofsky H, Fisher S. Psychological correlates of the development of amenorrhea in a stress situation. *Psychosom Med.* 1967;29:15–23.
18. Russel G. Premenstrual tension and "psychogenic" amenorrhea: Psychophysical interaction. *J Psychosom Res.* 1972;16:279–287.
19. Frisch RE, McArthur JW. Menstrual cycles: Fatness as a determinant of minimum weight for height necessary for their maintenance or onset. *Science.* 1974,185:949–954.
20. Vigersky BA, Andersen AE, Thompson RH, et al. Hypothalamic dysfunction in secondary amenorrhea associated with simple weight loss. *N Engl J Med.* 1977;297:1141–1153.
21. Gadpaille WJ, Sanborn CF, Wagner W Jr. Athletic amenorrhea, major affective disorders, and eating disorders. *Am J Psychiatry.* 1987;144:939–945.

22. Smith CG, Asch RH. Drug abuse and reproduction. *Fertil Steril.* 1987;48: 355–367.

23. Berga SL, Girton LG. The psychoneuroendocrinology of functional hypothalamic amenorrhea. *Psychiatr Clin North Am.* 1989;12:105–116.

24. Diedrichs P. The personality structure of women with secondary amenorrhea. In: Carenza L, Zichella L, eds. *Emotion and Reproduction.* London: Academic Press;1979: pp 133–136.

25. Ross GT, Van de Wiele RL. The ovaries. In: Williams RH, ed. *Textbook of Endocrinology.* Philadelphia: Saunders;1981: pp 355–399.

26. Knobil E, Natchiss J. The menstrual cycle and its neuroendocrine control. In: Knobil E, Neil JD, eds. *The Physiology of Human Reproduction.* New York: Raven Press;1988: pp 1971–1994.

27. Rivier C, Rivier J, Vale W. Stress-induced inhibition of reproductive functions: Role of endogenous corticotropin-releasing factor. *Science.* 1986;291: 607–618.

28. Khoury SA, Reame NE. Diurnal patterns of pulsatile luteinizing hormone secretion in hypothalamic amenorrhea: Reproducibility and response to opiate blockade and an alpha-2-adrenergic agonist. *J Clin Endocrinol Metab.* 1987;64:755–764.

29. Petraglia F, Porro C, Facchinetti F, Cicoli C, Bertelli E, Volpe A, Barbieri GC, Genazzani AR. Opioid control of LH secretion in humans: Menstrual cycle, menopause and aging reduce effect of naloxone but not of morphine. *Life Sci.* 1986;38:2103–2110.

30. Biller BMK, Federoff HJ, Koenig JI, Klibanski A. Abnormal cortisol secretion and responses to corticotropin-releasing hormone in women with hypothalamic amenorrhea. *J Clin Endocrinol Metab.* 1990;70:311–317.

31. Genazzani AD, Petraglia F, Fabbri G, Monzani A, Montanini V, Genazzani AR. Evidence of luteinizing hormone secretion in hypothalamic amenorrhea associated with weight loss. *Fertil Steril.* 1990;54:222–226.

32. Quigley ME, Sheehan KL, Casper RF, Yen SSC. Evidence for increased dopaminergic and opioid activity in patients with hypothalamic hypogonadotropic amenorrhea. *J Clin Endocrinol Metab.* 1980;50:949–957.

33. Berga SL, Mortola JF, Yen SSC. Amplification of nocturnal melatonin secretion in women with functional hypothalamic amenorrhea. *J Clin Endocrinol Metab.* 1988;66:242–255.

34. Fries H, Nillius SJ, Pettersson F. Epidemiology of secondary amenorrhea: A retrospective evaluation of etiology with regard to psychogenic factors and weight loss. *Am J Obstet Gynecol.* 1974;118:473–486.

35. Stracham GL, Skottowe I. Menstruation and the menopause in menstrual disease. *Lancet.* 1933;i:1058–1061.

36. Gregory BAJC. The menstrual cycle and its disorders in psychiatric patients. *J Psychosom Res.* 1957;2:199–244.

37. Fava G, Trombini G, Grandi S, Bernardi M, Pasquali Evangelisti L, Santarsiero G, Orlandi C. Depression and anxiety associated with secondary amenorrhea. *Psychosomatics.* 1984;25:905–908.

38. Reid RL, Yen SSC. Premenstrual syndrome. *Am J Obstet Gynecol.* 1981;85: 139–148.

39. O'Brien PMS. The premenstrual syndrome. *J Reprod Med.* 1985;30:113–126.

40. American Psychiatric Association. *Diagnostic and Statistical Manual of Mental Disorders.* 3rd ed. rev. Washington, DC: American Psychiatric Association; 1987.
41. Anderson M, Severino SK, Hurt SW, Williams NA. Premenstrual syndrome research: Using the NIMH guidelines. *J Clin Psychiatry.* 1988;49:484–486.
42. Harrison WM, Endicott J, Nee J, Glick H, Rabkin IG. Characteristics of women seeking treatment for premenstrual syndrome. *Psychosomatic.* 1989; 30:405–411.
43. Stout AL, Steege JF, Blazer DG, George LK. Comparison of lifetime psychiatric diagnoses in premenstrual syndrome clinic and community samples. *J Nerv Ment Dis.* 1986;174:517–522.
44. Pearlstein TB, Frank E, Rivera-Tovar A, Thoft JS, Jacobs E, Mieczkowsky TA. Prevalence of axis I and axis II disorders in women with late luteal phase dysphoric disorder. *J Affective Disord.* 1990;20:129–134.
45. Endicott J, Spitzer RL. A diagnostic interview: The Schedule for Affective Disorders and Schizophrenia. *Arch Gen Psychiatry.* 1978;35:837–844.
46. Rubinow DR, Byrne PR. Premenstrual syndrome: Overview from a methodologic perspective. *Am J Psychiatry.* 1984;141:163–176.
47. Muse KN, Cetel NS, Futterman LA, Yen SSC. The premenstrual syndrome, effects of medical ovariectomy. *N Engl J Med.* 1984;311:1345–1347.
48. Facchinetti F, Genazzani AD, Martignoni E, Fioroni L, Sances G, Genazzani AR. Neuroendocrine correlates of premenstrual syndrome: Changes in the pulsatile pattern of plasma LH. *Psychoneuroendocrinology.* 1990;4:269–277.
49. Dalton K. Premenstrual syndrome. *Br Med J.* 1980;137:1–4.
50. Carroll BJ, Steiner M. The psychobiology of premenstrual dysphoria: The role of prolactin. *Psychoneuroendocrinology.* 1978;3:171–179.
51. Facchinetti F, Nappi G, Petraglia F, Volpe A, Genazzani AR. Estradiol/ progesterone imbalance and the premenstrual syndrome. *Lancet.* 1983;ii:1302.
52. Facchinetti F, Martignoni E, Nappi G, Fioroni L, Sances G, Genazzani AR. Premenstrual failure of alpha-adrenergic stimulation on hypothalamus–pituitary response in menstrual migraine. *Psychosom Med.* 1989;51:550–558.
53. Facchinetti F, Romano G, Fava M, Genazzani AR. Lactate infusion induces panic attacks in patients with premenstrual syndrome. *Psychosom Med.* 1992; 54:288–296.
54. Stein MB, Schmidt PJ, Rubinow DR, Uhde TW. Panic disorder and the menstrual cycle: Panic disorder patients, healthy control subjects, and patients with premenstrual syndrome. *Am J Psychiatry.* 1989;146:1299–1303.
55. Smith S, Rinehart JS, Ruddock VE, Schiff I. Treatment of premenstrual syndrome with alprazolam: Results of a double-blind, placebo-controlled, randomized cross-over clinical trial. *Obstet Gynecol.* 1987;70:37–43.
56. Taylor JW. Psychological factors in the aetiology of premenstrual symptoms. *Aust NZ J Psychiatry.* 1979;13:35–41.
57. Kraft A, Palomobo J, Mitchell D, Dean C, Meyers S, Schidt A. The psychological dimensions of infertility. *Am J Orthopsychiatry.* 1980;50:618–628.
58. Freeman EW, Garcia C, Rickels K. Behavioral and emotional factors: Comparisons of anovulatory infertile women with fertile and other infertile women. *Fertil Steril.* 1983;40:195–201.

59. Mahlstedt PP, Macduff S, Verstein J. Emotional factors and the in vitro fertilization and embryo transfer process. *J In Vitro Fertil Embryo Transfer.* 1987;4:232–236.
60. Mai F, Monday R, Rum E. Psychiatric interview comparisons between infertile and fertile couples. *Psychosom Med.* 1972;34:430–440.
61. Downey J, Yingling S, McKinney M, Husami N, Jewelewics R, Maidman J. Mood disorders, psychiatric symptoms and distress in women presenting for infertility evaluation. *Fertil Steril.* 1989;52:425–432.
62. Hearn MT, Yuzpe AA, Brow SE, Caspar RF. Psychological characteristics of an in vitro fertilization participant. *Am J Obstet Gynecol.* 1987;156:269–274.
63. Haseltine FP, Mazure C, De L'Aune W, et al. Psychological interviews in screening couples undergoing in vitro fertilization. *Ann NY Acad Sci.* 1985; 442:504–520.
64. Garcia CR, Freeman EW, Rickels K, et al. Behavioral and emotional factors and treatment responses in a study of anovulatory infertile women. *Fertil Steril.* 1985;44:478–483.
65. Morse C, Dennerstein L. Infertile couples entering an in vitro fertilization program: A preliminary survey. *J Psychosom Obstet Gynecol.* 1985;4:207–219.
66. Nijis P, Koninckx PR, Verstraeten D, Mullens A, Nicazy H. Psychological factors of female infertility. *Eur J Obstet Gynecol Reprod Biol.* 1984;18:375–379.
67. Sarrel PM, De Cherney AH. Psychotherapeutic intervention for treatment of couples with secondary infertility. *Fertil Steril.* 1985;43:897–900.
68. Demyttenaere K, Nijis P, Oteeno O, Konicka PR, Evers-Kiebooms G. Anxiety and conception rates in donor insemination. *J Psychosom Obstet Gynaecol.* 1988;8:175–181.
69. Demyttenaere K, Nijis P, Evers-Kiebooms G, Koninckx PR. Personality characteristics influence the outcome of in vitro fertilization through psycho-endocrinological stress responses. *Psychoneuroendocrinology.* In press.
70. Weisberg E. Smoking and reproductive health. *Clin Reprod Fertil.* 1985;3:175–186.
71. Drake TS, Grunert GM. A cyclic pattern of sexual dysfunction in the infertility investigation. *Fertil Steril.* 1979;32:542–545.
72. Demyttenaere K, Ramon W, Nijis P. Sexual dysfunctions in IVF women: A perinatal risk for the psychosexual development of the coming child. *Int J Prenat Perinat Stud.* 1989;1:187–193.
73. Boivin J. *The Role of Psychosexual Factors in Postcoital Test Results.* Montreal: Concordia University;1990. Thesis.
74. Wagner G, Levin R. Human vaginal pH and sexual arousal. *Fertil Steril.* 1984;41:389–394.
75. Garner PR. The effect of body weight on menstrual function. *Curr Probl Obstet Gynecol.* 1984;7:1.
76. Ben-David J, Schenker JG. Transient hyperprolactinemia: A correctable cause of idiopathic female infertility. *J Clin Endocrinol Metab.* 1983;57:442–444.
77. Harrison RF, O'Moore RR, McSweeney J. Stress, prolactin and infertility. *Lancet.* 1979;i:209.
78. Koninckx PR. Stress hyperprolactinemia in clinical practice. *Lancet.* 1978;i:273.
79. Fruhstorfer B, Fruhstorfer H, Grass P, Milersky HG. Daytime noise stress and subsequent night sleep: Interference with sleep pattern, endocrine and neurocrine functions. *Int J Neurosci.* 1985;26:301–308.

80. Demyttenaere K, Nijis P, Evers-Kiebooms G, Koninckx PR. The effect of a specific emotional stressor on prolactin, cortisol, and testosterone concentrations in women varies with their trait anxiety. *Fertil Steril.* 1989;6:942–948.
81. Demyttenaere K, Nijis P, Evers-Kiebooms G, Koninckx PR. Coping, ineffectiveness of coping and the psychoendocrinological stress responses during in-vitro fertilization. *J Psychosom Res.* 1991;35:231–243.
82. Fateh M, Ben-Rafael Z, Benadiva CA. Cortisol levels in human follicular fluid. *Fertil Steril.* 1989;51:538–541.
83. Oldenhave A, Jaszmann LJB. The climacteric: Absence or presence of hot flushes and their relation to other complaints. In: Zichella L, Whitehead M, Van Keep PA, eds. *The Climacteric Hot Flushes.* Prog Basic Clin Pharmacol. Basel: Karger;1991:6: pp 6–39.
84. Greene JG. A factor analytic study of climacteric symptoms. *J Psychosom Res.* 1976;20:425–436.
85. Jaszmann L, van Lith ND, Zatt JCA. The perimenopausal symptoms: The statistical analysis of a survey. Part A and B. *Med Gynaecol Sociol.* 1969;4:268–275.
86. Holte A, Mikkelsen A. The menopausal syndrome: A factor analytic replication. *Maturitas.* 1991;13:191–203.
87. Rud T. Urogenital problems. In: Zichella L, Whitehead M, Van Keep PA, eds. *The Climacteric and Beyond.* London: Parthenon;1991: pp 145–153.
88. Hilton P, Stanton SL. The use of intravaginal oestrogen cream in genuine stress incontinence. *Br J Obstet Gynaecol.* 1983;4:940–944.
89. Hallstrom T. Sexuality in the climacteric. *Clin Obstet.* 1977;4:227–234.
90. Iddenden DA. Sexuality during the menopause. *Med Clin North Am.* 1987; 71:87–89.
91. Telinde RW. *Operative Gynecology.* 3rd ed. Philadelphia: Lippincott;1962: pp 244–265.
92. Bachmann GA. Correlates of sexual desire in postmenopausal women. *Maturitas.* 1985;7:211–217.
93. Neri I, Granella F, Nappi R, Manzoni GC, Facchinetti F, Genazzani AR. Features of headache at menopause: A clinicoepidemiologic study. *Maturitas.* In press.
94. Hunter M. Somatic experience of the menopause: A prospective study. *Psychosom Med.* 1990;52:357–367.
95. Barlow DH, Brockie JA, Rees CMP. Study of general practice consultations and menopausal problems. *Br Med J.* 1991;302:274–280.
96. Goldberg D. *The Detection of Psychiatric Illness by Questionnaire.* London: Oxford University Press;1972.
97. Ballinger SE. Psychosocial stress and symptoms of menopause: A comparative study of menopause clinic patients and nonpatients. *Maturitas.* 1985;7: 315–324.
98. Veeninga AT, Kraaimaat. Life stress and symptoms in menopause clinic patients and non-patients. *J Psychosom Obstet Gynaecol.* 1989;10:269–275.
99. Gitlin MJ, Pasnau RO. Psychiatric syndromes linked to reproductive function in women: A review of current knowledge. *Am J Psychiatry.* 1989;11: 146–153.
100. Weissman MM. The myth of involutional melancholia. *J Am Med Assn.* 1979;242:742–744.

101. Lindemann E. Observations on psychiatric sequelae to surgical operations in women. *Am J Psychiatry.* 1941;98:132–137.
102. Gath D, Cooper P, Bond A, et al. Hysterectomy and psychiatric disorder. II. Demographic, psychiatric and physical factors in relation to psychiatric outcome. *Br J Psychiatry.* 1982;140:343–350.
103. Utian WH. The mental tonic effect of estrogens administered to oophorectomized females. *S Afr Med J.* 1972;46:1979–1982.
104. Genazzani AR, Petraglia F, Facchinetti F, Genazzani AD, Bergamaschi M, Grasso A, Volpe A. Effects of Org OD 14 on pituitary and peripheral ß-endorphin in castrated rats and postmenopausal women. *Maturitas.* 1987; 7(suppl 1):35–48.
105. Sherwin BB, Gelfand MM. Sex steroids and affect in the surgical menopause: A double-blind, cross-over study. *Psychoneuroendocrinology.* 1985;10:325–335.
106. Campbell S. Double-blind psychometric studies on the effects of natural oestrogens on postmenopausal women. In: Campbell S, ed. *The Management of the Menopause and Postmenopausal Years.* Lancaster, U.K.: MTP Press;1976.
107. Dennerstein L, Burrows G. Psychological effects of progestogens in the postmenopausal years. *Maturitas.* 1986;8:101–106.
108. Holst J, Backstrom T, Hammarback S, Von Schoultz B. Progestogen addition during oestrogen replacement therapy effect on vasomotor symptoms and mood. *Maturitas.* 1989;11:13–20.
109. Ditkoff EC, Crary WG, Cristo M, Lobo AR. Estrogen improves psychological function in asymptomatic postmenopausal women. *Obstet Gynecol.* 1991;78: 991–995.

Chapter 20
Psychosomatic Medicine and Otorhinolaryngology

Ulrich Lamparter, Hans-Ulrich Schmidt

The Relevance
of Psychosomatic Medicine
in Otorhinolaryngology

The personal relationship between Sigmund Freud and the Berlin otorhinolaryngologist Wilhelm Fliess represented the initially close union between otorhinolaryngologic medicine and psychologic medicine with its rapid development since the beginning of the 20th century. But in the following period, the two specialties went separate ways. In the German-speaking countries, Lüscher[1] was the first to give a synopsis of psychosomatic aspects in otorhinolaryngology. As early as 1959, he stressed that inflammative diseases with demarcated foci as well as specific inflammations (lues, tuberculosis) had almost completely lost their practical relevance. At the same time he described a higher proportion of "functional disorders" like dysphagia or impaired voice and an undoubted increase in psychogenic disorders.

Today, ear, nose, and throat diseases have, with few exceptions, not yet been investigated continuously and systematically in terms

425

of their psychosomatic aspects. Thus, otorhinolaryngology owes its progress mainly to enormously refined diagnostic and operative techniques, whereas the functional or psychosomatic disorders of the ear, nose, and throat (ENT) are much less important in the research programs of university clinics. Nevertheless, according to Hoffmann,[2] two-thirds of the ENT patients suffer from psychogenic disorders. Especially in otorhinolaryngology, the time spent on anamnesis has been abbreviated in favor of a quick inspection. This shows the practical consequences of a research tradition which is mainly technically and instrumentally oriented. Such an abbreviated anamnesis increases the emotional resistance and the avoidance of conflicts by the patient, especially in functional disorders.[2]

The so far inadequate integration of psychosomatic medicine into otorhinolaryngology could also be caused by elements of the history of science. Early psychosomatic theories mainly related to the mechanism of "conversion" as an explanatory principle— the interpretation of symptoms was often based on the assumption of sexual conflict, a "shift from below to above"—but this could not explain all disorders of psychosomatic origin. The characteristics of ENT were seen as symbolic expressions, but their physiologic role was neglected. On the other hand, the extreme of overly organ-centered psychosomatic concepts (e.g., "nose reflex neurosis") represented the classic case of an organocentric misunderstanding (as if the nose was responsible for everything) of complex psychosomatic interrelations and was therefore rejected as obsolete.

Today, other attempts and explanations such as behavior equivalent, affect equivalent, conditioning, etc., provide an ample selection of psychopathogenetic concepts. What we know about the pathogenesis of functional disorders has come via psychophysiologic investigations. ENT are increasingly considered to be "border organs" responsible for communication with the outside world; therefore, their dysfunctions represent an incompatibility on the part of the patient to environmental conditions which are difficult to differentiate and are partly subjectively, partly objectively harmful.

THE NOSE

The sense of smell is—besides hearing and the tactile functions—one of the phylogenetically oldest sensory functions of the human being. Via connections with the thalamus, hypothalamus, and the limbic system, olfactory impressions lead to strong emotional stimulation. An example for this procedure is the activation of so-called early recollections, similar to phenomena caused by sound impressions. Numerous reflexes originating from the nose (nasocardial, nasoocular, nasopulmonal reflex) point to a close functional association with other organs and large parts of the autonomous nerve system.

PSYCHOSOMATIC PROBLEMS ASSOCIATED WITH THE SHAPE OF THE NOSE

The outer shape of the nose is significant for facial expression and therefore the nose becomes a partly conscious, partly unconscious symbol for its "owner." Conflicts regarding old age and loneliness, but above all conflicts regarding self-acceptance can focus on the shape of the nose and develop into hypochondria. Corrective surgery may not satisfy such a patient who may want the surgeon to redo the work. On the other hand, it has been observed that an originally satisfying surgical result can aggravate a depressive state. This paradox can be explained by the loss of the self-regulation mechanism—"if only I had another nose, everything would be different"—when the operation indeed did not change anything apart from the shape of the nose. Brunswick's[3] impressive description of the nose neurosis of the "Wolf Man" in 1926 provides a deep insight into the psychodynamics and the doctor–patient relation of this disorder. But there are, without doubt, patients who understandably suffer from the shape of their nose and the resulting objective changes of facial expression. They can be helped effectively by cosmetic surgery. It should be taken into account that somatic diseases (Wegner's disease, lues III, lupus erythematosus) can also lead to—mostly necrotic—changes in the nasal bones. In these cases, social stigmatization can occur; this also happens in persons with rhinophyma, caused by an alcohol-related hyperplasia of sebaceous glands and connective tissue.

ACUTE RHINITIS

Acute rhinitis as found in the common cold has so far rarely been the subject of systematic psychosomatic investigations. It is nevertheless a general experience that colds often happen after a stressful event or that they act as "psychosomatic valves" for suppressed regressive desires. If patients are sufficiently introspective, they often know the reason why they caught a cold. Lüscher[1] pointed out that it is difficult to differentiate between a disorder of the mucous membrane caused by viruses or bacteria and a hypersensitivity rhinopathia. He postulates frequent combinations, but mentions several publications which suggest a connection between emotional factors and the manifestation of rhinitis.[4,5] Saul[5] found that 15 of 60 psychoanalytically treated patients had frequent colds at the beginning of treatment, whereas this problem had practically disappeared by the end of the therapy. Kohut[6] stressed an important aspect regarding the interrelation between narcissistic offense and "cold"; in his opinion, the human ability to keep a constant body temperature is a fundamental regulative mode of the basic homeostasis of the "self." A threat or shock to this central psychic regulative system[7] seems to be able to cause "colds."

In a recently published study, Cohen and Tyrell[8] investigated the effect of "stress" on an outbreak of an infection of the respiratory tract. For this purpose, 394 healthy persons received rhinotropic viruses. They were asked about the "stress level" in their lives both in the past year and shortly before the examination. Cohen found a linear correlation between respiratory infections and clinically manifest colds on the one hand and previous stress situations on the other. Gay and Blager[9] did not find systematic studies on the connection between psychic factors and the development of acute rhinitis in adults. Regarding rhinitis in childhood, they report obvious psychic factors causative of colds, as well as a marked secondary epinosic gain. The children did not have an allergic disposition. These results were achieved by a meta-analysis of 53 cases described in the literature[10–15] and by the observation of four of their own patients.

CHRONIC RHINOPATHIA ("RHINITIS")

The conchae, which are a vegetatively innervated cavernous body, provide various ways of interaction with the airstream. Especially the temperature, but also the humidification of the inhaled air is regulated by the intensity of blood flow through the conchae. A parasympathetic innervation leads to a swelling of the nasal mucous membranes, whereas the sympathetic nerves cause a nasal vasoconstriction with an enlargement of the nasal cavity. Obstruction of the nose, rhinorrhea, sneezing, hyposmia, and "postnasal drip" (discharge of mucous in the pharynx) are the common principal symptoms of the chronic alteration of nasal regulative functions. Clinically, there are two different manifestations: *Allergic rhinopathia* caused by a previous immunization against house dust, animal hairs, etc., and *vasomotoric rhinopathia* mediated through entirely vegetative mechanisms.

ALLERGIC RHINOPATHIA ("RHINITIS")

There are two types of allergic rhinitis. The seasonal form represents the true hay fever and is caused by pollen from grasses, trees, or herbs. The perennial form is caused by house dust mites, animal hairs, or molds. The seasonal form usually shows all signs of serous rhinitis, whereas the perennial form often occurs without any pathological findings apart from a hyperplasia of the conchae. The pathogenesis of both types begins with an activation of the immune system. Specific antigens interact with IgE complexes, which are bound to mast cells or basophilic granulocytes. Intracellularly, a modified activity of cAMP and cGMP leads to the release of granules from the microtubules. The granules contain inflammation mediators like histamine and further chemotactic factors. Consecutively, the cells begin to synthesize leukotrienes (slowly

reacting substances of the anaphylactic reaction) and other acti-
vating substances which are released later. An increased vaso-
permeability is caused especially by kallikrein, bradykinin, and
histamine. Corresponding histamine receptors are located in the
blood vessels and glands of the nose as well as in the nerve end-
ings of sensory nasal nerves which trigger secretomotoric activities and sneezing via reflexes.[16]

The relevance of emotional factors for an allergic disposition
as well as for the sensitization and the acute onset of an allergic
reaction is variable; the development of an allergic disposition
seems in most cases to be caused by several factors, whereas psychic aspects are of great importance for sensitization and especially the triggering of acute episodes. As a rule, more introverted
persons tend to develop allergic phenomena, and depressive
persons apparently produce more allergen-specific immunoglobulin E against inhaled substances and food than schizophrenics,
alcoholics, or persons from a control group.[17] Bell[18] investigated
whether extremely introverted persons suffered more often from
allergic rhinitis; in contrast to other allergic diseases (bronchial
asthma), they found a very close connection. Other authors regard the role of psychic factors in the pathogenesis of classical
hay fever, which often occurs with fever, as less important.[19]

There is, however, no doubt that, at least in a subgroup of the
hay fever patients, the sight or even the visualization of certain flow-
ers, grasses, or pollen can trigger the characteristic symptoms. Thus,
the established pattern can become more and more explained in
psychological terms and develop into a conditioning reaction with
vegetative symptoms. In this context, Delius[20] introduced the term
allergovegetative disturbance; he pointed out that, empirically, striking
correlations can be observed between a "modified sensitivity with
antibody diathesis," vegetatively mediated vaso- and/or capillary lability on one hand, and psychic sensitivity on the other hand. The
generally observed increase in persons with allergic disposition can
possibly also be caused by changes in society: Mitscherlich[21] attributed the increase in the number of "allergies" to the general climate
of civilization, with collective and individual strains, impaired circa-
dian rhythm, unphysiological working conditions and stimulation,

increase of protectionistic dependencies with a concomitant loss of true protection. The effectiveness of a hyposensitization treatment after thorough allergologic diagnosis is generally agreed upon in seasonal allergic rhinitis.[22-24] A discussion as to whether this proceeding can prevent the transition to an allergic bronchial asthma is currently in progress. Zenner[25] points out that about 30% of nonhyposensitized children and juveniles with allergic rhinitis later develop bronchial asthma.

VASOMOTORIC RHINOPATHIA ("RHINITIS")

Vasomotoric rhinopathia is often caused by psychic stimuli. Suddenly, the nose is filled with watery secretions. Sayings like—"my nose is full" (which in German means "I'm fed up") or "I have the sniffles" show that this psychosomatic connection is part of general experience. Pathophysiologically, vasomotoric rhinopathia is generated by the release of mediators (histamine, leukotrienes, and substance P) from the mast cells.[26] Freeman[27] lists 100 causes for a vasomotoric attack. It can be caused by an unpleasant situation or merely by its expectation. Often the sight of a disliked person is sufficient.[28] The common denominator for all possible causes is that they lead to an unpleasant feeling.[1] They can occur in the context of an intra- or interpersonal conflict. This could be a serious ambivalence conflict, or conflicts between passive desires and a conscious, forced action to overcome these desires. Altogether, vasomotoric rhinitis can be explained as a somatization of a defense reaction. According to a theory of Hasegawa and Kern,[29] some patients with rhinitis experience even the physiologic nasal cycle as bothering (unilaterally "obstructed" nose); the anxious, excessive attention given to the nose and the subjective "overinterpretation" by far exceed the actual constriction of the lumen.

FUNCTIONAL IMPAIRMENT OF NASAL RESPIRATION

"*Sniffling*" is a quick, abbreviated inhalation of air which is in most cases unconscious. The more this procedure is automatized, the more the symptom can develop into a "sniffling tic." The main goal of therapy is to restitute the patient's self-observation regarding this procedure. *Nasal twang* is a pathologic nose resonance when speaking; especially the "open nasal twang" is often caused functionally.[28]

SINUSITIS

There are surprisingly few psychosomatic studies on acute and chronic sinusitis. Our own observations often showed a denied mourning reaction as psychosomatic background; "uncried tears" as an explanatory principle often helped to understand the cases. Some authors also described somatopsychic connections in patients with sinusitis: Mason[30] gives a case report of a 9-year-old girl showing a coincidence of sinusitis and modified behavior characterized by withdrawal, depression, and fear; these symptoms disappeared together with the sinusitis. Olness and Libbey[31] name sinusitis as a possible underlying disease in psychic changes in children.

MOUTH

GLOSSODYNIA

Glossodynia is a painful state of a macroscopically intact tongue which claims a lot of attention from the patient. Besides local mechanical or chemical irritations, the differential diagnosis comprises numerous, often subclinical, metabolically related causes (e.g., pernicious anemia, vitamin deficit, estrogen deficit), various skin diseases and disorders of the central nervous system (thalamic syndrome); but very often something literally "lies on the tip of the tongue" of the patient which can or must not be articulated. Psychiatric diseases (somatic projections in hyperthymic personalities, circumscript hypochondrias, coenesthetic misperceptions in psychoses) must also be taken into account.[32]

Dyschylia

A high sympathetic tone (fear!) makes the saliva more viscous and scanty. Mouth and pharynx become dry. This state is sometimes described as "glue tongue," "sticky gums," or "blotting paper throat" (direct translations of German terms), as strawy taste or bluntness of the teeth.[20]

Sialadenosis and Sialadenitis

Sialadenosis can occur in patients with bulivomia (bulimia nervosa). The otorhinolaryngologist is possibly the first contact person of (female) patients who try to conceal their true basis disorder. The pathogenesis of sialadenosis connected with bulimic eating–vomiting attacks has not been completely clarified.[33] It has so far not been investigated whether there are interrelations between *acute or chronic sialadenitis* and psychic phenomena (marked anxiousness). As a matter of principle, the regulation of salivation is so much dependent on psychic variables that psychosomatic factors can play a role even in the development of a local inflammation. The hypothesis can be formulated that a high sympathetic tone with consecutively reduced flow of saliva favors inflammatory changes.

Angina

Angina or acute tonsillitis is a good example for obvious connections between impaired immune competence on the one hand and stress or negative emotions on the other. In this context, Bräutigam and Christian[34] point out that most bacterial pathogens are also found in the pharynx of healthy persons; only the occurrence of additive noxae leads to the onset of angina. Pathologists class psychic factors among these additive causes. Lüscher[1] observed that psychic causes for the development of angina were rarely mentioned in the literature. In his own patients, he often found a conflict situation before the onset of acute angina. Especially relapses call for increased attention toward possible conflicts as psychogenic factors.

Regarding tonsillar focal infections, Lüscher points to the "tired man/woman" with a characteristic mixture of infections, neuro-dystonia, and neurotic disturbances.

According to Schellack,[35] psychic conflicts are in most cases based on conflicts concerning possessions and mirror situations characterized by oral-retentive temptations and their denial. In contrast to von Weizsäcker,[36] who observed that an acute angina can correlate with crises and disappointments in the "generative sphere" (e.g., ambivalent sexual desires), Schellack does not regard sexual causes as a frequent phenomenon. In a large study with 400 neurotic–depressive patients, Schellack[35] found 248 patients with recurring or chronic tonsillitis. Based on this observation, he postulated that tonsillitis could be the primordial symptom of a neurotic structure.

The psychogenesis of angina tonsillaris has very often been associated with situative terms like *examination angina, engagement angina, birthday angina, Christmas angina,* or *couvade-angina* (male childbed). In recent years, very little has been published about this matter, perhaps as a consequence of a good response to antibiotic treatment, which might render a psychological interpretation superfluous.

In a controlled study with 100 patients suffering from acute tonsillitis, Olson et al.[37] investigated the effect of the doctor–patient relationship. They compared a group of patients who had been thoroughly examined with another group. The patients of the second group received the same medication, but otherwise they were examined only briefly and had only a brief talk with the doctor, without being able to ask questions. Two days later, the patients of the first group stated significantly more often that they felt better and that the treatment had helped them. The authors judge this as a placebo effect. Unfortunately, the remission time of the infection was not documented in this study. Hoffmann[2] mentions the, meanwhile verified, connection between psychic tensions and the reduction of the immunologically important T-cell reactions in the lymphatic system. Among others, he refers to concepts described by Ader[38] and Adler[39] in connection with psychoimmunologic studies. These could also provide new aspects for the pathogenesis of recurring angina. Our own observations confirm that angina often develops after offenses to the patient, but also when there is an anxious expectation of an ambivalently experienced situation—in this case, the "angina" serves as a solution to the conflict.

PHARYNX

The lower pharynx from the base of the tongue to the entrance of the esophagus has a large number of motoric nerves and is thus characterized by complex movements. Some persons seem to pay an unusual amount of attention to these movements. In this context, Fleischer[40] points to the following contradiction: On the one hand, those with most severely damaged pharyngeal mucous membranes—among others, alcoholics, smokers, and steel workers— often do not report any symptoms; even progressive and decaying pharyngeal tumors seem to be tolerated without complaint. On the other hand, there are numerous patients who give emphatic portrayals of various ailments in the throat with obvious suffering, but without any or with almost no pathological findings in the mucous membrane.

GLOBUS FEELING

As early as 2500 years ago, the phenomenon of globus was described by Hippocrates; based on his "uterus theory" of hysteria, he interpreted the globus feeling as an ascended uterus pressing against the larynx. For Purcel,[41] the feeling of a hard ball in the throat was caused by a contraction of neck muscles leading to pressure against the thyroid cartilage. Today it is generally agreed upon that the term *globus hystericus* is obsolete[42] and that the globus complaint is a phenomenon which needs a more differentiated investigation. A common complaint is a subjective feeling of impairment and narrowing in the throat; these symptoms are reported by 3 to 4% of all patients consulting an otorhinolaryngologist for the first time, 75% of whom are female, primarily in the age group between 40 and 60 years. In most cases, the globus is sensed near the thyroid cartilage, and this feeling becomes stronger with excitement.[43] The *true globus feeling* is one of uneasiness sensed deeply in the pharynx, like a lump or like the feeling of narrowness which occurs at "empty swallowing" only.[44] The *globus equivalents* must be differentiated from the true globus feeling. They comprise nonspecific symptoms like "lump in the throat," feeling of narrowness, foreign body sensations, dryness, slimy feeling, scratchy throat, burning, compulsive throat-clearing and compulsive swallowing. The following symptoms are generally associated with organic disturbances and are not classified as being part of globus feeling or globus equivalents: unilateral occurrence, mechanical swallowing impediment, pain during swallowing, aspiration, regurgitation, burning when ingesting acid food or drinks, and respiratory obstruction.

In most cases, the true globus feeling corresponds with the perception of nonphysiologic tension of the muscles in the pharyngoesophageal transition zone. This tension decreases when solid or fluid food is swallowed and the swallowing reflex leads to an involuntary relaxation; but during "empty swallowing," this reflex is not triggered because there is no food bolus.[44] Very often, the increased muscle tension of the muscles responsible for swallowing is associated with increased tension of the whole muscular rigging of the neck. The data concerning the relevance of the gastroesophageal reflux in the genesis of globus complaints are inconsistent. A reflux presumably occurs in 15%[45] to 90% of all "globus patients"; nevertheless, the globus feeling does not necessarily disappear with the reflux symptoms. Besides reflux, other organic factors in the pathogenesis of globus complaints are mentioned; however, there is an inconsistent use of the term *globus* in the various publications: Edema of the arytenoid cartilage, cervical osteophytes, motility disturbances of the esophagus, cricopharyngeal dysfunctions. But even these somatic findings call for a psychological assessment. The mere awareness of the swallowing procedure which normally happens automatically can lead to increased self-observation and a broad range of sensations in the throat which cannot be explained by only organic causes. An exaggerated self-observation of the processes connected with swallowing and "throat awareness" can become even more intense when originally unconscious conflicts are represented in somatic symptoms.

Globus equivalents can be caused by various psychologic factors; very often, the continuous sensation occurs as a somatic complaint in depressive patients. Besides, it is a main or secondary symptom of many functional disorders which is often listed in tables referring to the subject. On the psychic level, there is often an unconscious defense against repressed oral–receptive, sexual, or nutritive desires. The corresponding ideas focus on "wanting to swallow" and "not being allowed to swallow" (often with oral-genital, less often with oral–nutritive contents), or at "having to swallow" and "not wanting to swallow." Besides, there are mourning equivalents, feelings of repressed aversions, and hypochondria.[46]

The *functional dysphagias.*, i.e., transportation disturbances of the food bolus with functional genesis, which are more than just a subjective sensation, and *organic dysphagias* which are caused by various factors which call for a thorough differential diagnosis and which sometimes are detected as a cause for an "unspecified weight loss," are to be distinguished from the term *globus.* Chronic pharyngitis leads to swallowing difficulties mainly when the patient is eating. Besides endogenous factors, environmental aspects must be taken into account, especially heat, welding smoke, and formaldehyde.[43] Nutritive factors are, among others, cigar smoke and distilled spirits. The therapy is aimed at the avoidance of these noxae; further, the viscosity of the mucus must be reduced. A good clinical and differential diagnostic rule is suggested by Ganz[43]: swallowing problems during eating are probably caused by an organic local disturbance such as pharyngitis; unpleasant sensations upon "empty swallowing" correspond to a functional disturbance (globus), and problems with swallowing fluids point to a neurologic disease (progressive bulbar paralysis). Some authors stress repeatedly[47] that the diagnosis of psychogenic globus or psychogenic dysphagia must be continually checked and reevaluated. According to Ravich et al.,[48] there is a danger of missing the development of an organic disease if the diagnosis "psychogenic swallowing disorder" is made too early.

On the other hand, Schnieder[49] reports a screening of 3200 patients for tumors in the ENT area. None of the patients had a malignoma, but 50% of the women and 40% of the men stated that they had experienced a globus feeling once or several times. The observation that globus feeling and carcinomas of the pharynx and larynx are not necessarily associated is also confirmed by Breuninger,[50] who stated that these malignancies often do not cause any globus feeling, even at an advanced stage.

FURTHER FUNCTIONAL DISORDERS OF THE PHARYNX

A special type of functional disorder of the pharynx is *aerophagia*, which can correspond with a severe protest reaction against a life situation which is not truly accepted.[46] In German colloquial speech, the term *armer Schlucker* is used.[20] Bräutigam and Christian[34] write that the emotional basis of this disorder is an unconscious rejection of any "ingestion," as this is experienced as the impulse to "gobble" and destroy. This symptom is not just a bad habit but a disease which must be taken seriously. The swallowed air can accumulate in the stomach, thus lifting the diaphragm with the possible induction of apparent cardiac symptoms (Roemheld's syndrome). The often self-induced *functional regurgitation* of food already swallowed can represent a complex method of quieting anxiety. Repeated chewing of regurgitated food can reduce anxious tension or loneliness and thus serve as a defense against fear. This symptom also occurs as a compromise phenomenon in bulivomia.

The *true psychogenic swallowing disorder* as equivalent of a habitualized protest in the sense of a conversion phenomenon occurs less often. It has been observed in children who had been forced to eat. Kanner,[51] cited by Gilbody,[52] reports the case of a young boy who developed disturbed swallowing of solid food after he had been beaten by his father because of bad table manners.

Conscious and unconscious ideas connected with the swallowing process can develop into a severe phobic fear of swallowing. Swallowing problems and fears can also coincide with certain social situations. Thus it is possible that the symptoms only occur when the patient is in company. Important diagnostic and therapeutic steps involve discussions with the patient so that he recognizes the anxiety hidden behind the somatic complaint "swallowing disorder." The psychotherapeutic approach is dependent on the basic psychic situation and/or conflict. In children, family therapy can be helpful. Good results with behavioral methods (relaxation exercises connected with a systematic desensitization, reduction of an aversive stimulus when the patient is swallowing, etc.) are described in case reports (a synopsis is provided by Klinger and Strang[53]). If the swallowing disorder occurs in connection with habitual vomiting in juveniles or in adolescence, a differential diagnosis of anorexia nervosa is important.

LARYNX

SNORING AND SLEEP APNEA SYNDROME

Snoring is caused by vibrations of the oropharyngeal soft tissues, when the upper respiratory tract is partly obstructed. There must be differentiation between the various types: (1) occasional snoring; (2) chronic or occasional snoring without pathologic apnea; and (3) snoring as a symptom of sleep apnea syndrome.[54] Snoring becomes more frequent with increasing age and is also associated with coronary heart disease. The psychosocial consequences of chronic or habitual snoring can be considerable (senior marriage, hospital wards) and require intense counseling. The sleep apnea syndrome frequently occurs in male persons around their 50th year of age. It is defined as the presence of at least 30 apnea episodes lasting for at least 10 seconds during a 7-hour period of sleep. This syndrome is associated with a pathologic coupling of vigilance and respiratory regulation caused by an impairment of central regulation or a collapse of the neck and laryngeal muscles. Patients suffer from symptoms provoked by sleep disturbances, but also from the physiologic consequences of hypoxia, e.g., hypertonus, arteriosclerosis, and arrhythmias. Ninety percent of the patients with sleep apnea show increased blood pressure. To those within earshot, the loud recommencement of respiration is usually perceived as "snoring." The apnea can result in panic awakening, which must not be misinterpreted as nonspecific sleeping disturbance or nocturnal "panic attack." A polysomnographic examination helps to find the correct diagnosis. Hypnotics, alcohol, or other types of sedation "in order to find continuous sleep at last" are contraindicated. Therapeutic possibilities are weight reduction and treatment with continuous positive airway pressure, as well as drug treatment with theophylline.

Voice Disorders

Functional Aphonia. The sudden "loss of voice" can often be exactly dated by the patient. This phenomenon is often caused by a psychic trauma. The patient literally "lost his speech." The psychodynamic interpretation is a "defense against the realization of unacceptable feelings."[55] Furthermore, a generalized inhibition of an archaic rage cry can be the cause of aphonia; the patient's fear maximally suppresses this cry. The symptom itself can easily be removed, for example, by suggestion.[56, 57] Nevertheless, it tends to come back when the basic conflict has not been dealt with.[58]

Functional Dysphonias. Hypofunctional voice disorders occur in connection with exhaustion and depression. *Hyperfunctional voice disorders* often develop in active persons who speak professionally and uneconomical use of the voice. In these cases, logopedic treatment aims not only at an isolated training of speech functions, but also at connections between phonation on the one hand and the expression of the patient's personality and his communicative behavior on the other hand.[59]

Spastic Dysphonia. Spastic dysphonia is a rare, but for the most part serious voice disorder with marked "spasms" of the respiratory and phonation muscles. When the voice is strained, the phonation appears pressed and the voice sounds like groaning. A hysterical genesis of this phenomenon is frequently suspected, but actually applies only to a small subgroup of patients. Today, the disorder is classified among the focal dystonias. The first manifestation can be triggered by psychologic factors. Under emotional stress, a prolonged deterioration can occur, and a temporary deterioration can happen in certain social situations, e.g., speaking on the phone or with authoritative persons. In unexpected situations, when the patient does not have time to think about the fact that he is speaking, the voice can be normal.[60] A psychic influence on the course of the disease could be understood as an insufficient or missing compensation of a disturbance of those subcortical feedback mechanisms which regulate the "dual function" of the larynx, i.e., its role as sound generator on the one hand and as "guard of the airstream" on the other hand. The disease, with its psychosocial consequences, cannot easily be approached with psychotherapeutic and/or logopedic measures. Thus, a symptomatic treatment with injection of botulinum toxin into the laryngeal muscles can be tried.

Psychosomatic Aspects of Laryngectomy. Today, the number of larynx carcinomas treated in German clinics is 10 times higher than in the thirties.[61] The average age of laryngectomized patients is around 46 years, which is relatively young. The excision of the larynx is an extreme operation; it is justified by the often favorable prognosis. Regional metastases can be controlled relatively well by surgery, and distant metastases often occur very late. Thus, the number of patients in whom rehabilitative surgery seems appropriate is quite large in comparison to other carcinomas.

On the other hand, such a surgical intervention appears to increase a tendency toward idealization and alexithymia in many of the affected[62]; this is a defense mechanism against the terrible condition of the often psychically indolent patients. They often become unable to both perceive and utter their deepest feelings. Schröder et al.[63] questioned laryngectomized patients and found that they described their psychosocial environment as being ideal, whereas their real situation was often characterized by loneliness and isolation; there is no person with whom they can talk about their most essential problem, that is, their cancer. Thus, even before they undergo surgery, patients should be acquainted with their life situation after laryngectomy: by making contact with an already laryngectomized patient who is actively coping with the disease, and by cooperating with family and friends. These psychotherapeutic measures have a health-promoting effect.

Laryngectomized patients usually cannot keep working after their 50th year of age. Maximally 10% of the patients succeed in keeping their jobs or changing to another occupation.[61] Besides the often disfiguring consequences of the operation, the accommodation to the "substitute voice" (esophagus speech, voice fistula, electronic help) is a special challenge to the patient. Plath[61] mentions that this problem should be discussed before surgery, too. In Germany, the psychosocial welfare of laryngectomized patients has been provided by special associations since 1972.

EAR

From the fetal stage, human beings have acoustic sensations which are not interrupted during sleep; these perceptions are carriers of the most important communicative element with the environment. In contrast to the eye, the ear cannot be "closed." Thus, it is one of the most stressed organs, especially in an industrialized and communications oriented society.

SUDDEN LOSS OF HEARING

It is generally agreed that sudden loss of hearing occurs with increasing frequency. This applies especially to the populations of the industrial nations in Western Europe, Japan, and the United States.[64] Byl[65] reported an incidence of 10.7 cases per 100,000 inhabitants in Northern California. With 4000 patients throughout the United States (1–2 patients per 100,000 inhabitants), Jaffe[66] gave a lower estimate. There are only a few comments on the incidence in Germany; about 20 cases per 100,000 inhabitants have been mentioned.[64]

Sudden loss of hearing is often understood as a stress reaction. In many cases, the acute idiopathic sudden loss of hearing can indeed be interpreted as a psychovegetatively mediated psychosomatic reaction to a stress or conflict situation occurring especially in industrialized societies. The pathogenesis includes a disturbed microcirculation in the cochlea with consecutive hypoxia of the sensory hair cells. The causative stress factors—often described as "pressure" by patients—can originate in the patient's work environment and are often aggravated by additional personal problems. Metaphors about the "blown fuse"[67] or the "blow in the inner ear," thus describe the sudden loss of hearing as a psychosomatic protective mechanism. The patients themselves mention a desire for quietness, or they clearly name what they do not want to hear anymore. Psychodynamically, one frequently finds superego conflicts (the voice of the conscience) and a preconscious, powerless protest attitude, combined with the experience of subjective helplessness. Typical traits of patients with sudden loss of hearing, which concern the primary personality and can be detected with psychological tests, are a strong sense of duty, an inhibited aggressiveness toward the outside, and an inclination toward mentally reliving the day's activities.

Our own observations have shown that the patients are often aware of their stress situation. Besides an early initiation of hemodilution therapy, protection from stimuli and stress avoidance are important therapeutic principles which, nevertheless, become effective only if the patient can experience the relaxation and safety provided by hospitalization. These therapeutic measures can be supported by appropriate psychologic interventions; there are clues that active psychologic relaxation methods and appropriate suggestions can result in marked improvement.[68]

If the patient's stress is provoked by neurotic and psychosocial complications, it is recommended to discuss the conflict situation with the patient and, if necessary, to initiate analytic psychotherapy.

Sudden loss of hearing is characterized by a relatively high spontaneous recovery rate,[64] but there is always a tendency for it to recur; a somatic pathway can develop as well as decreased hearing ability, and, finally, chronic tinnitus. For both therapeutic and prophylactic reasons it is sensible for the patient to use the sudden loss of hearing as a chance to change his or her life by seeking psychotherapeutic help.

PSYCHOGENIC HEARING DISTURBANCES

The variability of symptoms in purely psychogenic hearing disturbances comprises the situationally fluctuating hearing threshold and the rare, purely subjective deafness. Confrontational discussions with the often young patients should be avoided; it is better to build a bridge toward a "spontaneous remission without losing face." This can be achieved with an empathic attitude acknowledging the patient's trouble. On the other hand, there is also psychogenic acoustic hypersensitivity reaction (psychogenic hyperacusis)—frequently in crisis or conflict situations—representing exhaustion in the psychic confrontation with noise.

TINNITUS

Tinnitus aurium must be differentiated from central cerebral tinnitus and objective tinnitus. It is a frequent everyday phenomenon like pruritus or pain. Only an increase in intensity, combined with decompensating psychic processing, makes a disease of the troublesome symptom. Of 6804 randomly recruited persons from various British cities, 17% stated that they had suffered from tinnitus for some time; but for only 1%, this was connected with a decreased quality of life. The application of this percentage to the German population would result in a prevalence of 750,000 patients with tinnitus.[69] Pathophysiologically, tinnitus is the result of pathologic dislocation of the functioning of inner and outer hair cells in the organ of corti; central processes transform the stochastic spontaneous activity caused by the lesion into a procedure perceived as sound. A repetitive self-activating electrical activity (so-called oscillations) in the central auditory tract seem to play an additional role.[70] Tinnitus can also be interpreted as a consequence of an unnoticed sudden loss of hearing; this is plausible if one considers that at least 50% of the sensory epithelium must be damaged in order to cause a perceptible change in the hearing threshold. In this sense, tinnitus can be understood as a response to excessive psychophysic stress.[71] Sometimes the patient himself does not consciously experience his chronic emotional tension. Additional tension symptoms can increase the tinnitus and perpetuate a vicious circle: bruxism and mandibular dysfunctions, massive facial pain (Da Costa's syndrome), or cervical muscle tensions with functional blockade of the cervical vertebral arch joints. The tinnitus noise receives excessive attention by the patient and is finally experienced as a persecutor, if the patient's psyche cannot adequately cope with the disturbance. Besides, the patient loses the ability to imagine the noise as coming from the outside. A depressive reaction to the "loss of silence" has been observed as well.[72]

A first help is the generation of desired sounds with a radio or Walkman™ to cover the tinnitus noise. For the success of a special tinnitus masking agent it seems to be crucial that even with a relatively low volume (up to 10 dB), compared to the loudness of the tinnitus, a noticeable effect can be achieved.[73] Psychotherapeutic help is necessary, especially if a patient is lonely and the tinnitus becomes the only relevant "object" for him, even if it is a "persecutor." The decompensated tinnitus patient must never be cut loose by his doctor, for example, with the recommendation: "You will have to live with this problem." Differential research regarding tinnitus therapy is still very young; a good response to various measures—placebo treatment, relaxation methods, hypnotherapy, changes of attitude, and the use of antidepressive medication—does not justify therapeutic nihilism. Close cooperation with the patient is essential, leading the way to an individual form of therapy which helps to establish psychic recompensation. The experience that it is possible to diminish the intensity of the tinnitus reduces the feeling of being a victim; thus, the patient's fear is reduced and his relaxation increased.

Even the tinnitus noise itself can be reduced—within the biologic variability, based on the existing damage. The feeling of isolation often described by tinnitus patients ("Nobody who does not hear such noise can imagine how much I am suffering") can only be counteracted by contact with self-help groups (in Germany: Deutsche Tinnitus Liga e.V.). There are special tinnitus wards in psychosomatic clinics; there, patients can use a tinnitus diary to recognize their "personal" tinnitus as a phenomenon which signals tension or stress. Thus, the persecuting enemy can be changed into a protecting friend.

VESTIBULAR NEURONITIS ("VESTIBULAR CRISIS")

Vestibular neuronitis is characterized by sudden rotatory vertigo in connection with nystagmus, nausea, and vomiting, caused by viral inflammation or disturbed perfusion. So far, there are no systematic psychosomatic investigations on this disease, but single observations give hints of a previous irritation of the relation to the outer world and of the patient's inner orientation; another etiologic factor could be a somatized crisis in adolescence, which calls for psychotherapeutic intervention after improvement of the acute vertigo.

MÉNIÈRE'S DISEASE

The symptoms of Ménière's disease usually show an acute onset and consist of the triad, paroxysmal rotatory vertigo, loss of hearing, and tinnitus; this is accompanied by a feeling of destruction, panic, and vomiting. The incident is caused by bursting or leakage of the nedolymph tube in the inner ear, which is overextended due to an increased production or decreased absorption of endolymph. Psychovegetatively mediated influences may be made responsible especially for an increased production of endolymph. Psychodynamically oriented authors[74-77] have frequently found that the first attack especially was triggered by psychic factors. They often observed a high, suppressed aggressive tension in early adapted, always "nice" persons who had grown up without true affection (Nestwärme). Psychologic tests do not give any clues regarding specifity structure.[78] The trigger mechanism of the consequent attacks seems to become more and more independent of the amount of subjectively experienced stress. Instead, the disease itself develops into a stress factor with specific psychic consequences,[79] because the patient can never be sure, if there will not be another attack the next moment, deeply affecting and existentially shattering. In the attack-free interval, counseling, guidance, and support of the patient are important therapeutic measures: with this rare, but very dramatic disease, the patients often feel very lonely.

VERTIGO

Vertigo is one of the most frequent symptoms and points at a disturbed relation with space. In general, according to the mismatch theory, spatial orientation and perception of movement are disturbed by a conflict between stimuli, which do not correspond with expectations derived from earlier experiences.

The term *space* can mean both the outer, physical surroundings and the psychic, inner space, as well as the social space. Thus, the symptom *vertigo* can represent three different factors (this is also shown by the etymology of the German word for vertigo *Schwindel*): a somatic phenomenon, an emotional experience, and a social fact. Psychogenic vertigo as a single symptom yields a whole range of psychopathologic differentiations providing a nosologic classification. Thus, vertigo can be: A consequence of stimulus incompatibilities (phobic postural vertigo, mountain vertigo, motion sickness); a remembrance symbol (conversion); an anxiety equivalent (anxiety neurosis); an affect equivalent (for pleasure or aversion); a somatized depression, a psychic borderline phenomenon (schizoid crises); a latent awareness of one's own "eccentricity" (character disorders); and a social marker ("it's all a swindle"—the German word for vertigo also means *swindle*).[80]

Clinically, there is a very important and close relationship between vertigo and anxiety: patients with phobic posture vertigo often feel an anxiety to die and develop a secondary phobic avoidance-pattern, on the other side patients with panic attacks, agoraphobia, or acrophobia complain about unsteady feelings, dizziness or faintness.[81] Phobic postural vertigo is a clear indication for behavior therapy with gradual exposition training[82]; in other cases of psychogenic vertigo, the psychotherapeutic indication depends on the psychic findings and the conflict situation of the patient found in the therapeutic dialogue.

REFERENCES

1. Lüscher E. Psychische Faktoren bei Hals-Nasen-Ohrenleiden. *Arch Hals Nas Kehlk Heilk.* 1959;175:69–216.
2. Hoffmann SO. Psychosomatische Aspekte von Erkrankungen im Hals-Nasen-Ohrenbereich. *Arch Nas Ohr Kehlk Heilk.* 1986(suppl 2).
3. Brunswick RM. Ein Nachtrag zu Freuds "Geschichte einer infantilen Neurose." *Int Z Psychoanal.* 1929;15:1. Reprinted in: *Der Wolfsmann vom Wolfsmann.* Frankfurt: Fischer;1972.
4. Fowler EP. *Psychosom Med.* 1950;12:108 [cited in 1, p 159].
5. Saul LJ. Psychogenic factors in the etiology of the common cold and the related syndromes. *Int J Psychoanal.* 1938;19:451.
6. Kohut H. *Narzissmus.* Frankfurt: Suhrkamp;1973.
7. Deneke FW. Das Selbst-System. *Psyche.* 1989;43:577–608.
8. Cohen F, Tyrell D. Psychological stress and susceptibility to the common cold. *N Engl J Med.* 1991;325:606–612.
9. Gay M, Blager F. Psychogenic habit cough: Review and case report. *J Clin Psychiatry.* 1987;48:483–486.
10. Creer TL, Chai H. A single application of an aversive stimulus to eliminate chronic cough. *J Behav Ther Exp Psychiatry.* 1977;8:107–109. [cited in 9, p 483].
11. Alexander AB, Chai H. The elimination of chronic cough by response suppression shaping. *J Behav Ther Exp Psychiatry.* 1973;4:75–80 [cited in 9, p 483].
12. Cohlan SQ, Stone SM. The cough and the bedsheet. *Pediatrics.* 1984;74:11–15.
13. Shuper A, Mukamel M. Psychogenic cough. *Arch Dis Child.* 1983;58:745–747.
14. Weinberg EG. "Honking": Psychogenic cough tic in children. *S Afr Med J.* 1980;57:198–200.
15. Kravitz H, Gomberg RM. Psychogenic cough tic in children and adolescents. *Clin Pediatr.* 1969;8:580–583.
16. Kimmelmann MD, Gamal A. Vasomotor rhinitis. *Otolaryngol Clin North Am.* 1986;19:65–71.
17. Sugerman AA, Southern DL, Curan JF. A study of antibody levels in alcoholic, depressive and schizophrenic patients. *Ann Allergy.* 1982;48:166–171.

18. Bell I. Is allergic rhinitis more frequent in young adults with extreme shyness? A preliminary survey. *Psychosom Med.* 1990;52:517–525.
19. Czubalski K, Zawieza E. The role of psychic factors in patients with allergic rhinitis. *Acta Otolaryngol.* 1976;81:484–488.
20. Delius L. *Psychovegetative Syndrome.* Stuttgart: Thieme;1966.
21. Mitscherlich A. Psychosomatische Aspekte der Allergie. *Int Arch Allergy.* 1950;suppl 1:79.
22. Wahn U. Hyposensibilisierung bei allergischen Atemwegserkrankungen. *Dtsch Med Wochenschr.* 1991;116:701–704.
23. Varney VA, Gaga M. Usefulness of immunotherapy in patients with severe summer hay fever uncontrolled by antiallergic drugs. *Br Med J.* 1991;302:265.
24. Malling HJ. Immunotherapie. Position paper. *Allergy.* 1988;43:(suppl 6):9.
25. Zenner HP. Diagnostik und Therapie allergischer Erkrankungen der Schleimhaut des oberen Respirationstraktes. *Arch Ohr Nas Kehlk Heilk.* 1987(suppl 2).
26. Wolff P. Neue Aspekte zur Pathogenese und Therapie der hyperreflektorischen Rhinopathie. *Z Laryng Rhinol.* 1988;67:138.
27. Freeman J. *Hay-Fever.* London;1950.
28. Sopko H. Funktionelle Störungen in der HNO-Heilkunde. In: Uexküll Th., ed. *Psychosomatische Medizin.* Munich, Germany: Urban & Schwarzenberg; 1990:4.
29. Hasegawa M, Kern E. The human nasal cycle. *Mayo Clin Proc.* 1977;52:28–34. [Cited in 16, p 68].
30. Mason DE. Sinusitis with behavioral presentation. *J Am Acad Child Adolesc Psychiatry.* 1987;26:926–927.
31. Olness K, Libbey P. Unrecognized biologic bases of behavioral symptoms in patients referred for hypnotherapy. *Am J Clin Hypn.* 1987;30:1–8.
32. Renninghoff J, Lamparter U, Hörmann K. Psychosomatische Aspekte des Symptoms "Zungenbrennen." In: Majer EH, Zrunik M, eds. *Die Oto-Rhino-Laryngologie in Kooperation mit Nachbardisziplinen.* Vienna, Austria: Facultas;1987.
33. Maier H, Born IA, Bihl H, Küchenhoff A. Sialadenose bei Bulimia nervosa. In: Weidauer H, Maier H, eds. *Speicheldrüsenerkrankungen.* Berlin, Germany: Springer;1988: pp 47–51.
34. Bräutigam W. *Christian Psychosomatische Medizin.* Stuttgart, Germany: Thieme; 1986:4.
35. Schellack D. Angina tonsillaris. *Z Psychosom Med.* 1957;3:265.
36. Weizsäcker v V. *Studien zur Pathogenese.* Wiesbaden, Germany: Thieme;1946:2 [cited in 34].
37. Olson B, Olson B, Tibblin G. Effects of patients' expectations on recovery from acute tonsillitis. *Family Pract.* 1989;6:189–192.
38. Ader R. Verhalten und Immunsystem: Konditionierung und ihre Auswirkungen. In v Uexküll Th, ed. *Psychosomatische Medizin.* Munich, Germany: Urban & Schwarzenberg;1990; pp 171–183.
39. Adler R. Vorbemerkung zu R. Ader. In: v Uexküll Th, ed. *Psychosomatische Medizin.* Munich, Germany: Urban & Schwarzenberg;1990: pp 171–183.
40. Fleischer K. Differentialdiagnostische Überlegungen bei der chronischen Pharyngitis. *Dtsch Med Wochenschr.* 1980;105:283–284.
41. Purcel J. *A Treatise of Vapours or Hysteric Fits.* London;1707:2.

450 LAMPARTER—SCHMIDT

42. Malcomson KG. Globus hystericus vel pharyngis. *J Laryngol Otol.* 1968;82: 219–230.
43. Ganz H. Die chronische Pharyngitis. *HNO.* 1989;9:57–67.
44. Kellerhals B. Globus pharyngis? Eine Differentialdiagnose. *Ther Umsch.* 1991;48: 188–192.
45. Wilson JA, Maran AG, Ryde A, Pris J, Allan PL, Heading RC. Globus sensation is not due to gastrooesophageal reflux. *Clin Otolaryngol.* 1987;12:271–275.
46. Meyer AE. Psychosomatik der Kranken mit Störungen des oberen Verdauungstraktes. In: Jores A, ed. *Praktische Psychosomatik.* Bern, Switzerland: Huber;1976.
47. Stacher G. Differentialdiagnostik psychosomatischer Schluckstörungen. *Wien Klin Wochenschr.* 1986;98:658–663.
48. Ravich W, Wilson R, Bronwyn J, Donner M. Psychogenic dysphasia and globus: Reevaluation of 23 patients. *Dysphagia.* 1989;4:35–38.
49. Schnieder EA. Funktionelle Syndrome in der HNO-Heilkunde. In: v Uexküll Th, ed. *Psychosomatische Medizin.* Munich, Germany: Urban & Schwarzenberg; 1990: pp 1054–1071.
50. Breuninger H. Funktionelle Missempfindungen im Rachenraum. In: Berendes K, ed. Aktuelle Probleme der HNO-Heilkunde, Köln, Dt. Ärzteverlag, 1980: pp 215–228.
51. Kanner L. *Child Psychiatry.* Springfield, Ill: Charles Thomas;1935.
52. Gilbody JS. Errors of deglutition—real or imagined; or, don't forget the psyche. *J Laryngol Otol.* 1991;105:807–811.
53. Klinger R, Strang P. Psychiatric aspects of swallowing disorders. *Psychosomatics.* 1987;28:572–574.
54. Pirsig W. *Schnarchen—Ursachen, Diagnostik, Therapie.* Stuttgart, Germany: Hippokrates;1988.
55. Perkins W. In: Travis, ed. *Handbook of Speech Pathology.* New York: Appleton-Century-Croft;1957.
56. Schnitzler A. *Über die funktionelle Aphonie und deren Behandlung durch Hypnose und Suggestion.* Vienna, Germany: Braunmüller;1889.
57. Brodnitz FS. Funktionelle Aphonie. *HNO Praxis Heute.* 1985;5:127–137.
58. Berendes I. Psychologisches in der HNO-Praxis. *Z Laryng Rhinol.* 1972;51:1–11.
59. Stabenow L. Hals-Nasen-Ohren-Heilkunde einschliesslich Phoniatrie: Hahn P, ed. *Kindlers Psychologie des 20. Jahrhunderts.* Weinheim, Germany: Beltz;1983: 2:188–211.
60. Aaronson AE. *Clinical Voice Disorders.* Stuttgart, Germany: Thieme;1985.
61. Plath P. Rehabilitation von Kehlkopflosen. In: Ganz H, Schätzle W, eds. *HNO-Praxis Heute.* Berlin, Germany: Springer;1988: pp 123–146.
62. Hahn M, et al. Somatische, psychische und sprachliche Rehabilitation von Kehlkopflosen. *Laryng Rhinol Otol.* 1986;65:395–398.
63. Schröder M, et al. Psychosoziales Umfeld bei Patienten mit Malignomen im Kopf-Hals-Bereich. *Laryng Rhinol Otol.* 1989;68:122–127.
64. Weinaug P. Die Spontanremission beim Hörsturz. *HNO.* 1984;32:346–351.
65. Byl FM. Sudden hearing loss research clinic. *Otolaryngol Clin North Am.* 1978;11:71–79.
66. Jaffe BF. Clinical studies in sudden deafness. *Adv Otohrinolaryngol.* 1973;20: 221–228.

67. Greuel H. *Viel um die Ohren. Hörsturz-Schwindel-Ohrensausen.* Düsseldorf, Germany: VDG-Verlag;1988.
68. Greuel H. Suggestivbehandlung beim Hörsturz. *HNO.* 1983;31:136–139.
69. Scott B, Lindberg P. Tinnitus-Inzidenz und ihre Auswirkungen. In: Goebel G, ed. *Ohrgeräusche.* 1992.
70. Lenarz T. Probleme der Diagnostik und Therapie des chronischen Tinnitus aus HNO-ärztlicher Sicht. In: Goebel G, ed. *Ohrgeräusche.* 1992.
71. Böning J. Klinik und Psychopathologie von Ohrgeräuschen aus psychiatrischer Sicht. *Laryngol Rhinol.* 1981;60:101–103.
72. Goebel G, et al. Neue Aspekte des komplexen chronischen Tinnitus. *Psychother Psychosom Med Psychol.* 1991;41:123–133.
73. Vernon J, Griest S, Prest L. Attributes of tinnitus and the acceptance of masking. *Am J Otolaryngol.* 1990;11:44–50.
74. Fowler EP Jr, Zeckel A. Psychosomatic aspects of Ménière's disease. *JAMA.* 1952;148:1265–1271.
75. Hinchcliffe R. Emotion as a precipitating factor in Ménière's disease. *J Laryngol Otol.* 1967;81:471–475.
76. Basequaz G. Aspects psycho-dynamiques de la maladie de Ménière. *Lavae Med.* 1969;40:838–843.
77. Groen JJ. Psychosomatic aspects of Ménière's disease. *Acta Otolaryngol.* 1983; 35:407–416.
78. Hinchcliffe R. Personality profile in Ménière's disease. *J Laryngol.* 1967; 81:477–481.
79. Wechsler M, Crary WC. Ménière's disease. *Am J Otol.* 1986;7:93–95.
80. Brandt T, Dieterich M. Phobischer Attackenschwankschwindel. *Münch Med Wochenschr.* 1986;128:247–250.
81. Fava GA, Grandi S, Canestrari R, Grasso P, Pesarin F. Mechanisms of change of panic attacks with exposure treatment of agoraphobia. *J Affect Disord.* 1991;22:65–71.
82. Brandt T. *Vertigo. Its Multisensory Syndromes.* London: Springer;1991.

Chapter 21
Chronic Fatigue Syndromes in Clinical Practice

PETER MANU, THOMAS J. LANE,
DALE A. MATTHEWS

Fatigue is the chief complaint of at least 5% of patients in primary care and is responsible for over 10 million visits to primary-care physicians every year in the United States alone.[1] The symptom is variably described by patients and is not easily quantified in an objective manner or confirmed by physical examination or laboratory testing. Most patients complain of a state of abnormal exhaustion following usual activities, decreased energy for tasks requiring sustained effort or attention, and/or a global disturbance in the ability to act. Many patients also experience anticipatory fatigue as they contemplate performing levels of physical or mental activity which have led to fatigue in the past.

ETIOLOGIC CLASSIFICATION
OF FATIGUE SYNDROMES

The differential diagnosis of fatigue syndromes is extensive, but can be condensed into six principal categories: (1) physiologic states; (2) medical disorders; (3) psychiatric disorders; (4) adverse effects of prescribed, over-the-counter, or illegal drugs; (5) unhealthy life-styles or environments and severe psychosocial stressors in patients without well-defined medical or psychiatric disorders known to produce fatigue; and (6) the newly defined chronic fatigue syndrome.[2]

The physiological states producing an abnormal level of exhaustion include pregnancy, sleep deprivation, and excessive muscular activity performed by poorly conditioned individuals.

Among the many medical disorders causing marked tiredness are chronic inflammatory conditions (e.g., systemic lupus erythematosus and polymyalgia rheumatica); bacterial or viral infections (e.g., tuberculosis, acquired immune deficiency syndrome [AIDS], infectious mononucleosis, and Lyme disease); malignancies, endocrinopathies (hypothyroidism, hypopituitarism, adrenal insufficiency, and poorly controlled insulin-dependent diabetes mellitus); cardiovascular diseases with low-output heart failure; neurologic diseases (e.g., multiple sclerosis, extrapyramidal syndromes, and convulsive disorders); and primary sleep disorders (narcolepsy, obstructive sleep apnea, and periodic limb movements with frequent awakenings).

The psychiatric disorders characterized by fatigue or excessive fatigability include affective disorders (e.g., major depression and dysthymia), anxiety disorders (panic disorder, social phobia, obsessive–compulsive disorder, and generalized anxiety disorder), and somatoform disorders (hypochondriasis, conversion disorder, and somatization disorder).

A plethora of prescribed drugs create or contribute to the fatigue state, most notably cancer chemotherapeutic agents (e.g., α-interferon, high-dose corticosteroid therapy, vincristine, and cisplatinum); common drugs used for arterial hypertension (diuretics, calcium channel blockers, and adrenergic beta blockers); widely used anticonvulsants (phenobarbital and carbamazepine); most antihistaminics prescribed for seasonal allergy; and the majority of the benzodiazepines frequently prescribed for insomnia.

Unhealthy life-styles accompanied by fatigue may involve inappropriate levels of exercise, frequent disruptions of the normal wake–sleep cycle, as well as the excessive intake of alcohol or caffeine-containing beverages. Psychosocial stressors (aggressive pursuit of professional advancement or material wealth, marital miscommunication, family violence, prolonged bereavement, and unemployment) and the delayed effects of traumatic events (childhood sexual abuse, rape, or abortion) appear to be important contributing factors as well.

The newly defined chronic fatigue syndrome represents an effort to provide an operational definition to a syndrome of persistent, disabling fatigue, accompanied by symptoms resembling those of a viral infection. This illness has been called by many names in the past, including sporadic neuromyasthenia, benign myalgic encephalomyelitis, and chronic mononucleosislike syndrome. The condition is diagnosed in patients complaining of a fatigue state severe enough to reduce the premorbid activity by at least 50% for a period of at least 6 months. In addition, the diagnosis requires the presence of at least eight of the following symptoms or signs: feverishness, sore throat, painful or swollen lymph nodes in neck or armpit, muscle weakness, muscle pain, joint pain, protracted and severe postexercise fatigue, generalized headaches; neuropsychologic abnormalities (photophobia, scotomas, forgetfulness, irritability, confusion, depression); sleep disturbances; documented fever, nonexudative pharyngitis; and palpable and tender cervical or axillary lymph glands. Other clinical conditions that may produce chronic fatigue must be excluded by thorough medical evaluation.[2]

CLINICAL EPIDEMIOLOGY
OF FATIGUE SYNDROMES

PSYCHIATRIC DISORDERS

Although traditional medical training has tended to emphasize physical disorders as a likely cause of chronic fatigue syndromes, comprehensive evaluations of large numbers of patients with a chief complaint of persistent tiredness demonstrated that the majority suffer from psychiatric disorders.[3-6] In a prospective study conducted by us at the Chronic Fatigue Clinic of the University of Connecticut Health Center from November 1986 through January 1990, we had the opportunity to explore in depth the fatiguing illnesses of 327 nonselected patients (214 women and 113 men; mean age 38.8 years) whose major symptom was chronic fatigue. A standard medical or psychiatric disorder known to be associated with fatigue was identified in 267 patients (81%). Currently active psychiatric disorders were found in 249 patients (76%), physical disorders explained the fatigue syndrome of 4 patients (1%), and overlapping physical and mental disorders were responsible for the fatigue experienced by 13 patients (4%).

In our clinical experience, the most common cause of chronic fatigue is major depression, found in 56.5% of the patients with fatigue syndrome, a frequency five times greater than in the general population.[7] The disorder consists, in a majority of cases, of recurrent episodes of clinical depression clearly preceding the onset of the fatiguing illness for which these patients request medical treatment. A discriminant function analysis comparing patients who were depressed with those who had no psychiatric disorder, showed that the depressed patients were older, were more likely to report that they had lost their job due to fatigue symptoms, and were more likely to observe that their fatigue symptoms improved in the evening.[8]

Panic disorder ranked second among disorders seen in patients with chronic fatigue, being identified as etiologic in 13.5% of cases, a frequency 10 times greater than in the general population.[9] The disorder preceded or was coincidental with the onset of chronic fatigue in most of these patients. In comparison with the rest of the study cohort, significantly more patients with panic disorder had a history of severe depression, including persistent thoughts of death or suicide.[10]

The third most common diagnosis of this group of patients with chronic fatigue was somatization disorder, present in 11.9% of the patients, a frequency at least 100 times greater than in the general population.[11] Among the functional somatic symptoms reported significantly more frequently by these patients were muscle pain, joint pain, chest pain, shortness of breath, blurred vision, muscle weakness, and sexual indifference. These symptoms appeared to correlate with a perception by these patients of their inability to engage in habitual activities, a finding that could be useful when screening patients with chronic fatigue for somatization disorder.[12, 13] Somatization disorder was found to coexist quite often with major depression and sometimes also with panic disorder.

A less severe depressive syndrome, dysthymia, was found in 4.9% of the patients; a more severe one, bipolar disorder, accompanied the fatigue of 0.9% of the patients. Social phobia and agoraphobia without panic attacks (1.5% of patients each), generalized anxiety disorder (1.2% of cases), and obsessive–compulsive disorder (0.9%) completed the spectrum of anxiety disorders. Worth mentioning is also the fact that 28% of our patients with chronic fatigue had current or past substance use disorders, predominantly alcohol, cannabinoids, opioids, and amphetamine abuse or dependence. Although these disorders were not considered the direct cause of chronic fatigue, the patients with a lifetime history of a substance use disorder reported more lifetime depressive symptoms and were more likely to have had suicidal ideation and attempts.[14]

PHYSICAL DISORDERS

The medical disorders identified as the cause of illness among 327 patients with a chief complaint of chronic fatigue were obstructive sleep apnea (1% of cases), temporal lobe epilepsy (0.7%), polymyalgia rheumatica (0.7%), bronchial asthma (0.7%), hypopituitarism (0.3%), hypothyroidism (0.3%), systemic lupus erythematosus (0.3%), and chronic infections (Lyme disease in 1 case and prolonged recovery after Epstein-Barr virus infection, cytomegalovirus mononucleosis, and viral hepatitis A in 1 case each, for a total prevalence of 1.2%). Minor laboratory abnormalities (anemia, atypical lymphocytosis, elevations of the erythrocyte sedimentation rate, hypophosphatemia, decreased serum iron and total iron binding capacity, microscopic hematuria) were relatively common but produced diagnostic information relevant to fatigue in less than 5% of the patients.[15] Serologic evidence of reactivated Epstein-Barr virus was found in 23% of the patients, but physical examination and further laboratory testing did not provide support for a unique or specific physical, immunologic, or infectious ailment related to infectious mononucleosis. The prevalence of psychiatric morbidity in patients with elevated titers to Epstein-Barr virus was somewhat higher than that of age- and gender-matched control subjects with fatigue.[16] The presence of the so-called "systemic candidiasis" claimed by some 8% of our patients was not supported by objective findings; almost all the patients with this diagnostic belief were found to have a psychiatric disorder.[17]

Chronic Fatigue Syndrome

A substantial proportion of our patients believe that they suffer from the chronic fatigue syndrome. The diagnostic criteria already described in this text were recommended for both research and clinical applications, despite the fact that no data have been presented to demonstrate their reliability, validity, or prognostic usefulness and without consideration for the significant symptomatic overlap with depressive disorders.[18] When criteria are applied after the exclusion of psychiatric disorders, the frequency of the syndrome is less than 5% in our population of patients with chronic fatigue.[19] If psychiatric diagnoses are not considered exclusionary, approximately 30% of the patients with a chief complaint of chronic fatigue have the required number of additional subjective complaints. Compared with age- and gender-matched control subjects with chronic fatigue, the patients with the symptoms of the chronic fatigue syndrome had similar likelihoods of current psychiatric disorders (78 vs. 82%) and active mood disorders (73 vs. 77%). Patients with chronic fatigue syndrome were significantly more likely to have somatization disorder and to attribute their illness to a physical cause. In the majority of patients, the onset of their psychiatric disorder preceded the onset of the syndrome, usually by many years.[20]

Patients with the chronic fatigue syndrome reported more lifetime functional somatic symptoms than control subjects, with excess symptomatology in the gastrointestinal cluster (diarrhea, food intolerance), the menstrual cluster (excessive menstrual bleeding, irregular periods), and in the pain symptom cluster (abdominal pain, back pain). All patients reported depressed mood or anhedonia, and a majority had a history of prolonged periods of loss of interest in sexual activities, psychomotor retardation, and morbid preoccupation. The frequencies of the cognitive symptoms of depressive disorders (slow thinking, difficulty with concentration) were similar in chronic fatigue patients and controls. Only 20% of the chronic fatigue patients had any objective signs of the syndrome (i.e., fever, lymphadenopathy, or pharyngitis), a proportion no different from that of 13% found among control subjects.

We found little to distinguish patients with chronic fatigue syndrome from appropriate controls. The members of these two groups were demographically alike, had similar patterns of prior medical care, similar presentations of fatigue and related symptomatology, and similar physical findings. Our patients with chronic fatigue syndrome regarded their tiredness as due to an external cause (viral or immunologic) rather than to a mood disorder, possibly protecting themselves from feelings of guilt and worthlessness and loss of self-esteem.

The debate continues on role and primacy of mood disorders and somatization phenomena in the pathogenesis and maintenance of chronic fatigue syndrome. Many patients believe that depression is secondary to chronic fatigue syndrome and argue that depressive symptoms follow the onset of fatigue and are brought on by the frustration of having to deal with the disability produced by the fatigue. Our data do not support this contention; depression generally preceded fatigue or had a simultaneous onset, and we found no relationship between duration and severity of the symptoms of the chronic fatigue syndrome and the presence of major depressive disorders. Direct comparisons of the frequency of psychiatric disorders found among patients with chronic fatigue and in patients with a variety of chronic illnesses have supported our view that the excess of psychiatric morbidity identifiable in chronic fatigue syndrome is not a consequence of coping with a chronic, disabling condition. In one study, patients with chronic fatigue were shown to have a significantly higher lifetime prevalence of major depression (76 vs. 42%) and somatization disorders (46 vs. 0%) than did patients with seriously disabling rheumatoid arthritis.[21] In another recent study,[6] patients with chronic fatigue syndrome were compared with patients with peripheral neuromuscular fatiguing illnesses such as myasthenia gravis and chronic myopathies. Using criteria that excluded fatigue as a symptom, 72% of the chronic fatigue syndrome patients were classified as psychiatric cases as compared with 36% of the neuromuscular group.

Organic etiologies proposed for the chronic fatigue syndrome have centered on the role of chronic viral infections. In the past decade, consideration has been given to the role of the Epstein-Barr virus,[22-24] human herpesvirus type 6,[25-27] and enteroviruses,[28-30] but confirmatory evidence has not yet been produced. Recently published data[31] have demonstrated evidence for impaired activation of the hypothalamic–pituitary–adrenal axis in patients with chronic fatigue syndrome. Compared with normal subjects, patients showed an attenuated adrenocorticotropin response to ovine corticotropin-releasing hormone, an increased adrenocortical sensitivity to adrenocorticotropin, and an elevated basal evening adrenocorticotropin concentration, and reduced basal evening glucocorticoid levels. The results were interpreted to indicate a central nervous system defect, i.e., at or above the level of the hypothalamus, resulting in a deficiency in the release of corticotropin-releasing hormone and other secretagogues that are necessary for the normal activation of the pituitary–adrenal axis. In this context, it is worth mentioning that an attenuated adrenocorticotropin response to corticotropin-releasing hormone has been demonstrated in association with elevated basal cortisol levels in patients with major depression[32] and in association with normal basal cortisol levels during the depressed phase of seasonal affective disorders.[33] These data and those demonstrating that central administration of corticotropin-releasing hormone in animals is followed by a dose-dependent locomotor activation[34] suggest that quantitative or functional deficiencies of corticotropin-releasing hormone may contribute to the etiology of fatigue and may represent a common biological pathway responsible for the symptom in patients with typical and atypical depressive syndromes.

TREATMENT OF FATIGUE SYNDROMES

Four double-blind, placebo-controlled trials have been performed to date in patients with chronic fatigue. The antiviral agent acyclovir, which was chosen for its in vivo and in vitro effects against Epstein-Barr virus, was found to be ineffective and to have unacceptable toxicity.[35] A naturopathic extract of liver extract, folic acid, and cyanocobalamin was also ineffective.[36] In both of these studies, a significant placebo effect was noted. More recently, two studies using intravenous immunoglobulin therapy were published simultaneously. One study[37] demonstrated transient improvement but significant side effects in 43% of the patients who underwent high-dose (five times the usual amount) immunoglobulin therapy for 3 months. The second study[38] demonstrated no benefit from twice the usual dose given monthly for 6 months.

In view of the lack of efficacy of these treatments, as well as the frequency of psychiatric illnesses among patients with chronic fatigue syndromes, we suggest a comprehensive approach that takes into consideration all aspects of the patient's being and experience, including the physical, psychiatric, occupational, social, and spiritual dimensions of care. The patient's diagnostic beliefs should be acknowledged, addressed, and accepted as legitimate topics of discussion with the physician. The physician should attempt to "speak the language" of the patient's diagnostic belief, even if he or she believes that the patient's interpretation of the fatiguing illness is incomplete or erroneous. Attempts to dissuade patients from strongly held beliefs, particularly at the outset of the treatment, may be fruitless or even counterproductive. Although most patients resist a psychiatric explanation for their symptoms, they almost invariably accept the scientific evidence of neurotransmitter deficiency as a mechanism for the cognitive and affective symptoms of depression and the role of chloride channels and γ-aminobutyric dysregulation as mechanisms of anxiety. Often, following improvement with psychotropic medication, the patients are more willing to accept the contribution of their psychiatric disorder to their fatigue state. We believe this acceptance is important because it is often accompanied by a developing sense of internal control over the illness by the patient and is correlated highly with improvement on follow-up.[39]

Treatment of depression in patients with chronic fatigue includes psychotherapy and pharmacotherapy. Cognitive–behavioral therapy has shown substantial promise in these patients. The goals of cognitive–behavioral therapy are to identify, challenge, and change the negative all-or-nothing thinking characteristic for most of these patients and to promote more effective coping strategies and style of thinking. This form of therapy has led to substantial improvement in overall disability, fatigue, and somatic and psychiatric symptoms. The outcome was not affected by the length of illness, but improvement was less frequently noted among patients who attributed their symptoms to exclusively physical causes.[40]

We have found that the great majority of these patients are unwilling to accept referral for psychotherapy, but are willing to attempt a pharmacotherapeutic approach. The pharmacologic objectives are to relieve the main somatic symptoms, sleep and appetite disturbance, psychomotor retardation, or agitation, as well as to improve anhedonia and the mood disturbance. The improvement in the level of energy and in the ability to think and concentrate will usually follow the somatic improvement.

Tricyclic agents, monoamine oxidase inhibitors, and serotonin reuptake blocking agents are all useful in this regard. The side effects should be carefully explained and medications selected according to the most severe target symptoms. For example, for patients with fatigue associated with hypersomnia, psychomotor retardation, and weight gain, we suggest a serotonin reuptake blocking agent (e.g., fluoxetine). For patients with insomnia and restlessness, a tricyclic antidepressant with sedative properties (such as doxepin or nortriptyline) offers many advantages. Patients who complain of morning fatigue respond, in our experience, to moderate doses of desipramine administered in a single daily dose preferably early in the day. Patients whose fatigue is associated with muscle stiffness and muscle pain benefit from nightly doses of amitriptyline. For patients with a dual diagnosis of major depression and panic disorder, we obtained improvement after long-term treatment with monoamine oxidase inhibitors (e.g., phenelzine). We generally start with the lowest preparation available of the chosen drug and plan weekly increments until either therapeutic effects or unacceptable side effects are produced. Augmentation with lithium or thyroid hormones has occasionally been necessary.

Patients whose chronic fatigue is associated with panic disorder respond to three types of medication: high-potency benzodiazepines, tricyclic agents, and monoamine oxidase inhibitors. The side effect profile of high-potency benzodiazepines is quite favorable, but the risk of physical and psychological dependence must be carefully taken into consideration.

The chronic fatigue patients with somatization disorder are the most difficult to treat, because their symptoms are usually long-standing and recurrent and involve multiple-organ systems in addition to fatigue.[41] Frequent follow-up visits and setting limits with regard to phone calls to clinic and trips to the emergency room are essential. A brief, focused physical examination on each visit is expected and appreciated by the patient. The physician should acknowledge the symptoms as genuine expressions of suffering and should not dispute the reality of the complaint. It is important not to promise relief or cure with these patients, but to encourage verbalizations of problems and feelings, pay attention to and reward healthy behavior, and to avoid unnecessary laboratory investigations and diagnostic or therapeutic procedures while remaining vigilant for signs of organic illness.

Psychosomatic Evaluation
and Management of Chronic Fatigue

Although the major role of psychiatric disorders among most patients with chronic fatigue has been firmly established, a number of obstacles continue to hamper the use of this knowledge in clinical practice. First, most of these patients believe that their fatigue is due to a physical illness, and they expect (or demand) an exhaustive and costly array of laboratory or radiologic investigations. Second, many practitioners are insufficiently trained in the recognition of psychopathology contributing to the cause of fatigue syndromes. Third, establishing a psychiatric diagnosis and initiating the appropriate therapy is a time-consuming process, especially when dealing with a patient disappointed or doubtful about this diagnosis and treatment plan, and particularly amidst the hectic environment of a primary-care practice.

For nonpsychiatric physicians we suggest that the evaluation of patients complaining of persistent fatigue should proceed according to the following sequence. The initial visit would be dedicated to history and physical examination, routine laboratory investigations (e.g., complete blood cell count, erythrocyte sedimentation rate, thyroid-stimulation hormone, creatinine, serum aspartate aminotransferase, serum creatine phosphokinase, serum electrolytes, postprandial and fasting glucose, and urinalysis), and a screening interview for the presence of the basic features of major depression, panic disorder, and somatization disorder. The patients without abnormal findings on physical and laboratory evaluation who have screened positive for one or more of these psychiatric disorders should be scheduled for a detailed psychiatric interview. If confirmed, current psychiatric disorders can be effectively treated by the examining physician, or the patient can be referred for specialized psychiatric care. If there is no improvement after treatment, more extensive laboratory and radiologic investigations (e.g., nocturnal polysomnography, testing of neuroendocrine functioning, viral replication studies, and magnetic resonance imaging of the brain) should be performed when deemed necessary in the context of each patient's symptoms and history of illness.

CONCLUSIONS

Fatigue syndromes are common in clinical practice and represent a significant cause of occupational and social disability. Chronic psychiatric disorders (major depression, panic disorder, and somatization disorder) explain the fatigue syndrome in the vast majority of patients whose chief complaint is persistent tiredness, asthenia, or lethargy. A medical explanation for the chronic fatigue of patients without abnormalities on routine physical and laboratory evaluation will be found only in a distinct minority. The diagnosis and management requires a careful and focused psychiatric interview, restrained use of laboratory tests, and elicitation of patient's diagnostic beliefs. Specific pharmacologic interventions and cognitive–behavioral therapy are effective in most patients.

REFERENCES

1. U.S. Public Health Service. *The National Ambulatory Medical Care Survey, United States, 1975.* Vital Health Stat [13] No 36. DHEW Publication (PHS) 79–1787. Washington, DC: Public Health Service;1975.
2. Holmes GP, Kaplan JE, Gantz NM, Komaroff AL, Schonberger LB, Straus SE, Jones JF, Dubois RE, Cunningham-Rundles C, Pahwa S, Tosato G, Zegans LS, Purtilo DT, Brown N, Schooley RT, Brus I. Chronic fatigue syndrome: A working-case definition. *Ann Intern Med.* 1988;108:387–389.
3. Manu P, Matthews DA, Lane TJ. The mental health of patients with a chief complaint of chronic fatigue: A prospective evaluation and follow-up. *Arch Intern Med.* 1988;148:2213–2217.
4. Kruesi MJP, Dale J, Straus SE. Psychiatric diagnosis in patients who have chronic fatigue syndrome. *J Clin Psychiatry.* 1989;50:53–56.

5. Taerk GS, Toner BB, Salit IE, Garfinkel PE, Ozersky S. Depression in patients with neuromyasthenia (benign myalgic encephalomyelitis). *Int J Psychiatry Med.* 1987;17:49–56.
6. Wessely S, Powell R. Fatigue syndromes: A comparison of chronic "postviral" fatigue with neuromuscular and affective disorders. *J Neurol Neurosurg Psychiatry.* 1989;52:940–948.
7. Schulberg HC, Saul M, McClelland M. Assessing depression in primary medical and psychiatric practices. *Arch Gen Psychiatry.* 1985;12:1164–1170.
8. Manu P, Matthews DA, Lane TJ, Tennen H, Hesselbrock V, Mendola R, Afleck G. Depression among patients with a chief complaint of chronic fatigue. *J Affect Disord.* 1989;17:165–172.
9. Weissman MM. The epidemiology of anxiety disorders: Rates, risks, and familial patterns. *J Psychiatr Res.* 1988;22(suppl):99–114.
10. Manu P, Matthews DA, Lane TJ. Panic disorder among patients with chronic fatigue. *South Med J.* 1991;84:451–456.
11. Escobar JI, Canino G. Unexplained physical complaints: Psychopathology and epidemiologic correlates. *Br J Psychiatry.* 1989;154:24–27.
12. Manu P, Lane TJ, Matthews DA. Somatization disorder in patients with chronic fatigue. *Psychosomatics.* 1989;30:388–395.
13. Manu P, Lane TJ, Matthews DA, Escobar JI. Screening for somatization disorder in patients with chronic fatigue. *Gen Hosp Psychiatry.* 1989;11:294–297.
14. Kranzler HR, Manu P, Hesselbrock VM, Lane TJ, Matthews DA. Substance use disorders in patients with chronic fatigue. *Hosp Community Psychiatry.* 1991; 42:924–928.
15. Lane TJ, Matthews DA, Manu P. The low yield of physical examinations and laboratory investigations of patients with chronic fatigue. *Am J Med Sci.* 1990; 299:313–318.
16. Matthews DA, Lane TJ, Manu P. Antibodies to Epstein-Barr virus in patients with chronic fatigue. *South Med J.* 1991;84:832–840.
17. Renfro L, Feder HM, Lane TJ, Manu P, Matthews DA. Yeast connection among 100 patients with chronic fatigue. *Am J Med.* 1989;86:165–168.
18. Matthews DA, Lane TJ, Manu P. Definition of the chronic fatigue syndrome. *Ann Intern Med.* 1988;109:511–512.
19. Manu P, Lane TJ, Matthews DA. The frequency of the chronic fatigue syndrome in patients with symptoms of persistent fatigue. *Ann Intern Med.* 1988; 109:554–556.
20. Lane TJ, Manu P, Matthews DA. Depression and somatization in the chronic fatigue syndrome. *Am J Med.* 1991;91:335–344
21. Katon WJ, Buchwald DS, Simon GE, Russo JE, Mease PJ. Psychiatric illness in patients with chronic fatigue and those with rheumatoid arthritis. *J Gen Intern Med.* 1991;6:277–285.
22. Straus SE, Tosato G, Armstrong G, Lawley T, Preble OT, Henle W, Davey R, Pearson G, Epstein J, Brus I, Blaese RM. Persistent illness and fatigue in adults with evidence of Epstein-Barr virus infection. *Ann Intern Med.* 1985;102:7–16.
23. Straus SE. EB or not EB—That is the question. *JAMA.* 1987;257:2335–2336.
24. Gold D, Bowden R, Sixbey J, Riggs R, Katon WJ, Ashley R, Obrigewitch R, Corey L. Chronic fatigue: A prospective clinical and virologic study. *JAMA.* 1990;264:48–53.

25. Josephs SF, Henry B, Balachandran N, Strayer D, Peterson D, Komaroff AL, Ablashi DV. HHV-6 reactivation in chronic fatigue syndrome. *Lancet.* 1991; 337:1346–1347.

26. Levy JA, Ferro F, Greenspan D, Lennett ET. Frequent isolation of HHV-6 from saliva and the seroprevalence to the virus in the population. *Lancet.* 1990;335:1047–1050.

27. Buchwald D, Cheney PR, Peterson DL, Henry B, Wormsley SB, Geiger A, Ablashi DV, Salahuddin Z, Saxinger C, Biddle R, Kikinis R, Jolesz FA, Folks T, Balachandran N, Peter JB, Gallo RC, Komaroff AL. A chronic illness characterized by fatigue, neurologic and immunologic disorders, and active human herpesvirus type 6 infection. *Ann Intern Med.* 1992;116:103–113.

28. Yousef G, Bell E, Mann G, Murugesan V, Smith DG, McCartney RA, Mowbray JF. Chronic enterovirus infection in patients with postviral fatigue syndrome. *Lancet.* 1988;i:146–150.

29. Bell E, McCartney R, Riding M. Coxsackie B viruses and myalgic encephalomyelitis. *J R Soc Med.* 1988;81:329–333.

30. Miller NA, Carmichael HA, Calder BD. Antibody to Coxsackie B virus in diagnosing postviral fatigue syndrome. *Br Med J.* 1991;302:140–143.

31. Demitrack MA, Dale JK, Straus SE, Laue L, Listwak SJ, Kruesi MJP, Chrousos GP, Gold PW. Evidence for impaired activation of the hypothalamic–pituitary–adrenal axis in patients with chronic fatigue syndrome. *J Clin Endocrinol Metab.* 1991;73:1224–1234.

32. Gold PW, Loriaux L, Roy A, Kling M. Responses to corticotropin-releasing hormone in the hypercortisolism of depression and Cushing's disease. *N Engl J Med.* 1986;314:1329–1335.

33. Joseph-Vanderpool J, Rosenthal NE, Chrousos GP, Wehr T, Skwerer R, Kasper S, Gold PW. Abnormal pituitary-adrenal responses to corticotropin-releasing hormone in patients with seasonal affective disorder: Clinical and pathophysiological implications. *J Clin Endocrinol Metab.* 1991;72:1382–1387.

34. Sutton RE, Koob GF, LeMoal M, Rivier J, Vale W. Corticotropin releasing factor produces behavioural activation in rats. *Nature.* 1982;297:331–333.

35. Straus SE, Dale JK, Tobi M. Acyclovir treatment of the chronic fatigue syndrome. *N Engl J Med.* 1988;319:1692–1698.

36. Kaslow JE, Rucker L, Onishi R. Liver extract-folic acid-cyanocobalamin vs. placebo for chronic fatigue syndrome. *Arch Intern Med.* 1989;149:2501–2503.

37. Lloyd A, Hickie I, Wakefield D, Boughton C, Dwyer J. A double-blind, placebo-controlled trial of intravenous immunoglobulin therapy in patients with chronic fatigue syndrome. *Am J Med.* 1990;89:561–568.

38. Peterson PK, Shepard J, Macres M, Schenck C, Crosson J, Lurie N. A controlled trial of intravenous immunoglobulin G in chronic fatigue syndrome. *Am J Med.* 1990;89:554–560.

39. Matthews DA, Manu P, Lane TJ. Evaluation and management of patients with chronic fatigue. *Am J Med Sci.* 1991;302:269–277.

40. Butler S, Chalder T, Ron M, Wessely S. Cognitive behaviour therapy in chronic fatigue syndrome. *J Neurol Neurosurg Psychiatry.* 1991;54:153–158.

41. Escobar JI, Manu P, Matthews DA, Canino G, Swartz M. Medically unexplained physical symptoms, somatization disorder and abridged somatization: Studies with the Diagnostic Interview Schedule. *Psychiatr Dev.* 1989;3:235–245.

Chapter 22
Temporomandibular Joint Pain–Dysfunction Syndrome and Bruxism: Etiopathogenesis and Treatment from a Psychosomatic Integrative Viewpoint

M. BIONDI, A. PICARDI

The entities treated in this section, temporomandibular joint pain–dysfunction (TMJPD) syndrome and bruxism, have a major psychosomatic component among dental disorders. In the last 20 years several papers, appearing in specialized journals, underlined the role of stress, personality, and psychological factors in determining the above entities. In this paper, we will try to review them in an integrative manner, so that both medical and psychological aspects are taken into account.

TEMPOROMANDIBULAR JOINT PAIN–DYSFUNCTION SYNDROME

INTRODUCTION

The temporomandibular joint pain–dysfunction (TMJPD) syndrome[1] is characterized by pain and tenderness in the temporomandibular joint (TMJ) and the masticatory muscles, joint sounds (crepitus, popping, clicking) during mastication and opening, and restriction of mandibular movements. Other symptoms, like subluxation or dislocation of the mandible, tinnitus, dizziness, and pain radiating to the head, neck, and shoulder may also be present, but are not necessary for diagnosis. There are as yet no universally accepted standardized criteria for diagnosis of the TMJPD syndrome. TMJPD syndrome nomenclature underwent many changes and at times included different clinical pictures, only partially overlapping. In fact, this clinical entity has been labeled in many other ways, including Costen's syndrome, TMJ dysfunction (TMJD) syndrome, and myofascial pain-dysfunction (MPD) syndrome. These terms are not exactly synonyms; in their excellent review Moss and Garrett[2] tried to clarify the criteria for the differential diagnosis of TMJD or MPD syndromes (the term *Costen's syndrome* has fallen into disuse). They concluded that "a great deal of confusion exists regarding the differential diagnosis" and that the terms have been used synonymously by some authors, which present problems in cross-study comparisons. With this in mind, we decided to examine the literature on both syndromes, grouping the results together. We also decided to select, among the various available terms, the term *TMJ dysfunction pain syndrome*,[1] which highlights not only the mandibular dysfunction, but also pain, the most common complaint of patients.[3] However, it could be clinically useful for the reader to define the principal criteria for the diagnosis of TMJPD syndrome (Table 22.1) and better clarify the relationship between TMJD and MPD syndromes (Table 22.2). In the literature, the term *TMJD syndrome* is generally used to indicate cases of both probable organic and dysfunctional origin. The term *MPD syndrome* has been

TABLE 22.1
Criteria for the Diagnosis of Temporomandibular Joint Pain Dysfunction (TMJPD) Syndrome

---

Main Symptoms

Pain and tenderness in the temporomandibular joint and the masticatory muscles

Restriction of mandibular movements

Joint sounds during mastication and mouth opening

Accessory symptoms

Subluxation or dislocation of the jaw

Tinnitus

Dizziness

Pain radiating to the head, neck, or shoulder

The diagnosis may be made when one or more of the main symptoms are present; however, the diagnosis cannot be based on articular sounds alone [2].

---

originally proposed to indicate conditions in which the pain probably originates from myofascial structures, thereby excluding cases of evident organic joint origin.[4]

EPIDEMIOLOGY

Epidemiological studies have demonstrated that TMJPD syndrome is a common disorder, affecting a large portion of the population, up to 20 to 25%, without marked sex or age differences in the frequency of the syndrome (for a review[5]). In clinical populations, a number of studies have described the typical patient as a female, 20 to 40 years old.[6–8] The reason for this discrepancy may lie in the fact that women may seek professional help for this kind of problem more often than men.[9] In this respect, a recent epidemiological study is interesting: this study confirmed that objective signs of TMJD syndrome have no particular sex or age pattern of distribution. However, female and younger patients reported more subjective symptoms than male and older patients.[10]

TABLE 22.2
Relationship between TMJD and Myofascial Pain Dysfunction (MPD)

TMJD
Cases with an organic cause
Cases with a functional cause
MPD
Unilateral pain
Absence of evidence of organic changes in the TMJ
Lack of tenderness in the TMJ, palpated through the external auditory meatus
While the term TMJD syndrome is generally used to indicate cases of both probable organic and dysfunctional origin, the term MPD syndrome usually refers to a more definite clinical picture.

ETIOLOGY

Most probably, the etiology of the syndrome is multifactorial. Possible causes can be divided into two main categories: (1) structural, organic factors, and (2) functional factors. The possible organic causes are neurologic, vascular, or joint-related[11]: such causes will not be dealt with in detail here, as we focus mainly on psychosomatic aspects. When an organic factor is clearly present, the existence of a cause–effect relationship can be reasonably assumed. However, in a large percentage of patients there are only malocclusions, condylar displacement, or even no signs of structural damage: from now on, we will focus on this category of patients, in which pain is essentially myogenic. Basically, two models have been developed to explain the pathogenesis of TMJPD symptoms: a structural model, and a functional model.

The *structural model* emphasizes the role played by malocclusion, or by alterations in the maxillomandibular relationship. Support to this model is provided by the finding that many patients have occlusion mismatch[12] and that occlusion adjustment can have a therapeutic effect.[13, 14] It should be observed, however, that no significant differences in the frequency of malocclusion have been found between patients and controls.[15, 16] The structural model also postulates that malocclusion can produce an altered proprioceptive feedback, resulting in incoordination and spasm of the masticatory muscles. In this respect, it is true that many studies reported a high incidence of bruxism within the TMJPD population.[17–19] Nevertheless, as will be discussed later, occlusal interferences are not the only factor involved in the pathogenesis of bruxism: an important role is also played by stress and psychological factors. Moreover, neurophysiological studies do not support the view that malocclusion can induce, through proprioceptive reflexes, a hyperactivity of the jaw-closing muscles.[20] According to the *functional model* on the other hand, TMJPD syndrome is mainly the result of stress and emotional tension, which induce muscle spasm and fatigue. Experimental hyperactivity of the masticatory muscles has been shown to induce pain similar to that of the TMJPD syndrome.[21, 22]

Certain *personality characteristics* can render the individual more susceptible to the action of stress. Many studies have tried to determine personality correlates of patients with TMJPD syndrome. Pioneering work in this field has been carried out by Ruth Moulton.[23] She found that many patients were overtly dependent, while others tended to be obsessive, perfectionistic; in many patients symptoms of anxiety were present. Moulton hypothesized that patients developed oral habits, like grinding and clenching their teeth, to gain relief from tension: muscle spasm could then lead to pain, with a vicious pain–spasm–pain circle.[24] Another worker, Lupton,[25] found that patients were responsible, generous, managerial, and tended to deny feelings of submission and dependence. He inferred that they heavily relied on denial and repression, to maintain a posture of self-reliance: this would produce a strong somatic tension. A mechanism of denial and repression was also highlighted by Lefer[26]: in his opinion, jaw symptoms provided a way of keeping unacceptable feelings of dependence, depression or aggressiveness out of conscious awareness. McCall et al.[27] compared the Minnesota Multiphasic Personality Inventory (MMPI) profile of patients and healthy controls: they found that 48 items discriminated between the patient group and the control group. The patients appeared as frequently worried, restless, nervous, and irritable. Gross and Vacchiano[28] described patients as emotional, neurotic, easily worried, dissatisfied, overresponsible, and too conscientious. Schumann et al.,[19] comparing patients with normal controls, found a neurotic triad, with psychosomatic V, in the patients' MMPI profile (higher scores on hypochondria, depression, hysteria). Molin et al.,[29] using various personality inventories and a modified version of the Buss-Durkee Aggression Inventory, found that patients, compared to healthy subjects, had significantly higher scores in variables associated with emotional instability, nervous tension, tendencies to worry and feel insecure. Patients also appeared as more responsible, conscientious, serious, aggressive, and hostile. In another study, the MMPI profile of patients was within normal limits[15]; approximately half of the patients showed signs of anxiety, measured by the MMPI. However, the majority of these elevations did not exceed the normal limits, and only a weak relationship between anxiety and symptoms was observed. Malow et al.,[30] using the Spielberger State–Trait Anxiety Inventory, observed higher scores in patients, in comparison with healthy controls; however, the differences were not statistically significant.

Summing up, personality studies did not provide a clear personality profile of the TMJPD syndrome patient. Patients have been described as emotional, anxious, dependent, dominant, managerial, responsible, perfectionistic, hostile, worried, and insecure. Rugh and Solbergh[31] rightly emphasize that personality studies are correlational and thus cannot demonstrate causality: for example, it may be that the illness has caused the anxiety, and not the reverse.

Psychological stress appears to be closely linked to the TMJPD syndrome. Urinary concentrations of catecholamines and l 7-hydroxy steroids were found to be significantly higher in patients than in healthy controls.[32] The mechanism of action of stress is probably the induction of a state of excessive muscular tension, resulting in pain and possibly in structural damage to the stomatognathic system. It is well known that muscle activity increases in stress situations; some investigations also suggest the existence of a specific exaggerated response in the masseter and temporal muscles to anger and frustration.[33, 34] Patients affected by TMJPD syndrome tend to respond to stress with an increase in frontalis, temporalis, and masseter muscle activity.[35, 36] In a recent study, resting EMG activity of the masticatory muscles was found to be higher in patients than in healthy controls; furthermore, in response to mental load, EMG activity increased more in patients than in controls.[19]

After having critically examined the principal etiological theories, we attempt to draw some conclusions. However, it should be kept in mind that the TMJ can be viewed as a scale fulcrum, where the masticatory muscles and the dental system are functionally balanced[37]: consequently, the masticatory muscles, the dental system, and the TMJ form a functional unit. Therefore, joint dysfunction or malocclusion can be secondary to muscle spasm and hyperactivity, but the reverse can also occur.[14] With this in mind, the wisest conclusion about the etiopathogenesis of the TMJPD syndrome is that articular, occlusal, neurophysiological, and psychological factors are all involved, interacting in a complex way.[31, 38] A thorough physical and psychological examination can help to clarify which factor is predominant in a patient.

DIAGNOSIS

A good history taking is the first step towards a correct diagnosis. *Medical history* should investigate pain frequency, intensity, duration and quality, as well as worsening and relieving factors. As a general rule, pain results from, or is exacerbated by, function; often it is possible to notice a pattern of occurrence: for example, pain may be present in the mornings or evenings, or may be related to chewing. If the patient remains untreated for years, pain can become constant, with only variations in intensity.[39] Myogenic pain is usually described as dull; when the source of pain is located in the TMJ, or when there is a lesion somewhere, pain is more often acute.[40] The onset of pain can be related to trigger factors, such as emotional stress, trauma, or dental treatment. A complete dental history should be collected.[39] The presence of destructive oral habits, like bruxism, lip biting, fingernail biting, pen or pipe chewing, should be also investigated.

Psychosomatic history aims at evidentiating the presence of stressful events or situations temporally related with the onset or worsening of the disorder. It is useful to assess the patient's personality, as well as the presence of psychopathological symptoms such as anxiety and depression, using psychometric instruments if necessary. It is important to ask the patient about his life-style, his job, and his social relations: factors like these could play a role in pain onset and maintenance. The therapist should also pay attention to the patient's appearance, and to the way he reacts to the interview.[40, 41]

For diagnostic assessment it is appropriate to take advantage of a dentist's consultation; furthermore, it is advisable to have a TMJ radiographic examination performed. However, during *clinical examination,* it could be important to follow some useful criteria for the psychosomatic assessment of the case, suggesting the existence of a conspicuous myogenic component (Table 22.3). In this respect, if maximal mouth opening can be increased more than 2 mm with passive movement performed by the observer, the dysfunction is probably myogenic. It is also important to perform dynamic (active movements against a slight resistance) and static (the resistance opposed by the observer should be strong enough to prevent movement) tests. Pain evoked during a dynamic test can be myogenic or arthrogenic; instead, if isometric contraction is painful, pain is probably myogenic.[40]

Moulton[24] has given some advice for a *psychologically oriented approach* to the patient. The doctor should inquire into the nature of the situation with a thoughtful, nonjudgmental attitude; he should also manifest an interest in the patient as a person. It is important to carefully evaluate the degree of anxiety experienced by the patient, also paying attention to possible emotional meanings that physical symptoms may have. One should also try to make temporal correlations between the symptoms and life situations. The patient's reaction to pain should be investigated: for example, does he overreact or tend to be stoic? This type of approach can help to establish a good doctor–patient relationship; also, the doctor will gain an overall impression of the patient's problems, both from a physical and a psychological point of view.

TABLE 22.3
Differential Diagnosis between Arthrogenic and Myogenic Pain

Parameter	Myogenic	Arthrogenic
Quality of pain	dull	acute
Pain localization	poorly localized, referring to an extended area of the face	well localized
Relationship with stressful events and situations	generally present	inconsistent
Increase of passive movement mouth opening	greater than 2 mm	less than 2 mm
Pain during isometric contraction	usually present	usually absent
TMJ radiographic findings	alterations absent or not severe	possible presence of alterations
History of facial trauma	generally negative	positive in some cases

TREATMENT

The *classical dental treatment* is based on equilibration procedures and prostheses. Equilibration procedures involve the selective grinding and restoration of teeth, with the purpose of restoring optimal occlusion.[42] Prosthetic treatment can be subdivided into palliative or causative. Palliative treatment prostheses have simply the purpose of disengaging the teeth, interrupting the pain–spasm–pain cycle and relieving intrajoint symptoms caused by trauma, inflammation, or condylar displacement. Instead, when condylar displacement can be established as an important causative factor, prosthetic treatment has the aim of repositioning the jaw.[43] *Physiotherapy*, especially ultrasonic sound administration, can be effective;

"home remedies," like heat or a soft diet, are also frequently employed.[43]

Pharmacological therapy is mainly based on minor tranquilizers and analgesics: diazepam and aspirin are widely used.[43] In a double-blind study meprobamate was more effective than placebo in reducing symptoms.[44] Amitriptyline, a tricyclic antidepressant, has been reported to have a beneficial effect in some patients.[45] It is of considerable interest that a fairly high percentage of patients respond to *placebo treatment*. In two studies, approximately one-third to one-half of the patients improved after treatment with a placebo drug.[44, 46] Some sort of "dental placebos" also proved effective: 28 patients out of 71 reported improvement in symptoms after wearing a nonoccluding placebo splint for 2 to 6 weeks,[47] while 16 patients out of 25 reported a striking subjective improvement after two sessions of mock equilibration.[48] These positive placebo responses do not mean that pain is imaginary or that the patients are gullible; rather, they probably reflect the psychophysiologic impact of the doctor-patient relationship.[46]

In a functional perspective, psychotherapy may be the therapy of choice. Indeed, *psychotherapeutic and relaxation treatments* are widely used: group therapy,[49] relaxation training,[50, 51] assertive training, stress inoculation training, and rational–emotive therapy,[52] have all been reported to be fairly effective.

However, the only psychophysiological technique subjected to intense study is *EMG biofeedback training*. The use of this technique for the treatment of the TMJPD syndrome was first suggested by Budzynski and Stovya.[53] These authors showed that, within a single session, visual or auditory biofeedback was more effective than relaxation alone in reducing masseter EMG activity levels in normal volunteers. Recently, renewed interest in this technique has been provided by a study of Berry and Singh,[54] suggesting that masseter EMG biofeedback training can improve occlusal contacts. In a study, treatment with EMG biofeedback failed to relieve pain[55]; in a series of single case studies relaxation training appeared superior to masseter EMG biofeedback[56]; in patients unresponsive to drug and biteplate therapy, the combination of psychotherapy and biofeedback was more effective than biofeedback alone.[57] However, in the large majority of studies, treatment with EMG biofeedback proved effective, as can be seen from Table 22.4. Two studies have controlled for nonspecific effects. In the first, a group of 16 patients received 9 to 12 treatment sessions of masseter EMG biofeedback training, while a control group of 8 patients were "sham treated" with the same apparatus, supposedly receiving electrical stimulation for relaxing the muscles. Patients receiving biofeedback reported a significant improvement in pain, limitation of mouth opening, and tenderness; biofeedback appeared significantly more effective than sham treatment. Moreover, in the majority of patients the benefits gained from therapy lasted for a 1-year follow-up period.[63] In the second study, 10 patients were randomly assigned to treatment with 8 sessions of frontalis and masseter EMG biofeedback, while 9 patients received no treatment at all, but went through the same evaluations as the biofeedback group. Both groups reported subjective improvement in pain intensity and duration, but this improvement was significantly more pronounced in the biofeedback group; at a 6-month follow-up, improvement was still present.[67] A randomized, parallel study has compared the effect of masseter EMG biofeedback and splint therapy: biofeedback therapy proved as effective as splint therapy, and treatment results remained at the 12-month follow-up.[65] Summing up, EMG biofeedback training can be regarded as an interesting alternative to standard dental treatment.

Before starting a treatment, no matter whether a classical dental or a psychological one, it is important to assess the patient's expectations. The doctor should discuss rational treatment modalities with the patient: in this way the doctor's goals and those of the patient can more or less coincide.[24] Certain patients need pain as a protection against anxiety. It has been suggested that the more emotionally upset a patient is, the less physical treatment may be in order[24]; however, patients may demand radical procedures, desperately trying to find a physical answer to their emotional problems. In these cases, and generally in all nonresponding patients, it is important to proceed slowly with treatment, preferring reversible therapies. The doctor should avoid responding to the patient's demands with a radical escalation of therapy.[68] We conclude with

TABLE 22.4
Treatment of TMJPD Syndrome with EMG Biofeedback Training

Ref.	Pa-tients	Technique	Results	Follow-up
58	1	Sessions of masseter EMG BFB	Elimination of pain	Painfree for 6 months
45	23	Sessions of temporalis and masseter EMG BFB	Relief of symptoms in 15 patients	–
59	11	Sessions of masseter EMG BFB	Success with 8 patients	Improvement maintained after 4–15 months
55	6	Sessions of masseter EMB BFB	EMG levels decreased 2 patients slightly improved, 3 worsened	4 weeks
60	35	Sessions of masseter EMG BFB	Relief in 31 patients	–
61	7	Temporalis and masseter nocturnal EMG BFB	Marked reduction in facial pain	–
62	25	Sessions of frontalis EMG BFB	Reduction in EMG levels Improvement in the majority of patients	–
63	16	Sessions of masseter EMG BFB	Reduction in EMG levels Treatment successful in 15 patients	9 patients asymp-tomatic for a year
64	33	Sessions of temporalis or masseter EMG BFB	EMG levels reduced Improvement in all patients	–
65	15	Sessions of masseter EMG BFB	Improvement in 13 patients	Results maintained after a year
66	1	Sessions of masseter EMG BFB with bilateral equalisation training	EMG levels and pain ratings significantly reduced	Benefits maintained after 2 months
67	10	Sessions of frontalis or masseter EMG BFB	Frontalis EMG levels significantly reduced Improvement in the majority of patients	Results maintained after 6 months

BFB = Biofeedback.

a warning: in nonresponding patients a further careful physical examination has to be performed as well. In fact, long-lasting chronic pain from an unrecognized organic cause can induce emotional and behavioral changes that can cause secondary pain symptoms. As stated by Weinberg[39] in such cases labeling the patient as *psychosomatic* would have sad consequences.

BRUXISM

Bruxism can be defined as an involuntary, nonfunctional, excessive grinding or clenching of the teeth; this habit appears to serve no functional purpose, and is potentially destructive. In fact, if uncontrolled, it may lead to temporomandibular disorders, abrasive wear, and hypermobility of the teeth, pain in the periodontium, hypertrophy of the masticatory muscles, facial pain, and headaches.[69] According to conservative estimates, the *incidence* of bruxism in adult age ranges from 5 to 10%.[70] However, reports on the incidence and prevalence of bruxism vary widely[71-73]: this is not surprising, considering that many bruxers are not aware of their behavior, especially if it occurs during sleep.

Opinions regarding the *etiology* of bruxism are controversial. According to a *structural model*, bruxism is viewed mainly as the result of occlusal interferences: these interferences would trigger parafunctional jaw movements.[74] However, several lines of evidence suggest that bruxism is not exclusively related to occlusal interferences: a statistical correlation between the incidence of malocclusion and bruxism has not been found,[75] and in many cases occlusal adjustments do not stop bruxism.[76, 77] Also, in a recent study the experimental induction of occlusal discrepancies did not elicit nocturnal bruxism.[78]

Instead, according to a *functional model*, psychological factors and stress play a major role in promoting and perpetuating the habit. Many researchers tried to define the personality characteristics of bruxists. Vernallis,[79] using the MMPI and various projective tests, found a positive correlation between bruxism and measures of anxiety, hostility, and hyperactivity. Thaller[80] and Thaller et al.,[81] utilizing the Cornell Medical Index and the Rosenzweig Picture Frustration Test, found that bruxists, compared to controls, were more anxious and intrapunitive (i.e., they tended to turn aggressiveness toward themselves). Olkinuora[82] divided a group of bruxist patients into two subgroups: a subgroup of "strain bruxists," in which a connection between bruxism and mental strain was noted, and a subgroup of "nonstrain bruxists." The first subgroup was shown to be more aggressive, and to display a higher frequency of emotional disturbances. Molin and Levi[83] found a significantly higher level of anxiety in bruxist patients compared to controls. Another study[84] evaluated a group of 72 bruxers, comparing them to a normative nonbruxer group. Patients were found to perceive themselves as more internally controlled and to be more depressed, but less irritable and dysphoric; no significant differences in anxiety were observed between patients and controls. Recently, a correlation between type A behavior and bruxism has been pointed out.[85] It should be mentioned, however, that not all personality studies in bruxist patients have yielded significant results: Molin and Levi[83] did not find any correlation between aggressiveness and bruxism, nor did Frisch et al.[86] or Reding et al.[87]

Bruxism has been defined as "an anxiety response to environmental stress."[88] Indeed, in the last two decades a growing body of evidence has accumulated, suggesting an important correlation between stress and bruxism. An increase in tooth contacts during nonfunctional periods has been observed in people subjected to controlled physiologic stress.[89] Under experimental psychological stress, the electrical activity of the masseter muscle increased.[90] Marked bruxism seems to follow stressful or fatiguing days,[91] and increased levels of bruxism have been reported in patients who anticipated stress.[92] The perception of the desirability and controllability of life stress seems to be related to bruxism, and the effect of stress would be potentiated by the simultaneous presence of type A behavior.[85] Considering that the etiopathogenesis of bruxism is complex and probably multifactorial, we can suggest an integrated approach to the patient. When examining him, attention should be payed to his personality characteristics and his life-style, without neglecting, however, physical and mechanical factors that may be involved in his bruxism problem.

The *diagnosis* of bruxism can be very easy, if the patient is conscious of his or her habit, or has been informed of it by his or her sleeping partner. In the other cases, the presence of tooth wear, tooth hypermobility, fractured cusps, and masseter muscle hypertrophy can help to identify a bruxist patient.

The traditional *treatment* of bruxism is based on mechanical or pharmacological means. In Dawson's opinion, "regardless of whether the cause is emotional stress or occlusal triggers, the occlusion should be perfected ... the more perfect the occlusion, the less damage can be done to any of the structures of the masticatory system"[74] (p. 460). According to Ramfjord and Ash, occlusal adjustment results in "a marked reduction in muscle tonus, and harmonious integration of muscle action"[93] (p. 6). The occlusion can be perfected directly, by equilibration, occlusal restorations, and orthodontics, or indirectly, by occlusal splints.[74] It has been shown that splint therapy can induce a decrement in EMG-measured nocturnal bruxing activity; however, the effect disappears when the device is removed.[91, 94] Nevertheless, occlusal splints can be useful, particularly in severe nocturnal bruxers: in these patients, splints can provide good protection in the initial period of occlusal correction or psychological therapy. In acute conditions, short-term pharmacological treatment with diazepam[95] or methocarbamol[96] can be effective.

Alternatively, treatment strategy can be based on various forms of psychotherapy. Hypnosis has been used in bruxism for many decades.[97] In a recent study, suggestive hypnotherapy significantly reduced EMG activity in 8 bruxist patients, who also reported a decrease in facial pain.[98]

Behavioral techniques, like aversion therapy[99] and massed negative practice therapy,[100–102] have been utilized with success. Regarding massed practice therapy, however, other studies have provided negative or contradictory results.[94, 103] In the last two decades, nocturnal EMG biofeedback has been widely used for the treatment of bruxism, with good results: the most important

TABLE 22.5
Biofeedback Therapy in Bruxism

Ref.	Patients	Technique	Clinical response	Follow-up
104	9	masseter and temporalis EMG nocturnal BFB	< duration of bruxing episodes frequency not reduced	no
77	4	masseter and temporalis EMG nocturnal BFB	70% reduction of EMG activity	return to pretreatment levels after 3 months
105	5	masseter EMG nocturnal BFB	< duration of bruxing episodes frequency not reduced	no
106	2	masseter EMG nocturnal BFB	< rate and duration of bruxing episodes	no
107	12	masseter EMG nocturnal BFB	significant reduction of EMG activity subjective improvement reduction of pain	no
94	20	masseter EMG nocturnal BFB	< frequency and duration of bruxing episodes	return to baseline levels 2 weeks later
94	20	masseter EMG diurnal BFB	BFB not effective	–

BFB = Biofeedback.

studies are summarized in Table 22.5. Kardachi et al.[77] observed better results with biofeedback than with occlusal adjustment. Some reports suggest that biofeedback can be effective in subjects that have been refractory to standard dental treatment.[106, 108] Temporal analysis of bruxing behavior during biofeedback treatment has given contradictory results. In two studies, biofeedback induced a decrease in the duration but not the frequency of bruxing episodes[104, 105]: this suggests little evidence of learning. However, in other studies a reduction in both duration and number of bruxing episodes was observed.[94, 106] Further research is needed to clarify this point. A problem with biofeedback treatment is that in the majority of studies bruxing activity returns to pretreatment levels soon after discontinuing the treatment[77, 91, 94]; a possible explanation for this could lie in the short duration of therapy (1–2 weeks). In fact, when biofeedback therapy has a longer duration (2 months), improvement seems to be more lasting, and even better results can be obtained by gradually discontinuing the treatment for an additional period of 1 month.[107]

It should be remarked that standard dental treatment and psychotherapy are not mutually exclusive. They can successfully be associated in the same patient. For example, Robetti et al.[109] reported good results combining EMG biofeedback therapy with occlusal adjustment and splint therapy.

REFERENCES

1. Schwartz L. A temporomandibular joint pain–dysfunction syndrome. *J Chron Dis.* 1956;3:284.
2. Moss RA, Garrett JC. Temporomandibular joint dysfunction syndrome and myofascial pain dysfunction syndrome: A critical review. *J Oral Rehabil.* 1984; 11:3–28.
3. Greene CS, Lerman MD, Sutcher HD, Laskin DM. The TMJ paindysfunction syndrome: Heterogeneity of the patient population. *J Am Dent Assn.* 1969; 79:1168.
4. Laskin DM. Etiology of the pain-dysfunction syndrome. *J Am Dent Assn.* 1969:79:147.

5. Helkimo M. Epidemiological surveys of dysfunction of the masticatory system. In: Zarb GA, Carlsson GE, eds. *Temporomandibular Joint Function and Dysfunction.* Copenhagen, Denmark: Munksgaard;1979:chap 6, p 175.
6. Carraro JJ, Caffesse RG, Albano EA. Temporomandibular joint syndrome. *Oral Surg.* 1969;28:54.
7. Butler JH, Flke LE, Bandt CL. A descriptive survey of signs and symptoms associated with the myofascial pain dysfunction syndrome. *J Am Dent Assn.* 1975;90:635–690.
8. Heloe B, Heloe LA. Characteristics of a group of patients with temporomandibular joint disorders. *Community Dent Oral Epidemiol.* 1975;3:72–79.
9. Smith JP. The pain dysfunction syndrome. Why females? *J Dent.* 1976;4:283–286.
10. Rieder CE, Martinoff JT, Wilcox SA. The prevalence of mandibular dysfunction. Part I. Sex and age distribution of related signs and symptoms. *J Prosthet Dent.* 1983;50:81.
11. Weinberg LA. The etiology, diagnosis, and treatment of TMJ dysfunction-pain syndrome. Part I. Etiology. *J Prosthet Dent.* 1979;42:654–664.
12. Krogh-Poulsen WB, Olsson A. Management of the occlusion of the teeth. In: Schwartz A, Chayes CM, eds. *Facial Pain and Mandibular Dysfunction.* Philadelphia: Saunders;1968: pp 236–249.
13. Kopp S. Short-term evaluation of counseling and occlusal adjustment in patients with mandibular dysfunction involving the temporomandibular joint. *J Oral Rehabil.* 1979;6:101.
14. Weinberg LA. An evaluation of occlusal factors in TMJ dysfunction pain syndrome. *J Prosthet Dent.* 1979;41:198.
15. Solberg WK, Flint RT, Brantner JP. Temporomandibular joint pain and dysfunction: A clinical study of emotional and occlusal components. *J Prosthet Dent.* 1972;28:412–422.
16. Thomson H. The mandibular dysfunction syndrome. *Br Dent J.* 1971;130:187.
17. Ramfjord SP. Dysfunctional temporomandibular joint and muscle pain. *J Prosthet Dent.* 1961;11:353.
18. Franks AS. Masticatory muscle hyperactivity and temporomandibular joint dysfunction. *J Prosthet Dent.* 1965;15:1122.
19. Schumann NP, Zeiner U, Nebrich A. Personality and quantified muscular activity of the masticatory system in patients with temporomandibular joint dysfunction. *J Oral Rehabil.* 1988;15:35–47.
20. Yemm R. Neurophysiologic studies of temporomandibular joint dysfunction. *Oral Sci Rev.* 1976;7:31.
21. Christensen LV. Some effects of experimental hyperactivity of the mandibular locomotor system in man. *J Oral Rehabil.* 1975;2:169.
22. Scott DS, Lundeen TF. Myofascial pain involving the masticatory muscles: An experimental model. *Pain.* 1980;9:231.
23. Moulton RE. Oral and dental manifestations of anxiety. *Psychiatry.* 1955;18:261–273.
24. Moulton RE. Emotional factors in non-organic temporomandibular joint pain. In: Schwartz A, Chayes CM, eds. *Facial Pain and Mandibular Dysfunction.* Philadelphia: Saunders;1968: pp 318–334.
25. Lupton DE. Psychological aspects of temporomandiular joint dysfunction. *J Am Dent Assn.* 1969;79:131–136.

26. Lefer L. A psychoanalytic view of a dental phenomenon: Psychosomatics of the temporomandibular joint pain–dysfunction syndrome. *Contemp Psychoanal.* 1966;2:135–151.
27. McCall CM, Szmyd L, Ritter LM. Personality characteristics in patients with temporomandibular joint symptoms. *J Am Dent Assn.* 1961;62:694–698.
28. Gross SM, Vacchiano RB. Personality correlates of patients with temporomandibular joint dysfunction. *J Prosthet Dent.* 1973;30:326–329.
29. Molin C, Schalling D, Edman G. Psychological studies of patients with mandibular dysfunction syndrome. I Personality traits in patients and controls. *Swed Dent J.* 1973;66:1–11.
30. Malow RM, Grimm L, Olson RE. Differences in pain perception between myofascial pain dysfunction patients and normal subjects: A signal detection analysis. *J Psychosom Res.* 1980;24:303–309.
31. Rugh JD, Solberg WK. Psychological implications in temporomandibular pain and dysfunction. *Oral Sci Rev.* 1976;7:3–30.
32. Evaskus DS, Laskin DM. A biochemical measure of stress in patients with myofascial pain-dysfunction syndrome. *J Dent Res.* 1972;51:1464.
33. Perry HT, Lammie GA, Main J, Teuscher GW. Occlusion in a stress situation. *J Am Dent Assn.* 1960;60:626.
34. Yemm R. A comparison of the electrical activity of masseter and temporal muscles of human subjects during experimental stress. *Arch Oral Biol.* 1971; 16:269.
35. Kydd WL. Psychosomatic aspects of temporomandibular joint dysfunction. *J Am Dent Assn.* 1959;59:31–44.
36. Mercuri LG, Olson RE, Laskin DM. The specificity of response to experimental stress in patients with myofascial pain dysfunction syndrome. *J Dent Res.* 1979;58:1866–1871.
37. Pini P. *Schemi di gnatologia.* Milan, Italy: CIDES Odonto;1977.
38. Lerman MD. A unifying concept of the TMJ pain-dysfunction syndrome. *J Am Dent Assn.* 1973;86:833.
39. Weinberg LA. The etiology, diagnosis, and treatment of TMJ dysfunction-pain syndrome. Part II: Differential diagnosis. *J Prosthet Dent.* 1980;43:58–70.
40. Hansson T, Honee W, Hesse J, Bracchetti G. *Disfunzioni craniomandibolari.* Milan, Italy: Masson;1990.
41. Biondi M. La consulenza in medicina psicosomatica. In: Biondi M, ed. *La psicosomatica nella pratica clinica.* Rome: II Pensiero Scientifico;1992: pp 1–19.
42. Beyron H. Optimal occlusion. *Dent Clin North Am.* 1969;13:537.
43. Weinberg LA. The etiology, diagnosis, and treatment of TMJ dysfunction-pain syndrome. Part III. Treatment. *J Prosthet Dent.* 1980;43:186–196.
44. Greene CS, Laskin DM. Meprobamate therapy for the myofascial pain-dysfunction (MPD) syndrome: A double-blind evaluation. *J Am Dent Assn.* 1971;82:587–590.
45. Gessel AH. Electromyographic biofeedback and tricyclic antidepressants in myofascial pain-dysfunction syndrome: Psychological predictors of outcome. *J Am Dent Assn.* 1975;91:1048–1052.
46. Laskin DM, Greene CS. Influence of the doctor-patient relationship on placebo therapy for patients with myofascial pain-dysfunction (MPD) syndrome. A comparative study. *J Am Dent Assn.* 1972;85:892–894.

47. Greene CS, Laskin DM. Splint therapy for the myofascial pain-dysfunction (MPD) syndrome: A comparative study. *J Am Dent Assn.* 1972;84:624–628.

48. Goodman P, Greene CS, Laskin DM. Response of patients with myofascial pain-dysfunction syndrome to mock equilibration. *J Am Dent Assn.* 1976; 92:755–758.

49. Marbach JJ, Dworkin SF. Chronic MPD, group therapy and psychodynamics. *J Am Dent Assn.* 1975;90:827–833.

50. Gessel AH, Alderman MM. Management of myofascial pain-dysfunction syndrome of the temporomandibular joint by tension control training. *Psychosomatics.* 1971;12:302–309.

51. Moss RA, Wedding D, Sanders SH. The comparative efficacy of relaxation training and masseter EMG feedback in the treatment of TMJ dysfunction. *J Oral Rehabil.* 1983;10:9–17.

52. Steen PG, Mothersill KJ, Brooke RI. Biofeedback and a cognitive behavioral approach to treatment of myofascial pain dysfunction syndrome. *Behav Ther.* 1979;10:29.

53. Budzynski TH, Stovya JM. A biofeedback technique for teaching voluntary relaxation of the masseter. *J Dent Res.* 1973;52:116–119.

54. Berry DC, Singh BP. Effect of electromyographic biofeedback therapy on occlusal contacts. *J Prosthet Dent.* 1984;51:397–403.

55. Peck CL, Kraft GH. Electromyographic biofeedback for pain related to muscle tension. *Arch Surg.* 1977;112:889–895.

56. Moss RA, Wedding D, Sanders SH. The comparative efficacy of relaxation training and masseter EMG biofeedback in the treatment of TMJ dysfunction. *J Oral Rehabil.* 1983;10:9–17.

57. Olson RE. Biofeedback for MPD patients nonresponsive to drug and bite-plate therapy (abstract). *J Dent Res.* 1977;56:B61.

58. Carlsson SG, Gale EN, Ohman A. Treatment of temporomandibular joint syndrome with biofeedback training. *J Am Dent Assn.* 1975;91:602–605.

59. Carlsson SG, Gale EN. Biofeedback in the treatment of long-term temporomandibular joint pain. *Biofeedback Self Regul.* 1977;2:161.

60. Berry DC, Wilmot G. The use of a biofeedback technique in the treatment of mandibular dysfunction pain. *J Oral Rehabil.* 1977;4:255–260.

61. Clarke NG, Kardachi BJ. The treatment of myofascial pain-dysfunction syndrome using the biofeedback principle. *J Periodontol.* 1977;48:643–645.

62. Principato JJ, Barwell DR. Biofeedback training and relaxation exercises for treatment of temporomandibular joint dysfunction. *Otolaryngology.* 1978;86:766–769.

63. Dohrmann RJ, Laskin DM. An evaluation of electromyographic biofeedback for the treatment of myofascial pain-dysfunction syndrome. *J Am Dent Assn.* 1978;96:656–662.

64. Manns A, Miralles R, Adrian H. The application of audiostimulation and electromyographic biofeedback to bruxism and myofascial pain-dysfunction syndrome. *Oral Surg.* 1981;52:247–252.

65. Dahlstrom L, Carlsson SG. Treatment of mandibular dysfunction: The clinical usefulness of biofeedback in relation to splint therapy. *J Oral Rehabil.* 1984;11:277–284.

66. Klonoff EA, Janata JW. The use of bilateral EMG equalization training in the treatment of temporomandibular joint dysfunction: A case report. *J Oral Rehabil.* 1986;13:273–277.

67. Dalen K, Ellersen B, Espelid I, Gronningsaeter AG. EMG feedback in the treatment of myofascial pain dysfunction syndrome. *Acta Odontol Scand.* 1986;44:279–284.

68. Greene CS, Olson RE, Laskin DM. Psychological factors in the etiology, progression, and treatment of MPD syndrome. *J Am Dent Assn.* 1982;105:443–448.

69. Glaros AG, Rao SM. Effects of bruxism: A review of the literature. *J Prosthet Dent.* 1977;38:149–157.

70. Widgorowicz-Makowerowa N, Grodzi C. Frequency and etiopathogenesis of bruxism (English abstract). *Czasopismo Stomatol.* 1972;25:1109–1112.

71. Reding GR, Rubright WC, Zimmermann SO. Incidence of bruxism (abstract). *J Pent Res.* 1966;45:1198.

72. Nadler SC. Facts about dental bruxism. *NY J Dent.* 1973;43:153.

73. Glaros AG. Incidence of diurnal and nocturnal bruxism. *J Prosthet Dent.* 1981;45:545–547.

74. Dawson PE. *Evaluation, Diagnosis, and Treatment of Occlusal Problems.* St. Louis: Mosby;1989: pp 457–463.

75. Olkinuora M. Bruxism: A review of the literature on and a discussion of studies of bruxism and its psychogenesis and some new psychological hypotheses. *Suomen Hammaslaakaarin Toimituksia.* 1969;65:312–325.

76. Bailey JO Jr, Rugh JD. Effect of occlusal adjustment on bruxism as monitored by nocturnal EMG recordings (abstract 199). *J Dent Res.* 1980;59:317.

77. Kardachi BJR, Bailey JO Jr, Ash MM. A comparison of biofeedback and occlusal adjustment on bruxism. *J Periodontol.* 1978;49:367–372.

78. Rugh JD, Barghi H, Drago CJ. Experimental occlusal discrepancies and nocturnal bruxism. *J Prosthet Dent.* 1984;51:548.

79. Vernallis FF. Teeth-grinding: Some relationships to anxiety, hostility and hyperactivity. *J Clin Psychol.* 1955;11:389–391.

80. Thaller JL. Use of the Cornell Index to determine the correlation between bruxism and the anxiety state: A preliminary report. *J Periodontol.* 1960;31:138–140.

81. Thaller JL, Rosen G, Saltzman S. Study of the relationship of frustration and anxiety to bruxism. *J Periodontol.* 1967;38:193–197.

82. Olkinuora M. A psychosomatic study of bruxism with emphasis on mental strain and familiar predisposing factors. *Proc Finn Dent Soc.* 1972;68:110–123.

83. Molin C, Levi L. A psycho-odontologic investigation of patients with bruxism. *Acta Odontol Scand.* 1966; 24:373–391.

84. Pierce CJ, Gale EN. Psychometric evaluation of bruxers (abstract 752). *J Dent Res.* 1984;63:254.

85. Pingitore G, Chrobak V, Petrie J. The social and psychologic factors of bruxism. *J Prosthet Dent.* 1991;5:443–446.

86. Frisch J, Katz L, Ferreira AJ. A study on the relationship between bruxism and aggression. *J Periodontol.* 1960;31:409–412.

87. Reding GR, Zepelin H, Monroe LJ. Personality studies of nocturnal teeth-grinders. *Percept Motor Skills.* 1968;26:523–531.

88. Kristal L. Bruxism: An anxiety response to environmental stress. In: Spielberger CL, Sarason IG, eds. *Stress and Anxiety.* Washington, DC: Hemisphere;1979.

89. Butler JH, Stallard RE. Physiologic stress and tooth contact. *J Periodont Res.* 1969;4:152.

90. Yemm R. Variations in the electrical activity of the human masseter muscle occurring in association with emotional stress. *Arch Oral Biol.* 1969;14:873.

91. Rugh JD, Solberg WK. Electromyographic studies of bruxist behavior before and during treatment. *Calif Dent Assn J.* 1975;3:56–59.

92. Funch DP, Gale EN. Factors associated with nocturnal bruxism and its treatment. *J Behav Med.* 1980;3:385–397.

93. Ramfjord SP, Ash MM. *Occlusion.* Philadelphia: Saunders;1971.

94. Pierce CJ, Gale EN. A comparison of different treatments for nocturnal bruxism. *J Dent Res.* 1988;67:597–601.

95. Montgomery MT, Nishioka GJ, Rugh JD, Thrash WJ. Effect of diazepam on nocturnal masticatory muscle activity (abstract 96). *J Dent Res.* 1986;65:1980.

96. Chasins AI. Methocarbamal (Robaxin) as an adjunct in the treatment of bruxism. *J Dent Med.* 1959;14:166–170.

97. Glebred MB. Treatment of bruxism. A case report. *J Hypnos Psychol Dent.* 1958;1:18.

98. Clarke JH, Reynolds PJ. Suggestive hypnotherapy for nocturnal bruxism: A pilot study. *Am J Clin Hypn.* 1991;33:248–253.

99. Heller RF, Strang HR. Controlling bruxism through automated aversive conditioning. *Behav Res Ther.* 1973;11:327.

100. Ayer WA, Gale EN. Extinction of bruxism by massed practice therapy. *J Can Dent Assn.* 1969;35:492–494.

101. Ayer WA, Levin MP. Elimination of tooth grinding habits by massed practice therapy. *J Periodontol.* 1973;44:569–571.

102. Rugh JD, Solberg WK. Cognitive components of massed muscle exercise for bruxist subjects. *IADR Prog Abst.* 1974;53:464.

103. Heller RF, Forgione AG. An evaluation of bruxism control: Massed negative practice and automated relaxation training. *J Dent Res.* 1976;54:1120–1123.

104. Kardachi BJ, Clarke NG. The use of biofeedback to control bruxism. *J Periodontol.* 1977;48:639–642.

105. Rugh JD, Johnson RW. Temporal analysis of nocturnal bruxism during EMG biofeedback. *J Periodontol.* 1981;52:263–265.

106. Moss RA, Hammer D, Adams HE, Jenkins JO, Thompson K, Haber J. A more efficient feedback procedure for the treatment of nocturnal bruxism. *J Oral Rehabil.* 1982;9:125–131.

107. Hudzinski LG, Walters PJ. Use of a portable electromyogram integrator and biofeedback unit in the treatment of chronic nocturnal bruxism. *J Prosthet Dent.* 1987;58:698–701.

108. Feehan M, Marsh N. The reduction of bruxism using contingent EMG audible feedback A case study. *J Behav Ther Exp Psychiatry.* 1989;20:179–183.

109. Robetti I, Pellerey G, Montagnino E, Tiranti B. Un caso di applicazione del biofeedback in odontostomatologia. *Minerva Stomatol.* 1985;34:361–368.

Chapter 23
Body Image Disorders

PHILIP SNAITH

Attention to disturbances of the person's perception of his own body, its size and defects (real or imagined), has gained in prominence in the last decade. Professional focus upon eating disorders, especially anorexia nervosa with its characteristic gross distortion of self-perception of body size, has led to increasing awareness of milder and atypical presentations of eating disorders. The special relationship of body image disparagement to more general psychic disturbance, especially lowering of self-esteem with limitation of personal efficacy, has brought the subject out of the narrower clinical domain into the wider aspect of community survey.

The other major emphasis has been the recognition of psychopathological disorder and presentation of patients suffering from such disorders in the nonpsychiatric fields such as plastic surgery and dermatological clinics. The association of certain irrational beliefs or overvalued ideas to true delusions and the presence of later indubitable psychiatric disorder in some sufferers has led to a renewed interest in the specific disorder once termed *dysmorphophobia* but now, in the DSM-III-R, renamed *body dysmorphic disorder*.

Yet another influence on the development of disturbance of body image has been the bombardment of the public with so-called standards of personal "good looks" by the advertising industry, greatly enhanced by gigantic posters in the streets and invasion of living room space on the television screen. Through such influences it is extremely difficult to avoid perpetual reminders of one's

491

own not-so-good appearance with the constant exhortation to take corrective action, probably by purchasing and application of some medication or supposedly wholesome foodstuff.

This chapter will present a general overview of the field in the early 1990s with exclusion of those aspects related to clinical eating disorders. The specific characteristic concern with bodily appearance, which is a hallmark of the gender dysphoria state of transsexualism, will also be excluded from consideration here.

NONCLINICAL ASPECTS

The state of research into body image disturbance in nonclinical populations at the commencement of this decade is well summarized by Thompson.[1] In the 1980s alongside research into the phenomena of anorexia nervosa, there was increased interest in the extent of dissatisfaction with personal appearance in the population, the state for which the phrase "normative discontent" was coined. These aspects of body image were considered under the constructs of: (1) a perceptual component (the person's own concept of the size of the body or a part of the body); (2) a subjective component, i.e., the person's dissatisfaction and distress concerning body image; (3) a behavioral component that concerns the degree to which the person takes action, either in an attempt to alter bodily appearance or avoidance of situations involving self-exposure to observation by others.

The prevalence of discontent with body image is certainly high in the Western world: the proliferation of publications addressing the topic of "dieting" attests to this. Nielsen (quoted by Thompson) stated that over half of all females in the 25 to 54 years of age range were on a diet. There is a large cultural factor which makes it impossible to extrapolate findings from one culture to another or one ethnic group to another, even within a single geographical area. It appears to be generally true that people in the Third World, especially India and Africa hold opposite attitudes to Westerners and equate fatness with feminine beauty. Furnham and Alibhai[2] showed that Kenyan Asians rated larger figures more favorably than did white British women living in Britain, whereas Asian women born in Kenya but living in Britain had an intermediate attitude to their body shape. The study was conducted on small, possibly unrepresentative, samples, but the authors considered that their findings were in accord with other observations of cultural differences, i.e., that there was no disparagement of obesity in less affluent, developing countries. Within a Western society social class probably has an influence, with women of higher social status valuing slimness more than those in lower social strata. The greatest differential factor is gender, with men being on the whole more content with their bodily dimensions than women; these gender-related differences may commence at puberty or before. Salmons et al.[3] conducted a study in samples of schoolchildren of different gender and different age groups in Birmingham, England; subjects were instructed by a self-rated questionnaire, to assess the size of various aspects of their body (chest, stomach, hips, bottom, and thighs) as "much too big," "a bit big," "about right," or "too small." In all three age groups (11–13, 14–15, and 16–18) boys used the statement "much too big" less frequently than girls with respect to all parts of the body. In girls, apart from the bust, there was a distinct rise in estimation of all aspects of their body as too large. The authors commented that "girls become more deeply immersed in the slimness culture as they become young adults and meet peer pressure and media incitement to conform. They are likely to have dieted also, in response to these pressures and in striving for a sense of self-mastery" (p. 30).

The phenomenon of discontent with body image seems to be correlated with such features as low self-esteem and depression although no strong conclusions can be drawn owing to the paucity of studies in noneating disordered populations, poor definition of the concepts of self-esteem and "depression," and the overlap of constructs when assessing body image attitudes and "depression." With more rigorously defined constructs the field is ripe for further investigation, especially of the relation of attitudes to body image to emotional factors.

The onset of menstruation in girls appears to play an important part in body image[1]; the role of this developmental stage seems obviously related to the gain in weight and also to the girl's perception of herself as a sexual competitor.

Thompson[1] reviews the theories that have been advanced to explain body image dissatisfaction. The "self-ideal discrepancy" theory relates to the personal standards of perfection. Other theories, the "adaptive failure" and the "perceptual artefact" theory, relate particularly to the genesis of eating disorders and will not be reviewed here. In general, it may be stated that sociocultural factors play a large role in determining personal attitudes to, and dissatisfaction with, their own bodies. There not only are the ethnic and gender influences noted above but there is good evidence from survey of bodily configuration in fashion magazines and sexually titillating literature that, in the Western world, the "ideal" has changed over the last 100 years.[4]

Neurological Aspects

Gross neurological disorder leading to distortion of the body schema[5] involve lesions of the parietal lobes and somatosensory relay stations, and of the temporal lobes. The unilateral misperception of one's own body, so-called hemiasomatognosia form of anosognosia for hemiplegia, occurs in right cerebral hemisphere lesions leading to left-sided stroke. The side of the body may be neglected or even disowned. Lesions in either parietal lobe lead to hemi-inattention and hemispatial neglect. Another disturbance of body schema based on parietal lobe lesion is the Gerstmann syndrome with the triad of finger agnosia, acalculia, and right–left disorientation; the inability to name parts of the body may extend from the fingers alone to include other regions.

Other aspects of distortion of the body image based upon neurological disturbances are discussed by Trimble[6] who considers temporal lobe lesions in some detail. Depersonalization is the most pervasive of the body image disturbances and it may be limited to the experience of desomatization. There may be a rich array of other symptoms including perception of the distortion of the size of the body and perceptual disturbances which relate to the self, including hallucination of the self (autoscopy) or another (Doppelgänger). A peculiar and characteristic aspect of temporal lobe disturbance is the sensation of swelling passing through the body in a cephalic direction, a sensation which gave rise to the ancient notion of the uterus taking leave of its moorings in the pelvis and the concept of the globus hystericus.

PSYCHIATRIC DISORDERS

Undue concern with some aspect of personal appearance was called dysmorphophobia by Morselli in 1886.[7,8] The term persists although objection has been raised on the grounds that a phobic state is not an aspect of the disorder. The ICD-10 has no separate category but the DSM-III-R considers disorders under two categorical headings: (1) delusional disorder, somatic type; (2) body dysmorphic disorder. The distinction between these categories rests upon whether the bodily concern has the characteristics of a true delusion, but a clear distinction cannot always be made; moreover, the nondelusional state may progress to the delusional state in the course of time. It may be noted that the classificatory system recognizes the disturbances as being discrete categories but the view has been put forward that such disturbance is always symptomatic of some other psychiatric disorder.[9] The actual definitions in the DSM glossary[10] are as follows:

DELUSIONAL DISORDER, SOMATIC TYPE

Somatic delusions occur in several forms. Most common are convictions that the person emits a foul odor from his or her skin, mouth, rectum, or vagina; that he or she has an infestation of insects of or in the skin; that he or she has an internal parasite; that certain parts of his or her body (e.g., the large intestine) are not functioning; that certain parts of the body are, contrary to all evidence, misshapen or ugly. People with somatic delusions usually consult nonpsychiatric physicians for treatment of their perceived somatic condition. The age of onset is generally in middle or late adult life but can be younger.

BODY DYSMORHIC DISORDER

The essential feature is a preoccupation with some imagined defect in appearance in a normally appearing person. The most common complaints involve facial flaws such as wrinkles, spots on the skin, excessive facial hair, shape of the nose, mouth, jaw, or eyebrows, and swellings of the face. More rarely the complaint involves the appearance of the feet, hands, breasts, back, or some other part of the body. In some cases a slight physical anomaly is present but the person's concern is excessive. In the past this condition was called *dysmorphophobia*, but since the disturbance does not involve phobic avoidance that term was a misnomer. The term *dysmorphophobia* has been used to include cases in which the belief in a defect in appearance is of delusional intensity. It is unclear, however, whether the two different disorders can be distinguished by whether or not the belief is a delusion or whether there are merely two variants of the same disorder. In this manual a belief in the defect of delusional intensity is classified as delusional disorder, somatic type. The age of onset is most commonly between the ages of adolescence and the third decade. The disorder persists over several years.

It may be observed that this definition is not entirely satisfactory: it commences with the statement that the defect is "imagined" and later considers that a defect may be present but that the concern is excessive, and this of course entails a subjective judgment on the part of the examiner.

It may also be noted that the definition of body dysmorphic disorder makes no reference to the size of the genitals. Hay[11] recorded the concern with the size of the penis in 3 of 12 male patients considered to be suffering from dysmorphophobia. It is of course the focus of concern in the culture-bound condition of koro.

Aspect of bodily appearance may be singled out for disproportionate attention. The feature may "remind" the person of some disliked relative. Personal insecurity, low self-esteem, or emotional disorder may be managed by the intrapsychic defence of focus on a part of the body. In those patients who are not actually psychotic, personality traits of the sensitive and perfectionistic type may be prominent.[11] In other cases the concern may be a prelude to psychosis, and in such cases the concern may be expressed in a curious manner e.g., "the skin under my eyes meets the nose in a strange way."[7] It is possible to construct elaborate psychodynamic interpretations in any particular case; these may satisfy the psychiatrist but not relieve the patient.

Psychiatric examination will detect the presence of associated psychotic illness, obsessional disorder, excessive anxiety, and depression. It is important to distinguish between the concept of depression which is a state of demoralization consequent upon a chronic handicap or illness, a depression which is an aspect of low self-esteem, and the concept of depressive disorder which may be expected to respond to treatment by antidepressant drugs; the presence of pronounced anhedonia is probably the best clinical marker for the biogenic depressive state.[12]

A much quoted study[13] from a dermatological clinic found that a group of patients selected by the physician as having no adequate basis for their complaint had a high depression score on the Beck Depression Inventory. The problem with such instruments is that they cover a wide spectrum of disorder, including somatic concern and symptoms, and will therefore predictably show high scores in such samples. The use of the simple self-assessment device, the Hospital Anxiety and Depression Scale[14] may provide useful information in these patients since the depression subscale focuses on anhedonia.

The management of the importunate patient who persistently requests treatment for a bodily "abnormality" when such abnormality is either absent or minimal, is difficult. There are of course no absolute standards of "normality" of appearance. In doubtful cases good medical practice does require psychiatric opinion; emotionally disturbed or prepsychotic patients may become more dissatisfied by collusion with their demands. The malignant nature of body dysmorphic disorder has often been underlined (see above reviews for evidence).

In delusional disorder the treatment is obvious and antipsychotic medication is imperative. Even in nondelusional cases a trial of such medication is helpful, may sometimes lead to resolution of the complaint with sparing of years of misery and aggravation for both the patient and the medical advisers. Anhedonic depressive patients should be treated with an adequate dose of antidepressant medication. Patients whose complaint is a symptom of more pervasive anxiety state or neurotic disorder may respond to anxiety management techniques, congitive restructuring, or brief psychodynamic therapy.

The largest study of patients referred for plastic surgery was undertaken by Reich.[15] He concluded:

From the surgical point of view, the main indication for surgical alteration in appearance is the existence of correctable deformity. From the point of view of mental health, the existence of a psychiatric disorder is not a contraindication to operation as such, but should be viewed in relation to two criteria: (a) the realism of the patient's expectations, and (b) the likely ability of the patient to withstand an imperfect result. Psychiatric support is indicated if these criteria are not satisfied and if emotional problems exist which reinforce the patient's preoccupation with this deformity [p. 12].

REFERENCES

1. Thompson JK. *Body Image Disturbance: Assessment and Treatment*. New York: Pergamon Press;1990.
2. Furnham A, Alibhai N. Cross-cultural differences in the perception of female body shapes. *Psychol Med*. 1983;13:829–837.
3. Salmons PH, Lewis VJ, Rogers P, Gatherer AJH, Booth DA. Body shape dissatisfaction in schoolchildren. *Br J Psychiatry*. 1988;153(suppl 2):27–31.
4. Silverstein B, Peterson B, Perdue L. Some correlates of the thin standard of bodily attractiveness for women. *Int J Eating Disord*. 1986;5:895–906.

5. Cumming WJK. The neurobiology of the body schema. *Br J Psychiatry.* 1988; 153(suppl 2):7–11.

6. Trimble MR. Body image disturbance and the temporal lobes. *Br J Psychiatry.* 1988;153(suppl 2):12–14.

7. Birtchnell SA. Dysmorphophobia, a centenary discussion. *Br J Psychiatry.* 1988;153(suppl 2):41–43.

8. Phillips KA. Body dysmorphic disorder: The distress of imagined ugliness. *Am J Psychiatry.* 1991;148:1138–1149.

9. Bychowski G. Disorders of the body image in the clinical picture of psychoses. *J Nerv Ment Dis.* 1943;97:310–334.

10. American Psychiatric Association. *Diagnostic and Statistical Manual of Mental Disorders.* 3rd ed, rev. Washington, DC: American Psychiatric Association;1987.

11. Hay GG. Dysmorphophobia. *Br J Psychiatry.* 1970;116:399–406.

12. Snaith RP. Anhedonia. *Br Med J.* 1992;305:134.

13. Hardy GE, Cotterill JA. A study of depression and obsessionality in dysmorphophobic and psoriatic patients. *Br J Psychiatry.* 1982;140:19–22.

14. Zigmond A, Snaith RP. The hospital anxiety and depression scale. *Acta Psychiatr Scand.* 1983;67:361–370.

15. Reich J. The surgery of appearance: Psychological and related aspects. *Med J Austr.* 1969;2:5–13.

Chapter 24
Psychological Reactions to Medical Procedures

Jenifer Wilson-Barnett

Most nonsurgical medical procedures are undertaken as part of the diagnostic or therapeutic process. They usually involve techniques which aid visualization of parts of the body or biochemical analysis of certain fluids. Because they are undertaken so frequently, staff may consider them routine and fail to recognize patients' needs and reactions prior to and during such procedures. However, there is substantial evidence that anxiety and discomfort may be experienced for even those which are considered "minor." Clearly, staff communication skills need to be focused in this area because there is also reliable experimental work which provides guidance for good practice. Reducing psychological and physical discomfort through specific interventions should be possible in most cases, and it is now the challenge of helping to apply this in practice which should occupy researchers and clinicians alike.

The range of such medical procedures includes injections, biopsies, X rays, scans, and endoscopies. Despite the differences in these actual tests, certain common features pertain. Most involve a technician carrying out a physical "assault," either probing directly into the body with an invasive technique or "mapping" the interior to reveal or monitor abnormalities. Medical procedures involving repeated treatments are not discussed here. As more complex factors may be relevant over longer time periods involving patients' adjustment to illness and chronic symptoms, as well as the acute discomfort related to such treatments, more elaborate and sophisticated interventions by psychologists are often appropriate, and "training" for subjects to use such techniques is necessary. These have been well reviewed by Kendal and Epps.[1]

Patients have described their experiences during tests in particular ways.[2] They often feel vulnerable and exposed, feel they are being handled as a body rather than a person, and sense a lack of control in what is happening to them. Even for brief episodes such as simple X rays or blood tests, they may describe a feeling of "being explored physically." Their reliance on the technical competence of staff and their attention to detail evoke feelings of dependence and insecurity. Physical danger may only be imagined, for some tests, but there are known risks associated with even the most routine procedures which patients fear.

When specialized equipment and staff are needed, patients will be brought into an unfamiliar environment, often with heavy "space-aged" equipment. Dim lighting and noisy machinery, staff in protective clothing, and hard "clinical" surfaces do not serve to reassure patients. Their feelings of vulnerability and anxiety may also be compounded by physical symptoms and illness concerns. If tests are being undertaken in order to diagnose, fears of serious disease may heighten awareness and distort cues. Likewise, if tests are used for monitoring progress, results may have vital consequences for their future life.

All of these factors should alert staff to be sensitive, informative, and reassuring while undertaking such procedures. However, much of the underlying problem and reason for patients' stress associated with tests seems to stem from communication patterns, with a lack of information being given prior to, during, and also after tests are performed.[3, 4] Reasons for this professional "noncompliance"[5] are several, most relating to different priorities and lack of skill rather than ignorance that this is a necessary part of care. For the most advanced and highly complex procedures, nurses and doctors may be unaware of the detailed steps, but in these cases, information is likely to be more forthcoming from the specialists. It is perhaps the lack of staff's appreciation that, particularly the first time, any test, however routine, may be stressful for a patient, which probably leads to unnecessary distress and to dissatisfaction with communications in general.

The most common patient response to novel medically related events is "fear of the unknown."[6] Anxiety related to what might happen, and, if this is left unresolved, anticipated events, may become unrealistically threatening and ultimately unnecessarily complicated by such fear and physical arousal. However, provision of systematic information, carefully structured and tailored to the needs and questions of the individual, may prevent such feelings ever emerging. It is salutary to realize that patients are just as dissatisfied with information provision now as they were 2 decades ago when some of the early studies demonstrated the benefits of information-giving interventions prior to stressful episodes.[5] This general background serves to illustrate how important this field of research can be to clinical practice. For the whole range of procedures, general and particular information should be readily accessible. In the case of major tests, more sophisticated interventions can alleviate psychological and physical distress, but this should build on to a pattern of open communication with motivated staff aware of the importance of psychological care.

ORGANIZATION OF CARE PRIOR TO TESTS

Continuity in members of staff providing care may help to reassure individuals undergoing major tests. If one nurse could prepare and escort a patient during the test, patients may feel that their needs are more likely to be met. This should be possible for inpatients who may require physical preparation orders from doctors which need to be carried out by a nurse. Obviously, this member of staff should be responsible for ensuring that psychological preparation is also completed.

Physical preparation for some tests, while providing an obvious opportunity to discuss fears and give information, may in itself cause distress. Some bowel-cleansing agents are unnecessarily violent and may cause a sleepless and uncomfortable pretest period, and starvation may add to feelings of weakness. Likewise, depilation can sometimes be embarrassing and evoke feelings of dehumanization. However, skilled and careful attention should alleviate these reactions and in general motivate staff to evaluate whether some physical preparations are really necessary. For instance, complaints of stomach pains after evacuation enema prior to barium screening led De Lacey et al.[7] to evaluate and change to milder cleansing agents.

Both physical and psychological preparation needs to be scheduled as part of the plan of care. In the ward situation, intentional planning is necessary to effect this and prevent other apparently more immediate demands taking precedence. This should then be followed by the primary nurse, who has learned about the patient's thoughts or fears, accompanying the patient to the specialized department for the test. This is sometimes arranged but often not. The presence of a reassuring figure, known to the patient, with understanding of his or her needs can have a calming effect, although this has not been evaluated systematically to date. Early experiments on animal stress and others with humans demonstrated the buffering effects of a significant other.[8] Likewise, a nurse or relative could prevent adverse consequences during some major tests such as cardiac catheterization.

Continuity of care for those individuals coming for tests as outpatients has rarely been well achieved. Tests are often scheduled well in advance, allowing anxiety to mount over the interim period, and psychological preparation is limited to written information, in large measure containing instructions on physical preparation. Patients, thus, arrive not really knowing very much about the test, often only hearing from others the rather memorable and unfavorable aspects.[9] Outpatient nurses and technicians should be alert to this situation and attempt to compensate by spending time with each individual as he or she arrives. In future, written information should aim to incorporate useful strategies from research evidence which has been shown to be generally helpful.

PSYCHOLOGICAL INTERVENTIONS: PRINCIPLES OF INFORMATION GIVING

A systematic approach to information giving should be based on well-evaluated methods. Two decades of work in this area, reviewed by Ley,[5] provides guidelines for practice. This is relevant to the preparation of patients for tests, although research has covered a wide area of medical practice.

Clearly, the information requested by patients, as well as that shown to benefit them, should be included. Patients have reported that they wish to know more about the purpose of tests and when they will receive the results[10] rather than the details of the procedure. However, nurses recognizing the potential stress involved considered that patients should also be given the opportunity to learn about the procedure and rehearse their coping strategies. Balancing these aspects is important, as patients due for tests for the first time may have preconceived ideas which are not accurate. It is important, therefore, to ask what they have been told and what they understand will happen initially. Their own questions and concerns will then be elicited. Only by assessing their desire for information and their emotional state will judgments about appropriate information be possible and their participation in the process be achieved.

Principles of information giving, based on research, involve prioritizing and a logical structure. The most important aspects should be discussed first because most people's capacity for intake of new knowledge is limited. However, the clear chronology of the events leading up to and during the tests provides a logical structure. Ideally, both written and verbal information should be available. This was shown to be most appreciated by a majority of subjects due for barium X rays,[11] although earlier work by Wild and Evans[9] indicated an even preference for the two modes of information supply among a sample of outpatients. However, it does help to use a written sheet to provide this logical account, and subsequent reference by patients is then possible and usually appreciated. Written information should not be seen as a substitute for verbal explanations when there are opportunities for psychological preparation.

When discussing forthcoming tests, staff should adopt the main characteristics of "a good communicator." They should use a pleasant interactive style and constantly look for signs of worry or perplexity in their patients, taking time to sit comfortably, appearing "available" for discussion, and prepared to spend time with the patient to ensure their full participation. This may be facilitated by finding an interview room if there are too many distractions in the ward or outpatients' department.

Planning the content of such preparation to cover relevant aspects is important, but this can be provided in a way which leads on from questions. This gives a more natural, less didactic, format. Such obvious details as: why the test is being done; who will do it and where; how long this will take; what will this involve; when will the results be available, should always be covered and are familiar to most trained staff (assigning a person to do this has already been discussed). Prepepared leaflets can cover such details and should of course be updated when changes occur.

WRITTEN INFORMATION

Evidence abounds that much written material designed for patients is unsatisfactory.[12] Not only is the content more directive than informative but the physical production is inadequate. Style and presentation can be important and help to make information more accessible. Readability scores should be calculated, simply based on sentence and average word length. It is clear that an average reader may find many leaflets difficult. Given that a majority of patients having tests are likely to be over 65 years of age, it is also important to ensure that print size is adequate, tending to the larger sizes. Ley's[5] review shows that the amount of information does not have to be limited and that pictures do not necessarily help comprehension (however, for X rays these may be useful).

Sufficient copies of such leaflets should be available for patients to read at peace and retain. However, British hospitals seem unable to provide even simple leaflets in sufficient numbers for wards and departments.

OTHER PSYCHOLOGICAL INTERVENTIONS

When building on a good general system of information giving to offer further support to patients, it is important to select appropriate and feasible interventions. For instance, length of test and pretest admission may determine opportunities to provide more specific antistress strategies. For blood tests, although over in minutes still abhorred by some, extremely simple direct distraction or cognitive–behavioral techniques may be all that is possible. When repeated blood tests are needed for someone who is phobic, specialized help could be introduced, and when children are involved in groups, it may be possible to provide positive self-statements as well as procedural information, as in Klingman's[13] successful study.

For other major tests taking several minutes or hours, more elaborate interventions might be introduced and practiced beforehand. However, it is still necessary to match such an intervention with the test and chosen preference of patients. It is, for example, not appropriate to teach behavioral techniques such as muscle contraction and relaxation to those undergoing a test in which they are constantly required to move or breathe by the attending staff. Likewise, any technique that requires peace and quiet may not be suitable for investigations carried out in busy departments. Practice opportunities are necessary for many of the cognitive and behavioral interventions, and thus, outpatients may only benefit if special arrangements are made for such sessions. However, where particular major tests are undertaken frequently in particular areas, staff may benefit their patients by becoming proficient in such preparation and instruction. Cardiac wards having several cardiac catheterizations daily and gastroscopy clinics should provide specialists responsible for this type of preparation, able to teach other staff so that these interventions become established practice.

Although there was an effort in the research over the last 2 decades to isolate specific components within psychological interventions found to be associated with specific outcomes, it seems sensible in practice to be eclectic.[5] Use of a combined approach is inevitable to some extent, it is not possible to direct cognitive approaches away from unrealistic fears without a realistic account of anticipated events. Relaxation or deep breathing could also not be employed usefully, unless the subject knows when this should commence. It seems that many such techniques could usefully by seen as life skills for many patients—helpful during many episodes and likely to facilitate coping during health and illness. The efficacy and application of such interventions has been demonstrated at times of crisis, and certainly, major tests serve to illustrate how they can be applied to alleviate anxiety and physical discomfort. A brief review of evaluative studies is given below.

INSTRUCTIONS ON PHYSICAL COPING

It is difficult to find studies which evaluate interventions that do not include some components of behavioral or physical coping advice. As with research preparing subjects for surgery (in a review by Kincey and Saltmore),[14] most techniques build on a knowledge of what happens prior to and during tests and tend to indicate what to do to relieve discomfort. Requests for a rest, for analgesia, or for other comfort measures, should be generally solicited by staff and realistically included in psychological preparation. Nurses, for instance, would be failing in their duty not to suggest shifting pressure or weight during long periods of inactivity, and this is often accompanied by suggestions of breathing exercises or deep breathing to avoid chest infections, to which patients may be particularly vulnerable during hospitalization.

Studies evaluating specific information prior to barium studies,[11] cardiac catheterization,[15] and gastroscopy,[16] all contained information on physical coping in the intervention, although this was not seen as the prime and experimental component. This is probably an effective therapeutic aspect of preparation and one which patients have valued.[10]

SENSORY INFORMATION

This type of information has been shown as demonstrably anxiolytic during stressful medical procedures. Johnson's[6] review of studies directed by her provides the rationale and theoretical context for this intervention. This area of research was stimulated by a realization that much information given by staff may not be relevant to the actual experience of the patient during a stressful episode and that anticipation was therefore often not related to what happened in reality. Johnson's hypothesis directed research to establish that provision of sensory information, that is, an accurate and realistic understanding of what would occur and how it would feel, was associated with reduced anxiety and a greater feeling of control. A cognitive map of the procedure based on realistic descriptions from previous subjects provided greater reassurance than other kinds of information in several reliable studies.

One of the first major experiments by Johnson's team involved nasogastric intubation, or passing a tube to extract gastric contents for analysis which may be classified as a major diagnostic test. This is an anxiety-evoking and noxious incident: patients experience retching and soreness in the throat after extraction of the tube. Gastroscopy or endoscopy has been used as a model for a "stressful event" since the early 1970s. Johnson et al.[17] first demonstrated that more powerful anxiolytic effects could be achieved by providing sensory information than just by supplying the usual procedural details. Sensory information included details of what the patient would see, feel, hear, and smell. The researchers hypothesize that the more accurate the description, the more beneficial it will be in reducing stress.

Photographs and tapes were also used with a series of 99 patients in a gastroscopy clinic. The indicators of distress and fears used were: (1) dose of valium; (2) heart rate during examination; (3) hand and arm movements indicating tension during tube passage; (4) gagging during tube insertion; and (5) restlessness during the first 15 minutes. Three groups were compared on these measures, and baseline measurements were taken. The sensory message was played to the first (n = 34), procedural information to the second (n = 30), and the third group acted as controls (n = 35). Both intervention groups received less valium, but the sensory message was associated with less tension during tube passage, less restlessness during the examination, and also a lower rise in heart rate than all others.

When assessed and compared with other types of information, sensory information has been persistently superior in reducing anxiety; for instance, with female subjects undergoing pelvic examination, this was the case.[18] It was hypothesized that relaxation may prove more helpful than sensory information, as this procedure is particularly embarrassing and uncomfortable. With an intentional strategy such as relaxation, women might have prepared themselves physically and thus coped better with the passivity of the situation. However, sensory information was more helpful for this group.

Other researchers have also used sensory information in experimental studies, evaluating the effects positively. Early work with patients having barium X rays,[11, 19] showed that a combined information message significantly reduced the anxiety levels of patients enduring barium enema. Likewise, in a work by Finesilver,[15] it was demonstrated that comprehensive information on events and sensations experienced was helpful to patients (total sample = 40) in reducing the distress caused by the procedure and was associated with higher levels of satisfaction in the experimental group of 20 patients when compared with the 20 control patients receiving usual care.

When sensory information is combined with other forms of helpful advice or support, it seems to be most effective and probably suits the majority of patients' preference for preparation. This was demonstrated by Padilla et al.[20] when they tested four different film strips for 50 patients undergoing nasogastric intubation. They contained: (1) procedural information; (2) procedural information and sensory descriptions of common distressing sensations; (3) procedural information and suggestions of coping behavior to increase comfort; and (4) all three types of information. Each group contained both patients who had expressed a wish to feel in control by being more informed during the test and those who had not. Both from self-reports and for observer ratings, they all found "less distress on stressor impact" with the most complete package. Discomfort, pain, and anxiety were reduced. However, sensory information led to more people being willing to repeat the test. Preference for control had little effect on distress.

It is important to realize that sensory information requires carefully researched descriptions of the procedures. Patients' own reports need to be recorded, and the most usual value-free descriptions need to be employed. Adjectives such as "sharp," "pricking," "blown out," "tight," "pressing" are appropriate, whereas those reflecting an individual's appraisal of the intensity of the sensation, such as "quite painful" or "a little sore" may not be so useful, as others' appraisals may differ. Prepared tapes, photographs, and leaflets have been demonstrably beneficial and tend to be routinely employed now in some American clinics.

RELAXATION TECHNIQUES

In specific studies and for particular clinical situations or procedures, relaxation therapy can be valuable. Once learnt, this type of skill can be employed whenever needed.

However, in general for medical procedures, including surgery, results from this intervention are more equivocal than other strategies previously outlined. Only a few successful studies show this to be superior to other forms of support, particularly when specifically relevant to the actual details of the procedure.

Kaplan et al.[21] clearly demonstrated that brief relaxation training was associated with patients rating themselves as less anxious
during sigmoidoscopy and making fewer requests to stop the test,
although they also overestimated the duration of the test. It may
be that having employed the relaxation techniques they tended
to be too sleepy to ask the technician to cease and felt as though
they had been asleep and misjudged time. In failing to endorse
the findings of these researchers, Rice et al.[22] considered that relaxation did not help patients during cardiac catheterization. This
pilot study with 30 patients undergoing cardiac catheterization
attempted to assess a brief intervention by tape to teach a relaxation technique for use during the procedure. On neither self-
report measures of anxiety and distress nor observed behavior did
the intervention group differ from the controls. The authors concluded that the technique can be taught easily but doubted whether
it was actually employed by the sample. Once more, it may also have
been incompatible with the demands made by clinicians during
this procedure.

COGNITIVE COPING STRATEGIES

Various terms have been employed for describing these approaches,
but fundamentally, patients are encouraged to foresee and plan
for the stressful event and learn strategies that will help them
master their stress by thinking about it differently. Miller's[23] discussion about "controlling" responses to noxious events is relevant
to this work. Belief that discomfort can be reduced by the individual is seen as the most important aspect of control. This is then
associated with a reduction in both emotional and physical distress during the event. Through having it demonstrated to them
that stress can be experienced prior to the event and that cognitive approaches, such as employing positive statements and repeating controlling or optimistic phrases, can reduce this stress, patients
learn coping strategies. Positive reappraisal would encourage the

patient to remind himself of the benefit which could arise from going through the test, or to recall statements which emphasize that discomfort is "worthwhile in the end" and "will be over soon." For those tests which are fairly rapid but rather uncomfortable, such as a surface biopsy or a bone marrow puncture, "cognitive coping," may be particularly helpful. By emphasizing the value of the test, its accuracy and the prospect of correct treatment, patients could be led to feel better, or less "stressed." This may reduce the feeling of violation, or enhance a sense of control or choice in the matter.

However, some training for patients must be undertaken and involves discussing the procedure and necessary coping strategies or skills, which are rehearsed before application during the stressful episode. In the famous study of patients undergoing cardiac catheterization by Kendall et al.,[16] combined cognitive–behavioral approaches were employed. This was designed to compare the effects of a cognitive–behavioral intervention with an information or patient education package (with two control groups) on patients' experiences and physicians' ratings of patient adjustment to the procedure. Forty-four patients were randomly assigned to one of the four groups. The cognitive–behavioral intervention aimed to train patients to identify anxiety-producing cues and choose their own coping strategies in response. The intervention was designed in stages. Initially, patients were informed that the training was aimed to help them to feel less anxious and more comfortable during the cardiac catheterization. Relaxation and anxiety reduction was discussed, and the therapists discussed personal coping strategies in general, giving their own personal examples. Similar disclosures were then elicited from the patients and discussed in the light of successful means of coping which they had employed. Next, specific anxiety cues were mentioned in the context of the cardiac test and coping strategies discussed. Several rehearsals were then supervised with each patient, and patients were encouraged to employ them during the procedure.

Patient education was conducted for the other intervention group, with explanations of the procedure and an anatomical model. Both interventions took 45 minutes to complete. The two control groups either received additional attention or simply the usual care.

Outcome measures included self-reported anxiety ratings and a physician's rating of the patient's adjustment. Results of the study showed that both intervention groups were better adjusted to the procedure than either set of controls, and the cognitive–behavioral treatment was superior on both patients' self-reports and physician ratings.

Where repeated tests or stressful episodes are likely, this approach would certainly be worthwhile, as discussed by Kendall and Epps,[1] for medical treatments. This approach seems to accord with a new, more pragmatic, application of psychological experiments and to maximize the potential benefit for extremely distressed individuals.

CONCLUSION

Sufficient replication of studies and collated wisdom should give practitioners confidence to apply principles and specific interventions. Evidence that procedures can cause severe distress is strong, matched by research demonstrating therapeutic approaches to prevent and alleviate this. General implementation of good information-giving strategies and training for staff to include sensory descriptions is needed. More sophisticated approaches may also be applied by specialists, and, when frequent episodes justify this, nursing staff in particular should become proficient in the whole range of cognitive–behavioral techniques.

Future research should encourage field trials and inclusion of clinical staff as "therapists" or "interventionists." This might help to demonstrate the feasibility of greater dissemination and application. Less invasive but more modern tests (such as MRI and CAT scans), which are equally frightening, should also be studied. Written information on these is sometimes available for patients, but other staff need to know about sensation and experiences in order to help in preparation.

Despite the limited volume of intervention studies relating to any single test, it is interesting to extrapolate between them and with surgery. Similar features exist, and thus, psychological care needed to follow the same principles. Individual patients' preferences and choice should be paramount, and there seems to be general acceptance that the majority appreciate and benefit from either a behavioral, cognitive, or combined intervention. This need not necessarily take much effort or skill on behalf of staff and should be generally available. Greater partnership between patients, clinicians, and psychologists in this area of research in practice might reap real benefits for patients.

REFERENCES

1. Kendall PC, Epps J. Medical treatments. In: Johnstone M, Wallace L, eds. *Stress and Medical Procedures.* Oxford, U.K.: Oxford Medical Publications;1990: pp 99–119.
2. Wilson-Barnett J, Carrigy A. Factors influencing patients' emotional reaction to hospitalisation. *J Adv Nurs.* 1978;3:221–229.
3. Reynolds M. No news is bad news: Patients' views about communication in hospital. *Br Med J.* 1978;i:1673–1676.
4. Hawkins C. Patient's reactions to their investigations: A study of 504 patients. *Br Med J.* 1979;ii:638–640.
5. Ley P. *Communicating with Patients.* London: Chapman & Hall;1989.
6. Johnson JE. Preparing patients to cope with stress while hospitalised. In: Wilson-Barnett J, ed. *Patient Teaching. Recent Advances in Nursing Service.* Edinburgh: Churchill-Livingstone;1983;6:19–37.
7. De Lacey E, Benson M, Wilkins R, Spencer J, Cramer B. Routine colonic lavage is unnecessary for double-contrast barium enema in outpatients. *Br Med J.* 1982;284:1021–1022.
8. Nuckolls CB, Cassel J, Kaplan BH. Psychosocial assets, life crises and the prognosis of pregnancy. *Am J Epidemiol.* 1972;95:431–444.
9. Wild AA, Evans J. The patient and the X-ray department. *Br Med J.* 1968;iii: 607–609.
10. Schuster P, Jones S. Preparing the patient for a barium enema: A comparison of nurse and patient opinions. *J Adv Nurs.* 1982;7:523–527.
11. Wilson-Barnett J. Patients' emotional responses to barium X-rays. *J Adv Nurs.* 1978;3:37–46.

12. Spadaro C, Robinson LA, Smith LT. Assessing readability of patient information materials. *Am J Hosp Pharm.* 1980;37:215–221.
13. Klingman A. Mass inoculation in a community: The effect of primary prevention of stress reactions. *Am J Community Psychol.* 1985;13:323–332.
14. Kincey J, Saltmore S. Surgical treatments. In: Johnstone M, Wallace L, eds. *Stress and Medical Procedures.* Oxford, U.K.: Oxford Medical Publications;1990: pp 120–137.
15. Finesilver C. Preparation of adult patients for cardiac catheterization and coronary cineangiography. *Int J Nurs Stud.* 1979;16:211–221.
16. Kendall PC, Williams L, Pechaceck TF, Graham LE, Shisslak C, Herzoff N. Cognitive–behavioral and patient education interventions in cardiac catheterization procedures; The Palo Alto Medical Psychology Project. *J Consult Clin Psychol.* 1979;47:49–58.
17. Johnson JE, Morrissey JE, Leventhal H. Psychological preparation for an endoscopic examination. *Gastrointest Endosc.* 1973;19:180–182.
18. Fuller SS, Endress MP, Johnson JE. The effects of cognitive and behavioural control on coping with an aversive health examination. *J Hum Stress.* 1978;4: 18–25.
19. Johansen Hartfield M, Cason CL. Effect of information on emotional responses during barium enema. *Nurs Res.* 1981;30:151–155.
20. Padilla GV, Grant MM, Rains BL, Hansen RC, Bergstrom N, Wong H. Distress reduction and the effects of preparatory teaching films and patient control. *Res Nurs Health.* 1981;4:375–387.
21. Kaplan RM, Atkins CJ, Lenhard L. Coping with a stressful sigmoidoscopy: Evaluation of cognitive and relaxation preparation. *J Behav Med.* 1982;5:67–82.
22. Rice VH, Caldwell M, Butler S, Robinson J. Relaxation training and response to cardiac catheterisation: A pilot study. *Nurs Res.* 1986;35:39–43.
23. Miller S. Controllability and human stress: Method, evidence and theory. *Behav Res Ther.* 1979;17:287–304.

Part III

Treatment

Chapter 25
Behavioral Psychotherapy Applications in the Medically Ill

JEAN COTTRAUX

The evidence produced by clinical studies that psychological factors influence the body and vice versa has long been recognized from hippocratic teaching to modern psychoanalytically oriented psychosomatic medicine. More recently learning and cognitive theories have been applied to medical illnesses in order to overcome the mind–body dualism and propose new short-term therapies for modifying behaviors, emotions, and cognitions which are antecedents, or maintaining factors of health or illness. The evidence derived by epidemiological studies of the association of social and behavioral risk factors in physical diseases like cancer, alcoholism, heart disease, and obesity gave rise to numerous interventions and controlled studies. Hence, the classical psychosomatic medicine has been progressively prolonged by a new branch of psychology which has been called *behavioral medicine, health psychology, consultation liaison,* or *medical psychology,* depending on the country or theoretical orientation.

Behavioral medicine was defined by Schwartz and Weiss in 1978[1] as "the interdisciplinary field concerned with the development and integration of behavioral and biomedical science knowledge and techniques relevant to health and illness and the application of this knowledge and these techniques to prevention, diagnosis treatment, and rehabilitation"(p. 249). This widely accepted definition emphasizes the integration of biomedical and behavioral knowledge and techniques. It was further proposed to integrate relevant parts of epidemiology, anthropology, sociology, psychology, physiology, pharmacology, nutrition, neuroanatomy, endocrinology, immunology, and the various branches of medicine and public health, as well as related professions such as dentistry, social work, and health education. This integrating tendency has been recently presented as the ultimate goal in the field by Weiss.[2] The scope of behavioral medicine extends from research efforts to understand basic brain–body mechanism interactions to clinical diagnosis and intervention, public health disease prevention, and health promotion strategies. This definition underlines both the importance of studying psychosocial factors and the need for basic etiological research. The present paper will deal exclusively with the therapeutic part of the scope of behavioral medicine. Extensive discussions and reviews on the mind–body literature and etiological problems can be found elsewhere.[3-7]

BEHAVIORAL PSYCHOTHERAPY
PRACTICAL MANAGEMENT

As for psychiatric illnesses, nine criteria may define the clinical application of cognitive–behavior therapy to medical problems.

(1) The therapy is structured: an agenda is set for each session, patients and therapists interact on the basis of an empirical collaboration to solve psychological problems related to health and illness.

(2) The therapy is centered on current problems. Therapist and patient mutually agree on the selection of target behaviors and contract on the goals of the treatment.

(3) Functional analysis is carried out with the patient. It consists in isolating target problems to analyze their current antecedents, and consequences. Mediational cognitive variables: image, thought,

emotion, and belief systems are related to ongoing emotions and behaviors. While the main focus is on those factors maintaining current behavior, the past history of the patient is also noted if it has some relevance to here-and-now problems.

(4) Continuous measurement of target problem behaviors before, during, and after (following test and follow-up points) therapy usually up to 1 year after the end of the treatment. Other measures, especially cognitive or personality measures, should be used to complement the too restricted measurement of target behaviors.

(5) A written treatment program (usually 10–25 sessions) is defined with the patient. Its rationale and techniques are explained to the patient. The term of the therapy is fixed in advance. Sessions are given once or twice a week in individual sessions or a group format.

(6) The therapy aims at developing the patient's control over his or her own problem behaviors. Self-control is an important issue in most of the cases of medically ill patients. They must first monitor their risk behaviors, then self-record them, and finally implement a self-management program designed together with the therapist. The effects of such a program are then continuously positively reinforced by the patient (self-reinforcement).

(7) The therapy possesses a structured format. Each session starts with an agenda, and at the end of each session real-life homework is agreed on with the patient and its completion evaluated at the next session. Ongoing functional analysis is carried out to understand new or unexpected problems. At the last session patient and therapist agree on a maintenance program. Booster sessions are made if needed. The patient is, in general, followed up to 1 year after the end of the treatment to insure the quality of the outcomes and assess the durable effectiveness of the treatment.

(8) The techniques are designed to teach the patient new coping skills or improve old ones which are failing. Three basic techniques are used: (a) modification of emotional and psychophysiological responses, e.g., relaxation, implosion, biofeedback, stress management techniques; (b) behavior modification, e.g., one may use assertion training to cope with anger and learn how to decrease aggressive speech and behaviors toward others; (c) cognitive

modification, e.g., the therapist could question and challenge irrational anger and hostility thoughts in a patient suffering from
coronary prone pattern. He or she may also implement problem
solving techniques and relaxation induced by physical or psychological cues to cope with a difficult social encounter. At a deeper
level basic schemas about overachievement, or irrational beliefs,
about perfection and lovability and rejection should be discussed
in a socratic manner with the patients. This modification of the
way the patient sees himself, the outer world, and the future pur-
ports to change his or her life-style. For instance, a man with a type
A behavior pattern may change his philosophy of life and hence
will stop confronting other people with anger or hostility because
he always sees them as potential competitors.

(9) Techniques have to be empirically tested in single-case experimental designs, and at a later stage in controlled trials. They
are based on learning principles: classical and operant conditioning, social learning theory, but also on cognitive principles related
to an information-processing model.

Accountability of the Behavioral Psychotherapy Methods

A conference sponsored by the WHO was held in Geneva in the
fall of 1989 on the treatments in psychiatry. The WHO has published a book with the results from this conference.[8] The general
conclusions recommended that governments strengthen or establish research institutions which evaluate the effects of treatment
methods for mental disorders and their prevention. The group recommended also that any assessment of a treatment technique
should include seven components, especially quality of life evaluation. Table 25.1 represents the seven areas of assessment.

If we apply these criteria to the current status of behavioral
medicine, it is in a fairly respectable position, as will be shown by
a brief review of controlled studies.

TABLE 25.1
WHO: Seven Components of Treatment Evaluation

1 Effectiveness
Symptom reduction
Ability to perform social and occupational roles
Quality of life of the patients and their family
2 Safety
3 Side effects
4 Ethical issues
5 Cost-effectiveness compared to alternative treatments
6 Applicability in various settings and by different types of mental health professionals
7 Possibility of misuse of the treatment (i.e. drug dependence)

However, quality of life measurement should be added in future studies which have to deal not only with symptoms or risk factors modification but with life satisfaction. One may decrease a risk factor of coronary heart disease and build a perfect body with a severe diet, exhausting jogging, and aerobic exercise, but have as a consequence a constricted and unhappy life with few satisfying close relationships. Four areas are generally included in quality of life measurement[9]: self (health, self-regard, philosophy of life, standard of living); personal fulfillment (work, recreation, learning, creativity, social service, civic action); relationships (love, friendships, children, relatives); surroundings (home, neighborhood, community).

REVIEW OF THE CONTROLLED STUDIES

Application of cognitive behavior therapy principles and techniques to medical illness treatment and prevention started in the mid-1970s. We will briefly review some salient aspects of a now vast literature.

CARDIOVASCULAR PROBLEMS

A high proportion of coronary heart disease can be predicted from classic risk factors: cigarette smoking, lack of physical exercise, obesity, raised blood cholesterol, and high blood pressure. Various psychological risk factors such as type A behavior and hostility-anger have been identified. Behavior modification can be used as method of modifying the risk behavior in individuals, then in the community, and ultimately the nation's health.

TYPE A BEHAVIOR AND CORONARY HEART DISEASE

Type A behavior pattern has been characterized, after Osler at the turn of the century, by Friedman and Rosenman[10] as a complex of behavioral traits including excessive competitive drive, aggression, impatience, and time urgency, which suggested the presence of a chronic struggle against time and other people. This was a dimensional concept: the other end of the spectrum being represented by the relaxed and easy-going type B. Accordingly, type A is a statistical construct depending on an accurate evaluation with paper and pencil tests or a more sophisticated videotaped, structured interview validated by Friedman and Rosenman.

The modification of type A behavioral pattern has been proposed to prevent relapses and death after coronary heart disease. Following many years of research all over the world, it appears that the type A behavior pattern is a more than dubious concept. Today, researchers are considering that anger-hostility and aggression are the core risk factors inside the general picture of the type A behavior pattern. Epidemiological research shows, that these notions are factors, not only in cardiovascular illnesses, but also in sickness and mortality in general.

Fontaine[6] reported on a preliminary study that cast some doubts about the validity of the anger–hostility pattern. Series of behavioral sequences were designed to "stimulate" the hostility of subjects. Verbal, motor, and physiological behaviors were measured. The preliminary results suggested that there was no significant relation between objective measures of hostility and measures obtained through psychological testing. Subjects that described themselves as hostile may not be so at all in our experimental circumstances, and vice versa. Subjects classified as hostile by the tests had disturbed patterns of social relation, leading them either to reduce their social supports, or to undertake changes in their life-style. New cognitive and creative conceptualizations suggested recently that three dimensions were underlying the type A behavior pattern: hostility-competitiveness, low self-esteem, and low perceived control. Powell[11] hypothesized that low perceived control emerged from a belief of pure environmental determism and a related belief that environment can always be changed with persistence. The type A patient attempts to reduce his or her perceived low control in striving to overcontrol his or her social environment. In this respect the focus of the therapy should be to help the patient to switch from trying to impose his or her own wishes on the environment and to bring himself or herself in line with the environment. The effectiveness of such a stoical or Zen psychotherapeutic point of view has yet to be demonstrated by controlled studies.

What ever the case may be, there is controlled evidence of the effectiveness of modifying type A pattern and some controlled evidence of the positive effects of such a modification on recurrence of coronary events. In general the programs are presented in groups of 5 to 10 participants and include five modules which are completed over 12 sessions: relaxation, cognitive restructuring, social skill training, problem solving, and stress–anger management training.

The most important controlled study was run by Friedman et al.[12] and was positive. The study compared 270 patients who received simple medical counseling to 592 patients who received the same treatment plus type A behavior management (relaxation, cognitive therapy, life-style modification). At a 3-year follow-up both coronary heart disease relapses and type A behavior were found to be significantly decreased in the group receiving the behavior modification program. The effects of the behavior modification were superior to the effects of the simple medical counseling. Another important study showed that type A behavior can be readily modified[13] but did not clearly show if this actually reduced the incidence of myocardial infarction.

Nunes et al.,[14] in a meta-analytic literature review of 18 controlled studies, concluded that psychological interventions may have a positive effect on coronary heart disease prognosis and justify more research on their clinical applications. Combined reduction of coronary events was 50% after 3 years.

HYPERTENSION

Johnston[15] reported a literature review with positive outcome. There are at least 30 randomized controlled trials or relaxation-based procedures in the treatment of mild hypertension. A variety of procedures have been used but the most effective combines live (rather than tape-recorded) training in a systematic method of muscular relaxation, simple meditation, and advice on the management of stress. An analysis of all the published studies available showed that relaxation training was twice as effective in lowering blood pressure as a wide range of comparison procedures. Individual studies have shown relaxation to be more effective than no treatment, nondirective psychotherapy and an elaborate exercise-based comparison treatment. The effects persist for up to 4 years and may be associated with a reduction in coronary heart disease.

Jacob et al.[16] had a less optimistic appraisal of the outcome literature, especially regarding long-term outcomes. Relaxation and blood pressure feedback have been used in 13 controlled trials with stringent criteria. Their effectiveness was not comfirmed in several large scale trials: this fact was due to the improvement occurring in the control group. Physical exercise and restriction of sodium intake led to limited outcomes, in poorly controlled studies.

SMOKING

Smoking may produce lung and throat cancer and facilitate the development of cardiovascular diseases. Sixty controlled studies with a follow-up of at least 12 months have been conducted in the last 10 years and reviewed by Glasgow and Lichtenstein.[17] Behavioral approaches are superior to control conditions but do not differ from alternative interventions. We compared a short-term (three sessions) group program of stress management to placebo, acupuncture and waiting list did not show any difference between the four conditions at a 1-year follow-up in smokers recruited through advertisement.[18] However, more insistent behavioral treatment lasting 10 to 20 sessions with a strong maintenance program appeared more effective in motivated smokers.[17] Behavioral procedures appear to be less effective in preventing relapses among heavy than lighter smokers (< 20 cigarettes per day). To produce long-term maintenance an intervention must yield high rates of initial cessation. Relapse prevention strategies must be capable of reaching and involving a high percentage of recent quitters. No theory or relapse model of maintenance appears to be superior to another.

It is probably easier not to start smoking than to kick a habit with such a strong, quick, and positive effect both on attention and anxiety. Accordingly, prevention, through advertisement, against smoking and social pressure is the general behavior modification policy which has been adopted by most of the official health agencies in developed countries.

PREVENTION OF CARDIOVASCULAR RISK FACTORS IN THE COMMUNITY

Social learning-based interventions have been widely used to promote healthy life-style and reduce the risk factors of cardiovascular problems. The "five community study"[19] showed the effectiveness of TV health advertisement in addition to counseling on dietary behaviors, obesity, plasma cholesterol rates, blood pressure, and resting pulse rate at follow-ups ranging from 30 to 64 months. The mortality risk scores decreased by 15% and the coronary heart disease scores by 16%.

RAYNAUD'S DISEASE

Raynaud's disease is a disorder of the peripheral vasculature in which, under conditions of cold or, more rarely, emotional distress, extremely painful vasoconstriction occurs. Initial negative findings have been contradicted by Freedman et al.[20-22] who have shown that temperature feedback can lead to greater control of skin temperature than alternative procedures, and obtain long-term reductions in painful vasoconstrictive attacks. To date, replications by independent laboratories are needed.

TENSION HEADACHES, MIGRAINES, AND BIOFEEDBACK

Chronic headaches have been treated by behavioral techniques: relaxation, cognitive therapy, and biofeedback or their combination. Although physiological bases of biofeedback are less than established, therapeutic applications have shown a widespread dissemination in the last 25 years. Frontal surface electromyographic (EMG) feedback has been proposed to treat tension headaches, and thermistor-recorded hand temperature feedback to treat migraines by voluntary warming. The literature on headache suggests that biofeedback, although it is not a placebo, represents an additional technique, whose specificity, and modalities of action are still discussed.

Generally, relaxation appears as effective as biofeedback. But in one study galvanic skin reponse feedback was superior to tape-administered relaxation.[23] Relaxation appears as effective as biofeedback in migraines. Nonspecific factors play a significant role in the therapeutic process. Self-control and self-management techniques, and cognitive restructuring in everyday life, should be associated with biofeedback to maintain the therapeutic gains.

Blanchard[24] has reviewed 10 reports with at least a 12-months follow-up. The tentative conclusions were the following. (1) *Tension headache*: Headache relief from cognitive therapy and relaxation is maintained for 2 and 4 years, respectively. Initial headache reduction with frontal EMG feedback alone deteriorates progressively, but not to pretreatment level, after 2 or 3 years. (2) *Migraine headache*: There is good evidence for a maintenance of outcome at 12 months. (3) *Migraine and combined headache*: (vascular and tension headache) treated with relaxation and thermofeedback: there is a progressive deterioration over 4 years. (4) Blanchard even suggested that the effects of biofeedback may be less long lasting than alternative therapies.

A meta-analysis of 37 studies demonstrated that muscle activity (EMG) feedback used to reduce tension headache is better than no treatment but is not different from alternative procedures, such as relaxation training.[25]

A cognitively oriented form of stress management appeared more effective than EMG feedback in one controlled study and should be more thoroughly studied given the fact that headaches are often related to depression.[15] A meta-analysis of digital temperature feedback for migraine headache supported the same negative conclusions.[26]

To date, biofeedback, the experimental tenets of which have been challenged even by its early advocates,[27, 28] seems neither an experimentally based device nor a useful and handy therapeutic tool in general.

Clinically, we found biofeedback of some help in patients who had strong expectations in high technology, but no clear controlled study is supporting such a purely clinical impression.

It is interesting to note the shift occuring in the *Journal of Biofeedback and Self-Regulation* which intended this year to become the *Journal of Applied Psychophysiology*.[29]

CHRONIC PAIN

Pain clinics which use behavioral and cognitive methods have developed in the last 10 years to treat chronic pain, whether organic or psychogenic in origin. Most of the behavioral and cognitive approaches have been incorporated into multidisciplinary programs treating together various pain problems. One of the most studied single syndromes is chronic low-back pain. About 70% of the patients entering an operant conditioning program for chronic low-back pain demonstrated improvement after treatment and most of these patients maintained improvement at follow-up. While pain measurement problems limited the conclusions of the research literature, 15 controlled studies have been conducted which tested operant techniques or some kind of relaxation. Studies on operant techniques have shown an increase of activity levels, a decrease in consumption of medication, and improvement in mood and reported pain. Studies on relaxation showed mixed results. The status of cognitive variables and "pure" cognitive therapies is still unclear.[30]

STUTTERING

Since the initial work of Azrin and Nun, regulated breathing has been investigated in controlled studies showing its superiority over placebo conditions. The greater effectiveness of massed versus distributed practice and the necessity of maintenance programs have also been shown. In general, nine 1-hour sessions are necessary followed by a transfer maintenance phase of 3 months. The percentage of stuttered syllables is generally reduced from 45 to 5%.[31]

Andrews and Craig[32] demonstrated in several studies the objective value of a 50-hour speech retraining program using the smooth speech technique. The prediction of long-term outcomes was related to the degree of speech skill mastery, normal communication attitude, and internalization of the locus of control.

ALCOHOLISM

Chemical aversion and covert sensitization are adjunct techniques with limited effectiveness. Social skill training with cognitive restructuring which teaches the patient how to resist social pressure to drink are especially useful in preventing the relapse of socially anxious drinkers.[33] Controlled drinking versus total abstinence has been investigated: assignment to a goal of controlled drinking does not produce a better outcome than assignment to total abstinence. Controlled drinking seems to be more successful in less severe alcoholics in terms of duration of illness, physical dependence, and psychopathology.[34]

EATING DISORDERS

ANOREXIA NERVOSA

Bulimia and anorexia nervosa are chronic diseases with substantial morbidity and mortality. There is a nonchance cross-over between the two conditions. Operant conditioning in institutional settings is restricted to a quasi-emergency treatment for anorexia nervosa where the patient shows very significant and life-threatening weight loss. This behavioral technique has been used empirically for more than one century. Its effectiveness is well established but the long-term outcomes are not modified.[35] Nonbehavioral family therapy (following Minuchin's model) was better than individual supportive therapy at a 1-year follow-up in one study that included both bulimic and anorectic patients.[36] Longer follow-ups are obviously needed to establish the effectiveness of this first positive study of family therapy in this indication.

BULIMIA NERVOSA

Bulimia has been recently investigated by cognitive behavior therapists, who conceptualized bulimia as a compulsive behavior related to self-image disturbances. Cognitive restructuring associated with exposure to food and eating response prevention seems an effective approach in 1 uncontrolled and 2 controlled studies.[35] Another study by Pyle et al.[37] showed the superiority of a structured group cognitive behavioral therapy over imipramine. Modification of body image and depression appeared crucial in 2 controlled trials. They showed the superiority of stress management over nutritional management[38] and the superiority of cognitive behavior therapy over interpersonal therapy and a simplified behavioral therapy program.[39] Agras et al.[40] showed at a 4-month follow-up that cognitive behavior therapy associated with desipramine was equal to cognitive behavior therapy alone and superior to desipramine. But at an 8-month follow-up the combination was the better treatment. Cognitive behavior therapy has an effect on relapse prevention. Longer follow-ups are needed to ascertain a significant and lasting effect of the cognitive behavior therapy programs.

OBESITY

Apart from esthetical problems obesity is related to cardiovascular complications. Effectiveness of behavioral intervention for obesity has been proved in controlled studies. The outcomes are generally maintained at a 1-year follow-up, but beyond this point there is no evidence of maintenance. Adding pharmacotherapy to behavior therapy does not enhance the results. Long-term maintenance programs may improve the relapse rate.[41]

Research has clearly demonstrated that biological variables, especially genetic ones regulate body weight and shape. This sets limits on the possibility of individuals changing their bodies according to the "canons" of the current esthetical ideal: the myth of a perfectly slim and young body. This generates a conflict between the dominant culture widespread by the media and individual physiology. Accordingly, one of the goals of behavioral medicine should be to establish reasonable weight expectations. In this respect, three basic irrational beliefs have to be challenged (1) the body is infinitely malleable; (2) every person can reach the ideal body; (3) a person with an ideal body will achieve a more successful and happier life.[42]

Psychogeriatrics

The elderly will soon comprise 25% of the population. Behavioral gerontology represents an emerging field. An evaluation of the outcome literature suggests that the basic procedures that work with the young also work with the old. Dementia, depression, paranoia, anxiety disorders, institutional problems, social inactivity, dependence, alcohol abuse, impairment of memory and cognition have been treated with some success in uncontrolled case studies, quasi-experimental designs and a few controlled studies.[43] Fecal incontinence represents the only indication of choice for biofeedback.[44] Home health care and environmental modification for the growing segment of the population over 85 certainly represents a direction for behavioral intervention in the future.

Cancer, Aids, and Psychoneuroimmunology

Cancer

The application of behavioral methods to the treatment of cancer raised considerable interest but also strong methodological concerns.[45] Grossarth-Maticek et al.[45] claimed that the occurrence of cancer could be predicted from simple questionnaire measures. The cancer-prone individual is characterized by a strong need to achieve an unattainable goal, resulting in depression and hopelessness. This has some consistency with other descriptions of the psychological characteristics predictive of cancer. Grossarth-Maticek has developed a new therapy called "creative novation therapy," directed at altering these behavior patterns. Aspects of this new brand on the therapy market appear to have similarities to well-known procedures such as relaxation training, systematic desensitization, and self-control. Prospective randomized trials have shown a doubling of survival duration (from 1 to 2 years) in women with metastatic breast cancer following this therapy.[45] Similar results have been reported by a different group also treating patients with severe breast cancer.[46] But, before these claims achieve acceptance by the whole scientific community they will require many careful independent replications. Obviously we have to wait before raising hopes that may turn into bitter disillusions. One should remember that in a well-designed study by Cassileth et al.,[47] organic factors of a chronic nature were the key factors to determine the result in advanced malignant chronic disease.

PSYCHONEUROIMMUNOLOGY

Psychosocial stressors may have a direct influence on the immune function of the subject under stress as suggests a comprehensive and cautious review by Emmelkamp.[48] Bereavement following the death of a close family member led to reduced immune function in a study by Linn et al.[49] Kiecolt-Glaser et al.[50–52] showed immune function reduction after divorce, in cases of marital distress. The same responses were found by Glaser et al.[53] in students under the stressful condition of an examination period.

There is now some evidence, as suggested by Taylor et al.,[54] that relaxation training may lead to an improved immune function. A study by Pennebaker et al.[55] found that confronting negative experiences by writing about them on four consecutive days led to improved immune function. Fawzey et al.[56] showed that a behaviorally oriented group intervention consisting of health education, enhancement of problem-solving skills, and stress management led to positive changes in the immune system (natural killer lymphoid cell system) of patients with malignant melanoma.

AIDS

Despite evidence of an organic etiology one may wonder if it is possible to enhance the immune function of individuals suffering from the AIDS virus infection. There is already some evidence that psychosocial factors may contribute to its progression, although many confounding variables, such as drug addiction related to personality, and/or socioenvironmental problems like unemployment, may suggest a cautious approach to understanding this problem. Stress management and cognitive behavior therapy programs may help in restoring the immune functions of HIV-infected patients. It may also help in coping with depression related to a fatal illness, and support the patient in his or her adaptive efforts to a new way of life. One study by Coates et al.[57] showed no effects of cognitive behavior therapy on immunity but a diminuation of hazardous sex practice. Kiecolt-Glaser and Glaser[58] suggested that behavioral intervention may serve as an immunomodulator if prescribed in conjunction with an antiviral agent, and thus augment the bioavailability of medications while decreasing their toxicity. One of the goals could be the delay of immunologic decline by drugs combined with psychosocial intervention.

Moreover, social cofactors as anger-hostility related to a fatal illness may have serious consequences in the community, including the voluntary dissemination of AIDS by infected persons. Stress and social management provided by community mental health centers may help to prevent those desperate responses to AIDS in persons stricken by poverty, social rejection, and substance abuse.

CONCLUSION

Behavioral psychotherapy, otherwise called cognitive behavior therapy, may promote physical health and treat some behaviorally linked medical conditions. Prevention of risk factors, relapse through self-management, the development of a healthy life-style at a relatively low cost, and the possibility of using the technology of behavioral psychotherapy in the community are its main assets.

But the review we made shows also the limitations of these cognitive–behavioral approaches to medical illnesses, compared to their wide development in the field of anxiety disorders, depression, sexual and couple problems, and psychotic patient rehabilitation.

Another important issue is the training of nurses, social workers, and medical students in health psychology, to implement prevention programs which include psychosocial variables. More than that, it is needed to develop in medical staff members a more human attitude toward the patient in a field too often dominated by cold technology. Cognitive–behavioral models and intervention are easily teachable through clinical presentation, video, or role-play. Their systematic development in consultation–liaison settings may represent a significant progress toward the integration of psychology into medicine. A good example could be the psychological understanding of pain problems in units dealing with cancer patients.

To conclude this paper, we will address briefly the issue of scientific models in behavioral medicine. We underlined the failure of biofeedback to fulfill its promise. This failure is more than technical: it is the failure of a possible general self-control model for medical illnesses. To date, the development of basic research is needed to renew and establish more firmly the theoretical bases, and extend the practice of behavioral medicine. If not, behavioral medicine will become merely a special field of application for cognitive and behavioral methods which have been used successfully in anxiety disorders and depression and whose effectiveness has been demonstrated in controlled trials. The rationale behind this conception might be that depression and anxiety are frequent antecedents, concomitants, or consequences of physical illnesses.

We may guess that recent technological advances in cognitive sciences and neurosciences, such as neurometabolic imagery, may help to bridge the mind–body gap, and develop new theoretical models to understand health and medical illness.

REFERENCES

1. Schwartz GE, Weiss SM. Behavioral medicine revisited: An amended definition. *J Behav Med*. 1978;1:249.
2. Weiss SM. Behavioral medicine on the world scene: Toward the year 2000. *First Int Congr Behav Med*. Uppsala;1990.

3. Cottraux J. *Psychosomatique et médecine comportementale. Etudes de cas.* Paris: Masson;1981.
4. Cottraux J. *Les thérapies comportementales et cognitives.* Paris: Masson;1990.
5. Goldwurm GF. Keynote lecture: Behavioural medicine. In: Cottraux J, Légeron P, Mollard E, eds. *Which Psychotherapies for Year 2000?* Annual Series of European Research in Behaviour Therapy. Amsterdam, Netherlands: Swets & Zeitlinger;1992: pp 49–56.
6. Fontaine O. Behavioural medicine: Chairman's comments on G. F. Goldwurm's keynote lecture. In: Cottraux J, Légeron P, Mollard E, eds. *Which Psychotherapies for Year 2000?* Annual Series of European Research in Behaviour Therapy. Amsterdam, Netherlands: Swets & Zeitlinger;1992: pp 57–66.
7. Engel GL. How much longer must medicine's science be bound by a seventeenth century world view? *Psychother Psychosom.* 1992;57:3–16.
8. World Health Organization. *Scientific group on treatment of psychiatric disorders.* Geneva, Switzerland: WHO;November 1989.
9. Frisch MB. Use of quality of life inventory in problem assessment on treatment planning for cognitive therapy of depression. In: Freeman A, Dattilio F, eds. *Comprehensive Casebook of Cognitive Therapy.* New York: Plenum Press;1992: pp 27–52.
10. Friedman M, Rosenman RH. *Type A Behavior and Your Heart.* New York: Knopf;1974.
11. Powell L. The cognitive underpinnings of coronary prone behaviors. *Cogn Ther Res.* 1992;16:132–142.
12. Friedman M, Thoresen G, Gill J, Powell L, Ulmer D, Thomson L, Rabin D, Breall D, Dixon T, Levy R, Bourg E. Alteration of type A behavior and reduction in cardiac recurrences in postmyocardial infarction patients. *Am Heart J.* 1984;108:237–248.
13. Roskies E, Seraganian P, Oseasohn R, Hanley JA, Collu R, Martin N, Smilga C. The Montreal type A intervention project: Major findings. *Health Psychol.* 1986;5:45–69.
14. Nunes E, Frank K, Kornfeld D. Psychologic treatment for the type A behavior pattern and for coronary heart disease: A meta-analysis of the literature. *Psychosom Med.* 1987;48:159–173.
15. Johnston DW. Behavioural medicine. The application of behavior therapy to physical health. *Behav Psychother.* 1991;19:100–108.
16. Jacob R, Wing R, Shapiro A. The behavioral treatment of hypertension: Long-term effects. *Behav Ther.* 1987;18:325–352.
17. Glasgow R, Lichtenstein E. Long-term effects of behavioral smoking cessation interventions. *Behav Ther.* 1987;18:297–323.
18. Cottraux J, Harf R, Boissel JP, Schbath J, Bouvard M, Gillet J. Smoking cessation with behavior therapy or acupuncture: A controlled study. *Behav Res Ther.* 1983;21:417–424.
19. Farquhar J, Fortman S, Flora J, Barr-Taylor C, Haskell W, Williams P, Maccoby N, Wood P. Effects of community education on cardiovascular disease risk factors. The Stanford five-city project. *JAMA.* 1990;264:359–365.
20. Freedman RR, Lanni P, Wenig P. Behavioral treatment of Raynaud's disease: Long-term follow-up. *J Consult Clin Psychol.* 1985;53:136.

21. Freedman RR, Ianni P, Wenig P. Behavioral treatment of Raynaud's disease. *J Consult Clin Psychol.* 1983;51:539–549.
22. Freedman R, Sabarhava SC, Ianni P, Desai N, Wenig P, Mayes M. Noneural beta-adrenergic vasodilating mechanism in temperature biofeedback. *Psychosom Med.* 1988;50:394–401.
23. Collet L, Cottraux J, Juenet C. GSR feedback and Schultz relaxation in tension headache: A controlled study. *Pain.* 1986;25:205–213.
24. Blanchard E. Long-term effects of behavioral treatment of chronic headache. *Behav Ther.* 1987;18:387–400.
25. Holroyd KA, Penzien DB. Client variables and the behavioral treatment of recurrent tension headache: A meta-analytic review. *J Behav Med.* 1986;9: 515–536.
26. Blanchard EB, Andrasik F, Ahles TA, Teders SJ, O'Keefe D. Migraine and tension headache: A meta-analytic review. *Behav Ther.* 1980;11:613–631.
27. Miller N. Learning of visceral and glandular responses. 1969;68:434–445.
28. Miller N, Dworkin B. Visceral learning: Recent difficulties with curarized rats and significant problems for human research. In: Obrist PA, ed. *Cardiovascular Psychophysiology.* Chicago: Aldine;1974: pp 312–331.
29. Rosenfeld JP. New directions in applied psychophysiology. Biofeedback and self-regulation. *J Behav Med.* 1992;17(2):77–86.
30. Bono S, Zasa M. Chronic low back pain and therapy: A critical review and overview. *Behav Ther.* 1988;11:189–188.
31. Saint-Laurent L, Ladouceur R. Massed versus distributed application of the regulated breathing method for stutters and its long term effects. *Behav Ther.* 1987;18:38–50.
32. Andrews G, Craig A. Prediction of outcome after treatment for stuttering. *Br J Psychiatry.* 1988;153:235–240.
33. Emmelkamp P. Behavior therapy with adults. In: Garfield S, Bergin A. *Handbook of Psychotherapy and Behavior Change.* New York: Wiley;1986: pp 385–442.
34. Pelc I. Thérapie cognitivo-comportementale de l'alcoolisme. *Actual Psychiatr.* 1989;7:11–16.
35. Agras S. *Eating Disorders. Management of Obesity, Bulimia and Anorexia Nervosa.* New York: Pergamon Press;1987.
36. Russel G, Szmukler G, Dare C, Eisler M. An evaluation of family therapy in anorexia nervosa and bulimia. *Arch Gen Psychiatry.* 1987;44:1047–1056.
37. Pyle RL, Mitchell J, Eckert E, Hatsukami D, Pomeroy C, Zimmerman R. Maintenance treatment and 6-month outcome for bulimic patients who respond to initial treatment. *Am J Psychiatry.* 1990;147:871–875.
38. Laessle R, Beumont P, Butow P, Lennerts W, O'Connor M, Pirke K, Touyz S, Waadt S. A comparison of nutritional management with stress management in the treatment of bulimia nervosa. *Br J Psychiatry.* 1991;159:250–261.
39. Fairburn C, Jones R, Peveler R, Carr S, Solomon R, O'Connor M, Burton J, Hope R. Three psychological treatments in bulimia nervosa. A comparative trial. *Arch Gen Psychiatry.* 1991;48:463–469.
40. Agras S. Pharmacologic and cognitive–behavioral treatment for bulimia nervosa. A controlled comparison. *Am J Psychiatry.* 1992;149:82–87.
41. Wilson T, Brownell K. Behaviour therapy of obesity: An evaluation of treatment outcome. *Adv Behav Res Ther.* 1982;3:49–86.

42. Brownell K. Dieting and the search for a perfect body: Where physiology and culture collide. *Behav Ther.* 1991;22:1–12.
43. Carstensen L. The emerging field of behavioral gerontology. *Behav Ther.* 1988;19:259–281.
44. Wald A, Tunuguntla K. Anorectal sensorimotor dysfunction in fecal incontinence and diabetes mellitus. Modification with biofeedback therapy. *N Engl J Med.* 1984;310(20):1282–1288.
45. Grossarth-Maticek R, Eysenck HJ, Vetter H, Schmidt P. Psychosocial types and chronic disease: Results of the Heidelberg prospective psychosomatic intervention study. In: Maes S, Spielberger CD, Defares PB, Sarason IG, eds. *Topics in Health Psychology.* Chichester, U.K.: Wiley;1988: pp 57–75.
46. Spiegel D, Bloom JR, Kraemer HC, Gottlieb E. Effects of psychosocial treatment on survival of patients with metastatic breast cancer. *Lancet.* 1989;2:888–891.
47. Cassileth BR, Lusk EJ, Miller DS, Brown LL, Miller C. Psychosocial correlates of survival in advanced malignant disease. *N Engl Med.* 1985;312:1551–1555.
48. Emmelkamp P. Behaviour therapy in the "fin de siécle." In: Cottraux J, Légeron P, Mollard E, eds. *Which Psychotherapies for Year 2000?* Annual Series of European Research in Behaviour Therapy. Amsterdam, Netherlands: Swets & Zeitlinger;1992: pp 151–166.
49. Linn BS, Linn MW, Jensen J. Degree of depression and immune responsiveness. *Psychosom Med.* 1982;44:128–129.
50. Kiecolt-Glaser JK, Glaser R. Psychosocial modulators of immune function. *Ann Behav Med.* 1987;9:16–20.
51. Kiecolt-Glaser JK, Fisher L, Ogrocki P, Stout JC, Speicher CE, Glaser R. Marital quality, marital disruption and immune function. *Psychosom Med.* 1987;49:13–34.
52. Kiecolt-Glaser JK, Kennedy S, Malkoff S, Fisher L, Speicher CE, Glaser R. Marital discord and immunity in males. *Psychosom Med.* 1988;50:213–229.
53. Glaser R, Kennedy S, Lafuse WP, Bonneau RH, Speicher C, Hillhouse J, Kiecolt-Glaser JK. Psychological stress-induced modulation of interleukin 2 receptor gene expression and interleukin 2 production in peripheral blood leukocytes. *Arch Gen Psychiatry.* 1990;47:707–712.
54. Taylor CB, Ironson G, Burnett K. Adult medical disorders. In: Bellack AS, Hersen M, Kazdin AE, eds. *International Handbook of Behavior Modification and Therapy.* New York: Academic Press;1990; pp 371–397.
55. Pennebaker JW, Kiecolt-Glaser JK, Glaser R. Disclosure of trauma's and immune function: Health implications for psychotherapy. *J Consult Clin Psychol.* 1988;56:239–245.
56. Fawzey FI, Kemeny ME, Fawzey NW, Elashoff R, Morton D, Cousins N, Fahey JL. A structured psychiatric intervention for cancer patients. *Arch Gen Psychiatry.* 1990;47:729–735.
57. Coates TJ, Mc Kusick L, Stites DP, Kuno R. Stress management training reduced number of sexual partners but did not improve immune function in men infected with HIV. *Am J Public Health.* 1989;79:885–887.
58. Kiecolt-Glaser JK, Glaser R. Psychological influences on immunity implications for AIDS. *Am Psychol.* 1988;43:892–898.

Chapter 26
Hypnosis and Relaxation in the Medically Ill

NICHOLAS A. COVINO, FRED H. FRANKEL

It has become commonplace to assume that distressed and anxious patients fare less well in medical settings than those who are emotionally and psychologically more relaxed and adjusted. Whether the dependent measure is patient–physician interaction, medical compliance, surgical success, length of hospital stay, utilization of services, symptomatology, or prognosis, the anxious patient often has the less favorable outcome. Recent years have seen a variety of interventions offered to these patients despite the absence of a firm understanding of the mechanisms involved—why it is advantageous to one's health to be at ease emotionally has thus far been the subject only of speculation.

The method most commonly employed to achieve the desired peace of mind is pharmacological. This has its advantages and its obvious risks. In knowledgeable medical circles, a referral for stress management or psychological counseling might also occur. But it is our impression that only a very limited number of clinicians can include in their own therapeutic repertoire the verbal directions or psychological techniques that help achieve the state of relaxation that can be helpful to their patients. This is all the more remarkable because, in experienced hands, these measures can be accomplished in a few minutes.

Relaxation techniques are closely associated with hypnosis, which can be regarded as an accident in the history of medicine.

It was stumbled upon as animal magnetism by Mesmer over two centuries ago,[1] and is especially fascinating from this historical viewpoint. Its medical discovery is probably at the root of several psychotherapy models and hypnotic procedures of which relaxation therapy is the least complex. A search for the essentials of hypnosis rapidly exposes the multidimensional nature of the phenomenon.[2] It is used clinically, among other goals, to achieve relaxation, relieve pain, alleviate physical discomfort, relieve breathing difficulties, control eating habits, eliminate smoking, improve athletic capacity, and even slow down blood loss. It is also employed to minimize phobic behavior, alter moods, recover past memories, and restructure thinking. It is hardly likely that all of the above (plus several other possible accomplishments) can be explained by a single mental mechanism.

Induction procedures are generally employed to reach or create the basic experience described as hypnosis. The format varies widely, from simple and brief to complex and lengthy rituals. The goal is to prepare the patient, psychologically and physiologically, to be able to respond to the suggestions that mesh with the therapeutic strategy in his or her case. A standard induction procedure, one of many models, proceeds along the following lines. The therapist, having established a comfortable relationship with the patient, obtains consent to proceed. The patient then abdicates initiative and sits or lies comfortably waiting for directions. These generally lead to eye closure, a few slow deep breaths to foster relaxation and the relief of tension, and then the injunction to redistribute attention. This is directed either toward concentrating on a specific bodily sensation like an arm beginning to feel numb, tingling, or light, or on an environment of peace and quiet. Imagination is then encouraged to assist in the alteration of perceptions or in the achievement of involuntary movements; a forearm feeling light might be persuaded to move, as if on its own volition, in an upward direction, or the patient might experience in imagination the vivid perception of the sounds, smells, and feelings associated with a nurturing environment. With this baseline of relaxation and attentiveness established, the therapist is then in a position to proceed with the specifics of the more formalized strategy that will mesh with that particular patient's problems.

Regardless of the very different conceptual underpinnings of Mesmer's "animal magnetism" of two centuries ago, his goal was to persuade his patients that they would feel better as a consequence of the very suggestive and dramatic circumstances entailed in his procedures, one of which was sitting around the banquet. Much of what was accomplished by Mesmer was probably attributable to the effects of suggestion and suggestibility. Another important component of Mesmer's magnetism that belongs to the discourse on hypnosis was first noted by one of his disciples, the Marquis de Puysegur who described how one of his subjects had a complete amnesia for what had happened and what had been discussed during an episode of magnetism, once he came out of it. In a subsequent magnetic episode he was able to recall what had happened the first time. This manifestation of a different state of conscious awareness, with amnestic barriers between the states, is at the heart of the concept of dissociation that was developed by Janet[3] a century later to explain hypnosis. Now, a hundred years since Janet began to elaborate on this phenomenon, we are witness to a major resurgence of interest in dissociation. This is best understood by approaching it with the model of hypnosis in mind. The complex, controversial question in our current thinking about hypnosis is the extent to which its accomplishments are attributable to suggestibility or dissociation or a combination of the two.[4] The simpler tasks in hypnosis (e.g., achieving relaxation or altered physical sensations) are probably due to suggestibility, whereas the more complex negative hallucinations such as ignoring pain involve dissociation. An alternative view is that these might all be the result of varying combinations of suggestion and dissociation.

Clinical observations have confirmed over two centuries that patients vary in their degree of response to hypnotic suggestions, and this concept of stable individual differences among subjects is likewise generally accepted in the field. However, while many clinicians tend to respect these differences, there are those who claim that they have never failed to hypnotize a willing patient. The apparent paradox can probably be accounted for by acknowledging how differently "being hypnotized" is understood. The majority of motivated adults will be able to accomplish a level of relaxation as a result of an appropriate induction procedure, regardless of their hypnotic skills. This in itself can alleviate discomfort and pain to some extent. Achieving alterations in perception of a more dramatic kind requires a greater degree of hypnotic talent.

Scales that measure hypnotic capacity or skills were developed initially by the clinicians using hypnosis in the late 19th century. These have become more sophisticated and accepted over recent decades, largely as a result of convincing laboratory studies that have confirmed their validity.[5, 6] Tests of hypnotizability generally measure a range of hypnotic achievements that a subject is capable of in a graded fashion, following a standardized (often read) hypnotic induction procedure.[7, 8] On this basis it has become clear from a vast number of studies that roughly 5 to 10% of the population are very responsive, 25 to 30% are minimally responsive, and the remainder are distributed on a curve between the two extremes.[5] As stated above, the hypnotic skills that are measured depend on levels of suggestibility as well as the capacity to dissociate. Because the induction procedures of the scales generally achieve good levels of both relaxation and focused attention, even patients who score poorly in their final hypnotizability ratings can achieve levels of comfort, largely as a consequence of the induction ritual itself.

Psychological treatments generally, including hypnosis, were illuminated by the views of Frank[9] in the early 1960s. Frank suggested then that many psychological and healing procedures, as diverse as psychoanalysis on the one hand and Shamanism on the other, could be successful, and probably owed their effectiveness to a series of nonspecific therapeutic factors common to all such treatments. A trusting relationship with positive expectations, positive convictions about the treatment, the support of a plausible theory or religious belief, and culturally relevant rituals in an appointed locus, all contribute to improvement, regardless of the specifics of the therapy. This does not imply that all treatments are equal, or equally effective, but it does suggest that the nonspecific forces and rituals in all psychotherapies (including the hypnotic), play an important role in the achievement of improvements. Further gains then depend on the appropriateness of the specific concepts, procedures, and strategies to the demands of the individual case. Relaxation and hypnotic techniques can thus be seen to depend initially on elements present in any therapeutic relationship; they are then enhanced by the expectations of the patient even if his or her hypnotic capacity is limited; and they are probably increased still further if beneficial alterations in perception, cognition, and mood can be created, or if altered states of consciousness can be achieved. Most interested patients can therefore be candidates for a hypnotic procedure, provided they are not challenged to accomplish more than they are capable of.

The use of hypnosis and relaxation can be of considerable benefit to the medically ill. Therapeutic suggestions can be aimed at physiological dysfunction such as occurs in psychologically aggravated bronchospasm, as well as at the alleviation or relief of physical discomfort or pain. Even pathological entities such as warts and psoriasis appear to have responded, as well as the morbid process that follows severe burns.[10] Furthermore, cognitive and behavioral methods appear to be facilitated by the addition of hypnotic procedures and suggestions. Errors of exaggeration or generalization in thinking about the seriousness of the illness, noncompliance with the medication regimen, and habit disorders that involve smoking, overeating, or purging, are all subject to modifications that can be accomplished through the judicious use of direction, admonition, and encouragement in the context of the hypnotic situation.

The clinical and experimental literature involving hypnosis and medicine seems to divide into studies of the incidence of hypnotizability among patients with a particular clinical syndrome (e.g., bulimia) and those which utilize hypnosis as a therapeutic intervention. Due to the special nature of case reports and the limitations in generalizability associated with these, we have largely confined our review of this literature to empirical studies.

CLINICAL CATEGORIES

BRONCHIAL ASTHMA

Asthma is an old and interesting psychosomatic problem. Allergies, infections, and emotions are thought to be among the causes of asthma with age, culture, genetics, and learning history seen as moderating variables in the disease. Colloquialisms in our language (e.g., "panting with excitement," "breathless in anticipation") reflect the connections that we make between emotions and respiration. The immune system and the autonomic nervous system are both involved in asthma symptom production and exacerbation.[11]

Asthmatics run the gamut of personality types, including "normal."[12] However, elevations of patient anxiety have been implicated in symptom exacerbation and noncompliance with medical directives. Anxious-dependent patients often stay longer in chronic care facilities, receive higher doses of steroid medications than their nonanxious counterparts, and overutilize p.r.n. medications independent of pulmonary function tests.[13] Asthmalike symptoms have been conditioned in animals when allergenic sprays were repeatedly paired with neutral aerosols[14] or when humans have been led to believe they have had contact with an allergen[15, 16] or bronchoconstricting drug.[17–19]

Clinical trials with hypnosis for asthma relief have been encouraging. An early, large sample study by the British Tuberculosis Society[20] treated nonsteroid-dependent asthmatics with hypnosis or relaxation therapy. With bronchodilator use and self-report of days wheezing as dependent measures, they found a significant reduction for both groups on the latter variable, and hypnosis superior in assisting patients to reduce p.r.n. use of medication. Maher-Loughnan[21] compared a new bronchodilator drug with and without hypnosis. At the end of 18 months, the hypnosis group had no wheezing above baseline and showed a dramatic decrease in bronchodilator usage. The control group showed no significant change over a year of treatment.

In another test utilizing hypnosis and a bronchodilator medication, Ewen and Stewart[22] obtained measures of the subjects' level of hypnotizability along with pulmonary function tests. At the end of 6 weeks, the group receiving hypnosis showed a significant improvement in peak expiratory flow rates and a 74.9% improvement in bronchial hyperresponsiveness over baseline. Those highest in hypnotizability showed the best results. A similar study[23] found, after 1 year of hypnotic treatment, patients whose chronic asthma had been inadequately controlled by medication reported symptomatic relief along with a significant reduction in their medication use. This improvement, however, did not extend to measurable changes on pulmonary function tests.

In summary, several controlled studies demonstrate that hypnosis is more effective than relaxation or medication alone in the relief of symptoms and that it can be especially beneficial for those patients with hyperreactive personalities. Where it is assessed, those asthmatics with higher levels of hypnotizability seem to be most helped by hypnosis. Direct benefit of hypnotic treatment on pulmonary function requires further substantiation; however, the symptoms of asthma seem to be easily conditioned and suggestion has been shown to improve a patient's subjective experience, steroid use, frequency of wheezing and, potentially, hospitalization.

PAIN

Among the most common complaints of patients in primary care medical practices is pain. Research strongly supports the notion that psychological variables are involved in the perception and management of pain. Not only do attention from others and relief from responsibility serve to reinforce pain[24] but cognitive factors such as memories of past pain, anxiety, cultural beliefs, and dysfunctional ideas about the self serve to exacerbate it.[25]

The anesthesiologist Beecher[26, 27] was among the first to observe that pain reports and behaviors did not seem to relate directly to the degree of tissue damage. Soldiers with injuries more severe than those whom he saw as surgical patients in civilian life were more comfortable and required less pain medication than he expected.

The meaning of pain was different for these men who were "safe" and about to return home as "heroes."

Careful and meticulous work in this area has been done by the Hilgards.[28] They suggest that there is a linear relationship between the degree of noxious physical stimulation and the subject's report of pain, but that suggestion can alter it. In studies involving ischemic and cold-pressor stimuli, they were able to alter their subjects' physiological and psychological responses to pain.[28, 29] They found that highly hypnotizable patients were able to reduce their pain, when suggestions were made for analgesia, by as much as 33 vs. 13% among low hypnotizables exposed to the same stimuli.[29]

Other laboratory work supports the conclusion that cognitive factors involving perception seem to alter the pain experience. A number of studies indicate that hypnosis works better than stress inoculation,[28, 30] placebo control,[30, 31] distraction and relaxation[32, 33] in the control of pain. Furthermore, the patient's level of hypnotizability seems to be an important moderating variable.[28-30]

CARDIOLOGY

Unless the story is completely apocryphal, the diagnosis of type A Personality Behavior (TABP) was first made by a furniture reupholsterer who observed that the waiting room chairs in a cardiology practice were worn out only at the edges of the seat and armrests. These patients have been described as hard driving, competitive people with an inordinate amount of hostility.[34] Since that time, the role of psychological factors in heart disease has been the subject of much clinical and experimental research.

Among the well-known psychological interventions in this area is the work done by Benson and his colleagues.[35-38] Their work with the meditative technique they call "the relaxation response" has demonstrated the beneficial effect of relaxation on blood pressure, heart rate, oxygen consumption, and several neurotransmitters associated with heart disease. Their work follows that of Selye[39] and Cannon[40] who found a deleterious effect on the cardiovascular function and other organ systems from chronic stress. Most reviewers in this area conclude that pharmacotherapy is superior to psychological techniques in the management of hypertension.[41, 42] However, several studies[43-45] have found that relaxation strategies coupled with exercise training or a cognitive therapy can diminish cardiac events, hospital readmissions, and recurrent myocardial infarction in patients who have had a heart attack. Perhaps because of the great popularity and success of the work of those who considered relaxation and TABP as the most important psychological variables in heart disease, there are not many publications in this area utilizing hypnosis.

Treatment studies have favored cognitive interventions or some variation of relaxation technique. Suinn[46] suggests that appropriate interventions include: training in progressive relaxation; learning to link physiological tension to a stressful event; relaxation during the event and visualization of behaviors incompatible with TABP. Two large sample studies with patients who had documented heart attacks[47, 48] found an intervention similar to the above with an additional effort to change the type A behavior pattern attitudes and one utilizing groups were able to significantly reduce TABP and the recurrence of cardiac events after 2 years. In the group intervention[48] controls who did not receive the TABP counseling demonstrated an increase in cardiac events at a level three times their counterparts. A meta-analysis of 18 controlled interventions by Nunes et al.[49] found education, relaxation, support, TABP counseling, and cognitive therapy effective in reducing TABP, angina, subsequent MI, and deaths.

SURGICAL PREPARATION

Most surgical patients experience moderate to high degrees of anxiety. In a hospital system that views surgery as business as usual, these patients' anxieties can often be overlooked. Needles, absence from home and family, fears of pain, blood, death, dismemberment, and complications are frequent companions of the surgical patient. The degree to which these fears might interfere with successful surgery seems to be somewhat related to the procedure, state of disease, and the patient's personality style.[50] Psychological techniques seem to be helpful at many points in the course of surgery.[51]

Janis[52] was the first to write about the need for patients to do the "work of worrying" prior to surgery to master their anxiety. While the evidence does not support the universality of this as an intervention, Egbert et al.[53] found that even a 5-minute presurgery visit by the anesthesiologist significantly reduced the need for anesthesia during the procedure and that the "visited" patients were discharged 2 days earlier than expected. A group of patients undergoing a variety of gynecological surgical procedures were randomly offered hypnosis or a discussion group.[54] After surgery, patients in the hypnosis group were found to be significantly less anxious and to have required less anesthesia for the procedure.

In the clinical literature, physicians write that patients will ambulate and void more quickly when they are taught hypnosis for pain control and motivated to use it.[55] Flaherty and Fitzpatrick[56] found this to be true in a clinical experiment with their patients also requiring less pain medication and a shorter length of stay than their nonhypnosis counterparts. In this area, the anxiety of the surgical patient is soothed by the elements of suggestion and relaxation that hypnosis offers in a manner that requires less assistance from anesthesia. Absent are studies of hypnotizability among these patients that could demonstrate an association between frightening imagery and some negative outcome. Pain management techniques and behavioral rehearsal seem to be successful. As finances pressure surgical teams to complete their work with shorter hospital stays, hypnosis can be a very useful adjunct for treatment and recovery.

IRRITABLE BOWEL SYNDROME

Many of the patients seen in a gastroenterologist's office will be those with irritable bowel syndrome (IBS). Approximately 50% of the doctor's practice and 15% of the population[57, 58] will suffer from this disorder. Unfortunately, the exact cause of IBS remains unknown and factors such as diet, food allergy, and abnormal gut motility may create the symptoms of pain, abdominal distension, and constipation or diarrhea which are common to this condition. Abnormal activity in this area is not restricted to patients with gastrointestinal problems, since anxiety can create the familiar lump in the throat, appetite changes, and nervous diarrhea among normal people. Some work has demonstrated that the transit time of meals taken under stress is much more rapid than normal.[59] Under hypnosis, Beaugerie et al.[60] were able to modify the transit time of six healthy subjects. Although they did not assess the degree of hypnotizability, their subjects were able to significantly delay orocecal transit time following a meal and the injection of lactulose, when they were instructed to relax.

Patients with severe IBS who failed traditional medical therapies were the subjects of several treatment studies utilizing hypnosis.[57, 61, 62] These authors report a success rate of over 80% with patients who failed to respond to traditional medical treatments. In controlled experiments[57, 62] hypnosis was found to be superior in its results to supportive psychotherapy and placebo. They advise against utilizing this treatment with patients who have severe psychological problems and atypical IBS. Similar findings for hypnotherapy administered in a group setting were obtained by another British group.[58]

Although there are currently only a few research teams who are writing about their work in this area, they have reported on a large sample of subjects and have sparked some considerable enthusiasm for this approach.

PERSISTENT NAUSEA AND VOMITING

A number of medical conditions and treatments can elicit and maintain nausea and vomiting. Certain drugs used to treat cancer patients (e.g., cyclophosphamide) can cause emesis in more than 50% of this population. Furthermore, when the treatment is more intense or elicits severe posttreatment nausea and vomiting, the likelihood of anticipatory nausea and vomiting seems to increase.

Although the plurality of women have some mild form of nausea and vomiting during the first trimester of pregnancy, these symptoms can occur at a frequency of 10 to 15 times per day, in a condition called hyperemesis gravidarum. While this is a relatively uncommon malady (less than 1%), the serious problems associated with dehydration and electrolyte imbalance often mandate hospital admission.[63] After these medical problems are attended to, many women leave the hospital symptom free and remain so throughout the rest of the pregnancy.

A number of psychoanalytic interpretations have attempted to understand the presence of persistent nausea and vomiting as ambivalence about the pregnancy.[64] However, these symptoms can best be viewed as the result of classical conditioning. This theory posits some organic unconditioned stimulus (drug or hormone) is unwittingly paired with any number of neutral stimuli (CS) such as a particular food and a conditioned response (nausea, vomiting) quickly generates. Once established, this problem is often not helped by education, antiemetics, or other medical treatments, although pregnancy usually precludes the use of medications.

Apfel et al.[65] measured hypnotizability in patients with hyperemesis gravidarum. In a group of 28 women with mild to severe symptoms, they found a greater than expected incidence of hypnotizability. Furthermore, those with more severe symptoms were more hypnotizable than the less symptomatic.

Treatment studies using hypnosis for hyperemesis gravidarum and anticipatory emesis among cancer patients have shown very promising results. Fuchs et al.[66] used hypnosis in the treatment of 138 hyperemesis patients who were treatment failures with medication. Regardless of the treatment condition (group or individual), 122 patients reported symptomatic relief after only a brief treatment. Hypnosis was found to significantly reduce anticipatory emesis in patients with cancer when compared to counseling or no treatment.[67] In a study where patients served as their own controls,[68] 6 patients with cancer were asked to report their symptoms of emesis during and after chemotherapy. Each time at which the patients were treated with hypnosis, no emesis occurred. On three occasions where hypnosis was omitted, the emesis recurred despite previous success.

Although it is clear that a number of psychological issues can be associated with both pregnancy and cancer, the symptoms of persistent nausea and vomiting can probably be best explained by learning theory, with the patient's suggestibility providing a fertile ground for conditioning to take place. The use of hypnosis, which involves relaxation, distraction, and self-absorption seems to interfere with the conditioned associations long enough to permit extinction and relief.

EATING DISORDERS

Some literature suggests that hypnosis could be helpful to patients with anorexia nervosa.[69, 70] Unfortunately, very little empirical work has been done to support this claim. There are, however, a number of studies indicating the usefulness of hypnosis with bulimic patients. In support of this, current workers also cite the sense of spontaneous dissociation, involuntariness, feelings of depersonalization, and timelessness, often seen in such patients.[71–75]

In one of the earliest empirical efforts[76] bulimic patients were found to be significantly more hypnotizable than patients with anorexia nervosa. In addition, a subset of the anorexic group who purged where found to be more hypnotizable than those who did not. A similar finding came from a study of university women[77] where those who scored highly on a self-report measure of bulimia also had higher hypnotizability ratings than their nonbulimic counterparts. A recent controlled study of outpatient bulimics[78] found the same results on the Stanford Hypnotic Susceptibility Scale— Form:C (SHSS:C).

Some authors[75, 79] have reported that bulimic patients score high on measures of dissociation and have suggested that early childhood trauma may be implicated in the onset of the disorder.[80, 81] Our recent study[78] failed to find an increased incidence of dissociation in the bulimic group nor a correlation between the Dissociative Experiences Scale (DES) and the SHSS:C.

Other authors have found that bulimic women often rid themselves of negative emotions by binging and purging in a manner suggesting a negative reinforcement paradigm.[82, 83] If bulimic patients experience something akin to a trance state when they binge and if their suggestibility renders them more vulnerable to social pressures and conditioning principles, perhaps hypnosis can be a useful adjunct to their treatment. The success of cognitive–behavior therapy for bulimia is further encouragement for treatment programs to incorporate hypnosis.

HABIT DISORDERS

It seems that there have been more popular books and newspaper advertisements promoting the use of hypnosis for the treatment of cigarette smoking and weight control than for any other medical problems. It might be that these difficulties are still seen as the result of a lack of "will power" with clinicians and patients alike hoping that the right suggestion can be instrumental in providing sufficient motivation to stop these self-destructive behaviors. Unfortunately, the experimental support for the value of hypnosis per se in this area is weak, and such positive findings as there are have methodological weaknesses that limit our confidence in them.

Learning principles seem to be involved in important ways in both of these areas. Tomkins[84] suggests that problematic affects such as depression, boredom, and anxiety are diminished by cigarette smoking and that negative reinforcement principles govern this behavior. Addiction psychologists also cite the positive reinforcement properties of sudden repetitive bursts of nicotine in the blood and brain that serve as a stimulant. Likewise, Kaye et al.[82] and Abraham and Beaumont[83] find that depression and other burdensome emotions often precede a binge episode and are attenuated by the use of food. The positive reinforcement property of food is also evident.

A number of different psychological approaches seem to be required to help patients change these habits and maintain their abstinence. Patients seem to pass through several stages, often several times, in their efforts to make a change in a habit: contemplation, action, maintenance, and relapse.[85, 86] Each of these stages of change is unique and demands a different approach and intervention techniques (e.g., consciousness raising and motivation; stimulus control methods; relapse prevention). Thus far, interventions involving hypnosis seem to have ignored this literature and focused only on motivation and direct suggestions for behavioral change.

SMOKING

Although most studies fail to obtain a measure of hypnotizability on their subjects, there is some debate as to the role of hypnotizability in this work, with several authors asserting its irrelevance[87, 88] and others disagreeing. Among the latter is Berlin[89] who assessed the level of hypnotizability of 498 smokers in an experiment that had three conditions: (1) hypnosis with suggestion for smoking cessation; (2) hypnosis for relaxation with waking suggestions; (3) relaxation alone. The study found those who were most successful in smoking cessation were the highly hypnotizable patients who received the suggestions to stop smoking during trance. The next best performers were the highly hypnotizables who received the waking suggestions. Another larger sample study of family practice patients[90] found that hypnotizability predicted smoking abstinence at 3, but not at 6 months. This led the authors to conclude that hypnotizability might be very useful in assisting patients acutely, but not in the long run.

While methods vary considerably, most clinical reports and experimental studies claim similar success rates at somewhere between 20 and 30% although the similarity in the numbers might mask quite a diversity of patients. What is disconcerting about outcomes in this research is the overreliance on patient self-report and relative absence of physiological checks (e.g., serum thiocyanate, carbon monoxide levels) to validate abstinence. In studies which include compliant and suggestible patients, self-report data on smoking frequency is not the most credible.

WEIGHT CONTROL

The vast majority of papers on the use of hypnosis with obesity are clinical case studies and anecdotal reports. However, in a randomized trial, Andersen[91] found that obese persons were able to lose weight with hypnosis and that highly hypnotizable patients were the most successful. A similar finding occurred in a study of patients who were 28 to 74% above their ideal weight.[92] These subjects were told to lose 20 pounds in 90 days and were randomly assigned to an attention control condition or two treatments utilizing hypnosis. The best performers in this study were the highly hypnotizable patients and the best treatment offered individualized suggestions for weight loss. Cochrane and Friesen[93] studied people who were 20% over their ideal weight with hypnosis with or without an audiotape for weight control. At the end of 6 months, both hypnosis groups lost about 17 pounds versus the attention control group's net gain of ½ pound.

Although all of these studies indicate a statistically significant difference in favor of hypnosis, the weight loss achieved was quite modest. Moreover, the absence of longitudinal studies and follow-up data on these patients makes it very difficult for us to be confident of the permanence of the loss, and thus, the efficacy of hypnosis for weight control.

In addition to the psychological, there is a powerful physiological element to smoking and weight control. Cigarette smoking is clearly an addiction with smokers searching for cigarettes when they have been deprived of nicotine and smoking little when it is supplied by an alternate route.[94] Nicotine replacement seems to improve the likelihood that a patient will stop smoking, but it rarely is successful without psychological treatment. Kessey[95] suggests that there is a set point such that animals adjust their eating to compensate for starvation and forced feeding. Influences such as body temperature, serotonin, and other metabolic factors affect the rate at which patients are able to lose weight and contribute to their success in keeping it off. Unfortunately, very little has been done to join hypnotic interventions with other medical and psychological perspectives and treatments for smoking and obesity.

TRICHOTILLOMANIA

In survey studies, trichotillomania is not found to be a very common problem in mental health centers.[96] But, patients with bald spots in their hair often present to dermatology clinics and men can go easily unnoticed. Like nail biting, lip chewing, scratching, and other ritualistic behaviors, trichotillomania (i.e., the irresistible urge to pull hair), is an embarrassing habit that many patients use to diminish anxiety. In a fashion that follows negative reinforcement paradigm, patients are thought to discharge tension and distract themselves from unpleasant emotions successfully enough with this habit to continue its use.

Given the level of pain that these patients are able to tolerate and ignore in these behaviors, one would assume that their level of hypnotizability would be high. However, this has not been systematically tested. In order to maintain the symptom, these patients must ignore significant pain and often find themselves unaware of their habit. When they are asked to keep records, these people often note that the behaviors occur during periods when they feel they are in a trancelike state.

At the moment, we lack any studies of hypnotizability, or more than case reports of hypnosis among these patients. The nature of their symptom implies a certain capacity for dissociation which invites consideration of a hypnotic intervention, yet the literature in this area is scant.

INFECTION AND IMMUNITY

Considerable interest has been raised by occasional reports in the literature that allude to a relationship between psychosocial factors and cancer or infection. These not only have implied that stress factors can lead to the disease, but have also raised the possibility that procedures involving relaxation can promote healing.

Observations and studies attempting to substantiate the claims have focused largely on the incidence of infections among populations that appear to have been under stress, such as the bereaved, the depressed, students under academic stress, and prisoners. Other psychosocial variables that have attracted attention have included life changes and inhibited power motivation. Jemmott and Locke,[97] in a review of the subject report that the bulk of the empirical evidence indicates that people who have been exposed to a high degree of recent life stress have greater degeneration of overall health. Most reviewers have agreed.[98]

As we focus more precisely, it becomes clear that many difficulties remain. The definition of stress is not uniformly agreed upon;

it alludes to both the stimulus and the individual's response, and also the interaction between them. The nature of stress also reflects personal life-styles, personality characteristics, and the level of mental health. Comparisons among groups are therefore often methodologically less compelling.

In addition to these reports on vulnerability to disease, the hypnosis literature has included accounts of the opposite, improvements and even cures of cancer, attributed to relaxation and hypnoticlike procedures.[99, 100] For the most part these reports are regarded as methodologically weak. There is little doubt that quality of life has been improved by attention, support, and sustained faith, but whether or not that has prolonged life is not clear. A more recent study[101] reported prolonged survival in a group of women with breast cancer who participated in group therapy at weekly intervals for a year. The therapy included hypnotic techniques. This interesting finding awaits replication.

In attempts to understand the reports on the incidence of disease among the vulnerable and the therapeutic value of relaxation, other investigators have studied the parameters of immunocompetence. Despite the growing complexity of the field, it appears that immunologic functioning regulates susceptibility to cancer, infectious diseases, allergies, and autoimmune diseases. It is mediated hormonally, by antibodies, and by cells which influence delayed hypersensitivity reactions. These T lymphocytes and B lymphocytes are among the variables that have been studied. Whereas some studies have found a shift in the numbers of these cells in the expected direction, others have failed to replicate.

The literature reporting the effect of relaxation and hypnosis on skin disease and skin response illustrate the discrepancies in the findings thus far. For example, individual cases have been convincingly reported in which psoriasis responded successfully to hypnosis and relaxation therapy.[102, 103] However, in other instances, this procedure failed to work. Similarly, in the case of warts, Sinclair-Gieben and Chalmers[104] reported the disappearance of warts on one arm and not on the other, as a result of specific suggestions in hypnosis. Other studies failed to replicate the unilateral disappearance even though Surman et al.[105] did report that 17 of their 20 subjects lost 75% of their wart lesions bilaterally as a result of suggestion, compared with none in a control group. Because none of the studies on the effects of hypnosis on warts have explored the mechanisms that could be mediating the improvement, few can deny the possible role of placebo or relaxation.

Other studies have investigated the effects of hypnosis on the immunologic responses in human skin. Black[106] demonstrated an inhibition of both the immediate and delayed hypersensitivity responses to antigens by direct suggestion under hypnosis. These studies, and studies demonstrating the power of hypnotic suggestion in suppressing and creating contact dermatitis[107] have not been replicated.

Much of the evidence does support the notion that stress is associated with an increase in diseases against which the immune system defends, and that it is associated with diminished immunocompetence. The extent and the nature of the benefits that derive from relaxing or hypnotic interventions remain to be clarified.

SUMMARY STATEMENT

Despite the long tradition of the use of hypnosis in medical settings, we are still somewhat limited as to the conclusions that we can draw from this literature. To begin with, a number of the illnesses discussed have an unclear etiology (e.g., irritable bowel syndrome, bulimia) and comparisons among a variety of disease entities, symptoms, and habits are difficult to make. Likewise, physiological, environmental, and psychological factors contribute to varying degrees to these disorders which makes it hard to predict the likelihood for psychological interventions to facilitate change. The absence of large samples and prospective studies in the literature invites additional caution in generalizing from results. However, there are some conclusions that emerge from this review.

First, hypnosis seems to be quite helpful in the treatment of patients with: bronchial asthma[20-23]; pain[30-32]; and irritable bowel syndrome.[57, 58, 61, 62] The successful work of those who have treated cardiac patients with relaxation[35, 37, 38] and/or cognitive restructuring[46–48] leads us to think that hypnosis can be an effective treatment here as well. The mechanism for these effects is not evident.

Second, when studies have attempted to assess levels of hypnotizability, those with the highest scores tend to profit most from this intervention.[22, 23, 28, 31, 32, 89–91] Since those with high levels of hypnotizability are often found among those with the most refractory symptoms (e.g., bulimia, hyperemesis, phobia), it might be speculated that their capacity for vivid imagination and extreme receptivity to suggestions can be both an asset and a liability in their medical care.[108]

Third, several studies have found inordinate levels of hypnotizability among patients with conditions that are known to be caused or maintained by classical or instrumental learning principles. Those conditions mentioned in this review include: asthma[15–17, 19]; hyperemesis[65]; bulimia.[76–78] Previous work[109] found the same to be true among phobic patients.

Perhaps, suggestibility plays a role in the manner in which a patient makes associations uncritically (classical conditioning, stimulus generalization) or is easily influenced by operant reinforcers. It is also possible that those with unusual dissociative capacity will use it to escape problematic affects and subject their symptoms to negative reinforcement. Thus, symptoms such as bulimia, hyperemesis, and anticipatory nausea and vomiting can be unwittingly maintained by hypnotizable people, even when organic factors establish them initially.

Fourth, hypnosis has been able to effect more than symptom relief. Patients receiving hypnotic treatment for asthma have been able to reduce their medication use[20–23] and surgical patients have used less anesthesia,[54] ambulated more rapidly, and received earlier discharge from the hospital.[51, 53]

Fifth, in the several studies that tested these, hypnosis performed better than relaxation.[20, 30–33]

Sixth, since there seems to be an overlap between anxiety and hypnotizability in this area future studies would do quite well to obtain measures of both.

Seventh, when physiological factors contribute strongly to a condition, the role for hypnosis is diminished and/or should be linked with a pharmacological treatment. Thus, treatment of cigarette smokers, obesity, and other addictions should use hypnosis as part of a multidimensional treatment program.

While it is compelling to conclude that the mind can heal the body, we seem to be on the safest ground when psychological factors are seen as contributing to an illness or its symptoms in a significant fashion. When these factors include anxiety, dissociation, suggestion, and conditioning principles, our confidence in the efficacy of hypnosis seems to be justified; it can even be increased when the patient has demonstrated considerable capacity for hypnotizability.

REFERENCES

1. Ellenberger HF. *The Discovery of the Unconscious: The History and Evolution of Dynamic Psychiatry.* New York: Basic Books;1970.
2. Frankel FH. Hypnotizability and dissociation. *Am J Psychiatry.* 1990;147:823–829.
3. Janet P. *The Major Symptoms of Hysteria: Fifteen Lectures Given in the Medical School of Harvard University.* New York: Macmillan;1907.
4. Weitzenhoffer AM. *The Practice of Hypnotism.* New York: Wiley;1989.
5. Hilgard ER. *Hypnotic Susceptibility.* New York: Harcourt, Brace & World;1965.
6. Orne MT. On the simulating subject as a quasi-control group in hypnosis research: What, why and how. In: Fromm E, Shor RE, eds. *Hypnosis: Developments in Research and New Perspectives.* New York: Aldine;1979: pp 519–565.
7. Weitzenhoffer AM, Hilgard ER. *Stanford Hypnotic Susceptibility Scale, Forms A and B.* Palo Alto, CA: Consulting Psychologists Press;1959.
8. Shor RE, Orne EC. *The Harvard Group Scale of Hypnotic Susceptibility, Form A.* Palo Alto, CA: Consulting Psychologists Press;1962.
9. Frank JD. *Persuasion and Healing: A Comparative Study of Psychotherapy.* Baltimore: Johns Hopkins Press;1961.
10. Frankel FH. Significant developments in medical hypnosis during the past 25 years. *Int J Clin Exp Hypnosis.* 1987;35:231–247.
11. Weiss ST, Speizer. *Epidemiology of Asthma: Risk Factors and Natural History.* Boston: Little, Brown;1976.
12. Jones NF, Kinsma RA, Dirks JF, Dahlem NW. Psychological contributions to chronicity in asthma: Patient response styles influencing medical treatment and its outcome. *Med Care.* 1979;17:1103–1118.

13. Jones NF, Kinsman RA, Schum R, Resnikoff P. Personality profiles in asthma. *J Clin Psychol.* 1976;32:285–291.
14. Vachon L, Rich ES Jr. Visceral learning in asthma. *Psychosom Med.* 1976;38: 122–130.
15. MacKenzie JN. The production of "rose asthma" by an artificial rose. *Am J Med Sci.* 1886;91:45.
16. McFadden ER Jr, et al. The mechanisms of action of suggestion in the induction of acute asthma attacks. *Psychosom Med.* 1969;31:134.
17. Spector S, Luparello TJ, Kopetzky MT, Souhrada J, Kinsman RA. Response of asthmatics to methacholine and suggestion. *Am Rev Resp Dis.* 1976;113: 43–50.
18. Horton DJ, et al. Bronchoconstrictive suggestion in asthma: A role for hyperreactivity and emotions. *Am Rev Respir Dis.* 1978;117:1029.
19. Neild JE, Cameron IR. Bronchoconstriction in response to suggestion: Its prevention by an inhaled anticholinergic agent. *Br Med J.* 1985;290:646–674.
20. Report to Research Committee of the British Tuberculosis Association. Hypnosis for asthma: A controlled trial. *Br Med J.* 1968;4:71.
21. Maher-Loughnan GP. Hypnosis and autohypnosis for the treatment of asthma. *Int J Clin Exp Hypn.* 1970;18:1–14.
22. Ewer TC, Stewart DE. Improvement in bronchial hyperresponsiveness in patients with moderate asthma after treatment with a hypnotic technique: A randomized trial. *Br Med J.* 1986;293:1129–1134.
23. Morrison JB. Chronic asthma and improvement with relaxation by hypnotherapy. *J R Soc Med.* 1988; 81:701–704.
24. Roberts A. The operant approaches to the management of pain and accept disability. In: Holtzman A, Turk D, eds. *Pain Management: A Handbook of Psychological Treatment Approaches.* New York: Pergamon Press;1986.
25. Melzek R. Neuropsychological foundations of pain. In: Sternback RA, ed. *The Psychology of Pain.* New York: Raven Press;1986.
26. Beecher HK. The powerful placebo. *JAMA.* 1955;159:1602–1606.
27. Beecher HK. Relationship of significance of wound to the pain experienced. *JAMA.* 1956;161:1609–1613.
28. Hilgard ER, Hilgard JR. *Hypnosis in the Relief of Pain.* Los Altos, CA: Kaufman Press;1983.
29. Hilgard ER. Hypnosis in pain control. In: Langen D, ed. *Hypnose und psychosomatische Medizin.* Stuttgart, Germany: Hippokrates Verlag;1972.
30. Miller ME, Bowers KS. Hypnotic analgesia and stress inoculation in the reduction of pain. *J Abnorm Psychol.* 1986;95:6–14.
31. McGlashan TH, Evans FJ, Orne MT. The nature of hypnotic analgesia and placebo response to experimental pain. *Psychosom Med.* 1969;227:246.
32. Karlin R, Morgan D, Goldstein L. Hypnotic analgesia: A preliminary investigation of quantitated hemispheric electroencephalographic and attentional correlates. *J Abnorm Psychol.* 1980;89:591–594.
33. Zeltzer L, LeBaron S. Hypnosis and non-hypnotic techniques for reduction of pain and anxiety during painful procedures in children and adolescents with cancer. *J Pediatr.* 1982;101:1032–1035.
34. Friedman M, Rosenman. *Type A Behavior and Your Heart.* New York: Knopf; 1974.

35. Benson H. The relaxation response. History, physiological basis and clinical usefulness. *Acta Med Scand.* (suppl).1982;660:231–237.
36. Benson H, Greenwodd MM, Klemchuk H. The relaxation response: Psychophysiologic aspects and clinical applications. *Int J Psychiatry Med.* 1975;6:87–98.
37. Benson H, Rosner BA, Marzetta BR, Klemchuk HP. Decreased blood pressure in borderline hypertensive subjects who practiced meditation. *J Chronic Dis.* 1974;27:163–169.
38. Benson H, Frankel FH, Apfel R, Daniels MD, Schniewind HE, Nemiah JC, Sifneos PE, Crassweller KD, Greenwood MM, Kotch JB, Arns PA, Rosner B. Treatment of anxiety: A comparison of the usefulness of self-hypnosis and meditational relaxation technique. An overview. *Psychother Psychosom.* 1978;30:229–242.
39. Selye H. *The Stress of Life.* New York: McGraw-Hill;1956.
40. Cannon WB. *Wisdom of the Body.* New York: Norton;1932.
41. Blanchard E. Psychological treatment of cardiovascular disease. *Arch Gen Psychiatry.* 1977;34:1402–1413.
42. Schwartz GE, Shapiro AP, Redmond DP, Ragland DR, Weiss SM. Behavioral medicine approaches to hypertension: An integrative analysis of theory and research. *J Behav Med.* 1979;311–363.
43. Friedman M. The modification of type A behavior in post-infarction patients. *Am Heart J.* 1979;97:551–560.
44. Friedman M. Type A behavior: Its diagnosis, cardiovascular relation and the effect of its modification on recurrence of coronary artery disease. *Am J Cardiol.* 1989;64:12C–19C.
45. Friedman M, Thorensen CE, Gill JJ, Ulmer D, Powell LH, Price VA, Brown B, Thompson L, Rabin DD, Reall WS. Alteration of type A behavior and its effect on cardiac recurrences in post myocardial infarction patients: Summary results of the recurrent coronary prevention project. *Am Heart J.* 1986;23:653–665.
46. Suinn R. Intervention with type A behaviors. *J Consult Clin Psychol.* 1982;50:933–949.
47. Friedman M, Thoresen CD, Gill JJ, Ulmer D, Thompson I, Powell I, Price V, Elek SR, Rabin DD, Breall WS, Piaget G, Dixon T, Leavy R, Bourg E. Alterations of type A behavior and reduction in cardiac recurrences in post myocardial infarction patients. *Am Heart J.* 1984;108:237.
48. Friedman M. Type A behavior: Its diagnosis, cardiovascular relation and the effect of its modification on recurrence of coronary artery disease. *Am J Cardiol.* 1989;64:12C–19C.
49. Nunes E, Frank K, Kornfeld D. Psychologic treatment for the type A behavior pattern and for coronary heart disease: A meta-analysis of the literature. *Psychosom Med.* 1987;48:159–173.
50. Rogers M, Reich P. Psychological intervention with surgical patients: Evaluation outcome. *Adv Psychosom Med.* 1986;15:23–30.
51. Kaloupek D. Recommendations for psychological intervention with patients undergoing invasive medical procedures. *Behav Ther.* 1987;10:33–39.
52. Janis IL. *Psychological Stress: Psychoanalytic and Behavioral Studies of Surgery.* New York: J Wiley;1958.

53. Egben LD, Battit GE, Torndoff H, Beecher HK. Value of preoperative visit by an anaesthetist: A study in doctor-patient rapport. *JAMA.* 1963;185: 553–555.

54. Goldmann L, Ogg TW, Levey AB. Hypnosis and daycase anaesthesia: A study to reduce pre-operative anxiety and intra-operative anaesthetic requirements. *Anaesthesia.* 1988;43:466–469.

55. Matheson G, Drever JM. Psychological preparation of the patient for breast reconstruction. *Ann Plast Surg.* 1990;24:238–247.

56. Flaherty G, Fitzpatrick J. Relaxation technique to increase comfort levels of postoperative patients: A preliminary study. *Nurs Res.* 1987;27:352–355.

57. Whorwell PJ, Prior A, Faragher EB. Controlled trial of hypnotherapy in the treatment of severe refractory irritable-bowel syndrome. *Lancet.* 1984;ii: 1232–1234.

58. Harvey RF, Hinton RA, Gunary RM, Barry RE. Individual and group hypnotherapy in treatment of refractory irritable bowel syndrome. *Lancet.* 1989;i: 424–425.

59. Cann PA, Read NW, Brown C, Hobson N, Holdsworth CD. Irritable bowel syndrome: Relationship of disorders in the transit of a single solid meal to symptom patterns. *Gut.* 1983;24:405–411.

60. Beaugerie L, Burger AJ, Cadranel JF, Lamy P, Gendre JP, Le Quintrec Y. Modulation of orocaecal transit time by hypnosis. *Gut.* 1991;32:393–394.

61. Whorell PJ, Prior A, Colgan SM. Hypnotherapy in severe irritable bowel syndrome: Further experience. *Gut.* 1987;28:423–425.

62. Whorwell PJ. Use of hypnotherapy in gastrointestinal disease. *Br J Hosp Med.* 1991;45:27–29.

63. Kayton WJ, Reis RK, Bokan JA, Kleinman A. Hyperemesis Gravidarum: A biopsychosocial perspective. *Int J Psychiatr Med.* 1980;10:151–162.

64. Fairweather DV. Nausea and vomiting in pregnancy. *Am J Obstet Gynecol.* 1958;102:135–175.

65. Apfel RJ, Kelley SF, Frankel FH. The role of hypnotizability in the pathogenesis of and treatment of nausea and vomiting during pregnancy. *J Psychosom Obstet Gynecol.* 1985;5:179–186.

66. Fuchs K, Paldi E, Abramovici H, Peretz BA. Treatment of hyperemesis gravidarum by hypnosis. *Int J Clin Exp Hypn.* 1980;28:313–323.

67. Morrow GR, Morrell C. Behavioral treatment for the anticipatory nausea and vomiting induced by cancer chemotherapy. *N Engl J Med.* 1982;307: 1476–1480.

68. Redd WH, Andresen GV, Minagawa RY. Hypnotic control of anticipatory emesis in patients receiving cancer chemotherapy. *J Consult Clin Psychol.* 1982;50:14–19.

69. Baker EL, Nash MR. Applications of hypnosis in the treatment of anorexia nervosa. *Am J Clin Hypn.* 1987;29:185–193.

70. Vanderlinden J, Vandereycken W. The use of hypnotherapy in the treatment of eating disorders. *Int J Eating Disord.* 1988;7:673–679.

71. Torem MS. Dissociative states presenting as an eating disorder. *Am J Clin Hypn.* 1986;29:137–142.

72. Russell G. Bulimia nervosa: An ominous variant of anorexia nervosa. *Psychol Med.* 1979;9:429–448.

73. Sanders S. The perceptual alteration scale: A scale measuring dissociation. *Am J Clin Hypn.* 1986;29:95–102.

74. Chandarana P, Malla A. Bulimia and dissociative states: A case report. *Can J Psychiatry.* 1989;34:137–139.

75. Hall JR, McGill JC. Hypno-behavioral treatment of self-destructive behavior: Trichotillomania and bulimia in the same patients. *Am J Clin Hypn.* 1986;29:39–46.

76. Pettinati HM, Horne RL, Staats JM. Hypnotizability in patients with anorexia nervosa and bulimia. *Arch Gen Psychiatry.* 1985;42:1014–1016.

77. Barabasz M. Treatment of bulimia with hypnosis involving awareness and control in clients with high dissociative capacity. *Int J Psychosom.* 1989;36:104–108.

78. Covino NA, Jimerson DC, Walton B, Franko D, Frankel FH. Hypnotizability, dissociation and bulimia: An outpatient study. In preparation.

79. Demitrack MA, Putnam FW, Brewerton TD, Brandt HA, Gold PW. Relation of clinical variables to dissociative phenomena in eating disorders. *Am J Psychiatry.* 1990;147:1184–1188.

80. Goldfarb LA. Sexual abuse antecedent to anorexia nervosa, bulimia and compulsive over-eating: Three case reports. *Int J Eating Disord.* 1987;6:675–680.

81. Bulik CM, Sullivan PF, Rotry M. Childhood sexual abuse in women with bulimia. *J Clin Psychiatry.* 1989;50:460–464.

82. Kaye WH, Gwirtsman HE, George DT, Weiss SR, Jimerson DC. Relationship of mood alterations to binging behavior in bulimia. *Br J Psychiatry.* 1986;149:479–485.

83. Abraham SF, Beaumont PJ. How patients describe bulimia or binge eating. *Psychol Med.* 1982;12:625–635.

84. Tomkins SS. Psychological model for smoking behavior. *Am J Public Health Nation Health.* 1966;56:17–20.

85. Prochaska JO, DiClemente CC. Stages and processes of self-change of smoking: Toward an integrative model of change. *J Consult Clin Psychol.* 1983;51:390–395.

86. Brownell KD, Marlatt GA, Lichtenstein E, Wilson GT. Understanding and preventing relapse. *Am Psychol.* 1986;41:765–782.

87. Perry C, Mullen G. The effects of hypnotic susceptibility on reducing smoking behavior treated by an hypnotic technique. *J Clin Psychol.* 1975;31:498–505.

88. Perry C, Gelfand R, Marcovitch P. The relevance of hypnotic susceptibility in the clinical context. *J Abnorm Psychol.* 1979;88:592–603.

89. Berlin FS. Smoking decreased after hypnosis. *Arch Gen Psychiatry.* 1980;37:1200–1201.

90. Lambe R, Osier C, Franks P. A randomized controlled trial of hypnotherapy for smoking cessation. *J Fam Pract.* 1986;22(1):61–65.

91. Andersen MS. Hypnotizability as a factor in the hypnotic treatment of obesity. *Int J Clin Exp Hypn.* 1985;33:150–159.

92. Barabasz M, Spiegel D. Hypnotizability and weight loss in obese subjects. *Int J Eating Disord.* 1989;8:335–341.

93. Cochrane G, Friesen J. Hypnotherapy in weight loss treatment. *J Consult Clin Psychol.* 1986;54:489–492.

94. Henningfield JE, Nemeth-Coslett R. Nicotine dependence. Interface between tobacco and tobacco-related disease. *Chest.* 1988;93(2 suppl):37S–55S.

95. Keesey RE. A set point theory of obesity. In: Brownell K, Foreyt J, eds. *Handbook of Eating Disorders.* New York: Basic Books;1986.

96. Dean JT, Nelson E, Moss L. Pathologic hair pulling: A review of the literature and case reports. *Compr Psychiatry.* 1992;33:84–91.

97. Jemmott JB III, Locke SE. Psychosocial factors, immunologic mediation, and human susceptibility to infectious diseases: How much do we know? *Psychol Bull.* 1984;95:78–108.

98. Baker GHB. Invited review; Psychological factors and immunity. *J Psychosom Res.* 1987;31:1–10.

99. Meares A. A form of intensive meditation associated with the regression of cancer. *Am J Clin Hypn.* 1982/1983;25:114–121.

100. Newton BW. The use of hypnosis in the treatment of cancer patients. *Am J Clin Hypn.* 1982/1983;25:104–113.

101. Spiegel D, Kraemer HC, Bloom J, Gottheil L. Effect of psychologic treatment on survival of patients with metastatic breast cancer. *Lancet.* 1989;ii:888–891.

102. Frankel FH, Misch RC. Hypnosis in a case of long-standing psoriasis in a person with character problems. *Int J Clin Exp Hypn.* 1973;21:121–130.

103. Winchell SA, Watts RA. Relaxation therapies in the treatment of psoriasis and possible pathophysiologic mechanisms. *J Am Acad Dermatol.* 1988;18:101–104.

104. Sinclair-Gieben AHC, Chalmers D. Evaluation of treatment of warts by hypnosis. *Lancet.* 1959:480–482.

105. Surman OS, Gottlieb SK, Hackett TP, Silverberg EL. Hypnosis in the treatment of warts. *Arch Gen Psychiatry.* 1973;28:439–441.

106. Black S. Inhibition of immediate type hypersensitivity response by direct suggestion under hypnosis. *Br Med J.* 1963;925–929.

107. Ikemi Y, Nakagawa S. A psychosomatic study of contagious dermatitis. *Kyushu J Med Sci.* 1962;13:335–350.

108. Frankel FH. Hypnotic responsiveness—Clinically a mixed blessing? *Aust J Clin Exp Hypn.* 1979;7:117–123.

109. Frankel FH, Orne MT. Hypnotizability and phobic behavior. *Arch Gen Psychiatry.* 1976;33:1259–1269.

Chapter 27
Cognitive Interventions in Behavioral Medicine

PAUL M. G. EMMELKAMP, PATRICIA VAN OPPEN

CARDIOVASCULAR DISORDERS

The cardiovascular disorders, particularly hypertension and coronary heart disease, have received increasing attention from psychologists. Although there is a recent decline in the mortality figure, cardiovascular disease is still the leading cause of death in Western countries. Psychological interventions have focused on reducing blood pressure, quitting smoking, and changing type A behavior.

HYPERTENSION

Only in a minority of patients (3%) is hypertension due to a clear somatic cause, which suggests that psychological factors may be involved in one way or another in the majority of hypertensives. A number of studies have evaluated the effects of biofeedback and relaxation in reducing blood pressure. Results of these studies show that significant but modest improvements can be achieved with such behavioral methods. The better controlled studies found blood pressure reduction of 10 to 26 mm Hg systolic and 5 to 15 mm Hg diastolic.[1] It is curious that cognitive factors have hardly been investigated, although it is now widely acknowledged that apart from biological factors psychological factors may play an important role in determining blood pressure levels in a given individual. For example, recent studies show that blood pressure is dependent on the setting in which it is measured, e.g., clinic, work, or home.[2] There is increasing evidence that not only major stressors but also daily hassles may lead to an increase in hypertension.[3] This suggests that cognitive–behavioral stress management programs may have some value, but this has hardly been investigated. Bosley and Allen[4] found such a cognitive stress management program effective in reducing blood pressure, but further studies are needed before conclusions with respect to this particular approach can be drawn.

TYPE A BEHAVIOR

Type A individuals are characterized as hard-driving, time urgent, aggressive, hostile, impatient, and competitive. Such persons were believed to be at greater risk for coronary heart disease.[5] More recent studies, however, led to inconclusive results, which tempered enthusiasm for the relationship between type A behavior and coronary heart disease.[6] There is now increasing evidence that not type A behavior per se, but hostility is related to coronary heart disease, although other components of the type A cluster, such as impatience and time urgency, may also be important.[7]

Cognitive–behavioral programs have been found to be effective in changing elements of the type A pattern and have led to coronary changes.[6, 8–10] Such programs usually contain an amalgam of cognitive and behavioral interventions; thus, conclusions with respect to the specific contribution of cognitive elements are precluded.

Recently, a number of authors[11–13] have stressed the importance of cognitive factors, especially self-evaluative processes, in stimulating type A behavior as a coping style. Central in these conceptualizations are schemata concerning self and others related to type-A-related situations and emotional states. An example of such a schema is: "I am only worthy when I achieve more than others." Such schemata or core beliefs may lead to the competitive striving, hostile reactions, and impatience of type A persons. Such sche- mata may be the result of negative parental rearing practices, char- acterized by insufficient warmth and rejection.[14] Cognitive therapy that focuses more specifically on changing these schemata looks promising, but controlled studies have not yet been conducted.

SMOKING

Behavioral procedures, such as aversive smoking, stimulus control, and contingency management, have been found to be effective in about 60% of smokers.[15] Unfortunately, relapse is the rule rather than the exception. There is considerable evidence that relapse is often related to stress.[16] Based on the relapse prevention model of Marlatt and Gordon,[17] a number of studies have evaluated whether a cognitive–behavioral relapse prevention program would be more successful. In such programs subjects learn cognitive and behav- ioral coping skills for managing craving and smoking temptation situations. Unfortunately, most of these studies failed to show that such programs prevented relapse.[18]

OBESITY

Obesity is often associated with increased blood pressure and has been viewed as one of the risk factors for cardiovascular disease.[19] A number of interventions have been applied to reduce the weight of obese people, including restriction of high-fat diets, therapeu- tic starvation, medication, and exercise. For severely obese people even more radical interventions are used, such as the gastric bal- loon, jaw wiring, and bypass surgery. In behavioral procedures the emphasis is on reducing body weight. However, it is becoming increasingly clear that the long-term effects of behavioral therapy are rather disappointing. While behavioral programs are effective in reducing body weight in the mild to moderate obese individu- als up to 1 year follow-up,[20] results of long-term follow-up studies suggest that most patients will regain most of their weight after 4 to 5 years.[21] It is now increasingly acknowledged that most obese individuals cannot reduce the body weight substantially for a prolonged period of time due to a number of biological factors. First, genetic factors are involved in body shape and body weight,[22] which means that attempts to reduce body weight are limited by biological boundaries. Further, there is considerable evidence that displacement of body weight usually results in a homeostatic process of metabolic adjustment designed to return the organism to the body weight normally maintained.[21] Thus, the body appears to resist weight loss by making metabolic adjustments.

There is inconclusive evidence that cognitive interventions facilitate weight loss and maintenance. Although three studies[22-24] found that cognitive interventions did not enhance the effects of behavioral programs, two other studies[25, 26] found some support for the addition of a cognitive intervention. Thus, results are inconclusive.

There are a number of other developments that are relevant for treatment options with obese people. First, the health risks associated with obesity appear to have been exaggerated. In contrast with the prevailing opinion, recent prospective epidemiological studies provide no convincing evidence that obesity as an independent risk factor is associated with increased morbidity.[27] There is some evidence that not obesity but frequent weight fluctuations that occur with dieting and relapse may be related to the health risks and mortality. Garner and Wooley[21] suggest that initial successful weight reduction and subsequent regain of weight eventually may result in increased mortality. Apart from health risks, there is also some evidence that weight reduction programs lead to an increase in depression at follow-up. Given this state of affairs, it does seem warranted neither on empirical nor on ethical grounds to continue behavioral or dietary programs directed at weight reduction for most obese people.

There is increasing evidence that health risk factors are associated with other factors than obesity per se such as alcohol consumption, salt, sugar, fats, and inadequate exercise. Cognitive therapy can be of help to motivate obese people to exercise on a regular basis. Many obese individuals are ashamed of their bodies and fear ridicule when exercising, which can be reduced by means of cognitive therapy. Further, irrational beliefs can be dealt with in cognitive therapy. Such irrational beliefs include: (1) moderate obesity per se is associated with increased health risks; (2) one is only valuable as a person when one is thin; (3) consuming even small amounts of food is "bad"; and (4) drastic diets are necessary to reduce weight. Other targets for cognitive therapy are feelings of guilt associated with overeating. Finally, cognitive therapy may be directed at accepting the obese body and at teaching more adequate coping skills (than eating) to deal with emotional distress.

To date only a few studies have evaluated the effects of cognitive therapy. Roughan et al.[28] found a program focusing on coping skills and increasing acceptance of the obese body successful in changing body image, self-esteem and depression, but this study was uncontrolled. Cognitive therapy focusing on changing body image was also found to be successful in other studies.[29-31]

BULIMIA NERVOSA

In contrast with obesity, where only few studies have evaluated the effects of cognitive therapy, a number of studies have investigated the effects of cognitive therapy on bulimia nervosa. Only controlled studies will be discussed. Fairburn[32] was one of the first to develop a comprehensive cognitive–behavioral therapy program for bulimics. The behavioral part of the program consists of self-monitoring of food intake and vomiting and recommending a pattern of regular eating. Patients are instructed to engage in distracting (pleasant) activities when they have an urge to vomit. After there is some improvement in binge eating and vomiting, cognitive therapy is directed to irrational beliefs related to (binge) eating, body image, and weight. Further, patients are taught problem-solving skills to cope with emotional distress and to deal with relapse. A number of controlled studies have evaluated the effect of this and related cognitive–behavioral programs. Cognitive–behavioral therapy resulted in a reduction in vomiting of 100%[33] and 95%,[34] respectively. At 1 year follow-up, 55% of the patients in the study of Fairburn et al.[33] had completely stopped vomiting. In Kirkley et al.'s study[34] this figure was 38% at 3 months follow-up, but in this study subjects had chronic complaints (10 years). Further improvements were found on body image, depression, and self-esteem. Cognitive–behavioral therapy was found to be more effective than short-term structured psychotherapy along the lines of Bruch on a global rating of improvement[33] and more effective in terms of reduction in vomiting than nondirective psychotherapy.[34] Yates and Sambrailo[35] compared the effects of the behavioral and cognitive components of this program. Both methods were found to be equally effective, but results were less than those usually achieved in the comprehensive cognitive–behavioral program. However, Freeman et al.[36] found a comprehensive cognitive–behavioral program no more effective than behavioral therapy.

An alternative cognitive–behavioral program was developed by Leitenberg et al.[37] In this program exposure (to eating) and response prevention (of vomiting) are used. Weight gain following the consumption of food leads to anxiety in bulimics. Vomiting is considered an escape response that is reinforced by the momentary anxiety relief about weight gain. It is assumed that distorted cognitions are more easily modified when bulimics are eating frightening foods that cause a strong urge to vomit and vomiting is not allowed. The therapist stays with the patient until the urge to vomit is under control. During these exposure sessions therapists question the patient about thoughts underlying the anxiety. This program was found to be far more effective than no treatment.[37] Several studies compared cognitive–behavioral therapy with and without exposure plus response prevention and there is a trend favoring the package of cognitive–behavioral therapy with exposure plus response prevention.[38, 39]

In sum, cognitive–behavioral approaches have been found to lead to substantial changes in binge eating and vomiting, and there is some evidence that this package is more effective than each package on its own. Cognitive–behavioral therapy results in a substantial reduction in binging and purging and often in improvement in other problems as well, such as social relationships and depression. However, cognitive–behavioral therapy is still not the panacea for this condition, since only nearly half of the patients stopped vomiting completely.

ANOREXIA NERVOSA

Only few studies[40, 41] have evaluated the effects of cognitive–behavioral interventions in patients with anorexia nervosa, all of which were case studies. Controlled studies are lacking, presumably due to the paucity of patients. Thus, the status of cognitive–behavioral therapy for this condition cannot be assessed.

CHRONIC PAIN

The International Association for the Study of Pain[42] has defined pain as: "an unpleasant sensory and emotional experience associated with actual or potential tissue damage, or described in terms of such damage." Pain is usually considered chronic when it exceeds a period of 6 months.

Recently, cognitive factors have been emphasized in understanding chronic pain, which have clear treatment implications.[43] Cognitive–behavioral therapy for chronic pain focuses on modifying the patient's subjective experience of pain and cognitions while in pain and emphasizes the patient's acquisition of cognitive and behavioral skills for coping with pain.

The effects of cognitive–behavioral treatments have been examined in several studies. Turner[44] found the cognitive–behavioral condition, consisting of identifying cognitive and affective responses to pain and learning to use imagery techniques and coping self-statements to deal with pain and stress, combined with relaxation training to be superior to a waiting-list control condition. Patients involved in this study had low back pain. The patients receiving cognitive–behavioral treatment with relaxation training significantly improved on subjective pain ratings and had significantly reduced health care utilization at 18 months follow-up.

In another study,[45] a cognitive–behavioral treatment package was compared with a placebo medication condition for patients with low back pain. Cognitive–behavioral treatment led to significant reductions in pain and increases in internal locus of control, whereas the placebo medication did not.

Philips[46] compared the efficacy of a cognitive–behavioral treatment with a waiting-list control condition in patients suffering from a variety of pain complaints (head, back, facial, groin, or multiple). The cognitive–behavioral treatment was found to be significantly superior to the waiting-list condition with respect to changes in mood, affective reactions to pain, self-efficacy, avoidance behavior, drug intake, and exercise capacity. The clinically beneficial effects were even stronger at 1 year follow-up.

Keefe et al.[47] evaluated the effects of a cognitive–behavioral treatment versus an educational information intervention. Patients had osteoarthritic knee pain. These findings demonstrated that patients in the cognitive–behavioral treatment condition showed significantly lower levels of physical disability and pain as compared to patients receiving only the educational information. However, at 6 months follow-up patients receiving the cognitive–behavioral treatment failed to sustain the improvement in pain, but they were able to maintain improvement in psychological and in physical disability over time.[48]

Behavioral versus Cognitive–Behavioral Treatments

In recent years, three studies evaluated the relative effectiveness of a pure behavioral (operant) treatment and cognitive–behavioral treatments for chronic pain. Kerns et al.[49] demonstrated in a group of mixed pain patients that both treatments significantly reduced health care utilization in comparison with a waiting-list control condition. However, only the cognitive–behavioral condition showed reduction in pain, psychological distress, and dependence, and an increase in instrumental activities.

A second study, comparing the operant and cognitive–behavioral treatments for chronic low back pain, was reported by Turner and Clancy.[50] For both conditions significant improvement in physical and psychosocial disability was demonstrated at the posttest. The patients who received the operant treatment demonstrated a greater improvement than the cognitive–behavioral condition. However, at the follow-ups (6 months and 1 year) no differences between the two treatments were revealed, due to a steady improvement over time in the cognitive–behavioral condition.

Finally, a study reported by Nicholas et al.[51] compared the effectiveness of a cognitive treatment and a behavioral treatment versus physiotherapy in patients with chronic back pain. This study demonstrated that both the cognitive treatment and the behavioral treatment improved significantly more than the physiotherapy conditions. Moreover, the behavioral treatment led to significantly more improvement in the functional impairment than the cognitive treatments. However, this difference disappeared at the 6- and 12-month follow-ups.

RECENT DEVELOPMENTS

Two neglected problems in research into the treatment of chronic pain are the relapse rate and the noncompliance.[52] Usually, there exists a noncompliance rate with simple medical regimens of about 30% of the patients. The noncompliance rate of cognitive–behavioral treatments, which are more demanding of patients, can be expected to be larger and is estimated at between 30 and 60%.

An interesting recent development is the application of cognitive–behavioral prevention programs. Linton et al.[53] demonstrated the efficacy of a secondary prevention program for nurses having back pain who were at risk for chronic pain. This program included: (1) physical therapy; (2) cognitive–behavioral strategies; and (3) training in ways to avoid reinjury. Patients receiving this prevention program significantly improved in subjective pain, pain behavior, psychological distress, and fatigue, in contrast to the waiting-list control patients who did not show any significant improvement.

Taking together the results of the controlled studies in this area, there is firm evidence that cognitive–behavioral treatments are superior to no treatment and that the effects are maintained at follow-up. Since patients were treated with more than one method, conclusions with respect to the efficacy of the different treatment components are precluded. Another factor complicating the interpretation of the results concerns the heterogeneous samples, particularly with respect to the locus of pain. Further, a challenging task for further research is to reduce the relapse rate and the noncompliance.

Another area in need of research is the evaluation of prevention programs for patients with chronic pain. The results of the prevention program of Linton et al.[53] are encouraging, but further studies are needed to evaluate the effectiveness and the costs-benefits of such programs.

BENIGN HEADACHE

Two major forms of benign headache can be distinguished: (1) vascular headache (migraine or combined migraine and tension headache), and (2) chronic tension headache. Over the past decade, several controlled studies investigated whether benign headache would benefit from cognitive therapy. Most studies examined the effects of adding cognitive therapy components to progressive muscle relaxation and various forms of biofeedback training.

VASCULAR HEADACHE

Only a few controlled studies have investigated the value of cognitive therapy for vascular headache. Cognitive therapy for vascular headache sufferers consisted mostly of stress-inoculation training and cognitive restructuring, called cognitive stress-coping therapy.

A first attempt to study the effects of cognitive treatment in vascular headache was done by Lake et al.[54] The results of this study demonstrated that the addition of rational emotive therapy to biofeedback was no more effective than biofeedback alone.

Blanchard et al.[55, 56] demonstrated twice that the effects of biofeedback plus relaxation training with or without cognitive therapy, consisting of cognitive stress-coping therapy (once with a minimal therapist-contact format), were superior compared to an attention–placebo group with vascular headache.

Another study[57] evaluated the effects of a cognitive–behavioral therapy versus the same treatment using a minimal therapist-contact format. Both treatments showed a significant reduction in headache frequency, duration, and peak intensity.

Richter et al.[58] investigated the efficacy of two active treatments (relaxation and cognitive stress-coping therapy) compared with a placebo control group in the treatment of pediatric migraine. The migraine sufferers who received one of the active treatment reported significantly reduced headache activity and frequency, whereas the control group did not.

Finally, a number of studies[59–61] demonstrated no differences between the efficacy of cognitive treatment, other active treatments, and the combination of both for migraine headaches.

TENSION HEADACHE

Over the past decade, a number of studies have evaluated the effects of behavioral interventions for tension headache pain. Reviews of the efficacy of these interventions demonstrated that tension headache sufferers receiving biofeedback, relaxation, or a combination of both benefited equally from these interventions.[62–64] However, about 40% of tension headache sufferers do not improve after behavioral treatment. Therefore, several studies attempted to evaluate the effectiveness of cognitive therapy.

Usually, cognitive treatment for tension headache sufferers, called *stress-coping* training, focused on altering maladaptive cognitive responses assumed to result in tension headache. The results of a number of studies demonstrated that cognitive treatment, sometimes combined with relaxation or biofeedback, was superior compared to a waiting-list condition.[65-71]

In three studies it was found that cognitive therapy alone was superior to another active treatment (biofeedback or relaxation).[65, 67, 72] Further, the results of two studies revealed that cognitive therapy enhanced the effectiveness of relaxation.[70, 73] Finally, two studies[68, 74] showed that the combination of cognitive therapy with relaxation was superior to amitriptyline and to a supportive group therapy.

However, also negative results for cognitive therapy were reported. Four studies demonstrated that cognitive therapy alone or the addition of cognitive interventions to an active treatment did not yield an increase in therapy outcome.[66, 69, 71, 75]

Only one study[76] provided follow-up data up to 2 years. The follow-up data revealed that the cognitive therapy group was significantly more improved than the biofeedback group. No relapse occurred in the cognitive therapy group whereas a significant number of biofeedback patients relapsed.

CONCLUDING REMARKS

Summarizing the results of the controlled studies on the treatment of vascular headache, there is no evidence that cognitive therapy alone or adding cognitive therapy to active treatments is superior to biofeedback or relaxation training. These results are in contrast with the results of cognitive therapy in the treatment of chronic tension headache. The cognitive–behavioral intervention (alone or added to an active treatment) was found to be effective in a number of studies with tension headache sufferers. However, some studies demonstrated that cognitive therapy did not enhance the effectiveness of biofeedback or relaxation. Presumably, these differences are due to variation in the cognitive treatment protocols.

It seems worthwhile to investigate which patient with chronic tension headache profits from which form of cognitive therapy. Further, there is a pressing need for studies that evaluate the efficacy of cognitive therapy in a long-term follow-up.

AIDS AND HIV

AIDS and HIV disease provide a challenge for mental health workers. The possibility exists that psychosocial factors may affect the rate and degree of immunosuppression. Cognitive–behavioral therapy may help HIV-infected individuals to cope more adequately with the stress associated with the knowledge that one is seropositive. Perhaps, reduction of emotional distress and more adequate coping might directly improve immune function and alter the course of AIDS.[77]

There is some evidence that notification of positive HIV serostatus is associated with increased distress, depression, and somatic complaints.[78] Antoni et al.[79] followed healthy gay men from 5 weeks before notification of their positive serostatus. They found a cognitive–behavioral stress management to be effective in leading to significant increases in CD4 cells and natural killer cells, in contrast with no-treatment controls, who showed a slight decrement in CD4 cells.

Mulder et al.[80] recently compared the effects of cognitive–behavioral therapy with those of experiential therapy. Participants were male homosexuals in an asymptomatic stage of HIV infection. Subjects in the cognitive–behavioral therapy condition received training in cognitive restructuring, assertiveness skills, and coping strategies. Treatment in both conditions consisted of 15 sessions and was conducted in groups. Both treatments were found to be more effective than no treatment, but there was no evidence that one approach was more effective than the other. Treatment did not lead to an improvement in immune parameters.[81] However, the men who improved in psychological distress also had a relative increase in CD4 counts.

A related study was reported by Coates et al.[82] Cognitive–behavioral therapy led to improvement in psychological distress and a reduced number of sexual partners but not to improved immune functions.

There is a clear need for more controlled studies on the effects of cognitive–behavioral therapy on distress and immune functions.

The results of the three studies that have been published are encouraging, but further studies are needed before more firm conclusions can be drawn.

CANCER

Cognitive–behavioral studies on cancer can be divided in two major categories: first, studies that focus on managing aversive reactions to chemotherapy[83, 84] and, second, studies that focus on enhancement of quality of life and reduction of emotional distress. Here, only the latter studies will be discussed. To date, five studies have been published which evaluated a treatment package that included cognitive elements. We will discuss each study briefly.

Edgar et al.[85] evaluated the effects of a comprehensive coping skills treatment program in 205 subjects with a favorable survival prognosis. Half of the sample had breast cancer. Treatment was delivered individually. Treatment fostered active coping to improve a sense of personal control, relaxation training, cognitive restructuring, and problem solving. In cognitive restructuring patients were taught (1) that distress emerged not only from the facts but also from their cognitive appraisals of their illness, and (2) to reappraise catastrophic thoughts to make them more controllable and less distressing. Positive effects were found on anxiety, depression, and distress from intrusive thoughts about the illness. The effects were greatest for the most physically debilitated patients. Treatment consisted of five sessions and was conducted by nurses. There was some evidence that delayed treatment (4 months after diagnosis of cancer) was more effective than immediate treatment.

Fawzy et al.[86, 87] reported on a structured group support intervention (n = 35) including cognitive problem solving besides health education and stress management (relaxation). Subjects consisted of patients with primarily stage I melanoma (low mortality risk). At 6 months follow-up treatment resulted in significantly lower distress (POMS) than no treatment (n = 26). Interestingly, treated patients were found to use more active cognitive coping strategies than controls at 6 months follow-up. There was also some evidence that treatment affected immunological parameters. Most of the immunological changes were not found at the 6-week follow-up but had emerged 6 months later.

Heinrich and Coscarelli-Schag[88] compared the effectiveness of a program (n = 26) consisting of stress management, relaxation, cognitive therapy, and activity management with no treatment (n = 25). Patients had more severe disease than in the previous studies, suffering from lung, prostate, and colorectal cancer. Treatment consisted of six sessions and was conducted in groups. All patients (treated or not) improved on measures for social adjustment and emotional distress at the end of therapy. This study was quasi-experimental rather than controlled.

Two studies have been reported that compared the effects of a cognitive–behavioral program with another active treatment. Davis[89] compared the effects of cognitive–behavioral therapy (n = 5) with those of electromyography and temperature control biofeedback along with relaxation (n = 10) and with no-treatment control (n = 7). The cognitive–behavioral therapy consisted of self-instructional training (positive self-talk and positive problem-solving imagery) and of relaxation. Patients were females with early breast cancer with a low mortality risk. Treatment consisted of 13 sessions and was administered individually by a social worker. Although both treatment groups were found to improve in state anxiety in contrast to the no-treatment group, no differential improvements for conditions were found. Only on cortisol levels at 8 months follow-up did both intervention groups show significantly more improvement than no treatment. Numbers in each condition were rather small, precluding drawing firm conclusions.

Telch and Telch[90] evaluated the effects of group coping skills training (n = 13) and group support (n = 14). Both treatments involved six sessions. Patients consisted of a mixed sample, with primarily breast cancer and Hodgkin's disease with a moderate mortality risk. Coping skills training involved training in cognitive, behavioral, and affective coping strategies. Relaxation and stress management were also included. At the end of therapy, the coping skills patients were less distressed than the support and no-treatment control group (n = 14).

In sum, there is some evidence that a comprehensive cognitive–behavioral program may lead to a reduction in distress. It is unlikely that the positive effects found can be ascribed to social support provided by the group, since Telch and Telch[90] found the coping skills training more effective than a social support therapy. Since no study has been reported that evaluated the effects of a pure cognitive condition, it is unclear what the effects of cognitive therapy per se are. All programs consist of an amalgam of behavioral and cognitive interventions, thus precluding conclusions with respect to the contribution of cognitive and behavioral therapy respectively.

Often, treatment is rather short and not delivered by therapists versed in cognitive therapy (e.g., nurses and social workers). Further studies are needed in which cognitive therapy is administered over a longer period of time by well-trained, experienced cognitive therapists. The finding that cognitive therapy led to long-term benefits on cortisol and immunosuppression is interesting and there is a pressing need for further studies. One important caveat must be emphasized. In none of the studies were patients with a high mortality risk treated. Thus, whether cognitive therapy may help patients in coping with death has not yet been investigated. Finally, follow-up studies are certainly desirable.

ASTHMA

Asthma is a disorder characterized by increased hyperreactivity of the airways to stimuli, including (1) allergens; (2) nonspecific irritants such as cold air and exercise; and (3) infections. Asthma attacks may consist of (1) swelling of the bronchial walls; (2) constriction of the smooth muscle in the bronchial wall; (3) increased mucus secretion; (4) infiltration by inflammatory cells; or (5) a combination of these factors. Attacks usually occur intermittently and can reverse either with treatment or spontaneously.[91]

Psychosomatic views which hold that psychological factors are responsible in a causative sense are no longer tenable. There is, however, considerable evidence that stress exacerbates asthma. In a number of studies it has been demonstrated that threat of aversive stimulation leads to increases in airflow resistance in asthma patients. When asthma patients are led to believe that a bronchoconstriction is present but actually a neutral substance is present, many patients exhibit increases in airflow resistance. Such increased airflow resistance has also been demonstrated using a number of other stressors, including the imagination of fear and anger, watching stressful movies, and performing mental arithmetics.[92] As an aside, it should be noted that increased airflow resistance is not similar to asthma. Further, there is some evidence that such stressors may also lead to increased airflow resistance in nonasthmatic individuals.

Asthma is often associated with the experience of fear and panic. Asthmatic patients may develop phobias for situations in which they have had an attack or for the hospital setting. A number of studies have evaluated the effects of systematic desensitization and relaxation focusing on the anticipatory fear of attacks, but the evidence in favor of this approach for anxiety reduction and improved lung function is limited.[93] In patients with chronic obstructive pulmonary disease (COPD), a condition that is chronic and more severe, panic attacks are quite common.[94] There is some evidence that COPD patients who experience catastrophic cognitions in addition to the physiological sensations associated with COPD are more susceptible to panic.[95] While all COPD patients in this study experienced the physiological sensations associated with panic, only 37% experienced panic attacks, and these individuals reported more fear-provoking thoughts, i.e., catastrophic interpretations of body sensations. According to these authors, cognitive therapy is an important treatment option for these patients, since the physiological sensations are chronic. However, cognitive therapy has not yet been evaluated.

Another line of psychological research involves self-management. Self-management is a form of psychoeducation involving the transference of knowledge relating to asthma and often consists of a training in adequate self-management. These studies have been reviewed by Klingelhofer and Gershwin[96] and Lehrer et al.[97] Such programs lead to increased medication compliance, greater competence in managing symptoms, and decreased use of medical services. Recently, two studies have investigated the value of cognitive therapy in the training in self-management. Cognitive therapy consisted of rational emotive therapy and was conducted in groups. Cognitive therapy was directed at discovering and challenging irrational beliefs related to asthma and to inadequate coping. These studies[98, 99] found some evidence that such a cognitive self-management program led to improved coping (i.e., rational action in asthma attack situations). In addition, patients were less preoccupied with asthma in everyday life. Further, treatment led to increased medication compliance. These effects were established in comparison with a no-treatment control group. Unfortunately, this approach was not compared with a psychoeducational self-management program without a specific cognitive intervention. Hence, it is unclear whether cognitive therapy enhances the effects of routine psychoeducational self-management programs.

CONCLUDING REMARKS

Although the "cognitive revolution" is relatively new, by 1992 cognitive therapy had already made significant contributions to the field of behavioral medicine. Generally, it is difficult to speak of specific cognitive interventions since most cognitive interventions are embedded in behavioral programs. As noted throughout this report, it is often difficult to distangle the relative contribution of cognitive and behavioral components. In this report not all areas could be discussed. Another area in which cognitive approaches are promising is gastrointestinal disorder, i.e., the irritable bowel syndrome. Blanchard et al.[100–103] have shown that a cognitive–behavioral program consisting of education about the relationship between stress and bowel symptoms, relaxation and cognitive stress-coping techniques was effective in reducing bowel symptoms in about 60% of the patients. However, results are less promising for patients with inflammatory bowel disease (ulcerative colitis and Crohn's disease).[104, 105] Another area in which we may expect an important contribution from cognitive interventions is insomnia.[106, 107] New advances in the contribution of cognitive therapy undoubtedly will be made in the next few years.

REFERENCES

1. Weiss SM, Anderson RT, Weiss SM. Cardiovascular disorders: Hypertension and coronary heart disease. In: Sweet JJ, Rozensky RH, Tovian SM, eds. *Handbook of Clinical Psychology in Medical Settings.* New York: Plenum Press; 1991: pp 353–374.
2. Pickering T, Harshfield G, Kleinert H, Blank S, Laraugh J. Comparison of blood pressure during normal daily activities, sleep, and exercise. *JAMA.* 1982;247:992–996.
3. Linden W. *Psychological Perspectives of Essential Hypertension: Etiology, Maintenance and Treatment.* Karger Biobehavioral Medicine Series. Basel, Switzerland: Karger;1984:3.
4. Bosley F, Allen TW. Stress management training for hypertensives: Cognitive and physiological effects. *J Behav Med.* 1989;12:77–89.
5. Brand RJ, Rosenman RH, Sholtz RI, Friedman M. Multivariate prediction of coronary heart disease in the Western collaborative group study compared to the findings of the Framingham study. *Circulation.* 1976;53:348–355.
6. Thoresen CE, Powell LH. Type-A behavior pattern: New perspectives on theory, assessment, and intervention. *J Consult Clin Psychol.* 1992;60:595–604.
7. Matthews KA. CHD and type-A behaviors: Update on and alternative to the Booth-Kewley and Friedman quantitative review. *Psychol Bull.* 1988;104:373–380.
8. Nunes EV, Frank KA, Kornfeld DS. Psychological treatment for the type A behavior pattern and for coronary heart disease: A meta-analysis of the literature. *Psychosom Med.* 1987;48:159–173.
9. Levenkron JC, Moore L. Type A behavior pattern: Issues for intervention research. *Ann Behav Med.* 1988;10:78–83.
10. Price VA. Research and clinical issues in treating type A behavior. In: Houston BK, Snyder CR, eds. *Type A Behavior Pattern: Research, Theory and Intervention.* New York: Wiley;1988: pp 275–311.
11. Matthews KA. Psychological perspectives on the type A behavior pattern. *Psychol Bull.* 1982;91:293–323.

12. Price VA. *Type A Behavior Pattern: A Model for Research and Practice.* New York: Academic Press;1982.
13. Strube MJ. A self-appraisal model of the type A behavior pattern. *Perspect Pers.* 1987;2:201–250.
14. Emmelkamp PMG, Karsdorp EP. The effects of perceived parental rearing style on the development of type A pattern. *Eur J Pers.* 1987;1:223–230.
15. Hall SM, Hall SG, Ginsberg D. Pharmacological and behavioral treatment for cigarette smoking. *Prog Behav Modif.* 1990;25:87–119.
16. Cohen S, Lichtenstein E. Perceived stress, quitting smoking, and smoking relapse. *Health Psychol.* 1990;9:466–478.
17. Marlatt GA, Gordon JR. *Relapse Prevention: Maintenance Strategies in the Treatment of Addictive Behaviors.* New York: Guilford Press;1980.
18. Lichtenstein E, Glasgow RE. Smoking cessation: What have we learned over the past decade. *J Consult Clin Psychol.* 1992;60:518–527.
19. Weinsler RL, Norris DJ, Birch R. The relative contribution of body fat and fat pattern to blood pressure. *Hypertension.* 1985;7:578–585.
20. Brownell KD, Jeffery RW. Improving long-term weight loss: Pushing the limits of treatment. *Behav Ther.* 1987;18:353–374.
21. Garner DM, Wooley SC. Confronting the failure of behavioral and dietary treatments for obesity. *Clin Psychol Rev.* 1991;11:729–780.
22. Stunkard AJ, Harris JR, Pedersen NL, McLearn GE. A separated twin study of the body mass index. *N Engl J Med.* 1990;322:1483–1487.
23. DeLucia JL, Kalodner CR. An individualized cognitive intervention: Does it increase the efficacy of behavioral interventions for weight loss. *Addict Behav.* 1990;15:473–479.
24. Kalodner CR, DeLucia JL. The individual and combined effects of cognitive therapy and nutrition education as additions to a behavior modification program for weight loss. *Addict Behav.* 1991;16:255–263.
25. Collins RL, Rothblum ED, Wilson GT. The comparative efficacy of cognitive and behavioral approaches to the treatment of obesity. *Cogn Ther Res.* 1986;10:299–317.
26. Dunhel LD, Glaros AG. Comparison of self-instructional and stimulus control treatments for obesity. *Cogn Ther Res.* 1978;2:75–78.
27. Ernsberger P, Haskew P. Health implications of obesity: An alternative view. *J Obes Weight Regul.* 1987;6:58–137.
28. Roughan P, Seddon E, Vernon-Robberts J. Long-term effects of a psychologically-based group programme for women preoccupied with body weight and eating behavior. *Int J Obes.* 1990;14:135–147.
29. Butlers JW, Cash TF. Cognitive-behavioral treatment of women's body-image dissatisfaction. *J Consult Clin Psychol.* 1987;55:889–897.
30. Dworhin SH, Kerr BA. Comparison of interventions for women experiencing body image problems. *J Couns Psychol.* 1987;34:136–140.
31. Rosen JC, Saltzberg E, Srebnik D. Cognitive behavior therapy for negative body image. *Behav Ther.* 1989;20:393–404.
32. Fairburn CG. A cognitive behavioral approach to the treatment of bulimia. *Psychol Med.* 1981;11:707–711.
33. Fairburn CG, O'Connor M, Cooper PJ. A comparison of two psychological treatments for bulimia nervosa. *Behav Res Ther.* 1986;24:629–643.

34. Kirkley BG, Schneider JA, Agras WS, Bachman JA. Comparison of two group treatments for bulimia. *J Consult Clin Psychol.* 1985;53:43–48.

35. Yates AS, Sambrailo F. Bulimia nervosa: A descriptive and therapeutic study. *Behav Res Ther.* 1984;22:503–517.

36. Freeman C, Sinclair F, Turnbull J, Annadale A. Psychotherapy for bulimia: A controlled study. *J Psychiatr Res.* 1985;19:473–478.

37. Leitenberg H, Rosen JC, Gross J, Nudelman S, Vara LS. Exposure plus response prevention treatment of bulimia nervosa: A controlled evaluation. *J Consult Clin Psychol.* 1988;56:535–541.

38. Ordman AM, Kirschenbaum DS. Cognitive-behavioral therapy for bulimia: An initial outcome study. *J Consult Clin Psychol.* 1985;53:305–313.

39. Wilson GT, Rossiter E, Kleifeld EI, Lindholm L. Cognitive-behavioral treatment of bulimia nervosa: Controlled evaluation. *Behav Res Ther.* 1986;24:277–288.

40. Cooper PJ, Fairburn CG. Cognitive behavior therapy for anorexia nervosa: Some preliminary findings. *J Psychosom Res.* 1984;28:493–499.

41. Garner DM, Bemis KM. Cognitive therapy for anorexia nervosa. In: Garner DM, Garfinkel PE, eds. *Handbook of Psychotherapy for Anorexia Nervosa and Bulimia.* New York: Guilford Press;1985.

42. International Association for the Study of Pain (IASP). Pain terms: A list with definitions and notes on usage. *Pain.* 1979;6:249–252.

43. Keefe FJ, Dunsmore J, Burnett R. Behavioral and cognitive-behavioral approaches to chronic pain: Recent advances and future directions. *J Consult Clin Psychol.* 1992;60:528–536.

44. Turner JA. Comparison of group progressive-relaxation training and cognitive-behavioral group therapy for chronic low back pain. *J Consult Clin Psychol.* 1982;50:757–765.

45. Engstrom D. Cognitive behavioral therapy methods in chronic pain treatment. *Adv Pain Res Ther.* 1983;5:829–838.

46. Philips HC. The effects of behavioural treatment on chronic pain. *Behav Res Ther.* 1987;25:365–377.

47. Keefe FJ, Caldwell DS, Williams DA, Gil KM, Mitchell D, Robertson D, Robertson C, Martinez S, Nunley J, Beckham JC, Crisson JE, Helms M. Pain coping skills training in the management of osteoarthritic knee pain: A comparative study. *Behav Ther.* 1990;21:49–62.

48. Keefe FJ, Caldwell DS, Williams DA, Gil KM, Mitchell D, Robertson D, Robertson C, Martinez S, Nunley J, Beckham JC, Helms M. Pain coping skills training in the management of osteoarthritic knee pain. II. Follow-up results. *Behav Ther.* 1990;21:435–447.

49. Kerns RD, Turk DC, Holzman AD, Rudy TE. Comparison of cognitive–behavioral and behavioral approaches to the outpatient treatment of chronic pain. *Clin J Pain.* 1986;1:195–203.

50. Turner JA, Clancy S. Comparison of operant behavioral and cognitive–behavioral group treatment for chronic low back pain. *J Consult Clin Psychol.* 1988;56:261–266.

51. Nicholas MK, Wilson PH, Goyen J. Operant-behavioural and cognitive–behavioural treatment for chronic low back pain. *Behav Res Ther.* 1991;29:225–238.

52 Turk DC, Rudy TE. Neglected topics in the treatment of chronic pain patients—Relapse, noncompliance, and adherence enhancement. *Pain.* 1991; 44:5–28.

53. Linton SJ, Bradley LA, Jensen I, Spangfort E, Sundell L. The secondary prevention of low back pain: A controlled study with follow-up. *Pain.* 1989; 66:197–207.

54. Lake A, Rainey J, Papsdorf JD. Biofeedback and rational emotive therapy in the management of migraine headache. *J Appl Behav Anal.* 1979;12: 127–140.

55. Blanchard EB, Appelbaum KA, Nicholson NL, Radnitz CL, Morrill B, Michultka D, Kirsch C, Hillhouse J, Dentinger MP. A controlled evaluation of the addition of cognitive therapy to a home-based biofeedback and relaxation treatment of vascular headache. *Headache.* 1990;30:371–376.

56. Blanchard EB, Appelbaum KA, Radnitz CL, Morrill B, Michultka D, Kirsch C, Guarnieri P, Hillhouse J, Evans DD, Jaccard J, Barron KD. A controlled evaluation of thermal biofeedback and thermal biofeedback combined with cognitive therapy in the treatment of vascular headache. *J Consult Clin Psychol.* 1990;58:216–224.

57. Richarson GM, McGrath PJ. Cognitive-behavioral therapy for migraine headaches: A minimal-therapist-contact approach versus a clinic-based approach. *Headache.* 1989;29:352–357.

58. Richter IL, McGrath PJ, Humphreys PJ, Goodman JT, Firestone P, Keene D. Cognitive and relaxation treatment of paediatric migraine. *Pain.* 1986;25: 195–203.

59. Knapp TW, Florin I. The treatment of migraine headache by training in vasoconstriction of the temporal artery and a cognitive stress-coping training. *Behav Anal Modif.* 1981;4:267–274.

60. Birbaumer N, Gerber D, Miltner W, Lutzenberger W, Kluck M. Start with biofeedback and continue with behavior therapy in migraine. Proc 15th Annu Meet of the Biofeedback Society of America. Albuquerque. Biofeedback Society of America;1984.

61. Sorbi M, Tellegen B. Multimodel migraine treatment: Does thermal biofeedback add to the outcome? *Headache.* 1984;24:249–255.

62. Holroyd KA, Penzien DB. Client variables in the behavioral treatment of current tension headache: A meta-analytic review. *J Behav Med.* 1986;9: 515–536.

63. Blanchard EB. Long-term effects of behavioral treatment of chronic headache. *Behav Ther.* 1987;18:375–385.

64. Blanchard EB. Psychological treatment of benign headache disorders. *J Consult Clin Psychol.* 1992;60:537–551.

65. Holroyd KA, Andrasik F, Westbrook T. Cognitive control of tension headache. *Cogn Ther Res.* 1977;1:121–133.

66. Holroyd KA, Andrasik F. Coping and the self-control of chronic tension headache. *J Consult Clin Psychol.* 1978;5:1036–1045.

67. Holroyd KA, Andrasik F, Noble J. Comparison of EMG biofeedback and a credible pseudotherapy in treating tension headache. *J Behav Med.* 1980;3:29–39.

68. Figueroa JL. Group treatment of chronic tension headaches: A comparative treatment study. *Behav Modif.* 1982;6:229–239.

69. Bell NW, Abramowitz SI, Folkins CH, Spensley J, Hutchinson GL. Biofeedback, brief psychotherapy and tension headache. *Headache.* 1983;23:162–173.
70. Blanchard EB, Appelbaum KA, Radnitz CL, Michultka K, Morrill B, Kirsch C, Hillhouse J, Evans DD, Guarnieri P, Attanasio V, Andrasik F, Jaccard J, Dentinger MP. Placebo-controlled evaluation of abbreviated progressive muscle relaxation and of relaxation combined with cognitive therapy in the treatment of tension headache. *J Consult Clin Psychol.* 1990;58:210–215.
71. Appelbaum KA, Blanchard EB, Nicholson NL, Radnitz C, Kirsch C, Michultka D, Attansio V, Andrasik F, Dentinger MP. Controlled evaluation of the addition of cognitive strategies to a home-based relaxation protocol for tension headache. *Behav Ther.* 1990;21:293–303.
72. Murphy AI, Lehrer PM, Jurish S. Cognitive coping skills training and relaxation training as treatments for tension headaches. *Behav Ther.* 1990;21:89–98.
73. Tobin DL, Holroyd KA, Baker A, Reynolds RVC, Holm JE. Development and clinical trial of a minimal contact, cognitive–behavioral treatment for tension headache. *Cogn Ther Res.* 1988;12:325–339.
74. Holroyd KA, Nash JM, Pingel JD, Cordingley GE, Jerome A. A comparison of pharmacological (amitriptyline HCI) and nonpharmacological (cognitive-behavioral) therapies for chronic tension headaches. *J Consult Clin Psychol.* 1991;59:387–393.
75. Anderson NB, Lawrence PS, Olson TW. Within-subject analysis of autogenic training and cognitive coping training in the treatment of tension headache pain. *J Behav Ther Exp Psychiatry.* 1981;12:219–223.
76. Holroyd KA, Andrasik F. Do the effects of cognitive therapy endure? A two-year follow-up of tension headache sufferers treated with cognitive therapy or biofeedback. *Cogn Ther Res.* 1982;6:325–333.
77. Kiecolt-Glaser JK, Glaser R. Psychological influences on immunity: Implications for AIDS. *Am Psychol.* 1988;43:892–898.
78. Kelly JA, Murphy DA. Psychological interventions with AIDS and HIV: Prevention and treatment. *J Consult Clin Psychol.* 1992;60:576–585.
79. Antoni MH, Baggett L, Ironson G, LaPerriere A, August S, Klimas N, Schneiderman N, Fletcher MA. Cognitive behavioral stress management intervention buffers distress responses and elevates immunologic markers following notification of HIV-1 seropositivity. *J Consult Clin Psychol.* 1991;59:906–915.
80. Mulder C, Emmelkamp PMG, Antoni MH, Mulder CL, Sandfort TGM, de Vries MJ. Cognitive-behavioral and experiential group psychotherapy for HIV-infected homosexual men: A comparative study. Submitted.
81. Mulder CL, Antoni MH, Emmelkamp PMG, Mulder JW, Sandfort TGM, de Vries MJ. Cognitive-behavioral and experiential group psychotherapy for HIV-infected homosexual men. *Psychosom Med.* 1994;56:423–431.
82. Coates TJ, McKusick L, Stites DP, Kuno R. Stress management training reduced number of sexual partners but did not improve immune function in men infected with HIV. *Am J Public Health.* 1989;79:885–887.
83. Carnike CLM, Carey MP. Assessing nausea and vomiting in adult chemotherapy patients: Review and recommendation. *Ann Behav Med.* 1990:12:79–85.

84. Morrow GR, Dopkins PL. Anticipatory nausea and vomiting in cancer patients undergoing chemotherapy treatment: Prevalence, etiology, and behavioral interventions. *Clin Psychol Rev.* 1988;8:517–556.
85. Edgar L, Rosberger Z, Nowlis D. Coping with cancer during the first year after diagnosis: Assessment and intervention. *Cancer.* 1992;69:817–828.
86. Fawzy FI, Cousins N, Fawzy N, Kemeny ME, Elashoff R, Morton D. A structured psychiatric intervention for cancer patients. 1. Changes over time in methods of coping and affective disturbance. *Arch Gen Psychiatry.* 1990;47: 729–735.
87. Fawzy FI, Kemeny ME, Fawzy N, Elashoff R, Morton D, Cousins N, Fahey JL. A structured psychiatric intervention for cancer patients. II. Changes over time in immunological measures. *Arch Gen Psychiatry.* 1990;47:736–742.
88. Heinrich RL, Coscarelli-Schag C. Stress and activity management: Group treatment for cancer patients and their spouses. *J Consult Clin Psychol.* 1985;53:439–446.
89. Davis H. Effects of biofeedback and cognitive therapy on stress in patients with breast cancer. *Psychol Rep.* 1986;59:967–974.
90. Telch CF, Telch MJ. Group coping skills instructions and supportive group therapy for cancer patients: A comparison of strategies. *J Consult Clin Psychol.* 1986;54:802–808.
91. American Thoracic Society. Standards for the diagnosis and care of patients with chronic obstructive pulmonary disease (COPD) and asthma. *Am Rev Respir Dis.* 1987;136:225–244.
92. Kotses H, Himdi-Alexander M, Creer TL. A reinterpretation of psychologically-induced airway changes. *J Asthma.* 1989;26:53–63.
93. Vromans ISY. *Omgaan met Astma.* (Coping with asthma). Zeist, Netherlands: Kerkebosch;1990.
94. Yellowlees PM, Alpers JH, Bowden JJ, Ruffin RE. Psychiatric morbidity in patients with chronic airflow obstruction. *Med J Aust.* 1987;146:305–307.
95. Porzelius J, Kest M, Nochomovitz M. Respiratory function, cognitions, and panic in chronic obstructive pulmonary patients. *Behav Res Ther.* 1992;30: 75–77.
96. Klingelhofer EJ, Gershwin ME. Asthma self-management programs: Premises, not promises. *J Asthma.* 1988;25:89–101.
97. Lehrer PM, Sargunaraj D, Hochran S. Psychological approaches to the treatment of asthma. *J Consult Clin Psychol.* 1992;60:639–643.
98. Maes S, Schösser M. Changing health behavior outcomes in asthmatic patients: A pilot intervention study. *Soc Sci Med.* 1988;26:359–364.
99. Schlösser MG. *Self-Management and Asthma.* Leiden, Netherlands: Leiden University Press;1992.
100. Blanchard EB, Schwarz SP. Adaption of a multicomponent treatment for irritable bowel syndrome to a small-group format. *Biofeedback Self Regul.* 1987;12:63–69.
101. Blanchard EB, Schwarz SP, Suls JM, Gerardi MA, Scharff L, Greene B, Taylor AE, Berreman C, Malamood HS. Two controlled evaluations of a multicomponent psychological treatment of irritable bowel syndrome. *Behav Res Ther.* 1992;30:175–189.

102. Neff DF, Blanchard EB. A multicomponent treatment for irritable bowel syndrome. *Behav Ther.* 1987;18:70–83.
103. Schwarz SP, Taylor A, Scharff L, Blanchard EB. Behaviorally treated irritable bowel syndrome patients: A four-year follow-up. *Behav Res Ther.* 1990; 28:331–335.
104. Schwarz SP, Blanchard EB. Inflammatory bowel disease: A review of the psychological assessment and treatment literature. *Ann Behav Med.* 1990; 12:95–105.
105. Schwarz SP, Blanchard EB. Evaluation of a psychological treatment for inflammatory bowel disease. *Behav Res Ther.* 1991;29:167–177.
106. Borkovec TD. Insomnia. *J Consult Clin Psychol.* 1982;50:880–895.
107. Sanavio E. Pre-sleep cognitive intrusions and treatment of onset-insomnia. *Behav Res Ther.* 1988;26:451–459.

Chapter 28
Psychopharmacological Agents in Physical Disorders

JAMBUR ANANTH

Theoretically, the usefulness of psychotropic drugs in physical disorders is not surprising. Stress may lead to tachycardia, hypertension, irritable bowel syndrome, peptic ulcer, and tension headache. Such illnesses occur frequently and form the bulk of those treated by internists. Psychotropic drugs can alleviate stress and result in the improvement or prevention of the stress-related end organ disorders. Another assumption is that some physical illnesses are related to a particular area of the brain, intimately connected with emotions, on which psychotropic drugs act. By acting on neurohormones and on these specific brain areas, they can alleviate both psychiatric and physical disorders.

An intricate, complicated, and varied relationship exists between physical and mental illnesses. Physical illness may develop secondarily over many episodes of psychiatric illness or can be subliminal and undetectable over many years prior to the onset of a psychiatric illness.[1] For example, it has been well established that the earliest manifestation of cancer of the pancreas is depression. In addition, a common vulnerability to psychiatric and physical illness may exist. Eastwood and Trevelyan[2] noted that the number of physical conditions increased with the severity of the psychiatric illness. Furthermore, 17% of the more severely ill psychiatric patients suffered from 52% of the total major physical illnesses. These indicate that psychotropic drugs can influence both the physical and the psychiatric illnesses. Clinically, psychotropic drugs have been employed to treat a number of physical disorders of varied etiology. Such diverse clinical effects are based on the action of psychopharmacological agents on multiple organs, neurohormones, and receptors. For example, benzodiazepines have not only an anxiolytic action, but also amnesic, anticonvulsant, hypnotic, and muscle-relaxing activity. Similarly, antidepressants have norepinephrinergic, serotoninergic, antihistaminic, and anticholinergic actions. Lithium enhances colony-stimulating factor, and therefore has been employed to reverse leukopenia. Hence, the application of psychotropic drugs in treating a number of physical illnesses is of both practical and heuristic value.

ENURESIS

Through the years a variety of pharmacological agents have been used for the treatment of enuresis. A study[3] of 115 enuretics indicated no psychological disturbances and normal bladder functioning on urodynamic testing in nocturnal enuretic children. Despite the fact that many neurotics have an uninhibited detrusor with a decreased functional capacity of the bladder, treatment with belladonna and atropine derivatives are disappointing.

The effectiveness of imipramine in the treatment of nocturnal enuresis was first reported by MacLean[4] in an uncontrolled study. Since then, many reports have appeared providing good evidence to support the claim that the tricyclic drugs are helpful in some cases of nocturnal enuresis. Subsequently, a series of controlled studies have been reported, most of which confirm a statistically favorable effect of tricyclic antidepressants on nocturnal enuresis.[5-13] In a double-blind and crossover comparative study with placebo, the effects of amitriptyline were evaluated in 60 physically healthy children with nocturnal enuresis.[14] The children were aged 5 to 15 years, and about 35% were girls. Their randomly assigned treatment was changed to the other regimen after 4 weeks. Amitriptyline was considered better by 60% of the parents. After 8 weeks of treatment, all children were given amitriptyline at a dosage of 25 to 75 mg daily for 8 weeks and then gradually discontinued. After gradual withdrawal, 10% tended to be dry, 62% showed varied improvement, and 28% failed to benefit from treatment.

A later double-blind and placebo-controlled study with 62 children afflicted with nocturnal enuresis assessed the efficacy of two different dosage levels of imipramine and placebo, in order to determine the dose–effect relationship.[13] The results indicated that imipramine was markedly superior to placebo, but there was no difference between high (75 mg) and low dosage (50 mg). Drug withdrawal was almost always followed by a relapse, indicating that the drug was effective in controlling the condition, but was not a pharmacological cure. A pharmacokinetic study indicated that the optimum plasma level of imipramine and desipramine to be effective in nocturnal enuresis was 60μg/l.[15] Increasing the blood level of drugs did not produce any further improvement.

A well-designed study with a large sample was conducted in Spain.[16] One hundred forty children with enuresis aged between 5 and 14 years received imipramine from 12.5 to 100 mg/day. The response to treatment was considered as the percentage decrease in the frequency of enuresis. There was a statistically significant correlation of improvement with serum level, dose, compliance, and duration of treatment. In another 6-week, 41-children Turkish study,[17] 14 received imipramine, 8 amitriptyline, 10 chlordiazepoxide-clidinium, and 9 piracetam. Both antidepressants were given at 25 mg doses and chlordiazepoxide at 5 and clidinium at 0.5 mg. Piracetam was given at 400 mg doses. Imipramine produced a response far superior to that of other drugs within 2 weeks.

Studies describing the efficacy of behavioral methods at 80% and imipramine at 40% have been reported. However, only three studies have direct comparison. In one,[18] there were no baseline observations, it was not double-blind, and the patients were simultaneously receiving amphetamines. In the other study,[19] there was no baseline or placebo phase, and the amount of medication administered was too low. Children on alarm were seen weekly, while the ones on drugs were seen only twice during the study. In both the alarm was found to be more efficacious. Fournier et al.[20] attempted to assess the efficacy of imipramine, placebo, alarm device, and random awakening in 66 children (47 males and 17 females) during an 8-week period. Only imipramine and alarm were effective. Surprisingly, in both studies, the combination of the two was neither additive nor advantageous.

Other tricyclic antidepressant drugs, such as desipramine, amitriptyline, and nortriptyline, also have been reported to be equally effective.[21] Maprotiline was used in a study of 12 patients (mean age of 9 years) with functional enuresis and other behavioral disorders. The dosage of maprotiline ranged from 10 to 75 mg, with a mean of 63 mg. Enuresis improved in 11 and worsened in the rest.[22] This drug has been reported to be useful in a study of 100 children with various psychiatric disorders.[23] However as the diagnosis was not certain, the therapeutic effect might have been secondary to improvement of the primary psychiatric disorder.

Few studies on antidepressants report on the follow-up data. But the available evidence shows no carryover influence after the drug is withdrawn. Two follow-up studies[7, 13] did not find any difference between continuation of the drug or placebo. Three other studies[10, 11, 14] reported a 10 to 20% cure rate, but no control data are yet available. Two studies reported only a few relapses if the drug is continued.[24, 25]

Imipramine therapy should not be instituted until the evaluation is complete, as the drug can improve the condition even in the presence of an organic illness and thus delay recognition of the underlying cause and proper diagnosis. An appropriate dose of 50 to 70 mg for a period of 2 weeks is necessary to obtain the desired result. With the cessation of therapy, it is possible that the condition may recur. Trial cessation every 3 months after successful treatment is recommended. The disease has a spontaneous improvement rate which varies from 15[26] to 25% each year.[27] When imipramine is successful, a measurable increase in bladder capacity occurs.[28–30] The sleep-alerting effect of the drug may be useful in this disorder.[12] It has been observed that children treated for nocturnal enuresis also show improvement in areas of alertness, handwriting, reading, and behavior. It is not possible to predict who would benefit. However, the drug has been reported to be effective in girls for secondary enuresis and for severe cases of either sex.[13, 31] If the child wets the bed before midnight, it is better to administer the drug by 16.00 hours. Even though not the cure, the prospect of 14% completely losing the symptom during the ensuing year makes the treatment worthwhile.

Status Epilepticus

Diazepam even today remains the first drug of choice for status epilepticus.[32] It has also been employed in the management of acute ongoing seizures and in febrile seizures when used rectally. In a double-blind study,[33] the seizures were controlled in 76% of the episodes with diazepam (10 mg i.v.) and in 89% of the episodes with lorazepam (4 mg i.v.). Adverse effects occurred in 12.5% of the diazepam patients, with respiratory depression being the most important. A single bolus dose of diazepam (5–10 mg at a rate of 1–5 mg/min) has been reported to stop initial seizure activity in 88% of patients.[32, 34, 35] The clinical responses to 2 mg/minute diazepam was studied in detail.[36] The convulsions stopped in 32% after 3 minutes, in 68% after 5 minutes, and in 80% after 10 minutes. In those who failed to respond, acute metabolic disorders were noted. A recent prospective study on intravenously administered diazepam and phenytoin versus intravenous phenobarbital indicated that both regimens were equally effective with comparable safety.[37] A substantial number of responsive patients experience seizure recurrences 10 to 20 minutes later with only 50% seizure free 2 hours after a single injection.[38] The recurrence is considered to be due to the rapid redistribution of diazepam, resulting in an abrupt fall of its concentration in the brain. This leads to a significant loss of its anticonvulsant effect, necessitating additional treatment. A number of proposals have been made including intravenous continuous infusion of diazepam, phenobarbital, phenytoin, and lidocaine to overcome the recurrence of seizures.

CONTINUOUS INFUSION

This technique has not been studied in a double-blind fashion, and yet there are, however, convincing reports and uncontrolled observations. Single case reports have shown that refractory epileptics have improved with continuous diazepam infusions.[39, 40] The first prospective study of 6 patients reported 4 patients with complete or satisfactory control, 1 with temporary control, and 1 failure. The duration of treatment was 4 to 7 days with 140 to 200 mg of diazepam daily. Tolerance was seen only in those who received the infusion for more than a day. In a retrospective study of five patients, good seizure control in three, one breakthrough seizure, and one failure were noted with infusion of 10 to 48 mg/day, lasting for 12 to 24 hours.[38] A well-documented study of five children indicated adequate seizure control and no adverse effects when doses of 3 to 12 mg of diazepam per kilogram were given for 21 hours to 8 days.[41] Delgado-Escueta and Enrile-Bascal[36] suggest that patients with refractory status epilepticus be first given a trial of bolus diazepam injections of 10 to 20 mg at a rate of 2 mg/min, while simultaneously receiving an intravenous loading of 15 mg/kg phenytoin in the opposite arm. If seizure persists, a continuous infusion of diazepam 4 to 8 mg/hour with 50 mg of diazepam in 500 ml dextrose/water is recommended. Diazepam infusion has been reported to control another 25% of episodes.

Rectal solution of diazepam has been effectively used to control ongoing emergency seizure. This treatment was given at a home to 17 epileptic children with prolonged convulsions.[42] The drug was used 65 times and was given within 5 minutes of the start of a convulsion in 85% of the episodes. Convulsions were stopped within 15 minutes after the drug had been given in 80% of the episodes. In a prospective study,[43] 44 children aged 6 months to 5 years were treated with a rectal solution of diazepam during 59 convulsions. The drug was effective in 80% of the episodes. In 10%, rectal diazepam failed, and yet the intravenous administration of the same drug was effective.

PROPHYLAXIS

Several studies have explored the efficacy of diazepam in the prevention of febrile convulsions. In a study with a group of 289 children who had febrile convulsions,[44] randomly half of the group received diazepam whenever the temperature reached 38.5°C. The control group received diazepam only after the convulsions occurred. The total number of recurrence of febrile convulsions was reduced from 77 to 23 and the recurrence rate from 39 to 12% in the drug group. However, the risk of subsequent seizures was not lowered. Treatment of febrile seizures at home with diazepam, evaluated by a large Italian study with 601 children,[45] indicated that rectal administration by the parents was useful.

Oral diazepam is less effective than phenytoin or phenobarbital for grand mal seizures.[46] In resistant seizures, addition of diazepam 20 mg daily decreased the incidence of seizures.[47] Poor seizure control over long periods may be related to tolerance or to low blood levels.

Similarly, lorazepam has also been used for status epilepticus. Comer and Giesecke[48] found that lorazepam levels remained above 30 mg/ml for about 8 hours. A possible advantage of lorazepam over diazepam is its longer duration of action which is beneficial in controlling recurrences In addition, Leppik et al.[33] reported that the mean onset of action was 3 minutes, indicating its rapid onset of action. A review of 157 episodes of clinical status epilepticus treated with lorazepam in open trials[49-55] indicated that lorazepam is effective in status epilepticus. An open study[52] compared lorazepam and clonazepam in 50 adults with different seizures. The results indicated that both drugs were essentially identical in efficacy, but the former appeared to be superior to clonazepam in EEG improvement. In another study[56] comparing phenytoin and lorazepam in 80 patients with status epilepticus, lorazepam produced a resolution of status in 80% as compared with 56% by phenytoin. The only controlled study[33] indicated that lorazepam was as effective as, if not better than, diazepam.

PEPTIC ULCER

Peptic ulcer disease affects several million Americans annually and causes billions of dollars of economic loss due to morbidity and mortality. Historically, peptic ulcer disease has been treated with multiple modalities. Tricyclic antidepressants have been reported to be beneficial.[57-59] Interest in their antiulcer effect has increased ever since their H_2 receptor blocking effect was discovered. There are reports from Scandinavia,[60-62] England,[63] and South Africa[64] suggesting that trimipramine may enhance healing of duodenal ulcer. Statistically significant improvement ranging from 60 to 86% in the drug-treated group, as compared with 0 to 40% improvement in the placebo group has been reported.[62, 65-67] A study[64] indicated that tricyclic antidepressants were notably more effective than placebo at 4 weeks but not at 8 weeks. This study had a different population group, thereby accounting for the different result. A more recent double-blind placebo-controlled study from Scotland[68] entered endoscopically proven active duodenal ulcer patients. Fifteen patients received trimipramine and 16 placebo. Endoscopy at 4 weeks showed ulcer healing in 11 patients on trimipramine (73%) and in 6 patients on placebo.[38] Overall, these studies provide sufficient proof that trimipramine is statistically significantly superior to placebo in healing peptic ulcers.

Since then, four studies[69-72] have compared tricyclic antidepressants with cimetidine or ranitidine for ulcer-healing efficacy and one other[73] has reported successful treatment with trimipramine after cimetidine has failed. Berstad et al.[70] compared three different groups of patients in a double-blind study: 35 were treated with 25 mg of trimipramine at bedtime, 30 with 400 mg of cimetidine at bedtime, and 26 with 200 mg of cimetidine three times a day. After 6 weeks of treatment, 86% of the trimipramine group, 85% of the low-cimetidine group, and 100% of the high-cimetidine group were noted to have their ulcer healed by endoscopic examination. However, high-dosage antacid therapy is an artifact in this study. When the completely healed patients were observed without medication for 1 year, with immediate endoscopy for recurrent symptoms,[71] 64% of the trimipramine group, 48% of the low-cimetidine group, and 54% of the high-cimetidine group had ulcer relapse. Another study[69] attempted ulcer prevention by randomly allocating 83 patients initially healed after treatment with 1000 mg of cimetidine or 50 mg of trimipramine to maintenance treatment with either cimetidine 400 mg or trimipramine 25 mg or placebo daily for 6 months. After 6 months of treatment, 88% of the cimetidine group, 55% of the trimipramine group, and 53% of the placebo group remained in remission. After a follow-up of further 6 months, cimetidine patients were statistically significantly better than the other two groups. The results implied that trimipramine was not better than placebo. However, the dosage of trimipramine was only 25 mg which could have acted as placebo.

Hoff et al.,[73] in an open study, compared the efficacy of 1000 mg of cimetidine daily with that of 50 mg of doxepin daily in 50 patients. After 6 weeks of treatment, 84% of the cimetidine-treated group and 78% of the doxepin-treated group had healed ulcers on endoscopy. Another study[72] compared the efficacy of ranitidine 300 mg daily with trimipramine 50 mg daily or placebo in a double-blind design for a period of 6 weeks. The ranitidine-treated group consisted of 32 patients, the placebo group of 34 patients, and the trimipramine-treated group of 30 patients. There was a significant difference between the placebo and the ranitidine group (67 vs. 97%), with a healing rate of 79% in the trimipramine-treated group.

Generally ulcers are treated using a dose of 50 mg of trimipramine, a lower dose than required to treat depression (150–300 mg daily). The side effect profile needs consideration. Drowsiness is the most common side effect,[64] occurring in half of the patients.[63]

ULCERATIVE COLITIS

Imipramine is recommended for the treatment of ulcerative colitis based on the supposition that these are depressed patients.[74]

Supporting such a hypothesis are the reports showing that severe ulcerative colitis patients without any evidence of depression have responded to imipramine and methamphetamine.[75] Irritable bowel syndrome, a related condition,[76, 77] has been reported to improve with tricyclic antidepressants. Lithium use in the treatment of ulcerative colitis is an unsettled issue. Liss et al.[78] reported that 23 of their 25 ulcerative colitis patients had a concomitant affective disorder. This finding gives credibility for the use of lithium in ulcerative colitis patients with associated endogenous depressive features. In addition, the transmucosal potential difference across the rectal mucosa was found to be greater in lithium-treated patients which may be of potential use in ulcerative colitis.[79] Clinically, lithium has been found to be useful in a case of ulcerative colitis.[80] On the other hand, Varsamis and Wand[81] reported exacerbation of diarrhea in a patient with regional ileitis and affective disorder while on lithium. Diarrhea is a common complication of lithium therapy and intoxication. Ulcerative colitis patients are susceptible to develop these side effects as a result of electrolyte imbalance. Hence, it is better to avoid using this drug in the management of ulcerative colitis.

HICCUPS

The term *hiccup* refers to sudden contraction of the inspiratory muscles, terminated by abrupt contraction of the glottis to produce the characteristic sound. Most hiccups are often brief and self-limited episodes, involving one half of diaphragm, often the left. Overdistention of stomach, excitement, ingestion of very hot or cold food, or alcohol consumption are some of the common causes of this entity. Persistent hiccups lasting for more than 24 hours often imply an underlying serious organic disorder of either central or peripheral origin.[82–84] The hiccup intensity does not correlate with the severity in organic group. The neural pathway is described as a reflex arc, the afferent portion of which is the vagus nerve, the phrenic nerve, and the sympathetic chain arising from T_6–T_{12}. The efferent limb is the phrenic nerve.[82, 85] A reflex center in the upper cervical region (C_3 and C_5), along with a higher center near the respiratory center,[86, 87] has been established.

The drug most widely accepted as the treatment of choice for hiccups is chlorpromazine.[87–91] In various controlled studies, it has been found to cure 80% of hiccups, with an additional 10% experiencing temporary relief.[92–94] There are, however, some reports of its ineffectiveness[95, 96] which can be explained on the basis of its heterogeneity. Haloperidol orally[97–101] or intramuscularly has also been reported to be useful.

ASTHMA

The asthmatic state is, in essence, an increased sensitivity of the bronchial system which has become excessively reactive both to bronchoconstricting and dilating stimuli, with edema of the bronchial mucosa and accumulation of mucus as additional factors in obstruction of the airway. Beumer[102] reported that 25 mg of imipramine afforded partial protection against the effects of histamine administered by the intramuscular route in a histamine challenge test. Alcock,[103] based on projective tests, and Green,[104] by anecdotal report, provided evidence of a relationship between asthma and depression. Thus, antidepressants can improve asthma by improving depression, by protecting against the effects of histamine, or by anticholinergic action.

Many investigators[105–109] have reported on the usefulness of imipramine in asthmatic patients. This drug has been generally used as an adjuvant medication[110] in combination with prednisone.[111] Twenty asthmatics were treated successfully with amitriptyline 50 mg daily.[112] This agent was reported to be effective in the treatment of asthma in 37 of the 60 patients as judged by clinical evaluation.[113] These findings are supported by additional case reports.[114, 115] Spiegelberg[116] has noted imipramine or promethazine, or a combination of both to be useful in the treatment of asthmatic patients. A between-patient double-blind study,[117] during which 25 asthmatic patients received a daily dose of 75 mg of imipramine for 10 days, failed to reveal any difference in the prevention of attacks between imipramine and placebo. However, the period of 10 days may not be enough to study prevention. Double-blind studies with antidepressants may be of value to determine whether these drugs have a curative or a prophylactic value in asthmatics. Furthermore, by evaluating sedating, antihistaminic, and anticholinergic antidepressants with those which are not, their mode of action in asthma can be clarified.

Hydroxyzine was found to be effective in the treatment of asthma.[118, 119] Shah et al.[120] treated 84 patients with 75 mg daily over 1 month. Analysis indicated that 58 patients showed complete symptomatic relief, 25 attained partial relief, and 1 did not improve. A later study[121] revealed that hydroxyzine increased the airway conductance by 50% of the central values in asthmatic patients, indicating its mechanism of action in asthma. Some others have reported successful treatment of asthma with this agent.[122-124] Kahn and Jokl[125] observed that metaproterenol sulfate with oxazepam was superior to the former drug alone in treating asthmatics. Chlorpromazine may sometimes be life saving in status asthmaticus.[126, 127] Risks of treating asthmatics with tricyclic antidepressants are the combined anticholinergic effect of antiasthmatic and antidepressant drugs as well as hypertension due to interaction of sympathomimetics with antidepressants. Depressed or anxious asthmatics can be treated with antidepressants, with careful monitoring.

ARTHRITIS

Recent evidence indicates that tricyclic antidepressants have anti-inflammatory effects in chronic adjuvant induced arthritis in rats.[128] This effect reduces the physical signs of arthritis, increases mobility, and reduces pain-associated behaviors.[129] Six placebo-controlled studies have evaluated the effects of imipramine as an adjunct to nonsteroidal anti-inflammatory drugs for relief of arthritic symptoms. A study[130] compared the effects of imipramine 75 mg daily to placebo in 22 arthritic patients in a double-blind crossover study. Each treatment was given for 3 weeks. Compared to the baseline scores, 13 patients improved with imipramine, and only 2 improved on placebo. Grip strength as an indicator of improvement was better in 7 patients on imipramine and in only 1 on placebo. A multicenter crossover study[131] also compared imipramine 75 mg daily with placebo in 55 nondepressed arthritic patients along adjunctive standard analgesic therapy. Each treatment lasted for 4 weeks. Only imipramine produced a statistically significant improvement in pain relief, grip strength, and early-morning stiffness. Saarialho-Kere et al.[132] in a crossover comparison of dextropropoxyphene, dextropropoxyphene plus amitriptyline, indomethacin, and placebo noted that amitriptyline alone or in combination with dextrapropoxyphene was significantly superior to dextrapropoxyphene alone. Sarzi Puttini et al.[133] compared dothiepin and placebo and noted that dothiepin was statistically significantly superior in improving pain in arthritis. Another 8-week study[134] which compared the efficacy of clomipramine 25 mg daily to placebo in 49 patients with joint pain along with standard analgesic treatment did not find any difference between the two groups. However, rightly, the authors questioned whether 25 mg of clomipramine was an adequate dose. Only one study reported no effect.[135]

CANCER CHEMOTHERAPY

The relationship between cancer and psychotropic drugs is intriguing. Long ago, Snow[136] and Guy[137] reported that women who suffer from depression were more prone to cancer. Kerr et al.[138] noted a higher than expected mortality among men followed up for primary affective disorders. Varsamis et al.[139] in a 6-year follow-up noted a high incidence of malignant disease in 24 affective disorder patients. Whitelock and Siskind[140] found that male cancer rates were significantly higher among depressed patients. Hence, as depression and cancer are related, antidepressants may be of value in cancer patients.

Chlorpromazine uncouples oxidative phosphorylation and inhibits DNA synthesis in the bone marrow.[141] It also inhibits the virus-induced Brown Pearce carcinoma in rabbits[142] and mammary adenocarcinoma in rats[143] and other animals. Levit and Polliak[144] observed regression of squamous cell carcinoma with high-dosage chlorpromazine.

Taking mortality as a criterion, Katz et al.[145] noted that between 1955 and 1961 the cancer mortality among patients in New York mental hospitals was significantly lower than that in a matched group of general population. Similarly, Rassidakis et al.[146, 147] confirmed the same, indicating that less psychiatric patients die of cancer. Ananth and Burnstein[148] noted that while cancer-related deaths were lower, the prevalence of cancer was higher among psychiatric patients. This finding may simply mean that phenothiazines prevent cancer mortality, but not their occurrence. Even though very preliminary, low cancer rates in mental hospitals and the possible implication of neuroleptics producing such an effect is a fertile field to explore.

The magnitude of the problem of cancer is great, and some 15% of the nonmetastatic cancer patients[149–151] and 60 to 90% of advanced cancer patients[152, 153] report significant pain. Appropriate care for pain is an essential ingredient of cancer management. Psychotropic drugs may be useful in cancer by alleviating pain, decreasing the concern of the patient, potentiating the action of analgesics, and alleviating chemotherapy-induced nausea and vomiting.

Phenothiazines are useful as adjuncts to alleviate pain and chemotherapy-induced nausea.[154] Tricyclic antidepressants are particularly useful in pancreatic carcinoma because of a high incidence of depression. Benzodiazepines have been used as adjuncts to alleviate anxiety, anticipation, nausea, and vomiting. Derogatis et al.,[155] in a survey of five major centers, noted that half the patients receive psychotropic drugs, and half of those who receive them obtain benzodiazepines. They are prescribed to 16% of terminal patients.[156]

Lorazepam[157–163] and diazepam[164–166] have been evaluated in clinical trials for chemotherapy-induced nausea and vomiting. Either of them was given within 2 hours after various chemotherapy. The reports indicate that about 80% were anxiety free after the injection,[158, 160] and 80% were sedated but rouseable.[161] Bishop et al.,[157] in a randomized double-blind crossover prospective design, noted that benzodiazepines were beneficial in reducing chemotherapy-induced nausea and vomiting. Even though these drugs did not prove to be superior to metaclopramide, they have the advantage of not inducing extrapyramidal symptoms. Gagen et al.,[159] in a randomized crossover study of 44 patients receiving multiple cancer chemotherapy, compared the effects of lorazepam 2 to 4 mg intravenously along with dexamethasone with metaclopramide. Lorazepam and dexamethasone were significantly superior to metaclopramide. Natale,[162] in a double-blind study of 14 patients, noted that metaclopramide combined with dexamethasone was better than lorazepam alone. Luesley et al.[164] did not find any difference in emetic control when diazepam combined with prochlorperazine or metaclopramide was used. The sedation and memory loss produced by benzodiazepines are also beneficial in alleviating their suffering. As many as 25% of the patients who have been on chemotherapy may develop anticipatory anxiety.[167, 168] With lorazepam it was noted that many patients who had chemotherapy and vomiting did not remember it[160, 166] and hence had no anticipation, and those that did remember were not disturbed.[159, 162] In chronic pain, benzodiazepines have not been proven to be useful.

In cancer patients antidepressants are used to treat the depression, antianxiety drugs to treat anticipatory anxiety, and both benzodiazepines and neuroleptics to prevent chemotherapy induced nausea and vomiting.

PAIN SYNDROMES

The relationship between pain and depression is complex. Pain can be a symptom (masked depression or atypical depression) of depression, or it can secondarily lead to depression. If antidepressants indeed exert antipain effects, it is vital to ascertain whether such an action is related to, or independent of, its antidepressant action. Like other psychotropic drugs, antidepressants lack specificity in their action, acting on multiple neurotransmitters such as histamine, serotonin, norepinephrine, and acetylcholine. As antidepressant and antipain mechanisms overlap, it is difficult to separate these two mechanisms. The discovery of endogenous opioids have linked depression and pain. Sternbach[169] suggested that pain itself can inhibit serotonin, and thus chronic pain can deplete serotonin and induce depression. Therefore, opiates may be ineffective in the absence of adequate serotonin. Pain has both norepinephrine and serotonin mechanisms. Norepinephrine is involved in those who are depressed. The effect of tricyclics on pain is supported by the fact that pain and not depression improves within 3 to 4 days of drug administration, while depression improves after 2 weeks.[170-172] Chronic pain relief has also been reported despite lack of antidepressant response.[173-178]

ACUTE PAIN

Studies using animal paradigms for acute pain demonstrate that tricyclic antidepressants provide species-specific analgesia for acute pain.[179] Antidepressants are hypothesized to potentiate the analgesic effects of morphine.[180, 181] Imipramine, amitriptyline, and clomipramine have been often employed as analgesics in man.[182] One careful report[183] indicated that doxepin in single doses did not alter laboratory-induced dental pain threshold in 18 normal adult males who were repeatedly tested in a double-blind and placebo-controlled study over a 4-week period. However, experimental induction of pain and duration of the study are in question. Another equally well-controlled study[184] indicated that imipramine reduced pain ratings in response to an intracutaneous electrical stimulus by 40%, comparable to the effect of meperidine and superior to placebo. With regard to clinical pain, neither amitriptyline nor desipramine given preoperatively for 1 week at 25 to 75 mg daily provided analgesia after dental extraction. Here, the drug did not prove to have preventive action.[185] In one study, desipramine and not amitriptyline had antinociceptive effect.[171] Hence, antidepressants are generally used as analgesic adjuvants in acute-pain management with variable results.

CHRONIC PAIN

Neuropathic pains are thought to arise from spontaneous neuronal hyperactivity or disturbed inhibition following central nervous system or peripheral nerve injury. Such disorders as postherpetic neuralgia,[186–188] diabetic peripheral neuropathy,[189, 190] trigeminal neuralgia,[191] thalamic pain,[192–194] and neuralgia from lesions of plexus or peripheral nerves,[195] have been reported to respond to tricyclic antidepressants. Treatment is effective in both depressed or nondepressed patients. Tricyclic antidepressants have also been used as analgesics against facial pain[196] and phantom limb pain.[197–198] Two double-blind controlled studies have found that antidepressants are the most useful drugs for postherpetic neuralgia. Watson et al.[187] demonstrated, in a placebo-controlled study, the therapeutic effect of amitriptyline in a sample of elderly nondepressed patients with persistent postherpetic neuralgia. Two-thirds had moderate pain relief even without a change in depression. Serum tricyclic antidepressant levels were low, but increases in levels had a paradoxical effect, suggesting a therapeutic window for dosage to relieve pain. Max et al.[199, 200] reported that amitriptyline and not lorazepam relieves this pain. In some, there was recurrence of pain, casting doubt on the long-term effects, while in others, there was a complete relief from pain, permitting discontinuing of medication without recurrence.

Controlled studies indicate that tricyclic antidepressants are effective in relieving the pain of diabetic neuropathy without depressive symptoms. Kvinesdal et al.[201] used imipramine for peripheral neuropathy in insulin-requiring diabetes with good blood sugar control. Analgesic effect was achieved whithin 2 weeks with one-half of the blood concentration required to treat depression. On the other hand, Turkington[202] evaluated 59 diabetic-documented depressed patients treated with imipramine, diazepam, and amitriptyline. Both antidepressants produced equivalent pain relief, while diazepam did not. On a 2-year follow-up, after discontinuation of therapy, pain recurred in 26% of the patients and again remitted with antidepressants. Davis et al.[189] reported the beneficial effects of a combination of amitriptyline and fluphenazine within 5 days in three diabetic neuropathy patients. Response in an additional eight patients with a similar combination has been reported.[203] Taub,[204] in a series of case reports, documented five treatment-resistant patients who received amitriptyline 75 to 100 mg daily and fluphenazine 4 mg or thioridazine 100 mg and found a marked decrease in pain 1 to 2 weeks after initiation. Rascal et al.[205] noted that there was no correlation between plasma levels and clinical improvement. These results provide substantial proof for the efficacy of tricyclic antidepressants in chronic pain disorders. The role of the new serotonin uptake inhibitors is yet to be established. Benzodiazepines have also been employed for postoperative pain.[206]

INFECTIONS

There is preliminary evidence that lithium may have a role in the treatment of herpes simplex.[207, 208] Several studies have suggested improvement of genital herpes with lithium treatment and its exacerbation following withdrawal. Leib[209, 210] reported remissions of genital herpes in six bipolar patients receiving lithium, and the response corresponded to the adequacy of the lithium level. Skinner[211] conducted a double-blind placebo-controlled pilot study of lithium ointment for genital herpes. Seventy-three patients self-administered either 8% or placebo ointments for 7 days. Swabs taken indicated that virus excretion was decreased in the lithium group. Further exploration is needed.

LEUKOPENIA

A favorable response to lithium is dependent on the integrity of stem cell precursors. In those disorders where the number of target cells for enhancing colony-stimulating factor is decreased and in those where this factor is in optimal quantity, lithium may not exert a beneficial effect. Lithium has been employed in a variety of chronic neutropenias.[212, 213] It is in Felty's syndrome that greatest success has been reported.[214] Lithium has been prescribed to reduce the occurrence of fever and infections in patients receiving cancer chemotherapy. In addition, adding lithium produced fewer leukopenia and infection-related chemotherapeutic reductions.[215, 216] A group of investigators from the South Eastern Cancer Study Group[217] noted that lithium did not decrease the duration of cancer chemotherapy induced leukopenia, infections, or remission rate. In fact, the remission rate was lower in lithium-treated patients which was not explainable. On the other hand, lithium has been used in Felty's syndrome and neuroleptic- as well as carbamazepine-induced[218] leukopenia with positive results.

CLUSTER HEADACHES AND MIGRAINE

Uncontrolled studies also report that amitriptyline is useful in migraine.[219–221] Couch et al.[222] reported that amitriptyline was superior to placebo in preventing migraine and in decreasing the severity of the attacks that occurred in nondepressed patients. On the other hand, in depressed patients with mild headache, there was some response, and with severe headache, there was no response.

A controlled study of 340 migraine patients[223] compared the effects of amitriptyline with that of propranolol and biofeedback. Ergot and conventional analgesics formed the control groups. Amitriptyline was found to be significantly superior to conventional treatment and placebo, but inferior to propranolol. Addition of antidepressants to propranolol was of no particular advantage. With regard to mixed migraine and contraction headache prophylaxis,[223] comparison of amitriptyline, propranolol, ergotamine, biofeedback, and combination of these drugs with biofeedback, indicated that amitriptyline was superior to other single agents, and the combination of amitriptyline, biofeedback, and propranolol was by far the best. The response to amitriptyline correlated with the initial depression score, but occurred with a subtherapeutic dose. In a double-blind and placebo-controlled study[220] with 20 patients for a period of 27 weeks on a dosage of 30 to 60 mg of amitriptyline daily, the frequency of migraine attacks decreased significantly in 16 of the 20 patients. The total number of attacks recorded during the study period was 207 for the drug group and 356 for the placebo group.

TENSION HEADACHES

Low-dosage amitriptyline was found superior to imipramine[224] or to placebo[225] for the relief of chronic tension headache, and both antidepressants were superior to barbiturates.[224] Oshaka et al.[226] found that amitriptyline and doxepin were superior to diazepam. Interestingly, doxepin relieved both headache and depression, while amitriptyline improved only the mood. Edmeads et al.[227] reported that amitriptyline, at half the dose used for depression, is the most effective for tension headaches. There are also reports of improvement of cluster headaches as well. A double-blind, randomized, and crossover study compared the efficacy of doxepin, starting with 25 mg at bedtime and increasing to 100 mg daily, to that of placebo in 23 mixed-tension vascular headaches.[228] During doxepin treatment, there was a significant reduction in the headache index defined as the product of headache days times severity. In a single report,[229] trazodone 100 mg daily was effective in the treatment of chronic intractable mixed-tension headache.

Neiper[230] used lithium orotate to treat 44 patients who had constant headache, migraine, and hemicrania. Sixteen had previously been treated unsuccessfully with lithium carbonate or citrate. Lithium orotate was effective in 39 patients at doses of 750 to 900 mg/week; serum lithium levels were not reported. Neiper[230] speculated that orotic acid forms a complex with lithium and enters the brain via a specific carrier mechanism. Chazot et al.,[231] employing a crossover design with 2 months each of lithium gluconate and placebo, found lithium gluconate to be significantly more effective in reducing the number of migraine attacks in 25 patients. In contrast, in an open study, Peatfield and Rose[232] showed exacerbation of migraine in all five of their patients. Three refused to complete the 4-week trial, and the remaining two had more migraine attacks than before. Medina and Diamond[233] treated 22 patients with cyclic migraine for 13 weeks and noted that headache disappeared in five, and in 14 it became less severe. In three who discontinued therapy, headaches recurred. A further study[234] confirmed the results. Thus, the current data on the usefulness of lithium in headaches are inconsistent.

REFERENCES

1. Ananth J. Physical illness in psychiatric disorders. *Compr Psychiatry.* 1984;25: 586–593.
2. Eastwood MR, Trevelyan MG. Relationship between physical and psychiatric disorder. *Psychol Med.* 1972;2:363–372.
3. Kass EJ, Diokno AC, Montealegre A. Enuresis: Principles of management and result of treatment. *J Urol.* 1979;121:794–796.
4. MacLean REG. Imipramine hydrochloride (Tofranil) and enuresis. *Am J Psychiatry.* 1960;117:551.
5. Blackwell B, Currah J. The pharmacology of nocturnal enuresis. In: Kolvin I, Mackeith RC, Meadow SR, eds. *Bladder Control and Enuresis.* London: Heinemann;1973: pp 231–257.
6. Dinello FA, Champelli J. The use of imipramine in the treatment of enuresis: A review of the literature. *Can Psychiatr Assn J.* 1968;13:237.
7. Forsythe WI, Merrett JD. A controlled trial of imipramine (Tofranil) and nortriptyline (Allergon) in the treatment of enuresis. *Brit J Clin Pract.* 1969;23:210–215.

8. Harrison JS, Albino VJ. An investigation into the effects of imipramine hydrochloride on the incidence of enuresis in institutionalized children. *S Afr Med J.* 1970;44:253.

9. Kardash S, Hillman ES, Werry J. Efficacy of imipramine in childhood enuresis: A double blind study with placebo. *Can Med Assn J.* 1968;99:263.

10. Kunin SA, Limbert DJ, Plastzker ACG, Platzker AC, McGinley J. The efficacy of imipramine in the management of enuresis. *J Urol.* 1970;104:612–615.

11. Martin GI. Imipramine pamoate in the treatment of childhood enuresis. A double blind study. *Am J Dis Child.* 1971;122:42.

12. Miller PR, Campelli JW, Dinello FA. Imipramine in the treatment of enuretic school children. *Am J Dis Child.* 1968;115:17–20.

13. Shaffer D, Costello AJ, Hill ID. Control of enuresis with imipramine. *Arch Dis Child.* 1968;43:665–671.

14. Pouissaint AF, Ditman KS, Greenfield R. Amitriptyline in childhood enuresis. *Clin Pharmacol Ther.* 1966;7:21–25.

15. Jorgensen OS, Lober M, Christiansen J, Gram LF. Plasma concentration and clinical effect in imipramine treatment of childhood enuresis. *Clin Pharmacokinet.* 1980;5:386–393.

16. Fernandez De Gatta MM, Galindo P, Rey F, Gutierrez J, Tamayo M, Garcia MJ, Dominguez-Gil A. The influence of clinical and pharmacological factors on enuresis treatment with imipramine. *Br J Clin Pharmacol.* 1990;30: 693–698.

17. Yurdakok M, Kinik E, Beduk Y, Guvenc H, Onder US. Treatment of enuresis: A study with imipramine, amitriptyline, chlordiazepoxideclidinium and pirecetam. *Turk J Pediatr.* 1986;28:171–175.

18. McConaghy N. A controlled trial of imipramine, amphetamine pad and bell conditioning and random awakening in the treatment of nocturnal enuresis. *Med J Aust.* 1969;ii:237–239.

19. Wagner W, Johnson SB, Walker D, Carter R, Wittner J. A controlled comparison of two treatments for nocturnal enuresis. *Pediatrics.* 1982;101: 302–307.

20. Founrier JP, Garfinkel BD, Bond A, Beauchesne H, Shapiro SK. Pharmacological and behavioral management of enuresis. *J Am Acad Child Adolesc Psychiatry.* 1987;26:849–853.

21. Liderman PC, Wasserman DH, Lieberman VR. Desipramine in the treatment of enuresis. *J Urol.* 1966;101:314.

22. Simeon J, McGuire J, Lawrence S. Maprotiline effects in children with enuresis and behavioral disorders. *Prog Neuropsychopharmacol.* 1981;5:495–498.

23. Kuhn-Gebbardt V. Results obtained with a new antidepressant in children, In: Kielholz P, ed. *Depressive Illness: Diagnosis, Assessment, Treatment.* Bern, Switzwerland:1972; pp 229–233.

24. Dische S. Management of enuresis. *Br Med J.* 1971;iii:33–36.

25. McGregor HG. Enuresis in children: A report of 70 cases. *Brit Med J.* 1937;1: 1061–1063.

26. Forsythe WI, Redmond A. Enuresis and spontaneous cure rate. Study of 1129 enuretics. *Arch Dis Child.* 1974;49:259.

27. Oppel WC, Harper PA, Rider RV. The age of attaining bladder control. *Pediatrics.* 1968;42:614–626.

28. Esperanca M, Gerrard JW. Nocturnal enuresis: Comparison of the effect of imipramine and diet restriction on bladder capacity. *Can Med Assn J.* 1969;101:324–327.
29. Hagglund TB, Parkkulainen KV. Enuretic children treated with imipramine (Tofranil): A cystometric study. *Ann Paediatr Fenn.* 1965;11:53.
30. Hagglund TB. Enuretic children treated with fluid restriction or forced drinking: A clinical and cystometric study. *Ann Paediatr Fenn.* 1965;11:84.
31. Kolvin I, Garside RF, Taunch J, Currah J, Macnay RA. Feature clustering and prediction of improvement in nocturnal enuresis. In: Kolvin I, Mackeith RC, Meadow SR, eds. *Bladder Control and Enuresis.* London: Heinemann;1973: p 258.
32. Schmidt D. Benzodiazepines: An update. *Recent Adv Epilepsy.* 1985;2:125–136.
33. Leppik IE, Derivan AT, Homan RW, Walker J, Ramsay RE, Partick B. Double-blind study of lorazepam and diazepam in status epilepticus. *JAMA.* 1983; 249:1452–1454.
34. Brown TR, Perry JK. Benzodiazepines in the treatment of epilepsy. *Epilepsia.* 1973;14:277–310.
35. Schmidt D. Benzodiazepines: Diazepam. In: Woodbury DM, Penny JK, Pipenger CE, eds. *Antiepileptic Drugs.* 2nd ed. New York: Raven Press;1982: pp 711–735.
36. Delgado-Escueta AV, Enrile-Bascal F. Combination therapy for status epilepticus: Intravenous diazepam and phenytoin. *Adv Neurol.* 1983;34:477–485.
37. Shaner DM, McCurdy SA, Herring MO, Gabor AJ. Treatment of status epilepticus: A prospective comparison of diazepam and phenytoin versus phenobarbital and optimal phenytoin. *Neurology.* 1988;38:202–207.
38. Prensky AL, Raff MC, Moore MJ, Schwab RSI. Intravenous diazepam in the treatment of prolonged seizure activity. *N Engl J Med.* 1967;267:779–784.
39. Grattini S, Marcucci F, Morselli J, Mussini E. The significance of measuring blood levels of benzodiazepines; in Davis DS, Prichard BNC, eds. *Biological Effects of Drugs in Relation to Their Plasma Concentrations.* London: Macmillan; 1973: pp 211–226.
40. Nicol C, Tutton IC, Smith BH. Parenteral diazepam in status epilepticus. *Neurology.* 1969;19:332–334.
41. Thong YH, Abramson DC. Continuous infusion of diazepam in infants with severe recurrent convulsions. *Med Ann DC.* 1974;43:63–65.
42. Hoppu K, Cantavouri P. Diazepam rectal solution for home treatment of acute seizures in children. *Acta Paediatr Scand.* 1981;70:369–372.
43. Knudsen FU. Rectal administration of diazepam in solution in the acute treatment of convulsions in infants and children. *Arch Dis Child.* 1979;54: 855–857.
44. Knusden FU. Effective short term diazepam prophylaxis in febrile convulsions. *J Pediatr.* 1975;106:487–490.
45. Ventura A, Basso T, Bortolan G, Gardini A, Guidobaldi G, Lorusso G, Marinoni S, Merli A, Messi G, Mussi G, Nuner M, Patamia F, Rabusin P, Sacher B, Ulliana A. Home treatment of seizures as a strategy for the long term management of febrile convulsions in children. *Helv Paediatr Acta.* 1982;37:581–587.

46. Chien C, Keegan D. Diazepam as an oral long-term anticonvulsant for epileptic mental patients. *Dis Nerv Syst.* 1972;33:100–104.
47. Milligan NM, Dhillon S, Griffith A, Oxley J. A clinical trial of single dose rectal and oral administration of diazepam for the prevention of serial seizures in adult epileptic patient. *J Neurol Neurosurg Psychiatry.* 1984;47: 235–331.
48. Comer WH, Giesecke AH Jr. Injectable lorazepam (Ativan). *Semin Anesthesiol.* 1972;1:33–39.
49. Amand G, Evrard P. Le lorazépam injectable dans état de mal épileptiques. *Rev Electroencéphalogr Neurophysiol Clin.* 1976;6:532–533.
50. Griffith PA, Karp HR. Lorazepam therapy for status epilepticus. *Ann Neurol.* 1980;7:493.
51. Levy RJ, Krall RL. Treatment of status epilepticus with lorazepam. *Arch Neurol.* 1984;41:605–611.
52. Sorel L, Mechler L, Harmant J. Comparative trial of intravenous lorazepam and clonazepam in status epilepticus. *Clin Ther.* 1981;4:326–336.
53. Lacey DJ, Singer WD, Horwitz SJ, Gilmore H. Clinical and laboratory observations: Lorazepam therapy in status epilepticus in children and adolecents. *J Pediatr.* 1986;108:771–774.
54. Walker JE, Homan RW, Vasko MR, Crawford IL, Bell RD, Tasker WG. Lorazepam in status epilepticus. *Ann Neurol.* 1979;6:207–213.
55. Waltregny A, Dargent J. Preliminary study of parenteral lorazepam in status epilepticus. *Acta Neurol Belg.* 1985;75:219–229.
56. Treiman DM, De Giorgio CM, BenMenachem E, Gehret D, Nelson L, Salisbury S, Barber KO, Wickboldt CL. Lorazepam versus phenytoin in the treatment of generalized convulsive status epilepticus: Report of an ongoing study. *Neurology.* 1985;35(suppl 1):284.
57. Racoma A, Brown RP. Nocturnal ulcer pain relief from tricyclic antidepressants (letter). *JAMA.* 1987;257:485.
58. Ries RK, Gilbert DA, Katon W. Tricyclic antidepressant therapy for peptic ulcer disease. *Arch Intern Med.* 1984;144:566–569.
59. Singh DA, Sunder S, Tripathi KK. Tricyclic antidepressant therapy in duodenal ulcer. *J Indian Med Assn.* 1987;85:265–267.
60. Valnes K, Skaug OE, Larsen S, Myren JI. Trimipramine and duodenal ulcer. *Scand J Gastroenterol.* 1980;15(suppl):71–78.
61. Valnes K, Wetterhus S, Ellekjaer E, Halvorsen L, Hovdenak N, Larsen S, Skaug OE, Tonder M, Myren J. Trimipramine in the treatment of duodenal ulcer: A multicenter open study. *Scand J Gastroenterol.* 1980;15(suppl): 6–70.
62. Wetterhus S, Aubert E, Bjrekeset T, Berg CE, Holvorsen L, Hovdenak N, Myren J, Roland M, Sigstad H, Guldahl M. Effect of trimipramine on symptoms and healing of peptic ulcer. *Scand J Gastroenterol.* 1977;12(suppl): 33–38.
63. Daneshmend TK, Homeida M, Mountford RA, Brown P, Neumann PSI. Clinical trial value of trimipramine versus placebo in duodenal ulcer healing. *Gut.* 1981;22:1045–1047.
64. Moshal MG, Kahn F. Trimipramine in the treatment of gastric ulcer. *Scand J Gastroenterol.* 1981;16:295–298.

65. Guldahl M. The effect of trimipramine on masked depression in patients with duodenal ulcer: A double blind study. *Scand J Gastroenterol.* 1978; 12(suppl):27–31.

66. Nitter L Jr, Haraldsson A, Holck P, Myren JI. The effect of trimipramine on the healing of peptic ulcer. A double blind study. Multicenter investigation. *Scand J Gastroenterol.* 1978;12(suppl):39–41.

67. Valnes K, Myren J, Ovigstad T. Trimipramine in the treatment of gastric ulcer. *Scand J Gastroenterol.* 1978;13:497–500.

68. Mackay HP, Pickard WR, Mitchell KG, Green GP. A double-blind study of trimipramine in the treatment of active duodenal ulceration. *Scand J Gastroenterol.* 1984;19:190–193.

69. Becker U, Faurschou P, Jensen J, Lindorff K, Ranlov PJ. Relapse prevention of duodenal ulcers with trimipramine, cimetidine, or placebo. *Scand J Gastroenterol.* 1984;19:405–410.

70. Berstad A, Bjerke K, Carlsen E, Aadland E. Treatment of duodenal ulcer with an antacid in combination with trimipramine or cimetidine. *Scand J Gastroenterol.* 1977;12(suppl):46–52.

71. Berstad A, Aadland E, Bjerke K, Carlsen E. Relapse of duodenal ulcer after treatment with trimipramine/antacid or cimetidine/antacids. *Scand J Gastroenterol.* 1981;16:933–936.

72. Stave R, Myren J, Osnes M. Prevention of recurrent ulcer bleeding. *Scand J Gastroenterol.* 1986;21(suppl 124):55–62.

73. Hoff GS, Ruud TE, Tonder M, Holter O. Doxepin in the treatment of duodenal ulcer: An open clinical and endoscopic study comparing doxepin and cimetidine. *Scand J Gastroenterol.* 1981;16:1041–1042.

74. Kirshner JB. Drug therapy of ulcerative colitis. *Mod Med Minneap.* 1966; 34:115.

75. Spiegelberg U. *Kombinierte Behandlung psychosomatischer Krankheitszustände: Probleme der pharmacopsychiatrischen Kombinations- und Langzeitbehandlung. Rothenburger Gespräch 1965.* Basel, Switzerland: Karger;1966: pp 198–207.

76. Cunha UV. Antidepressants: Their uses in nonpsychiatric disorders of aging. *Geriatrics.* 1988;41:63–74.

77. Greenbaum DS, Mayle JE, Vangeren LE, Jerome JA, Mayer JW, Greenbaum RB, Matson RW, Stein GE, Dean HA, Halversen NA. Effects of desipramine on irritable bowel syndrome compared with atropine and placebo. *Dig Dis Sci.* 1987;32:257–266.

78. Liss JL, Alpers D, Woodruff RA. The irritable colon syndrome and psychiatric illness. *Dis Nerv Syst.* 1973;34:151–157.

79. Rask-Madsen J, Baastrup PC, Schwartz P. Lithium induced hyperpolarization of the human rectum in vitro. *Br Med J.* 1972;ii:496–498.

80. Zibook S. Ulcerative colitis: A case responding to treatment with lithium carbonate. *JAMA.* 1972;219:755.

81. Varsamis J, Wand RR. Severe diarrhea associated with lithium carbonate therapy in regional ileitis. *Lancet.* 1972;ii:1322.

82. Bellingham-Smith E. The significance and treatment of obstinate hiccough. *Practitioner.* 1938;140:166–171.

83. Mayo C. Hiccup. *Surg Gynecol Obstet.* 1932;55:700–708.

84. Noble E. Hiccup. *Can Med Assn J.* 1934;31:38–41.

85. Travell J. A trigger point for hiccup. *J Am Osteopath Assn.* 1977;77:2039–2044.
86. Newsome Davis J. An experimental study of hiccups. *Brain.* 1970;93:851–872.
87. Wagner M, Stapezynski J. Persistent hiccups. *Ann Emerg Med.* 1982;11:24–26.
88. Laing T, Marariu M, Malik GI. Intractable hiccups and posterior fossa arteriovenous malformations: A case report. *Henry Ford Hosp Med J.* 1981;29: 145–147.
89. Lewis J. Hiccups: Causes and cures. *J Clin Gastroenterol.* 1985;7:539–552.
90. Nathan M, Leshner R, Keller A. Intractable hiccups. *Laryngoscope.* 1980;90: 1612–1618.
91. Williamson B, MacIntyre I. Management of intractable hiccup. *Br Med J.* 1977;ii:501–503.
92. Davignon A, Laurieux G, Genest J. Chlorpromazine in the treatment of persistent hiccough. *Union Med Can.* 1955;84:282.
93. Efrati P. Obstinate hiccup as a prodromal symptom in thoracic herpes zoster. *Neurology.* 1956;6:601–602.
94. Friedgood C, Ripstein C. Chlorpromazine (Thorazine) in the treatment of persistent hiccough. *Union Med Can.* 1955;84:282.
95. Obis P. Remedies for hiccups. *Nursing.* 1974;4:88.
96. Salem M, Baraka A, Rattenborg C, Holliday DAI. Treatment of hiccup by pharyngeal stimulation in anesthetized and conscious subjects. *JAMA.* 1967;202:126–130.
97. Driscoll C. Symptom control in terminal illness. *Prim Care.* 1987;14:353–363.
98. Ives T, Fleming M, Weart C. Treatment of intractable hiccups with intramuscular haloperidol. *Am J Psychiatry.* 1985;142:1368–1369.
99. Korcyzn AD. Hiccup. *Br Med J.* 1971;ii:590–591.
100. Lamphier T. Methods of management of persistent hiccup. *Md Med J.* 1977;11:80–81.
101. Scarnati RA. Intractable hiccups (singultus): Report of a case. *J Am Osteopath Assn.* 1979;79:127–129.
102. Beumer HH. Untersuchungen über den Antihistamin- Effekt von Imipramin beim Menschen. *Arzneimittelforschung.* 1966;10:1352–1353.
103. Alcock T. Some personality characteristics of asthmatic children. *Br Med J.* 1960;iii:133.
104. Green R. Asthma and manic depressive psychosis: Simultaneously incompatible or coexistent. *J Nerv Ment Dis.* 1965;140:64.
105. Cordova Castro A. Aspectos psyquiatricos del asma bronquial. *Rev Cubana Med.* 1962;1:33–38.
106. Godfarb AA, Venutolu F. The use of an antidepressant drug in chronically allergic individuals. *Ann Allergy.* 1963;21:667–676.
107. Malhov E, Diaz A, Greiding L, Mazzolli RE. Acción de un derivado iminodibencitico en pacientes con asma grave irreductible. *Diabetic Med.* 1962;34: 1766.
108. Sanger MD. The use of tranquilizers and antidepressants in allergy. *Ann Allergy.* 1962;20:705–709.
109. Staehelin B, Kägi P, Schupp M, Vogelsanger G. Behandlungsergebnisse mit dem Iminobenzylderivat Tofranil bei 136 Fällen von Rhinitis vasomotoria, Rhinitis pollinosa und Asthma bronchiale. *Pyract Otorhinolaryngol.* 1960;22: 289–307.

110. Kaplan M, Kravitz RS, Ross WD. The effects of imipramine on depressive components of medical disorders. *Proc 3rd World Congr of Psychiatry, Montreal;* 1961;2:1362–1367.

111. Fels H. Theoretische und praktische Gesichtspunkte zu einer kombinierten Behandlung des Asthma Bronchiale. *5th Int Congr of Allergy, Madrid;* 1964: p 155.

112. Meares RA, Mills JE, Horvak TB, Atkinson JM, Dunn LQ, Rand MJ. Amitriptyline and asthma. *Med J Aust.* 1971;ii:25–28.

113. Sugihara H, Ishihara K, Noguchi H. Clinical experience with amitriptyline (Tryptanol) in bronchial asthma. *Ann Allergy.* 1965;23:422–429.

114. Ananth J. Antiasthmatic effect of amitriptyline. *Can Med Assn J.* 1974;110:1131.

115. Wilson C. Effect of amitriptyline. *Can Med Assn J.* 1974;111:212.

116. Spiegelberg U. Pharmacotherapy and psychosomatics. *Int Pharmacopsychiatry.* 1968;1:87–111.

117. Robin AA, Langley GE. A controlled trial of imipramine. *Br J Psychiatry.* 1964;110:419–422.

118. Eisenberg BC. Relief of allergic symptoms with tranquilizers in combinations with other drugs. *Clin Med.* 1978;5:897.

119. Kessler F. Hydroxyzine HCI in the management of allergic conditions. *Clin Med.* 1967;74:37–45.

120. Shah JR, Talivakar CV, Karkanis V. Observations on the study of antiasthmatic preparation containing hydroxyzine. *Indian J Chest Dis.* 1970;12:116–120.

121. Heurich AM, Souza-Poza M, Lyons HA. Bronchodilator effects of hyroxyzine hydrochloride. *Respiration.* 1972;29:135–138.

122. Barlow PB, Barger JH. MEFP and FEV marase. *Mich Med.* 1967;66:1259–1262.

123. Britt LS. The response of acute asthmatics to a single drug. *J Tenn Med Assn.* 1966;59:459–461.

124. Paul K. Clinical experiences with a new bronchodilator agent (Marax). *Wien Med Wochenschr.* 1969;119:252–253.

125. Kahn J, Jokl H. Treatment of asthmatic dyspnea. *Med Klin.* 1968;63: 1814–1818.

126. Baum GL, Schotz SA, Gumpel RS, Osgood C. The role of chlorpromazine in the treatment of bronchial asthma and chronic pulmonary emphysema. *Dis Chest.* 1957;32:547–579.

127. Robinson KC, Zuck D. Chlorpromazine in status asthmaticus. *Lancet.* 1954; i:1349.

128. Ananth J. Rheumatoid arthritis. In: Kaplan HI, Sadock BJ, eds. *Comprehensive Textbook of Psychiatry.* 5th ed. Baltimore: Williams & Wilkins;1989;vol 2: pp 1225–1231.

129. Butler SH, Weil-Fugazza J, Godefroy F, Besson JM. Reduction of arthritis and pain behavior following chronic administration of amitriptyline or imipramine in rats with adjuvant-induced arthritis. *Pain.* 1985;23:159–175.

130. Scott WAM. The relief of pain with an antidepressant in arthritis. *Practitioner.* 1969;202:802–805.

131. Gingras M. A clinical trial of Tofranil in rheumatic pain in general practice. *J Int Med Res.* 1976;4(suppl 2):41–49.

132. Saarialho-Kere U, Julkunen H, Mattila MJ, Seppälä T. Psychomotor performance of patients with rheumatoid arthritis: Crossover comparison of dextropropoxyphene, dextropropoxyphene plus amitriptyline, indomethacin and placebo. *Pharmacol Toxicol.* 1988:63:286–292.

133. Sarzi Puttini P, Cazzola M, Boccassini L, Ciniselli G, Santanrea S, Caruso I, Benvenuti C. A comparison of dothiepin versus placebo in treatment of pain in rheumatoid arthritis and the association of pain and depression. *J Int Med Res.* 1988;16:331–337.

134. Ganvir P, Beaumont G, Seldrup J. A comparative trial of clomipramine and placebo as adjunctive therapy in arthralgia. *J Int Med Res.* 1973;8(suppl 3):60–66.

135. MacNeill Al, Dick WC. Imipramine and rheumatoid factor. *J Int Med Res.* 1976;4(suppl 2):23–27.

136. Snow H. *Cancer and the Cancer Process.* London: Churchill;1893.

137. Guy R. *An Essay on Scirrous Tumors and Cancer.* London: Churchill;1759.

138. Kerr TA, Schapira K, Roth M. The relationship between premature death and affective disorder. *Br J Psychiatry.* 1969;115:1277–1282.

139. Varsamis J, Zuckhowski T, Maini KK. Survival rates of death in geriatric psychiatric patients: A six year follow up. *Can Psychiatr Assn J.* 1972;7:17–22.

140. Whitelock FA, Siskind M. Depression and cancer: A follow up study. *Psychol Med.* 1979;9:747–752.

141. Pisciotta AV. Agranulocytosis induced by certain phenothiazine derivatives. *JAMA.* 1968;208:1862–1868.

142. Pudov VI. Effect of aminazine on metastatic dissemination of Brown Pearce tumor. *Farmakol Toksikol.* 1971;34:454–456.

143. Hill R, Bell C, Goldberg H, Hilf R, Bell C, Goldenberg H, Michel I. Effect of fluphenazine hydrochloride on R3230 AC mammary gland carcinoma and mammary glands of the rat. *Cancer Res.* 1971;31:1111–1127.

144. Levijt IS, Polliak A. Inhibition of chemical carcinogenesis in the hamster cheek pouch by topical chlorpromazine. *Nature.* 1970;228:1096–1097.

145. Katz J, Kunofsky S, Patton REI. Cancer mortality among patients in New York mental hospitals. *Cancer.* 1967;20:2194–2199.

146. Rassidakis NC, Kelleporis M, Fox S. Malignant neoplasm as a cause of death among psychiatric patients. *Int Ment Health Res Newslett.* 1971;13:6.

147. Rassidakis NC, Kelleporis M, Karaiossefidis K. Malignant neoplasms as a cause among psychiatric patients. *Int Ment Health Res Newslett.* 1972;14:1–3.

148. Ananth J, Burnstein M. Cancer: Less common in psychiatric patients? *Psychosomatics.* 1977;18(2):44–47.

149. Daut RL, Cleeland CS. The prevalence and severity of pain in cancer. *Cancer.* 1982;50:1913–1918.

150. Foley KM. The treatment of cancer pain. *N Engl J Med.* 1981;313:84–95.

151. Kanner RM, Fley KM. Patterns of narcotic use in a cancer pain clinic. *Ann NY Acad Sci.* 1981;362:161–172.

152. Cleeland CS. Nonpharmacologic management of cancer pain. *J Pain Symptom Manage.* 1987;2(suppl 2):23–28.

153. Twycross RG, Lack SA. *Symptom Control in Far Advanced Cancer: Pain Relief.* London: Pitman;1983: pp 3–14.

154. Landa L, Breivik H, Husebo S, Elgen A, Rennemo F. Beneficial effects of flupenthixol on cancer pain patients. *Pain.* 1984;20(suppl 2):253.

155. Derogatis LR, Feldstein M, Morrow G, Shhmale A, Schmitt M, Gates C, Murawski B, Holland J, Penman D, Melisaratos N, Enelow AJ, Adler LM.

A survey of psychotropic drug prescriptions in an oncology population. *Cancer.* 1979;44:1919–1929.

156. Goldberg RJ, Mor V. A survey of psychotropic use in terminal cancer patients. *Psychosomatics.* 1985;26:745–751.

157. Bishop JF, Oliver IN, Wolf MM, Matthews JP, Long M, Bingham J, Hillcoat BL, Cooper IA. Lorazepam: A randomized double blind cross over study of a new antiemetic in patients receiving cytotoxic chemotherapy and chlorperazine. *J Clin Oncol.* 1984;2(6):691–695.

158. Bowcock SJ, Stockdale AD, Bolton JAR, Bolton JA, Kang AA, Retsas S. Antiemetic prophylaxis with high dose metaclopramide or lorazepam in vomiting induced by chemotherapy. *Br Med J.* 1984;288:1879.

159. Gagen M, Gochnour D, Young D, Gaginella T, Neidhart J. A randomized trial of metaclopramide and a combination of dexamethasone and lorazepam for prevention of chemotherapy induced vomiting. *J Clin Oncol.* 1984;2: 696–701.

160. Laszlo J, Clark RA, Hanson DC, Tyson L, Crumpler L, Gralla R. Lorazepam in cancer patients treated with cisplastin: A drug having antiemetic, amnesic and anxiolytic effects. *J Clin Oncol.* 1985;8:864–869.

161. Maher J. Intravenous lorazepam to prevent nausea and vomiting associated with cancer chemotherapy. *Lancet.* 1981;i:91–92.

162. Natale RB. Current evaluation of efficacy: The University of Michigan experience. *Oncol Times.* 1985;7(suppl):13–14.

163. Semard NF, Leuchter RS, Townsend DE, Wade ME, Lagasse LD. A pilot study of lorazepam induced amnesia with cisplatinum containing chemotherapy. *Gynecol Oncol.* 1984;17:277–280.

164. Luesley DM, Terry PB, Chan KK. High dose intravenous metaclopramide and intermittent intramuscular prochlorperazine and diazepam in the management of emesis induced by cis-chlorodiammineplatinum. *Cancer Chemother Pharmacol.* 1985;14:250–252.

165. Plezia PM, Alberts DS, Kessler J, Aapro MS, Graham V, Surwit EA. Immediate termination of intractable vomiting induced by cisplatin combination chemotherapy using an intensive five drug antiemetic regimen. *Cancer Treat Rep.* 1984;68:1693–1695.

166. Rohins HI, Ershler WB, De Jough L, Chang YC, Frosdowicz PM, Carr BI, Meyer DK. Antiemetic effect of intravenous diazepam in patients receiving cis-diamminedichloroplatinum: Pilot study. *Med Pediatr Oncol.* 1979;7: 247–249.

167. Morrow GR, Arseneau JC, Asbury RF, Bennett JM, Boros L. Anticipatory nausea and vomiting in chemotherapy patients. *N Engl J Med.* 1982;305: 431–432.

168. Wilcox PM, Fetting JH, Nettesheim KM, Abeloff MD. Anticipatory vomiting in women receiving cyclophosphamide, methotrexate and 5–FU adjunct chemotherapy for breast carcinoma. *Cancer Treat Rep.* 1982;66:1601–1604.

169. Sternbach RA. *Pain Patients: Traits and Treatment.* New York: Academic Press;1974.

170. Hameroff SR, Weiss JL, Lerman JC, Cork RC, Watts KS, Crago BR, Neuman CP, Womble JR, Davis TP. Doxepin's effects on chronic pain and depression: A controlled study. *J Clin Psychiatry.* 1984;45:45–52.

171. Levine JD, Gordon NC, Smith R, McBryde R. Desipramine enhances opiate postoperative analgesia. *Pain.* 1986;25:245–257.
172. Smoller B. The use of dexamethasone test as a marker of efficacy in the treatment of myofacial syndrome with amitriptyline. *Pain.* 1976;2(suppl):250.
173. Gourlay GK, Cherry DA, Cousins MF, Cousine MJ, Love I. A controlled study of serotonin uptake blocker zimelidine in the treatment of chronic pain. *Pain.* 1986;25:35–52.
174. Jenkins DG, Ebbut AF, Evans CD. Tofranil in the treatment of low back pain. *J Int Med Res.* 1976;4(suppl 2):28–40.
175. Lascelles RG. Atypical facial pain and depression. *Br J Psychiatry.* 1966;112:651–659.
176. Pheasant H, Bursk A, Goldfarb J, Weiss JN, Borelli L. Amitriptyline and chronic low back pain: A randomized double blind cross over study. *Spine.* 1983;8:552–557.
177. Ward N, Bokan JA, Phillips M, Benedetti C, Butler S, Spengler D. Antidepressants in concomitant chronic back pain and depression. Doxepin and desipramine compared. *J Clin Psychiatry.* 1984;45:54–57.
178. Ward NG. Tricyclic antidepressants for chronic low back pain: Mechanisms of action and predictors of response. *Spine.* 1986;11:661–665.
179. Saarnivaara L, Mattila MJ. Comparison of tricyclic antidepressants in rabbits: Antinociception and potentiation of the noradrenaline pressore responses. *Psychopharmacology.* 1974;35:221–236.
180. Paoli F, Darcourt G, Corsa P. Note préliminaire sur l'action de l'imipramine dans les états douloureux. *Rev Neurol (Paris).* 1960;102:530–534.
181. France RD, Houpt JL, Ellinwood EH. Therapeutic effects of antidepressants in chronic pain. *Gen Hosp Psychiatry.* 1984;296:712–715.
182. Lee R, Spencer PSJ. Antidepressants and pain: A review of the pharmacological data supporting the use of certain tricyclics in chronic pain patients. *J Int Med Res.* 1977;5:146–156.
183. Chapman CR, Butler SH. Effects of doxepin on perception of laboratory induced pain in man. *Pain.* 1978;5:253–262.
184. Bromm B, Meier W, Scharein E. Imipramine reduces experimental pain. *Pain.* 1986;24:245–257.
185. Murphy DL, Seiver LJ, Insel TR. Therapeutic responses to tricyclic antidepressants and related drugs in nonaffective disorder patient populations. *Prog Neuropsychopharmacol Biol Psychiatry.* 1985;9:3–13.
186. Ho CY. Treatment of post-herpetic neuralgia. *Med J Aust.* 1965;ii:869–872.
187. Watson CPN, Evans RJ, Reed K, Mersky H, Goldsmith L, Warsh JI. Amitriptyline versus placebo in post-herpetic neuralgia. *Neurology.* 1982;32: 671–673.
188. Woodlorde JM, Dwyer B, McEwan BW. Treatment of postherpetic neuralgia. *Med J Austr.* 1969;ii:869–872.
189. Davis IL, Lewis SB, Gerich JE, Kaplan RA, Schwartz TA, Wallin JD. Peripheral diabetic neuropathy treated with amitriptyline and fluphenazine. *JAMA.* 1977;238:2291–2292.
190. Mandel CM, Klein RF, Chappel DA, Dere WH, Gertz BJ, Karam JH, Lavin TN, Grunfeld C. A trial of amitriptyline and fluphenazine in the treatment of painful diabetic neuropathy A double blind cross over study. *JAMA.* 1986;255:637–639.

191. Dalessio DJ. Chronic pain syndromes and disordered cortical inhibitions: Effects of tricyclic compounds. *Dis Nerv Syst.* 1967;28:325–328.
192. Agnew DC. Thalamic pain. *Bull Clin Neurosci.* 1984;49:93–98.
193. Koppel BS. Amitriptyline in the treatment of thalamic pain. *South Med J.* 1986;79:759–761.
194. Kocher R. The use of psychotropic drugs in the treatment of cancer pain: Recent results. *Cancer Res.* 1984;89:118–126.
195. Langohr HD, Stohr M, Petruch F. An open and double blind cross over study on the efficacy of clomipramine (Anafranil) in patients with painful mono- and polyneuropathies. *Eur Neurol.* 1982;21:309–317.
196. Sharav Y, Singer E, Schmidt E, Dionne RA, Dubner R. Analgesic effects of amitriptyline on chronic facial pain. *Pain.* 1987;31:199–209.
197. Sherman RA, Sherman CJ, Parker L. Chronic phantom and stump pain among American veterans: Results of a survey. *Pain.* 1984;18:83–95.
198. Urban BJ, France RD, Steinberger EK, Scott DL, Maltbie AA. Long term use of narcotic/antidepressant medication in the management of phantom limb pain. *Pain.* 1986;24:191–196.
199. Max MB, Schafer SC, Culnane M, Smoller B, Dubner R, Gracely RH. Amitriptyline but not lorazepam relieves postherpetic neuralgia. *Neurology.* 1988;38:1427–1432.
200. Max MB, Culnane M, Schafer SC, Gracely RH, Walther DJ, Smoller B, Dubner R. Amitriptyline relieves diabetic neuropathy pain in patients with normal or depressed mood. *Neurology.* 1987;37:589–596.
201. Kvinesdal B, Molin J, Froland A, Gram LFI. Imipramine treatment of painful diabetic neuropathy. *JAMA.* 1980;251:1727–1730.
202. Turkington RW. Depression masquerading as diabetic neuropathy. *JAMA.* 1980;243:1147–1150.
203. Young RJ, Clark BF. Pain relief in diabetic neuropathy: The effectiveness of imipramine and related drugs. *Diabetic Med.* 1985;2:363–366.
204. Taub A. Relief of postherpetic neuralgia with psychotropic drugs. *J Neurosurg.* 1973;39:235–239.
205. Rascal O, Tran MA, Bonnevialle P. Lack of correlation between plasma levels of amitriptyline and nortriptyline and clinical improvement of chronic pain of peripheral origin. *Clin Neuropharmacol.* 1987;10:560–564.
206. Singh PN, Sharma P, Gupta PK, Pandey K. Clinical evaluation of diazepam for relief of post-operative pain. *Br J Anaesth.* 1981;53:831–836.
207. Horrobin DF. Lithium in the control of herpes virus infections. In: Bach RO, ed. *Lithium: Current Applications in Science, Medicine and Technology.* New York: Wiley;1985: pp 397–406.
208. Skinner GRB, Hartley C, Buchanan A, Harper L, Gallimore P. The effect of lithium chloride on the replication of herpes simplex virus. *Med Microbiol Immunol* (Berl). 1980;168:139–148.
209. Leib J. Remission of recurrent herpes infection during lithium therapy. *N Engl J Med.* 1979;301:942.
210. Leib J. Immunopotentiation and inhibition of herpes virus activation during therapy with lithium carbonate. *Med Hypotheses.* 1981;7:885–890.
211. Skinner GRB. Lithium ointment for genital herpes. *Lancet.* 1983;ii: 288.

212. Barrett AJ. Hematological effects of lithium and its use in treatment of neutropenia. *Blut.* 1980;40:1–6.
213. Rosoff AH, Robinson WA. Lithium effects on granulopoiesis and immune functions. *Adv Exp Med Biol.* 1980;127:281–291.
214. Kaplan RA. Lithium in Felty's syndrome. *Ann Intern Med.* 1976;84:342.
215. Anderson T. Lithium carbonate stimulation of granulopoiesis in hematologic and oncologic disease. *Ariz Med.* 1979;36:762–763.
216. Lee M, Hopkins LE. Attenuation of chemotherapy induced neutropenia with lithium carbonate. *Am J Hosp Pharm.* 1980;37:1066–1071.
217. Stein RS, Vogel WR, Lefante J. Failure of lithium to limit neutropenia significantly during induction therapy of acute myelogenous leukemia. *Am J Clin Oncol.* 1984;7:365–369.
218. Brewerton TD. Lithium counteracts carbamazepine induced leukopenia while increasing its therapeutic effect. *Biol Psychiatry.* 1986;21:677–685.
219. Friedman AP. The migraine syndrome. *Bull NY Acad Med.* 1968;44:45–62.
220. Gomersall JD, Stuart A. Amitriptyline in migraine prophylaxis. *J Neurol Neurosurg Psychiatry.* 1973;36:648–690.
221. Mahloudji M. Prevention of migraine. *Br Med J.* 1969;i:182–183.
222. Couch JR, Ziegler DK, Hassanein R. Amitriptyline in migraine prophylaxis. *Arch Neurol.* 1979;36:695–699.
223. Mathew NT. Prophylaxis of migraine and mixed headache. A randomized controlled study. *Headache.* 1981;21:105–109.
224. Lance JW, Curran DA, Anthony M. Investigation into the mechanism and treatment of chronic tension headache. *Med J Aust.* 1965;ii:909–914,
225. Lance JW, Curran DA. Treatment of chronic tension headache. *Lancet.* 1964;i:1236–1239.
226. Oshaka A, Ghaleb HA, Sadek A. A double blind trial for the clinical management of psychogenic headache. *Br J Psychiatry.* 1973;122:181–183.
227. Edmeads JS, Raskin NH, Rothner AD. Modern management of headache: Mechanisms and therapeutics. In: *Annual Courses of the American Academy of Neurology. Minneapolis, American Academy of Neurology;*1985;2:1–132.
228. Morland TJ, Storli VO, Mogstad TE. Doxepin in the prophylactic treatment of mixed vascular and tension headaches. *Headache.* 1979;19:382–383.
229. Pies R. Trazodone and intractable headaches (letter). *J Clin Psychiatry.* 1983;44:317.
230. Neiper HA. The clinical application of lithium orotate: A two-year study. *Agressologie.* 1973;14:407–411.
231. Chazot G, Chauplannaz G, Biron A, Schott B. Migraine: Treatment with lithium. *Presse Méd.* 1979;8:2836–2837.
232. Peatfield RC, Rose FC. Exacerbation of migraine by treatment with lithium. *Headache.* 1981;21:140–142.
233. Medina JL, Diamond S. Cyclical migraine. *Arch Neurol.* 1981;38:343–344.
234. Medina JL. Cyclic migraine: A disorder responsive to lithium carbonate. *Psychosomatics.* 1982;23:625–637.

Chapter 29
Compliance

BARRY BLACKWELL

Ever since Eve ate the forbidden fruit it has been metaphorically clear that people sometimes prefer not to follow instructions. Public ambivalence about this topic is apparent from its semantics; some cultures (where authority is less often questioned) lack words to convey the concept of compliance. In more egalitarian countries consumer advocates have complained that the word is coercive. This has led to the tongue-in-cheek observation[1] that "adherence seems too sticky, fidelity has too many connotations and maintenance suggests a repair crew." So whatever its shortcomings, *compliance* continues to be the most popular term in use today.

Socially sanctioned authority figures such as physicians know the accuracy of Hippocrates' aphorism that "patients often lie when they state they have taken certain medicines," but they have been slow to acknowledge or examine the failure of their own prescriptive behavior. The word *compliance* did not even enter the official medical lexicon until 1975 when it replaced the term *patient drop-out* in the Index Medicus.

In spite of this slow start, during the past two decades compliance has become a topic of intense investigation and debate. The first two international conferences on compliance at McMaster University in 1977 and 1979 defined the parameters of the field and documented an exponential increase in the number of research studies and reviews on the topic.[2] This

625

was later followed by the appearance of several texts.[3, 4] This abrupt interest in such an ancient issue can be attributed to at least three factors. First, the discovery of modern major pharmaceuticals including antibiotics, anti-inflammatory agents, steroids, synthetic analgesics, and psychotropic drugs brought many diseases under control. As the acute treatable disorders were managed and the population aged, interest shifted to more chronic conditions, and the emphasis was less on cure and more on risk reduction, disease prevention, and life-style change. This resulted in treatment regimens that were long-term, complex, and which created quality of life considerations for the consumer.

Second, midcentury saw a pervasive shift in the sociopolitical climate which shaped people's expectations toward autonomy and self-care.[5] During the 18th and 19th centuries in the pre-scientific era of medicine, the public largely took care of its own health. They were exhorted to do so by social and religious leaders such as John Wesley, whose popular text *Primitive Physic* chastized the medical profession for mystifying its work in order to distance itself from people. The rise of scientific medicine in the early 20th century reinforced medical authority and marked what Paul Starr called "the retreat of private judgment."[6] Patient acquiescence was assumed and compliance taken for granted. Following the Second World War, the pendulum began to swing back with a growing distrust of authoritarianism. The move toward individual autonomy was epitomized by the civil rights, women's rights, and patients' rights movements. Distrust of a purely biomedical approach was expressed, the biopsychosocial model was espoused, and both public and professional opinions began to advocate active patient participation and partnership in treatment.

Third, and finally, as these scientific and social changes took place, the physician's unique prerogative to prescribe was increasingly eroded. A variety of other health professionals became more actively involved in understanding and participating in the treatment process. These included pharmacists, nurses, psychologists, educators, sociologists, epidemiologists, and anthropologists.

As long as treatments were largely panaceas, neglect of compliance was hardly surprising; now that so much therapy is effective, the individual and social costs compel our interest. Overall estimates are that half of outpatients and a quarter of inpatients default significantly from prescribed regimens and that up to one in 10 hospital and one in four nursing home admissions are a direct result. An individual denied a scarce kidney or heart transplant because of suspected compliance problems receives a death sentence; a society that shuns preventative methods to check the spread of HIV infection embraces genocide. Despite such persuasive examples, the benefits and consequences of our contemporary interest in compliance are open to question and interpretation.

Precisely because effective remedies may also be toxic, one expert[7] has argued that:

[S]ome sort of rough and ready natural law seems to be at work. The physician will be expected to prescribe with only approximate accuracy, and the patient will be expected to comply with only modest fidelity. Thus, has mankind been able to survive bleeding, cupping, leeches, mustard plasters, turpentine stupes and Panalba.

The questionable social cost benefit of a zealous pursuit of better compliance is best illustrated by the ongoing controversy concerning early intervention in mild to moderate hypertension.[8] The fact that treatment can reduce an individual's blood pressure is clear but an unexpected consequence has been that an increase in that person's sense of vulnerability may result in illness behavior and absenteeism from work. The annual cost of blood pressure screening in lost productivity in the United States alone is estimated to be in the millions of dollars.

DEFINITIONS, MEASUREMENT, AND RESEARCH

While every area of inquiry has its own evaluative problems, compliance has more than most. Compliance has been defined as the extent to which a person's behavior in terms of taking medications, following diets, or executing life-style changes coincides with medical or health advice. This simple sounding phrase conceals a host of possibilities. First it is necessary to define which behavior is involved, beginning with the reluctance to initiate treatment, including rejection of screening procedures, not filling prescriptions, or failure to attend an initial appointment ("no shows"). After engagement in therapy, compliance problems may include irregular attendance, premature termination (dropouts or against medical advice), or failure to follow recommendations. The latter may involve diet, life-style, or prescriptions. Faulty compliance with medication may include errors of purpose, timing, or dosage as well as total or partial omission or use of inadvertent combinations.

The outcome of compliance can also be defined in a number of ways. The simplest is categorical statements such as "good," "fair," or "poor." More scientific or quantitative evaluations include the percentage of a regimen that is adhered to. Perhaps the most pertinent outcome measure is change in health status or behavior. However, a major problem is the lack of a fixed relationship between the degree of compliance and health change. For example, 80% compliance may result in weight gain on a diet while the same degree of compliance will attain good blood pressure control on an antihypertensive regimen. Furthermore, these are average outcomes; an individual who takes 100% of their antihypertensive medication may fail to obtain blood pressure control if it is the wrong medication, they fail to absorb it, or if other factors including morbid obesity or stress render them treatment refractory. These difficulties can be resolved by the use of an index or composite outcome measure which takes into account selection of the appropriate treatment regimen, adequate compliance, and achievement of desired health change.

Beyond definition lies the equally complex question of measurement. It has been noted that in the compliance field simple measures are not accurate and accurate measures are not simple. Both patients and providers are prone to overestimate compliance and physicians are particularly inaccurate at predicting it.

Methods of measurement include biological assays, pill counts, interviews, and microchip monitoring devices that record when a container is opened or a dropper is tilted. A major problem of all these methods is that compliance problems diminish under scrutiny. The fact that people modify their behavior in response to being observed or visiting a health care provider is known as the "toothbrush" or "white coat" effect. This makes it almost impossible to study compliance in ways that relate to real life. These twin problems of reactivity and lack of generalizability are difficult to surmount and contribute to the large number of negative or inconsistent research findings. Because of these problems, it has been recommended that studies of compliance use more than one measure and that observations should be random, extended, and unobtrusive to minimize reactivity. The recent introduction of microchip computers is a significant advance because they permit observation with subterfuge, although the need to obtain informed consent obviously undermines this potential advantage.

Given these problems of definition and measurement, research on compliance is difficult. An early review of over 500 studies found that only 16% had adequate design and only 10% had reliable objective measures of outcome.[2] More than 50 different diseases have been studied with the focus primarily on chronic long-term conditions, particularly those that are silent or symptom free and which therefore present the greatest challenge. Hypertension is sometimes considered the "Mount Everest," with glaucoma a close second.

An equally wide range of outcome factors have been studied including disease characteristics, aspects of the regimen or treatment setting, patient variables, and the therapeutic interaction. Over half of these studies have failed to reveal any association between compliance and more than 200 variables. Those factors most easily observed (such as patient demographics and disease characteristics) have been the least rewarding, while the subtler variables (such as psychological and interactional factors) have been more predictive.[9]

In addition to these specific difficulties, research on compliance suffers from generic problems such as ascertainment biases (how subjects are selected for study) and retrospective or correlational designs.

Much research is pragmatic, although five major theoretical approaches can be identified.[10] The oldest and most basic is the biomedical approach, which focuses on the more technical or mechanistic problems and potential solutions. It emphasizes the various aspects of the treatment regimen and aims to find particular personality attributes in noncompliant patients but it ignores the more subtle, social, and interpersonal determinants of behavior. The second is the operant behavioral model, which evolved alongside the compliance field. It emphasized the structuring of the environment and its reward systems, as well as the teaching of specific skills needed to make compliance easier. This model often lacks an individualized approach and fails to consider less conscious cognitions that are not linked to immediate rewards. A third model is the educational one which aims to enhance communication between provider and patient. It stresses the significance of timing, instruction, and comprehension of information but tends to ignore the powerful attitudinal, motivational, and interpersonal factors that distort or disrupt the transfer of knowledge into action. The fourth and particularly popular model is the Health Belief Model which views compliance as being based on a rational appraisal of the balance between the perceived benefits of treatment and barriers to obtaining it. While the model yields modest associations between its assumptions and compliance behavior in some situations, it fails to do so in others, particularly in risk reduction behaviors that are linked to more socially determined or unconscious motivations. A fifth and final model is the self-regulatory systems approach. This considers both the cognitive and emotional response to a perceived threat of illness, the actions taken as a result, and the individual's appraisal of their own behavior. In addition, this model examines the congruence between patient and practitioner with respect to each of the three stages of the model (illness representation, coping behavior, and appraisal of action). While this model is the most comprehensive, it is difficult to apply because of its multivariate and transactional nature and lack of standardized measuring instruments.

TABLE 29.1
Factors that Increase or Decrease the Likelihood of Compliance

Increase	Decrease
Patient satisfaction	Asymptomatic illness
Level of supervision	Duration of therapy
Patient's view of disease	Complexity of regimen
Patient's compliance strategy	Side effects
Family influence/stability	Social isolation
	Anxiety/drug or alcohol abuse

DETERMINANTS OF COMPLIANCE

Although it is clear that noncompliance is a common problem, physicians consistently underestimate its prevalence among their own patients and overestimate their personal ability to detect or predict its occurrence. This difficulty is contributed to by the fact that there is no stereotypical noncompliant person or situation.

To a limited extent the literature has identified some features which can be viewed as risk factors for increasing or decreasing compliance.[11] They are listed in Table 29.1. Compliance is most likely when the patient has a satisfactory relationship with a trusted physician who displays a sustained interest in compliance and control of the illness. A treatment regimen will be adhered to more faithfully if the patient views the disease as a serious one to which they are personally susceptible but also believes that treatment can control symptoms. Better compliance can be expected if the patient has strategies for fitting treatment into their life-style and family members share an interest in their well-being.

On the negative side, compliance may be lessened in illnesses which have no obvious symptoms, particularly when they are chronic. Compliance is also hampered by treatment with multiple medications, particularly if they require frequent dosing or have unpleasant side effects. Those living alone or without concerned relatives are at additional risk while anxiety, alcohol or drug abuse can impair memory or motivation and therefore reduce the ability to comply.

It is a myth that people with psychiatric illness differ significantly in the size or scope of compliance problems compared to other chronic conditions such as arthritis, diabetes, epilepsy, or glaucoma.[12] Patients with hypertension who have minimal social support overlap in degree of noncompliance with patients who suffer from chronic schizophrenia.

While identifying these positive and negative influences can be helpful in indicating which individuals may be at risk, the actual determinants of compliance are often kaleidoscopic and may change from one situation to another or over time. For example, a juvenile onset diabetic may take pride in parental approval of perfect compliance during latency but later on may act out adolescent conflicts by neglect of the regimen. In midlife, crippled by complications of disease, the same neglect may serve either as a form of passive suicide or as a stoic refusal to let illness dictate lifestyle. This kind of subtle and longitudinal interplay between person, disease, and treatment over the course of a lifetime often eludes more superficial, cross-sectional studies.

The truly significant factors that influence compliance often elude simple inquiry and are found in attitudes, beliefs, and value judgments concerning the quality of life and appropriateness of personal or professional care. People may decide to stop medication to give their body a rest, or because they believe their life is in the hands of God. A shorter life without treatment may be preferred to a lingering existence with its inconveniences. Understanding such behaviors may be partially illuminated by Levanthal et al.'s[13] cognitive model of people's commonsense representations of illness and by Becker's Health Beliefs Model.[14] An interesting example is the manner in which patients who have so-called "silent" diseases such as hypertension or glaucoma monitor the progress of their condition and its treatment through their own bodily sensations.[15] Although physicians do not believe that it is possible for individuals to tell when their blood pressure is elevated, at least 80% of patients who are in treatment for hypertension believe they can do so because of such sensations as bodily warmth, muscle tension, or headaches. About a third of patients with glaucoma report similar sensations which indicate to them when their ocular pressure is elevated. The fact that patients take medications in response to such body sensations often results in faulty compliance and poor control of the disorder.

These models may be too highly rational to fully explain some patterns of seemingly self-destructive behavior (often attributed by doctors to "denial"). In such matters art may inform us more readily than science. The author James Dickey[16] has written a poem describing his personal experience with diabetes. The first stanza entitled "Sugar" describes the advice about treatment he receives from his physician.

> Moderation, moderation
> My friend, and exercise. Each time the barbell
> Rose. . . . each time a foot fell
> Jogging, it counted itself
> One death . . . two death . . . three death and resurrection
> For a little while.

The second stanza entitled "Under Buzzards" sets forth Dickey's decision not to comply with the prescribed regimen:

> But something is gone from me, Friend.
> This is too sensible. Really it is better
> To know when to die . . . better for my blood
> To stream with the death-wish of birds.
> You know, I had just as soon crush
> This doomed syringe
> Between two mountain rocks, and bury this needle in needles
> Of trees. Companion, open that beer.

MANAGEMENT

Management of compliance can be viewed as a two-stage process. The first involves education of the patient to a full understanding of their condition and its treatment. The second includes a variety of interventions to assist the patient in which their own role may vary from being a relatively passive participant with professional supervision to complete autonomy and self-care.

EDUCATION

Most patients are surprisingly poorly informed about their own condition or its treatment, frequently fail to question physicians, and obtain much of their information from lay sources. Efforts to remedy this focus more often on the patient's shortcomings than the professional's responsibility to apply the principles of adult education.[17] Comprehension and recall of information are inhibited by the anxiety of an office visit and the traditionally passive role of the patient. Both are made worse if the physician adopts an authoritarian stance and uses fear as an aid to ensuring compliance. Information transfer is facilitated when it is given in short, clear sentences, the patient is encouraged to ask questions, and is invited to repeat back the information at the end of an interview. Verbal or written repetition facilitate retention. Traditional medical encounters are distressingly unidirectional with little attempt to elicit the patient's attitudes, beliefs, or feelings about their condition or its treatment. Compliance is facilitated when the physician strives for congruence with the patient concerning the cause and significance of symptoms, expectations about treatment, and agreement on the degree of mutual involvement in its implementation.

James Dickey's first encounter with his physician is sadly stereotypical of the kind of educational interaction that lays a foundation for future noncompliance.

> The doctor was young
> And nice. He said, I must tell you,
> My friend, that it is needless moderation
> And exercise. You don't want to look forward

To gangrene and kidney
Failure boils blindness infection skin trouble falling
Teeth coma and death.

INTERVENTION

Education is necessary but not sufficient for compliance to occur; some other intervention is almost always necessary. Several studies have shown that the improvement which occurs when compliance is being observed returns to baseline when the intervention is over even though the subjects have been educated to a criterion about their condition and the consequences of poor compliance.[18, 19]

As such studies also suggest, probably the most significant contribution to good compliance is the involvement of another interested person. This ubiquitous influence, loosely defined as "social support," may include health care providers, significant others, patient support groups, or community workers who make home visits. Much still remains unclear about the specific ingredients of this factor and how to titrate the optimal amount of attention.[20]

There is also much that the treating physician can do to facilitate compliance. This may include regular appointments with a familiar person at convenient times and places (sometimes the work site). Minimizing side effects, simplifying the regimen, and tailoring it to the patient's life-style are basic strategies. The use of pill containers and identifying compliance reminders can be valuable adjuncts.

These strategies place the patient in a passive role and do not address the issues of how to assist them to become more actively involved and autonomous. To succeed at this requires that the patient desires to be independent and the physician is willing to relinquish control. This begins with a dialogue in which mutual goals are agreed upon; in establishing the severity of the condition and the significance of compliance, the physician should administer only the proper dose of fear, sufficient to arouse the patients' sense of susceptibility but not their vulnerability, while allowing them to do the work of worrying. This latter is accomplished when the patient achieves a belief in the efficacy of the treatment often as a result of self-monitoring their own condition and its response to therapy or lifestyle adjustment. Examples include self-monitoring of blood pressure and blood sugar levels in hypertension and diabetes and recording the response to taking medication, exercise, or diet. When compliance is less than adequate to achieve desired treatment goals, keeping a behavioral diary may assist the patient to identify the barriers to successful outcome.

Finally, the physician should resist the temptation to blame only the patient. Time taken once again to understand the patient's inner attitudes and beliefs may be rewarding. Good compliance is seldom achieved at the first attempt. As Mark Twain noted, "you can't throw a habit out of the window; you have to coax it down the stairs, one step at a time."

OUTCOME EVALUATION

Outcome evaluation in compliance has produced few significant and reproducible findings.[9] This is a consequence of both the multiply determined nature of the problem and the difficulties of research. In earlier studies, interventions to improve compliance tended to be atheoretical and pragmatic, often focusing on single strategies for altering factors that were easy to manipulate (i.e., treatment regimens, waiting lists, educational packages, pill containers). Such interventions were fairly easy to control for, and trial methodology or analysis was relatively conventional and uncomplicated. As the limitations of single, relatively simple approaches became clear, more complex and often multiple interventions were attempted. Design, analysis, and interpretation became more complicated but the conclusions remain few. Except in short-term illnesses, single interventions are seldom effective, and while strategies with multiple components usually fare better than controls, the differences are often small (in the range of 20–30% improvement). Those factors that are effective are difficult to distinguish from those that are not and they may differ between individuals. The benefits obtained are usually independent of type of provider or place of intervention.

CONCLUSION

Despite its complexity, or perhaps because of it, compliance is a challenging and intriguing area of inquiry particularly for psychiatrists to apply their biomedical training, psychological insights, and their social awareness. This is because there is no stereotypical noncompliant person or situation. Each individual must be analyzed to assess both the superficial mechanical aspects of the treatment regimen as well as the person's underlying attitudes, beliefs, and quality of life concerns. Success is seldom complete and is often based on the achievement of congruence between physician and patient about the nature, treatment and progress of the illness and the relative role of each in its management. Psychiatrists equipped with this knowledge are in a unique position to consult with colleagues about a problem that is ubiquitous in the practice of medicine and has profound personal and societal impact.

REFERENCES

1. Feinstein AR. On white-coat effects and the electronic monitoring of compliance (editorial). *Arch Intern Med.* 1990;150:1377–1378.
2. Haynes RB, Taylor DW, Sackett DL, eds. *Compliance with Therapeutic and Preventive Regimens.* Baltimore: Johns Hopkins University Press;1979.
3. Cramer JA, Spilker B, eds. *Patient Compliance in Medical Practice and Clinical Trials.* New York: Raven Press;1991.
4. DiMatteo MR, DiNicola DD. *Achieving Patient Compliance: The Psychology of the Medical Practitioner's Role.* New York: Pergamon Press;1982.

5. Steele D, Blackwell B, Gutmann M, Jackson TC. Beyond advocacy: A review of the active patient concept. *Patient Educ Couns.* 1987;10:3–23.
6. Starr P. *The Social Transformation of American Medicine.* New York: Basic Books; 1982.
7. Charney E. Compliance and prescribance. *Am J Dis Child.* 1975;129:1009–1010.
8. Alderman MH, Lamport B. Labelling of hypertensives: A review of the data. *J Clin Epidemiol.* 1990;43:195–200.
9. Blackwell B. Compliance, measurement and intervention. *Curr Opin Psychiatry.* 1989;2:787–789.
10. Leventhal H, Cameron L. Behavioral theories and the problem of compliance. *Patient Educ Couns.* 1987;10:117–138.
11. Blackwell B, Gutmann M. Compliance. In: Bulpitt CJ, ed. *Handbook of Hypertension, Epidemiology of Hypertension.* New York: Elsevier;1985:6.
12. Barofsky I, Bulson RD. *The Chronic Psychiatric Patient in the Community: Principles of Treatment.* Jamaica, NY: Spectrum Publications;1980.
13. Leventhal H, Nerenz D, Steele DJ. Illness representations and coping with health threats. In: Baum A, Taylor S, Singer J, eds. *Handbook of Psychology and Health.* Hillsdale. NJ: Lawrence Erlbaum;1984:4.
14. Becker MH. Sociobehavioral determinants of compliance. In: Sackett DL, Haynes RB, eds. *Compliance with Therapeutic Regimens.* Baltimore: Johns Hopkins University Press;1976.
15. Gutmann MC, Meyer D, Leventhal H, et al. Medical- versus patient-oriented interviewing (abstract). *Clin Res.*1979;27:278A.
16. Dickey J. *Diabetes. In the Eye Beaters.* Garden City, NY: Doubleday;1970.
17. Ley P. Psychological studies of doctor-patient communication. In: Rachman S, ed. *Contributions to Medical Psychology.* Oxford, U.K.: Pergamon Press;1977.
18. Wilber JA, Barrow JG. Reducing elevated blood pressure. *Minn Med.* 1969; 52:1303.
19. McKenney JM, Slining JG, Henderson HR, et al. The effect of clinical pharmacy services on patients with essential hypertension. *Circulation.* 1973;48: 1104.
20. Levy RL. The role of social support in patient compliance. A selective review. In: Haynes RB, Mattson ME, Engebretson TO, eds. *Patient Compliance to Prescribed Antihypertensive Medication Regimens.* Bethesda, MD: National Institute of Health Publication No. 81–2102;1980: p 139.

Chapter 30
Supportive Psychotherapy

Hellmuth Freyberger, Harald J. Freyberger

Theoretical Considerations

"Nonspecific Curative" Supportive Work Relationship in Analytical Psychotherapy

According to Luborsky,[1] "supportive" denotes that aspect of analytical psychotherapy which may be "helpful–supportive" for the patient in his relationship with the therapist. In the therapist's view this supportive aspect is aimed less at psychoanalytically specific listening, understanding, intervening, and listening again, but rather represents an additional nonspecific curative factor. However, according to Luborsky this helpful–supportive relationship should not prevail to such a degree within analytical psychotherapy as to impair the effectiveness of the analytical treatment techniques, for these techniques subsequently make possible the ultimate goal of analytical psychotherapy, i.e., conflict-oriented enlightenment. On the basis of his analytical psychotherapeutic concept, Luborsky formulated the additional concept of the "nonspecific curative supportive work relationship." This work relationship supports the patient in achieving his main conflict-oriented treatment aim.

Exclusive–Supportive Psychotherapy

We distinguish between "nonspecific curative" supportive work relationship within analytical psychotherapy and exclusive–supportive

639

psychotherapy which is not an additional part of analytical psychotherapy. This independent supportive psychotherapeutic treatment
is particularly indicated in those patients who do not sufficiently
utilize interpretative and comprehension-oriented interventions;
e.g., patients suffering from very low anxiety tolerance and difficulties concerning their self-reflective ability.

The clinical interest in supportive–psychotherapeutic aspects
was considerably advanced as a consequence of the Menninger
Foundation's long-term psychotherapy study from 1952 to 1972
which concerned certain groups of patients suffering from borderline syndrome. On the basis of this Topeka research not only psychoanalytical and analytical techniques were applied but also exclusive–
supportive psychotherapy. Starting from their extensive research
experience and with special regard to supportive–psychotherapeutic
aspects, the Menninger Foundation researchers concluded from
their (psycho-)analytical treatment results that additional supportive treatment characteristics and their additional effectivity
concerning patients' psychic changes played a more important
role than they had originally expected.[2] Particularly the so-called
genuine psychic changes may be achieved to a limited extent
by exclusive–supportive psychotherapy, even without the occurrence of intrapsychic conflict solutions. Supplementary to their
conclusions the Topeka people emphasized that exclusive–
supportive psychotherapy would be most effective if it was applied
"with the greatest possible psychoanalytical competence."[3]

Practical Procedures

Indications concerning Exclusive–Supportive Psychotherapy in Psychosomatic Medicine

Considerations on the Patient's Condition. Besides the patients who
are primarily suitable for (psycho-)analytical therapy, we may clearly
differentiate in psychosomatic medicine between certain groups

of patients where (psycho-)analytical techniques are not (yet) indicated because of the patients' great emotional fragility (in the sense of a marked ego weakness). The marked ego weakness in these two patient groups may be characterized as follows: (1) Strongly reduced psychic frustration tolerance, very low narcissistic tonus, profound aggressive inhibition, intensively dependent on outside interhuman resources, respectively orientations and increased vulnerability with regard to object loss. (2) Clearly impaired perceptive faculty, particularly reduced introspective and self-reflecting ability. (3) Insufficient defense mechanisms, particularly prevailing of denial in comparison with the more differentiated psychic process of repression.

Apart from the traits of marked ego weakness as a precondition for supportive psychotherapy, the patient must be characterized by a certain potential for dependency wishes (on the basis of a dependency–independency conflict) so that the therapist will be able to build up a close contact with his patient on the basis of an oral–narcissistic object relationship (in the sense of an initial supportive psychotherapeutic step). In contrast to this, indication for supportive psychotherapy is considerably more difficult if a marked proximity–distance conflict prevails in the patient. Now the patient's great difficulty is to accept therapeutic proximity.

The number of patients who are not motivated to take the initial supportive psychotherapeutic steps because of a marked proximity–distance conflict does not seem to be a small one. On the basis of our own wide-ranging examination of 274 Hannover consultation–liaison patients, a psychotherapeutic indication could not be formulated in 37.5%.[4]

Special Indications. Starting from the above described traits of ego weakness and the potential for dependency wishes in psychosomatic medicine, the special indications with regard to exclusive–supportive psychotherapy particularly concern the following two patient groups:

(1) Psychosomatic patients: This group includes those psychosomatic patients who are originally not interested in psychotherapy in spite of their considerable (psycho-)somatic dilemmas as well

as their showing the typical traits of ego weakness. Therefore, the therapist's way of handling their neurotic problems is to motivate these patients for conflict-oriented enlightenment psychotherapy. Characteristic examples in this connection may be patients suffering from cardiac neurosis, irritable bowel syndrome, tibromyalgia syndrome, peptic ulcer, chronic inflammatory bowel diseases, and bronchial asthma, who simultaneously show a lack of introspective capacity and ego strength as well as a proximity–distance conflict. Included in this group are those patients who are suffering from organic diseases in a psychosomatic sense and who are suitable for the motivation work concerning conflict–oriented enlightenment psychotherapy.

(2) Chronically medically ill patients: These patients show clear psychic impairments particularly with regard to the secondary psychic reactions due to the perception of their bodily disease and/or of their neurotic problems. We here define the concept "chronically medically ill patient" in two different ways, namely: (a) as a chronic development of disease, and (b) as the determination of disease by somatic organic factors. However, as concerns a patient's assignment to this group we did not consider relevant whether psychosomatic factors concerning disease manifestation and further development were evident. We also included in this group those patients whose physical disease could have been caused by psychic factors but who were simultaneously unsuitable for the motivation work concerning conflict-oriented enlightenment psychotherapy. Therefore these patients, who are strictly speaking psychosomatic cases, may not see any psychological dimension of their physical disease and must—in the case of an indication supplementary to medical therapy—be treated with supportive psychotherapy like chronically medically ill patients whose disease is not determined by psychic factors either. A typical example with regard to the patients who are strictly speaking psychosomatic but not suitable for psychotherapy may be the majority of ulcerative colitis and Crohn patients. The development of their bowel disease is both serious, with repeated relapses, and obstinately chronically strengthened as well as characterized by an unusually large pathological–anatomical stretching of their intestinal wall.

These two psychosomatic and chronically medically ill patient groups who show the corresponding traits of marked ego weakness and dependency wishes are particularly frequently seen by the clinical psychosomaticist on the basis of the consultation–liaison service. Therefore the psychodynamically oriented development of our supportive psychotherapeutic techniques was particularly based on extensive experience in dealing with patients within the scope of consultation–liaison activities.

SUPPORTIVE PSYCHOTHERAPEUTIC PROCEDURES

THE GROUP OF PSYCHOSOMATIC PATIENTS

The psychosomatic patient's motivation for conflict-oriented enlightenment psychotherapy takes place on the basis of three well-characterized interview and treatment steps which start from typical supportive–psychotherapeutic principles.

The First Interview and Treatment Step. The first step, which includes two to three sessions, may be particularly characterized by the patient's ability to talk about himself.

Initially the therapist's function in taking up and maintaining the contact in the sense of an oral–narcissistic object relationship may be very difficult. Frequently considerable emotional involvement is necessary on the part of the therapist. But it should be remembered that this involvement is not experienced by the patient as a pressing or demanding one. This therapy situation may be partially compared to that described by Winnicott[5] as a facilitating environment in the sense of an environment by which psychic development may be inspired. The further therapy steps are aimed at the patient's regular and intensive preoccupation with his physical troubles, pathological organ fantasies, and medical treatment details. These preoccupations, which show traits of anxiety, depression, and narcissistic insults, include a very important specific communicative interest of the patient toward his key figures. Therefore the therapist too is interested in bringing the patient's hypochondriacal concerns into the center of his interview sessions. Now the patient may talk about himself in consequence of the therapist's emphatic presence. The resulting verbal and emotional expression of the hypochondriacal contents represents for the patient not only a considerable psychic release but also the decisive initial step toward building a firm object relationship with his therapist. The patient is now able to freely expand his ability for expressing himself in dialogue including the crucial point of the hypochondriacal content.

As a consequence of these verbal abreactions of hypochondriacal contents, circumscribed psychic capacity (for the ego functions) may be freed in the patient. This patient's psychic free capacity includes a very important condition with regard to his or her ability to experience with more discrimination feelings and thoughts for the very first time. A further characteristic of supportive–psychotherapeutic intervention is the therapist's supplying information and advice in the sense of psychoeducative measures.[3] The effectiveness of this intervention may be intensified by the therapeutically very efficacious principle of the patient's so-called corrective emotional experience with his therapist.[6] A positive transference relationship will become evident now for the first time, and will continue during the following two interview and treatment steps. In view of this transference reaction, which is experienced by the patient as gratifying, the therapist does without interpretations. On the basis of a stabilization of this positive transference relationship, the effectiveness of the supportive–psychotherapeutic interventions is strongly promoted.[3] In this connection, Fürstenau[7] speaks of the adequate representation not only of healthy adult responsibility in the relationship but also the sufficient stability giving professional parents' replacement function in the sense of Freud's concept of "subsequent education" (Table 30.1).

The patients who may not be ready for work in the following interview and for the second treatment step can remain in the first supportive–psychotherapeutic setting based on supportive long-term psychotherapy.

TABLE 30.1
Key Words Concerning First Supportive Psychotherapeutic Step

1   Talking about himself
2   Psychoeducative measures
3   Correcting emotional experience
4   Subsequent education

The Second Interview and Treatment Step. The second interview and
treatment step, which includes one to three sessions, aims at encouraging the patient to experience personal feelings in somewhat
greater detail than has been the case up to now. Therapeutically
the following two processes prevail: offering and talking over the
patient's experience, examples which concern nonhypochondriac
contents on the one hand as well as the doctor's encouraging his
patient to reflect and to describe his genuine feelings in more
detail on the other hand. If the patient is able to attain these two
goals, both the perception and display of well-characterized feelings may become manifest in him or her. These feelings concern
experiences of object loss which the patient had suffered and not
mastered in the recent or distant past. If the patient is able to spontaneously present the initial situation of his object loss, then his
offer for contact to his therapist becomes manifest. However, if the
patient is not able to present spontaneously his initial situation,
then the therapist should consider the systematic elaboration of
the nonmastered object loss in the sense of an optimal interview
entry. The initial situation may be relatively new to the patient and
therefore both introspectively easily available and potentially,
vis-à-vis the therapist's interventions, better available for self-reflection. If the patient is able to see more clearly the topic of his object
loss, he may subjectively perceive more clearly the feelings related
to this object loss which he had suppressed up to that time, namely
particular separation anxieties as well as feelings of inner and outer
isolation. Furthermore, because of the patient's inability to master

TABLE 30.2
Key Words Concerning Second Supportive Psychotherapeutic Step

1   More differentiated object loss feelings experience
2   'New learning'
3   Understanding communication

his narcissistic insult due to object loss—at least on a preconscious level—the mobilization of frustration–aggressive tendencies, which were previously suppressed, is also evident. This frustration–aggressive mobilization as well as feelings of a narcissistic insult are clearly perceived by the therapist. But the patient is only able, little by little, to mention his frustration-aggression, particularly because of his (fantasied) anxiety that his therapist would not tolerate even discrete feelings of hostility on the part of his patient.

If the patient is able to deal increasingly with the topic of "nonmastered object loss" in a discriminating manner, then a form of "new learning" may take place, for now the decisive condition for a possible development of improved introspective and self-reflective abilities may be given. This realization is an expression of what was called "understanding-communication"[7] on the basis of an emotionally stable doctor–patient relationship (Table 30.2).

This "understanding-communication" could have "an important supportive function if it were experienced by the patient as suitable."[7] Success at this level of communication may provide evidence for the patient that his therapist will be able to help him.[1] The patient who has insufficient motivation for the work at the next interview and treatment level can remain on this second psychotherapy level in the sense of supportive long-term psychotherapy.

The Third Interview and Treatment Step. The associative anamnestic approach[8] prevails in the third interview and treatment step which includes two to three sessions on an average. This approach particularly helps the therapist to motivate his patient for conflict-oriented enlightenment psychotherapy. This approach which is called the clinical interview[8] includes an interview technique by which the therapist attempts to create a situation which also has psychodynamic elements. Gradually a transition from plain supportive psychotherapeutic techniques to psychodynamically oriented techniques takes place. Now the therapist deals with the patient's present conflict situation which may be particularly characterized by the causes and consequences of the nonmastered object loss. At the beginning of the associative anamnesis he brings in the so-called "key words" whose contents are of subjectively high relevance to the patient's personal experience. The patient reacts with suitable associations whereupon the associative anamnestic modality is continued by the therapist's renewed bringing in of similar suitable associations. By this procedure, which takes the form of a conducted associative route, highly important patient-oriented nodal points will finally become manifest. These nodal points come from the current chains of association which were associatively/ anamnestically produced by the doctor and his patient. If, based on these current chains of association, sufficiently enriched associative anamnestic material is available, we may make an effort to confront the patient cautiously with his needs and behavior modalities. The patient may then be able to express more differentiatedly the correlation between psychic and somatic troubles as well as psychodynamically relevant initial details concerning the beginning of his object loss.

These expressed fantasies may signal the beginning of constructive self-reflection and therefore the beginning of a conflict-oriented enlightenment. The achievement of these aims, which should include the patient's subjectively somewhat more competent conflict orientation, was defined by Wallerstein[3] on the basis of his psychoeducative view as "the patient's education to realistically oriented resolving of problems" (Table 30.3).

With regard to the psychosomatic patient, conflict-enlightenment psychotherapy is purposefully introduced on an inpatient basis and continued in an outpatient setting by procedures following psychoanalytically oriented techniques which can take place on an individual or a group basis.

TABLE 30.3
Key Words Concerning Third Supportive Psychotherapeutic Step

1   Associative anamnesis
2   Education to problem solving

Effectiveness Criteria. Starting from an empirically substantiated interdisciplinary project, Kunsebeck et al.[9] examined 29 Crohn patients who were both hospitalized in a gastroenterological inpatient ward and suffering from an acute disease course. These 29 Crohn patients were treated by supportive psychotherapy supplementary to the gastroenterological interventions in contrast to a Crohn patient group of the same size which did not receive additional psychotherapy. At the beginning and at the end of the inpatient gastroenterological therapy, as well as 4 and 13 months later, the variables "depression" and "anxiety" showed a significant decrease in the psychotherapeutically treated patients contrary to the control group. Furthermore, during follow-up 1 year after hospital discharge it could be proved that the psychotherapeutically treated patients showed significantly less medical inpatient treatment and less frequent consultation contacts with their general practitioners. Eight of the psychotherapeutically treated patients could be motivated to undergo conflict-enlightenment psychotherapy on an inpatient basis.

DISCUSSION

Our findings with regard to indication and patients' motivation for supportive psychotherapy correspond largely with the results of Schneider et al.,[10] who examined empirically the motivation for psychotherapy in four different patient groups. Starting from their group comparison the authors found that in psychoneurotic patients who were treated in a psychodynamically oriented psychiatric inpatient setting the most pronounced motivation for psychotherapy existed. No preceding indication concerning supportive psychotherapy existed in these patients, for usually they were directly motivated for psychodynamically oriented psychotherapy. In contrast to this, the second patient group, those with chronic (psycho-)somatic symptoms, who were hospitalized in a general psychosomatic clinic, showed distinctly lower values concerning their psychotherapy motivation. Initially these patients may be seen in a supportive psychotherapeutic setting, but as frequently the indication for psychotherapy in the sense of conflict-oriented enlightenment exists. With regard to the extent of motivation for psychotherapy, Schneider et al.[10] placed in the third position those patients with functional somatic disorders who were examined by primary care physicians. These patients showed strong fixations to somatic processes. Finally, the authors found the lowest psychotherapy motivation in a group of patients with urticaria, psoriasis, or neurodermatitis who were hospitalized in a dermatology clinic. The third and fourth patient groups are typical examples of indications for supportive psychotherapy as well as for the following three interview and treatment steps.

ADDITIONAL SYSTEMIC PSYCHOTHERAPEUTIC PROCEDURES

According to our extensive experience concerning systemic psychotherapeutic interviews in the sense of the "Mailänder Model" and the "New Heidelberg School," which can be arranged in addition to the described individual interview and treatment steps, may be suitable to stimulate the patient's motivation for conflict-enlightenment psychotherapy. This motivation for psychotherapy seems to particularly promote both the patient's interest concerning the initial individual interviews and the transition from the second to the third interview and treatment step. In our experience these effects can be explained as follows:

(1) The patient sees his family or partner relationship more clearly defined and outlined if not only the therapist but also family members or partners are present.

(2) Circular questioning, which is typical of systemic psycho-therapy, favors the production of additional information which may rarely be got in individual interviews, and from which all interview partners (including the therapist) can clearly profit.

(3) Systemic interventions seem to considerably reduce resistance with regard to psychosomatic medicine and psychotherapy, which is not infrequently evident in family members or partners of patients who are seen on the consultation–liaison service. This resistance, which may be carried over to the patient, stems from the key figures' marked fear that psychosomatic–psychotherapeutic approaches could lead to a loosening of family structures as well as direct or indirect feelings of guilt (e.g., that the older family members could have made mistakes concerning the education of both the patient and his siblings). Systemic psychotherapeutic interventions on the basis of sessions in the presence of the patient and family members or partners could therefore result in a weakening of the patient's and the family members' or partners' resistance to psychotherapy as well as preventing an interruption of therapy on the part of the patient.

THE GROUP OF CHRONICALLY MEDICALLY ILL PATIENTS

PSYCHODYNAMIC PROCESSES

Typical initial situations, particularly on the basis of nonmastered object loss, may precede both the disease manifestation and relapse in chronically medically ill patients. These patients can be characterized by typical psychic adaptation processes by which they should be able to tolerate their disease and to deal with it in inter-human relationships. Patients' psychic decompensations should be prevented in this way.

The subjective perception of a chronic physical disease is experienced by the patient as a secondary marked object loss, the loss of his own somatic functions. The somatic processes are perceived both in respect to subjectively threatening dysfunctions and as no longer feeling in command. Subsequently, the patient reacts with an emotional shock by which both the considerable insult to his narcissistic tonus and marked dependency wishes are determined. Strong (separation) anxiety (even fear of death) and/or strong emotional exhaustion become evident. Both the anxieties and the emotional exhaustion represent adaptively oriented modalities in the sense of outwardly oriented signals by which doctors', nurses', and relatives' medical and psychic help should be mobilized as soon as possible. Now the patient concentrates upon his diseased organ in the sense of a medically oriented self-concern (secondary hypochondria). From an adaptive view this secondary hypochondria represents a manner of fearful depression-oriented self-reflection which particularly includes details of the traumatically experienced disease process. Furthermore this secondary hypochondria finds its expression not only in the patients' frequently unending "disease dialogues" but also in disease dialogues between the patient and his family members or/and partners. Additional object relationships may be mobilized in these two dialogical ways. In the view of the patient these continuously fantasized secondary hypochondriac contents and their subsequent verbal abreaction represent, at least transiently, a considerable psychic relief. Finally, the chronically medically ill patients show a continuous idea which is characteristic of their state: Why am *I* so ill and not others? As a consequence of this continuously impairing idea, a strong conglomeration of secondary frustration–aggressive thoughts and feelings becomes evident on the patient's preconscious level. Further sources of these frustration–aggressive tendencies are feelings of disappointment as a consequence of object loss as well as the regular frustrations in medical and/or family- or partner-related everyday life unavoidable in chronically medically ill patients. For the purpose of his own psychic relief, these secondary frustration–aggressive tendencies must at least partially be suppressed by the patient. The patient fears that direct expression of his frustration–aggression could lead to the emotional retreat of both doctors and nurses group as well as family members or partners.

TABLE 30.4
Psychodynamic Key Words in Chronically Medically Ill Patients

1 Object loss in own somatic functions
2 Secondary hypochondria
3 Secondary frustration-aggression
4 Denial work

Therefore the suppression of these frustration–aggressive tendencies is the most important determinant with regard to the depressive feelings and anxieties which represent leading psychic symptoms of the chronically medically ill patient (Table 30.4).

A further relevant psychodynamic process in medically ill patients is denial work. Here we differentiate between three variants in close connection with the patient's psychic adaptation modalities. First the realistically adapted denial work affords the patient so much self-reflecting freedom that he may sufficiently perceive both the relevance of the doctor–patient or patient–family relationship as well as the absolute necessity of treatment programs. In contrast to this realistically adapted denial the too weakly developed denial work includes, in the patient's experience, the subjective overestimation of both the seriousness of the disease and the stress of treatment. Now complaining and accusing modalities as well as a restricted compliance ability prevail in the patient. Third, the too strongly developed denial includes both marked suppression of relevant perceptions concerning disease experience and treatment understanding, as well as restriction of compliance ability.

PSYCHOTHERAPY

Indications. The indication for supportive psychotherapy exists particularly when the denial work does not function in a realistically adapted manner. Therefore psychic adaptation processes may be labilized. Then the doctors and nurses as well as the family- and/or partner or related key figures experience themselves frequently as psychically overburdened and may therefore fail in their function as supportively effective key figures. Denial work that is either too weak or too strong is particularly determined by object loss. Somatic crisis situations lead to an increase in the experience of object loss in the patient's own somatic function. Moreover, object loss may be determined by narcissistic insults, particularly on the basis of subjectively and objectively frustrating interventions on the part of the doctors and nurses and/or the family members or the partners.

Techniques. The supportive psychotherapeutic steps in chronically medically ill patients concern initially the building up of an oral–narcissistic object relationship. Further intervention techniques deal with the patient's secondary frustration–aggression and his present conflict situation.

(1) *Dealing with the secondary frustration–aggression.* The repeated highlighting of frustration–aggression by the therapist is mainly aimed at making the patient aware of the accompanying subjectively distressing contents. Now the therapist makes the central theme vis-à-vis the patient his continuing question: "Why am I ill and not the others?" Thus the patient is offered ample opportunity to psychically relieve and express himself. But an interpretative dealing with this topic should not take place yet, for the patient's frustration-tolerance is not sufficient for this purpose. This noninterpretative dialogue can be tolerated by the patient only if an emotionally firm relationship exists with his therapist.

(2) *Dealing with the present conflict situation.* Dealing with conflict situations starts from the experience that acute or long-lasting conflicts may considerably strain chronically medically ill patients. But frequently these patients are not able to spontaneously name the contents of their conflict. More often the patients may only verbalize these conflicts if therapist and/or emphatically involved family members or partners are present. The selective structuring of the conflict-oriented themes has a particular function in this connection. If the therapist is able to select the themes which may be tolerated by the patient then a common problem-oriented dialogue can be set in motion, but without more intensive

confrontation or even interpretative dealing with the conflict top-ics. These latter procedures are not (yet?) indicated because of the patient's insufficient psychic frustration-tolerance. More often a superficial explanation of the conflicts is indicated.

In our clinicopsychosomatic experience dealing with frustration–aggression and conflict situations represents the most effective supportive psychotherapeutic intervention with regard to chroni-cally medically ill patients.

Psychotherapeutic Effects. The supportive psychotherapeutic approach may be experienced by the chronically medically ill patient as anxiety-resolving, depression-alleviating, and stabilizing concern-ing his narcissistic tonus. Furthermore reality-adapted denial work is favored. Finally the patients may show traits of an increased abil-ity for relationship as a consequence of the narcissistic gratifica-tion which is mediated by the doctor.

ADDITIONAL SYSTEMIC PSYCHOTHERAPEUTIC PROCEDURES

Systemic psychotherapeutic approaches which can be arranged in addition to individual psychotherapy in the chronically medically ill patient concern the following indications:

(1) The possibility of gaining supplementary productive infor-mation.

(2) The necessity of a decrease in intensity concerning symbi-otic functions of family members or partners with regard to the patient. The too intensive symbiotic fusions which may exist be-tween the patient and his key figures, particularly as a consequence of a family member's or partner's being affected, lead to a too in-tensive proximity between these and the patient. As a consequence the function of the key figures as supportive presence can be con-siderably impaired because of the reduction of their self-autonomy. Due to this intensely close symbiotic fusion the systemic psycho-therapeutic approach includes the therapist's aim to make pos-sible a new emotional equilibrium with regard to the polarities of proximity and distance vis-à-vis the patient on the one hand and the family members or partners on the other hand.

(3) Approach in the sense of problem solving. This well-aimed approach is indicated if the patient is interested in addressing emotionally stressful topics which the family members or partners tend to negate or to minimize.

(4) Individual systemic psychotherapy of the key figures. If the family members and/or partners are not able to tolerate the emotional confrontation with the patient, the individual systemic psychotherapeutic approach (in the sense of "family therapy without family") is indicated for the key figure(s).

Conclusion Concerning the Rating of Supportive and Systemic Psychotherapy in the Scope of Consultation–Liaison Activities

With regard to the above-described psychosomatic and chronically medically ill patients we lay particular emphasis on systemic-psychotherapeutic interventions supplementary to individual supportive psychotherapeutic procedures. On the one hand, universal clinicopsychosomatic relevance is too rarely attached to the organizational structure of consultation–liaison services. On the other hand, our empirical findings based on our own wide-ranging examination of 274 Hannover consultation–liaison patients (including catamnestic findings) speak unequivocally for the superiority of the combination of individual supportive psychotherapy and additional systemic interventions in comparison to supportive psychotherapy alone.[4]

References

1. Luborsky L. *Principles of Psychoanalytic Psychotherapy.* New York: Basic Books; 1984.

2. Kernberg O, Burstein E, Coyne L, Applebaum A, Horowitz L, Voth H. Psychotherapy and Psychoanalysis: Final report of the Menninger Foundation's psychotherapy research project. *Bull Menninger Clinic.* 1972;36:1–275.

3. Wallerstein R. *Forty-Two Lives in Treatment.* New York: Guilford;1986.

4. Freyberger H, Brinker M. Die supportiv-psychotherapeutische Arbeitsbeziehung bei psychosomatischen Patienten und chronisch körperlich Kranken. In: Meyer AE, Strauss B, eds. *Psychoanalytische Psychosomatik.* Stuttgart, Germany: Schattauer. In press.

5. Winnicott DW. *The Maturational Processes and the Facilitating Environment.* London: Hogarth Press;1965.

6. Alexander F. *Psychosomatic Medicine.* Berlin: Gruyter;1971.

7. Fürstenau P. *Entwicklungsförderung durch Therapie (Grundlagen psychoanalytisch-systemischer Psychotherapie).* Münich, Germany: Pfeiffer;1992.

8. Deutsch F. Training in psychosomatic medicine. In: Jores A, Stokvis B, Freyberger H, Stunkard A, eds. *Training in Psychosomatic Medicine.* Adv. Psychosom. Med. Basel, Switzerland: Karger;1964:4:35–46.

9. Kunsebeck HW, Lempa W, Freyberger H: Kurz- und Langzeiteffekte ergänzender Psychotherapie bei Patienten mit Morbus Crohn. In: Lamprecht F, ed. *Spezialisierung und Integration in Psychosomatik und Psychotherapie.* Heidelberg, Germany: Springer;1987: pp 253–262.

10. Schneider W, Beisenherz B, Freyberger HJ. Therapy expectation in different groups of patients with chronic diseases. *Psychother Psychosom.* 1990;54:1–7.

Chapter 31
Inpatient and Ward Psychosomatic Psychotherapy: Concepts, Effectiveness, and Curative Factors

BERNHARD STRAUSS, MANUELA BURGMEIER-LOHSE

THEORETICAL FRAMEWORK

Inpatient and ward psychosomatic psychotherapy can be defined as the application of various *defined psychological interventions,* planned with the consent of the patient, the therapeutic institution, and the patient's reference group, in a *specifically organized clinical setting to treat a psychosomatic, neurotic, or personality disorder in an intensive manner* with the aim of improving or healing it.[1]

Although this definition excludes several other psychotherapeutic approaches in a hospital (such as psychotherapy for somatic and psychiatric patients), it includes the most important features of inpatient psychotherapy. Whilst other authors use slightly different models,[2, 3] this definition takes into account the particular characteristics which distinguish inpatient settings from outpatient psychotherapy.

INPATIENT AND WARD PSYCHOSOMATIC PSYCHOTHERAPY
AS PART OF THE CARE SYSTEM: THE SITUATION IN GERMANY

Compared with other countries, the Federal Republic of Germany has a very large number of beds in psychotherapeutic units. Schepank[1] reports that there are more beds in special units for inpatient psychosomatics and psychotherapy in Germany than in the whole rest of the world put together. Recent estimates indicate that there are more than a hundred units or hospitals offering inpatient psychosomatic psychotherapy, comprising approximately 9000 beds, including some for adolescents.[4] This surprisingly high total, nevertheless, corresponds to a mere 0.7% of *all* hospital beds in Germany.[5] Out of 104 units listed in a survey of psychotherapy/psychosomatic units by Neun,[4] 75 are mainly psychodynamically oriented, 11 mainly behavioral, and a further 18 work along systemic or other lines.

This unique situation does not mean that Germans are particularly prone to psychosomatic or psychoneurotic disorders, or that there is a lack of outpatient psychotherapists. Social circumstances and in particular historical reasons have made inpatient psychotherapy an important element in the psychotherapeutic care system.[1]

Schepank[1] mentions the following social and cultural aspects which have led to the current situation: (1) relatively widespread prosperity; (2) the health insurance scheme; (3) a long tradition of psychoanalytically oriented theory and practice; (4) the parallel development of psychoanalysis alongside traditional psychiatric care systems; (5) the democratic political system; and (6) in contrast to other wealthy Western countries a clear division between church and state which has made it possible to set up inpatient units with the support of the general public.

The historical aspects of inpatient and ward psychosomatic psychotherapy have been extensively reviewed by Senf[2] and Schepank.[1] Their roots reach back to the 1920s. One of the most important steps was the foundation by Simmel[6] of a hospital in Berlin offering psychoanalytic treatment, a move which helped to establish inpatient psychotherapy in Germany. After he emigrated, Simmel, whose ideas on organizing and running an inpatient psychotherapy unit still remain valid, inspired the foundation of similar institutions in the United States, for instance the Menninger Clinic in Topeka.[2] Nowadays there are treatment programs to be found in several American hospitals providing day treatment approaches similar to the inpatient and ward psychosomatic psychotherapy offered in Germany.[7] Although Simmel's hospital only survived for a few years (like other hospitals with a psychotherapeutic bias, such as Groddeck's sanatorium in Baden-Baden), the idea of inpatient psychotherapy was taken up again after the Second World War, resulting in several hospitals which offered different forms of treatment (see below) ranging from pure psychoanalysis to psychoanalytically oriented psychosomatic treatment and internal-psychosomatic medical units. Such figures as Wiedemann, Schwidder, Kühnel, Jores, Curtius, and Mitscherlich are closely linked with the institutionalization of inpatient psychotherapy in Germany during the postwar period. At the beginning of the 1960s many hospitals which had offered "cures" (i.e., health spas) were converted into rehabilitation clinics with a psychotherapeutic and/or psychosomatic focus, a change encouraged by the health insurance companies who realized that providing psychosomatic care reduced their costs. A government survey of all the psychosocial care systems in Germany made between 1970 and 1975 (the Psychiatry Enquete), coupled with general acknowledgment that neuroses and psychosomatic disturbances are illnesses to be treated within the general health insurance system, and the inclusion of psychotherapy and psychosomatics as a standard part of the curriculum for medical students, have all contributed to the current state of inpatient psychotherapy and psychosomatics in Germany.

This brief summary of the history of inpatient psychotherapy highlights the complexity of the factors favoring the development of this kind of psychotherapeutic care. Accordingly, the past years have seen the growth of a variety of models for inpatient care of psychosomatic disorders, accompanied by a lively discussion on the theories underlying such treatment.

As far as organization is concerned, there are three distinct types of inpatient and ward psychosomatic psychotherapy currently available:

(1) Psychosomatic/psychotherapeutic wards in university hospitals (some focusing on internal medicine, others on psychoanalysis and psychotherapy). They often have very limited resources for inpatient treatment since the number of beds is very restricted.

(2) Hospitals for psychosomatics or psychotherapy (most of them private or financed by the insurance companies). They can usually admit more patients (50–300 beds) and offer a broader range of treatment and therapies. Psychosomatically oriented rehabilitation is one of their strong points; as well as reintegrating chronically ill patients into their families and professions again they aim at enhancing their patients' lives by increasing their self-confidence and improving their skills, which is an effective preventive measure against relapse.

(3) Psychosomatic units within general hospitals. They are usually equipped with 5 to 40 beds, and their advantage lies in cooperating with other wards. They also offer consultation and liaison services.

To illustrate how one such internal-psychosomatic model works, here is a brief description of the Ulm unit set up by Köhle et al.[8] According to the classical interpretation of psychosomatic disease,[9] later developed by von Uexküll,[10] every illness consists of somatic, psychical and social aspects. Köhle et al.[8] put this concept into practice in the form of an "internal–psychosomatic ward." Treatment is centered around two focal points, the relationship between nurse and patient on the one hand and the relationship between the patient and the intern and/or psychosomatic physician on the other. The doctor's visit functions as a therapeutic setting in which patient and doctor can talk about the patient's adaptability and defense mechanisms, and where supportive psychotherapeutic techniques can be brought into play. The nurses themselves also visit the patients, which means that they too have an active and independent therapeutic function. It is important that the patient has a working relationship with both nurses and doctor, as this encourages his or her coping abilities. Regular supervision in the form of Balint groups for both doctors and nurses is available.

Despite a tremendous increase in the number of behaviorally oriented psychosomatic clinics practicing behavioral medicine,[11] most hospitals still work along psychoanalytical and psychodynamic lines, a fact which has had a considerable impact on our thinking.

Theoretical Ideas on Inpatient Psychotherapy

Initially psychotherapy in hospital was divided into two schools of thought: (1) anthropological medicine, including psychotherapeutic approaches and techniques used in conjunction with traditional internal, neurological, psychiatric, or other forms of treatment, and (2) psychoanalysis, which during the 1960s was influenced and extended by the concept of a "therapeutic community" and group therapy. The aim in those days was to establish independent psychosomatic or psychotherapeutic wards or whole hospitals with specialized staff providing a therapeutic environment.

Anthropological medicine, introduced by Victor von Weizsäcker,[9] was based on the premise that psychotherapists and hospital staff cooperate closely with one another, giving more priority to "a mutual understanding between patient and doctor than to any single-handed activity on the doctor's part, and preferring to open up new horizons by including biographical and social background information to simply concentrating on the patient's physical state"[12] (p. 31). Weizsäcker's ideas represented a fundamental turnaround in medical thinking, challenging the apparently self-evident conclusions drawn by scientific medicine.

Ernst Simmel[6] was the first to formulate and put into practice a new and independent form of inpatient psychoanalytic therapy. He realized that for many patients the protective framework of the hospital was vital, especially for those who could not be given psychoanalysis as outpatients. Nowadays these patients would be diagnosed as having an ego structure defect/disorder. They are overtaxed by the psychoanalytic rules, such as abstinence, free association, and transference, and by being admitted to the hospital they are freed from the pathological relationships in their daily lives. Simmel[6] grasped that offering "multiple transferences" in in-patient psychotherapy could be therapeutically effective and enhance the effect of a single analysis. These ideas were extended to include the concept therapeutic community. This originated in the so-called Northfield experiment where Bion[13] treated soldiers suffering from anxiety neuroses in group settings because he lacked the funds to treat them singly. The idea was taken up by Main[14]; in the Cassell Hospital near London he ran therapeutic communities on the following lines: (1) the hospital is a therapeutic field where the therapeutic process is essentially influenced by the group situation, and (2) therapy is undertaken by a group of therapeutic employees who build up and maintain the therapeutic field by close cooperation and coordinated therapeutic measures; the patients' potential is enhanced since they themselves take part in the therapeutic process in an active and personally responsible way. These guidelines link the individual perspective, interpreted along psychoanalytic lines, with the wider social context, an approach which in the 1980s became the integrative model for inpatient psychotherapy.

From the very start it proved difficult to integrate psychoanalytic therapy into hospital life since essential rules such as anonymity, neutrality, and abstinence were contradicted by the demands of the day-to-day routine. It looked as though the only role the hospital played was providing shelter to assist individual analyses. This changed at the beginning of the 1970s with the realization that every coworker in a ward actually takes part and plays a role in the therapeutic process. The whole clinical field has to be organized in such a way that different kinds of treatment, such as analytic group therapy, concentrative movement therapy, and creative therapy—to name only a few—are regarded as equally worthwhile. The aim is to adapt psychoanalytic methods to the special needs of patients with severe neurotic or psychosomatic disorders instead of trying and failing to adapt them to the hospital's routine.

Generally speaking there are three main approaches to inpatient psychoanalytic psychotherapy: quasi-outpatient therapy, bipolar therapy, and integrative therapy.

Quasi-outpatient therapy makes a clear distinction between therapeutic sessions and the inpatient field, which means that therapy is designed along the lines used for outpatients and the ward only has a neutral protective function ("hotel"). One example for this kind of hotel hospital was the private hospital Chestnut Lodge in the United States.[15]

The bipolar approach distinguishes between "therapeutic space" and "real-life space." Enke[16] suggests centering the therapeutic process in the group therapy sessions and building up a so-called house group to work on the social problems which arise from the patients living together. This means that therapeutic work and social reality are kept formally separate but the therapeutic space is linked to the social reality of life in the ward since the therapist is kept informed about both spaces.[17]

As mentioned above, the idea of a therapeutic community provides a transition to an integrated model, where the entire clinical field is seen as a therapeutic space. Every relationship between the patient and others on the ward is used for therapeutical purposes, every coworker, whether doctor, therapist, or nursing staff, passes on and receives information, so that the dualism between therapeutic space and real-life space ceases to exist, and the patient is offered multiple transferences.[18]

One such integrative treatment model is used in the clinic for psychotherapy and psychosomatics at the Kiel University Hospital; here is a brief description of it. The inpatient department can accommodate a maximum of eight patients who usually live at close quarters with one another for 6 to 7 months, forming a slow open group. The patients are neurotic persons too disturbed to be treated as outpatients, persons with narcissistic and borderline personality disorders, and persons with psychosomatic symptoms.

Treatment for this group consists of several integrated activities such as creative therapy, dance therapy, painting, and sports, all on a group level, including a psychoanalytically oriented 90-minute group therapy five times a week (Table 31.1). In line with the hypothesis that a psychotherapeutic ward acts as a "dynamic unit," staff all exchange information daily on every patient and all therapeutic activities. In addition the group therapist and the nursing staff have separate external supervision once a week.

TABLE 31.1
Weekly Plan of Therapeutic Activities

Time	Monday	Tuesday	Wednesday	Thursday	Friday
7.30–8.00	Sports	Sports		Sports	Sports
9.00–10.30	*Group therapy*	*Group therapy*	*Group therapy*	*Group therapy*	*Group therapy*
11.30–13.15			Creative therapy		
15.00–16.30	Painting	Group activity		*Dance therapy*	Discussion group with team
17.00–19.00	Creative therapy	Creative therapy		Creative therapy	Creative therapy
From 19.30	Time for group activities in- and outside the ward				

Practical Issues and Research Results

Indication for Inpatient Psychosomatic Treatment

Patients with psychosomatic disorders often have a long career as patients behind them before they finally obtain adequate treatment. Several large-scale studies have confirmed that between 30 and 60% of all patients who regularly visit general practitioners or specialists of various kinds are suffering from neurotic or psychosomatic disorders.[19] As Stuhr and Haag[20] have recently shown, the same applies to a similar proportion of patients undergoing treatment in general hospitals. On average between 5 and 8 years elapse between the appearance of the first symptoms and the beginning of adequate treatment. It is very likely that in the meantime the disorder has become chronic, often fostered by purely somatic treatment (Zielke and Mark[19] describe this as "iatrogenic chronification"). These data indicate how important it is for patients with psychosomatic disorders to be offered proper treatment, including the forms of treatment offered on psychotherapy units.

More specifically, more clarity is needed on the indication for hospitalizing such patients. Looked at from a psychoanalytical point of view, the approach so far in inpatient psychotherapy has focused on object relations (as described by Kernberg[21]) rather than on psychodynamics. In the United States these concepts have been applied in the long-term treatment of patients with borderline personality disorders.[7, 21, 22] This group of patients—similar to those suffering from psychosomatic disorders—find it difficult to establish a bond with the therapist, and some have a history of dropping out of outpatient treatment. Poor introspective ability, or lack of psychological mindedness, problems in communicating and verbalizing emotions, and difficulties in getting in contact with their inner needs, affective states, anxieties, and feelings of well-being,[2] all features which are supposed to be typical for patients with psychosomatic disorders, are said to indicate inpatient treatment. Similarly, patients with structural ego disorders are commonly referred to inpatient wards on the assumption that an outpatient setting would put too much strain on them and their therapists. In short, the characteristics of the problematic patient are thought to be an indication for inpatient treatment.

So far, empirical investigations have not shown that these patients benefit in a specific way from integrated inpatient treatment. In a study of our own, designed to weigh the advantages and disadvantages of this setting, all the patients treated within a 2-year period were carefully examined on admission and discharge using several questionnaires and an interview. It turned out that those who benefited most from 6 months of inpatient treatment (Strauss et al., unpubl. data) were those with fairly pronounced somatic symptoms (measured on the SCL 90R) on admission, a marked tendency to rationalize their condition (gauged on a modified version of the Defense Mechanism Inventory), and relatively poor autonomy in the initial interview (rated according to the Vanderbilt scales for psychotherapy[23]).

As Senf[2] points out, no inpatient psychotherapy ward would be able to endure an undiluted mixture of this kind of patients, especially as they tend to reveal their pathological sides and become highly labile when they find themselves in such a regression-provoking setting as an inpatient ward. In practice, patients with psychosomatic disturbances (belonging to the ICD-10 categories F45 and F54), and personality and eating disorders (ICD-10 F60/F50) are usually treated in conjunction with neurotic patients (ICD-10 F40–44/48) who have slightly more mature personalities. Nevertheless, at least in psychosomatic units which are not attached to university hospitals, the proportion of patients suffering from psychosomatic (or somatopsychic) disorders approaches 50 to 60%. A lot of neurotic patients also show symptoms of further psychophysiological disorders.[5]

The general indications for inpatient psychotherapy have been described by Heigl,[24] recommending hospital treatment for (1) patients who for somatic or psychiatric reasons need the permanent support and control offered by a clinic; (2) those who need the shelter of the hospital (for their own safety or that of their relatives); (3) patients who may benefit from the set timetable of psychotherapy within a ward as opposed to an outpatient setting; (4) patients who need the variety of psychotherapeutic offers available in a hospital; (5) those who may benefit from the suggestive atmosphere of a psychosomatic/therapeutic ward which can motivate patients with organic fixations to join in psychotherapy; and (6) those who otherwise cannot find a therapist in their home town (geographical indication[25]) or cannot afford outpatient treatment[24] (pp. 225ff).

Attempts to describe the characteristics of patients treated in psychosomatic inpatient wards in a systematic way are still in their infancy. One project is under way in Germany to set up a common documentation system for inpatient psychosomatics and psychotherapy (Schors et al., unpubl. data). Recently, von Rad[25] described some of the traits of inpatients being treated in a psychosomatic ward attached to a general hospital. His findings reveal that this clientele is highly selected compared with other inpatient populations: out of a total of more than 700 patients treated in this ward, two-thirds were female, patients aged over 60 were the exception, two-thirds of all the patients were unable to work at the time of admission, and approximately 70% belonged to the middle classes. Von Rad[25] concluded from these data that "inpatient psychosomatics has to open up its therapeutic boundaries in the future," especially to male patients, older patients, the chronically ill, and those from lower class backgrounds. A similar report was made by Schmidt[26] on patients in a private psychosomatic rehabilitation clinic. Sixty percent were diagnosed as neurotic, 20% were suffering from psychosomatic disorders, and a further 10% from functional disorders. The total sample was very like von Rad's[25]: two-thirds were female, average age was between 41 and 50 years, and 90% were in a psychosomatic clinic for the first time, although more than 50% of them had had psychiatric care before. Schmidt[26] concluded that a hospital "marks a different point in the psychotherapeutic care system than any outpatient institution."

RESEARCH RESULTS

As already mentioned, various strands in the history of inpatient psychotherapy have resulted in a variety of theories and settings; there is no standard form of treatment. This may be one of the reasons why empirical research has so far steered clear of inpatient treatment. Few authors have attempted to formulate the aims such research might have. Colson et al.[27] discussed three possible strategies:

(1) An organizational perspective on hospital treatment: "A shot-gun approach in which many treatment and setting characteristics are measured—for example the degree of organization on the ward . . .";

(2) An objective dose approach describing or quantifying in a "relatively objective manner a few conventional treatment variables, such as the length of inpatient stay, types of medication used, or number of hours the patients are in the various kinds of treatment meetings," and

(3) A subjective dose approach:

These are assessments designed to capture the treaters' or patients' experience of treatment or the treatment setting as in assessments of the ward atmosphere. Such measures tend to bypass those dimensions of treatment that are the primary focus of hospital treaters—for example protective or restrictive group structure, the patients' participation in group or individual modalities, medication, involvement in a variety of activities in the milieu[27] (pp. 281–282).

The few efforts made so far to look into inpatient settings in a systematic way have used this last approach, focusing on the effects and effectiveness of different kinds of treatment.

Effects and Effectiveness of Inpatient and Ward Psychosomatic Psychotherapy. Most investigations, most of them *uncontrolled* studies, so far have looked into how the patients and staff assess treatment as a whole, or compared their reactions of admission, on dismissal, and at follow-up. Janssen[28] has summarized the results of all these studies. Senf[29] concluded from more than 30 investigations that roughly three-quarters of the patients report improvements after inpatient treatment. This is supported by two large-scale studies carried out recently in Germany, the "Heidelberg follow-up project"[29, 30] and the "Magic Mountain Study."[26, 31] Schmidt[26] also reported that 60% of all the patients treated in a psychosomatic hospital were either satisfied or very satisfied with the results of their treatment, and that at follow-up these proved to be stable, as confirmed by standardized questionnaires on personality traits. The Heidelberg study showed that even patients with structural ego disturbances showed an improvement in their symptoms and related changes in psychosocial variables (70%) approximating those in patients without such deficits (80%).[2]

In addition to these findings from questionnaires, there is an increasing amount of evidence that inpatient psychotherapy has a positive effect on more objective variables, such as the ability to work, highly relevant to health insurance companies anxious to reduce the costs of psychological disorders.

Lamprecht,[5] for instance, reported that, although 95% of the patients in his clinic had a history of psychological problems lasting longer than 5 years, the following variables showed that treatment had had a positive effect: at follow-up visits to doctors were down by 20%, sick leave by 47%, stays in hospital by up to 59%, and 64% reported much reduced medication. Similarly, Zielke and Mark[19] reported that 78.7% of patients who previously had been unable to work were able to do so after inpatient treatment in a behaviorally-oriented hospital.

Predicting the Outcome of Treatment. Compared with outpatient psychotherapy, research into the outcome of hospital psychotherapy is meager. The figures available suggest that the degree of chronification diminishes the effects of inpatient psychotherapy,[29] and that the patient's motivation has an effect on the outcome.[32]

The Magic Moutain Study, a large-scale investigation into the effects of treatment in a private psychosomatic hospital, has shown that the long-term effects of treatment can be negatively predicted by the number of psychological problems the patient has when admitted, how long his or her main symptoms have persisted, how often he or she has had psychiatric care, the type of employment involved, and whether the patient is capable of working.

Studies on the Process in Inpatient Psychotherapy. In many inpatient settings, group psychotherapy is a central factor in the treatment program, and in some, like that described above, it is the basic constituent. The reasons are sometimes economic ones, but there is also strong evidence that the long-term effects of inpatient treatment are even better if group therapy is included.[33, 34] Some authors[2] assume that all inpatient psychotherapy is a type of group therapy, since the process in the ward is always influenced by the whole group of patients and the therapeutic team. It is, therefore, not surprising that among the studies into the relation between process and outcome many have focused on group psychotherapy.

A summary of their results was recently presented by Strauss,[35] showing that the therapeutic factors[36] in an inpatient setting do not differ from those in an outpatient group, at least if one takes the patients' answers as criteria. Catharsis, insight, interpersonal learning, and experiencing group cohesion are the most significant factors in both settings. Looking at the relation between treatment and outcome, the following variables have been shown to be positive predictors of success in inpatient group therapy: a high degree of emotional relatedness to the group, positive experiences within the group, social integration, affective discomfort, activity and resonance, recapitulation of family experiences, increasing openness to disagreements, and more realistic attitudes.

One basic assumption behind inpatient psychotherapy for psychosomatic disorders is that this setting offers a convenient combination of various therapeutic measures in a suitably organized institution, making it possible to treat patients who could not be given outpatient treatment or if so with little hope of success. As mentioned above, most inpatient programs consist of a mixture of interventions on an interpretative, supportive, and nonverbal level. The subjective importance of the nonverbal aspect has been demonstrated by several authors. Kordy and Schöneberg,[37] for instance, reported that in the Heidelberg follow-up the patients regarded "concentrative movement therapy" as just as important as verbal (i.e., individual and group) psychotherapy. Table 31.2 shows the order in which inpatients in the therapy program in Kiel graded the single components. It also shows how important the therapeutic community and nonverbal treatment were felt to be. Research into this aspect is sparse mainly because new methods are required to measure the effects.

TABLE 31.2
Rank Order of the Single Treatment Elements
(Patients' Evaluation, Kiel University Hospital)

---

1 Therapeutic community
2 Group psychotherapy
3 Talking with other patients
4 Dance therapy
5 Talking with nurses
6 Individual sessions (admission/dismissal)
7 Creative therapy
8 Painting
9 Other group activities
10 Sports

Carl et al.[38] tried to compare the dynamics of verbal analytical group treatment and concentrative movement therapy, using qualitative methods. They showed that the two forms of treatment are related in terms of thematic continuity and a "complementary of persons and expressions." Interestingly, some psychodynamic processes appeared earlier in the nonverbal treatment than in the verbal group therapy.

The question whether there is any relation between specific elements in a setting and the outcome of treatment has been systematically investigated by Kordy and Schöneberg.[37] Put briefly, they discovered that patients apparently choose those components on the "menu" which they find individually relevant to their current development. It was assumed that the choice available might be particularly important for the patients' benefit, but in fact the pre–post success rates were hardly linked to specific components. Inpatient psychotherapy only failed if the patient did not find any of the components helpful. Similarly, Bräutigam et al.[39] have shown that the subjective importance of the therapeutic factors "regression," "new insights," and "positive interpersonal experiences," could not predict the patients' satisfaction with treatment. Only those patients who did not rate any of these three factors as helpful were less satisfied with treatment than the rest of the sample.

Towards a Theory of Inpatient
Psychosomatic Psychotherapy

As mentioned above, inpatient and ward psychotherapy for psychosomatic patients has become a significant part of the care system, at least in Germany. Despite its practical relevance, however, its theoretical foundations are still shaky.[40] The most widespread assumption in discussions on this form of treatment is that it is convenient for "problematic patients."[2, 28] This attitude was already outlined by Groddeck[41] who founded a psychoanalytic hospital for somatically ill patients in Baden-Baden in the 1920s; in a letter to Freud he writes: "I have a sanatorium accommodating people who would not recover elsewhere. Sometimes I succeed with this difficult treatment, sometimes I don't" (translated by the authors).

To be able to pinpoint the reasons why some patients benefit from this setting and others do not, we need more research. Looking at the data available so far, including our results in Kiel, several specific factors can be *tentatively* identified which contribute to the success of inpatient psychotherapy for patients suffering from psychosomatic, neurotic or personality disorders:

(1) Undoubtedly time is one important factor. Several studies, including the Heidelberg follow-up project, have confirmed that the duration of a therapy predicts the outcome especially in patients suffering from psychosomatic and personality disorders.[42]

(2) It is well known that nonverbal techniques augmenting verbal psychotherapy are especially important for patients who tend to somatize. In a study of our own (Strauss and Burgmeier-Lohse, unpubl. data), this was confirmed by the observation that the patients who benefited most rated the nonverbal, body-oriented elements of treatment more highly than the other patients did.

(3) Whilst other authors have confirmed that nonverbal forms of treatment play an important part, the success or failure of the whole therapy program depends on other factors as well. As the results of Kordy and Schöneberg[37] indicate, one important feature of successful treatment is a broad range of components, a big "menu" for the patients to choose from.

(4) The therapeutic community, fostered by the way the ward is organized, the length of stay, and the therapy program itself, offering the patients a reliable structure and a chance to act out their difficulties, gains considerable importance; this was reflected in our own study by the high rating the satisfied patients gave to it. Everyday life on the ward provides a milieu where patients can make all kinds of interpersonal experience with one another and the staff which are much more intense than in short-term or out-patient therapy. In fact, our study showed that a high proportion of the quarrels and misunderstandings discussed in the verbal group sessions were triggered by the patients' problems in dealing with one another, and represented a repetition of experiences they had gone through with members of their family or other significant people.

Our sample rated this factor—working through family relationships—more highly than groups in other settings have done. In fact, the more and less "successful" patients could be distinguished by how highly they rated this factor. Allied factors were the perception that they could verbalize their problems and act as they chose within the group even if the others did not approve, and that the group therapist brought to light important and painful topics with his or her interventions. These factors, reflecting insight, conscious experience of recurrent maladaptive interpersonal behaviors, and the permissiveness of the group, seem to enable the patients to reappraise their introjections.

(5) Our results suggest that patients who benefited more were able to make use of other factors provided by the setting, such as group cohesion and so on, but that they managed to make their most important learning steps independently of the atmosphere on the ward or the degree of group cohesion.

Ratings of the individual patients' interactions during selected group sessions using the Structural Analysis of Social Behavior (SASB),[43] also showed that the more successful patients were able to dissociate themselves from the group during the final phase of treatment, when they tend to let their thoughts wander "outside." These interaction patterns were apparently acceptable to the group, for the patient in question was hardly drawn into conversation during these sessions despite being rated as highly influential in a sociogram (Strauss and Burgmeier-Lohse, in preparation).

(6) All in all, we have reason to conclude that the treatment program in an inpatient setting provides something one could call a framework for gaining autonomy. The explicit rules in the patients' community and the implicit rules in psychotherapy offer a context in which the patients are invited to develop their resources and insights by discovering their potential and their limits.

These factors highlight the specific qualities of inpatient psychotherapy for psychosomatic patients, showing that it is well suited to be part of the general mental health care system as well as a good training ground for therapists and a fruitful field for research into what really happens in psychotherapy.

REFERENCES

1. Schepank H. Die stationäre Psychotherapie in der Bundesrepublik Deutschland. In: Schepank H, Tress W, eds. *Die stationäre Psychotherapie und ihr Rahmen.* Heidelberg, Germany: Springer;1987: pp 13–38.
2. Senf W. Theorie der stationären Psychotherapie. In: Becker H, Senf W, eds. *Praxis der stationären Psychotherapie.* Stuttgart, Germany: Thieme;1988: pp 2–34.
3. von Rad M. Die Gruppe als therapeutisches Element in der stationären Psychotherapie. In: Lang H, ed. *Wirkfaktoren der Psychotherapie.* Heidelberg, Germany: Springer;1990: pp 78–93.
4. Neun H. *Psychosomatische Einrichtungen.* Göttingen, Germany: Vandenhoeck & Ruprecht;1990.
5. Lamprecht F. Stationäre Psychosomatik: Luxus oder Notwendigkeit. *Dtsch Ärztebl.* 1990;87:B-753–755.
6. Simmel E. Die psychoanalytische Behandlung in der Klinik. *Int Z Psychoanal.* 1927;14:352–370.
7. Karterud S, Vaglum S, Friis S, Irion T, Johns S, Vaglum P. Day hospital treatment community treatment for patients with personality disorders. *J Nerv Ment Dis.* 1992;180:238–243.
8. Köhle K, Böck D, Grauhan A. *Die internistisch-psychosomatische Krankenstation. Ein Werkstattbericht.* Basel, Switzerland: Rocom;1977.
9. Weizsäcker V von. *Grundfragen medizinischer Anthropologie.* Tübingen, Germany: Furche;1948.

10. Uexküll Th von. Psychosomatische Medizin gestern, heute und morgen. *Therapiewoche.* 1982;31:838–852.
11. Broda M, Engelhardt W. Stationäre verhaltensmedizinische Psychosomatik. In: Neun H, ed. *Psychosomatische Einrichtungen.* Göttingen, Germany: Vandenhoeck & Ruprecht;1990: pp 46–54.
12. Bräutigam W. Medizinisch-psychologische Anthropologie. Darmstadt, Germany: Wiss. Buchgesellschaft;1980.
13. Bion WR. *Erfahrungen in Gruppen.* Stuttgart, Germany: Klett;1971.
14. Main TF. The hospital as a therapeutic institution. *Bull Menninger Clin.* 1946;10:66–70.
15. Foudraine J. *Wer ist aus Holz?* Münich, Germany: Piper;1973.
16. Enke H. Bipolare Gruppenpsychotherapie als Möglichkeit psychoanalytischer Arbeit in der stationären Psychotherapie. *Z Psychother Med Psychol.* 1965;15:116–121.
17. Beese F. Klinische Psychotherapie. In: Hahn P, ed. *Die Psychologie des 20. Jahrhunderts.* Zürich, Switzerland: Kindler;1977:3:1144–1160.
18. Arfsten A-J, Hoffmann SO. Stationäre psychoanalytische Psychotherapie als eigenständige Behandlungsform. *Prax Psychother.* 1978;23:233–245.
19. Zielke M, Mark N. Effizienz und Effektivität stationärer psychosomatischer Behandlungen. *Prax Klin Verhaltensmed Rehabil.* 1989;7:132:147.
20. Stuhr U, Haag A. Eine Prävalenzstudie zum Bedarf an psychosomatischer Versorgung in den allgemeinen Krankenhäusern Hamburgs. *Psychother Med Psychol.* 1989;39:273–281.
21. Kernberg O. *Severe Personality Disorders.* New Haven, CT: Yale University Press; 1984.
22. Koenigsberg H. Indications for hospitalization in the treatment of borderline patients. *Psychiatr Q.* 1984;56:247–254.
23. Suh CS, Strupp HH, O'Malley SS. The Vanderbilt process measures. In: Greenberg LS, Pinsof WM, eds. *The psychotherapeutic process.* New York: Guilford Press;1986: pp 285–324.
24. Heigl F. *Indikation und Prognose in Psychoanalyse und Psychotherapie.* Göttingen, Germany: Vandenhoeck & Ruprecht;1972.
25. von Rad M. Psychosomatische Medizin und stationäre Psychotherapie in einem Allgemeinkrankenhaus—Ansprüche und Wirklichkeit. In: Tress W, ed. *Psychosomatische Medizin und Psychotherapie in Deutschland.* Göttingen, Germany: Vandenhoeck & Ruprecht;1992: pp 167–177.
26. Schmidt J. *Evaluation einer psychosomatischen Klinik.* Frankfurt, Germany: VAS;1991.
27. Colson DB, Coyne L, Pollack WS. Scales to assess the emphasis of psychiatric hospital treatment. *Psychiatry.* 1985;51:281–290.
28. Janssen PL. *Psychoanalytische Therapie in der Klinik.* Stuttgart, Germany: Klett; 1987.
29. Senf W. Stationäre psychoanalytische Psychotherapie. In: Neun H, ed. *Psychosomatische Einrichtungen.* Göttingen, Germany: Vandenhoeck & Ruprecht;1990: pp 37–45.
30. Kordy H, von Rad M, Senf W. Success and failure in psychotherapy: Hypotheses and results from the Heidelberg follow-up project. *Psychother Psychosom.* 1983;40:211–227.

31. Bernhard P, Lamprecht F, Schmidt J. Stationäre Psychotherapie: Möglichkeiten und Grenzen. In: Lamprecht F, ed. *Spezialisierung und Integration in der Psychosomatik und Psychotherapie.* Heidelberg, Germany: Springer;1987: pp 391–398.

32. Riedel WP, Schoof M. Diagnosenspezifische Therapieergebnisse in der stationären Psychotherapie. *Z Psychosom Med.* 1992;38:169–181.

33. Mentzel C, Mentzel G. Die Patienten einer psychosomatischen Kurklinik. *Psychosom Med.* 1976;23:56–72.

34. Lamprecht F, Schmidt J. Das Zauberberg-Projekt: Zwischen Verzauberung und Ernüchterung. In: Ahrens St, ed. *Entwicklung und Perspektiven der Psychosomatik.* Heidelberg, Germany: Springer;1990: pp 204–236.

35. Strauss B. Empirische Untersuchungen zur stationären Gruppenpsychotherapie. *Gruppenpsychother Gruppendyn.* 1992;28:125–149.

36. Yalom I. *Gruppenpsychotherapie.* Munich, Germany: Kindler;1975.

37. Kordy H, Schöneberg O. Differential relevance of therapeutic factors in inpatient psychotherapy. Paper presented at Ann Meet of the Society for Psychotherapy Research, Wintergreen;1990.

38. Carl A, Fischer-Antze R, Gaedtke H, Hoffmann SO, Wendler W. Vergleichende Darstellung gruppendynamischer Prozesse bei konzentrativer Bewegungstherapie und analytischer Gruppentherapie. *Gruppenpsychother Gruppendyn.* 1976;21:52–72.

39. Bräutigam W, Senf W, Kordy H. Wirkfaktoren psychoanalytischer Therapie aus der Sicht des Heidelberger Katamneseprojekts. In: Lang H, ed. *Wirkfaktoren der Psychotherapie.* Heidelberg, Germany: Springer;1989: pp 172–185.

40. Kneschke M. Neurosentherapie Erwachsener im Kontext von Kleingruppe und therapeutischer Gemeinschaft. In: Hess H, ed. *Soziale Beziehung und Krankheit.* Leipzig, Germany: Barth;1991: pp 111–123.

41. Groddeck G. *Briefe über das Es.* Munich, Germany: Kindler;1930/1974.

42. Kordy H, Senf W. Überlegungen zur Evaluation psychotherapeutischer Behandlungen. *Psychother Psychosom Med Psychol.* 1985;35:207–212.

43. Benjamin L. Structural analysis of social behavior. *Psychol Rev.* 1974;81:392–425.

Appendix:
Diagnostic Criteria for Use
in Psychosomatic Research

Giovanni A. Fava, Harald J. Freyberger,
Per Bech, George Christodoulou, Tom Sensky,
Töres Theorell, Thomas N. Wise

The past two decades have witnessed a renaissance in psychiatric diagnosis, and this progress has resulted in DSM-IV[1] and ICD-10[2] classifications of mental disorders. Such methods, or their precursors, are used as the main tools to characterize psychosocial problems in the medically ill. An analysis of their codes most relevant to psychosomatic medicine, however, may reveal the conceptual flaws and clinical inadequacies of diagnostic categories such as adjustment disorders, psychological factors affecting physical conditions, and somatoform disorders.[3, 4] These inadequacies also extend to the ICD-10 category describing psychological symptoms which are not severe enough to fulfill the diagnostic criteria of a specific diagnostic category. Measurement of psychological distress and well-being in the medically ill frequently involves symptoms whose severity is considerably less than what is generally found in psychiatric settings.[5] A considerable body of evidence which has accumulated in psychosomatic medicine and relates to concepts such as quality of life, stressful life events, somatization and personality, has not resulted in operational tools whereby psychosocial aspects of medical disease can be differentiated. Psychosomatic investigators have attempted to demonstrate that a certain psychological characteristic X is more prevalent in condition A compared to condition B. Even when they do find a significant difference by reliable statistical and psychometric methods, this does not mean that every patient with A also presents with X, and that a patient with B may not present with X features. Replication attempts are often disappointing as one would expect from characteristics of modest sensitivity and low specificity in heterogenous medical entities. One may wonder whether a quite different strategy may be endorsed: to translate psychosocial characteristics observed in various medical diseases in diagnostic criteria, which may entail clinical (prognostic and therapeutic) value, and may be studied across disorders.

These characteristics are defined as "psychosomatic syndromes," to emphasize the varieties of associated somatic and mental responses that individuals offer to life situations. The term—unlike the classic concept of psychosomatic disease or disorder[3]—is devoid of pathogenetic implications. Particularly in the field of medical disorders not explained by organic disease, the identification of these psychosomatic syndromes may bring together "a larger number of seemingly unrelated facts" as Halliday wished half a century ago.[6] A patient with functional medical illness A, for instance, may be judged to be quite different from a patient with B. Yet, the presence of X in both may be clinically far more important than suffering from disorders belonging to different headings of anatomical systems. Psychosomatic syndromes can thus be studied across different medical disorders as categorical variables. Their settings (different medical disorders) may or may not prove of clinical value. The modification of these psychosomatic syndromes by psychotherapeutic or pharmacologic means may provide new prospects for psychosomatic research.

In 1972 Feighner et al.[7] introduced diagnostic criteria for use in psychiatric research. Their initial statement was as follows:

These criteria are not intended as final for any illness. The criteria represent a distillation of our clinical research experience, and of the experiences of others cited in the references. This communication is meant to provide common ground for different research groups so that diagnostic definitions can be emended constructively as further studies are completed[7] (p. 57).

It is our aim to provide such ground for psychosomatic medicine and psychotherapy research. We will provide a description of psychosomatic syndromes. Such descriptions are intended only as screening diagnoses in the setting of medical disease, once the patient has seen a physician for somatic symptoms, or where the symptoms were disabling enough to interfere with everyday life, or the somatic symptoms led the patient to take medications for them. The psychological characterizations are clinically meaningful only if and when somatic disturbances are associated, and are therefore subsumed under the rubric of psychosomatic syndromes, which is different from psychiatric disorders. Their relationships with current psychiatric nosology (DSM-IV or ICD-10) will be briefly outlined. These diagnostic criteria are to be used across patient characteristics (medical diagnoses, age, sex, etc.) and can be integrated by dimensional variables, to be obtained by psychological rating scales and inventories. (e.g., Eysenck's neuroticism and extraversion dimensions).

The criteria can also be used in a multiaxial approach, as outlined by Mezzich and Schmolke.[8] They may provide either supplementary diagnoses for the first or second axes of DSM-IV classification or they may pave the way for an additional axis for psychosomatic research. These psychosomatic syndromes may also occur in the setting of other psychiatric disorders, i.e., psychiatric comorbidity may occur.[9]

Psychosomatic Syndromes

Alexithymia

Alexithymia, a concept introduced by Sifneos[10] to describe impoverished fantasy life with a resulting utilitarian way of thinking and a characteristic inability to use appropriate words to describe emotions, has stimulated two decades of psychosomatic research.[11] It has been found that alexithymia is more common in patients with

TABLE A.1
Diagnostic Criteria for Alexithymia (A through B Are Required)

A At least 3 of the following 6 characteristics should
  be present:
  (1) inability to use appropriate words to describe
      emotions
  (2) tendency to describe details instead of feelings
      (e.g., circumstances surrounding an event rath-
      er than the feelings)
  (3) lack of a rich fantasy life
  (4) thought content associated more with external
      events rather than fantasy or emotions
  (5) unawareness of the common somatic reactions
      that accompany the experience of a variety of
      feelings
  (6) occasional but violent and often inappropriate
      outbursts of affective behavior

B Alexithymia does not occur only in the course of a
  mood disorder, social phobia or organic mental disorder

  Specify type:
  (1) pervasive
  (2) situational (restricted to inhibition of anger
      and/or assertive behavior)

---

long-lasting psychosomatic conditions than in other subjects. The
inhibition of emotional expression and particularly a life-
long tendency to suppress anger, have been found to involve an
increased risk for a variety of health problems both using the alexithymia[11] or similar[12, 13] psychological constructs. Table A.1 summarizes the most salient alexithymic features.[10, 14] We differentiated
pervasive and situational alexithymia, on the basis that in some
patients alexithymia involves all emotions and situations, whereas
in other patients it is limited to specific affects and/or situations.
Self-rating scales, such as the Toronto Alexithymia Scale,[11] lack
some of the most important pieces of information which can only

TABLE A.2
Diagnostic Criteria for Type A Behavior (A through C Are Required)

A At least 5 of the following 9 characteristics should be present:
   (1) excessive degree of involvement in work and other activities subject to deadlines
   (2) steady and pervasive sense of time urgency
   (3) display of motor-expressive features (rapid and explosive speech, abrupt body movements, tensing of facial muscles, hand gestures) indicating sense of being under the pressure of time
   (4) hostility and cynicism
   (5) irritable mood
   (6) tendency to speed up physical activities
   (7) tendency to speed up mental activities
   (8) high intensity of desire for achievement and recognition
   (9) high competitiveness

B The behavior elicits stress-related physiologic responses that precipitate or exacerbate symptoms of a medical condition

C The behavior does not occur in the course of manic or hypomanic syndromes

be obtained by interviews focused on emotions and emotional coping. Yet, they may add further data.

Type A Behavior

A large number of studies have been conducted in the past 3 decades on the pathogenic role of type A behavior in coronary heart disease.[15] The search for these characteristics in noncardiac conditions has been neglected. Various methods of assessment have been used and the results have been rather controversial; hostility and time urgency have appeared to be two key components.[15] Table A.2

lists the most relevant clinical features of type A behavior pattern.[15, 16]

ABNORMAL ILLNESS BEHAVIOR

It was defined by Pilowsky[17] as the persistence of a maladaptive mode of perceiving, experiencing, evaluating, and responding to one's health status, despite the fact that a doctor has provided a lucid and accurate appraisal of the situation and management to be followed (if any), with opportunities for discussion, negotiation, and clarification, based on adequate assessment of all relevant biological, psychological, social, and cultural factors.

There are considerable overlaps between the concept of abnormal illness behavior and the DSM categories of somatoform disorders, which have been discussed in detail elsewhere.[3] Pilowsky differentiates somatically and psychologically focused abnormal illness behavior. Within the somatic one there are two broad categories: illness affirming and illness denying. The illness-affirming abnormal behavior includes disorders which are listed in DSM-IV as factitious disease, somatization disorder, conversion disorder, hypochondriasis, and pain disorder[1] and in ICD-10 as feigning of symptoms or disabilities, somatization disorder, hypochondriacal disorder, somatoform autonomic dysfunction, and somatoform pain disorder.[2] There are differences in the two classification systems which are likely to increase confusion among psychosomatic researchers and whose discussion is beyond the aims of this paper. In particular, the DSM-IV lacks the ICD-10 category of somatoform autonomic dysfunction, which includes symptoms of autonomic arousal (e.g., palpitations, sweating, tremor, flushing) without evidence of a significant disturbance of structure or function of the involved system or organ. There are obvious problems with this heterogeneous category which lacks adequate boundaries with the somatic manifestations of psychiatric disorders and with hypochondriasis, and combines long-lasting disturbances with short-lived symptoms. The psychosomatic problems entailed by this category will be discussed under the heading of somatization. A major problem

TABLE A.3
Diagnostic Criteria for Disease Phobia (A through D Are Required)

A Persistent, unfounded fear of suffering from a specific disease (e.g., AIDS, cancer), with doubts remaining despite adequate examination and reassurance

B Fears tend to manifest themselves in attacks rather than in constant, chronic worries as in hypochondriasis; panic attacks may be an associated feature

C The object of fears does not change with time and duration of symptoms exceeds 6 months

D Fears are not secondary to mood or anxiety disorders

with the DSM-IV and ICD-10 classification of hypochondriacal fears and attitudes is that they only define the most severe end of the spectrum (hypochondriasis, characterized by resistance to medical reassurance and multiple fears). There is evidence[3, 18] that other worries are worthy of clinical attention: disease phobia (Table A.3), thanatophobia (Table A.4) and health anxiety (Table A.5). Further, the illness-denying category of abnormal illness behavior[17] provides room for various psychosomatic situations occurring in medical and surgical settings (Table A.6).

SOMATIZATION

Somatization, defined by Lipowski[19] as the tendency to experience and communicate psychological distress in the form of physical symptoms and to seek medical help for them, is a widespread clinical phenomenon which cuts across diagnostic categories, both of psychiatric and medical type. Psychosomatic research in the field of functional symptoms has suggested a high percentage of psychiatric comorbidity[3] and a primary–secondary distinction has been found to be feasible,[20] as outlined in Table A.7.

TABLE A.4
Diagnostic Criteria for Thanatophobia (A through D Are Required)

A Attacks with the sense of impending death and/or conviction of dying soon, even though there is no objective medical reason for such fear

B Marked and persistent fear and avoidance of news which reminds of death (e.g., funerals, obituary notices); exposure to these stimuli almost invariably provokes an immediate anxiety response

C The avoidance, anxious anticipation and distress interfere significantly with the person's level of functioning

D Thanatophobia is not secondary to mood or anxiety disorders; attacks do not meet diagnostic criteria for panic

---

TABLE A.5
Diagnostic Criteria for Health Anxiety (A through C Are Required)

A Generic worry about illness, concern about pain and bodily preoccupations (tendency to amplify somatic sensations) of less than 6 months' duration

B Worries and fears readily respond to appropriate medical reassurance, even though new worries may ensue after some time

C Worries and fears are not secondary to mood or anxiety disorders

---

Kellner[21] summarized some characteristics of patients suffering from various functional medical disorders, such as nonulcer dyspepsia, urethral syndrome, and irritable bowel syndrome. Unlike in the DSM-IV definition of somatization disorder or

TABLE A.6
Diagnostic Criteria for Illness Denial (A through C Are Required)

A Persistent denial of having a physical disorder and of the need of treatment (e.g., lack of compliance, delayed seeking of medical attention for serious and persistent symptoms, counterphobic behavior), as a reaction to the symptoms, signs, diagnosis or medical treatment of a physical illness

B The patient has been provided a lucid and accurate appraisal of the medical situation and management to be followed

C The reaction is not part of a mood or neurologic disorder (anosognosia)

TABLE A.7
Diagnostic Criteria for Functional Somatic Symptoms Secondary to a Psychiatric Disorder (A through D Are Required)

A Symptoms of autonomic arousal (e.g., palpitations, sweating, tremor, flushing) or functional medical disorder (e.g., irritable bowel syndrome, fibromyalgia, neurocirculatory asthenia), causing distress, or repeated medical care, or resulting in impaired quality of life

B Appropriate medical evaluation uncovers no organic pathology to account for the physical complaints

C A psychiatric disorder (which includes the involved somatic symptoms within its manifestations) preceded the onset of functional somatic symptoms (e.g., panic disorder and cardiac symptoms)

D Even though health anxiety may occur, the patient does not meet the criteria for hypochondriasis or disease phobia

TABLE A.8
Diagnostic Criteria for Persistent Somatization (A through C Are Required)

A Functional medical disorder (e.g., fibromyalgia, fatigue, esophageal motility disorders, nonulcer dyspepsia, irritable bowel syndrome, neurocirculatory asthenia, urethral syndrome), whose duration exceeds 6 months, causing distress, or repeated medical care, or resulting in impaired quality of life
B Additional symptoms of autonomic arousal (involving also other organ systems) and exaggerated side effects from medical therapy are present, indicating low sensation or pain thresholds and high suggestibility
C Somatic symptoms do not occur in the course of a mood, anxiety or organic mental disorder

conversion, such symptoms occur in the setting of known psychophysiological mechanisms. Kellner suggested that it may be advantageous to conceptualize a somatizing patient as someone in whom psychophysiological symptoms have clustered, as outlined in Table A.8. The DSM-IV differentiates between somatization disorder and conversion. The distinction is mainly based on the number of symptoms instead of more precise clinical features. Table A.9 outlines the diagnostic criteria for conversion symptoms (regardless of their number) based on Engel's[22] stringent criteria. Such diagnosis overlaps with the ICD-10 category of dissociative (conversion) disorders. Table A.10 describes the diagnostic criteria for anniversary reaction, which may be a special form of conversion as well as other types of somatization.

IRRITABLE MOOD

A considerable body of evidence has suggested a pathogenetic role for anger, hostility, and irritable mood in physical illness, both of

TABLE A.9
Diagnostic Criteria for Conversion Symptoms (A through D Are Required)

A One or more symptoms or deficits affecting voluntary motor or sensory function, characterized by lack of anatomical or physiological plausibility, and/or absence of expected physical signs or laboratory findings, and/or inconsistent clinical characteristics; if symptoms of autonomic arousal or functional medical disorder are present, conversion symptoms should be prominent, causing distress, or repeated medical care, or resulting in impaired quality of life

B At least 2 of the following features are present:
   (1) ambivalence in symptom reporting (e.g. the patient appears relaxed or unconcerned as he describes distressing symptoms)
   (2) hystrionic personality features (colorful and dramatic expression, language and appearance; demanding dependency; high suggestibility; rapid mood changes)
   (3) precipitation of symptoms by psychological stress, the association of which the patient is unaware
   (4) history of similar physical symptoms experienced by the patient, or observed in someone else, or wished on someone else

C Appropriate medical evaluation uncovers no organic pathology to account for the physical complaints

D Somatic symptoms do not occur in the course of a mood, anxiety or organic mental disorder

organic and functional nature.[23] Table A.11 outlines the diagnostic criteria for irritable mood, largely based on the work of Snaith and Taylor.[24] Irritability can covary but differs from depressed mood. It may be part of the type A personality associated with hostile cynicism.

TABLE A.10
Diagnostic Criteria for Anniversary Reaction (A through C Are Required)

A   Symptoms of autonomic arousal (e.g., palpitations, sweating, tremor, flushing) or functional medical disorder (e.g., irritable bowel syndrome, fibromyalgia, neurocirculatory asthenia) or conversion symptoms causing distress, or repeated medical care, or resulting in impaired quality of life

B   Appropriate medical evaluation uncovers no organic pathology to account for the physical complaints

C   Symptoms began when the patient reached the age or on the occasion of the anniversary when a parent or very close family member developed a life-threatening illness and/or died; the patient is unaware of such association

TABLE A.11
Diagnostic Criteria for Irritable Mood (A through D Are Required)

A   A feeling state characterized by irritable mood which may be experienced as brief episodes, in particular circumstances, or it may be prolonged and generalized; it requires an increased effort of control over temper by the individual or results in irascible verbal or behavioral outbursts

B   The experience of irritability is always unpleasant for the individual and overt manifestation lacks the cathartic effect of justified outbursts of anger

C   The feeling elicits stress-related physiologic responses that precipitate or exacerbate symptoms of a medical disorder

D   Irritable mood is not secondary to a psychiatric disorder (such as major depression or panic disorder) and to type A behavior

TABLE A.12
Diagnostic Criteria for Demoralization (A through D Are Required)

A A feeling state characterized by the patient's consciousness of having failed to meet his or her own expectations (or those of others) or being unable to cope with some pressing problems; the patient experiences feelings of helplessness, or hopelessness, or giving up

B The feeling state should be prolonged and generalized (at least 1-month duration)

C The feeling closely antedated the manifestations of a medical disorder or exacerbated its symptoms

D Demoralization is not secondary to a psychiatric disorder (such as major depression or panic disorder)

DEMORALIZATION

Several clinical observations have substantiated a psychological state characterized by the giving-up complex,[25] helplessness and hopelessness, demoralization,[26] as a facilitating factor for the onset of disease to which the individual was predisposed. Such a subsyndromal state cannot be identified with psychiatric categories[5] and is described in Table A.12.

CONCLUSION

The diagnostic criteria presented in this paper are obviously tentative in the sense that they may change and become more precise with new data and with endorsement by psychosomatic investigators. They supplement DSM-IV or ICD-10 criteria, even though in some cases they substitute for them. We hope that this first set of criteria will result in progress in nosological aspects of psychosomatic research. A first field trial is currently in preparation and clinicians who are interested can contact the corresponding author of this paper. Not only the diagnostic descriptions which are given here are likely to be refined, but further syndromes will possibly join those listed. Clinicians working at the interface between medicine and psychiatry[27] can provide important phenomenological grounds for such developments, and their suggestions and observations are welcome as well.

REFERENCES

1. American Psychiatric Association. *Diagnostic and Statistical Manual of Mental Disorders*. 4th ed. Washington, DC: American Psychiatric Press;1994.
2. World Health Organization. *The ICD-10 Classification of Mental and Behavioural Disorders*. Geneva, Switzerland: WHO;1992.
3. Fava GA. The concept of psychosomatic disorder. *Psychother Psychosom*. 1992;58:1–12.
4. Sensky T. Somatization: Syndromes or processes? *Psychother Psychosom*. 1994;61:1–3.
5. Bech P. Measurement of psychological distress and well-being. *Psychother Psychosom*. 1990;54:77–89.
6. Halliday JL. The significance of the concept of a psychosomatic affection. *Psychosom Med*. 1945;7:240–245.
7. Feighner JP, Robins E, Guze SB, Woodruff RA, Winokur G, Munoz R. Diagnostic criteria for use in psychiatric research. *Arch Gen Psychiatry*. 1972;26:57–63.
8. Mezzich JE, Schmolke MM. Multiaxial diagnosis and psychotherapy planning. *Psychother Psychosom*. 1995;63:71–80.
9. Freyberger HJ, Schneider W, Malchow CP. The concept of comorbidity in the diagnosis of psychosomatic and neurotic disorder. *Psychother Psychosom*. In press.
10. Sifneos PE. The prevalence of "alexithymic" characteristics in psychosomatic patients. *Psychother Psychosom*. 1973;22:255–262.
11. Sifneos PE. Affect, emotional conflict, and deficit. An overview. *Psychother Psychosom*. 1991;56:116–122.
12. Greer J. Cancer and the mind. *Br J Psychiatry*. 1983;143:535–543.
13. Berry DS, Pennebaker JW. Nonverbal and verbal emotional expression and health. *Psychother Psychosom*. 1993;59:11–19.
14. Nemiah JC, Freyberger H, Sifneos PE. Alexithymia. A view of the psychosomatic process. In: Hill OW, ed. *Modern Trends in Psychosomatic Medicine*. London: Butterworths;1976: pp 430–439.

15. Littman AB. Review of psychosomatic aspects of cardiovascular disease. *Psychother Psychosom.* 1993;60:148–167.
16. Friedman M, Powell LH. The diagnosis and quantitative assessment of type A behavior. *Integrative Psychiatry.* 1984;2:123–129.
17. Pilowsky I. Abnormal illness behavior. *Psychother Psychosom.* 1986;46:76–84.
18. Fava GA, Grandi S. Differential diagnosis of hypochondriacal fears and beliefs. *Psychother Psychosom.* 1991;55:114–119.
19. Lipowski ZJ. Somatization. *Psychother Psychosom.* 1987;47:160–167.
20. Fava GA, Magelli C, Savron G, Conti S, Bartolucci G, Grandi S, Semprini F, Saviotti FM, Belluardo P, Magnani B. Neurocirculatory asthenia. *Acta Psychiatr Scand.* 1994;89:314–319.
21. Kellner R. Psychosomatic syndromes, somatization and somatoform disorders. *Psychother Psychosom.* 1994;61:4–24.
22. Engel GL. Conversion symptoms. In: Mac Bryde CM, Blacklow RS, eds. *Signs and Symptoms.* Philadelphia: Lippincott;1970: pp 650–659.
23. Fava GA. Irritable mood and physical illness. *Stress Med.* 1987;3:293–299.
24. Snaith RP, Taylor CM. Irritability. *Br J Psychiatry.* 1985;147:127–136.
25. Schmale AH. Giving up as a final common pathway of changes in health. *Adv Psychosom Med.* 1972;7:20–40.
26. Frank JD, Frank JB. *Persuasion and Healing.* Baltimore: Johns Hopkins University Press;1991.
27. Wise TN. Consultation-liaison research: The use of differing perspectives. *Psychother Psychosom.* 1995;63:9–21.

Name Index

Exley, P., 324
Extein, I., 324
Eyles, E., 32
Eysenck, H. J., 206, 208, 227, 366, 533–534
Eysenck, S. B., 227
Eysenck, S. B. G., 208
Ezrachi, O., 358–359, 360

Fabbri, G., 397
Faber, J., 241
Fabrega, H. Jr., 97
Facchinetti, F., 395, 397, 402, 404, 415, 417
Fahey, J. L., 534, 580
Faillace, L. A., 251
Fair, P. L., 300
Fairburn, C. G., 532, 571, 572, 573
Fairweather, D. V., 552
Falcone, C., 279
Fallo, F., 168, 317, 318, 322, 323, 330, 331
Fallowfield, L. J., 366
Faragher, E. B., 135, 550, 551, 560
Farega, H. Jr., 93
Farmer, C. J., 299, 300
Farmer, R., 133
Farquhar, C. M., 141–142
Farquhar, J., 527
Fateh, M., 410
Faurschou, P., 600
Fava, G. A., xvii, xviii, 93, 134, 148, 161, 162–163, 164, 165, 166, 167–169, 170, 172, 173, 174, 175, 176, 177, 232, 243, 303, 317, 318, 319, 320, 321, 322, 323, 326, 329, 330, 331, 373, 386, 398, 448, 677, 678, 682, 683, 686–687
Fava, M., 280, 283, 325, 326, 404
Fawzey, F. I., 534
Fawzey, N. W., 534
Fawzy, F. I., 361, 580
Fawzy, N., 361–362, 580

Feder, H. M., 458
Federoff, H. J., 397
Fediao, R., 351
Fedoravicius, A. S., 135
Feehan, M., 485
Feeny, D., 303, 304
Feigenbaum, H., 301
Feighner, J. P., 275, 678
Feinglass, E. J., 182
Feinleib, M., 268
Feinstein, A. R., 162, 207, 625
Feldman, M., 241, 243
Feldstein, M., 343, 607
Fellner, C. H., 306
Fels, H., 603
Felson, D. T., 127, 128
Fenton, S., 300
Fenton, S. S. A., 304
Fenwick, J. W., 262
Ferguson, B., 185t
Ferguson, C. W., 299
Fergusson, D. M., 197
Fergusson, J., 351
Fernadez, E., 356
Fernandez, P., 194
Fernandez De Gatta, M. M., 595
Ferney, D. M., 132
Ferraccioli, G., 128
Ferrante, J., 328
Ferraro, K. F., 302
Ferreira, A. J., 482
Ferreira, J. M., 325
Ferrell, B. R., 342
Ferro, F., 460
Feting, J., 345, 348, 349
Fetting, J. H., 355, 607
Ficarra, B. J., 323
Field, T., 71
Field, T. M., 194, 195, 198
Fielding, B., 303
Figueroa, J. L., 578
Fine, P. G., 128
Fine, P. R., 148

Subject Index

751